# ASEAN ENVIRONMENTAL LAW, POLICY AND GOVERNANCE

## Selected Documents

Volume I

# Errata

ASEAN Environmental Law, Policy and Governance: Selected Documents (Volume I) *compiled and edited by Kheng-Lian Koh*

- Acknowledgements, page xi, paragraph 3, line 5, the phrase "another Foreword" should read "the Preface".

# ASEAN ENVIRONMENTAL LAW, POLICY AND GOVERNANCE

## Selected Documents

Volume I

*Compiled and Edited by*

Koh Kheng-Lian

*Emeritus Professor,*
*National University of Singapore, Singapore*

World Scientific

NEW JERSEY • LONDON • SINGAPORE • BEIJING • SHANGHAI • HONG KONG • TAIPEI • CHENNAI

*Published by*

World Scientific Publishing Co. Pte. Ltd.

5 Toh Tuck Link, Singapore 596224

*USA office:* 27 Warren Street, Suite 401-402, Hackensack, NJ 07601

*UK office:* 57 Shelton Street, Covent Garden, London WC2H 9HE

**British Library Cataloguing-in-Publication Data**
A catalogue record for this book is available from the British Library.

**ASEAN ENVIRONMENTAL LAW, POLICY AND GOVERNANCE**
**Selected Documents**
**(Volume 1)**



ISBN-13 978-981-4261-18-0
ISBN-10 981-4261-18-1

Typeset by Stallion Press
Email: enquiries@stallionpress.com

Printed in Singapore by B & Jo Enterprise Pte Ltd

# FOREWORD

In the Charter of the Association of Southeast Asian Nations (ASEAN), which came into force in December 2008, one of the purposes of ASEAN is stated as:

> "To promote sustainable development so as to ensure the protection of the region's environment, the sustainability of its natural resources, the preservation of its cultural heritage and the high quality of life of its peoples."

Indeed, the ASEAN region has an abundance of natural resources. Its biodiversity is immensely rich and unique. Its ecology is still being explored, and new organizms just discovered. At the same time, this lush and varied geography is heavily populated by many nations with long histories and traditions.

Civilizations have come and gone in Southeast Asia. Yet, globalization and the modern age have brought dynamic economic development with the relentless exploitation of the natural wealth. Through the years, Southeast Asians have endeavoured to balance progress and sustainability. This has now acquired urgency, as climate change is no longer an academic pursuit.

The challenges faced in protecting the natural resources and advancing the material well-being of society, are tackled in different ways by the different member states of ASEAN. Some governments focus on enacting new laws and regulations at the national level. Others establish or strengthen requisite institutions. Joining international organizations and signing on to international agreements and conventions, is another strategy which has been used. The contents of this book clearly demonstrate the efforts of the ASEAN policy-makers. Nonetheless, all these actions encountered various problems and it is a remarkable accomplishment to have arrived at this stage.

It is time-consuming to work through any one particular measure. The domestic considerations are now intertwined with transnational concerns. With the increasing transcendence of country boundaries, no walls separate or contain environmental disasters such as air and water pollution. Neither are there demarcations to discriminate the exploitation of forests and underwater assets. There is no quick solution to environmental degradation and unsustainable use of the natural resources.

Since 1977, ASEAN as a collective, has nevertheless embarked on regional initiatives aimed at tacking such challenges. Several agreements and frameworks have been drawn up. They are part of the process of regional cooperation and community building. However, implementing ASEAN's agenda on the environment has been patchy. The pressures of feeding a large population, coupled with the incessant demands of the market, make any enforcement of laws and protection, imperfect. Several ASEAN member states have also to grapple with many bureaucratic and anti-social habits, which further complicate the management of natural resources and the promotion of environmental protection.

A case in point on the ASEAN process is the ratification of the ASEAN Agreement on Transboundary Haze Pollution. Given ASEAN's diversity in culture and politics, the regional organisation adheres to the practice of non-interference in the differing governance systems. While this has given rise to peace and intensified economic collaboration within the ASEAN region, the practice has also led to criticisms of ASEAN being a stumbling block, hindering progress on the environmental front. Despite many in ASEAN having a strong desire for laws and regulations, which enable more protection for the environment in ASEAN, we have to recognise the need for the ASEAN process to run its course. ASEAN would have to approach environmental sustainability in a balanced and step-by-step manner.

A concrete example of progress is encapsulated in the ASEAN Socio-Cultural Community (ASCC) Blueprint that will be endorsed by the ASEAN Leaders at the 14$^{th}$ ASEAN Summit in 2009. This Blueprint serves as a common denominator, which will help guide the development of ASEAN member states towards environmental sustainability and thereafter aid work in harmonizing environmental laws and regulations. Acknowledging the diversity in ASEAN, the ASCC Blueprint is an open declaration of ASEAN's commitment and determination towards achieving environmental sustainability for the region.

As we seek more laws and regulations for the ASEAN environmental landscape, it is imperative that we recognise that ASEAN works primarily on the basis of trust and cordiality. As such, laws and regulations that are of a regional nature would certainly have to be guided by the capability and capacity of each ASEAN country. There is no one-size-fits-all approach in managing the environment and sustainable development in ASEAN. Ultimately, all ASEAN member states share a common but differentiated responsibility in the protection and conservation of Southeast Asia's special and valuable environmental heritage.

*ASEAN Environmental Law, Policy and Governance: Selected Documents*, in two volumes, covers a wide range of topics and will be a boon to capacity building and in promoting awareness in environmental sustainability in the ASEAN region and beyond.

*Ambassador Ong Keng Yong*
*Director, Institute of Policy Studies,*
*Lee Kuan Yew School of Public Policy, Singapore*
*Ambassador-At-Large in the Singapore Ministry of Foreign Affairs (MFA)*
*Singapore's Non-Resident Ambassador to Iran*
*Former Secretary-General of ASEAN*

# PREFACE

In this book, Professor Koh Kheng-Lian, judiciously and perceptively, invites us to witness the maturing of the Association of Southeast Asian Nations (ASEAN) as a regional socio-economic and cultural integration organization. Here Professor Koh gathers the constituent decisions that incrementally define the ASEAN consensus and provides insights into the emergence how peoples across many languages and traditions find a common path toward sustainable development.

ASEAN has advanced its programs for sustaining natural resources, biodiversity, public health, and nature conservation in important ways. These efforts have been in tandem with growing collaboration in many other sectors, such as finance, transport, and commerce. What makes the environmental agenda so important is the region's enormous richness in biodiversity, as well as its habitats for many migratory species whose range encompasses the ASEAN area as a key link in pathways that extend from as far away as the Arctic or Australia and Antarctic. ASEAN constituencies know intimately that their nations have accepted the obligation under the United Nations Convention on the Law of the Sea to protect and preserve the marine environment; all ASEAN nations share a direct association with the oceans. In like vein, the ASEAN States have important, common but differentiated duties to stabilize the climate of the Earth. The typhoons and floods at one extreme, and the welcome rainfall for freshwater resources at another extreme, evidence the region's dependence on climatic conditions.

No one nation can provide for environmental stewardship in Southeast Asia. Only the sort of transnational cooperation can ensure a sound environment for all the peoples of the region. By harmonizing programs, standards, and sharing in capacity building, the region is building the foundation for effective cooperation and performance. This work is not accomplished suddenly. There can be no true capacity-building transnationally without confidence building. This happens gradually, through successive programs and plans of action, and reassessment and reappraisals. Much international development assistance focuses on external economic indicators and seeks a short-term burst in productivity; such patterns of development repeatedly deteriorate, are subject to corrupt manipulation or lack the personnel to sustain them over time.

ASEAN has pursued a more effective model, working on harmonization and integration through pragmatic and effective common endeavors. Much of what works in ASEAN is grounded on a confidence-building model. To be sure, the European Union, from the earliest work of European Communities and the Council of Europe, has also demonstrated that regional confidence building is key to socio-economic well-bring. The EU has been focused inwardly, on its own political integration, and like other regions has not seen how ASEAN has been cultivating its own distinctive kind of regional harmonization and integration.

Professor Koh facilitates the study of ASEAN in important ways. Without this compendium, comparative regional studies would be difficult. She has been a close watcher as well as a leader in building ASEAN's environmental conservation cooperation, and brings her unique insights to the editing of this work.

All those who strive to build environmental cooperation across nations are indebted to Professor Koh for her scholarly work over one decade in the study and analysis of ASEAN's environmental programs. Her leadership in the Asia-Pacific Centre for Environmental Law at the Faculty of Law of the National University of Singapore has been a beacon to government officials in Asia, to scholars around the world, and to institutions such as the Asian Development Bank, that build the framework for sustainable development. Her role as a Vice-Chair for South and East Asia for the Commission on Environmental Law of the International Union for the Conservation of Nature (IUCN) has enabled her to bring ASEAN's leadership to the attention of other regions.

ASEAN's environmental laws and programs are building, almost in an organic and evolutionary way. To discern this growth requires detailed attention to what some dismiss as a bureaucratic meeting or a routine administrative act. The genius of this work is in linking these small — sometimes imperceptible — environmental legal measures to reveal their maturation over time and their morphing into new patterns. This book can only remind us how indebted we all are to Professor Koh Kheng-Lian for her dedicated scholarship as one of Asia's pioneers in environmental law.

*Nicholas A. Robinson*
*Gilbert & Sarah Kerlin Distinguished Professor of Environmental Law*
*Pace University School of Law (New York, USA)*
*Former IUCN Chair, IUCN Commission on Environmental Law*

# ACKNOWLEDGEMENTS

I am very grateful to His Excellency Dr Surin Pitsuwan, Secretary-General of the ASEAN, and the ASEAN Secretariat for permission to reproduce documents and for useful comments during the preparation of the manuscript.

I am deeply indebted to His Excellency Ong Keng Yong, former Secretary-General of the ASEAN Secretariat, currently Director of the Institute of Policy Studies and Singapore's Ambassador-at-Large, for the *Foreword.* Given his first-hand knowledge of ASEAN, he has made insightful comments on the complexities of achieving a balance between progress and sustainability, and how Southeast Asians have endeavoured in this regard to meet the challenges ahead.

My heartfelt appreciation to Professor NA Robinson, Gilbert & Sarah Kerlin Distinguished Professor of Environmental Law, Pace University School of Law (New York, USA), and former Chair of the IUCN Commission for Environmental Law, and Co- Director of the Center for Environmental Legal Studies of the Pace University, for another *Foreword.* A legal luminary in the environmental world, Professor Robinson emphasizes that no one nation can provide for environmental stewardship, and only transnational cooperation can ensure a sound environment. This includes harmonizing standards, integrating programmes and capacity building. He keenly observes that these areas are maturing and are still in the process of morphing into new patterns, even from small measures, which may be imperceptible but must be linked.

*Dr Koh Kheng-Lian*
*Emeritus Professor*
*Faculty of Law*
*National University of Singapore;*
*Founding Director, Asia- Pacific Centre for Environmental Law;*
*Former Regional Vice Chair (1996–2004)*
*IUCN Commission on Environmental Law (CEL) for South and East Asia*
*and member of its Steering Committee*

*1 March 2009*

# CONTENTS

# INTRODUCTION

Over a decade has elapsed since my first compilation, *Selected ASEAN Documents on the Environment* was published in 1996. It was launched in conjunction with the official opening on 1 July 1996 of the Asia-Pacific Centre of Environmental Law (APCEL), established by the Faculty of Law, National University of Singapore (NUS) in partnership with the International Union for the Conservation of Nature (IUCN) and in collaboration with the United Nations Environment Programme (UNEP). That publication was prepared for use in the APCEL/IUCN/UNEP 'Training the Trainers Course on Capacity Building for Environmental Legal Education in Asia and the Pacific' which was held in 1997 and 1998 at the Faculty of Law, NUS. Those two courses, which were sponsored by the ADB (Asian Development Bank) and NUS, attracted environmental law professors from some 15 countries in the Asia-Pacific region and were designed to help develop and hone participants' pedagogical skills to teach what was then a 'new subject' back home in their respective universities.

Back then and more so now, environmental law was and is becoming increasingly important, complex and dynamic. The course we organized was significant in that APCEL answered the call of the 1992 United Nations Conference on Environment and Development's Agenda 21 (paragraph 8.20) that "competent international and academic institutions … cooperate to provide … training … in environmental and developmental law." The materials used for the course were those relevant to the region and included environmental instruments emanating from ASEAN.

Since the publication of *Selected ASEAN Documents on the Environment*, ASEAN has incrementally developed more instruments on environmental law, policy and governance to augment and refine existing ones. New areas such as climate change and energy, freshwater water resources and zoonotic diseases (for example, avian influenza and SARS) have also been addressed over the years. As Agenda 21's call for promoting environmental education is being implemented throughout the world, ASEAN is taking up this crucial challenge by strengthening its capacity to work towards the development of environmental sustainability. Strategy 4 of the ASEAN Strategic Plan of Action on the Environment, 1994–1998 states:

> … as environmental issues now transcend beyond regional boundaries, the need to develop these capabilities in order to implement international agreements on environment as well as effectively participate in the negotiation of new international treaties and the review of existing ones, cannot be over emphasized .... ASEAN from a regional standpoint should strengthen its regional capacities.

One recent landmark of ASEAN cooperation is the ASEAN Environmental Education Action Plan, 2000–2005. It has now been succeeded by the ASEAN Environmental Education Action Plan II 2008–2012. More recently, the Charter of the Association of Southeast Asian Nations, 2007 (ASEAN Charter) has called for the development of human resources through cooperation in education, the enhancement of good governance and the promotion of a "people-oriented ASEAN".

*ASEAN Environmental Law, Policy and Governance: Selected Documents*, in two volumes, is a compilation of a selection of over 150 documents. The scope of environmental law is wide-ranging and straddles the three "ASEAN pillars", namely, security, economic and socio-cultural communities — with the environment being subsumed under the third of these mutually reinforcing pillars. It is not always easy to discern the interconnectedness of environment with other disciplines. For example, what has, ASEAN's interfaith initiatives to do with the environment? Not everyone knows that the Earth Charter, which is the ethical foundation of environmental sustainability, has had significant inputs and endorsement worldwide including from interfaith religious organizations. What is the relevance of the Treaty on the Southeast Asia Nuclear Weapon Free Zone, the ASEAN Convention on Counter Terrorism, cyber crime, the rights of women and migrants to the environment? They do have an impact on the environment in direct or tangential ways. The list goes on, so I will not belabour the point.

Volume I consists of two parts: Part I, *Setting the Stage for ASEAN Environmental Cooperation, Harmonization and Integration*-contains documents which are directly or indirectly related to or have a real or potential impact on the various aspects of environment. This section gives an overview of the various mutual reinforcing and interrelated documents on the environment. Part II, *General Legal Frameworks on the Environment:* Part A, deals with the general programmes, strategies, plans of action and blueprints; Part B covers general declarations, resolutions and accord. These are soft law instruments.

Volume II deals with sectoral areas including nature conservation and biodiversity; transboundary pollution; water resources management; animal and human health; and energy and climate change.

ASEAN has a vital role to play in shaping environmental law, policy and governance. It can facilitate and has facilitated the implementation of multinational environmental agreements. This requires greater cooperation and collaboration among its members, but is not easy for many reasons — not least because of new, emerging, and unchartered environmental issues, new scientific discoveries about the interconnectedness of environmental issues. There is inadequate coordination among ASEAN member states, as they still lack the experience in tackling environmental issues. However, the ASEAN legal frameworks such as programmes, plans of action, strategies, policies and a host of other initiatives in these two volumes provide the roadmap of the progress ASEAN has made over the last thirty years since environment was put on the agenda in 1978. These documents can point the way to the future and provide guidance for ASEAN to achieve its *Vision* 2020 of an ASEAN Community "clean and green … with fully established mechanisms for sustainable development to ensure the protection of the region's environment, the sustainability of its natural resources, and the high quality of life of its peoples." At the12th ASEAN Summit in 2006 it was decided to accelerate the ASEAN Community by 2015.

To achieve this *Vision,* capacity-building and research are critical to galvanize action to meet the challenges of sustainable development. The ASEAN Charter demonstrates that there is the political will to forge ahead with the three pillars, which include environment. If ASEAN is to play a meaningful role in the dynamics of participatory regionalism not only at the national level of its members but in a multi-polar world, we need to lay a strong foundation for understanding the ecological problems that ASEAN and the world faces today.

This publication is timely as the ASEAN Charter has entered into force since 15 December 2008. The $14^{th}$ ASEAN Summit was held from 27 February to 1 March 2009 in Cha-Am Hua Hin, Thailand. Some of the relevant documents from this Summit were just in time to be included in this volume I.

I hope this compilation will serve as a useful reference book and demonstrate the progressive development of environmental law in the areas of cooperation, harmonization and integration before ASEAN moves forward. Having these documents easily available is the first step in facilitating access to the materials now extant and in promoting awareness and interest in this area. In 2007, the ASEAN Declaration on Environmental Sustainability stated that ASEAN would contribute to the UN Decade on Education for Sustainable Development through the ASEAN Environmental Education Plan. Capacity-building and research are crucial, and for a start I will be offering an elective course by the same title at the Law Faculty, National University of Singapore, beginning in the second semester, January 2009.

# PART I

# SETTING THE STAGE FOR ASEAN ENVIRONMENTAL COOPERATION, HARMONIZATION AND INTEGRATION

# CHAPTER 1

# THE ASEAN DECLARATION

## (Bangkok Declaration)

### Bangkok, 8 August 1967

The Presidium Minister for Political Affairs/Minister for Foreign Affairs of Indonesia, the Deputy Prime Minister of Malaysia, the Secretary of Foreign Affairs of the Philippines, the Minister for Foreign Affairs of Singapore and the Minister of Foreign Affairs of Thailand:

**MINDFUL** of the existence of mutual interests and common problems among countries of South-East Asia and convinced of the need to strengthen further the existing bonds of regional solidarity and cooperation;

**DESIRING** to establish a firm foundation for common action to promote regional cooperation in South-East Asia in the spirit of equality and partnership and thereby contribute towards peace, progress and prosperity in the region;

**CONSCIOUS** that in an increasingly interdependent world, the cherished ideals of peace, freedom, social justice and economic well-being are best attained by fostering good understanding, good neighbourliness and meaningful cooperation among the countries of the region already bound together by ties of history and culture;

**CONSIDERING** that the countries of South-East Asia share a primary responsibility for strengthening the economic and social stability of the region and ensuring their peaceful and progressive national development, and that they are determined to ensure their stability and security from external interference in any form or manifestation in order to preserve their national identities in accordance with the ideals and aspirations of their peoples;

**AFFIRMING** that all foreign bases are temporary and remain only with the expressed concurrence of the countries concerned and are not intended to be used directly or indirectly to subvert the national independence and freedom of States in the area or prejudice the orderly processes of their national development;

## DO HEREBY DECLARE:

**FIRST**, the establishment of an Association for Regional Cooperation among the countries of South-East Asia to be known as the Association of South-East Asian Nations (ASEAN).

**SECOND**, that the aims and purposes of the Association shall be:

1. To accelerate the economic growth, social progress and cultural development in the region through joint endeavours in the spirit of equality and partnership in order to strengthen the foundation for a prosperous and peaceful community of South-East Asian Nations;
2. To promote regional peace and stability through abiding respect for justice and the rule of law in the relationship among countries of the region and adherence to the principles the United Nations Charter;
3. To promote active collaboration and mutual assistance on matters of common interest in the economic, social, cultural, technical, scientific and administrative fields;
4. To provide assistance to each other in the form of training and research facilities in the educational, professional, technical and administrative spheres;
5. To collaborate more effectively for the greater utilization of their agriculture and industries, the expansion of their trade, including the study of the problems of international commodity trade, the improvement of their transportation and communications facilities and the raising of the living standards of their peoples;
6. To promote South-East Asian studies;
7. To maintain close and beneficial cooperation with existing international and regional organizations with similar aims and purposes, and explore all avenues for even closer cooperation among themselves.

**THIRD**, that to carry out these aims and purposes, the following machinery shall be established:

(a) Annual Meeting of Foreign Ministers, which shall be by rotation and referred to as ASEAN Ministerial Meeting. Special Meetings of Foreign Ministers may be convened as required.
(b) A Standing committee, under the chairmanship of the Foreign Minister of the host country or his representative and having as its members the accredited Ambassadors of the other member countries, to carry on the work of the Association in between Meetings of Foreign Ministers.
(c) Ad-Hoc Committees and Permanent Committees of specialists and officials on specific subjects.

(d) A National Secretariat in each member country to carry out the work of the Association on behalf of that country and to service the Annual or Special Meetings of Foreign Ministers, the Standing Committee and such other committees as may hereafter be established.

**FOURTH**, that the Association is open for participation to all States in the South-East Asian Region subscribing to the aforementioned aims, principles and purposes.

**FIFTH**, that the Association represents the collective will of the nations of South-East Asia to bind themselves together in friendship and cooperation and, through joint efforts and sacrifices, secure for their peoples and for posterity the blessings of peace, freedom and prosperity.

**DONE** in Bangkok on the Eighth Day of August in the Year One Thousand Nine Hundred and Sixty-Seven.

**For the Republic of Indonesia :**

**ADAM MALIK**
**Presidium Minister for Political**
**Minister for Foreign Affairs**

**For the Republic of Singapore :**

**S. RAJARATNAM**
**Minister of Foreign Affairs**

**For Malaysia :**

**TUN ABDUL RAZAK**
**Deputy Prime Minister,**
**Minister of Defence and**
**Minister of National Development**

**For the Kingdom of Thailand :**

**THANAT KHOMAN**
**Minister of Foreign Affairs**

**For the Republic of the Philippines :**

**NARCISO RAMOS**
**Secretary of Foreign Affairs**

Source: http://www.aseansec.org/1212.htm
Accessed date: 26 January 2006
Publisher: ASEAN Secretariat
Country: Jakarta
Date of Publication: 2004

# CHAPTER 2

# DECLARATION OF ASEAN CONCORD

**Indonesia, 24 February 1976**

The President of the Republic of Indonesia, the Prime Minister of Malaysia, the President of the Republic of the Philippines, the Prime Minister of the Republic of Singapore and the Prime Minister of the Kingdom of Thailand:

**REAFFIRM** their commitment to the Declarations of Bandung, Bangkok and Kuala Lumpur, and the Charter of the United Nations;

**ENDEAVOUR** to promote peace, progress, prosperity and the welfare of the peoples of member states;

**UNDERTAKE** to consolidate the achievements of ASEAN and expand ASEAN cooperation in the economic, social, cultural and political fields;

## DO HEREBY DECLARE:

ASEAN cooperation shall take into account, among others, the following objectives and principles in the pursuit of political stability:

1. The stability of each member state and of the ASEAN region is an essential contribution to international peace and security. Each member state resolves to eliminate threats posed by subversion to its stability, thus strengthening national and ASEAN resilience.
2. Member states, individually and collectively, shall take active steps for the early establishment of the Zone of Peace, Freedom and Neutrality.
3. The elimination of poverty, hunger, disease and illiteracy is a primary concern of member states. They shall therefore intensify cooperation in economic and social development, with particular emphasis on the promotion of social justice and on the improvement of the living standards of their peoples.
4. Natural disasters and other major calamities can retard the pace of development of member states. They shall extend, within their capabilities, assistance for relief of member states in distress.

5. Member states shall take cooperative action in their national and regional development programmes, utilizing as far as possible the resources available in the ASEAN region to broaden the complementarity of their respective economies.
6. Member states, in the spirit of ASEAN solidarity, shall rely exclusively on peaceful processes in the settlement of intra-regional differences.
7. Member states shall strive, individually and collectively, to create conditions conducive to the promotion of peaceful cooperation among the nations of Southeast Asia on the basis of mutual respect and mutual benefit.
8. Member states shall vigorously develop an awareness of regional identity and exert all efforts to create a strong ASEAN community, respected by all and respecting all nations on the basis of mutually advantageous relationships, and in accordance with the principles of self-determination, sovereign equality and non-interference in the internal affairs of nations.

## AND DO HEREBY ADOPT

The following programme of action as a framework for ASEAN cooperation:

### A. Political

1. Meeting of the Heads of Government of the member states as and when necessary.
2. Signing of the Treaty of Amity and Cooperation in Southeast Asia.
3. Settlement of intra-regional disputes by peaceful means as soon as possible.
4. Immediate consideration of initial steps towards recognition of and respect for the Zone of Peace, Freedom and Neutrality wherever possible.
5. Improvement of ASEAN machinery to strengthen political cooperation.
6. Study on how to develop judicial cooperation including the possibility of an ASEAN Extradition Treaty.
7. Strengthening of political solidarity by promoting the harmonization of views, coordinating position and, where possible and desirable, taking common actions.

### B. Economic

1. Cooperation on Basic Commodities, particularly Food and Energy

   i) Member states shall assist each other by according priority to the supply of the individual country's needs in critical circumstances, and priority to the acquisition of exports from member states, in respect of basic commodities, particularly food and energy.

ii) Member states shall also intensify cooperation in the production of basic commodities particularly food and energy in the individual member states of the region.

2. Industrial Cooperation

i) Member states shall cooperate to establish large-scale ASEAN industrial plants particularly to meet regional requirements of essential commodities.
ii) Priority shall be given to projects which utilize the available materials in the member states, contribute to the increase of food production, increase foreign exchange earnings or save foreign exchange and create employment.

3. Cooperation in Trade

i) Member states shall cooperate in the fields of trade in order to promote development and growth of new production and trade and to improve the trade structures of individual states and among countries of ASEAN conducive to further development and to safeguard and increase their foreign exchange earnings and reserves.
ii) Member states shall progress towards the establishment of preferential trading arrangements as a long term objective on a basis deemed to be at any particular time appropriate through rounds of negotiations subject to the unanimous agreement of member states.
iii) The expansion of trade among member states shall be facilitated through cooperation on basic commodities, particularly in food and energy and through cooperation in ASEAN industrial projects.
iv) Member states shall accelerate joint efforts to improve access to markets outside ASEAN for their raw material and finished products by seeking the elimination of all trade barriers in those markets, developing new usage for these products and in adopting common approaches and actions in dealing with regional groupings and individual economic powers.
v) Such efforts shall also lead to cooperation in the field of technology and production methods in order to increase the production and to improve the quality of export products, as well as to develop new export products with a view to diversifying exports.

4. Joint Approach to International Commodity Problems and Other World Economic Problems

i) The principle of ASEAN cooperation on trade shall also be reflected on a priority basis in joint approaches to international commodity problems and other world economic problems such as the reform of international trading system, the reform on international monetary system and transfer of real resources, in the United Nations and other relevant multilateral fora, with a view to contributing to the establishment of the New International Economic Order.

ii) Member states shall give priority to the stabilisation and increase of export earnings of those commodities produced and exported by them through commodity agreements including bufferstock schemes and other means.

5. Machinery for Economic Cooperation

Ministerial meetings on economic matters shall be held regularly or as deemed necessary in order to:

i) formulate recommendations for the consideration of Governments of member states for the strengthening of ASEAN economic cooperation;
ii) review the coordination and implementation of agreed ASEAN programmes and project on economic cooperation;
iii) exchange views and consult on national development plans and policies as a step towards harmonizing regional development; and
iv) perform such other relevant functions as agreed upon by the member Governments.

## C. Social

1. Cooperation in the field of social development, with emphasis on the well being of the low-income group and of the rural population, through the expansion of opportunities for productive employment with fair remuneration.
2. Support for the active involvement of all sectors and levels of the ASEAN communities, particularly the women and youth, in development efforts.
3. Intensification and expansion of existing cooperation in meeting the problems of population growth in the ASEAN region, and where possible, formulation of new strategies in collaboration with appropriate international agencies.
4. Intensification of cooperation among member states as well as with the relevant international bodies in the prevention and eradication of the abuse of narcotics and the illegal trafficking of drugs.

## D. Cultural and Information

1. Introduction of the study of ASEAN, its member states and their national languages as part of the curricula of schools and other institutions of learning in the member states.
2. Support of ASEAN scholars, writers, artists and mass media representatives to enable them to play an active role in fostering a sense of regional identity and fellowship.

3. Promotion of Southeast Asian studies through closer collaboration among national institutes.

## E. Security

Continuation of cooperation on a non-ASEAN basis between the member states in security matters in accordance with their mutual needs and interests.

## F. Improvement of Asean Machinery

1. Signing of the Agreement on the Establishment of the ASEAN Secretariat.
2. Regular review of the ASEAN organizational structure with a view to improving its effectiveness.
3. Study of the desirability of a new constitutional framework for ASEAN.

**DONE** at Denpasar, Bali this Twenty-Fourth Day of February in the year One Thousand Nine Hundred and Seventy-Six.

**For the Republic of Indonesia:**

**SOEHARTO**
**President**

**For the Republic of Singapore:**

**LEE KUAN YEW**
**Prime Minister**

**For Malaysia:**

**DATUK HUSEIN ONN**
**Prime Minister**

**For the Kingdom of Thailand:**

**KUKRIT PRAMOJ**
**Prime Minister**

**For the Republic of the Philippines:**

**FERDINAND E. MARCOS**

Source: http://www.aseansec.org/1216.htm
Accessed date: 26 January 2006
Publisher: ASEAN Secretariat
Country: Jakarta
Date of Publication: 2004

# CHAPTER 3

# TREATY OF AMITY AND COOPERATION IN SOUTHEAST ASIA

**Indonesia, 24 February 1976**

The High Contracting Parties:

**CONSCIOUS** of the existing ties of history, geography and culture, which have bound their peoples together;

**ANXIOUS** to promote regional peace and stability through abiding respect for justice and the rule or law and enhancing regional resilience in their relations;

**DESIRING** to enhance peace, friendship and mutual cooperation on matters affecting Southeast Asia consistent with the spirit and principles of the Charter of the United Nations, the Ten Principles adopted by the Asian-African Conference in Bandung on 25 April 1955, the Declaration of the Association of Southeast Asian Nations signed in Bangkok on 8 August 1967, and the Declaration signed in Kuala Lumpur on 27 November 1971;

**CONVINCED** that the settlement of differences or disputes between their countries should be regulated by rational, effective and sufficiently flexible procedures, avoiding negative attitudes which might endanger or hinder cooperation;

**BELIEVING** in the need for cooperation with all peace-loving nations, both within and outside Southeast Asia, in the furtherance of world peace, stability and harmony;

**SOLEMNLY AGREE** to enter into a Treaty of Amity and Cooperation as follows:

## CHAPTER I: PURPOSE AND PRINCIPLES

### Article 1

The purpose of this Treaty is to promote perpetual peace, everlasting amity and cooperation among their peoples which would contribute to their strength, solidarity and closer relationship.

### Article 2

In their relations with one another, the High Contracting Parties shall be guided by the following fundamental principles:

a. Mutual respect for the independence, sovereignty, equality, territorial integrity and national identity of all nations;
b. The right of every State to lead its national existence free from external interference, subversion or coersion;
c. Non-interference in the internal affairs of one another;
d. Settlement of differences or disputes by peaceful means;
e. Renunciation of the threat or use of force;
f. Effective cooperation among themselves.

## CHAPTER II: AMITY

### Article 3

In pursuance of the purpose of this Treaty the High Contracting Parties shall endeavour to develop and strengthen the traditional, cultural and historical ties of friendship, good neighbourliness and cooperation which bind them together and shall fulfill in good faith the obligations assumed under this Treaty. In order to promote closer understanding among them, the High Contracting Parties shall encourage and facilitate contact and intercourse among their peoples.

## CHAPTER III: COOPERATION

### Article 4

The High Contracting Parties shall promote active cooperation in the economic, social, technical, scientific and administrative fields as well as in matters of common ideals and aspirations of international peace and stability in the region and all other matters of common interest.

### Article 5

Pursuant to Article 4 the High Contracting Parties shall exert their maximum efforts multilaterally as well as bilaterally on the basis of equality, non-discrimination and mutual benefit.

## Article 6

The High Contracting Parties shall collaborate for the acceleration of the economic growth in the region in order to strengthen the foundation for a prosperous and peaceful community of nations in Southeast Asia. To this end, they shall promote the greater utilization of their agriculture and industries, the expansion of their trade and the improvement of their economic infrastructure for the mutual benefit of their peoples. In this regard, they shall continue to explore all avenues for close and beneficial cooperation with other States as well as international and regional organisations outside the region.

## Article 7

The High Contracting Parties, in order to achieve social justice and to raise the standards of living of the peoples of the region, shall intensify economic cooperation. For this purpose, they shall adopt appropriate regional strategies for economic development and mutual assistance.

## Article 8

The High Contracting Parties shall strive to achieve the closest cooperation on the widest scale and shall seek to provide assistance to one another in the form of training and research facilities in the social, cultural, technical, scientific and administrative fields.

## Article 9

The High Contracting Parties shall endeavour to foster cooperation in the furtherance of the cause of peace, harmony, and stability in the region. To this end, the High Contracting Parties shall maintain regular contacts and consultations with one another on international and regional matters with a view to coordinating their view, actions and policies.

## Article 10

Each High Contracting Party shall not in any manner or form participate in any activity which shall constitute a threat to the political and economic stability, sovereignty, or territorial integrity of another High Contracting Party.

## Article 11

The High Contracting Parties shall endeavour to strengthen their respective national resilience in their political, economic, socio-cultural as well as security fields in conformity with their respective ideals and aspirations, free from external interference as well as internal subversive activities in order to preserve their respective national identities.

## Article 12

The High Contracting Parties in their efforts to achieve regional prosperity and security, shall endeavour to cooperate in all fields for the promotion of regional resilience, based on the principles of self-confidence, self-reliance, mutual respect, cooperation and solidarity which will constitute the foundation for a strong and viable community of nations in Southeast Asia.

# CHAPTER IV: PACIFIC SETTLEMENT OF DISPUTES

## Article 13

The High Contracting Parties shall have the determination and good faith to prevent disputes from arising. In case disputes on matters directly affecting them should arise, especially disputes likely to disturb regional peace and harmony, they shall refrain from the threat or use of force and shall at all times settle such disputes among themselves through friendly negotiations.

## Article 14

To settle disputes through regional processes, the High Contracting Parties shall constitute, as a continuing body, a High Council comprising a Representative at ministerial level from each of the High Contracting Parties to take cognizance of the existence of disputes or situations likely to disturb regional peace and harmony.

## Article 15

In the event no solution is reached through direct negotiations, the High Council shall take cognizance of the dispute or the situation and shall recommend to the parties in dispute appropriate means of settlement such as good offices, mediation, inquiry or conciliation. The High Council may however offer its good offices, or upon agreement of the parties in dispute, constitute itself into a committee of mediation, inquiry or conciliation. When deemed necessary, the High Council shall recommend appropriate measures for the prevention of a deterioration of the dispute or the situation.

### Article 16

The foregoing provision of this Chapter shall not apply to a dispute unless all the parties to the dispute agree to their application to that dispute. However, this shall not preclude the other High Contracting Parties not party to the dispute from offering all possible assistance to settle the said dispute. Parties to the dispute should be well disposed towards such offers of assistance.

### Article 17

Nothing in this Treaty shall preclude recourse to the modes of peaceful settlement contained in Article 33(l) of the Charter of the United Nations. The High Contracting Parties which are parties to a dispute should be encouraged to take initiatives to solve it by friendly negotiations before resorting to the other procedures provided for in the Charter of the United Nations.

## CHAPTER V: GENERAL PROVISION

### Article 18

This Treaty shall be signed by the Republic of Indonesia, Malaysia, the Republic of the Philippines, the Republic of Singapore and the Kingdom of Thailand. It shall be ratified in accordance with the constitutional procedures of each signatory State. It shall be open for accession by other States in Southeast Asia.

### Article 19

This Treaty shall enter into force on the date of the deposit of the fifth instrument of ratification with the Governments of the signatory States which are designated Depositories of this Treaty and the instruments of ratification or accession.

### Article 20

This Treaty is drawn up in the official languages of the High Contracting Parties, all of which are equally authoritative. There shall be an agreed common translation of the texts in the English language. Any divergent interpretation of the common text shall be settled by negotiation.

IN FAITH THEREOF the High Contracting Parties have signed the Treaty and have hereto affixed their Seals.

**DONE** at Denpaser, Bali, this twenty-fourth day of February in the year one thousand nine hundred and seventy-six.

**For the Republic of Indonesia:**

**SOEHARTO**
**President**

**For the Republic of Singapore:**

**LEE KUAN YEW**
**Prime Minister**

**For Malaysia:**

**DATUK HUSEIN ONN**
**Prime Minister**

**For the Kingdom of Thailand:**

**KUKRIT PRAMOJ**
**Prime Minister**

**For the Republic of the Philippines:**

**FERDINAND E. MARCOS**

Source: http://www.aseansec.grg/1217.htm
Accessed date: 25 January 2006
Publisher: ASEAN Secretariat
Country: Jakarta
Date of Publication: 2004

# PROTOCOL AMENDING THE TREATY OF AMITY AND COOPERATION IN SOUTHEAST ASIA

**Philippines, 15 December 1987**

The Government of Brunei Darussalam
The Government of the Republic of Indonesia
The Government of Malaysia
The Government of the Republic of the Philippines
The Government of the Republic of Singapore
The Government of the Kingdom of Thailand

**DESIRING** to further enhance cooperation with all peace-loving nations, both within and outside Southeast Asia and, in particular, neighbouring States of the Southeast Asia region

**CONSIDERING** Paragraph 5 of the preamble of the Treaty of Amity and Cooperation in Southeast Asia, done at Denpasar, Bali, on 24 February 1976 (hereinafter referred to as the Treaty of Amity) which refers to the need for cooperation with all peace-loving nations, both within and outside Southeast Asia, in the furtherance of world peace, stability and harmony.

## HEREBY AGREE TO THE FOLLOWING:

### Article 1

Article 18 of the Treaty of Amity shall be amended to read as follows:

> "This Treaty shall be signed by the Republic of Indonesia, Malaysia, the Republic of the Philippines, the Republic of Singapore and the Kingdom of Thailand. It shall be ratified in accordance with the constitutional procedures of each signatory State.
>
> It shall be open for accession by other States in Southeast Asia.
>
> States outside Southeast Asia may also accede to this Treaty by the consent of all the States in Southeast Asia which are signatories to this Treaty and Brunei Darussalam."

## Article 2

Article 14 of the Treaty of Amity shall be amended to read as follows:

> "To settle disputes through regional processes, the High Contracting Parties shall constitute, as a continuing body, a High Council comprising a Representative at ministerial level from each of the High Contracting Parties to take cognizance of the existence of disputes or situations likely to disturb regional peace and harmony.
>
> However, this article shall apply to any of the States outside Southeast Asia which have acceded to the Treaty only in cases where that state is directly involved in the dispute to be settled through the regional processes."

## Article 3

This Protocol shall be subject to ratification and shall come into force on the date the last instrument of ratification of the High Contracting Parties is deposited.

**DONE** at Manila, the fifteenth day of December in the year one thousand nine hundred and eighty-seven.

For Brunei Darussalam :

**PRINCE HAJI MOHAMED BOLKIAH**
Minister of Foreign Affairs

For the Republic of the Philippines :

**RAUL S. MANGLAPUS**
Secretary for Foreign Affairs

For the Republic of Indonesia :

**PROF. DR. MOCHTAR KUSUMAATMADJA**
Minister of Foreign Affairs

For the Republic of Singapore :

**S. DHANABALAN**
Minister of Foreign Affairs

For Malaysia :

**DATO HAJI ABU HASAN HAJI OMAR**
Minister of Foreign Affairs

For the Kingdom of Thailand :

**AIR CHIEF MARSHALL SIDDHI SAVETSILA**
Minister of Foreign Affairs

Source: http://www.aseansec.org/1218.htm
Accessed Date: 19 May 2006
Publisher: ASEAN Secretariat
Country: ASEAN Member States
Date of Publication: 2004

# SECOND PROTOCOL AMENDING THE TREATY OF AMITY AND COOPERATION IN SOUTHEAST ASIA

**Manila, Philippines, 25 July 1998**

The Government of Brunei Darussalam
The Government of the Kingdom of Cambodia
The Government of the Republic of Indonesia
The Government of the Lao People's Democratic Republic
The Government of Malaysia
The Government of the Union of Myanmar
The Government of the Republic of the Philippines
The Government of the Republic of Singapore
The Government of the Kingdom of Thailand
The Government of the Socialist Republic of Vietnam
The Government of Papua New Guinea

Hereinafter referred to as the High Contracting Parties:

**DESIRING** to ensure that there is appropriate enhancement of cooperation with all peace-loving nations, both within and outside Southeast Asia and, in particular, neighboring States of the Southeast Asia region;

**CONSIDERING** Paragraph 5 of the preamble of the Treaty of Amity and Cooperation in Southeast Asia, done at Denpasar, Bali, on 24 February 1976 (hereinafter referred to as the Treaty of Amity) which refers to the need for cooperation with all peace-loving nations, both within and outside Southeast Asia, in the furtherance of world peace, stability and harmony.

## HEREBY AGREE TO THE FOLLOWING:

### Article 1

Article 18, Paragraph 3, of the Treaty of Amity shall be amended to read as follows:

> "States outside Southeast Asia may also accede to this Treaty with the consent of all the States in Southeast Asia, namely, Brunei Darussalam,

the Kingdom of Cambodia, the Republic of Indonesia, the Lao People's Democratic Republic, Malaysia, the Union of Myanmar, the Republic of the Philippines, the Republic of Singapore, the Kingdom of Thailand and the Socialist Republic of Vietnam."

## Article 2

This Protocol shall be subject to ratification and shall come into force on the date the last instrument of ratification of the High Contracting Parties is deposited.

**DONE** at Manila, the twenty-fifth day of July in the year one thousand nine hundred and ninety-eight.

**For Brunei Darussalam :**

**PRINCE MOHAMED BOLKIAH**
**Minister of Foreign Affairs**

**For the Kingdom of Cambodia :**

**CHEM WIDHYA**
**Special Envoy of the**
**Royal Government of Cambodia**

**For the Republic of Indonesia :**

**ALI ALATAS**
**Minister for Foreign Affairs**

**For the Lao People's Democratic Republic :**

**SOMSAVAT LENGSAVAD**
**Deputy Prime Minister and**
**Minister of Foreign Affairs**

**For Malaysia :**

**DATUK SERI ABDULLAH**
**HAJI AHMAD BADAWI**
**Minister of Foreign Affairs**

**For the Union of Myanmar :**

**U OHN GYAW**
**Minister for Foreign Affairs**

**For the Republic of the Philippines :**

**DOMINGO L SIAZON, JR.**
**Secretary of Foreign Affairs**

**For the Republic of Singapore :**

**S JAYAKUMAR**
**Minister for Foreign Affairs**

**For the Kingdom of Thailand :**

**SURIN PITSUWAN**
**Minister of Foreign Affairs**

**For the Socialist Republic of Vietnam :**

**NGUYEN MANH CAM**
**Deputy Prime Minister and**
**Minister of Foreign Affairs**

**For Papua New Guinea :**

**ROY YAKI**
**Minister of Foreign Affairs**

Source: http://www.aseansec.org/702.htm
Accessed date: 3 March 2009
Country: Jakarta
Date of Publication: 2007

# CHAPTER 4

## MANILA DECLARATION

**Philippines, 15 December 1987**

The Sultan and Yang Di-Pertuan of Negara Brunei Darussalam, the President of the Republic of Indonesia, the Prime Minister of Malaysia, the President of the Republic of the Philippines, the Prime Minister of the Republic of Singapore, and the Prime Minister of the Kingdom of Thailand;

**REAFFIRMING** their commitment to the ASEAN Declaration, the Declaration of ASEAN Concord, the Declaration of the Zone of Peace, Freedom and Neutrality of 1971, and the 1977 accord of Kuala Lumpur;

**ENCOURAGED** by the achievements of ASEAN in the last two decades, particularly in creating a political environment conducive to the development of its members, and in carving out a distinct identity recognized and respected in the community of nations;

**HAVING** reviewed the current international political and economic situation and having considered the implications for ASEAN of changes over the last decade;

**CONVINCED** that economic development and progress are fundamental to the stability and security of the region;

**MOVED** by an abiding faith in the capabilities of their peoples and the potentials for growth of their nations, and by a deep hope in the future of ASEAN;

**ENDEAVOURING** to advance the achievements of ASEAN as a dynamic and cohesive, regional association of states for the well-being of its peoples;

### DO HEREBY DECLARE:

1. Member states shall strengthen national and regional resilience to ensure security, stability and growth in the ASEAN region.
2. ASEAN regionalism founded upon political, economic, and cultural cohesion is more vital than ever for the future of Southeast Asia.

3. ASEAN shall pursue regional solidarity and cooperation under all circumstances, especially whenever pressures and tensions of any kind, arising from within the region or from without, challenge the capacities, resourcefulness, and goodwill of the ASEAN nations.
4. Intra-regional disputes shall be settled by peaceful means in accordance with the spirit of the Treaty of Amity and Cooperation in Southeast Asia and the United Nations Charter.
5. While each member state shall be responsible for its own security, cooperation on a non-ASEAN basis among the member states in security matters shall continue to accordance with their mutual needs and interests.
6. Member states shall strengthen intra-ASEAN economic cooperation to maximize the realization of the region's potential in trade and development and to increase ASEAN's efficacy in combating protectionism and countering its effects.
7. Member states shall encourage an environment in which the private sector can play an increasing role in economic development and in intra-ASEAN cooperation.
8. ASEAN functional cooperation shall promote, increased awareness of ASEAN, wider involvement and increased participation and cooperation by the peoples of ASEAN, and development of human resources.

## AND DO HEREBY AGREE AS FOLLOWS:

### Political cooperation

1. ASEAN solidarity shall be strengthened through the adoption of common stands an collective actions on matters vital to ASEAN cohesion and resilience and through coordination on matters of common interest at the international level.
2. ASEAN shall intensify all efforts towards achieving the early realization of a Zone of Peace, Freedom and Neutrality in Southeast Asia (ZOPFAN) in consultation with states outside ASEAN.
3. ASEAN shall intensify its efforts toward early establishment of a Southeast Asia Nuclear Weapon Free Zone (SEANWFZ), including continuation of the consideration of all as relating to the establishment of the Zone and of an appropriate instrument to establish the Zone.
4. ASEAN shall promote and develop cooperation with states in the Pacific region, both the industrialized and developing states, in recognition of

its increasing dynamism and potential. Relations with the developing countries in the region could also be fostered in the context of Soutt-South cooperation.

## Economic cooperation

5. To intensify efforts toward significant expansion of intra-ASEAN trade, ASEAN shall adopt and carry out a package of measures for the improvement of the Preferential Trading Arrangements (PTA). Such measures shall include the progressive reduction in the number of items in the member-countries' exclusion lists and the deepening of the margin of preference for items currently in the PTA. ASEAN shall also relax ASEAN-content requirement in the Rules of Origin on a case-by-case basis. The standstill of non-tariff barriers (NTBs) shall be implemented and the rollback of NTBs negotiated as soon as possible after the Manila Meeting of Heads of Government.
6. In the area of intra-ASEAN cooperate commodities, ASEAN shall take joint action to address problems of structural surpluses, seek greater market shares, develop indigenous resource-based industries, intensify research and development (R&D) programmes and encourage the establishment of producer associations, regional trade associations and commodity exchanges.
7. ASEAN shall encourage intra-ASEAN travel and develop a viable and competitive tourist industry. The year 1992, the 25th Anniversary Year of ASEAN, is declared as "Visit ASEAN Year".
8. ASEAN shall enhance cooperation in the field of energy, including energy planning, exchange of information, transfer of technology, research and development, manpower training, conservation and efficiency, and the exploration production and supply of energy resources.

....

10. ASEAN cooperation in food, agriculture and forestry shall be aimed at improving the standard of living in the agricultural and forestry sectors; sustaining adequate supply of basic agricultural and forestry commodities to meet regional needs; and reducing the differences in agricultural and forestry structures in the region. Future cooperative efforts shall be geared towards greater private sector involvement and more emphasis on human resources development of farmers, fishermen and forestry workers.

## Relationship with dialogue partners

11. While ASEAN's dialogues with Australia, Canada, the European Community, Japan, New Zealand and the United States have covered wide areas, member states shall further emphasize market access, trade and tourism promotion, investments, flow of resources, industrial development, transfer of technology, human resources development, and support for ASEAN positions in international fora. ASEAN's dialogues with these countries should be kept under review to meet these objectives.

## Functional cooperation

12. Member states shall, through education, institutional linkages, and improved flow of information, seek to enhance awareness of ASEAN, inculcate in the people the common socio-economic values and heritage, and promote mutual understanding of the culture, traditions and ways of life of their nations.
13. Intra-ASEAN functional cooperation shall be designed for a wider involvement and increased participation by the women and youth, as well as Non-Governmental Organizations, Inter-Governmental Organizations and ASEAN Inter-Parliamentary Organization.
14. ASEAN shall intensify its cooperation on health, drug abuse prevention and combatting illicit trafficking in drugs, labour, law, population, child survival and welfare, socio-cultural programmes, and science and technology.
15. In the area of environment, ASEAN shall cooperate in promoting the principle of sustainable development and systematically integrating it into all aspects of development and shall focus on the need for policy guidelines to protect ASEAN's common resources and environment.
16. ASEAN shall emphasize developing an intelligent and highly productive workforce by increasing investment in science and technology and by providing effective training in order to facilitate effective transfer of technology.

## Machinery for ASEAN Cooperation

17. The ASEAN organizational structure will continually be improved with a view to enhancing its effectiveness.

**DONE** in the City of Manila of the Philippines, this Fifteenth Day of December in the Year One Thousand Nine Hundred and Eighty-Seven, the twentieth year of the Association of Southeast Asian Nations.

**For Negara Brunei Darussalam :**

**SULTAN HAJI HASSANAL BOLKIAH**
**Sultan and Yang Di-Pertuan**

**For the Republic Of Indonesia :**

**SOEHARTO**
**President**

**For Malaysia :**

**DATUK SERI DR. MAHATHIR MOHAMAD**
**Prime Minister**

**For the Repuublic of the Philippines :**

**CORAZON C. AQUINO**
**President**

**For the Republic of Singapore :**

**LEE KUAN YEW**
**Prime Minister**

**For the Kingdom of Thailand**

**GENERAL PREM TINSULANONDA**
**Prime Minister**

Source: http://www.aseansec.org/5117.htm
Accessed date: 3 March 2006
Publisher: ASEAN Secretariat
Country: Jakarta
Date of Publication: 2003

# CHAPTER 5

# CHAIRMAN'S STATEMENT OF THE FIRST MEETING OF THE ASEAN REGIONAL FORUM

**Bangkok, 25 July 1994**

1. The First Meeting of the ASEAN Regional Forum (ARF) was held in Bangkok on 25 July 1994 in accordance with the 1992 Singapore Declaration of the Fourth ASEAN Summit, whereby the ASEAN Heads of State and Government proclaimed their intent to intensify ASEAN's external dialogues in political and security matters as a means of building cooperative ties with states in the Asia-Pacific region.
2. Attending the Meeting were the Foreign Ministers of ASEAN, ASEAN's Dialogue Partners, ASEAN's Consultative Partners, and ASEAN's Observers or their representatives. The Minister of Foreign Affairs of Thailand, served as Chairman of the Meeting.
3. Being the first time ever that high-ranking representatives from the majority of states in the Asia-Pacific region came to specifically discuss political and security cooperation issues, the Meeting was considered a historic event for the region. More importantly, the Meeting signified the opening of a new chapter of peace, stability and cooperation for Southeast Asia.
4. The participants of the Meeting held a productive exchange of views on the current political and security situation in the Asia-Pacific region, recognizing that developments in one part of the region could have an impact on the security of the region as whole. It was agreed that, as a high-level consultative forum, the ARF had enabled the countries in the Asia-Pacific region to foster the habit of constructive dialogue and consultation on political and security issues of common interest and concern. In this respect, the ARF would be in a position to make significant contributions to efforts towards confidence-building and preventive diplomacy in the Asia-Pacific region.
5. Bearing in mind the importance of non-proliferation of nuclear weapons in the maintenance of international peace and security, the Meeting welcomed the continuation of US-DPRK negotiation and endorsed the early resumption of inter-Korean dialogue.

6. The Meeting agreed to:

   - convene the ARF on an annual basis and hold the second meeting in Brunei Darussalam in 1995; and
   - endorse the purposes and principles of ASEAN's Treaty of Amity and Cooperation in Southeast Asia, as a code of conduct governing relations between states and a unique diplomatic instrument for regional confidence-building, preventive diplomacy, and political and security cooperation.

7. The Meeting also agreed to entrust the next Chairman of the ARF Brunei Darussalam, working in consultation with ARF participants a appropriate, to:

   - collate and study all papers and ideas raised during the ARF Senior Officials Meeting and the ARF in Bangkok for submission to the second ARF through the second ARF-SOM, both of which to be held in Brunei Darussalam. Ideas which might be the subjects of such further study including confidence and security building, nuclear non-proliferation, peacekeeping cooperation including regional peacekeeping training centre, exchanges of non classified military information, maritime security issues, and preventive diplomacy;
   - study the comprehensive concept of security, including its economic and social aspects, as it pertains to the Asia-Pacific region;
   - study other relevant internationally recognized norms and principles pertaining to international and regional political and security cooperation for their possible contribution to regional political and security cooperation;
   - promote the eventual participation of all ARF countries in the UN Conventional Arms Register; and
   - convene, if necessary, informal meetings of officials to study all relevant papers and suggestions to move the ARF process forward.

8. Recognizing the need to develop a more predictable constructive pattern of relationships for the Asia-Pacific region, the Meeting expressed its firm conviction to continue to work towards the strengths and the enhancement of political and security cooperation within the region as a means of ensuring a lasting peace, stability, and prosperity for the region and its peoples.

## NOTE

ASEAN consists of Brunei Darussalam, Indonesia, Malaysia, Philippines, Singapore, and Thailand. ASEAN's Dialogue Partners are: Australia, Canada, the European Union, Japan, New Zealand, Republic of Korea, and the United States.

ASEAN's Consultative Partners are China and Russia. And, ASEAN's Observers are Laos, Papua New Guinea, and Vietnam.

Source: http://www.aseansec.org/3621.htm
Accessed date: 13 November 2008
Publisher: ASEAN Secretariat
Country: Jakarta
Date of Publication: 2004

# ANNEX

## PROCEDURE FOR A FACT-FINDING MISSION

1. The State Party requesting a fact-finding mission as provided in Article 13, hereinafter referred to as the "requesting State", shall submit the request to the Executive Committee specifying the following:

   (a) the doubts or concerns and the reasons for such doubts or concerns;
   (b) the location in which the situation which gives rise to doubts has allegedly occurred;
   (c) the relevant provisions of this Treaty about which doubts of compliance have arisen; and
   (d) any other relevant information.

2. Upon receipt of a request for a fact-finding mission, the Executive Committee shall:

   (a) immediately inform the State Party to which the fact-finding mission is requested to be sent, hereinafter referred to as the "receiving State", about the receipt of the request; and
   (b) not later than 3 weeks after receiving the request, decide if the request complies with the provisions of Paragraph 1 and whether or not it is frivolous, abusive or clearly beyond the scope of this Treaty. Neither the requesting nor receiving State Party shall participate in such decisions.

3. In case the Executive Committee decides that the request does not comply with the provisions of Paragraph 1, or that it is frivolous, abusive or clearly beyond the scope of this Treaty, it shall take no further action on the request and inform the requesting State and the receiving State accordingly.
4. In the event that the Executive Committee decides that the request complies with the provisions of Paragraph 1, and that it is not frivolous, abusive or clearly beyond the scope this Treaty, it shall immediately forward the request for a fact-finding mission to the receiving State, indicating, inter alia, the proposed date for sending the mission. The proposed date shall not be later than 3 weeks from the time the receiving State receives the request for a fact-finding mission. The Executive Committee shall also immediately set up a fact-finding

mission consisting of 3 inspectors from the IAEA who are neither nationals of the requesting nor receiving State.

5. The receiving State shall comply with the request for a fact-finding mission referred to in Paragraph 4. It shall cooperate with the Executive Committee in order to facilitate the effective functioning of the fact-finding mission, inter alia, by promptly providing unimpeded access of the fact-finding mission to the location in question. The receiving State shall accord to the members of the fact-finding mission such privileges and immunities as are necessary for them to exercise their functions effectively, including inviolability of all papers and documents and immunity from arrest, detention and legal process for acts done and words spoken for the purpose of the mission.
6. The receiving State shall have the right to take measures to protect sensitive installations and to prevent disclosures of confidential information and date not related to this Treaty.
7. The fact-finding mission, in the discharge of its functions, shall:

   (a) respect the laws and regulations of the receiving State;
   (b) refrain from activities inconsistent with the objectives and purposes of this Treaty;
   (c) submit preliminary or interim reports to the Executive Committee; and
   (d) complete its task without undue delay and shall submit its final report to the Executive Committee within a reasonable time upon completion of its work.

8. The Executive Committee shall:

   (a) consider the reports submitted by the fact-finding mission and reach a decision on whether or not there is a breach of this Treaty;
   (b) immediately communicate its decision to the requesting State and the receiving State; and
   (c) present a full report on its decision to the Commission.

9. In the event that the receiving State refuses to comply with the request for a fact-finding mission in accordance with Paragraph 4, the requesting State through the Executive Committee shall have the right to request for a meeting of the Commission. The Executive Committee shall immediately request the Commission to convene a meeting in accordance with Paragraph 3(e) of Article 9.

## PROTOCOL TO THE TREATY ON SOUTHEAST ASIA NUCLEAR WEAPON-FREE ZONE

The States Parties to this Protocol,

Desiring to contribute to efforts towards achieving general and complete disarmament of nuclear weapons, and thereby ensuring international peace and security, including in Southeast Asia;

Noting the Treaty on the Southeast Asia Nuclear Weapon-Free Zone, signed at Bangkok on the fifteenth day of December, one thousand nine hundred and ninety-five;

Have agreed as follows:

### Article 1

Each State Party undertakes to respect the Treaty on the Southeast Asia Nuclear Weapon-Free Zone, hereinafter referred to as the "Treaty", and not to contribute to any act which constitutes a violation of the Treaty or its Protocol by States Parties to them.

### Article 2

Each State Party undertakes not to use or threaten to use nuclear weapons against any State Party to the Treaty. It further undertakes not to use or threaten to use nuclear weapons within the Southeast Asia Nuclear Weapons-Free Zone.

### Article 3

This Protocol shall be open for signature by the People's Republic of China, the French Republic, the Russian Federation, the United Kingdom of Great Britain and Northern Ireland and the United States of America.

### Article 4

Each State Party undertakes, by written notification to the Depositary State, to indicate its acceptance or otherwise of any alteration to its obligation under this Protocol that may be brought about by the entry into force of an amendment to the Treaty pursuant to Article 19 thereof.

## Article 5

This Protocol is of a permanent nature and shall remain in force indefinitely, provided that each State Party shall, in exercising its national sovereignty, have the right to withdraw from this Protocol if it decides that extraordinary events, related to the subject-matter of this Protocol, have jeopardized its supreme national interests. It shall give notice of such withdrawal to the Depositary State twelve months in advance. Such notice shall include a statement of the extraordinary events it regards as having jeopardized its supreme national interests.

## Article 6

This Protocol shall be subject to ratification.

## Article 7

This Protocol shall enter into force for each State Party on the date of its deposit of its instrument of ratification with the Depositary State. The Depositary State shall inform the other States Parties to the Treaty and to this Protocol on the deposit of instruments of ratification.

IN WITNESS WHEREOF the undersigned, being duly authorized by their Governments, have signed this Protocol.

DONE at Bangkok this fifteenth day of December, one thousand nine hundred and ninety-five, in one original in the English language.

# CHAPTER 6

# TREATY ON THE SOUTHEAST ASIA NUCLEAR WEAPON-FREE ZONE

**Bangkok, Thailand 15 December 1995**

The States Parties to this Treaty:

**DESIRING** to contribute to the realization of the purposes and principles of the Charter of the United Nations;

**DETERMINED** to take concrete action which will contribute to the progress towards general and complete disarmament of nuclear weapons, and to the promotion of international peace and security;

**REAFFIRMING** the desire of the Southeast Asian States to maintain peace and stability in the region in the spirit of peaceful coexistence and mutual understanding and cooperation as enunciated in various communiques, declarations and other legal instruments;

**RECALLING** the Declaration on the Zone of Peace, Freedom and Neutrality (ZOPFAN) signed in Kuala Lumpur on 27 November 1971 and the Programme of Action on ZOPFAN adopted at the 26th ASEAN Ministerial Meeting in Singapore in July 1993;

**CONVINCED** that the establishment of a Southeast Asia Nuclear Weapon-Free Zone, as an essential component of the ZOPPAN, will contribute towards strengthening the security of States within the Zone and towards enhancing international peace and security as a whole;

**REAFFIRMING** the importance of the Treaty on the Non-Proliferation of Nuclear Weapons (NPT) in preventing the proliferation of nuclear weapons and in contributing towards international peace and security;

**RECALLING** Article VII of the NPT which recognizes the right of any group of States to conclude regional treaties in order to assume the total absence of nuclear weapons in their respective territories;

**RECALLING** the Final Document of the Tenth Special Session of the United Nations General Assembly which encourages the establishment of nuclear weapon-free zones;

**RECALLING** the Principles and Objectives for Nuclear Non-Proliferation and Disarmament, adopted at the 1995 Review and Extension Conference of the Parties to the NPT, that the cooperation of all the nuclear-weapon States and their respect and support for the relevant protocols is important for the maximum effectiveness of this nuclear weapon-free zone treaty and its relevant protocols.

**DETERMINED** to protect the region from environmental pollution and the hazards posed by radioactive wastes and other radioactive material;

**HAVE AGREED as follows:**

## ARTICLE 1

### Use of term

For the purposes of this Treaty and its Protocol:

(a) "Southeast Asia Nuclear Weapon-Free Zone", hereinafter referred to as the "Zone", means the area comprising the territories of all States in Southeast Asia, namely, Brunei Darussalam, Cambodia, Indonesia, Laos, Malaysia, Myanmar, Philippines, Singapore, Thailand and Viet Nam, and their respective continental shelves and Exclusive Economic Zones (EEZ);
(b) "territory" means the land territory, internal waters, territorial sea, archipelagic waters, the seabed and the sub-soil thereof and the airspace above them;
(c) "nuclear weapon" means any explosive device capable of releasing nuclear energy in an uncontrolled manner but does not include the means of transport or delivery of such device if separable from and not an indivisible part thereof;
(d) "station" means to deploy, emplace, implant, install, stockpile or store;
(e) "radioactive material" means material that contains radionuclides above clearance or exemption levels recommended by the International Atomic Energy Agency (IAEA);
(f) "radioactive wastes" means material that contains or is contaminated with radionuclides at concentrations or activities greater than clearance levels recommended by the IAEA and for which no use is foreseen; and

(g) "dumping" means

(i) any deliberate disposal at sea, including seabed and subsoil insertion, of radioactive wastes or other matter from vessels, aircraft, platforms or other man-made structures at sea, and

(ii) any deliberate disposal at sea, including seabed and subsoil insertion, of vessels, aircraft, platforms or other man-made structures at sea, containing radioactive material, but does not include the disposal of wastes or other matter incidental to, or derived from the normal operations of vessels, aircraft, platforms or other man-made structures at sea and their equipment, other than wastes or other matter transported by or to vessels, aircraft, platforms or other man-made structures at sea, operating for the purpose of disposal of such matter or derived from the treatment of such wastes or other matter on such vessels, aircraft, platforms or structures.

## ARTICLE 2

## Application of the Treaty

1. This Treaty and its Protocol shall apply to the territories, continental selves, and EEZ of the States Parties within the Zone in which the Treaty is in force.
2. Nothing in this Treaty shall prejudice the rights or the exercise of these rights by any State under the provisions of the United Nations Convention on the Law of the Sea of 1982, in particular with regard to freedom of the high seas, rights of innocent passage, archipelagic sea lanes passage or transit passage of ships and aircraft, and consistent with the Charter of the United Nations.

## ARTICLE 3

## Basic undertakings

1. Each State Party undertakes not to, anywhere inside or outside the Zone:

   (a) develop, manufacture or otherwise acquire, possess or have control over nuclear weapons;
   (b) station or transport nuclear weapons by any means; or
   (c) test or use nuclear weapons.

2. Each State Party also undertakes not to allow, in its territory, any other State to:

   (a) develop, manufacture or otherwise acquire, possess or have control over nuclear weapons;
   (b) station nuclear weapons; or
   (c) test or use nuclear weapons.

3. Each State Party also undertake not to:

   (a) dump at sea or discharge into the atmosphere anywhere within the Zone any radioactive material or wastes;
   (b) dispose radioactive material or wastes on land in the territory of or under the jurisdiction of other States except as stipulated in Paragraph 2(e) of Article 4; or
   (c) allow, within its territory, any other State to dump at sea or discharge into the atmosphere any radioactive material or wastes.

4. Each State Party undertakes not to:

   (a) seek or receive any assistance in the Commission of any act in violation of the provisions of Paragraphs 1, 2 and 3 of this Article; or
   (b) take any action to assist or encourage the Commission of any act in violation of the provisions of Paragraphs 1, 2 and 3 of this Article.

## ARTICLE 4

### Use of nuclear energy for peaceful purposes

1. Nothing in this Treaty shall prejudice the right of the States Parties to use nuclear energy, in particular for their economic development and social progress.
2. Each State Party therefore undertakes:

   (a) to use exclusively for peaceful purposes nuclear material and facilities which are within its territory and areas under its jurisdiction and control;
   (b) prior to embarking on its peaceful nuclear energy programme, to subject its programme to rigorous nuclear safety assessment conforming to guidelines and standards recommended by the IAEA for the protection of health and minimization of danger to life and property in accordance with Paragraph 6 of Article III of the Statute of the IAEA;
   (c) upon request, to make available to another State Party the assessment except information relating to personal data, information protected by intellectual property rights or by industrial or commercial confidentiality, and information relating to national security;
   (d) to support the continued effectiveness of the international non-proliferation system based on the Treaty on the Non-Proliferation of Nuclear Weapons (NPT) and the IAEA safeguard system; and
   (e) to dispose radioactive wastes and other radioactive material in accordance with IAEA standards and procedures on land within its territory or on land within the territory of another State which has consented to such disposal.

3. Each State Party further undertakes not to provide source or special fissionable material, or equipment or material especially designed or prepared for the processing, use or production of special fissionable material to:

   (a) any non-nuclear-weapon State except under conditions subject to the safeguards required by Paragraph 1 of Article III of the NPT; or
   (b) any nuclear-weapon State except in conformity with applicable safeguards agreements with the IAEA.

## ARTICLE 5

### IAEA safeguards

Each State Party which has not done so shall conclude an agreement with the IAEA for the application of full scope safeguards to its peaceful nuclear activities not later than eighteen months after the entry into force for that State Party of the Treaty.

## ARTICLE 6

### Early notification of a nuclear accident

Each State Party which has not acceded to the Convention on Early Notification of a Nuclear Accident shall endeavour to do so.

## ARTICLE 7

### Foreign ships and aircraft

Each State Party, on being notified, may decide for itself whether to allow visits by foreign ships and aircraft to its ports and airfields, transit of its airspace by foreign aircraft, and navigation by foreign ships through its territorial sea or archipelagic waters and overflight of foreign aircraft above those waters in a manner not governed by the rights of innocent passage, archipelagic sea lanes passage or transit passage.

## ARTICLE 8

### Establishment of the commission for the Southeast Asia nuclear weapon-free zone

1. There is hereby established a Commission for the Southeast Asia Nuclear Weapon-Free Zone, hereinafter referred to as the "Commission".

2. All States Parties are ipso facto members or the Commission. Each State Party shall be represented by its Foreign Minister or his representative accompanied by alternates and advisers.
3. The function of the Commission shall be to oversee the implementation of this Treaty and ensure compliance with its provisions.
4. The Commission shall meet as and when necessary in accordance with the provisions of this Treaty including upon the request of any State Party. As far as possible, the Commission shall meet in conjunction with the ASEAN Ministerial Meeting.
5. At the beginning of each meeting, the Commission shall elect its Chairman and such other officers as may be required. They shall hold office until a new Chairman and other officers are elected at the next meeting.
6. Unless otherwise provided for in this Treaty, two-thirds of the members of the Commission shall be present to constitute a quorum.
7. Each member of the Commission shall have one vote.
8. Except as provided for in this Treaty, decisions of the Commission shall be taken by consensus or, failing consensus, by a two-thirds majority of the members present and voting.
9. The Commission shall, by consensus, agree upon and adopt rules of procedure for itself as well as financial rules governing its funding and that of its subsidiary organs.

## ARTICLE 9

### The executive committee

1. There is hereby established, as a subsidiary organ of the Commission, the Executive Committee.
2. The Executive Committee shall be composed of all States Parties to this Treaty. Each State Party shall be represented by one senior official as its representative, who may be accompanied by alternates and advisers.
3. The functions of the Executive Committee shall be to:

   (a) ensure the proper operation of verification measures in accordance with the provisions on the control system as stipulated in Article 10;
   (b) consider and decide on requests for clarification and for a fact-finding mission;
   (c) set up a fact-finding mission in accordance with the Annex of this Treaty;
   (d) consider and decide on the findings of a fact-finding mission and report to the Commission;

(e) request the Commission to convene a meeting when appropriate and necessary;
(f) conclude such agreements with the IAEA or other international organizations as referred to in Article 18 on behalf of the Commission after being duly authorized to do so by the Commission; and
(g) carry out such other tasks as may, from time to time, be assigned by the Commission.

4. The Executive Committee shall meet as and when necessary for the efficient exercise of its functions. As far as possible, the Executive Committee shall meet in conjunction with the ASEAN Senior Officials Meeting.
5. The Chairman of the Executive Committee shall be the representative of the Chairman of the Commission. Any submission or communication made by a State Party to the Chairman of the Executive Committee shall be disseminated to the other members of the Executive Committee.
6. Two-thirds of the members of the Executive Committee shall be present to constitute a quorum.
7. Each member of the Executive Committee shall have one vote.
8. Decisions of the Executive Committee shall be taken by consensus or, failing consensus, by a two-thirds majority of the members present and voting.

## ARTICLE 10

## Control system

1. There is hereby established a control system for the purpose of verifying compliance with the obligations of the States Parties under this Treaty.
2. The Control System shall comprise:

   (a) the IAEA safeguards system as provided for in Article 5;
   (b) report and exchange of information as provided for in Article 11;
   (c) request for clarification as provided for in Article 12; and
   (d) request and procedures for a fact-finding mission as provided for in Article 13.

## ARTICLE 11

## Report and exchange of information

1. Each State Party shall submit reports to the Executive Committee on any significant event within its territory and areas under its jurisdiction and control affecting the implementation of this Treaty.

2. The States Parties may exchange information on matters arising under or in relation to this Treaty.

## ARTICLE 12

### Request for clarification

1. Each State Party shall have the right to request another State Party for clarification concerning any situation which may be considered ambiguous or which may give rise to doubts about the compliance of that State Party with this Treaty. It shall inform the Executive Committee of such a request. The requested State Party shall duly respond by providing without delay the necessary information and inform the Executive Committee of its reply to the requesting State Party.
2. Each State Party shall have the right to request the Executive Committee to seek clarification for another State Party concerning any situation which may be considered ambiguous or which may give rise to doubts about compliance of that State Party with this Treaty. Upon receipt of such a request, the Executive Committee shall consult the State Party from which clarification is sought for the purpose of obtaining the clarification requested.

## ARTICLE 13

### Request for a fact-finding mission

A State Party shall have the right to request the Executive Committee to send a fact-finding mission to another State Party in order to clarify and resolve a situation which may be considered ambiguous or which may give rise to doubts about compliance with the provisions of this Treaty, in accordance with the procedure contained in the Annex to this Treaty.

## ARTICLE 14

### Remedial measures

1. In case the Executive Committee decide in accordance with the Annex that there is a breach of this Treaty by a State Party, that State Party shall, within a reasonable time, take all steps necessary to bring itself in full compliance with this Treaty and shall promptly inform the Executive Committee of the action taken or proposed to be taken by it.

2. Where a State Party fails or refuses to comply with the provisions of Paragraph 1 of this Article, the Executive Committee shall request the Commission to convene a meeting in accordance with the provisions of Paragraph 3(e) of Article 9.
3. At the meeting convened pursuant to Paragraph 2 of this Article, the Commission shall consider the emergent situation and shall decide on any measure it deems appropriate to cope with the situation, including the submission of the matter to the IAEA and, where the situation might endanger international peace and security, the Security Council and the General Assembly of the United Nations.
4. In the event of breach of the Protocol attached to this Treaty by a State Party to the Protocol, the Executive Committee shall convene a special meeting of the Commission to decide on appropriate measures to be taken.

## ARTICLE 15

### Signature, ratification, accession, deposit and registration

1. This Treaty shall be open for signature by all States in Southeast Asia, namely, Brunei Darussalam, Cambodia, Indonesia, Laos, Malaysia, Myanmar, Philippines, Singapore, Thailand and Vietnam.
2. This Treaty shall be subject to ratification in accordance with the constitutional procedure of the signatory states. The instruments of ratification shall be deposited with the Government of the Kingdom of Thailand which is hereby designated as the Depositary State.
3. This Treaty shall be open for accession. The instruments of accession shall be deposited with the Depositary State.
4. The Depositary State shall inform the other States Parties to this Treaty on the deposit of instruments of ratification or accession.
5. The Depositary State shall register this Treaty and its Protocol pursuant to Article 102 of the Charter of the United Nations.

## ARTICLE 16

### Entry into force

1. This Treaty shall enter into force on the date of the deposit of the seventh instrument of ratification and/or accession.
2. For States which ratify or accede to this Treaty after the date of the seventh instrument of ratification or accession, the Treaty shall enter into force on the date of deposit of its instrument of ratification or accession.

## ARTICLE 17

### Reservations

This Treaty shall not be subject to reservations.

## ARTICLE 18

### Relations with other international organizations

The Commission may conclude such agreements with the IAEA or other international organizations as it considers likely to facilitate the efficient operation of the control system established by this Treaty.

## ARTICLE 19

### Amendments

1. Any State Party may propose amendments to this Treaty and its Protocol and shall submit its proposals to the Executive Committee, which shall transmit them to all the other States Parties. The Executive Committee shall immediately request the Commission to convene a meeting to examine the proposed amendments. The quorum required for such a meeting shall be all the members of the Commission. Any amendment shall be adopted by a consensus decision of the Commission.
2. Amendments adopted shall enter into force 30 days after the receipt by the Depositary State of the seventh instrument of acceptance from the States Parties.

## ARTICLE 20

### Review

Ten years after this Treaty enters into force, a meeting of the Commission shall be convened for the purpose of reviewing the operation of the Treaty. A meeting of the Commission for the same purpose may also be convened at anytime thereafter if there is consensus among all its members.

## ARTICLE 21

### Settlement of disputes

Any dispute arising from the interpretation of the provisions of this Treaty shall be settled by peaceful means as may be agreed upon by the States Parties to the dispute. If within one month, the parties to the dispute are unable to achieve a peaceful settlement of the dispute by negotiation, mediation, enquiry or conciliation, any of the parties concerned shall, with the prior consent of the other parties concerned, refer the dispute to arbitration or to the International Court of Justice.

## ARTICLE 22

### Duration and withdrawal

1. This Treaty shall remain in force indefinitely.
2. In the event of a breach by any State Party of this Treaty essential to the achievement of the objectives of the Treaty, every other State Party shall have the right to withdraw from the Treaty.
3. Withdrawal under Paragraph 2 of Article 22, shall be effected by giving notice twelve months in advance to the members of the Commission.

**IN WITNESS WHEREOF**, the undersigned have signed this Treaty.

**DONE** at **Bangkok**, this fifteenth day of December, one thousand nine hundred and ninety-five, in one original in the English language.

FOR BRUNEI DARUSSALAM

HAJI HASSANAL BOLKIAH
Sultan of Brunei Darussalam

FOR THE REPUBLIC OF INDONESIA

SOEHARTO
President

FOR THE KINGDOM OF CAMBODIA

Samdech Krom Preah NORODOM RANARIDH
First Prime Minister

Samdech HUN SEN
Second Prime Minister

FOR THE LAO PEOPLE'S DEMOCRATIC REPUBLIK

KHAMTAY SIPHANDONE
Prime Minister

FOR MALAYSIA

DR MAHATHIR BIN MOHAMAD
Prime Minister

FOR THE UNION OF MYANMAR

SENIOR GENERAL THAN SHWE
Chairman of the State Law and Order Restoration Council
and Prime Minister

FOR THE REPUBLIC OF THE PHILIPPINES

FIDEL V. RAMOS
President

FOR THE REPUBLIC OF SINGAPORE

GOH CHOK TONG
Prime Minister

FOR THE KINGDOM OF THAILAND

BANHARN SILPA-ARCHA
Prime Minister

FOR THE SOCIALIST REPUBLIC OF VIETNAM

VO VAN KIET
Prime Minister

Source: http://www.aseansec.org/2082.htm
Accessed date: 2 October 2008
Publisher: ASEAN Secretariat
Country: Jakarta
Date of Publication: 2006

# CHAPTER 7

# THE ASEAN REGIONAL FORUM: A CONCEPT PAPER

## INTRODUCTION

1. The Asia-Pacific region is experiencing an unprecedented period of peace and prosperity. For the first time in a century or more, the guns are virtually silent. There is a growing trend among, the states in the region to enhance dialogue on political and security cooperation. The Asia-Pacific is also the most dynamic region of the world in terms of economic growth. The centre of the world's economic gravity is shifting into the region. The main challenge of the ASEAN Regional Forum (ARF) is to sustain and enhance this peace and prosperity.
2. This is not an easy challenge. The region has experienced some of the most disastrous wars of the twentieth century. It is also a remarkably diverse region where big and small countries co-exist. They differ significantly in levels of development. There are cultural, ethnic, religious and historical differences to overcome. Habits of cooperation are not deep-seated in some parts of the region.
3. ASEAN has a pivotal role to play in the ARF. It has a demonstrable record of enhancing regional cooperation in the most diverse sub-region of the Asia-Pacific. It has also fostered habits of cooperation and provided the catalyst for encouraging regional cooperation in the wider Asia-Pacific region. The annual ASEAN Ministerial Meetings have contributed significantly to the positive regional environment today. There would be great hope for the Asia-Pacific if the whole region could emulate ASEAN's record of enhancing the peace and prosperity of its participants.
4. Although ASEAN has undertaken the obligation to be the primary driving force of the ARF, a successful ARF requires the active participation and cooperation of all participants. ASEAN must always be sensitive to and take into account the interests and concerns of all ARF participants.

## THE CHALLENGES

5. To successfully preserve and enhance the peace and prosperity of the region, the ARF must dispassionately analyse the key challenges facing the region. Firstly, it should acknowledge that periods of rapid economic growth are often

accompanied by significant shifts in power relations. This can lead to conflict. The ARF will have to carefully manage these transitions to preserve the peace. Secondly, the region is remarkably diverse. The ARF should recognise and accept the different approaches to peace and security and try to forge a consensual approach to security issues. Thirdly, the region has a residue unresolved territorial and other differences. Any one of these could spark conflagration that could undermine the peace and prosperity of the region. Over time, the ARF will have to gradually defuse these potential problems.

6. It would be unwise for a young and fragile process like the ARF to tackle all these challenges simultaneously. A gradual evolutionary approach is required. This evolution can take place in three stages:

   Stage I: Promotion of Confidence-Building Measures
   Stage II: Development of Preventive Diplomacy Mechanisms
   Stage III: Development of Conflict-Resolution Mechanisms

7. The participants of the first ARF Ministerial Meeting in Bangkok in July 1994 agreed on "the need to develop a more predictable and constructive pattern of relations for the Asia-Pacific region". In its initial phase, the ARF should therefore concentrate on enhancing, the trust and confidence amongst participants and thereby foster a regional environment conducive to maintaining the peace and prosperity of the region.

## Stage I: Promotion of confidence-building measures

8. In promoting confidence-building measures, the ARF may adopt two complementary approaches. The first approach derives from ASEAN's experience, which provides a valuable and proven guide for the ARF. ASEAN has succeeded in reducing, tensions among, its member states, promoting region cooperation and creating a regional climate conducive to peace and prosperity without the implementation of explicit confidence-building measures, achieving conditions approximating those envisaged in the Declaration of Zone of Peace, Freedom and Neutrality (ZOPFAN). The concepts of ZOPFAN and its essential component, the Southeast Asia Nuclear Weapons-Free Zone (SEANFWZ), are significantly contributing to regional peace and stability. ASEAN's well established practices of consultation and consensus (musyawarah and mufakat) have been significantly enhanced by the regular exchanges of high-level visits among ASEAN countries. This pattern of regular visits has effectively developed into a preventive diplomacy channel. In the Asian context, there is some merit to the ASEAN approach. It emphasises the need to develop trust and confidence among neighbouring states.

9. The principles of good neighbourliness, which are elaborated in the concept of ZOPFAN, are enshrined in the 1976 Treaty of Amity and Cooperation in Southeast Asia (TAC). One simple concrete way of expanding the ASEAN experience is to encourage the ARF participants to associate themselves with the TAC. It is significant that the first ARF meeting in Bangkok agreed to "endorse the purposes and principles of ASEAN Treaty of Amity and Cooperation in Southeast Asia as a code of conduct governing relations between states and a unique diplomatic instrument for regional confidence-building, preventive diplomacy, and political and security cooperation."
10. The second approach is the implementation of concrete confidence-building measures. The first ARF meeting, in Bangkok entrusted the next Chairman of the ARF, Brunei Darussalam, to study all the ideas presented by ARF participants and to also study other relevant internationally recognized norms, principles and practices. After extensive consultations, the ASEAN countries have prepared two lists of confidence-building measures. The first list (Annex A) spells out measures which can be explored and implemented by ARF participants in the immediate future. The second list (Annex B) is an indicative list of other proposals which can be explored over the medium and long-term by ARF participants and also considered in the immediate future by the Track Two process. These lists include possible preventive diplomacy and other measures.
11. Given the delicate nature of many of the subjects being considered by the ARF, there is merit in moving, the ARF process along two tracks. Track One activities will be carried out by governments. Track Two activities will be carried out by strategic institutes and non-government organisations in the region, such as ASEAN-ISIS and CSCAP. To be meaningful and relevant, the Track Two activities may focus, as much as possible, on the current concerns of the ARF. The synergy between the two tracks would contribute greatly to confidence-building measures in the region. Over time, these Track Two activities should result in the creation of a sense of community among participants of those activities.

## *Moving beyond Stage 1*

12. There remains a residue of unresolved territorial and other disputes that could be sources of tension or conflict. If the ARF is to become, over time, a meaningful vehicle to enhance the peace and prosperity of the region, it will have to demonstrate that it is a relevant instrument to be used in the event that a crisis or problem emerges. The ARF meeting in Bangkok demonstrated this by taking a stand on the Korean issue at the very first meeting. This was a signal

that the ARF is ready to address any challenge to the peace and security of the region.

13. Over time, the ARF must develop its own mechanisms to carry preventive diplomacy and conflict-resolution. In doing so, the ARF will unique challenges. There are no established roads or procedures for it to follow. Without a high degree of confidence among ARF participants, it is unlikely that they will agree to the establishment of mechanisms which are perceived to be intrusive and/or autonomous. This is a political reality the ARF should recognize. However, it would be useful in the initial phase for the Track Two process to consider and investigate a variety of preventive diplomacy and conflict-resolution mechanisms. A good start was made with the three workshops organized by International Studies Centre (Thailand) and Institute of Policy Studies (Singapore) on ASEAN-UN Cooperation for Peace and Preventive Diplomacy, and the Indonesia-sponsored series off workshops on the South China Sea.

### Stage II: Development of preventive diplomacy

14. Preventive diplomacy would be a natural follow-up to confidence building measures. Some suggestions for preventive diplomacy measures are spelled out in Annexes A and B.

### Stage III: Conflict resolution

15. It is not envisaged that the ARF would establish mechanisms conflict resolution in the immediate future. The establishment of such mechanisms is an eventual goal that ARF participants should pursue as they proceed to develop the ARF as a vehicle for promoting regional peace and stability.

## ORGANISATION OF ARF ACTIVITIES

16. There shall be an annual ARF Ministerial Meeting, in an ASEAN capital just after the ASEAN Ministerial Meeting. The host country will chair the meeting. The incoming Chairman of the ASEAN Standing Committee will chair all inter-sessional Track One activities of the ARF.
17. The ARF shall be apprised of all Track Two activities through the current Chairman of the Track One activities, who will be the main link between Track One and Track Two activities.
18. In the initial phase of the ARF no institutionalization is expected. Nor should a Secretariat be established in the near future. ASEAN shall be the repository

of all ARF documents and information and provide the necessary support to sustain ARF activities.

19. The participants of the ARF comprise the ASEAN member states, the observers, and consultative and dialogue partners of ASEAN. Applications to participate in the ARF shall be submitted to the Chairman of the ARF who will then consult the other ARF participants.
20. The rules of procedure of ARF meetings shall be based on prevailing, ASEAN norms and practices. Decisions should be made by consensus after careful and extensive consultations. No voting will take place. In accordance with prevailing ASEAN practices, the Chairman of the ASEAN Standing Committee shall provide the secretarial support and coordinate ARF activities.
21. The ARF should also progress at a pace comfortable to all participants. The ARF should not move "too fast for those who want to go slow and not too slow for those who want to go fast".

## CONCLUSION

22. ARF participants should not assume that the success of the ARF can be taken for granted. ASEAN's experience shows that success is a result of hard work and careful adherence to the rule of consensus. ARF participants will have to work equally hard and be equally sensitive to ensure that the ARF process stays on track.
23. The ARF must be accepted as a "sui generis" Organization. It has no established precedents to follow. A great deal of innovation and ingenuity will be required to keep the ARF moving forward while at the same time ensure that it enjoys the support of its diverse participants. This is a major challenge both for the ASEAN countries and other ARF participants. The UN Secretary-General's "Agenda for Peace" has recognized that "just as no two regions or situations are the same, so the design of cooperative work and its division of labour must adjust to the realities of each case with flexibility and creativity".

Source: http://www.aseansec.org/3635.htm
Accessed date: 2 October 2008
Publisher: ASEAN Secretariat
Country: Jakarta
Date of Publication: 2006

# CHAPTER 8

# ASEAN VISION 2020

We, the Heads of State/Government of the Association of Southeast Asian Nations, gather today in Kuala Lumpur to reaffirm our commitment to the aims and purposes of the Association as set forth in the Bangkok Declaration of 8 August 1967, in particular to promote regional cooperation in Southeast Asia in the spirit of equality and partnership and thereby contribute towards peace, progress and prosperity in the region.

We in ASEAN have created a community of Southeast Asian nations at peace with one another and at peace with the world, rapidly achieving prosperity for our peoples and steadily improving their lives. Our rich diversity has provided the strength and inspiration to us to help one another foster a strong sense of community.

We are now a market of around 500 million people with a combined gross domestic product of US$600 billion. We have achieved considerable results in the economic field, such as high economic growth, stability and significant poverty alleviation over the past few years. Members have enjoyed substantial trade and investment flows from significant liberalization measures.

We resolve to build upon these achievements.

Now, as we approach the 21st century, thirty years after the birth of ASEAN, we gather to chart a vision for ASEAN on the basis of today's realities and prospects in the decades leading to the Year 2020.

That vision is of ASEAN as a concert of Southeast Asian nations, outward looking, living in peace, stability and prosperity, bonded together in partnership in dynamic development and in a community of caring societies.

## A CONCERT OF SOUTHEAST ASIAN NATIONS

We envision the ASEAN region to be, in 2020, in full reality, a Zone of Peace, Freedom and Neutrality, as envisaged in the Kuala Lumpur Declaration of 1971.

ASEAN shall have, by the year 2020, established a peaceful and stable Southeast Asia where each nation is at peace with itself and where the causes for conflict have been eliminated, through abiding respect for justice and the rule of law and through the strengthening of national and regional resilience.

We envision a Southeast Asia where territorial and other disputes are resolved by peaceful means.

We envision the Treaty of Amity and Cooperation in Southeast Asia functioning fully as a binding code of conduct for our governments and peoples, to which other states with interests in the region adhere.

We envision a Southeast Asia free from nuclear weapons, with all the Nuclear Weapon States committed to the purposes of the Southeast Asia Nuclear Weapons Free Zone Treaty through their adherence to its Protocol. We also envision our region free from all other weapons of mass destruction.

We envision our rich human and natural resources contributing to our development and shared prosperity.

We envision the ASEAN Regional Forum as an established means for confidence-building and preventive diplomacy and for promoting conflict-resolution.

We envision a Southeast Asia where our mountains, rivers and seas no longer divide us but link us together in friendship, cooperation and commerce.

We see ASEAN as an effective force for peace, justice and moderation in the Asia-Pacific and in the world.

## A PARTNERSHIP IN DYNAMIC DEVELOPMENT

We resolve to chart a new direction towards the year 2020 called, ASEAN 2020: Partnership in Dynamic Development which will forge closer economic integration within ASEAN.

We reiterate our resolve to enhance ASEAN economic cooperation through economic development strategies, which are in line with the aspiration of our respective peoples, which put emphasis on sustainable and equitable growth, and enhance national as well as regional resilience.

We pledge to sustain ASEAN's high economic performance by building upon the foundation of our existing cooperation efforts, consolidating our achievements, expanding our collective efforts and enhancing mutual assistance.

We commit ourselves to moving towards closer cohesion and economic integration, narrowing the gap in the level of development among Member Countries, ensuring that the multilateral trading system remains fair and open, and achieving global competitiveness.

We will create a stable, prosperous and highly competitive ASEAN Economic Region in which there is a free flow of goods, services and investments, a freer flow of capital, equitable economic development and reduced poverty and socio-economic disparities.

We resolve, inter alia, to undertake the following:

- maintain regional macroeconomic and financial stability by promoting closer consultations in macroeconomic and financial policies.
- advance economic integration and cooperation by undertaking the following general strategies: fully implement the ASEAN Free Trade Area and accelerate liberalization of trade in services, realize the ASEAN Investment Area by 2010 and free flow of investments by 2020; intensify and expand sub-regional cooperation in existing and new sub-regional growth areas; further consolidate and expand extra-ASEAN regional linkages for mutual benefit cooperate to strengthen the multilateral trading system, and reinforce the role of the business sector as the engine of growth.
- promote a modern and competitive small and medium enterprises (SME) sector in ASEAN which will contribute to the industrial development and efficiency of the region.
- accelerate the free flow of professional and other services in the region.
- promote financial sector liberalization and closer cooperation in money and capital market, tax, insurance and customs matters as well as closer consultations in macroeconomic and financial policies.
- accelerate the development of science and technology including information technology by establishing a regional information technology network and centers of excellence for dissemination of and easy access to data and information.
- establish interconnecting arrangements in the field of energy and utilities for electricity, natural gas and water within ASEAN through the ASEAN Power Grid and a Trans-ASEAN Gas Pipeline and Water Pipeline, and promote

cooperation in energy efficiency and conservation, as well as the development of new and renewable energy resources.

- enhance food security and international competitiveness of food, agricultural and forest products, to make ASEAN a leading producer of these products, and promote the forestry sector as a model in forest management, conservation and sustainable development.
- meet the ever increasing demand for improved infrastructure and communications by developing an integrated and harmonized trans-ASEAN transportation network and harnessing technology advances in telecommunication and information technology, especially in linking the planned information highways/multimedia corridors in ASEAN, promoting open sky policy, developing multimodal transport, facilitating goods in transit and integrating telecommunications networks through greater interconnectivity, coordination of frequencies and mutual recognition of equipment-type approval procedures.
- enhance human resource development in all sectors of the economy through quality education, upgrading of skills and capabilities and training.
- work towards a world class standards and conformance system that will provide a harmonized system to facilitate the free flow of ASEAN trade while meeting health, safety and environmental needs.
- use the ASEAN Foundation as one of the instruments to address issues of unequal economic development, poverty and socio-economic disparities.
- promote an ASEAN customs partnership for world class standards and excellence in efficiency, professionalism and service, and uniformity through harmonized procedures, to promote trade and investment and to protect the health and well-being of the ASEAN community.
- enhance intra-ASEAN trade and investment in the mineral sector and to contribute towards a technologically competent ASEAN through closer networking and sharing of information on mineral and geosciences as well as to enhance cooperation and partnership with dialogue partners to facilitate the development and transfer of technology in the mineral sector, particularly in the downstream research and the geosciences and to develop appropriate mechanism for these.

## A COMMUNITY OF CARING SOCIETIES

We envision the entire Southeast Asia to be, by 2020, an ASEAN community conscious of its ties of history, aware of its cultural heritage and bound by a common regional identity.

We see vibrant and open ASEAN societies consistent with their respective national identities, where all people enjoy equitable access to opportunities for total human development regardless of gender, race, religion, language, or social and cultural background.

We envision a socially cohesive and caring ASEAN where hunger, malnutrition, deprivation and poverty are no longer basic problems, where strong families as the basic units of society tend to their members particularly the children, youth, women and elderly; and where the civil society is empowered and gives special attention to the disadvantaged, disabled and marginalized and where social justice and the rule of law reign.

We see well before 2020 a Southeast Asia free of illicit drugs, free of their production, processing, trafficking and use.

We envision a technologically competitive ASEAN competent in strategic and enabling technologies, with an adequate pool of technologically qualified and trained manpower, and strong networks of scientific and technological institutions and centers of excellence.

We envision a clean and green ASEAN with fully established mechanisms for sustainable development to ensure the protection of the region's environment, the sustainability of its natural resources, and the high quality of life of its peoples.

We envision the evolution in Southeast Asia of agreed rules of behaviour and cooperative measures to deal with problems that can be met only on a regional scale, including environmental pollution and degradation, drug trafficking, trafficking in women and children, and other transnational crimes.

We envision our nations being governed with the consent and greater participation of the people with its focus on the welfare and dignity of the human person and the good of the community.

We resolve to develop and strengthen ASEAN's institutions and mechanisms to enable ASEAN to realize the vision and respond to the challenges of the coming century. We also see the need for a strengthened ASEAN Secretariat with an enhanced role to support the realization of our vision.

## AN OUTWARD-LOOKING ASEAN

We see an outward-looking ASEAN playing a pivotal role in the international fora, and advancing ASEAN's common interests. We envision ASEAN having an intensified relationship with its Dialogue Partners and other regional organizations based on equal partnership and mutual respect.

## CONCLUSION

We pledge to our peoples our determination and commitment to bringing this ASEAN Vision for the Year 2020 into reality.

Kuala Lumpur
15 December 1997

Source: http://www.aseansec.org/1814.htm
Accessed date: 7 February 2006
Publisher: ASEAN Secretariat
Country: Jakarta
Date of Publication: 2004

# CHAPTER 9

# JOINT COMMUNIQUE OF THE 34TH ASEAN MINISTERIAL MEETING

**Hanoi, 23–24 July 2001**

We, the Foreign Ministers of the ten ASEAN Member Countries, met in Ha Noi, Viet Nam, on 23–24 July 2001 under the chairmanship of His Excellency Mr. Nguyen Dy Nien, Minister for Foreign Affairs of the Socialist Republic of Viet Nam. The Meeting was also attended by the Secretary-General of ASEAN. Present at the Opening Ceremony of the Meeting were the representative for Papua New Guinea as Observer and the representative of the United Nations. Transitional Administration in East Timor as guest of the host country. His Excellency Mr. Phan Van Khai, Prime Minister of the Socialist Republic of Viet Nam delivered the Keynote Address at the Opening Ceremony of the Meeting.

....

2. We discussed the challenges facing ASEAN, in particular the global economic outlook, the impact of globalization and the region's political and economic situation that could undermine ASEAN's development and progress.
3. We expressed concern over the global economic outlook, especially the economic downturn in the U.S., Japan and Europe, which in turn could hamper the prospects for continued growth in the ASEAN region. We resolved to accelerate existing cooperative endeavours to enhance ASEAN's dynamism and competitiveness.
4. We exchanged views on how ASEAN could best position itself to reap the benefits and meet the challenges of globalization including the need to address the development gap and digital divide. We also discussed the need to promote regional stability, sustain economic growth enhance ASEAN's competitiveness and strengthen cooperation within ASEAN and between ASEAN and the rest of the world. We shared the view that in order to effectively meet these challenges, the ASEAN Member Countries must continue to be stable, united, integrated and outward-looking. We reaffirmed the fundamental principles of ASEAN and the importance of working together to meet the challenges and further enhance mutual trust and confidence. In line with these we also reaffirmed our commitment to accelerate the implementation of the Hanoi Plan of Action (HPA) with a view to realizing the ASEAN Vision 2020.

## IMPLEMENTATION OF THE INITIATIVE FOR ASEAN INTEGRATION (IAI)

5. We were gratified to see good progress in the follow-up to the Initiative for ASEAN Integration (IAI) which ASEAN Leaders put forth at the 4th ASEAN Informal Summit in Singapore last November. We commended the IAI Task Force and the ASEAN Standing Committee for taking the lead in the coordination and implementation of the IAI. On our part we adopted at this 34th AMM the Ha Noi Declaration on Narrowing Development Gap for closer ASEAN Integration, which reiterates the common commitment in ASEAN to integrate Cambodia, Laos, Myanmar and Viet Nam into ASEAN economic mainstream and prescribes concrete measures for this crucial and long-term process focusing on three priority areas namely infrastructure. Information and communication technology and human resource development. In this connection, we expressed our appreciation for all the assistance that ASEAN's friends and partners have extended to the IAI endeavor and expressed our strong belief that progress in the IAI would continue to contribute significantly to peace, prosperity and progress in the region.
6. To complement existing bilateral assistance extended to CLMV and facilitate request for funding support from interested Dialogue Partners and other sources, we agreed that the Member Countries of ASEAN should jointly initiate "ASEAN IAI Projects" based on the priority areas identified by the IAI Task Force.

## ASEAN FOREIGN MINISTERS' RETREATS

7. We stressed the importance of engaging in frank and open discussion as well as enhancing mutual trust and confidence with a view to further strengthening cooperation among ASEAN Member Countries in order to seek avenues to address the above mentioned challenges. In this connection, we agreed to meet more often in a less formal atmosphere. Following the United Nations Millennium Summit we held an ASEAN Ministerial Meeting in informal retreat style in New York on 18 September 2000 to coordinate ASEAN position at the UN.
8. We held, for the first time, a Retreat separate from the regular ASEAN Ministerial Meetings, in Yangon, Myanmar, on 30 April 2001. We had frank discussions on regional and international developments, and renewed ASEAN's commitment to further deepen cooperation and play a more important role in enhancing regional security.
9. We also held a Retreat in Ha Noi on 23 July 2001, during the 34th ASEAN Minister Meeting; We discussed the future direction of ASEAN and measures

to enhance the Association's contribution and active role in cooperation with its Dialogue Partners and other parties.

10. We noted, with appreciation. Thailand's offer to host the next ASEAN Foreign Ministers' Retreat in the first quarter of 2002.

## POLITICAL AND SECURITY COOPERATION

11. We reiterated the importance of the Treaty of Amity and Cooperation (TAC), which serves as a framework governing relations within ASEAN and between ASEAN and countries in other parts of the world. We welcomed the entry into force of the Second Protocol to the TAC following the ratification of the Protocol by Papua New Guinea (PNG). We adopted the Rules of Procedure of the High Council of the TAC and renewed our call for extra-regional states, particularly the major powers, to accede to the TAC.
12. We welcomed the progress in the implementation of the SEANWFZ Treaty, stressed the importance of direct consultation between ASEAN, and the Five Nuclear Weapon States (NWS) and considered this a significant progress towards encouraging the accession of the Nuclear Weapon States to the Protocol to the SEANWFZ Treaty. In this connection, we welcomed the first direct consultation between ASEAN and the NWS in Ha Noi on 19 May 2001, reaffirmed our support to this process and called for continued consultations with the NWS. We also welcomed the participation for the first time of the Philippines as a full member of the SEANWFZ Commission, having recently deposited its instrument of ratification.

....

## REGIONAL AND INTERNATIONAL ISSUES

....

24. We welcomed the successful outcome of the United Nations Millennium Summit held in New York on 6–8 September 2000. We were of the view that the Summit was a success since it reaffirmed the UN Member Countries' commitment to the UN process and to the implementation of the Millennium Declaration adopted by the Summit in which the world leaders pledged to make the right to development a reality for all. We agreed that ASEAN should work with the rest of the world community to implement the Millennium Declaration.
25. We exchanged views on the reform of the United Nations and reiterated that the reform of the UN and the UN Security Council should be undertaken in conformity with the principles of strengthening representativeness, effectiveness,

transparency and accountability with a view to enhancing the role of the UN in the service of all nations, particularly developing ones.

26. We stressed the importance of achieving universal adherence to the Comprehensive Nuclear Test Ban Treaty (CTBT) and the Nuclear Non-Proliferation Treaty (NPT) and called on the Nuclear Weapon States to make further efforts towards the elimination of all nuclear weapons.
27. We noted the progress that has been made in negotiating a Protocol on the verification of the Biological Weapon Convention (BWC) and looked forward to the 5th Review of the BWC in November 2001.
28. We also noted the outcome of the UN Conference on Small and Light Weapons in all its aspects held in New York on 9–20 July 2001 and expressed our hope that the Program of Action adopted by this conference would be implemented effectively.
29. We noted the recent dialogues among the major powers and concerned states on the NMD and expressed our hope that such dialogues would narrow down the differences and bring new constructive approaches to address the issues related to the NMD in the interest of maintaining world security and stability.
30. We recalled the decision made by the 26th ASEAN Ministerial Meeting held in Singapore on 13–14 July 1993 to consider the establishment of an appropriate regional mechanism on human rights and noted the consultations between the ASEAN Senior Officials and the Working Group for an ASEAN Human Rights Mechanism. We acknowledged the efforts of the Working Group in realizing this objective, including the convening of a Workshop for an ASEAN Human Rights Mechanism in Jakarta, Indonesia on 5–6 July 2001. In this connection, we agreed that ASEAN-ISIS should also be involved in the discussions especially in the broader context of a People's ASEAN.
31. We should endeavour to find a common position in the regional and international form. On the WTO, we recognized the need for a balanced and broad-based agenda for a new round of multilateral trade negotiations, taking into account the interests of developing countries. The agenda should include capacity building for developing countries to better cope with the challenges of liberalization and carry out the various commitments under WTO. We refined our conviction that cooperation in a rule-based multilateral trading system plays a vital role in alleviating poverty of ASEAN. Furthermore, we reiterated ASEAN's wish to see the WTO speed up the process for the accession of Cambodia, Laos and Viet Nam to the organization. We were likewise of the view that the early accession of China to the WTO would be a significant contribution to the multilateral trading system.

32. We expressed our concern over the decline of commodity prices in the international market. Recalling the importance of the commodity sector to the economies of Member Countries, we expressed our support for efforts by ASEAN to continue to formulate a common stand and course of action to effectively address trade distorting practices of developed countries, such as export subsidies and domestic support measures, that continue to plague international trade in commodities.
33. We reiterated ASEAN's call for support for the participation of Cambodia, Laos and Myanmar in APEC's Working Groups pending their eventual admission into APEC. We welcomed China's APEC chairmanship for the year 2001 and expressed our full support for the realization of the theme "Meeting New Challenges in the New Century: Achieving Common Prosperity through Participation and Cooperation".
34. We noted the successful conclusion of 3rd Asia-Europe Foreign Ministers' Meeting (ASEM FMM) in Beijing, China, on 14–25 May 2001, and reaffirmed our commitment to ASEM process. We reiterated our support for the early admission of Cambodia. Laos and Myanmar into ASEM. We agreed to work towards a more interactive and informal dialogue at future ASEM meetings in order to reinvigorate the comprehensive Asia-Europe Partnership in the post crisis era. In this context, we looked toward to the 4th ASEM FMM in Spain in June 2002 and the ASEM IV Summit in Copenhagen in September 2002.
35. We attached high importance to the Greater Mekong Sub-regional Cooperation Program (GMS), which aims to increase intra-regional cross border trade through better physical linkages to create more positive investment climate; and to strengthen labour force and markets through human resource development initiatives. In this regard, we noted that there is a natural complementarily between the aims of the GMS programs and the ASEAN's interest and activities in the Mekong sub-region including through the ASEAN Mekong Basin Development Cooperation (AMBDC). Which underlines the need for closer cooperation and coordination between the two bodies.
36. Welcoming the success of the First Ministerial Meeting on Mekong-Ganga Cooperation in Vientiane on 11–13 November 2000, we considered this cooperation as complementary efforts to exploit the potential of the region and expressed the hope that this cooperation, which in the initial stage would focus on tourism promotion and development, would bring about tangible results, contributing to the efforts to integrate the Mekong sub-region to the region. We looked forward to the success of the 2nd Ministerial Meeting on Mekong-Ganga cooperation, in Hanoi, on 18 July 2001.

## ECONOMIC COOPERATION

37. We were encouraged by the continued economic recovery in ASEAN, but also recognized the urgent need to continue with structural refines in view of the slowdown in the global economy. We emphasized the importance of continuing regional economic integration as a measure to reduce costs and attract investment.
38. We welcomed the efforts to expedite the accomplishment of AFTA and emphasized the important milestone it represents for regional economic integration. We lauded the important move by the original signatories in accelerating the implementation of the CEPT scheme. We expressed support for efforts to publicize AFTA and welcomed the CEPT Outreach Program conducted from 21 March 2001–6 April 2001 in five ASEAN capitals to disseminate information on the benefits of AFTA to the business community.
39. We were encouraged by significant progress in the implementation of AICO. We stressed the importance of ASEAN's trade facilitation initiatives. Particularly in terms of customs and standards for intra-ASEAN trade. We recalled that the Sixth ASEAN Summit in December 1998 had called for a second round of negotiations in services. We strongly urged the relevant ASEAN bodies to ensure that substantive otters in air transport, business services, construction, finance, maritime transport, telecommunications and tourism be made before the end of this year. We urged an early implementation of the Framework Agreement on the ASEAN Investment Area (AlA).
40. We noted the significant progress made in the implementation of the regional financing arrangements particularly the enlargement of the ASEAN Swap Arrangement and its expansion to include all 10 ASEAN Member Countries, and the conclusion of several substantial agreements on bilateral swap arrangements among ASEAN Member Countries, China, Japan and the Republic of Korea under the Chiang Mai Initiative.
41. We lauded the decision taken by the ASEAN Economic Ministers to establish an ASEAN-GSP Scheme to accord preferential treatment to export goods from Cambodia, Laos, Myanmar and Viet Nam on a bilateral basis, and expressed our belief that this would bring immediate trade benefits to these newer Member Countries.
42. We were pleased with the progress in the implementation of e-ASEAN Framework Agreement signed by ASEAN Leaders at the 4th ASEAN Informal Summit in Singapore last November, particularly the development of a reference framework for e-commerce legal infrastructure. We welcomed the holding of the e-ASEAN Business leaders Forum in April 2001 to validate the Framework Agreement's attractiveness to leading ICT multinational corporations

and invite their active participation. We were pleased with the successful outcome of the First ASEAN Telecommunication Ministers' Meeting (TELMIN) in Kuala Lumpur on 13–14 July 2001 including its decision to participate actively in the realization of e-ASEAN and other ICT related activities in ASEAN.

43. We stressed the importance of the tourism industry to the economies of Member Countries and reiterated our support for the Visit ASEAN Campaign (VAC) launched in Brunei Darussalam and expressed our hope that the VAC would give ASEAN a stronger brand name as a single tourism destination.
44. We recognized the importance of those sub-regional groupings/growth areas such as BIMP-EAGA. IMT-GT, IMS-GT, the AMBDC and the West-East Corridor in hastening regional integration and believed that a well-balanced development in sub-regional groupings/growth areas could serve as a solid foundation for ASEAN Economic Integration. In this regard, we lauded the convening of a seminar in Brunei Darussalam aimed at developing a common strategy for revitalizing these sub-regional groupings/growth areas. We appreciated the support and assistance being given to newer Member Countries including those through development projects/programs in the AMBDC. We reiterated our call to gather support and assistance from ASEAN Member Countries and from the rest of the international community for the development of ASEAN sub-regional cooperation.

## FUNCTIONAL COOPERATION

45. We noted that the ASEAN-Australia Safety Nets Project commenced implementation in May 2001 and expressed appreciation to Australia for its support for ASEAN's endeavour. We considered this an important step forward in improving the region's capacity to design social safety nets and to assess the social impact of economic and other setbacks. We also noted that two activities under the Framework ASEAN Plan of Action on Rural Development and Poverty Eradication were being implemented with support from the UNDP.
46. We welcomed the measures taken by the ASEAN Health Ministers to improve the competitiveness of health service and health-related products in ASEAN, and to provide the people or ASEAN with a better access to cheaper drugs.
47. We noted with satisfaction the progress in the preparation for the special session on HIV/AIDS on the occasion of 7th ASEAN Summit in November 2001 in Brunei Darussalam. Including the active participation of UNAIDS and other parties in the formulation of the ASEAN Work Program on HIV/AIDS II (2001–2004). We also noted that the ASEAN regional response to HIV/AIDS was in line with the Declaration of commitments on HIV/AIDS

adopted by the United Nations General Assembly Special Session on HIV/AIDS on 25–27 June 2001 in New York.

48. We welcomed the Yangon 2000 Declaration on Preparing ASEAN Youth For the Challenges of Globalization, announced at the 3rd ASEAN Ministerial Meeting on Youth (AMMY), held in Yangon in November 2000, which provided guidance for preparing and empowering the region's youth to make use of the opportunities and meet challenges created by globalization.
49. We noted the importance of the on-going efforts to combat forest fires and haze problems in the region. These include the implementation of the Regional Haze Action Plan and Iimmediate Action Plan; monitoring of forest fifes and haze; and negotiations on the ASEAN Agreement on Transboundary Haze Pollution, which was expected to be concluded by the end of this year. We emphasized the importance of strong commitments among the Member Countries, increased public and community awareness and participation, and continued support from donors to ensure success and sustainability of activities. In this regard, we expressed our appreciation for the assistance of the Asian Development Bank (ADB), some international organizations and Dialogue Countries.

....

51. Recalling the recommendations of the ASEAN Eminent Persons Group to develop more and broader linkages among educational institutions at all levels and to raise the standards of education in the whole of ASEAN, we reaffirmed the importance of student and academic exchanges among the universities of the ASEAN Member Countries. In this connection, we recognized the important role of the ASEAN University Network (AUN) as a pillar of the human resource development in the region. and requested the AUN to explore the acceleration of credit transfer among its member universities. We also requested relevant ASEAN bodies to continue to explore the establishment of common professional and technical standards in ASEAN and the setting up of benchmarks in the field of education.
52. We expressed support for efforts of the Committee on Science and Technology (COST) to develop cooperation with China, Japan and the Republic of Korea within the ASEAN + 3 framework.

....

55. We welcomed the endorsement of the ASEAN and China Cooperative Operations in Response to Dangerous Drugs (ACCORD) Plan of Action by the International Congress in Pursuit of a Drug-Free ASEAN 2015, which was jointly organized by Thailand, ASEAN and the United Nations Office for Drug Control and Crime Prevention on 11–13 October 2000 in Bangkok,

Thailand. We are gratified by the agreement to strengthen coordination in proactively advocating awareness of the danger of drugs and response building consensus and sharing best practices on demand reduction, strengthening the rule of law through improved law enforcement cooperation and legislative review, and eliminating the supply of illicit drugs by boosting alternative development program and community participation in the eradication of illicit crops. Mindful that illegal drugs and narcotics trafficking is not only of concern to each ASEAN Member Country and ASEAN as a whole, but also to the entire international community, we agreed to designate 2002–2003 as "ASEAN Drugs Awareness Years" in order to help raise the awareness of the peoples of ASEAN on the danger of illicit drugs and narcotics trafficking and mobilize their support for further strengthening the region's efforts in the fight against narcotic drugs. In this regard, we agreed to request the ASEAN Senior Officials on Drug Matters (ASOD) to consider how to implement such measures. including the possibility of establishing an appropriate ASEAN mechanism to combat illegal drugs and narcotics trafficking.

## EXTERNAL RELATIONS

56. We expressed our satisfaction with the progress of cooperation within the framework of ASEAN + 3 with China, Japan and the Republic of Korea in all fields, particularly trade, investment and finance. Considering that the enhancement of these cooperative activities was of great significance in restoring economic dynamism in East Asia in general and South East Asia in particular, we encouraged further cooperative efforts with priority to be given to infrastructure, ICT and human resource development. In this connection we welcomed the establishment of the East Asia Study Group (EASG) and initiatives to boost this cooperation. We also encouraged the participation of China, Japan and the Republic of Korea and other Dialogue Partners in the implementation of ASEAN initiatives such as the IAI and measures highlighted in the Hanoi Declaration on Narrowing Development Gap for Closer ASEAN Integration.
57. We reaffirmed that ASEAN's relations with its Dialogue Partners are the most significant aspect of ASEAN's external relations and expressed appreciation for their support for the implementation of the HPA and other ASEAN plans of action. We called upon the Dialogue Partners to continue the assistance especially after the review of the HPA by the ASEAN Summit in November 2001 in Brunei Darussalam, which would identify priority areas that ASEAN should focus on.
58. In the context of ASEAN overall development cooperation with Dialogue partners, we reiterated that the principle of non-discrimination should be

upheld and respected in the Dialogue Partners relations with ASEAN and agreed that development cooperation activities in the dialogue process should involve ASEAN as one regional entity.

59. We recalled the successful convening of the 13th ASEAN-European Union Ministerial Meeting (AEMM) on 11–12 December 2000 in Vientiane. We expressed ASEAN's desire to further strengthen its relations and to promote dialogue with the EU in all sectors of mutual interest. We looked forward to the next AEMM in Europe.
60. We stressed ASEAN's continued interest in enhancing closer cooperation with the United Nations, inter-governmental and regional organizations and welcomed the ASEAN Secretariat's efforts to coordinate closer cooperation with these organizations.

Source: http://www.aseansec.org/3045.htm
Accessed date: 8 October 2008
Publisher: ASEAN Secretariat
Country: Jakarta
Date of Publication: 2007

# CHAPTER 10

# JOINT STATEMENT OF THE MINISTERS RESPONSIBLE FOR ENVIRONMENT OF THE MEMBER STATES OF ASEAN TO THE WORLD SUMMIT ON SUSTAINABLE DEVELOPMENT

**Bali, Indonesia, 4 June 2002**

1. We the Ministers responsible for environment of Brunei Darussalam, Cambodia, Indonesia, Lao PDR, Malaysia, Union of Myanmar, Republic of the Philippines, Singapore, Thailand and Viet Nam of the Association of Southeast Asian Nations (ASEAN) met in Bali, Indonesia on 4 June 2002 to review the progress, constraints and challenges on the implementation of Agenda 21 in the region and to consider the key issues to be discussed at the World Summit on Sustainable Development (WSSD).
2. We in ASEAN are committed to pursuing sustainable development in the region and have demonstrated this commitment through ASEAN's Vision 2020 as "a concert of Southeast Asian nations, outward looking, living in peace, stability and prosperity, bonded in partnership in dynamic development and in a community of caring societies". The Vision also calls for "a clean and green ASEAN with fully established mechanisms for sustainable development to ensure the protection of the region's environment, the sustainability of its natural resources and the high quality of life of its peoples". In particular, the Hanoi Plan of Action calls for the protection of the environment and promotion of sustainable development.
3. ASEAN has a well-established governance structure for the Southeast Asian region to effectively develop, coordinate and implement regional programs. ASEAN also provides the forum to facilitate the development and implementation of integrated regional sustainable development policies, strategies and action plans, such as Vision 2020 and the Hanoi Plan of Action, which are consistent with the global framework and the needs of the member countries.
4. We note that the UN General Assembly, in launching the World Summit on Sustainable Development, called for a reinvigoration of the global commitment to sustainable development. Implicit in this decision is the clear message that not much has been accomplished since Rio. In fact, environmental

conditions and the world's natural resource base have deteriorated over the last ten years. The situation in ASEAN is no exception. In fact the impact has been felt on a larger scale because of the region's unique and diverse natural resources.

5. We are of the view that established principles, strategies and action plans for sustainable development as contained in the Rio Declaration and Agenda 21 are as valid as they were ten years ago. We are concerned that the commitments in financial assistance, technology transfer and capacity building have not been fully realized. We therefore call upon developed countries to immediately fulfill those commitments in line with the principle of common but differentiated responsibilities.
6. We emphasize that the declarations and commitments such as those contained in the Millennium Declaration and the Monterrey Consensus on Financing for Development should be implemented expeditiously.
7. We, therefore, are confident that the WSSD presents a unique opportunity to pull together all these resolutions to provide the impetus for holistic, action-oriented implementation measures for real progress towards sustainable development.
8. We believe that WSSD should set in place targeted, time-bound, practical and implementable actions for achieving specific sustainable development goals. In particular, the use of regional governance structures, regional goals and plans as a vehicle to implement these efforts at the national and regional levels should be emphasized.
9. We recognize the important role of the civil society and other major groups in the implementation of Agenda 21. We acknowledge the need for their participation and contribution, and fully support meaningful processes that would effectively engage them in the implementation of sustainable development agenda.
10. We call for the further enhancement of the international economic and trading systems to complement ASEAN's efforts to open trade and investment environment in the region through the implementation of the ASEAN Free Trade Area (AFTA) and the ASEAN Investment Area (AIA). In particular, we call for the improved market access for developing countries' exports, eliminating trade-distorting subsidies and barriers to trade for agricultural products. The provision of special and differential treatment to developing countries should also at the same time be tackled with urgency.
11. We recognize the opportunities for expanded trade, but are concerned about the possible constraints for trade based on genuine or ostensible environmental grounds. We oppose the use of environmental measures for protectionist purposes.

12. We call for measures to strengthen the international financial architecture which includes a review of the roles of the international financial institutions as well as international regulatory bodies in order to enhance their capacity to contain and resolve financial crises. Other measures include closer and more coordinated monitoring of short-term capital flows and a global agreement on disclosure requirements for such flows and closer collaboration and information sharing among national and international regulators. We emphasize that the global effort in this aspect should recognize the diverse circumstances and priorities of individual economies at different stages of development. Due priority should, therefore, be accorded to measures to protect the poor and most vulnerable segments of society.
13. Heavy debt burden has hampered the implementation of sustainable development. Therefore, debt relief measures should be pursued immediately and expeditiously. We support the efforts to develop and apply innovative mechanisms to comprehensively address debt problems in developing countries through, among others, the use of special drawing rights, debt swaps for nature and development programs. We welcome efforts to deal comprehensively and effectively with the debt problems of developing countries through various national and international measures designed to make the management of their debt sustainable in the long term.
14. We call for international support to eliminate absolute poverty in ASEAN and to further reduce the level of poverty (almost half the people in ASEAN still earn less that US$2 a day), in accordance with the vision and development goals set by ASEAN.
15. ASEAN welcomes international collaboration to help realize the goals of Healthy ASEAN 2020, through implementation of the relevant programs and activities.
16. We call for the speedy implementation of the provisions of the Convention on Biological Diversity, giving emphasis to issues that are of particular importance to resource-rich countries. These include mechanisms for the fair and equitable sharing of benefits derived from research and development and use of biological resources and the protection, promotion and equitable use of traditional knowledge. They also include mechanisms for the improvement, generation, development and sustainable use of biotechnology and its safe transfer, particularly to developing countries.
17. We call upon the international community to promote the management, conservation and sustainable development of all kinds of forests; address the underlying causes of deforestation and forest degradation, including linking forestry issues with anti-poverty measures; and to promote trade policies that

are transparent, and support sustainable forest management, including better market access and fair pricing for forestry products.

18. We call for international support to enhance ASEAN's effort in improving regional coordination for the integrated protection and management of its coastal and marine areas. We are also committed to addressing pollution from land- and sea-based activities through the development of a regional action plan for the protection of its marine environment.
19. ASEAN has experienced recurrent episodes of transboundary haze from land and forest fires and has taken several measures to address this problem. Such problems are not only occurring in the ASEAN region, but also in other developed and developing countries. While the global impacts of forest damaged in terms of biodiversity loss or emissions of carbon dioxide are obvious, member countries have largely been left to tackle these problems by themselves. The ASEAN Agreement on Transboundary Haze Pollution will provide the legal and institutional framework to tackle this problem on national as well as regional basis, including prevention, monitoring, coordination, disaster relief, and research and development. We therefore call for sustained international support to deal with the problem in the long term.
20. We call upon the international community to extend their support to developing countries who are parties and those who have yet to become parties to the multilateral environmental agreements to assist them to strengthen their legislative, institutional and administrative capability and capacity to mitigate and address the specific environmental problems. We further call for concerted efforts to foster synergy and coordination among the multilateral environmental agreements. We support the early entry into force of the Kyoto Protocol.
21. We call for the strengthening of the sustainable development governance and institutional frameworks, including enhancing the capacity of national and regional institutions and the development of human resources. The existing frameworks for regional inter-governmental governance should be fully utilized as part of the international governance structure. Greater use should be made of regional inter-governmental organizations to promote coordinated sustainable development initiatives for that region.
22. Adequate and predictable financing provides the means to ensure the effective implementation of sustainable development initiatives. We note with concern that the agreed target of 0.7% of GNP for ODA has yet to be achieved, but in fact has been declining since Rio. We therefore call for specific pledges, including time frames for achieving this target, to be made at WSSD.
23. We call upon the Global Environment Facility to enhance its effectiveness by improving its operational procedures to be more responsive to the identified

needs of developing countries. We further invite the Global Environment Facility to accord priority to regional projects developed within the ASEAN institutional framework.

24. We urge developed countries to facilitate transfer of environmentally sound technology on preferential terms to enable developing countries to implement sustainable development initiatives as agreed upon, such as, in the various multilateral environmental agreements.
25. We welcome the initiatives on partnerships (Type II Outcomes), as this will lead to concrete, implementable, and time-bound actions for sustainable development. We urge interested parties to explore such partnerships in the key programs areas that have been outlined in the ASEAN Report to the World Summit on Sustainable Development. However, we stress that such partnerships should not prevent member states from fulfilling the agreed political commitments, based on the principle of common but differentiated responsibilities, in terms of technology transfer, financial support, capacity building and human resource development.

Source: http://www.aseansec.org/10200.htm
Accessed date: 22 January 2009
Publisher: ASEAN Secretariat
Country: Jakarta
Date of Publication: 2007

# CHAPTER 11

# DECLARATION OF ASEAN CONCORD II (BALI CONCORD II)

The Sultan of Brunei Darussalam, the Prime Minister of the Kingdom of Cambodia, the President of the Republic of Indonesia, the Prime Minister of the Lao People's Democratic Republic, the Prime Minister of Malaysia, the Prime Minister of the Union of Myanmar, the President of the Republic of the Philippines, the Prime Minister of the Republic of Singapore, the Prime Minister of the Kingdom of Thailand and the Prime Minister of the Socialist Republic of Viet Nam;

**RECALLING** the Declaration of ASEAN Concord adopted in this historic place of Bali, Indonesia in 1976, the Leaders of the Association of Southeast Asian Nations (ASEAN) expressed satisfaction with the overall progress made in the region;

**NOTING** in particular the expansion of ASEAN to ten countries in Southeast Asia, the deepening of regional economic integration and the impending accession to the Treaty of Amity and Cooperation (TAC) by States outside Southeast Asia;

**CONSCIOUS** of the need to further consolidate and enhance the achievements of ASEAN as a dynamic, resilient, and cohesive regional association for the well-being of its member states and people as well as the need to further strengthen the Association's guidelines in achieving a more coherent and clearer path for cooperation between and among them;

**REAFFIRMING** their commitment to the principles enshrined in the ASEAN Declaration (Bangkok, 1967), the Declaration on Zone of Peace, Freedom, and Neutrality (Kuala Lumpur, 1971), the Treaty of Amity and Cooperation in Southeast Asia (Bali, 1976), the Declaration of ASEAN Concord (Bali, 1976), and the Treaty on the Southeast Asia Nuclear Weapons Free Zone (Bangkok, 1995);

**COGNIZANT** that the future of ASEAN cooperation is guided by the ASEAN Vision 2020, the Hanoi Plan of Action (1999–2004), and its succeeding Plans of Action, the Initiative for ASEAN Integration (IAI), and the Roadmap for the Integration of ASEAN (RIA);

**CONFIRMING** further that ASEAN Member Countries share primary responsibility for strengthening the economic and social stability in the region and ensuring their peaceful and progressive national development, and that they are determined to ensure their stability and security from external interference in any form or manner in order to preserve their national interest in accordance with the ideals and aspirations of their peoples;

**REAFFIRMING** the fundamental importance of adhering to the principle of non-interference and consensus in ASEAN cooperation;

**REITERATING** that the Treaty of Amity and Cooperation in Southeast Asia (TAG) is an effective code of conduct for relations among governments and peoples;

**RECOGNIZING** that sustainable economic development requires a secure political environment based on a strong foundation of mutual interests generated by economic cooperation and political solidarity;

**COGNIZANT** of the interdependence of the ASEAN economies and the need for ASEAN member countries to adopt "Prosper Thy Neighbour" policies in order to ensure the long-term vibrancy and prosperity of the ASEAN region;

**REITERATING** the importance of rules-based multilateral trading system that is equitable and that contributes towards the pursuit of development;

**REAFFIRMING** that ASEAN is a concert of Southeast Asian nations, bonded together in partnership in dynamic development and in a community of caring societies, committed to upholding cultural diversity and social harmony;

## DO HEREBY DECLARE THAT:

1. An ASEAN Community shall be established comprising three pillars, namely political and security cooperation, economic cooperation, and socio-cultural cooperation that are closely intertwined and mutually reinforcing for the purpose of ensuring durable peace, stability and shared prosperity in the region;
2. ASEAN shall continue its efforts to ensure closer and mutually beneficial integration among its member states and among their peoples, and to promote regional peace and stability, security, development and prosperity with a view to realizing an ASEAN Community that is open, dynamic and resilient;
3. ASEAN shall respond to the new dynamics within the respective ASEAN Member Countries and shall urgently and effectively address the challenge of translating ASEAN cultural diversities and different economic levels into equitable development opportunity and prosperity, in an environment of solidarity, regional resilience and harmony;

4. ASEAN shall nurture common values, such as habit of consultation to discuss political issues and the willingness to share information on matters of common concern, such as environmental degradation, maritime security cooperation, the enhancement of defense cooperation among ASEAN countries, develop a set of socio-political values and principles, and resolve to settle long-standing disputes through peaceful means;
5. The Treaty of Amity and Cooperation in Southeast Asia (TAC) is the key code of conduct governing relations between states and a diplomatic instrument for the promotion of peace and stability in the region;
6. The ASEAN Regional Forum (ARF) shall remain the primary forum in enhancing political and security cooperation in the Asia Pacific region, as well as the pivot in building peace and stability in the region. ASEAN shall enhance its role in further advancing the stages of cooperation within the ARF to ensure the security of the Asia Pacific region;
7. ASEAN is committed to deepening and broadening its internal economic integration and linkages with the world economy to realize an ASEAN Economic Community through a bold, pragmatic and unified strategy;
8. ASEAN shall further build on the momentum already gained in the ASEAN + 3 process so as to further draw synergies through broader and deeper cooperation in various areas;
9. ASEAN shall build upon opportunities for mutually beneficial regional integration arising from its existing initiatives and those with partners, through enhanced trade and investment links as well as through IAI process and the RIA;
10. ASEAN shall continue to foster a community of caring societies and promote a common regional identity;

## DO HEREBY ADOPT:

The framework to achieve a dynamic, cohesive, resilient and integrated ASEAN Community:

### A. Asean Security Community (ASC)

1. The ASEAN Security Community is envisaged to bring ASEAN's political and security cooperation to a higher plane to ensure that countries in the region live at peace with one another and with the world at large in a just, democratic and harmonious environment. The ASEAN Security Community members shall rely exclusively on peaceful processes in the settlement of intra-regional differences and regard their security as fundamentally linked to one another and bound by geographic location, common vision and objectives.

2. The ASEAN Security Community, recognizing the sovereign right of the member countries to pursue their individual foreign policies and defense arrangements and taking into account the strong interconnections among political, economic and social realities, subscribes to the principle of comprehensive security as having broad political, economic, social and cultural aspects in consonance with the ASEAN Vision 2020 rather than to a defense pact, military alliance or a joint foreign policy.
3. ASEAN shall continue to promote regional solidarity and cooperation. Member Countries shall exercise their rights to lead their national existence free from outside interference in their internal affairs.
4. The ASEAN Security Community shall abide by the UN Charter and other principles of international law and uphold ASEAN's principles of non-interference, consensus-based decision-making, national and regional resilience, respect for national sovereignty, the renunciation of the threat or the use of force, and peaceful settlement of differences and disputes.
5. Maritime issues and concerns are transboundary in nature, and therefore shall be addressed regionally in holistic, integrated and comprehensive manner. Maritime cooperation between and among ASEAN member countries shall contribute to the evolution of the ASEAN Security Community.
6. Existing ASEAN political instruments such as the Declaration on ZOPFAN, the TAC, and the SEANWFZ Treaty shall continue to play a pivotal role in the area of confidence building measures, preventive diplomacy and the approaches to conflict resolution.
7. The High Council of the TAC shall be the important component in the ASEAN Security Community since it reflects ASEAN's commitment to resolve all differences, disputes and conflicts peacefully.
8. The ASEAN Security Community shall contribute to further promoting peace and security in the wider Asia Pacific region and reflect ASEAN's determination to move forward at a pace comfortable to all. In this regard, the ARF shall remain the main forum for regional security dialogue, with ASEAN as the primary driving force.
9. The ASEAN Security Community is open and outward looking in respect of actively engaging ASEAN's friends and Dialogue Partners to promote peace and stability in the region, and shall build on the ARF to facilitate consultation and cooperation between ASEAN and its friends and Partners on regional security matters.
10. The ASEAN Security Community shall fully utilize the existing institutions and mechanisms within ASEAN with a view to strengthening national and regional capacities to counter terrorism, drug trafficking, trafficking of persons and other transnational crimes; and shall work to ensure that the

Southeast Asian Region remains free of all weapons of mass destruction. It shall enable ASEAN to demonstrate a greater capacity and responsibility of being the primary driving force of the ARF.

11. The ASEAN Security Community shall explore enhanced cooperation with the United Nations as well as other international and regional bodies for the maintenance of international peace and security.
12. ASEAN shall explore innovative ways to increase its security and establish modalities for the ASEAN Security Community, which include, inter alia, the following elements: norms-setting, conflict prevention, approaches to conflict resolution, and post-conflict peace building.

## B. ASEAN Economic Community (AEC)

1. The ASEAN Economic Community is the realization of the end-goal of economic integration as outlined in the ASEAN Vision 2020, to create a stable, prosperous and highly competitive ASEAN economic region in which there is a free flow of goods, services, investment and a freer flow of capital, equitable economic development and reduced poverty and socio-economic disparities in year 2020.
2. The ASEAN Economic Community is based on a convergence of interests among ASEAN members to deepen and broaden economic integration efforts through existing and new initiatives with clear timelines.
3. ASEAN Economic Community shall establish ASEAN as a single market and production base, turning the diversity that characterizes the region into opportunities for business complementation making the ASEAN a more dynamic and stronger segment of the global supply chain. ASEAN's strategy shall consist of the integration of ASEAN and enhancing ASEAN's economic competitiveness. In moving towards the ASEAN Economic Community, ASEAN shall, inter alia, institute new mechanisms and measures to strengthen the implementation of its existing economic initiatives including the ASEAN Free Trade Area (AFTA), ASEAN Framework Agreement on Services (AFAS) and ASEAN Investment Area (AIA); accelerate regional integration in the priority sectors; facilitate movement of business persons, skilled labour and talents; and strengthen the institutional mechanisms of ASEAN, including the improvement of the existing ASEAN Dispute Settlement Mechanism to ensure expeditious and legally binding resolution of any economic disputes. As a first step towards the realization of the ASEAN Economic Community, ASEAN shall implement the recommendations of the High Level Task Force on ASEAN Economic Integration as annexed.
4. The ASEAN Economic Community shall ensure that deepening and broadening integration of ASEAN shall be accompanied by technical and development cooperation in order to address the development divide and accelerate

the economic integration of Cambodia, Lao PDR, Myanmar and Viet Nam through IAI and RIA so that the benefits of ASEAN integration are shared and enable all ASEAN Member Countries to move forward in a unified manner.

5. The realization of a fully integrated economic community requires implementation of liberalization and cooperation measures. There is a need to enhance cooperation and integration activities in other areas. These will involve, among others, human resources development and capacity building; recognition of educational qualifications; closer consultation on macroeconomic and financial policies; trade financing measures; enhanced infrastructure and communications connectivity; development of electronic transactions through e-ASEAN; integrating industries across the region to promote regional sourcing; and enhancing private sector involvement.

## C. ASEAN Socio-Cultural Community (ASCC)

1. The ASEAN Socio-cultural Community, in consonance with the goal set by ASEAN Vision 2020, envisages a Southeast Asia bonded together in partnership as a community caring society.
2. In line with the programme of action set by the 1976 Declaration of ASEAN Concord, the Community shall foster cooperation in social development aimed at raising the standard of living of disadvantaged groups and the rural population, and shall seek the active involvement of all sectors of society, in particular women, youth, and local communities.
3. ASEAN shall ensure that its work force shall be prepared for, and benefit from, economic integration by investing more resources for basic and higher education, training, science and technology development, job creation, and social protection. The development and enhancement of human resources is a key strategy for employment generation, alleviating poverty and socio-economic disparities, and ensuring economic growth with equity. ASEAN shall continue existing efforts to promote regional mobility and mutual recognition of professional credentials, talents, and skills development.
4. ASEAN shall further intensify cooperation in the area of public health, including in the prevention and control of infectious diseases, such as HIV/AIDS and SARS, and support joint regional actions to increase access to affordable medicines. The security of the Community is enhanced when poverty and diseases are held in check, and the peoples of ASEAN are assured of adequate health care.
5. The Community shall nurture talent and promote interaction among ASEAN scholars, writers, artists and media practitioners to help preserve and promote ASEAN's diverse cultural heritage while fostering regional identity as well as cultivating people's awareness of ASEAN.

6. The Community shall intensify cooperation in addressing problems associated with population growth, unemployment, environmental degradation and transboundary pollution as well as disaster management in the region to enable individual members to fully realize their development potentials and to enhance the mutual ASEAN spirit.

We hereby pledge to our peoples our resolve and commitment to bring the ASEAN Community into reality and, for this purpose, task the concerned Ministers to implement this Declaration.

**DONE** in Bali, Indonesia, on the Seventh Day of October in the Year Two Thousand and Three.

| | |
|---|---|
| For Brunei Darussalam<br>HAJI HASSANAL BOLKIAH<br>Sultan of Brunei Darussalam | For the Kingdom of Cambodia<br>SAMDECH HUN SEN<br>Prime Minister |
| For the Republic of Indonesia<br>MEGAWATI SOEKARNOPUTRI<br>President | For the Lao People's Democratic Republic<br>BOUNNHANG VORACHITH<br>Prime Minister |
| For Malaysia<br>DR. MAHATHIR BIN MOHAMAD<br>Prime Minister | For the Union of Myanmar<br>GENERAL KHIN NYUNT<br>Prime Minister |
| For the Republic of the Philippines<br>GLORIA MACAPAGAL-ARROYO<br>President | For the Republic of Singapore<br>GOH CHOK TONG<br>Prime Minister |
| For the Kingdom of Thailand<br>DR. THAKSIN SHINAWATRA<br>Prime Minister | For the Socialist Republic of Viet Nam<br>PHAN VAN KHAI<br>Prime Minister |

Source: http://www.aseansec.org/15159.htm
Accessed date: 7 February 2006
Publisher: ASEAN Secretariat
Country: Jakarta
Date of Publication: 2004

# CHAPTER 12

# CHAIRMAN'S STATEMENT OF THE 11$^{TH}$ ASEAN SUMMIT "ONE VISION, ONE IDENTITY, ONE COMMUNITY"

**Kuala Lumpur, 12 December 2005**

1. The 11$^{th}$ ASEAN Summit, with the theme "One Vision, One Identity, One Community", was chaired by The Honourable Dato' Seri Abdullah Ahmad Badawi, the Chairman of the 11$^{th}$ ASEAN Summit and the Prime Minister of Malaysia. The Leaders of ASEAN had a productive meeting, which was held in plenary, and in retreat for the first time allowing for candid and frank discussions.
2. A total of 10 documents listed in the Annex, were issued as the outcome of the 11$^{th}$ ASEAN Summit.

## ASEAN INTEGRATION AND COMMUNITY BUILDING

3. We welcomed the progress in ASEAN integration and the ongoing community building efforts. We underscored the importance of ASEAN's cohesion in dealing with issues and challenges facing the region to enhance ASEAN's credibility, transparency and solidarity to protect and nurture the collective interest of ASEAN.

## ASEAN Charter

4. We signed the Kuala Lumpur Declaration on the Establishment of the ASEAN Charter, which will be a landmark constitutional document embodying fundamental principles, goals, objectives and structures of ASEAN cooperation capable of meeting the needs of the ASEAN Community and beyond. In this connection, we agreed to establish an Eminent Persons Group (EPG), comprising highly distinguished and well respected citizens from ASEAN Member Countries with a mandate to examine and provide practical recommendations on the directions for ASEAN and nature of the ASEAN Charter. We further tasked our Ministers to establish, as necessary, a High Level Task Force to carry out the drafting of the ASEAN Charter based on the Declaration and the recommendations of the EPG.

## Vientiane Action Programme

5. We noted the reports on the progress in the implementation of the Vientiane Action Programme (VAP) and the follow-up to the previous ASEAN and Related Summits. We acknowledged the steady progress made in the implementation of the VAP and our decisions and initiatives. We welcomed the establishment of the ASEAN Development Fund (ADF) and urged the ASEAN Member Countries and our Dialogue Partners to consider contributing to the Fund to support ASEAN's integration. We called on our Ministers and Senior Officials to study the bottlenecks in the implementation and to find creative solutions to carry out pending measures in the VAP and our decisions and initiatives taken at previous Summits. We requested the Secretary-General of ASEAN to update us with the progress made at our next Summit.

## ASEAN Security Community

6. We noted the steady progress made in the implementation of the ASEAN Security Community (ASC) related activities through the VAP and the ASC Plan of Action (PoA). We noted the accomplishments in implementing the ASC, including the establishment of the Inter-Sessional Support Group on Confidence Building and Preventive Diplomacy and the revival of the Inter-Sessional Meeting on Disaster Relief under the ASEAN regional Forum (ARF); the setting up of the ASEAN-China Joint Working Group on the Implementation of the Declaration on the Conduct of Parties in the South China Sea; and the promotion of greater public awareness about ASEAN through holding activities on the occasion of ASEAN day.
7. We welcomed the efforts towards enhancing ASEAN's cooperation in combating terrorism and other transnational crimes through the implementation of agreements among ASEAN Members Countries and the revitalisation and re-ordering of priorities of existing work plans and programmes to give sharper focus to meeting the challenges posed by such crimes. We recognised the important role of inter-faith dialogue in fighting the spread of terrorism and promoting understanding among our people.

## ASEAN Economic Community

....

15. We stand committed to the common goals of eradicating poverty and hunger in ASEAN as pledged at the World Food Summit and Millennium

Declarations, and reiterated in the VAP. We, therefore, strongly support further resource mobilisation for agriculture and rural development in the ASEAN Member Countries as agriculture plays a pivotal role in improving food security and poverty reduction. We acknowledged that more and better investment in the sector will create additional employment opportunities, enhance competitiveness and ensure sustainable economic growth. In this regard, we welcomed a number of national and ASEAN initiatives and plans of action and cooperation with various regional and international organisations, including those within the United Nations system such as the Food and Agriculture Organisation and the Economic and Social Commission for Asia and the Pacific to bolster projects and activities in agriculture and propose practical modalities for financing the cooperative programmes.

## ASEAN Socio-Cultural Community

16. We were satisfied with the overall progress made in the implementation of the ASEAN Socio-Cultural Community (ASCC)-related measures and activities of the VAP and the ASCC PoA, particularly, in the areas of disaster management and emergency relief; prevention and control of the diseases such as HIV and AIDS and avian influenza; combating transnational crimes; promoting social, women and child development; and poverty eradication. We agreed to further enhance cooperation in these areas to move towards the realisation of the ASCC by 2020.
17. We welcomed the responsive action and coordinative efforts by ASEAN Member Countries to control and eradicate the spread of Highly Pathogenic Avian Influenza (HPAI) in the region. We called for further institutional linkages and partnerships among all stakeholders in public and private sectors and civil society. We reaffirmed the commitment and support of our countries to the various initiatives undertaken by HPAI Taskforce and ASEAN Expert Group on Communicable Diseases, through the Regional Framework for Control and Eradication of HPAI, establishment of ASEAN Animal Health Trust Fund, and ASEAN Plus Three Emerging Infectious Diseases Programme. We emphasised the importance of ASEAN's collective strength in coordinating a common regional approach and sharing resources to address transboundary threats, including the setting up of a regional network of antiviral drugs stockpile. We called upon our Dialogue Partners, international organisations, and other relevant donors to work closely with ASEAN and all concerned parties in combating avian influenza.
18. We agreed on the need to work closely and collaborate in the area of avian influenza. We noted Malaysia's intention to establish the Regional Avian

Influenza Research and Reference Centre (NAIRRC) as well as the Regional WHO Collaborating Centre for Influenza. The two centres will share their respective experience in virological surveillance and diagnostic capabilities for the benefit of this region.

19. We noted with encouragement the progress made in addressing the HIV transmission and AIDS treatment through the implementation of the ASEAN Work Programme (AWP) on HIV/AIDS II and look forward to the agenda for future action through a strategic framework for AWP III, which we endorsed. We strongly believe that ASEAN's strength in fighting the HIV and AIDS lies in joint action and coordination among the Member Countries. We looked forward to convening the Second Special Session on HIV and AIDS in conjunction with the 12th ASEAN Summit in 2006, to signal ASEAN's commitment in combating the AIDS pandemic and to give impetus to regional responses in taking urgent action to eradicate this threat to our future generations. We agreed to promote a higher profile and voice for ASEAN's work in this area with the international community, particularly in global decision-making on fund allocation for HIV and AIDS prevention and control.
20. We recalled with sorrow the loss of lives and devastation caused by the Tsunami of 26 December 2004 last year, and resolved to prevent the recurrence of such devastation. In this regard, we underlined the importance of establishing a regional early warning system.
21. We welcomed the signing of the ASEAN Agreement on the Disaster Management and Emergency Response in July 2005 in Vientiane, Lao PDR, which inter-alia provides for a stand by regional military and civilian capacity to deal with disasters, to further intensify cooperation in this area among ASEAN Member Countries as well as between ASEAN, and other countries and regional and international organisations.
22. We expressed serious concern over the impact of land and forest fires and the resulting transboundary haze pollution that affects our region almost annually. While noting the various measures that have been undertaken at the national level over the years, and at the regional level guided by the ASEAN Agreement on Transboundary Haze Pollution, we recognised the need to further intensify and undertake coordinated action, particularly to address the underlying causes of land and forest fires. We noted with satisfaction the concerted action taken by ASEAN Member Countries during the recent severe haze episode by mobilising personnel, aircraft and equipment to suppress the fires and stand ready to provide such assistance during critical periods in the future. We called for swift and more effective inter-agency collaboration and coordination at the national and regional levels to deal comprehensively with the transboundary haze pollution. Recognising also its transboundary nature

and widespread impact on various sectors, we have directed our relevant Ministers and agencies to deal collectively with this issue.

23. We also noted the efforts to establish a transboundary network of sanctuaries on the island of Borneo involving Malaysia, Brunei Darussalam and Indonesia. Such sanctuaries would protect the biological diversity of plants and animals in the green Heart of Borneo and would play a vital role in protecting all of the island major water catchment.
24. We welcomed the decision of the ASEAN Ministers of Education to convene the ASEAN Ministerial Meeting on Education on a regular basis. This is a significant development given the important role of education in ASEAN's social and economic development and its community building efforts including raising the awareness of ASEAN, instilling the 'we feeling' and creating a sense of belonging to the ASEAN Community. We also agreed that the Meeting should focus on enhancing regional cooperation in education matters among Member Countries as well as to cooperate closely with other ASEAN sectoral bodies in the context of the building the ASEAN Socio-Cultural Community (ASCC) and implementing the Plan of Action of the ASCC.
25. We agreed to establish ASEAN university games, ASEAN youth peace corps, ASEAN computer games and ASEAN science olympiad to promote greater interaction and understanding among the youths in the region. We tasked our ministers to look into the possibility of synchronising the university vacation period so as to enable students to partake in the activities.
26. We exchanged views the utilising information communication technology (ICT) to promote interaction among our people, including the possibility of an e-ASEAN community.

## Bridging the Development Gap

27. We reiterated that bridging the development gap is critical to regional integration. We noted ASEAN's efforts to bridge the development gap through the Initiative for ASEAN Integration (IAI) in the past few years focusing on human resources development, infrastructure (transport and energy), regional economic integration and information technology. We were encouraged by the steady progress in the implementation of the IAI projects and expressed our appreciation to the ASEAN Member Countries, Dialogue Partners and regional and international organisations for their support and contribution.
28. We noted the mid-term review report of the IAI, in particular the recommendations put forward in the report. We acknowledged the need to further broaden the scope of the IAI to meet the urgent needs of the CLMV countries, the need

for participation in IAI activities by other underdeveloped sub-regions in ASEAN and the need to mobilise resources to support IAI implementation.

....

30. We recognised the important contribution of various sub-regional arrangements to ASEAN integration and noted the substantial progress made in the implementation of the initiatives and programmes under such arrangements. In this regard, we welcomed the successful convening of the Second Brunei-Indonesia-Malaysia-Philippine East Asia Growth Area (BIMP-EAGA) Summit and the BIMP-EAGA Roadmap to Development, which will guide the stakeholders in the implementation of doable, practical and sustainable strategies, programs and projects that will benefit the communities of member countries in BIMP-EAGA. We also welcomed the First Indonesia-Malaysia-Thailand Growth Triangle (IMT-GT) Summit, and the Second Cambodia-Laos-Myanmar-Viet Nam (CLMV) Summit on 11 December 2005 in Kuala Lumpur, Malaysia.
31. We also appreciated the valuable contribution of sub-regional cooperation framework aimed at narrowing the development gap and accelerating the integration of new members, as such as the Greater Mekong Sub-region (GMS) and Ayeyawady-Chao Phraya-Mekong Economic Cooperation Strategy (ACMEC).

## ASEAN Foundation

32. We noted the Report of the Executive Director of the ASEAN Foundation. We agreed that the Foundation should further intensify its efforts in promoting awareness of ASEAN among the peoples of ASEAN, and addressing issues related to poverty alleviation and socio-economic disparities in the region.

## Aceh, Indonesia

33. We welcomed the positive developments in the solution of the conflict in Aceh, Indonesia, through the dialogue leading to the conclusion of the Memorandum of Understanding between the Government of Indonesia and GAM. We also welcomed the efforts made to keep member states of ASEAN informed of such developments. We supported the cooperation between Indonesia and ASEAN contributing countries to the Aceh Monitoring Mission as a model for cooperation between ASEAN Member Countries in conflict resolution as provided for in the ASEAN Security Community, as well as a model for cooperation between regions, in this case with the European Union.

## Myanmar

34. We noted the increased interest of the international community on developments in Myanmar. In this context, we took note of the briefing by Myanmar on the latest developments in the implementation of its Roadmap to Democracy. We encouraged Myanmar to expedite the process and welcomed the invitation by Myanmar to the Foreign Minister of Malaysia in his capacity as Chairman of the ASEAN Standing Committee to visit Myanmar to learn first-hand of the progress. We also called for the release of those placed under detention.

## EXTERNAL RELATIONS

## ASEAN Plus Three Cooperation

35. We were pleased with the overall progress made in our cooperation within the ASEAN Plus Three framework, including the steady implementation of the short-term and some of the medium and long term East Asia Study Group measures. We looked forward to the signing of the Kuala Lumpur Declaration on the ASEAN Plus Three Summit on 12 December 2005 to reaffirm our commitment to the ASEAN Plus Three cooperation. We reiterated our commitment to ensuring that the ASEAN Plus Three process would be the main vehicle for the realisation of the East Asian community in the future, and would work closely with our Plus Three partners on this common objective.

## Cooperation with Dialogue Partners

36. We noted the encouraging progress in ASEAN's cooperation with its Dialogue Partners. We also noted the Report of the ASEAN-China Eminent Persons Group, in particular their recommendations to strengthen the ASEAN-China partnership, which we will discuss with the Premier of China on 12 December 2005. We also look forward to the adoption of the Joint Statement with Japan to further enhance the partnership for a stable and prosperous region.
37. We welcomed the ASEAN-Russian Federation Joint Declaration on Progressive and Comprehensive Partnership and the Comprehensive Program of Action for 2005–2015 to strengthen ASEAN-Russia relations, which we will conclude with the President of the Russian Federation on 13 December 2005. We will adopt a Plan of Action with the President of the Republic of Korea to implement the Joint Declaration on Comprehensive Partnership on 13 December 2005.

38. We also welcomed the recent accession of Australia, Mongolia and New Zealand to the Treaty of Amity and Cooperation in Southeast Asia, which will further enhance the role of the Treaty as a code of conduct governing inter-state relations in the region for the promotion of peace and stability.
39. We noted the progress in the free trade area (FTA) negotiations with China, India, the Republic of Korea, Japan, and the Australia New Zealand. We underscored the importance of these arrangements in collectively strengthening ASEAN's trade and economic cooperation with our Dialogue Partners and contributing to the progress, prosperity and development of the region. We encouraged all partners to work with ASEAN towards the realisation of the FTAs with the longer-term benefits of such FTAs in mind. We looked forward to the signing of the Framework Agreement on Comprehensive Economic Cooperation with the Republic of Korea on 13 December 2005 and welcomed the other agreements pertaining to the ASEAN-ROK FTA signed by our Economic Ministers with the ROK on 9 December 2005. We further welcomed the signing of the ASEAN-Russian Federation Economic and Development Cooperation Agreement by the ASEAN Foreign Ministers and the Minister of Foreign Affairs of the Russian Federation on 10 December 2005, which will strengthen the economic and development cooperation dimensions of the relations as both sides work towards a progressive and comprehensive partnership.

## East Asia Summit

40. We welcomed the convening of the East Asia Summit (EAS) on 14 December 2005, as an open and inclusive forum with ASEAN as the driving force for broad strategic, political, economic issues of common interest. We also agreed that the EAS should be a "top-down" forum for Leaders to exchange views. We looked forward to the signing of the Kuala Lumpur Declaration on the East Asia Summit. We agreed that the efforts of the EAS to promote community building in this region will be consistent with and reinforce the realisation of the ASEAN Community, and will form an integral part of the evolving regional architecture.
41. We agreed that the EAS and the ASEAN Plus Three process should move on parallel tracks without overlapping and complement one another as well as other regional processes.

....

## REGIONAL AND INTERNATIONAL POLITICAL AND SECURITY AND ECONOMIC ISSUES

43. We exchanged views on the regional and international situation and acknowledged that our regional environment continues to be peaceful and stable. We are aware that the region is being confronted with challenges such as the threat of terrorism, the outbreak of avian influenza, and the rise in oil prices which have direct negative impact on regional economic development and public health. We agreed that ASEAN should step up efforts to address these challenges at the bilateral, regional and multilateral levels in accordance with our obligations under international law and with respect for national sovereignty, territorial integrity and the principle of non-interference in the internal affairs of other countries.
44. We were outraged at the series of terrorist attacks in our region and other parts of the world that resulted in the loss of innocent lives. We strongly condemned such acts of terror and extended our sympathies to the victims and their families. We condemned acts of terrorism in all its forms and manifestations, and emphasised the need to maintain and intensify cooperation among states in the region to combat terrorism and seriously address the root causes of terrorism. We continue to reject any attempt to associate terrorism with any race, religion, nationality or ethnic group.
45. We reaffirmed our support for the denuclearization of the Korean Peninsula and support the efforts made by the Six Party Talks to find a peaceful and comprehensive solution to the nuclear issue on the Korean Peninsula. In this connection, we welcomed the fourth and fifth rounds of the Six-Party Talks held in July and November 2005 in Beijing, China, and called on all concerned parties to exert utmost efforts to move towards a peaceful resolution to the nuclear issue on the Korean Peninsula.

...

## WTO

50. We recognized that a successful outcome of the WTO Doha Development Agenda (DDA) negotiations would crucially contribute towards further strengthening of the multilateral trading system, promoting global economic growth and in particularly enhancing economic development in developing countries. For this reason, it is important to maintain the level of ambition established in the Doha Declaration and ensure that the objectives of the DDA are pursued to a successful conclusion.

51. An ambitious and overall balanced outcome at the end of the Round must include, among others; a comprehensive package in agriculture to ensure substantial reductions in trade distorting domestic support, substantial improvements in market access for all products by significantly lowering tariffs and reducing quantitative restrictions, and the elimination of all forms of export subsidies of developed Members by 2010; an agreement on non-agricultural market access through a Swiss formula with ambitious coefficients and sectoral agreements on a voluntary basis that will ensure real market access improvements for all WTO Members; an agreement in services that will create commercially meaningful and real market access opportunities in all WTO Members; clarification and improvement of the WTO rules for securing and enhancing benefits in market access that will ensure clearer and more predictable trade disciplines; and clearer and improved WTO rules for trade facilitation that will contribute to further expediting the movement, release and clearance of goods.
52. We stressed that the development dimension of the Round should be embodied in all negotiating areas and deliver real, effective and operational development benefits to all developing country members and in particularly, take into account the special needs of the least developed countries (LDCs).
53. We called on all WTO Members, especially those that have the largest stake in the global trading system and derive the biggest benefits from it, to make all necessary contributions and additional efforts to ensure that the upcoming Ministerial Conference in Hong Kong provides a substantial platform to move the DDA negotiations forward to a successful completion of the round by the end of 2006.
54. We also noted the progress made so far in WTO membership negotiations of Lao PDR and the Socialist Republic of Viet Nam. We called on WTO members to turn their strong support for the WTO membership of these countries into concrete actions by accelerating the negotiations and by not posing excessive requests beyond their capacities so that these countries become WTO members soon. Early accession to the WTO of these countries will facilitate their full integration into the international economy and further strengthen and enrich the multilateral trading system.

## OTHER MATTERS

55. We noted with appreciation the ASEAN Business Advisory Council (ABAC) report and agreed to continue to support its role in the overall strategy of increasing the private sector engagement in ASEAN economic policy deliberations. We also underscored the need for closer coordination and regular

engagement between the private sector and relevant public agencies in the implementation of ABAC's recommendations as well as the ASEAN economic initiatives and programmes.

56. We welcomed the convening of the ASEAN Tourism Investment Forum on 9 December 2005 in Kuala Lumpur, Malaysia, which would contribute to our countries' efforts to attract more tourism-related investment into the region and to developing ASEAN as an attractive tourist destination.
57. We took note of the Report of the ASEAN Civil Society Conference (ACSC) which was held on 7–9 December 2005. We recognised that the civil society will play an increasing important role in ASEAN as we develop a people-centred ASEAN Community. Thus, we supported the holding of the Conference annually on the sidelines of the ASEAN Summit and that its report be presented to the Leaders.

Source: http://www.aseansec.org/18039.htm
Accessed date: 22 January 2009
Publisher: ASEAN Secretariat
Country: Jakarta
Date of Publication: 2005

# CHAPTER 13

# KUALA LUMPUR DECLARATION ON THE EAST ASIA SUMMIT

**Kuala Lumpur, 14 December 2005**

**WE**, the Heads of State/Government of the Member Countries of the Association of Southeast Asian Nations (ASEAN), Australia, People's Republic of China, Republic of India, Japan, Republic of Korea and New Zealand, on the occasion of the historic First East Asia Summit on 14 December 2005 in Kuala Lumpur, Malaysia;

**RECALLING** the decision of the 10th ASEAN Summit and supported by the 8th ASEAN Plus Three Summit held on 29 November 2004 in Vientiane, Lao PDR, to convene the First East Asia Summit in Malaysia in 2005;

**REITERATING** our commitment to the purposes and principles of the Charter of the United Nations, the Treaty of Amity and Cooperation in Southeast Asia and other recognized principles of international law;

**ACKNOWLEDGING** that in a rapidly changing international environment, our economies and societies have become increasingly interlinked and interdependent;

**REALISING** the increasing range of challenges facing the world and the need for concerted regional and global efforts to respond to these challenges;

**RECOGNISING** our shared interests in achieving peace, security and prosperity in East Asia and the world at large;

**DESIROUS** of creating a peaceful environment by further enhancing cooperation and strengthening the existing bonds of friendship among our countries in keeping with the principles of equality, partnership, consultation and consensus thereby contributing to peace, security and economic prosperity in the region and the world at large;

**CONVINCED** of the importance of strengthening bilateral and multilateral interactions and cooperation among the participating countries of the East Asia Summit and the world at large on issues of common interest and concern in order to enhance peace and economic prosperity;

**REITERATING** the conviction that the effective functioning of multilateral systems will continue to be indispensable for advancing economic development;

**RECOGNISING** that this region is today a source of dynamism for the world economy;

**SHARING** the view that the East Asia Summit could play a significant role in community building in this region;

**FURTHER RECOGNISING** the need to support efforts to build a strong ASEAN Community which will serve as a solid foundation for our common peace and prosperity;

## DO HEREBY DECLARE:

**FIRST**, that we have established the East Asia Summit as a forum for dialogue on broad strategic, political and economic issues of common interest and concern with the aim of promoting peace, stability and economic prosperity in East Asia.

**SECOND**, that the efforts of the East Asia Summit to promote community building in this region will be consistent with and reinforce the realization of the ASEAN Community, and will form an integral part of the evolving regional architecture.

**THIRD**, that the East Asia Summit will be an open, inclusive, transparent and outward-looking forum in which we strive to strengthen global norms and universally recognized values with ASEAN as the driving force working in partnership with the other participants of the East Asia Summit.

**FOURTH**, we will focus, among others, on the following:

- Fostering strategic dialogue and promoting cooperation in political and security issues to ensure that our countries can live at peace with one another and with the world at large in a just, democratic and harmonious environment;
- Promoting development, financial stability, energy security, economic integration and growth, eradicating poverty and narrowing the development gap in East Asia, through technology transfer and infrastructure development, capacity building, good governance and humanitarian assistance and promoting financial links, trade and investment expansion and liberalization; and

- Promoting deeper cultural understanding, people-to-people contact and enhanced cooperation in uplifting the lives and well-being of our peoples in order to foster mutual trust and solidarity as well as promoting fields such as environmental protection, prevention of infectious diseases and natural disaster mitigation.

**FIFTH**, that:

- Participation in the East Asia Summit will be based on the criteria for participation established by ASEAN;
- The East Asia Summit will be convened regularly;
- The East Asia Summit will be hosted and chaired by an ASEAN Member Country that assumes the ASEAN Chairmanship and held back-to-back with the annual ASEAN Summit; and
- The modalities of the East Asia Summit will be reviewed by ASEAN and all other participating countries of the East Asia Summit.

**SIGNED** at Kuala Lumpur, Malaysia, on the Fourteenth Day of December in the Year Two Thousand and Five.

For Brunei Darussalam:

**HAJI HASSANAL BOLKIAH**
Sultan of Brunei Darussalam

For the Kingdom of Cambodia:

**SAMDECH HUN SEN**
Prime Minister

For the Republic of Indonesia:

**DR. SUSILO BAMBANG YUDHOYONO**
President

For the Lao People's Democratic Republic:

**BOUNNHANG VORACHITH**
Prime Minister

For Malaysia:

**DATO' SERI ABDULLAH AHMAD BADAWI**
Prime Minister

For the Union of Myanmar:

**GENERAL SOE WIN**
Prime Minister

For the Republic of the Philippines:

**GLORIA MACAPAGAL-ARROYO**
President

For the Republic of Singapore:

**LEE HSIEN LOONG**
Prime Minister

For the Kingdom of Thailand:

**DR. THAKSIN SHINAWATRA**
Prime Minister

For the Socialist Republic of Viet Nam:

**PHAN VAN KHAI**
Prime Minister

For Australia:

**JOHN HOWARD**
Prime Minister

For the People's Republic of China:

**WEN JIABAO**
Premier

For the Republic of India:

**DR. MANMOHAN SINGH**
Prime Minister

For Japan:

**JUNICHIRO KOIZUMI**
Prime Minister

For the Republic of Korea:

**ROH MOO-HYUN**
President

For New Zealand:

**HELEN CLARK**
Prime Minister

Source: http://www.aseansec.org/18098.htm
Accessed date: 7 February 2006
Publisher: ASEAN Secretariat
Country: Jakarta
Date of Publication: 2005

# CHAPTER 14

# CHAIRMAN'S STATEMENT OF THE FIRST EAST ASIA SUMMIT

**Kuala Lumpur, 14 December 2005**

1. The First East Asia Summit was held successfully on 14 December 2005 in Kuala Lumpur, Malaysia. The Meeting was chaired by The Honourable Dato' Seri Abdullah Ahmad Badawi, Prime Minister of Malaysia, and was attended by Heads of State/Government of ASEAN, Australia, the People's Republic of China, the Republic of India, Japan, the Republic of Korea and New Zealand. Russia was invited as Guest of the Government of Malaysia. Malaysia was privileged to host and chair this historic Summit.
2. We had a productive exchange of views on regional and international political and economic issues as well as on the challenges facing the region and the world.
3. Understanding that the de-nuclearisation of the Korean Peninsula in a peaceful and verifiable manner will greatly contribute to the peace, stability, and prosperity of the Asia Pacific region, we strongly endorsed the Joint Statement adopted at the Fourth Round of the Six-party Talks on September 19, 2005. We also shared the view that the Fifth Round of the Talks should be resumed as soon as possible, as agreed upon, to enable the Parties to the Talks to continue their discussion on ways to faithfully and expeditiously implement the commitments stated in the Joint Statement.
4. We exchanged views on the recent developments in the region, international terrorism, maritime security as well as the need to address the threat of infectious diseases. In this context we adopted the East Asia Summit Declaration on Avian Influenza Prevention, Control and Response. Leaders acknowledged the ongoing threat that terrorism poses to the region and stressed the continuing need for comprehensive efforts, including at national and regional levels, to combat it.
5. Recognizing the fact that our economies are dependent upon stable fuel supplies and in the light of the uncertainty of global fuel prices, we supported cooperation in the energy field including development of fuel efficient technologies and alternative energy sources.
6. We recognized the increasing inter-linkages and growing inter-dependence among our countries and agreed to deepen integration and cooperation in order to promote the creation of a harmonious prosperous community of nations.

7. We discussed development issues which include among others, issues such as sustainable development, technology transfer, trade and investment related issues, challenges to socio-economic development namely poverty, development gap, capacity building and issues related to good governance and promotion of human rights and democracy. We reiterated our commitment for concerted regional and global efforts to respond to these challenges.
8. We reaffirmed our abiding commitment to the objectives of the Doha Development Agenda of the World Trade Organization and the importance of the Hong Kong WTO Ministerial establishing a clear roadmap for completion of the Doha round in 2006. We reiterated our strong preference that all WTO members must achieve an ambitious and balanced outcome in the Doha Round that is development-orientated and delivers real gains for trade in agriculture, non-agricultural market access and services.
9. We also had an exchange of views on the effort at community building being undertaken in the East Asian region. In this regard we expressed our full support for ASEAN's efforts to realize the ASEAN Community. We also recognized that the East Asian community is a long term goal that would contribute to the maintenance of peace, security, prosperity and progress in the region and beyond.
10. We had extensive and in-depth discussions on the East Asia Summit and its role in the evolving Regional architecture. We agreed that the East Asia Summit with ASEAN as the driving force is an integral part of the overall evolving regional architecture. We also agreed that the East Asian region had already advanced in its efforts to realize an East Asian community through the ASEAN + 3 process. In this context we believed that the EAS together with the ASEAN + 3 and the ASEAN + 1 processes could play a significant role in community building in the region.
11. We reiterated our agreement that the East Asia Summit should remain open and outward looking, with ASEAN as the driving force working in partnership with the other participants of the East Asia Summit. In this context, we welcomed the Russian Federation's expression of interest to participate in the East Asia Summit and agreed to consider its participation in future East Asia Summits based on the criteria established by ASEAN.
12. We agreed that the EAS would continue to be a leaders' led Summit for strategic discussions on key issues affecting the region and the evolving regional architecture. We appreciated the informal, retreat style format of our first meeting which enabled us to discuss issues in a frank, spontaneous and free-flowing manner.
13. We also noted that some form of mechanism may be desirable to facilitate follow-up action of the EAS and to coordinate and implement the areas of cooperation we had identified. In this regard we agreed that the officials and the ASEAN Secretariat follow through with the decisions of the EAS.

14. We signed the Kuala Lumpur Declaration on the East Asia Summit outlining its principles and purposes, areas of cooperation and primary modalities.
15. We agreed that the East Asia Summit will be convened annually. In this context we agreed to convene the Second East Asia Summit in Cebu, Philippines on 13 December 2006.

Source: http://www.aseansec.org/18104.htm
Accessed date: 7 February 2006
Publisher: ASEAN Secretariat
Country: Jakarta
Date of Publication: 2005

# CHAPTER 15

# KUALA LUMPUR DECLARATION ON THE ESTABLISHMENT OF THE ASEAN CHARTER

**Kuala Lumpur, 12 December 2005**

**WE**, the Heads of State/Government of Brunei Darussalam, Kingdom of Cambodia, Republic of Indonesia, Lao People's Democratic Republic, Malaysia, Union of Myanmar, Republic of the Philippines, Republic of Singapore, Kingdom of Thailand and Socialist Republic of Viet Nam, Member Countries of ASEAN, on the occasion of the 11th ASEAN Summit in Kuala Lumpur;

**CONSCIOUS** of the unity and diversity in ASEAN and the existing ties of history, geography and culture that have bound their peoples together;

**RECOGNISING** the ASEAN Declaration (Bangkok Declaration) of 1967 as the founding document of ASEAN that represents the collective will of the nations of Southeast Asia to bond themselves together in friendship and cooperation and, through joint efforts and sacrifices, secure for their peoples and for posterity the blessings of peace, freedom and prosperity;

**ACKNOWLEDGING** that the vision, strategy and initiative of ASEAN over the years have made an important contribution to the maintenance of peace, security and stability of the region;

**COGNISANT** that mutual respect for the independence, sovereignty, equality, territorial integrity and national identity of ASEAN Member Countries has fostered a positive environment for the steady development of an ASEAN Community to meet the challenges of the future;

**DESIRING** to realize an ASEAN Community as envisaged in the Declaration of ASEAN Concord II (Bali Concord II) and its Plans of Action and Roadmap, and the ASEAN Vision 2020 which envision ASEAN as a concert of Southeast Asian nations, outward-looking, living in peace, stability and prosperity, bonded together in partnership in dynamic development and in a community of caring societies;

**RECOGNISING** that the global and regional economic and political environment has changed and is constantly changing thereby requiring ASEAN and its community building efforts to evolve and adapt to these changes and challenges;

**RECOGNISING** the importance of having an appropriate institutional framework of ASEAN that is able to meet the challenges of realizing an ASEAN community;

**CONVINCED** of the need for an ASEAN Charter to serve as a firm foundation for ASEAN in the years ahead and to facilitate community building towards an ASEAN Community and beyond;

## DO HEREBY DECLARE:

**FIRST**, we are committed to establish the ASEAN Charter.

**SECOND**, the ASEAN Charter will serve as a legal and institutional framework of ASEAN to support the realization of its goals and objectives.

**THIRD**, the ASEAN Charter will codify all ASEAN norms, rules, and values and reaffirm that ASEAN agreements signed and other instruments adopted before the establishment of the ASEAN Charter shall continue to apply and be legally binding where appropriate.

**FOURTH**, the ASEAN Charter will reaffirm principles, goals and ideals contained in ASEAN' s milestone agreements, in particular the ASEAN Declaration (1967), the Treaty of Amity and Cooperation in Southeast Asia (1976), the Treaty on Southeast Asia Nuclear Weapon Free Zone (1995), the ASEAN Vision 2020 (1997) and the Declaration of ASEAN Concord II (2003) as well as the principles of inter-state relations in accordance with the UN Charter and established international law that promote and protect ASEAN community interests as well as inter-state relations and the national interests of the individual ASEAN Member Countries. These include among others:

- Promotion of community interest for the benefit of all ASEAN Member Countries;
- Maintaining primary driving force of ASEAN;
- Narrowing the development gaps among Member Countries;
- Adherence to a set of common socio-cultural and political community values and shared norms as contained in the various ASEAN documents;

- Continuing to foster a community of caring societies and promote a common regional identity;
- Effective implementation as well as compliance with ASEAN's agreements;
- Promotion of democracy, human rights and obligations, transparency and good governance and strengthening democratic institutions;
- Ensuring that countries in the region live at peace with one another and with the world at large in a just, democratic and harmonious environment;
- Decision making on the basis of equality, mutual respect and consensus;
- Commitment to strengthen ASEAN's competitiveness, to deepen and broaden ASEAN's internal economic integration and linkages with the world economy;
- Promotion of regional solidarity and cooperation;
- Mutual respect for the independence, sovereignty, equality, territorial integrity and national identity of all nations;
- Renunciation of nuclear weapons and other weapons of mass destruction and avoidance of arms race;
- Renunciation of the use of force and threat to use of force; non-aggression and exclusive reliance on peaceful means for the settlement of differences or disputes;
- Enhancing beneficial relations between ASEAN and its friends and partners;
- Upholding non-discrimination of any ASEAN Member Countries in ASEAN's external relations and cooperative activities;
- Observance of principles of international law concerning friendly relations and cooperation among States; and
- The right of every state to lead its national existence free from external interference, subversion or coercion and non-interference in the internal affairs of one another.

**FIFTH**, the ASEAN Charter will confer a legal personality to ASEAN and determine the functions, develop areas of competence of key ASEAN bodies and their relationship with one another in the overall ASEAN structure.

## AND DO HEREBY AGREE:

**TO** establish an Eminent Persons Group (EPG), comprising highly distinguished and well respected citizens from ASEAN Member Countries, with the mandate to examine and provide practical recommendations on the directions and nature of the ASEAN Charter relevant to the ASEAN Community as envisaged in the Bali Concord II and beyond, taking into account, but not limited to, the principles, values and objectives as contained in this Declaration.

**TO** consider their recommendations at our subsequent meetings.

**TO** task our Ministers to establish, as necessary, a High Level Task Force to carry out the drafting of the ASEAN Charter based on the Kuala Lumpur Declaration on the Establishment of the ASEAN Charter and the recommendations of the EPG.

**DONE** in Kuala Lumpur, Malaysia, on the Twelfth Day of December in the Year Two Thousand and Five.

For Brunei Darussalam:

**HAJI HASSANAL BOLKIAH**
Sultan of Brunei Darussalam

For the Kingdom of Cambodia:

**SAMDECH HUN SEN**
Prime Minister

For the Republic of Indonesia:

**DR. SUSILO BAMBANG YUDHOYONO**
President

For the Lao People's Democratic Republic:

**BOUNNHANG VORACHITH**
Prime Minister

For Malaysia:

**DATO' SERI ABDULLAH AHMAD BADAWI**
Prime Minister

For the Union of Myanmar:

**GENERAL SOE WIN**
Prime Minister

For the Republic of the Philippines:

**GLORIA MACAPAGAL-ARROYO**
President

For the Republic of Singapore:

**LEE HSIEN LOONG**
Prime Minister

For the Kingdom of Thailand:

**DR. THAKSIN SHINAWATRA**
Prime Minister

For the Socialist Republic of Viet Nam:

**PHAN VAN KHAI**
Prime Minister

Source: http://www.aseansec.org/18030.htm
Accessed date: 7 February 2006
Publisher: ASEAN Secretariat
Country: Jakarta
Date of Publication: 2005

# CHAPTER 16

# ASEAN OBTAINS OBSERVER STATUS IN THE UNITED NATIONS

On Monday, 4 December 2006, the United Nations General Assembly unanimously granted observer status to ASEAN. The Philippines, as the current chair of ASEAN, had tabled the resolution for ASEAN's observer status on 10 October 2006. The Sixth Committee adopted the resolution before it was sent to the General Assembly. More than 70 countries co-sponsored the resolution.

The General Assembly also adopted another resolution on "Cooperation between the United Nations and the Association of Southeast Asian Nations" on the same day.

The two resolutions mark a strengthening of ASEAN-UN cooperation. ASEAN can now participate in the sessions and work of the General Assembly in the capacity of an observer. The UN and ASEAN will also look to hold more regular summits.

ASEAN does not have a permanent office in New York. As such, the current ASEAN Chair's Permanent Mission to the UN will represent ASEAN's interests in the General Assembly.

....

Source: http://www.aseansec.org/18992.htm
Accessed date: 16 January 2008
Publisher: ASEAN Secretariat
Country: Jakarta
Date of Publication: 2006

# CHAPTER 17

# JOINT COMMUNIQUE OF THE 39TH ASEAN MINISTERIAL MEETING (AMM)

**Kuala Lumpur, 25 July 2006**

## FORGING A UNITED, RESILIENT AND INTEGRATED ASEAN

## INTRODUCTION

....

## OPENING ADDRESS

3. The Honourable Dato' Seri Abdullah Ahmad Badawi, Prime Minister of Malaysia, delivered an Opening Address at the Opening Ceremony of the 39th ASEAN Ministerial Meeting. The Honourable Prime Minister of Malaysia emphasized the need for ASEAN to be steadfast in keeping its solidarity and to remain focused on achieving its common mission of fostering greater regional integration. ASEAN should adopt the approach of proceeding step-by-step, instrument-by-instrument, institution-by-institution in its community building efforts. This is the only way to ensure that ASEAN achieves true consensus on establishing a set of common values, perceptions and outlook.
4. On the building of the ASEAN Community, he underlined three overarching principles, whereby there should be a universal acceptance that community interests would prevail over national interests on issues affecting the community and that ASEAN has to do better in giving national effect to wider international treaties and conventions, including ASEAN treaties and agreements by putting in place capacities for enforcing community decisions. In addition, Member Countries must adhere to a common set of community values, though universal in nature, but are distinctly ASEAN in character. Topping the list of values must be acceptance of good governance in our respective countries and societies.
5. He looked forward to receiving the report of the Eminent Persons Group on the ASEAN Charter which would be a major leap forward in ASEAN's work of placing the building blocks for the ASEAN Community.

....

## THE ASEAN COMMUNITY

7. We were pleased with the progress made in moving towards the realization of the ASEAN Community by the year 2020, through the implementation of the Vientiane Action Programme (VAP), and based on the three pillars, namely the ASEAN Security Community (ASC), ASEAN Economic Community (AEC) and ASEAN Socio-Cultural Community (ASCC), as enshrined in the Bali Concord II. We agreed that it was important for ASEAN to strengthen our integration efforts for all three pillars of the ASEAN community. As a follow-up to our Leaders' discussions at the 11th ASEAN Summit in Kuala Lumpur, we exchanged views on how to bring forward the realisation of the ASEAN Community from 2020–2015 and the possible ways of achieving this objective. We reiterated the importance of maintaining ASEAN centrality in the context of ASEAN related regional architectures to support the attainment of the objectives of the establishment of the ASEAN Community.
8. We welcomed the ongoing historic mission of the Eminent Persons Group on the ASEAN Charter to propose bold and visionary ideas for the future direction of ASEAN and provide practical recommendations on the nature of the ASEAN Charter, as mandated by the Kuala Lumpur Declaration on the Establishment of the ASEAN Charter, which was signed by our Leaders at the 11th ASEAN Summit in Kuala Lumpur, Malaysia on 12 December 2005.
9. We commended the EPG for its consultative and inclusive approach in engaging all pertinent stakeholders in ASEAN, including meetings with representatives of ASEAN Inter-Parliamentary Organization (AIPO), Working Group for an ASEAN Human Rights Mechanism, ASEAN Institutes of Strategic and International Studies (ASEAN-ISIS), civil society organizations, ASEAN Chambers of Commerce and Industry (ASEAN-CCI) and the private sector. We reiterated our support for the EPG to continue to "think out of the box" and explore all bold and visionary ideas for the strengthening of ASEAN and its institutional framework. We are confident that the EPG's report and recommendations, which would be presented for consideration by our Leaders at the 12th ASEAN Summit in Cebu, the Philippines, would enable the Leaders to decide on the drafting of the Charter. The EPG report represents a significant contribution to the building of the ASEAN Community that is more people-centred and resilient to challenges. In this context, we agreed to establish the High Level Task Force to carry out the drafting of the ASEAN Charter after the 12th ASEAN Summit, based on the Kuala Lumpur Declaration on the Establishment of the ASEAN Charter.
10. We underlined the need to enhance the effectiveness and efficiency of ASEAN for improved coordination in its endeavours to achieve the goals and objectives of the ASEAN Community.

## VIENTIANE ACTION PROGRAMME (VAP)

11. In ensuring the expeditious implementation of the VAP, we reiterated that the implementation of the three pillars of the ASEAN Community should be mutually reinforcing. We agreed to undertake greater efforts to enhance the coordination mechanism in its implementation to help us realise the goals of the ASEAN Community. We also agreed that Member Countries should take into account the need to integrate the VAP into their national development plans. In this regard, we welcomed the convening of the 5th ASEAN Senior Officials Meeting on Development Planning (SOMDP) in Kuala Lumpur on 6–7 July 2006, in facilitating the integration of ASEAN's goals, objectives and implementation of the VAP into national development plans of Member Countries. We further agreed that the Plans of Action with the respective Dialogue Partners should be in tangent with the VAP.
12. We welcomed the ASEAN Baseline Report as a crucial instrument in the evaluation of the achievements of the VAP and successor action programmes. In this regard, we reiterated the importance of regular review of the VAP to ensure that all the programmes and activities are responsive to ASEAN needs and priority.
13. We appreciated the contributions by several ASEAN Dialogue Partners to the ASEAN Development Fund (ADF), which serves as a common pool of financial resources for the implementation of the VAP. We called upon other Dialogue Partners, countries as well as international organizations to support and contribute to the ADF.
14. We underscored the importance of narrowing the development gap among ASEAN Member Countries, which is essential for the regional integration of ASEAN. We agreed that in undertaking capacity-building projects, focus should also be given to developing policy environment that is conducive to support trade, investment and infrastructure sectors in the CLMV countries. We expressed our appreciation to our Dialogue Partners, donor countries, institutions and ASEAN Member Countries for their contributions and assistance towards ASEAN integration.

## Initiative for ASEAN Integration (IAI)

15. We stressed the need for effective implementation of the recommendations in the Report of the Mid-term Review of the IAI Work Plan, which was adopted by our Leaders at the 11th ASEAN Summit in December 2005 in Kuala Lumpur. The Report has broadened the scope of the IAI to meet the urgent needs of the CLMV countries and to improve the coordination mechanism. We underlined the need to further explore innovative sources of funding to

support the efforts, including through private and public initiatives and welcomed Thailand's offer to prepare a paper on this matter.

16. We welcomed the sustained efforts taken by the ASEAN-6 countries and Dialogue Partners to implement the IAI Work Plan (2002–2008) and look forward to their further support and assistance. We believed that there is a need to harmonize the IAI Work Plan projects within the framework of the 7 focus areas and to ensure that the IAI projects support the realization of the 11 priority integration sectors under the AEC.

....

## ASEAN SECURITY COMMUNITY (ASC)

....

22. We noted the outcome of the Fifth Workshop on an ASEAN Regional Mechanism on Human Rights held on 29–30 June 2006 in Kuala Lumpur and viewed it as an important forum for continuous dialogue on the establishment of a regional human rights mechanism in ASEAN. We also noted the work carried out by the non-governmental Working Group for an ASEAN Human Rights Mechanism, including the meeting between the open-ended ASEAN SOM Troika and the Working Group at the sidelines of the 39th AMM with the objective to facilitate the implementation of the activities under the promotion of human rights component of the VAP. We further noted that the National Human Rights Commissions of Indonesia, Malaysia, the Philippines and Thailand are prepared to collaborate with the Working Group and other civil society organizations, with the view to facilitating the establishment of an ASEAN Human Rights Mechanism.
23. In accordance with the Plan of Action to implement the ASEAN Security Community, the Ministers also agreed to begin discussions on the elaboration of an ASEAN Instrument on the Protection and Promotion of the Rights of Migrant Workers.

### Treaty of Amity and Cooperation in Southeast Asia

24. We reaffirmed the importance of the Treaty of Amity and Cooperation in Southeast Asia (TAC) as an instrument of peace, security and cooperation in inter-state relations. We were gratified that a growing number of countries outside ASEAN have either acceded or expressed their interest to accede to the TAC. We regarded this as further testimony of the continued relevance of the TAC in contributing to regional peace, security and stability. In this context, we welcomed the accession of Australia on 10 December 2005 at the margins of the 11th ASEAN Summit.

25. We welcomed the decision by France to accede to the TAC. However, we noted that France was not able to accede to the Treaty during the 39th AMM/PMC/13th ARF in Kuala Lumpur due to the situation in the Middle East. We expressed the hope that France would be able to accede to the TAC soon.
26. We also reiterated our call to other Dialogue Partners and countries to accede to the TAC in the near future so as to create a favourable environment conducive for development in the region which will be beneficial not only to ASEAN but all its partners and friends as well.

## South China Sea

....

## Transnational Crimes and Counter Terrorism

29. We reiterated our strong condemnation against terrorism in all its forms and manifestations and emphasised the need to address the root causes of terrorism. We reaffirmed our commitment to prevent, suppress and eliminate international terrorism in accordance with the Charter of the United Nations and international law.
30. We underscored the significant role of the ASEAN Ministers Meeting on Transnational Crime (AMMTC) in combating transnational crimes and called on the AMMTC to heighten cooperation in these areas including other relevant ASEAN bodies and ASEAN Dialogue Partners. In this regard, we also look forward to the convening of the 6$^{th}$ AMMTC in Brunei Darussalam in 2007.
31. We noted the successful conclusion of the Treaty on Mutual Legal Assistance in Criminal Matters (MLAT) by all ASEAN Member Countries, which would improve the effectiveness of cooperation in combating transnational crime and terrorism through mutual legal assistance in criminal matters, and expressed hope that the Treaty would be ratified by all ASEAN Member Countries. We also recalled the proposal to work towards the immediate establishment of an ASEAN extradition treaty as envisaged by the 1976 Declaration of ASEAN Concord as stipulated in the VAP, and the consequent decision by the 6$^{th}$ ASEAN Law Ministers Meeting (ALMM) that ASLOM would examine modalities for a model ASEAN extradition treaty.
32. We welcomed efforts to enhance the capacity of the ASEAN Member Countries in counter-terrorism including through the elaboration of an ASEAN Convention on Counter terrorism as provided for under the VAP, and the

consequent decision of the 6th SOMTC in Bali in 2006 to create a joint experts working group (EWG), comprising representatives from SOM, SOMTC and ASLOM, to work out the terms of reference and guiding principles of an ASEAN Convention on Counter Terrorism.

33. We also noted the need to pursue cooperation to prevent and combat corruption as mandated by the VAP and look forward to the convening of the ad-hoc working group meeting piror to the 7th SOMTC in Lao PDR in 2007 to further follow-up on this initiative.
34. We called for continued close cooperation between security-related bodies, such as Interpol, ASEANAPOL and the relevant national authorities particularly relating to intelligence information sharing on terrorism. We also called upon all Member Countries to strengthen the existing technical cooperation for the development of capacity and capability of counter terrorism-related agencies and officials. In this connection, we further called for continued cooperation between the regional centres, in particular, the Southeast Asia Regional Centre for Counter-Terrorism (SEARCCT) in Kuala Lumpur, the International Law Enforcement Academy (ILEA) in Bangkok and the Jakarta Centre for Law Enforcement Cooperation (JCLEC) in Semarang.

## Treaty on the Southeast Asia Nuclear Weapon-Free Zone (SEANWFZ)

35. We reaffirmed the importance of vigorous efforts to further strengthen cooperation in supporting the implementation of the Treaty on the Southeast Asia Nuclear Weapon-Free Zone (SEANWFZ). We urged the nuclear weapons States to become parties to the Protocol of the SEANWFZ Treaty as soon as possible.
36. We recalled Article 20 of the SEANWFZ Treaty of 15 December 1995, which states that "Ten years after this Treaty enters into force, a meeting of the Commission shall be convened for the purpose of reviewing the operation of the Treaty". We directed the Executive Committee of the SEANWFZ to look into the implementation of Article 20.

## ASEAN Regional Forum (ARF)

37. We reaffirmed the roles of ASEAN as the primary driving force of the ARF process and the ARF as the primary forum in enhancing political and security dialogue and cooperation in the wider Asia-Pacific region as well as the pivot for building peace and security in the region. We welcomed Bangladesh's participation at the 13th ARF on 28 July 2006 as the 26th participating country

in the ARF, which would contribute to further enhance political and security dialogue and cooperation in the region.

38. We commended the important progress made in the implementation of the ARF activities, which had to a great extent contributed to political stability, security, and cooperation in the Asia-Pacific region. We recognized the need to forge concrete cooperation among ARF countries in building capacity and capabilities in order to better cope with numerous challenges. While emphasizing that confidence building would continue to play a vital role in the ARF process, we welcomed the ARF's progress towards Preventive Diplomacy (PD) and look forward to the development of concrete measures in PD at a pace comfortable to all. We noted with satisfaction the progress made in the implementation of the agreed ARF activities for the Inter-Sessional year 2005–2006.

## ASEAN ECONOMIC COMMUNITY (AEC)

....

43. We supported the initiative taken to further broaden and enhance economic relations with the European Union and the United States of America. In this respect, we noted the recommendations made in the Report of the ASEAN-EU Vision Group on Enhanced Partnership on the establishment of an ASEAN-EU FTA to foster and diversify trans-regional trade and investment flows and to deepen economic integration between the two regions in a sustainable manner. We were pleased to note that ASEAN and EU would undertake domestic consultations before any decision could be made to launch an FTA. The initiatives in pursuing these engagements are consistent with the principle of open regionalism that ASEAN has always advocated.

....

### Energy Cooperation

46. We recognized the adverse impact of rising international oil prices on the economy of Member Countries and hence underscored the importance of finding ways to enhance energy efficiency and increase the share of renewable energy sources in power generation and energy consumption. We called for greater regional cooperation in sharing experience, knowledge and expertise to help promote energy efficiency and development of new and renewable energy sources in the region. In this respect, we commended the efforts by the ASEAN Ministers of Energy and the ASEAN Senior Energy Officials in

expediting the conclusion of the Memorandum of Understanding (MoU) on the ASEAN Power Grid and the ASEAN Petroleum Security Agreement (APSA) 2005, as well as the progressive implementation of the Memorandum of Understanding (MoU) on the Trans-ASEAN Gas Pipeline (TAGP).

## Sub-regional Cooperation

47. We were pleased with the substantial progress made in the implementation of the initiatives and programmes under various sub-regional arrangements. In this regard, we recalled the successful convening of the 2nd Summit of the Ayeyawady-Chao Phraya-Mekong Economic Cooperation Strategy (ACMECS) held in Thailand on 1–3 November 2005. We also recalled the successful convening of the Second Brunei-Indonesia-Malaysia-Philippine East ASEAN Growth Area (BIMP-EAGA) Summit, the First Indonesia-Malaysia-Thailand Growth Triangle (IMT-GT) Summit, the Second Cambodia-Laos-Myanmar-Viet Nam (CLMV) Summit and the Second Cambodia-Laos-Viet Nam Growth Triangle (CLV-GT) Summit on 11 December 2005 in Kuala Lumpur, Malaysia. We reaffirmed the importance that ASEAN attaches to the various sub-regional cooperation frameworks in enhancing the efforts of narrowing the development gap among all Member Countries as well as accelerating the integration of ASEAN.

## ASEAN SOCIO-CULTURAL COMMUNITY (ASCC)

....

49. We commended the holding of the Civil Society Conference at the sidelines of the 11th ASEAN Summit on 7–9 December 2005 in Kuala Lumpur. The involvement of civil society is a vital component of developing a people-centred ASEAN Community. In this regard, we were pleased to note that the Philippines will continue the engagement with civil society groups during its chairmanship on the regional level. An opportunity for the civil society representatives to report to the Leaders will be arranged during the 12th ASEAN Summit.
50. We supported the continued efforts by the ASEAN Foundation in generating public awareness of ASEAN and fostering a sense of belonging to ASEAN among its peoples through its various activities. We noted the Report of the Executive Director of the ASEAN Foundation on the Foundation's activities. We encouraged other countries and regional and international organizations as well as the private sector from ASEAN Member Countries to cooperate

closely with the ASEAN Foundation and assist it to carry out its activities aimed at realizing its goals and objectives.

## Sectoral Cooperation

....

### *Environment*

52. We recalled the concerns expressed by our Leaders at the 11th ASEAN Summit held in Kuala Lumpur on 12 December 2005, on the issue of transboundary haze pollution resulting from land and forest fires that affects some of the Member Countries annually. We reiterated our commitment to further intensify and undertake coordinated action by our relevant Ministries and agencies at the national and regional levels, to deal collectively with the transboundary haze pollution, guided by the ASEAN Agreement on Transboundary Haze Pollution. In this regard, we noted the on-going process of ratification by Member Countries which have yet to ratify the Agreement and expected this to be finalised soon in order to ensure effective regional cooperation in this area.
53. We commended the initiative to commemorate 2006 as the ASEAN Environment Year with the theme: "Biodiversity: Our Life, Our Future", which was launched in Bogor, Indonesia on 18 May 2006. We urged all Member Countries and our collaborating partners to showcase ASEAN's efforts, and promote awareness and ownership, in promoting environmental protection, in particular sustainable management of our rich and diverse biological diversity. In this respect, we welcomed the establishment of the ASEAN Centre for Biodiversity based in Los Banos, the Philippines, which was launched on 27 September 2005 to further promote collaboration on biodiversity. We expressed our appreciation to the EU for providing financial support for the first three years of operation of the Centre, and called upon Member Countries and our collaborating partners to continue to lend support to the activities of the Centre.
54. We reaffirmed the importance of the Heart of Borneo initiative, as stated in the Chairman's Statement of the 11th ASEAN Summit, as a collective effort to promote sustainable forest management.
55. We reiterated the importance of concrete implementation of UNFCCC and Kyoto Protocol and called for further concrete implementation and commitment to pursue efforts for parties, particularly those in Annex I of the

Convention and its Kyoto Protocol to address climate change. Therefore, we urged the Annex I Parties to increase their commitment in implementing the Clean Development Mechanism (CDM) activities particularly in the ASEAN region.

## Disaster Management

56. We expressed our deepest condolences to the Governments and the peoples of the Republic of the Philippines and the Republic of Indonesia over the tremendous loss of lives and property as a result of the mudslide disaster which struck Guinsaugon St. Bernard, Southern Leyte, Philippines on 17 February 2006; the earthquake which struck Yogyakarta and Central Java, Indonesia, on 27 May 2006; and the tsunami which struck Western and Central Java, Indonesia, on 17 July 2006 respectively. We expressed our appreciation for the expeditious relief efforts of ASEAN Member Countries, friendly countries, international organizations and other relief organisations and called upon them to continue to provide their support for rehabilitation and reconstruction activities to enable speedy recovery of those affected.
57. We recalled the ASEAN Agreement on Disaster Management and Emergency Response (AADMER), which was signed on 26 July 2005 in Vientiane, Lao PDR. We welcomed the ratification of the Agreement by Member Countries and further called upon Member Countries that have yet to ratify the Agreement to do so in order to ensure effective regional cooperation in this area. In this regard, we noted the offer by Indonesia to host the ASEAN Coordinating Centre for Humanitarian Assistance on disaster management (AHA Centre).
58. We emphasized the importance of developing effective multi-nodal and multi-hazard early warning systems to save lives and minimise damages. We recognized the existing efforts such as the establishment of the UNESCAP Multi-Donor Voluntary Trust Fund for Tsunami Early Warning Arrangements in the Indian Ocean and Southeast Asia, with Thailand and Sweden contributed a total of US$12.5 million. In this regard, we encouraged the contribution and utilisation of the fund to enhance the capacity of the early warning systems. In addition, those efforts to strengthen disaster preparedness of local communities should be promoted.
59. We reaffirmed our commitment to strengthen ASEAN standby arrangements for disaster relief and emergency response and to enhance linkages with other regional and global standby arrangements through the sharing of earmarked assets, joint exercises in search and rescue and expediting the establishment of

common guidelines and standard operating procedures as well as regional disaster early warning and monitoring capacities through real time information sharing in order to ensure rapid responses to emergencies.

## *Health*

60. We recalled our Leaders' decision at the 11th ASEAN Summit to strengthen regional institutional linkages and partnership among all stakeholders in ASEAN Member Countries to control and eradicate the spread of Highly Pathogenic Avian Influenza (HPAI) in the region. In this regard, we expressed our deep concern over the negative effects of the avian influenza on economy and society and called for greater cooperation among Member Countries and others, through information exchange and best practices, to prevent and control the spread of the disease. We noted the progress in stockpiling vaccines and antiviral drugs to meet the immediate needs of affected countries and underlined the importance to prepare for containment when human cases occur; and meet pandemic preparedness needs.
61. We commended the work of the ASEAN HPAI Taskforce and the ASEAN+3 Emerging Infectious Diseases (EID) Programme to conduct and coordinate effective and comprehensive plans to combat emerging and re-emerging diseases. We also welcomed endeavours from donor countries and international organizations to help keep ASEAN free from emerging diseases. In particular, we appreciated the funding support of Japan and the Asian Development Bank (ADB) to assist ASEAN in combating the avian influenza in the region.
62. We commended the efforts made by the ASEAN Health Ministers to ensure regional cooperation and unity in health emergencies, and in providing the necessary guidance for development of an operation plan for the Third ASEAN Work Programme on HIV and AIDS (2006–2010). We welcomed their preparations to convene a Second Special Session on HIV and AIDS for ASEAN Leaders in December 2006 alongside the 12th ASEAN Summit. We also underlined the need for a higher profile of ASEAN cooperation on the issue to be highlighted to the international community, such as through the convening of ASEAN panels at the International Conferences on AIDS in Asia and the Pacific (ICAAP) since 2001. We noted that ASEAN's commitment to address the issue together with like-minded partners has also resulted in a cooperation agreement with the Joint United Nations Programme on HIV/AIDS (UNAIDS).

### *Education*

63. We welcomed the convening of the First ASEAN Education Ministers Meeting (ASED) held in Singapore on 21 March 2006 and its Joint Statement. As education is an important tool in engendering the ASEAN identity and promoting the development of the ASEAN Socio-Cultural Community, we welcomed the initiative by ASED to lay a strategic framework for education collaboration in the region which among others, highlighted the importance of education, particularly in primary and basic education, in developing a regional identity. This is relevant to the emphasis placed by ASEAN Leaders to establish an ASEAN Community imbued with a sense of awareness and belonging.

....

### *Labour*

....

### *Women*

....

### *Youth*

67. We reiterated the need to involve ASEAN youth in our various mainstream and sectoral programmes and activities as part of the regional effort to empower and shape our youth into useful citizens with strong national and regional identity, features that are essential as we strive towards realising the ASEAN Community. We welcomed the initiative taken to establish a youth development fund in ASEAN, to address the VAP's call for increased participation of youth in the productive workforce, and encourage their entrepreneurship and employability, leadership and regional awareness. We further called upon the different ASEAN sectoral bodies to link their respective efforts in addressing priorities for the youth.

### *Science and Technology*

68. We reaffirmed that human resource and technology developments have played a vital role in sustaining economic growth and enhancing community well-being in ASEAN. We welcomed the initiative of the 11th ASEAN Ministerial Meeting on Science and Technology (S&T) held on 11–12 August 2005 in

Jakarta to focus the regional science and technology cooperation on human resource and development and research in emerging fields and enabling technologies such as renewable and alternative energy, development of information technology application particularly on open source systems, biotechnology and food science, materials science and nanotechnology and disaster management. In this regard, we look forward to the convening of the 4th Informal ASEAN Ministerial Meeting on Science and Technology on 28–29 August 2006 in Kuala Lumpur.

69. We welcomed the continued efforts by ASEAN Member Countries to implement new activities under the ASEAN-help-ASEAN Programme to promote S&T development in ASEAN. We were pleased to note that since its launching by the ASEAN S&T Ministers in 2002, joint activities implemented under the Programme have benefited ASEAN Member Countries and also contributed in narrowing the development gap.

## EXTERNAL RELATIONS

70. We expressed satisfaction with the progress achieved in ASEAN's relations with the Dialogue Partners, namely, Australia, Canada, China, the European Union, India, Japan, New Zealand, the Republic of Korea, the Russian Federation, the United States of America, the United Nations Development Programme and the increasing interest of Sectoral Dialogue Partner Pakistan to engage more with ASEAN. We also expressed our commitment to intensify cooperation in various fields with ASEAN Dialogue Partners for the mutual benefit of our peoples and region. We further expressed our appreciation to our Dialogue Partners for their continued support in ASEAN's efforts towards establishing the ASEAN Community by 2020.
71. In this regard, we look forward to the signing of the Framework Document for the Plan of Action to Implement the ASEAN-US Enhanced Partnership on 27 July 2006.

. . . .

72. On ASEAN-Russia relations, we are pleased to note the successful convening of the First ASEAN-Russian Federation Summit held in Kuala Lumpur on 13 December 2005, and the endorsement of the ASEAN-Russia Joint Declaration on Progressive and Comprehensive Partnership.

. . . .

75. We welcomed the interest expressed by several non-regional countries and international institutions to extend technical assistance and financial support for the

implementation of ASEAN's development agenda. As an outward-looking organization, ASEAN recognised the need to establish other forms of formal relations with other non-regional countries and international institutions to assist its development agenda. In this context, we tasked the ASEAN Directors-General and the ASEAN Secretariat to develop new categories of partnership with non-regional countries and international institutions while maintaining the moratorium on new Dialogue Partnership. We also welcomed the offer of the Philippines to work with the ASEAN Secretariat in identifying ways to strengthen cooperation with the Shanghai Cooperation Organisation (SCO).

76. We renewed our commitment to the ASEAN Plus Three (ASEAN+3) cooperation and reiterated our long-term goal of developing an East Asian community. We agreed that the ASEAN Plus Three process would remain as the main vehicle with ASEAN as the driving force for East Asian community building. Pursuant to the signing of the Kuala Lumpur Declaration on the ASEAN Plus Three Summit in Kuala Lumpur on 12 December 2005, we noted that the ASEAN Plus Three Senior Officials and the Directors-General, in their meetings on 18 May 2006 in Karambunai, Sabah and 8 June 2006 in Seoul, ROK, respectively, had had initial discussions in preparation of the drafting of the Second Joint Statement on East Asia Cooperation, and the accompanying Work Plan, to be issued by our Leaders in 2007 to commemorate the 10th anniversary of the ASEAN Plus Three cooperation.

77. We recalled the successful convening of the First East Asia Summit (EAS) in Kuala Lumpur on 14 December 2005 attended by all Leaders of ASEAN Member Countries, Australia, China, India, Japan, Republic of Korea and New Zealand. While emphasising ASEAN as the driving force, we reaffirmed that the EAS, as an open, inclusive, transparent and outward-looking forum, would serve as a platform for dialogue on broad strategic, political and economic issues of common interest to promote peace and economic prosperity in East Asia. We reaffirmed the efforts of the East Asia Summit to promote community building in this region and its integral part of the evolving regional architecture. We viewed this 'Leaders-led' Summit as an important event of historical significance to ASEAN and agreed to cooperate using existing mechanisms to implement the decisions of the Summit and the 17 areas of cooperation mentioned by the Leaders.

78. We recalled the successful holding of the Second ASEAN-UN Summit on 13 September 2005 in New York wherein it was agreed that ASEAN-UN cooperation needs to be further broadened with the involvement of the various UN specialised agencies to encompass all areas related to community building,

including key issues related to development, in particular, poverty eradication and the Millennium Development Goals, prevention and control of infectious diseases, disaster management, transnational issues, trade and investment as well as peace and security. We noted that the Summit also agreed to convene future ASEAN-UN Summits on a regular basis. In this context, the Philippines proposed to explore the possibility of having an ASEAN-UN Summit in 2007.

## DEVELOPMENTS IN MYANMAR

....

## REGIONAL AND INTERNATIONAL ISSUES

81. We exchanged views on the following issues:

....

- ***World Trade Organization (WTO)***

93. We reemphasized the importance of a rule-based multilateral trading system. We expressed regret on the failure to agree to the negotiating modalities on agriculture and non-agriculture market access (NAMA) at the Informal Ministerial Meeting held on 29 June–1 July 2006 in Geneva. We called on all WTO Members, especially the major ones, to redouble their efforts in line with their commitment to the objectives of the Doha Development Agenda (DDA) and to ensure that the negotiations would come to a successful conclusion by the end of 2006. We reiterated that the Doha Round must achieve an ambitious and balanced outcome that is development-oriented with particular emphasis on ensuring real, effective and operational development benefits to developing countries.
94. We reiterated our support to the early accession of the Lao PDR and Viet Nam to the WTO. In this connection, we congratulated Viet Nam on her conclusion of all her bilateral negotiations and supported the earliest completion of the multilateral negotiation process to enable Viet Nam to join the WTO before November 2006.

- ***Asia-Middle East Dialogue (AMED)***

....

### • *Asia-Cooperation Dialogue (ACD)*

96. We also welcomed the outcome of the 5th ACD Ministerial Meeting on 23–24 May 2006 in Doha, Qatar. We commended the progress that has been made with respect to the promotion of closer cooperation in the area of energy, which is to put priority on such areas as energy security, research and assessment on energy, energy infrastructure and development and exploring the possibility of reinvesting revenues that accrue from the energy in the ACD countries to enhance sustainable growth and development in Asia. We look forward to the 2nd ACD Energy Forum to be hosted by Pakistan in November 2006 to further discuss this and other important energy issues. We also commended the progress that has been made in the area of financial cooperation, especially with regard to making productive use of Asia's substantial savings, including revenues that accrue from the energy trade, and invest these through the Asian Bond Market mechanism for the benefit of the region.

### • *Asia-Africa Cooperation*

97. We noted the progress on the follow up of the outcome of the Asia-Africa Summit toward the realisation of the New Asia-Africa Strategic Partnership (NAASP) and look forward for the development of concrete programme and project cooperation by the Senior Officials' Meeting to be held in Durban on 1–3 September 2006.

### • *Asia-Pacific Economic Cooperation (APEC)*

98. We welcomed the progress achieved by APEC member economies towards facilitating and liberalizing trade and investment as well as towards economic and technical cooperation in the Asia-Pacific region. We believed ASEAN and APEC share a common vision of promoting regional sustainable growth and shared prosperity. We also believed that greater collaboration between ASEAN and APEC through the exchange and sharing of information, expertise and best practices and capacity building programmes would contribute towards this vision and that the ASEAN-APEC partnership would also benefit the business sector and other sectors through the various trade facilitation initiatives to address business concerns and impediments to cross border trade, investment and cooperation. In this regard, we expressed our full support for Viet Nam to successfully hold the 14th APEC Economic Leaders' Meeting in November 2006 with a view to

contributing to the building of a dynamic community for sustainable development and prosperity. We also supported Cambodia's intention to seek membership in APEC.

## • *Asia-Europe Meeting (ASEM)*

99. We stressed the need for ASEM to provide a foundation and framework for fostering the Asia-Europe comprehensive partnership in the 21st century. We look forward to a successful convening of the 6th ASEM Summit on 10–11 September 2006 in Helsinki, Finland and the commemoration of the 10th anniversary of ASEM as an important benchmark of a ten-year process linking Asia and Europe. We hoped that the 6th ASEM Summit would further strengthen a mutually beneficial and forward looking Asia-Europe partnership.

    We hoped further it would reflect in its vision on the future directions of ASEM cooperation in areas of mutual concern and interest such as strengthening multilateralism; addressing security threats; sustainable development; dialogue among cultures and civilisations; and globalization and competitiveness.
100. We welcomed the initiative to establish the ASEM Virtual Secretariat (AVS) at the ASEAN Secretariat as an information-sharing device to facilitate coordination and cooperation among its partners. In this context, we look forward to contributions to the ASEAN Secretariat by all ASEM partners to ensure the effective operation of the AVS.

## • *United Nations (UN)*

101. We reaffirmed our support for multilateralism and international law as embodied in the UN Charter. In reviewing the status of the implementation of the 2005 World Summit Outcome Document, adopted at the conclusion of the High-level Plenary Meeting of the General Assembly held from 14–16 September 2005, we supported a comprehensive reform of the United Nations and underlined the need to enhance the voice and the role of the developing countries within the UN system. We believed that to ensure that the UN remains relevant and effective, it is imperative that it be democratized efficient, transparent, accountable, and truly reflective of the will and interest of all Member States. We also welcomed the establishment of the UN Human Rights Council and the UN Peacebuilding Commission.

102. We reaffirmed ASEAN's support for Indonesia, Viet Nam, Thailand, Cambodia and Malaysia's candidature to become non-permanent members of the UN Security Council for the year 2007–2008, 2008–2009, 2011–2012, 2013–2014, 2015–2016 respectively. In this context, we also reaffirmed our collective endeavour to support Indonesia's bid for the non-permanent seat for the UNSC for 2007–2008, in the election to be held at the 61st Session of the UN General Assembly and requested Indonesia to coordinate this endeavour with the Permanent Representatives of ASEAN Member Countries in New York.

## ASEAN Candidature for the UNSG

....

## Cooperation with Regional Organizations

104. We recalled the outcomes of the ASEAN-South Asia Association for Regional Cooperation (SAARC), ASEAN-Gulf Cooperation Council (GCC) and ASEAN-Economic Cooperation Organization (ECO) Foreign Ministers Meetings in September 2005 in New York where several areas were identified for cooperation between ASEAN and these organisations. We recognized the potential of these cooperation arrangements to generate mutual benefits.

## 40th AMM

....

Source: http://www.aseansec.org/18561.htm
Accessed date: 8 October 2008
Publisher: ASEAN Secretariat
Country: Jakarta
Date of Publication: 2006

# CHAPTER 18

# CHAIRPERSON'S STATEMENT OF THE 12$^{TH}$ ASEAN SUMMIT H.E. THE PRESIDENT GLORIA MACAPAGAL-ARROYO

## "ONE CARING AND SHARING COMMUNITY"

**Cebu, Philippines, 13 January 2007**

1. We, the Heads of State and/or Government of ASEAN Member Countries, had a very productive 12$^{th}$ ASEAN Summit Meeting, on 13 January 2007 in Cebu, Philippines.
2. We exchanged views on regional and international developments, focusing on how we may deepen ASEAN integration to better foster the region's sustainable development, stability, security and prosperity for the benefit of all our peoples.
3. We resolved to uphold the centrality of ASEAN and to enhance its standing as an effective driving force for regional initiatives and collective responses to the challenges and opportunities facing our region, countries and peoples. We stressed that the ASEAN community we are building shall be a community of peoples caring for and sharing their human, natural and cultural resources and strengths for their common good and mutual benefit.

## CEBU DECLARATION ON THE BLUEPRINT OF THE ASEAN CHARTER

4. We recognized that ASEAN must manage the key challenges of regional integration, globalization, economic growth and new technologies. In doing so, we acknowledged that ASEAN must remain cohesive with strong institutions and responsive policies for regional community building. To help realize this vision, we signed the Cebu Declaration on the Blueprint of the ASEAN Charter to endorse the Report of the Eminent Persons Group (EPG) on the ASEAN Charter as one of the basis of the drafting of the ASEAN Charter together with our views and directives given at the 11$^{th}$ and 12$^{th}$ ASEAN Summit. We also directed the High Level Task Force to complete the drafting of the ASEAN Charter in time for the 13$^{th}$ Summit in Singapore in 2007.

## AN ASEAN SOCIO-CULTURAL COMMUNITY

5. We recognized ASEAN's progress in creating a caring environment that prioritizes the quality of life of its peoples. We agreed to address the special needs of the vulnerable and disadvantaged, through people-centered integration. To reinforce this environment in the context of building a stronger regional identity, we agreed to hold ASEAN Day commemorative activities in each our countries.
6. We agreed to strengthen the protection and promotion of the rights and welfare of women and children within and between our countries. Towards this end, we will mainstream their concerns in our national and regional plans.
7. We recognized the contributions of our migrant workers to the development and prosperity of our region. We, therefore, issued the ASEAN Declaration on the Protection and Promotion of the Rights of Migrant Workers as a concrete manifestation of our collective commitment to attain this objective. We directed our officials to implement the Declaration and to develop, in accordance with its provisions, effective mechanisms to safeguard our migrant workers, including an ASEAN instrument to protect and promote the rights of migrant workers, consistent with our vision of building a just, humane and democratic ASEAN Community. We also instructed the Secretary General to report annually on the progress of these directives.
8. We convened the Second Special Session on HIV and AIDS to stem and reverse the spread of HIV and AIDS in the region. We agreed to strengthen national AIDS policies and programs to protect persons living with HIV and AIDS, as well as other affected groups, from social stigma. We agreed to remove obstacles in the access of quality products and medicines for HIV and AIDS prevention and treatment. We adopted the Third ASEAN Work Program on HIV and AIDS (AWP III) for 2006–2010. We expressed support for the work of the ASEAN Task Force on AIDS (ATFOA) in strengthening regional responses to HIV and AIDS through multi-sectoral participation. We expressed appreciation for the assistance extended by UNAIDS to ASEAN in implementing regional HIV and AIDS initiatives.
9. We agreed to strengthen our efforts to achieve our common goals of eradicating poverty and hunger in ASEAN, as determined by the World Food Summit, the U.N. Millennium Development Goals (MDGs) and the VAP. We undertook to support further resource mobilization for agriculture and rural development in the ASEAN. We adopted the ASEAN Statement calling upon the Paris Club to seriously consider the Philippine proposal, raised at the ASEAN Inter-Parliamentary Assembly, for debt-equity arrangements to fund MDG projects.

10. We agreed to support the operations of the ASEAN Center for Biodiversity, based in the Philippines to actively promote biodiversity conservation in the region. We also agreed to pursue marine biodiversity projects in the region.
11. We discussed the transboundary haze pollution in the region and noted the work of the ASEAN Environment Ministers in developing effective strategies to address this problem and in mobilizing resources to implement the Plans of Action in dealing with Transboundary Haze Pollution. We stressed the importance of bringing the Haze issue to the attention of other countries and international organizations. We noted that the ASEAN Environment Ministers had adopted the Cebu Resolution on Sustainable Development to address critical and persistent environmental problems that generate economic and social dislocations. We also agreed to work on an ASEAN Leaders Declaration on Environmental Sustainability to be issued at our next Summit in Singapore.
12. We welcomed the progress in implementing the VAP and decisions from previous ASEAN and Related Summits. We urged Member Countries and Dialogue Partners to continue contributing to the ASEAN Development Fund to support ASEAN's integration. We tasked our Ministers to take steps to fully implement the VAP and other ASEAN action plans and decisions, and we directed the Secretary-General to update us on these matters at our next Summit.

## AN ASEAN COMMUNITY BY 2015

13. We affirmed our strong commitment to accelerate the establishment of an ASEAN Community by 2015 as envisioned in the ASEAN Vision 2020 and the ASEAN Concord II and agreed to sign the Cebu Declaration on the Establishment of the ASEAN Community by 2015.

## ASEAN SECURITY COMMUNITY

14. We welcomed the steady progress made in implementing ASEAN Security Community (ASC) — related activities through the VAP and the ASC Plan of Action, including the convening of the First ASEAN Defense Ministers Meeting, as well as advances in the work of the ASEAN Regional Forum (ARF) and the ASEAN-China Joint Working Group on the Implementation of the Declaration on the Conduct of Parties in the South China Sea.
15. We signed the ASEAN Convention on Counter Terrorism to enhance the region's capacity to confront terrorism in all its forms and manifestations, and to deepen counter-terrorism cooperation among our law enforcement and other relevant authorities. We also recognized the importance of inter-faith

dialogue in fostering greater understanding among our peoples and pledged to increase cooperation in this area.

## ASEAN ECONOMIC COMMUNITY

16. We agreed to hasten the establishment of the ASEAN Economic Community by 2015 and to transform ASEAN into a region with free movement of goods, services, investment, skilled labour, and freer flow of capital.
17. We expressed serious concern over the negative impact that prolonged high oil prices have on economic growth and development in the region. To address this problem in a strategic manner, we agreed to deepen ASEAN energy cooperation, especially for key ASEAN infrastructure projects, including the ASEAN power grid and Trans-ASEAN Gas Pipeline. Our ultimate aim is to create an open energy market. We`also stressed that ASEAN must improve energy use efficiency, and must diversify its energy supply by developing such alternative energy sources as biofuels and civilian nuclear power. In this regard, we agreed to pay close attention to the security, environmental, health and safety dimensions of the energy sector and we tasked our officials to look into a regional nuclear safety regime.

## NARROWING DEVELOPMENT GAP

18. We noted that the Mid-term Review of the Initiative for ASEAN Integration (IAI) Work Plan has recommended new project areas to benefit the ASEAN New Members, Cambodia, Laos, Myanmar and Vietnam. We recognized that the IAI needs more resources to meet their urgent needs and those of the ASEAN sub-regions. We also called for developing a coherent and integrated approach to infrastructure development, particularly transport linkages, in order to narrow development gaps.
19. We agreed to promote greater education cooperation among our countries and to strengthen education within them, in order to narrow our region's development gaps, to prepare our youth for regional leadership, and to increase the competitiveness of our peoples. We commended the contribution of the ASEAN University Network (AUN) towards this effort and called for the strengthening of the Network to facilitate educational access.

## MYANMAR

20. We took note of the briefing by Myanmar on the latest developments in the implementation of its Roadmap to Democracy. We encouraged Myanmar to

make greater progress towards national reconciliation. In this regard, we called for the release of those placed under detention and for effective dialogue with all parties concerned. Furthermore, we agreed on the need to preserve ASEAN's credibility as an effective regional organization by demonstrating a capacity to manage important issues within the region.

## ASEAN'S EXTERNAL RELATIONS

21. We appreciated the dynamism and diversity of our cooperation with each of our Dialogue Partners, particularly for integration and the narrowing of development gaps. We looked forward to their continued engagement with ASEAN.
22. We welcomed the accession of France and Timor Leste to the Treaty of Amity and Cooperation in Southeast Asia during our Summit. Their accession enhances the Treaty as our principal regional instrument governing peaceful inter-state relations, and should be followed by closer peace and security cooperation with ASEAN in the region and in the United Nations and other international fora.
23. We welcomed the progress of free trade agreement (FTA) negotiations with China, Japan, the Republic of Korea, India, Australia and New Zealand. We underscored the importance of FTA's in strengthening ASEAN's global competitiveness and its cooperation with its Dialogue Partners. We encouraged all Dialogue Partners to work with ASEAN on the early conclusion of their respective FTA's. These FTA's, taken together, will deepen East Asian economic integration, which will benefit the peoples of the region.

## EAST ASIA SUMMIT

24. We looked forward in convening the Second East Asia Summit (EAS) on 15 January 2007. Reaffirming that ASEAN should consolidate its leading and central role in the evolving regional architecture; we are committed to ensuring that our meeting will build on the success of the First EAS. We looked forward to signing the Cebu Declaration on East Asian Energy Security which would help shape a common regional policy for energy issues, including the development and use of alternative and renewable forms of energy, promotion of energy efficiency and resource and infrastructure development through greater private sector involvement. We tasked our officials to continue working with our EAS partners in coming up with concrete projects to enhance our energy security.
25. We exchanged views on the future of East Asian cooperation. We agreed on the need to strengthen cooperation with other EAS partners and reaffirmed

that the ASEAN Plus Three process would be the main vehicle towards achieving an East Asian community.

## ASEAN — SHANGHAI COOPERATION ORGANIZATION (SCO)

26. We welcomed the Philippine initiative to forge closer cooperation with the Shanghai Cooperation Organization (SCO), which is ASEAN's immediate neighbor and a potential partner in promoting peace, security and prosperity in the region. We tasked our officials to identify means of strengthening our linkages with the SCO, in addition to the existing arrangement between our Secretariats.

## REGIONAL AND INTERNATIONAL ISSUES

27. We agreed to continue our cooperation to maintain security, stability and peace in our region. Towards this end, we will continue collective action to address the challenges posed by such serious threats as terrorism and transnational crime, avian influenza and other major infectious diseases, environmental degradation, natural disasters, destabilizing increases in oil prices, and the negative impact of rapid globalization and growth.
28. We reaffirmed that the denuclearization of the Korean Peninsula is an international priority. We, therefore, urged the DPRK to desist from conducting further nuclear tests, to take concrete and effective steps to implement the 19 September 2005 Joint Statement, and to rejoin, at an early date, the Nuclear Non-Proliferation Treaty. We emphasized that DPRK must effectively address the humanitarian concerns of the international community.
29. We fully support the Six-Party Talks and other diplomatic efforts to resolve the Korean Peninsula issue. At the same time, we agreed that the international community must convey in clear terms to the DPRK that the latter must denuclearize in a verifiable manner. We, therefore, reaffirmed our commitment to the full implementation of UNSC Resolutions 1695 and 1718 for this purpose,
30. We expressed our continuing concern over instability in Iraq and the Middle East. We called for dialogue between all contending sides, to secure national reconciliation in Iraq, and a durable and equitable settlement between Israel and Palestine, consistent with the relevant United Nations resolutions.
31. We reaffirmed our commitment to the United Nations and our support for its comprehensive reform, including the enhancement of the voice and role of developing countries in its structure and processes. We welcomed the message

to ASEAN of the new United Nations Secretary General, Ban Ki-moon, and expressed our pride that he is from our own region and our best wishes for his success in his important tasks.

## WTO

32. We took note of the message from WTO Director General Pascal Lamy on the status of the negotiations on the WTO talks and the Doha Development Round. We adopted the ASEAN Statement on the WTO to express support for the resumption of the Doha Round.
33. We welcomed Viet Nam's accession to the WTO and reiterated our support for early accession of Lao PDR into the WTO.

## PAKISTAN

34. We noted the Proposal by the Prime Minister of Malaysia for Pakistan to be accorded the status of full Dialogue Partner of ASEAN as per the latter's request. We agreed that the request be given due consideration.

## OTHER MATTERS

35. We supported the continued efforts of the ASEAN Foundation to foster a greater sense of regional identity among our peoples. We noted the Report of the Executive Director of the ASEAN Foundation and agreed to ensure full private sector involvement in our community building activities.
36. We welcomed the report of the ASEAN Business Advisory Council (ABAC) and expressed our continuing support for its role in enhancing private sector engagement in ASEAN economic policy discussions. We also underscored the need for closer coordination and regular engagement between the private sector and relevant public agencies in the implementation of the ABAC recommendations and ASEAN's economic initiatives and programmes.
37. We were pleased with the innovative proposals made by the President of the 27th ASEAN Inter-Parliamentary Organization (AIPO) Assembly on making ASEAN more effective and meaningful for Asia and the world, and on enhancing ASEAN-AIPO interaction.
38. We welcomed the report of the Chair of the 5th ASEAN People's Assembly (APA) on the outcome of the 5th APA that was held in Manila on 8–9 December 2006. We took into consideration the 5th APA's recommendations on how to strengthen cooperation between ASEAN and the region's civil society organizations.

Source: http://www.aseansec.org/19280.htm
Accessed date: 8 October 2008
Publisher: ASEAN Secretariat
Country: Jakarta
Date of Publication: 2007

# CHAPTER 19

# CEBU DECLARATION TOWARDS ONE CARING AND SHARING COMMUNITY

**WE**, the Heads of State/Government of Brunei Darussalam, the Kingdom of Cambodia, the Republic of Indonesia, the Lao People's Democratic Republic, Malaysia, the Union of Myanmar, the Republic of the Philippines, the Republic of Singapore, the Kingdom of Thailand, the Socialist Republic of Viet Nam, Member Countries of the Association of Southeast Asian Nations, hereinafter referred to as ASEAN;

**RECALLING** the goals and objectives of the ASEAN Vision 2020, which sets out a broad vision of the ASEAN becoming "a concert of Southeast Asian Nations, outward looking, living in peace, stability and prosperity, bonded together as partners in dynamic development and in a community of caring and sharing societies";

**RECALLING FURTHER** the Declaration of ASEAN Concord II (Bali Concord II), adopted during the 9$^{th}$ ASEAN Summit in Bali, Indonesia, on 7 October 2003, which aims to realise the establishment of the ASEAN Community comprising three pillars, namely the ASEAN Security Community (ASC), ASEAN Economic Community (AEC), and ASEAN Socio-Cultural Community (ASCC) that are closely intertwined and mutually reinforcing for the purpose of ensuring durable peace, stability and shared prosperity in the region;

**REAFFIRMING** the core elements of the ASEAN Socio-Cultural Community Plan of Action of the Vientiane Action Programme (VAP), which aims to build a community of caring and sharing societies to address issues of poverty, equity and human development; manage the social impact of economic integration by building a competitive human resource base and adequate systems of social protection; enhance environmental sustainability and sound environmental governance; and strengthen the foundations of regional social cohesion towards an ASEAN Community;

....

**REAFFIRMING FURTHER** the ASEAN Plan of Action on Rural Development and Poverty Eradication (RDPE), which aims to formulate strategies and implement programmes and projects based on the vision to eradicate poverty and respond to challenges of globalisation, trade liberalisation and regional integration;

**EXPRESSING** the need to accelerate the implementation of agreed ASEAN activities to address the development gap among ASEAN Member Countries, and to facilitate the pace of economic integration of ASEAN into one community of nations;

## HEREBY DECLARE TO:

1. Reaffirm our commitment to realise the MDGs and the four strategic thrusts of the ASEAN Socio-Cultural Community (ASCC), particularly in reducing poverty and inequality and in improving the standard and quality of life of our people.
2. Direct our relevant ASEAN Sectoral Ministerial bodies to accelerate ASEAN cooperation under the socio-cultural pillar through closer consultation and synergy of cooperation in realising the goals of the ASEAN Socio-Cultural Community (ASCC) with clear timelines.

....

4. Encourage equitable and effective participation of women in all fields in the ASEAN community-building process.
5. Encourage greater institutional collaboration in promoting ASEAN awareness particularly among the younger generation, and promote the increased involvement of ASEAN youth and students at national and regional level activities, so that they can make valuable contributions to the achievement of the ASEAN Community.
6. Commit to improve our standard of education to build a more competitive workforce.
7. Expand the participation of ASEAN parliamentarians, private sector and civil society organisations in line with the goal toward a people-centred ASEAN.
8. Promote ASEAN identity building in support of an ASEAN Community by undertaking initiatives and activities to increase the level of ASEAN awareness and "we feeling" among the peoples of ASEAN. We also reaffirm our efforts in preserving and promoting the region's rich and vast cultural heritage and living traditions, which reflect the ASEAN spirit of unity in cultural diversity and social harmony.

**DONE** at Cebu, Philippines, this Thirteenth Day of January in the Year Two Thousand and Seven, in a single original copy in the English Language.

For Brunei Darussalam:

**HAJI HASSANAL BOLKIAH**
Sultan of Brunei Darussalam

For the Kingdom of Cambodia:

**SAMDECH HUN SEN**
Prime Minister

For the Republic of Indonesia:

**DR. SUSILO BAMBANG YUDHOYONO**
President

For the Lao People's Democratic Republic:

**BOUASONE BOUPHAVANH**
Prime Minister

For Malaysia:

**DATO' SERI ABDULLAH AHMAD BADAWI**
Prime Minister

For the Union of Myanmar:

**GENERAL SOE WIN**
Prime Minister

For the Republic of the Philippines:

**GLORIA MACAPAGAL-ARROYO**
President

For the Republic of Singapore:

**LEE HSIEN LOONG**
Prime Minister

For the Kingdom of Thailand:

**GENERAL SURAYUD CHULANONT (RET.)**
Prime Minister

For the Socialist Republic of Viet Nam:

**NGUYEN TAN DUNG**
Prime Minister

Source: http://www.aseansec.org/19254.htm
Accessed date: 22 January 2009
Publisher: ASEAN Secretariat
Country: Jakarta
Date of Publication: 2007

# CHAPTER 20

# CHAIRMAN'S STATEMENT OF THE 13TH ASEAN SUMMIT "ONE ASEAN AT THE HEART OF DYNAMIC ASIA"

**Singapore, 20 November 2007**

1. On the occasion of the 40th Anniversary of ASEAN, we, the Heads of State/Government of ASEAN Member Countries gathered in Singapore for the 13th ASEAN Summit on 20 November 2007. We had candid and fruitful discussions under our 40th Anniversary theme of "One ASEAN at the Heart of Dynamic Asia", and our substantive theme of "Energy, Environment, Climate Change and Sustainable Development".

## ASEAN CHARTER

2. We celebrated the signing of the ASEAN Charter as a historic milestone for ASEAN, representing our common vision and commitment to the development of an ASEAN Community as a region of lasting peace, stability, sustained economic growth, shared prosperity and social progress. We commended the Eminent Persons Group and High Level Task Force on the Drafting of the ASEAN Charter for their inspired contributions.
3. We agreed that implementation will be the key to the realisation of the vision outlined in the ASEAN Charter. With the Singapore Declaration on the ASEAN Charter, we pledged to undertake all measures necessary to ensure expeditious ratification and implementation of the Charter. We welcomed Thailand's offer to host a special ceremony to celebrate the entry into force of the ASEAN Charter during the next Summit, at the Saranrom Palace, where the ASEAN Declaration was signed in 1967.

## ENERGY, ENVIRONMENT, CLIMATE CHANGE AND SUSTAINABLE DEVELOPMENT

4. We recognised that the issues of energy security, environment, climate change and sustainable development are interrelated and complex, and represents

a serious global challenge that must be addressed in a comprehensive manner through individual, regional and concerted international action. In particular, the adverse effects of climate change, such as rising sea levels and changing weather patterns, would have direct impact on the security, livelihood and well-being of the peoples of ASEAN, and thus necessitated urgent action. We underscored the importance of establishing a comprehensive post-2012 international climate change arrangement, based on the principles of equity, flexibility, effectiveness, common but differentiated responsibilities and respective capabilities. We declared our commitment to the UNFCCC process and pledged our support for Indonesia's hosting of the UNFCCC meeting in December 2007, and its efforts to work with all parties to adopt the "Bali Roadmap" towards negotiations for a post-2012 international agreement.

5. We agreed that ASEAN, as a region, must do its part in addressing these issues. Through the ASEAN Declaration on Environmental Sustainability, we pledged to deepen cooperation in a wide range of activities, including combating transboundary environmental pollution, and ensuring the conservation and sustainable management of natural resources. We also agreed to explore the safe and sustainable use of alternative energies, such as hydropower, biofuels and solar power. Through the ASEAN Declaration on the 13th Session of the Conference of the Parties (COP) to the UNFCCC and the 3rd Session of the Meeting of the Conference of the Parties serving as the Meeting of the Parties (CMP) to the Kyoto Protocol, we commit to support Indonesia for the successful conclusion of the climate change conference in Bali.
6. We noted in particular that ASEAN's rich endowment of forestry resources meant our region could contribute in a major way to the global reduction of greenhouse gas through the preservation of carbon sinks. In this regard, we are committed to increasing forest cover in our region, and welcomed concrete initiatives such as the Heart of Borneo conservation plan being undertaken by Brunei, Indonesia and Malaysia. We pledged to tackle and guard against unsustainable practices, such as illegal logging, preventing slash-and-burn practices and forest fires, through cooperation to implement robust enforcement, education and increased bilateral and regional cooperation. We also called upon the international community to participate in and contribute to such efforts. In addition, we support other relevant initiatives such as the Forestry Eleven Forum, and the Coral Triangle Initiative on Coral Reefs, Fisheries and Food Security.
7. Given the need to explore alternative sources of energy, we stressed the need to ensure that these sources are sustainable and safe. In this regard, we welcomed our Energy Ministers' work in following up on our discussions at the

12th ASEAN Summit in Cebu, in particular the move to establish a Nuclear Energy Safety Sub-Sector Network (NES-SSN) to discuss civilian nuclear energy safety and security issues, and to develop a nuclear safety regime at the regional level that meets international standards. There should also be stronger and better cooperation on the development of renewable sources of energy in an effort by ASEAN to address climate change. Building an ASEAN Community

## ASEAN ECONOMIC COMMUNITY

8. We welcomed the finalisation of the Blueprint for the ASEAN Economic Community (AEC) and the signing of the Declaration on the AEC Blueprint, which will serve as the roadmap for transforming ASEAN into a single market and production base, highly competitive and fully integrated into the global community by 2015. We emphasised the importance of equitable economic development, and the reduction of poverty and socio-economic disparities. We urged that the benefits of economic integration be quickly accrued to all people of ASEAN through timely implementation of the provisions of the Blueprint, which should be monitored through the development of an AEC Scorecard mechanism. We tasked the ASEAN Economic Ministers to ensure that we follow-through with our commitments in the Blueprint, and we designated 2008 to be the year for promoting ASEAN Economic Community Awareness.
9. We reiterated the commitment of our Transport Ministers to ensure the timely implementation of the ASEAN Roadmap for Integration of Air Travel Sector (RIATS), and pledged to work towards the expeditious signing of the implementing texts of the RIATS in February 2008, which will pave the way for fully liberalised air services among ASEAN capitals by December 2008. We agreed that fully liberalised air services within ASEAN would contribute positively on our region's competitiveness and accelerate our integration efforts.

## ASEAN POLITICAL-SECURITY COMMUNITY

10. We applauded our sectoral ministers for their contributions and relentless efforts to enhance peace rid security in the region through active cooperation and consultations in forums such as the AMM, AMMTC and ASEAN Regional Forum (ARF). We also commended the spirit of cooperation of our Defence Ministers and militaries in forging practical cooperation to address the range of transnational security issues facing the region. We noted the

ADMM's aspiration to establish a robust, effective, open and inclusive regional security architecture, which would enhance regional peace and stability, and contribute to the realisation of the ASEAN Political-Security Community.

11. In the spirit of realising the ASEAN Community by 2015, we tasked our Ministers and officials to draft a Blueprint for the ASEAN Political Security Community (APSC), which would be adopted at the 14th ASEAN Summit.

## ASEAN SOCIO-CULTURAL COMMUNITY

12. We underlined the need to enhance education and to hone the skills and talents of our peoples as ASEAN moves towards closer integration, in order to ensure the region's competitiveness, and to reap the benefits of globalisation while minimising the social impacts. We underscored the importance of promoting greater understanding and friendship among our people through the building of stronger people-to-people linkages, especially our youths. We expressed appreciation for the setting up of the SGD 5 million Singapore-ASEAN Youth Fund, and also applauded the efforts of ASEAN member countries in promoting greater ASEAN awareness, through a series of commemorative activities to celebrate ASEAN's $40^{th}$ Anniversary, suggestions such as the inclusion of ASEAN studies into our national curricula and Thailand's proposal to establish ASEAN Friendship Associations. We designated ASEAN Day (8 August) as a Special Day.
13. In order to ensure that concrete actions are undertaken to promote the establishment of an ASEAN Socio-Cultural Community, we tasked our Ministers and officials to draft a Blueprint for the ASEAN Socio-Cultural Community (ASCC), which would be adopted at the 14th ASEAN Summit.

## NARROWING THE DEVELOPMENT GAP

14. We agreed that narrowing the development gap remains an important task which will ensure that benefits of ASEAN's integration efforts are fully realised. We noted that our efforts to narrow the development gap, such as through the Initiative for ASEAN Integration (IAI), should be aligned with the broader objectives of ASEAN's integration efforts. We thanked Singapore for its pledge of a third tranche of IAI contributions amounting to SGD 30 million from 2009–2011. .... We also expressed appreciation to Singapore's voluntary contribution of US$500,000 to the ASEAN Development Fund, which will provide financial resources to support the implementation of the Vientiane Action Programme.

## STRENGTHENING THE ASEAN SECRETARIAT

15. We recognised that with the increasing scope of ASEAN cooperation, the Secretariat's infrastructure and facilities should be upgraded to meet this additional workload. In this connection, we welcome Singapore's contribution of US$240,500 to the Secretariat to upgrade its Information Technology and archival and depository systems.

## MYANMAR

16. We had an extensive and open discussion on Myanmar. We were given a comprehensive briefing by Myanmar PM Thein Sein, where he emphasised that the situation in Myanmar was a domestic affair, and that Myanmar was fully capable of handling the situation by itself. He reaffirmed that Myanmar had every confidence in managing the good offices of the UN. As ASEAN Chair, Singapore issued a statement to clarify ASEAN's role and stand. We reiterated that the Myanmar Government should continue to work with the UN in order to open up a meaningful dialogue with Daw Aung San Suu Kyi and the National League for Democracy (NLD); make full use of the good offices of the UN Secretary-General and Professor Gambari in this process; lift restrictions on Daw Aung San Suu Kyi and release all political detainees; work towards a peaceful transition to democracy; and address the economic difficulties faced by the people of Myanmar. We emphasised that we will strive to prevent the Myanmar issue from obstructing ASEAN's integration efforts, especially the ASEAN Charter and the establishment of the ASEAN Community.

## ASEAN'S EXTERNAL RELATIONS

17. We are pleased with the overall progress of our cooperation within the ASEAN Plus Three framework, and looked forward to the celebration of the 10th Anniversary of ASEAN Plus Three cooperation with our Plus Three Dialogue Partners. We reiterated that ASEAN Plus Three cooperation will continue to support ASEAN integration with the objective to realise the ASEAN Community, and play a key role in regional community building efforts for the long-term goal of realising an East Asian community with ASEAN as the driving force. We looked forward to the adoption of the Second Joint Statement on East Asia Cooperation and its accompanying ASEAN Plus Three Cooperation Work Plan (2007–2017), which would provide strategic guidance for the future direction of ASEAN Plus

Three cooperation, with the aim of building an open regionalism connected to the world.

18. We reiterated that the dynamic and diverse cooperation with our Dialogue Partners have played a crucial role in facilitating our integration efforts and the narrowing of development gaps. We welcomed our Dialogue Partners' vigorous engagement with ASEAN and encouraged them to further deepen and broaden cooperation to achieve a stable, prosperous and outward-looking region. However, we regretted that some of our dialogue relations have been strained as a result of the Myanmar issue. We urged our dialogue partners to take a strategic and comprehensive view of our relations.
19. We also underscored the importance of Free Trade Agreements (FTAs) in strengthening ASEAN's global competitiveness and its cooperation with its Dialogue Partners. We encouraged all partners to work with ASEAN towards the speedy realisation of the FTAs with the longer-term benefits of such FTAs in mind. These FTAs, taken collectively, will deepen our economic integration and widen our web of trade and investment links with the world, thereby contributing to the overall development and benefit of the people of the region. In this regard, we welcomed the significant achievements in our FTA negotiations with China, Japan, and ROK, and looked forward to further progress in our FTA talks with India, Australia and New Zealand, as well as the European Union.
20. We noted that ASEAN and the EU will be holding a Commemorative Summit to mark 30 years of cooperation in Singapore on 22 November 2007, and looked forward to having a substantive discussion with our partners from Europe.
21. We recognised and supported the mutually reinforcing and complementary roles of the ASEAN plus Three process and the East Asia Summit (EAS), and such regional forums as the ASEAN Regional Forum, to promote East Asian cooperation. We reaffirmed our desire to continue developing the EAS as a high-level strategic forum for dialogue, and a means to catalyse regional cooperation among its participating countries. We looked forward to signing the Singapore Declaration on Climate Change, Energy and the Environment at the EAS, which will set out important common ground among the EAS participating countries on the key principles which can help pave the way to a more effective post-2012 agreement.
22. We reiterated our strong commitment towards an expeditious and successful conclusion of the Doha Development Round. Concluding the Round is essential to promote growth, opportunity, and prosperity. The primacy of the rules-based multilateral trading system is also vital to ensure a fair and

predictable global market in which we can all participate. We firmly believe that a successful outcome is within our collective grasp if we all make the necessary sacrifices. ASEAN is prepared to make our contribution. We each know what we must do, and we call on all WTO Members to do the same at this critical juncture. We have come too far to fail. ASEAN also reiterated their strong support to Lao PDR's early accession to the WTO.

## INCOMING SECRETARY-GENERAL OF ASEAN

23. We endorsed Thailand's nomination of H.E. Dr. Surin Pitsuwan as the incoming Secretary-General of ASEAN. We thanked outgoing Secretary-General H.E. Ong Keng Yong for his outstanding contributions to ASEAN.

## OTHER MATTERS

24. We noted the reports from the ASEAN Inter-Parliamentary Assembly, ASEAN Foundation and the ASEAN Civil Society Conference 2007 which was held in Singapore in October 2007. We renewed our commitment to build a people-oriented ASEAN that is responsive to the needs of its peoples, and welcomed the ongoing efforts to institutionalise a genuine process of dialogue between the Leaders and all quarters of society, with the ASEAN Secretariat playing a key role as facilitator. We noted the comments and suggestions made by the civil society groups, including the need to deepen economic integration and community-building efforts, pay attention to well-being and livelihood of vulnerable groups in society, promote democracy, good governance and human rights, effectively resolve the transboundary environmental pollution, including haze, and ensure that in the development of nuclear power as an alternative energy source of power generation and civilian nuclear energy use, international nuclear safety and security standards are upheld.

....

26. We recognised the importance of highlighting ASEAN's economic opportunities to the world business community, and looked forward to attending the ASEAN Event at the World Economic Forum (WEF) in Davos in January 2008.
27. We expressed support for the Philippines' hosting of the 2nd Meeting of the Global Forum on Migration and Development in 2008, and urged all member

countries to participate actively in the drawing up of concrete initiatives that promote and harness the link between migration and development.

Source: http://www.aseansec.org/21093.htm
Accessed date: 16 January 2008
Publisher: ASEAN Secretariat
Country: Jakarta
Date of Publication: 2007

# CHAPTER 21

# JOINT STATEMENT ON THE COMMISSION FOR THE TREATY ON THE SOUTHEAST ASIA NUCLEAR WEAPON-FREE ZONE

**Manila, 30 July 2007**

We, the Foreign Ministers of the State Parties to the Treaty of the Southeast Asia Nuclear Weapon Free Zone, met in Manila, the Philippines on 29 July 2007, to review the implementation of the Treaty and to consider a plan of action to further enhance cooperation among State Parties as well as non-states parties, particularly the Nuclear Weapon States.

We conducted a thorough review of the implementation of the Treaty during the 10 years since it entered into force in 1997. We expressed appreciation for the ASEAN Secretariat's work in preparing the Stocktaking Paper on the Implementation of the SEANWFZ Treaty, and are pleased to note that the State Parties have abided by their responsibilities and obligations under the Treaty.

We reaffirmed our commitment to further enhance and promote the Southeast Asia Nuclear Weapon-Free Zone and resolved to undertake the following measures under the Plan of Action for the period 2007–2012:

- Ensure compliance with our undertakings under the SEANWFZ Treaty, including accession to the International Atomic Energy Agency (IAEA) safeguards agreements and related instruments;
- Continue close consultations to pursue the accession of all five nuclear weapon states;
- Seek cooperation with the IAEA, other international and regional bodies, other Nuclear Weapon-Free Zones, Dialogue Partners and other friendly states, in developing legal framework to meet international standards on nuclear safety, establishing regional networks for early notification of nuclear accidents, developing a regional emergency preparedness and response plan and strengthening capacity building in the region on nuclear safety issues;
- Jointly draw up specific work programmes/projects to implement the Plan of Action.

We expressed our appreciation to the Secretary of Foreign Affairs of the Philippines, H.E. Alberto G. Romulo, for organising and hosting the Meeting of the SEANWFZ Commission and for ably steering, as Chairman of the Commission, the conduct of the review of the SEANWFZ Treaty and the adoption of the Plan of Action for the SEANWFZ for 2007–2012.

We welcomed the election of the Minister for Foreign Affairs of Singapore, H.E. George Yeo, as the incoming Chairman of the Commission of the SEANWFZ on 30 July 2007 and expressed our confidence that the Plan of Action to Strengthen the implementation of the Treaty on the Southeast Asia Nuclear Weapon-Free Zone would be vigorously pursued under his able chairmanship.

Source: http://www.aseansec.org/20775.htm
Accessed date: 2 October 2008
Publisher: ASEAN Secretariat
Country: Jakarta
Date of Publication: 2007

# CHAPTER 22

# CEBU DECLARATION ON THE ACCELERATION OF THE ESTABLISHMENT OF AN ASEAN COMMUNITY BY 2015

**WE**, the Heads of State/Government of Brunei Darussalam, the Kingdom of Cambodia, the Republic of Indonesia, the Lao People's Democratic Republic, Malaysia, the Union of Myanmar, the Republic of the Philippines, the Republic of Singapore, the Kingdom of Thailand and the Socialist Republic of Viet Nam, Member Countries of ASEAN, on the occasion of the 12th ASEAN Summit in Cebu;

**ACKNOWLEDGING** the prescience of ASEAN Vision 2020 and the significant and important progress that ASEAN has made towards the goals of that visionary declaration;

**RECALLING** the proposal made at the 11th ASEAN Summit in Kuala Lumpur in December 2005, on accelerating the establishment of an ASEAN Community, as well as the exchange of views at the 39th ASEAN Ministerial Meeting in July 2006 in Kuala Lumpur and the recommendation from the 38th ASEAN Economic Ministers Meeting in August 2006;

**RECOGNIZING** that different levels of development within ASEAN require some flexibility as ASEAN moves towards a more integrated and interconnected future;

**WELCOMING** the concrete outcomes of the First Coordinating Conferences for the ASEAN Security Community Plan of Action (ASCCO) and ASEAN Socio-Cultural Community Plan of Action (SOC-COM), as well as the Consultative Meetings for the Priority Integration Sectors (COPS) under the ASEAN Economic Community;

**BUILDING UPON** our commitment to the Vientiane Action Programme in November 2004 as successor to the Hanoi Plan of Action to realise the aims of ASEAN Vision 2020 and the Declaration of ASEAN Concord II, and welcoming the establishment of the ASEAN Development Fund in 2005 as a positive step towards integration;

**EXPRESSING SATISFACTION** with the progress towards narrowing the development gap under the Initiative for ASEAN Integration and other programmes and acknowledging the need to enhance efforts to achieve this goal;

**DETERMINED** to deal more effectively with the increasing range of transboundary concerns which ASEAN faces in this rapidly changing world since the articulation of Vision 2020 in 1997 and the Declaration of ASEAN Concord II in 2003 through better coordination and increased cooperation within ASEAN;

**ENCOURAGED** by ASEAN's deepening relations with our Dialogue Partners in various areas including our FTA negotiations, comprehensive plans of action and the convening of the East Asia Summit, and our Dialogue Partners' engagement of ASEAN as a reliable and substantive partner in the development of a larger community in the region;

**CONSCIOUS** also that the strengthening of ASEAN integration through the accelerated establishment of an ASEAN Community will reinforce ASEAN's centrality and role as the driving force in charting the evolving regional architecture;

**BELIEVING** that at the core of ASEAN's response to the increasing number of regional challenges must be its efforts to build a strong ASEAN Community premised on a closely integrated, dynamic and vibrant regional economy, deeper political and security cooperation and stronger socio-cultural linkages;

## DO HEREBY DECLARE

**FIRST**, ASEAN's strong commitment towards accelerating the establishment of an ASEAN Community by 2015 along the lines of ASEAN Vision 2020 and the Declaration of ASEAN Concord II, in the three pillars of the ASEAN Security Community, ASEAN Economic Community and ASEAN Socio-Cultural Community;

**SECOND**, ASEAN's strong determination to accelerate the full implementation of the ASEAN Community's programme areas, measures and principles, with appropriate flexibility;

**THIRD**, ASEAN's determination to create a stronger, more united and cohesive ASEAN that can better manage the challenges posed by the evolving regional architecture and economic climate; and

**FOURTH**, that ASEAN remains committed to further expanding our engagement with our Dialogue Partners and other parties, and believes that such interaction will assist ASEAN in its integration efforts to achieve the ASEAN Community by 2015.

**DONE** at Cebu, Philippines, this Thirteenth Day of January in the Year Two Thousand and Seven, in a single original copy in the English Language.

For Brunei Darussalam:

**HAJI HASSANAL BOLKIAH**
Sultan of Brunei Darussalam

For the Kingdom of Cambodia:

**SAMDECH HUN SEN**
Prime Minister

For the Republic of Indonesia:

**DR. SUSILO BAMBANG YUDHOYONO**
President

For the Lao People's Democratic Republic:

**BOUASONE BOUPHAVANH**
Prime Minister

For Malaysia:

**DATO' SERI ABDULLAH AHMAD BADAWI**
Prime Minister

For the Union of Myanmar:

**GENERAL SOE WIN**
Prime Minister

For the Republic of the Philippines:

**GLORIA MACAPAGAL-ARROYO**
President

For the Republic of Singapore:

**LEE HSIEN LOONG**
Prime Minister

For the Kingdom of Thailand:

**GENERAL SURAYUD CHULANONT (RET.)**
Prime Minister

For the Socialist Republic of Viet Nam:

**NGUYEN TAN DUNG**
Prime Minister

Source: http://www.aseansec.org/19260.htm
Accessed date: 2 October 2008
Publisher: ASEAN Secretariat
Country: Jakarta
Date of Publication: 2007

# CHAPTER 23

# ASEAN CONVENTION ON COUNTER TERRORISM

Member Countries of the Association of Southeast Asian Nations (ASEAN) — Brunei Darussalam, the Kingdom of Cambodia, the Republic of Indonesia, the Lao People's Democratic Republic, Malaysia, the Union of Myanmar, the Republic of the Philippines, the Republic of Singapore, the Kingdom of Thailand, and the Socialist Republic of Viet Nam, hereinafter referred to as "the Parties";

**RECALLING** the Charter of the United Nations and relevant principles of international law, the relevant international conventions and protocols relating to counter terrorism and relevant resolutions of the United Nations on measures aimed at countering international terrorism, and reaffirming our commitment to protect human rights, fair treatment, the rule of law, and due process as well as the principles enshrined in the Treaty of Amity and Cooperation in Southeast Asia done at Bali on 24 February 1976;

**REAFFIRMING** that terrorism cannot and should not be associated with any religion, nationality, civilisation or ethnic group;

**RECALLING** also the ASEAN Declaration on Joint Action to Counter Terrorism and the Declaration on Terrorism adopted at the ASEAN Summits in 2001 and 2002 respectively;

**REAFFIRMING** our commitment to the Vientiane Action Programme done at Vientiane on 29 November 2004, particularly its thrust on "shaping and sharing of norms" and the need, among others, to work towards the conclusion of an ASEAN Mutual Legal Assistance Agreement, and an ASEAN Convention on Counter Terrorism, and the establishment of an ASEAN Extradition Treaty as envisaged by the 1976 Declaration of ASEAN Concord;

**DEEPLY CONCERNED** over the grave danger posed by terrorism to innocent lives, infrastructure and the environment, regional and international peace and stability as well as to economic development;

**REALISING** the importance of identifying and effectively addressing the root causes of terrorism in the formulation of any counter terrorism measures;

**REITERATING** that terrorism, in all its forms and manifestations, committed wherever, whenever, and by whomsoever, is a profound threat to international peace and security and a direct challenge to the attainment of peace, progress and prosperity for ASEAN and the realisation of ASEAN Vision 2020;

**REAFFIRMING** our strong commitment to enhance cooperation in countering terrorism which covers the prevention and suppression of all forms of terrorist acts;

**REITERATING** the need to improve regional cooperation on counter terrorism and undertake effective measures through deepening cooperation among ASEAN law enforcement agencies and relevant authorities in countering terrorism;

**ENCOURAGING** the Parties to become parties as soon as possible to the relevant international conventions and protocols relating to counter terrorism;

Have agreed as follows:

## ARTICLE I

### Objective

This Convention shall provide for the framework for regional cooperation to counter, prevent and suppress terrorism in all its forms and manifestations and to deepen cooperation among law enforcement agencies and relevant authorities of the Parties in countering terrorism.

## ARTICLE II

### Criminal Acts of Terrorism

1. For the purposes of this Convention, "offence" means any of the offences within the scope of and as defined in any of the treaties listed as follows:
   a. Convention for the Suppression of Unlawful Seizure of Aircraft, signed at The Hague on 16 December 1970;
   b. Convention for the Suppression of Unlawful Acts Against the Safety of Civil Aviation, concluded at Montreal on 23 September 1971;

   c. Convention on the Prevention and Punishment of Crimes Against Internationally Protected Persons, Including Diplomatic Agents, adopted in New York on 14 December 1973;
   d. International Convention Against the Taking of Hostages, adopted in New York on 17 December 1979;
   e. Convention on the Physical Protection of Nuclear Material, adopted in Vienna on 26 October 1979;
   f. Protocol for the Suppression of Unlawful Acts of Violence at Airports Serving International Civil Aviation, supplementary to the Convention for the Suppression of Unlawful Acts Against the Safety of Civil Aviation, done at Montreal on 24 February 1988;
   g. Convention for the Suppression of Unlawful Acts Against the Safety of Maritime Navigation, done at Rome on 10 March 1988;
   h. Protocol for the Suppression of Unlawful Acts Against the Safety of Fixed Platforms Located on the Continental Shelf, done at Rome on 10 March 1988;
   i. International Convention for the Suppression of Terrorist Bombings, adopted in New York on 15 December 1997;
   j. International Convention for the Suppression of the Financing of Terrorism, adopted in New York on 9 December 1999;
   k. International Convention for the Suppression of Acts of Nuclear Terrorism, adopted in New York on 13 April 2005;
   l. Amendment to the Convention on the Physical Protection of Nuclear Material, done at Vienna on 8 July 2005;
   m. Protocol of 2005 to the Convention for the Suppression of Unlawful Acts Against the Safety of Maritime Navigation, done at London on 14 October 2005; and
   n. Protocol of 2005 to the Protocol for the Suppression of Unlawful Acts Against the Safety of Fixed Platforms Located on the Continental Shelf, done at London on 14 October 2005.

2. On depositing its instrument of ratification or approval, a Party which is not a Party to a treaty listed in paragraph 1 of this Article may declare that, in the application of this Convention to that Party, that treaty shall be deemed not to be included in paragraph 1 of this Article. This declaration shall cease to have an effect as soon as the treaty enters into force for the Party having made such a declaration, which shall notify the depositary as stated in paragraph 2 of Article XX of this entry into force.
3. When a Party ceases to be a party to a treaty listed in paragraph 1 of this Article, it may make a declaration as provided for in this Article, with respect to that treaty.

## ARTICLE III

### Sovereign Equality, Territorial Integrity and Non-Interference

The Parties shall carry out their obligations under this Convention in a manner consistent with the principles of sovereign equality and territorial integrity of States and that of non-interference in the internal affairs of other Parties.

## ARTICLE IV

### Preservation of Sovereignty

Nothing in this Convention entitles a Party to undertake, in the territory of another Party, the exercise of jurisdiction or performance of functions which are exclusively reserved for the authorities of that other Party by its domestic laws.

## ARTICLE V

### Non-Application

This Convention shall not apply where the offence is committed within a single Party, the alleged offender and the victims are nationals of that Party, the alleged offender is found in the territory of that Party and no other Party has a basis under this Convention to exercise jurisdiction.

## ARTICLE VI

### Areas of Cooperation

1. The areas of cooperation under this Convention may, in conformity with the domestic laws of the respective Parties, include appropriate measures, among others, to:

    a. Take the necessary steps to prevent the commission of terrorist acts, including by the provision of early warning to the other Parties through the exchange of information;
    b. Prevent those who finance, plan, facilitate, or commit terrorist acts from using their respective territories for those purposes against the other Parties and/or the citizens of the other Parties;
    c. Prevent and suppress the financing of terrorist acts;
    d. Prevent the movement of terrorists or terrorist groups by effective border control and controls on issuance of identity papers and travel documents,

and through measures for preventing counterfeiting, forgery or fraudulent use of identity papers and travel documents;

e. Promote capacity-building including trainings and technical cooperation and the holding of regional meetings;
f. Promote public awareness and participation in efforts to counter terrorism, as well as enhance inter-faith and intra-faith dialogue and dialogue among civilisations;
g. Enhance cross-border cooperation;
h. Enhance intelligence exchange and sharing of information;
i. Enhance existing cooperation towards developing regional databases under the purview of the relevant ASEAN bodies;
j. Strengthen capability and readiness to deal with chemical, biological, radiological, nuclear (CBRN) terrorism, cyber terrorism and any new forms of terrorism;
k. Undertake research and development on measures to counter terrorism;
l. Encourage the use of video conference or teleconference facilities for court proceedings, where appropriate; and
m. Ensure that any person who participates in the financing, planning, preparation or perpetration of terrorist acts or in supporting terrorist acts is brought to justice.

2. Subject to the consent of the Parties concerned, Parties shall cooperate to address the root causes of terrorism and conditions conducive to the spread of terrorism to prevent the perpetration of terrorist acts and the propagation of terrorist cells.

## ARTICLE VII

## State Jurisdiction

1. A Party shall take such measures as may be necessary to establish its jurisdiction over the offences covered in Article II of this Convention when:

   a. The offence is committed in the territory of that Party; or
   b. The offence is committed on board a vessel flying the flag of that Party or an aircraft which is registered under the laws of that Party at the time the offence is committed; or
   c. The offence is committed by a national of that Party.

2. A Party may also establish its jurisdiction over any such offence when:

   a. The offence is committed against a national of that Party; or

b. The offence is committed against a state or government facility of that Party abroad, including its embassy or other diplomatic or consular premises; or
c. The offence is committed in an attempt to compel that Party to do or to abstain from doing any act; or
d. The offence is committed by a stateless person with habitual residence in the territory of that Party.

3. A Party shall likewise establish its jurisdiction over the offences covered in Article II of this Convention in cases where the alleged offender is present in its territory and it does not extradite that person to any of the Parties that have established their jurisdiction in accordance with paragraph 1 or 2 of this Article.
4. This Convention does not exclude the exercise of any criminal jurisdiction established by a Party in accordance with its domestic laws.

## ARTICLE VIII

### Fair Treatment

1. Any person who is taken into custody or regarding whom any other measures are taken or proceedings are carried out pursuant to this Convention shall be guaranteed fair treatment, including enjoyment of all rights and guarantees in conformity with the laws of the Party in the territory of which that person is present and applicable provisions of international law, including international human rights law.
2. Upon receiving information that a person who has committed or who is alleged to have committed an offence covered in Article II of this Convention may be present in its territory, the Party concerned shall take such measures as may be necessary under its domestic laws to investigate the facts contained in the information.
3. Upon being satisfied that the circumstances so warrant, the Party in whose territory the offender or alleged offender is present shall take the appropriate measures under its domestic laws so as to ensure that person's presence for the purpose of prosecution or extradition.
4. Any person regarding whom measures referred to in paragraph 3 of this Article are being taken shall be entitled:

   a. To communicate without delay with the nearest appropriate representative of the State of which that person is a national or which is otherwise entitled to protect that person's rights;
   b. To be visited by a representative of that State;
   c. To be informed of that person's rights under subparagraphs (a) and (b) of paragraph 4 of this Article.

5. The rights referred to in paragraph 4 of this Article shall be exercised in conformity with the laws and regulations of the Party in the territory of which the offender or alleged offender is present, subject to the provision that the said laws and regulations must enable full effect to be given to the purposes for which the rights accorded under paragraph 4 of this Article are intended.
6. When a Party, pursuant to the present Article, has taken a person into custody, it shall immediately notify, directly or through the Secretary-General of ASEAN, the Parties which have established jurisdiction in accordance with paragraph 1 or 2 of Article VII, and, if it considers it advisable, any other interested Parties, of the fact that such person is in custody and of the circumstances which warrant that person's detention. The Party which is carrying out the investigation referred to in paragraph 2 of this Article shall promptly inform the said Parties of its findings and shall indicate whether it intends to exercise jurisdiction over the said person.

## ARTICLE IX

## General Provisions

1. The Parties shall adopt such measures as may be necessary, including, where appropriate, national legislation, to ensure that offences covered in Article II of this Convention, especially when it is intended to intimidate a population, or to compel a government or an international organisation to do or to abstain from doing any act, are under no circumstances justifiable by considerations of a political, philosophical, ideological, racial, ethnic, religious or other similar nature.
2. Pursuant to Article VI of this Convention, the Parties shall, where possible, establish channels of communication between their competent agencies to facilitate the exchange of information to prevent the commission of offences covered in Article II of this Convention.
3. The Party where the alleged offender is prosecuted shall, upon the request of the other Parties claiming jurisdiction over the same, communicate the status of the case at any stage of the proceedings to those other Parties.

## ARTICLE X

## Status of Refugees

The Parties shall take appropriate measures, in conformity with the relevant provisions of their respective domestic laws and applicable international law, including international standards of human rights, before granting refugee status, where the Parties recognise and grant such status, for the purpose of ensuring that the asylum seeker has not planned, facilitated or participated in the commission of terrorist acts.

## ARTICLE XI

### Rehabilitative Programmes

The Parties shall endeavour to promote the sharing of best practices on rehabilitative programmes including, where appropriate, social reintegration of persons involved in the commission of any of the offences covered in Article II of this Convention with the objective of preventing the perpetration of terrorist acts.

## ARTICLE XII

### Mutual Legal Assistance in Criminal Matters

1. The Parties shall, in conformity with their respective domestic laws, afford the widest measure of assistance in connection with investigations or criminal proceedings brought in respect of the offences covered in Article II of this Convention.
2. The Parties shall, where they are parties to the Treaty on Mutual Legal Assistance in Criminal Matters done in Kuala Lumpur on 29 November 2004, carry out their obligations under paragraph 1 of this Article in conformity with that Treaty.

## ARTICLE XIII

### Extradition

1. The Party in the territory of which the alleged offender is present shall, in cases to which Article VII of this Convention applies, if it does not extradite that person, be obliged, without exception whatsoever and whether or not the offence was committed in its territory, to submit the case without undue delay to its competent authorities for the purpose of prosecution, through proceedings in accordance with the domestic laws of that Party. Those authorities shall take their decision in the same manner as in the case of any other offence of a grave nature under the domestic laws of that Party.
2. The offences covered in Article II of this Convention shall be deemed to be included as extraditable offences in any extradition treaty existing between any of the Parties before the entry into force of this Convention. The Parties

undertake to include such offences as extraditable offences in every extradition treaty to be subsequently concluded between them.

3. When a Party which makes extradition conditional on the existence of a treaty receives a request for extradition from another Party with which it has no extradition treaty, the requested Party may, at its option, and in conformity with its domestic laws, consider this Convention as a legal basis for extradition in respect of the offences covered in Article II of this Convention.

## ARTICLE XIV

### Political Offences Exception

None of the offences covered in Article II of this Convention shall be regarded for the purposes of extradition under Article XIII of this Convention or mutual legal assistance in criminal matters under Article XII of this Convention as a political offence or as an offence connected with a political offence or as an offence inspired by political motives. Accordingly, a request for extradition or for mutual legal assistance in criminal matters based on such an offence may not be refused on the sole ground that it concerns a political offence or an offence connected with a political offence or an offence inspired by political motives.

## ARTICLE XV

### Designation of Central Authorities or Coordinating Structures

Each Party shall designate, as appropriate, a central authority or coordinating structure to enhance cooperation under this Convention.

## ARTICLE XVI

### Implementation, Monitoring and Review

The relevant ASEAN sectoral bodies involved in ASEAN cooperation on countering terrorism shall be responsible for monitoring and reviewing the implementation of this Convention.

## ARTICLE XVII

### Confidentiality

1. Each Party shall preserve the confidentiality and secrecy of documents, records and other information received from any other Party, including the source thereof.

2. No document, record or other information obtained pursuant to this Convention shall be disclosed to or shared with any other Party, State or person except with the prior written consent of the Party which provided such document, record or information.

## ARTICLE XVIII

### Relationship with Other International Instruments

This Convention shall not derogate from obligations subsisting between the Parties pursuant to other international agreements nor, where the Parties agree, shall it prevent the Parties from providing assistance to each other pursuant to other international agreements or the provisions of their respective domestic laws.

## ARTICLE XIX

### Settlement of Disputes

Any difference or dispute between the Parties arising from the interpretation or application of the provisions of this Convention shall be settled amicably through consultation and negotiation between the Parties through diplomatic channels or any other peaceful means for the settlement of disputes as agreed upon between the Parties.

## ARTICLE XX

### Ratification, Approval and Depositary

1. This Convention shall be subject to ratification or approval in accordance with the internal procedures of the Parties.
2. The instruments of ratification or approval shall be deposited with the Secretary-General of ASEAN who shall promptly inform the other Parties of such deposit.

## ARTICLE XXI

### Entry into Force and Amendment

1. This Convention shall enter into force on the 30$^{th}$ (thirtieth) day following the date of the deposit of the 6$^{th}$ (sixth) instrument of ratification or approval with

the Secretary-General of ASEAN in respect of those Parties that have submitted their instruments of ratification or approval.

2. For any Party ratifying or approving this Convention after the deposit of the 6th (sixth) instrument of ratification or approval, but before the day the Convention enters into force, the Convention shall also apply to that Party on the date the Convention enters into force.
3. In respect of a Party ratifying or approving this Convention subsequent to its entry into force pursuant to paragraph 1, it shall enter into force for that Party on the date its instrument of ratification or approval is deposited.
4. This Convention may be modified or amended at any time by mutual written consent of the Parties. Such modification or amendment shall enter into force on such date as shall be mutually agreed upon by Parties and shall form part of this Convention.
5. Any modification or amendment shall not affect the rights and obligations of the Parties arising from or based on the provisions of this Convention before the entry into force of such modification or amendment.

## ARTICLE XXII

## Withdrawal

1. Any Party may withdraw from this Convention at any time after the date of the entry into force of this Convention for that Party.
2. The withdrawal shall be notified by an instrument of withdrawal to the Secretary-General of ASEAN.
3. The withdrawal shall take effect 180 (one hundred and eighty) days after the receipt of the instrument of withdrawal by the Secretary-General of ASEAN.
4. The Secretary-General of ASEAN shall promptly notify all the other Parties of any withdrawal.

## ARTICLE XXIII

## Registration

This Convention shall be registered by the Secretary-General of ASEAN to the United Nations Secretariat pursuant to Article 102 of the Charter of the United Nations.

**DONE** at Cebu, Philippines, this Thirteenth Day of January in the Year Two Thousand and Seven, in a single original copy in the English language.

For Brunei Darussalam:

**HAJI HASSANAL BOLKIAH**
Sultan of Brunei Darussalam

For the Kingdom of Cambodia:

**SAMDECH HUN SEN**
Prime Minister

For the Republic of Indonesia:

**DR. SUSILO BAMBANG YUDHOYONO**
President

For the Lao People's Democratic Republic:

**BOUASONE BOUPHAVANH**
Prime Minister

For Malaysia:

**DATO' SERI ABDULLAH AHMAD BADAWI**
Prime Minister

For the Union of Myanmar:

**GENERAL SOE WIN**
Prime Minister

For the Republic of the Philippines:

**GLORIA MACAPAGAL-ARROYO**
President

For the Republic of Singapore:

**LEE HSIEN LOONG**
Prime Minister

For the Kingdom of Thailand:

**GENERAL SURAYUD CHULANONT (RET.)**
Prime Minister

For the Socialist Republic of Viet Nam:

**NGUYEN TAN DUNG**
Prime Minister

Source: http://www.aseansec.org/19250.htm
Accessed date: 20 February 2009
Publisher: ASEAN Secretariat
Country: Jakarta
Date of Publication: 2007

# CHAPTER 24

# CEBU DECLARATION ON THE BLUEPRINT OF THE ASEAN CHARTER

**WE**, the Heads of State/Government of Brunei Darussalam, the Kingdom of Cambodia, the Republic of Indonesia, the Lao People's Democratic Republic, Malaysia, the Union of Myanmar, the Republic of the Philippines, the Republic of Singapore, the Kingdom of Thailand and the Socialist Republic of Viet Nam, Member Countries of ASEAN, on the occasion of the 12th ASEAN Summit in Cebu;

**INSPIRED** by One Vision, One Identity, the creation of One Community for ASEAN by the year 2020;

**EMBARKING** on a momentous undertaking of establishing an ASEAN Community and facilitating its realisation by adopting an ASEAN Charter as stated in the Kuala Lumpur Declaration on the Establishment of the ASEAN Charter adopted at the 11th ASEAN Summit on 12 December 2005 in Kuala Lumpur;

**CONSCIOUS** that ASEAN has matured into a regional organisation and is expanding its role as an integrated regional economy and a dynamic force in maintaining regional peace and stability as envisaged in the Declaration of ASEAN Concord II (Bali Concord II) and its plans of action, roadmaps, and the ASEAN Vision 2020 which envisions ASEAN as a concert of Southeast Asian nations, outward-looking, living in peace, stability and prosperity, bonded together in partnership in dynamic development and in a community of caring societies;

**MINDFUL** of the immense opportunities and key challenges posed by ASEAN's regional integration process, rapid globalisation and impact of new technologies, as well as the pressing need to strengthen and reinforce further the existing institutions of ASEAN by providing ASEAN with a legal personality and an efficient structure, which will facilitate the attainment of community objectives;

**RECALLING** our decision in the Kuala Lumpur Declaration on the Establishment of the ASEAN Charter at the 11th ASEAN Summit to establish the

Eminent Persons Group (EPG) on the ASEAN Charter, whom we mandated to examine and provide practical recommendations on the directions and nature of the ASEAN Charter relevant to the ASEAN Community as envisaged in the Bali Concord II and beyond, taking into account, but not limited to, the principles, values and objectives as contained in the Kuala Lumpur Declaration on the Establishment of the ASEAN Charter, and to consider their recommendations at our subsequent meetings;

**NOTING** that our Ministers have established a High Level Task Force to carry out the drafting of the ASEAN Charter based on the Kuala Lumpur Declaration on the Establishment of the ASEAN Charter and the recommendations of the EPG;

**RECOGNIzING** the outstanding and comprehensive work of the EPG and its dedication and the efficiency with which it has carried out its mandate, producing the Report of the EPG on the ASEAN Charter;

**ACKNOWLEDGING** the earnest efforts of the EPG in actively consulting various ASEAN sectors and stakeholders, including civil society organisations, businessmen, academics and parliamentarians on their views regarding what should be the key components of an ASEAN Charter and the changes necessary to support the realisation of ASEAN's community building;

## WE DO HEREBY AGREE

**FIRST**, we are committed to establish an ASEAN Charter as a crowning achievement of 40 years of ASEAN to enable ASEAN to meet future challenges and opportunities;

**SECOND**, we reiterate our conviction that an ASEAN Charter will serve as a firm foundation in achieving one ASEAN Community by providing an enhanced institutional framework as well as conferring a legal personality to ASEAN;

**THIRD**, we endorse the Report of the EPG on the ASEAN Charter and agree that the High Level Task Force should commence the drafting of the ASEAN Charter based on our directions given at the 11th and 12th ASEAN Summits, the relevant ASEAN documents, together with the EPG recommendations, to be completed in time for the 13th ASEAN Summit in Singapore in November 2007.

**DONE** at Cebu, Philippines, this Thirteenth Day of January in the Year Two Thousand and Seven, in a single original copy in the English language.

For Brunei Darussalam:

**HAJI HASSANAL BOLKIAH**
Sultan of Brunei Darussalam

For the Kingdom of Cambodia:

**SAMDECH HUN SEN**
Prime Minister

For the Republic of Indonesia:

**DR. SUSILO BAMBANG YUDHOYONO**
President

For the Lao People's Democratic Republic:

**BOUASONE BOUPHAVANH**
Prime Minister

For Malaysia:

**DATO' SERI ABDULLAH AHMAD BADAWI**
Prime Minister

For the Union of Myanmar:

**GENERAL SOE WIN**
Prime Minister

For the Republic of the Philippines:

**GLORIA MACAPAGAL-ARROYO**
President

For the Republic of Singapore:

**LEE HSIEN LOONG**
Prime Minister

For the Kingdom of Thailand:

**GENERAL SURAYUD CHULANONT (RET.)**
Prime Minister

For the Socialist Republic of Viet Nam:

**NGUYEN TAN DUNG**
Prime Minister

Source: http://www.aseansec.org/19257.htm
Accessed date: 2 October 2008
Publisher: ASEAN Secretariat
Country: Jakarta
Date of Publication: 2007

# CHAPTER 25

# CHARTER OF THE ASSOCIATION OF SOUTHEAST ASIAN NATIONS

**Singapore, 20 November 2007**

## PREAMBLE

**WE, THE PEOPLES** of the Member States of the Association of Southeast Asian Nations (ASEAN), as represented by the Heads of State or Government of Brunei Darussalam, the Kingdom of Cambodia, the Republic of Indonesia, the Lao People's Democratic Republic, Malaysia, the Union of Myanmar, the Republic of the Philippines, the Republic of Singapore, the Kingdom of Thailand and the Socialist Republic of Viet Nam:

**NOTING** with satisfaction the significant achievements and expansion of ASEAN since its establishment in Bangkok through the promulgation of The ASEAN Declaration;

**RECALLING** the decisions to establish an ASEAN Charter in the Vientiane Action Programme, the Kuala Lumpur Declaration on the Establishment of the ASEAN Charter and the Cebu Declaration on the Blueprint of the ASEAN Charter;

**MINDFUL** of the existence of mutual interests and interdependence among the peoples and Member States of ASEAN which are bound by geography, common objectives and shared destiny;

**INSPIRED** by and united under One Vision, One Identity and One Caring and Sharing Community;

**UNITED** by a common desire and collective will to live in a region of lasting peace, security and stability, sustained economic growth, shared prosperity and social progress, and to promote our vital interests, ideals and aspirations;

**RESPECTING** the fundamental importance of amity and cooperation, and the principles of sovereignty, equality, territorial integrity, non-interference, consensus and unity in diversity;

**ADHERING** to the principles of democracy, the rule of law and good governance, respect for and protection of human rights and fundamental freedoms;

**RESOLVED** to ensure sustainable development for the benefit of present and future generations and to place the well-being, livelihood and welfare of the peoples at the centre of the ASEAN community building process;

**CONVINCED** of the need to strengthen existing bonds of regional solidarity to realise an ASEAN Community that is politically cohesive, economically integrated and socially responsible in order to effectively respond to current and future challenges and opportunities;

**COMMITTED** to intensifying community building through enhanced regional cooperation and integration, in particular by establishing an ASEAN Community comprising the ASEAN Security Community, the ASEAN Economic Community and the ASEAN Socio-Cultural Community, as provided for in the Bali Declaration of ASEAN Concord II;

**HEREBY DECIDE** to establish, through this Charter, the legal and institutional framework for ASEAN,

**AND TO THIS END**, the Heads of State or Government of the Member States of ASEAN, assembled in Singapore on the historic occasion of the 40th anniversary of the founding of ASEAN, have agreed to this Charter.

## CHAPTER I

## Purposes and Principles

### Article 1

Purposes

The Purposes of ASEAN are:

1. To maintain and enhance peace, security and stability and further strengthen peace-oriented values in the region;
2. To enhance regional resilience by promoting greater political, security, economic and socio-cultural cooperation;

3. To preserve Southeast Asia as a Nuclear Weapon-Free Zone and free of all other weapons of mass destruction;
4. To ensure that the peoples and Member States of ASEAN live in peace with the world at large in a just, democratic and harmonious environment;
5. To create a single market and production base which is stable, prosperous, highly competitive and economically integrated with effective facilitation for trade and investment in which there is free flow of goods, services and investment; facilitated movement of business persons, professionals, talents and labour; and freer flow of capital;
6. To alleviate poverty and narrow the development gap within ASEAN through mutual assistance and cooperation;
7. To strengthen democracy, enhance good governance and the rule of law, and to promote and protect human rights and fundamental freedoms, with due regard to the rights and responsibilities of the Member States of ASEAN;
8. To respond effectively, in accordance with the principle of comprehensive security, to all forms of threats, transnational crimes and transboundary challenges;
9. To promote sustainable development so as to ensure the protection of the region's environment, the sustainability of its natural resources, the preservation of its cultural heritage and the high quality of life of its peoples;
10. To develop human resources through closer cooperation in education and life-long learning, and in science and technology, for the empowerment of the peoples of ASEAN and for the strengthening of the ASEAN Community;
11. To enhance the well-being and livelihood of the peoples of ASEAN by providing them with equitable access to opportunities for human development, social welfare and justice;
12. To strengthen cooperation in building a safe, secure and drug-free environment for the peoples of ASEAN;
13. To promote a people-oriented ASEAN in which all sectors of society are encouraged to participate in, and benefit from, the process of ASEAN integration and community building;
14. To promote an ASEAN identity through the fostering of greater awareness of the diverse culture and heritage of the region; and
15. To maintain the centrality and proactive role of ASEAN as the primary driving force in its relations and cooperation with its external partners in a regional architecture that is open, transparent and inclusive.

## Article 2

Principles

1. In pursuit of the Purposes stated in Article 1, ASEAN and its Member States reaffirm and adhere to the fundamental principles contained in the

declarations, agreements, conventions, concords, treaties and other instruments of ASEAN.

2. ASEAN and its Member States shall act in accordance with the following Principles:

   (a) respect for the independence, sovereignty, equality, territorial integrity and national identity of all ASEAN Member States;
   (b) shared commitment and collective responsibility in enhancing regional peace, security and prosperity;
   (c) renunciation of aggression and of the threat or use of force or other actions in any manner inconsistent with international law;
   (d) reliance on peaceful settlement of disputes;
   (e) non-interference in the internal affairs of ASEAN Member States;
   (f) respect for the right of every Member State to lead its national existence free from external interference, subversion and coercion;
   (g) enhanced consultations on matters seriously affecting the common interest of ASEAN;
   (h) adherence to the rule of law, good governance, the principles of democracy and constitutional government;
   (i) respect for fundamental freedoms, the promotion and protection of human rights, and the promotion of social justice;
   (j) upholding the United Nations Charter and international law, including international humanitarian law, subscribed to by ASEAN Member States;
   (k) abstention from participation in any policy or activity, including the use of its territory, pursued by any ASEAN Member State or non-ASEAN State or any non-State actor, which threatens the sovereignty, territorial integrity or political and economic stability of ASEAN Member States;
   (l) respect for the different cultures, languages and religions of the peoples of ASEAN, while emphasising their common values in the spirit of unity in diversity;
   (m) the centrality of ASEAN in external political, economic, social and cultural relations while remaining actively engaged, outward-looking, inclusive and non-discriminatory; and
   (n) adherence to multilateral trade rules and ASEAN's rules-based regimes for effective implementation of economic commitments and progressive reduction towards elimination of all barriers to regional economic integration, in a market-driven economy.

## CHAPTER II

## Legal personality

### Article 3

Legal Personality of ASEAN

ASEAN, as an inter-governmental organisation, is hereby conferred legal personality.

## CHAPTER III

## Membership

### Article 4

Member States

The Member States of ASEAN are Brunei Darussalam, the Kingdom of Cambodia, the Republic of Indonesia, the Lao People's Democratic Republic, Malaysia, the Union of Myanmar, the Republic of the Philippines, the Republic of Singapore, the Kingdom of Thailand and the Socialist Republic of Viet Nam.

### Article 5

Rights and Obligations

1. Member States shall have equal rights and obligations under this Charter.
2. Member States shall take all necessary measures, including the enactment of appropriate domestic legislation, to effectively implement the provisions of this Charter and to comply with all obligations of membership.
3. In the case of a serious breach of the Charter or non-compliance, the matter shall be referred to Article 20

### Article 6

Admission of New Members

1. The procedure for application and admission to ASEAN shall be prescribed by the ASEAN Coordinating Council.
2. Admission shall be based on the following criteria:

    (a) location in the recognised geographical region of Southeast Asia;
    (b) recognition by all ASEAN Member States;

(c) agreement to be bound and to abide by the Charter; and
(d) ability and willingness to carry out the obligations of Membership.

3. Admission shall be decided by consensus by the ASEAN Summit, upon the recommendation of the ASEAN Coordinating Council.
4. An applicant State shall be admitted to ASEAN upon signing an Instrument of Accession to the Charter.

## CHAPTER IV

## Organs

### Article 7

ASEAN Summit

1. The ASEAN Summit shall comprise the Heads of State or Government of the Member States.
2. The ASEAN Summit shall:

   (a) be the supreme policy-making body of ASEAN;
   (b) deliberate, provide policy guidance and take decisions on key issues pertaining to the realisation of objectives of ASEAN, important matters of interest to Member States and all issues referred to it by ASEAN Coordinating Council, the ASEAN Community Councils and ASEAN Sectoral Ministerial Bodies;
   (c) instruct the relevant Ministers in each of the Councils concerned to hold ad hoc inter-Ministerial meetings, and address important issues concerning ASEAN that cut across the Community Councils. Rules of procedure for such meetings shall be adopted by the ASEAN Coordinating Council;
   (d) address emergency situations affecting ASEAN by taking appropriate actions;
   (e) decide on matters referred to it under Chapters VII and VIII;
   (f) authorise the establishment and the dissolution of Sectoral Ministerial Bodies and other ASEAN institutions; and
   (g) appoint the Secretary-General of ASEAN, with the rank and status of Minister, who will serve with the confidence and at the pleasure of the Heads of State or Government upon the recommendation of the ASEAN Foreign Ministers Meeting.

3. ASEAN Summit Meetings shall be:

   (a) held twice annually, and be hosted by the Member State holding the ASEAN Chairmanship; and

(b) convened, whenever necessary, as special or ad hoc meetings to be chaired by the Member State holding the ASEAN Chairmanship, at venues to be agreed upon by ASEAN Member States.

## Article 8

ASEAN Coordinating Council

1. The ASEAN Coordinating Council shall comprise the ASEAN Foreign Ministers and meet at least twice a year.
2. The ASEAN Coordinating Council shall:

   (a) prepare the meetings of the ASEAN Summit;
   (b) coordinate the implementation of agreements and decisions of the ASEAN Summit;
   (c) coordinate with the ASEAN Community Councils to enhance policy coherence, efficiency and cooperation among them;
   (d) coordinate the reports of the ASEAN Community Councils to the ASEAN Summit;
   (e) consider the annual report of the Secretary-General on the work of ASEAN;
   (f) consider the report of the Secretary-General on the functions and operations of the ASEAN Secretariat other relevant bodies;
   (g) approve the appointment and termination of the Deputy Secretaries-General upon the recommendation of the Secretary-General; and
   (h) undertake other tasks provided for in this Charter or such other functions as may be assigned by the ASEAN Summit.

3. The ASEAN Coordinating Council shall be supported by the relevant senior officials.

## Article 9

ASEAN Community Councils

1. The ASEAN Community Councils shall comprise the ASEAN Political-Security Community Council, ASEAN Economic Community Council, and ASEAN Socio-Cultural Community Council.
2. Each ASEAN Community Council shall have under its purview the relevant ASEAN Sectoral Ministerial Bodies.
3. Each Member State shall designate its national representation for each ASEAN Community Council meeting.

4. In order to realise the objectives of each of the three pillars of the ASEAN Community, each ASEAN community Council shall:

   (a) ensure the implementation of the relevant decisions of the ASEAN Summit;
   (b) coordinate the work of the different sectors under its purview, and on issues which cut across the other Community Councils; and
   (c) submit reports and recommendations to the ASEAN Summit on matters under its purview.

5. Each ASEAN Community Council shall meet at least twice a year and shall be chaired by the appropriate Minister from the Member State holding the ASEAN Chairmanship.
6. Each ASEAN Community Council shall be supported by the relevant senior officials.

## Article 10

ASEAN Sectoral Ministerial Bodies

1. ASEAN Sectoral Ministerial Bodies shall:

   (a) function in accordance with their respective established mandates;
   (b) implement the agreements and decisions of the ASEAN Summit under their respective purview;
   (c) strengthen cooperation in their respective fields in support of ASEAN integration and community building; and
   (d) submit reports and recommendations to their respective Community Councils.

2. Each ASEAN Sectoral Ministerial Body may have under its purview the relevant senior officials and subsidiary bodies to undertake its functions as contained in Annex 1. The Annex may be updated by the Secretary-General of ASEAN upon the recommendation of the Committee of Permanent Representatives without recourse to the provision on Amendments under this Charter.

## Article 11

Secretary-General of ASEAN and ASEAN Secretariat

1. The Secretary-General of ASEAN shall be appointed by the ASEAN Summit for a non-renewable term of office of five years, selected from among nationals of the ASEAN Member States based on alphabetical rotation, with due

consideration to integrity, capability and professional experience, and gender equality.

2. The Secretary-General shall:

   (a) carry out the duties and responsibilities of this high office in accordance with the provisions of this Charter and relevant ASEAN instruments, protocols and established practices;
   (b) facilitate and monitor progress in the implementation of ASEAN agreements and decisions, and submit an annual report on the work of ASEAN to the ASEAN Summit;
   (c) participate in meetings of the ASEAN Summit, the ASEAN Community Councils, the ASEAN coordinating Council, and ASEAN Sectoral Ministerial Bodies and other relevant ASEAN meetings;
   (d) present the views of ASEAN and participate in meetings with external parties in accordance with approved policy guidelines and mandate given to the Secretary-General; and
   (e) recommend the appointment and termination of the Deputy Secretaries-General to the ASEAN Coordinating Council for approval.

3. The Secretary-General shall also be the Chief Administrative Officer of ASEAN.
4. The Secretary-General shall be assisted by four Deputy Secretaries-General with the rank and status Deputy Ministers. The Deputy Secretaries-General shall be accountable to the Secretary-General in carrying out their functions.
5. The four Deputy Secretaries-General shall be of different nationalities from the Secretary-General and shall come from four different ASEAN Member States.
6. The four Deputy Secretaries-General shall comprise:

   (a) two Deputy Secretaries-General who will serve a non-renewable term of three years, selected from among nationals of the ASEAN Member States based on alphabetical rotation, with due consideration to integrity, qualifications, competence, experience and gender equality; and
   (b) two Deputy Secretaries-General who will serve a term of three years, which may be renewed for another three years. These two Deputy Secretaries-General shall be openly recruited based on merit.

7. The ASEAN Secretariat shall comprise the Secretary-General and such staff as may be required.
8. The Secretary-General and the staff shall:

   (a) uphold the highest standards of integrity, efficiency, and competence in the performance of their duties;

(b) not seek or receive instructions from any government or external party outside of ASEAN; and
(c) refrain from any action which might reflect on their position as ASEAN Secretariat officials responsible only to ASEAN.

9. Each ASEAN Member State undertakes to respect the exclusively ASEAN character of the responsibilities of the Secretary-General and the staff, and not to seek to influence them in the discharge of their responsibilities.

## Article 12

Committee of Permanent Representatives to ASEAN

1. Each ASEAN Member State shall appoint a Permanent Representative to ASEAN with the rank of Ambassador based in Jakarta.
2. The Permanent Representatives collectively constitute a Committee of Permanent Representatives, which shall:

   (a) support the work of the ASEAN Community Councils and ASEAN Sectoral Ministerial Bodies;
   (b) coordinate with ASEAN National Secretariats and other ASEAN Sectoral Ministerial Bodies;
   (c) liaise with the Secretary-General of ASEAN and the ASEAN Secretariat on all subjects relevant to its work;
   (d) facilitate ASEAN cooperation with external partners; and
   (e) perform such other functions as may be determined by the ASEAN Coordinating Council.

## Article 13

ASEAN National Secretariats

Each ASEAN Member State shall establish an ASEAN National Secretariat which shall:

(a) serve as the national focal point;
(b) be the repository of information on all ASEAN matters at the national level;
(c) coordinate the implementation of ASEAN decisions at the national level;
(d) coordinate and support the national preparations of ASEAN meetings;
(e) promote ASEAN identity and awareness at the national level; and
(f) contribute to ASEAN community building.

## Article 14

ASEAN Human Rights Body

1. In conformity with the purposes and principles of the ASEAN Charter relating to the promotion and protection of human rights and fundamental freedoms, ASEAN shall establish an ASEAN human rights body.
2. This ASEAN human rights body shall operate in accordance with the terms of reference to be determined by the ASEAN Foreign Ministers Meeting.

## Article 15

ASEAN Foundation

1. The ASEAN Foundation shall support the Secretary-General of ASEAN and collaborate with the relevant ASEAN bodies to support ASEAN community building by promoting greater awareness of the ASEAN identity, people-to-people interaction, and close collaboration among the business sector, civil society, academia and other stakeholders in ASEAN.
2. The ASEAN Foundation shall be accountable to the Secretary-General of ASEAN, who shall submit its report to the ASEAN Summit through the ASEAN Coordinating Council.

# CHAPTER V

# Entities Associated with ASEAN

## Article 16

Entities Associated with ASEAN

1. ASEAN may engage with entities which support the ASEAN Charter, in particular its purposes and principles. These associated entities are listed in Annex 2.
2. Rules of procedure and criteria for engagement shall be prescribed by the Committee of Permanent Representatives upon the recommendation of the Secretary-General of ASEAN.
3. Annex 2 may be updated by the Secretary-General of ASEAN upon the recommendation of the Committee of Permanent Representatives without recourse to the provision on Amendments under this Charter.

## CHAPTER VI

## Immunities and Privileges

### Article 17

Immunities and Privileges of ASEAN

1. ASEAN shall enjoy in the territories of the Member States such immunities and privileges as are necessary for the fulfilment of its purposes.
2. The immunities and privileges shall be laid down in separate agreements between ASEAN and the host Member State.

### Article 18

Immunities and Privileges of the Secretary-General of ASEAN and Staff of the ASEAN Secretariat

1. The Secretary-General of ASEAN and staff of the ASEAN Secretariat participating in official ASEAN activities or representing ASEAN in the Member States shall enjoy such immunities and privileges as are necessary for the independent exercise of their functions.
2. The immunities and privileges under this Article shall be laid down in a separate ASEAN agreement.

### Article 19

Immunities and Privileges of the Permanent Representatives and Officials on ASEAN Duties

1. The Permanent Representatives of the Member States to ASEAN and officials of the Member States participating in official ASEAN activities or representing ASEAN in the Member States shall enjoy such immunities and privileges as are necessary for the exercise of their functions.
2. The immunities and privileges of the Permanent Representatives and officials on ASEAN duties shall be governed by the 1961 Vienna Convention on Diplomatic Relations or in accordance with the national law of the ASEAN Member State concerned.

## CHAPTER VII

## Decision-Making

### Article 20

Consultation and Consensus

1. As a basic principle, decision-making in ASEAN shall be based on consultation and consensus.
2. Where consensus cannot be achieved, the ASEAN Summit may decide how a specific decision can be made.
3. Nothing in paragraphs 1 and 2 of this Article shall affect the modes of decision-making as contained in the relevant ASEAN legal instruments.
4. In the case of a serious breach of the Charter or non-compliance, the matter shall be referred to the ASEAN Summit for decision.

### Article 21

Implementation and Procedure

1. Each ASEAN Community Council shall prescribe its own rules of procedure.
2. In the implementation of economic commitments, a formula for flexible participation, including the ASEAN Minus X formula, may be applied where there is a consensus to do so.

## CHAPTER VIII

## Settlement of Disputes

### Article 22

General Principles

1. Member States shall endeavour to resolve peacefully all disputes in a timely manner through dialogue, consultation and negotiation.
2. ASEAN shall maintain and establish dispute settlement mechanisms in all fields of ASEAN cooperation.

## Article 23

Good Offices, Conciliation and Mediation

1. Member States which are parties to a dispute may at any time agree to resort to good offices, conciliation or mediation in order to resolve the dispute within an agreed time limit.
2. Parties to the dispute may request the Chairman of ASEAN or the Secretary-General of ASEAN, acting in an ex-officio capacity, to provide good offices, conciliation or mediation.

## Article 24

Dispute Settlement Mechanisms in Specific Instruments

1. Disputes relating to specific ASEAN instruments shall be settled through the mechanisms and procedures provided for in such instruments.
2. Disputes which do not concern the interpretation or application of any ASEAN instrument shall be resolved peacefully in accordance with the Treaty of Amity and Cooperation in Southeast Asia and its rules of procedure.
3. Where not otherwise specifically provided, disputes which concern the interpretation or application of ASEAN economic agreements shall be settled in accordance with the ASEAN Protocol on Enhanced Dispute Settlement Mechanism.

## Article 25

Establishment of Dispute Settlement Mechanisms

Where not otherwise specifically provided, appropriate dispute settlement mechanisms, including arbitration, shall be established for disputes which concern the interpretation or application of this Charter and other ASEAN instruments.

## Article 26

Unresolved Disputes

When a dispute remains unresolved, after the application of the preceding provisions of this Chapter, this dispute shall be referred to the ASEAN Summit, for its decision.

## Article 27

Compliance

1. The Secretary-General of ASEAN, assisted by the ASEAN Secretariat or any other designated ASEAN body, shall monitor the compliance with the findings, recommendations or decisions resulting from an ASEAN dispute settlement mechanism, and submit a report to the ASEAN Summit.
2. Any Member State affected by non-compliance with the findings, recommendations or decisions resulting from an ASEAN dispute settlement mechanism, may refer the matter to the ASEAN Summit for a decision.

## Article 28

United Nations Charter Provisions and Other Relevant International Procedures

Unless otherwise provided for in this Charter, Member States have the right of recourse to the modes of peaceful settlement contained in Article 33(1) of the Charter of the United Nations or any other international legal instruments to which the disputing Member States are parties.

# CHAPTER IX

# Budget and Finance

## Article 29

General Principle

1. ASEAN shall establish financial rules and procedures in accordance with international standards.
2. ASEAN shall observe sound financial management policies and practices and budgetary discipline.
3. Financial accounts shall be subject to internal and external audits.

## Article 30

Operational Budget and Finances of the ASEAN Secretariat

1. The ASEAN Secretariat shall be provided with the necessary financial resources to perform its functions effectively.
2. The operational budget of the ASEAN Secretariat shall be met by ASEAN Member States through equal annual contributions which shall be remitted in a timely manner.

3. The Secretary-General shall prepare the annual operational budget of the ASEAN Secretariat for approval by the ASEAN Coordinating Council upon the recommendation of the Committee of Permanent Representatives.
4. The ASEAN Secretariat shall operate in accordance with the financial rules and procedures determined by the ASEAN Coordinating Council upon the recommendation of the Committee of Permanent Representatives.

## CHAPTER X

## Administration and Procedure

### Article 31

Chairman of ASEAN

1. The Chairmanship of ASEAN shall rotate annually, based on the alphabetical order of the English names of Member States.
2. ASEAN shall have, in a calendar year, a single Chairmanship by which the Member State assuming the Chairmanship shall chair:

   (a) the ASEAN Summit and related summits;
   (b) the ASEAN Coordinating Council;
   (c) the three ASEAN Community Councils;
   (d) where appropriate, the relevant ASEAN Sectoral Ministerial Bodies and senior officials; and
   (e) the Committee of Permanent Representatives.

### Article 32

Role of the Chairman of ASEAN

The Member State holding the Chairmanship of ASEAN shall:

(a) actively promote and enhance the interests and well-being of ASEAN, including efforts to build an ASEAN Community through policy initiatives, coordination, consensus and cooperation;
(b) ensure the centrality of ASEAN;
(c) ensure an effective and timely response to urgent issues or crisis situations affecting ASEAN, including providing its good offices and such other arrangements to immediately address these concerns;
(d) represent ASEAN in strengthening and promoting closer relations with external partners; and
(e) carry out such other tasks and functions as may be mandated.

## Article 33

Diplomatic Protocol and Practices

ASEAN and its Member States shall adhere to existing diplomatic protocol and practices in the conduct of all activities relating to ASEAN. Any changes shall be approved by the ASEAN Coordinating Council upon the recommendation of the Committee of Permanent Representatives.

## Article 34

Working Language of ASEAN

The working language of ASEAN shall be English.

# CHAPTER XI

# Identity and Symbols

## Article 35

ASEAN Identity

ASEAN shall promote its common ASEAN identity and a sense of belonging among its peoples in order to achieve its shared density, goals and values.

## Article 36

ASEAN Motto

The ASEAN motto be: "*One Vision, One Identity, One Community*"

## Article 37

ASEAN Flag

The ASEAN flag shall be as shown in Annex 3.

## Article 38

ASEAN Emblem

The ASEAN emblem shall be as shown in Annex 4.

## Article 39

ASEAN Day

The eighth of August shall be observed as ASEAN Day.

## Article 40

ASEAN Anthem

ASEAN shall have an anthem.

# CHAPTER XII

## External Relations

## Article 41

Conduct of External Relations

1. ASEAN shall develop friendly relations and mutually beneficial dialogue, cooperation and partnerships with countries and sub-regional, regional and international organisations and institutions.
2. The external relations of ASEAN shall adhere to the purposes and principles set forth in this Charter.
3. ASEAN shall be the primary driving force in regional arrangements that it initiates and maintain its centrality in regional cooperation and community building.
4. In the conduct of external relations of ASEAN, Member States shall, on the basis of unity and solidarity, coordinate and endeavour to develop common positions and pursue joint actions.
5. The strategic policy directions of ASEAN's external relations shall be set by the ASEAN Summit upon the recommendation of the ASEAN Foreign Ministers Meeting.
6. The ASEAN Foreign Ministers Meeting shall ensure consistency and coherence in the conduct of ASEAN's external relations.
7. ASEAN may conclude agreements with countries or sub-regional, regional and international organisations and institutions. The procedures for concluding such agreements shall be prescribed by the ASEAN Coordinating Council in consultation with the ASEAN Community Councils.

## Article 42

Dialogue Coordinator

1. Member States, acting as Country Coordinators, shall take turns to take overall responsibility in coordinating and promoting the interests of ASEAN in its relations with the relevant Dialogue Partners, regional and international organisations and institutions.
2. In relations with the external partners, the Country Coordinators shall, inter alia:

   (a) represent ASEAN and enhance relations on the basis of mutual respect and equality, in conformity with ASEAN's principles;
   (b) co-chair relevant meetings between ASEAN and external partners; and
   (c) be supported by the relevant ASEAN Committees in Third Countries and International Organisations.

## Article 43

ASEAN Committees in Third Countries and International Organisations

1. ASEAN Committees in Third Countries may be established in non-ASEAN countries comprising heads of diplomatic missions of ASEAN Member States. Similar Committees may be established relating to international organisations. Such Committees shall promote ASEAN's interests and identity in the host countries and international organisations.
2. The ASEAN Foreign Ministers Meeting shall determine the rules of procedure of such Committees.

## Article 44

Status of External Parties

1. In conducting ASEAN's external relations, the ASEAN Foreign Ministers Meeting may confer on an external party the formal status of Dialogue Partner, Sectoral Dialogue Partner, Development Partner, Special Observer, Guest, or other status that may be established henceforth.
2. External parties may be invited to ASEAN meetings or cooperative activities without being conferred any formal status, in accordance with the rules of procedure.

## Article 45

Relations with the United Nations System and Other International Organisations and Institutions

1. ASEAN may seek an appropriate status with the United Nations system as well as with other sub-regional, regional, international organisations and institutions.
2. The ASEAN Coordinating Council shall decide on the participation of ASEAN in other sub-regional, regional, international organisations and institutions.

## Article 46

Accreditation of Non-ASEAN Member States to ASEAN

Non-ASEAN Member States and relevant inter-governmental organisations may appoint and accredit Ambassadors to ASEAN. The ASEAN Foreign Ministers Meeting shall decide on such accreditation.

# CHAPTER XIII

## General and Final Provisions

## Article 47

Signature, Ratification, Depository and Entry into Force

1. This Charter shall be signed by all ASEAN Member States.
2. This Charter shall be subject to ratification by all ASEAN Member States in accordance with their respective internal procedures.
3. Instruments of ratification shall be deposited with the Secretary-General of ASEAN who shall promptly notify all Member States of each deposit.
4. This Charter shall enter into force on the thirtieth day following the date of deposit of the tenth instrument of ratification with the Secretary-General of ASEAN.

## Article 48

Amendments

1. Any Member State may propose amendments to the Charter.
2. Proposed amendments to the Charter shall be submitted by the ASEAN Coordinating Council by consensus to the ASEAN Summit for its decision.
3. Amendments to the Charter agreed to by consensus by the ASEAN Summit shall be ratified by all Member States in accordance with Article 47.

4. An amendment shall enter into force on the thirtieth day following the date of deposit of the last instrument of ratification with the Secretary-General of ASEAN.

## Article 49

Terms of Reference and Rules of Procedure

Unless otherwise provided for in this Charter, the ASEAN Coordinating Council shall determine the terms of reference and rules of procedure and shall ensure their consistency.

## Article 50

Review

This Charter may be reviewed five years after its entry into force or as otherwise determined by the ASEAN Summit.

## Article 51

Interpretation of the Charter

1. Upon the request of any Member State, the interpretation of the Charter shall be undertaken by the ASEAN Secretariat in accordance with the rules of procedure determined by the ASEAN Coordinating council.
2. Any dispute arising from the interpretation of the Charter shall be settled in accordance with the relevant provisions in Chapter VIII.
3. Headings and titles used throughout the Charter shall only be for the purpose of reference.

## Article 52

Legal Continuity

1. All treaties, conventions, agreements, concords, declarations, protocols and other ASEAN instruments have been in effect before the entry into force of this Charter shall continue to be valid.
2. In the case of inconsistency between the rights and obligations of ASEAN Member States under such instruments and this Charter, the Charter shall prevail.

### Article 53

Original Text

The signed original text of this Charter in English shall be deposited with the Secretary-General of ASEAN, who shall provide a certified copy to each Member State.

### Article 54

Registration of the ASEAN Charter

This Charter shall be registered by the Secretary-General of ASEAN with the Secretariat of the United Nations, pursuant to Article 102, paragraph 1 of the Charter of the United Nations.

### Article 55

ASEAN Assets

The assets and funds of the Organisation shall be vested in the name of ASEAN.

**DONE** in Singapore on the Twentieth Day of November in the Year Two Thousand and Seven, in a single original in the English language.

For Brunei Darussalam:

**HAJI HASSANAL BOLKIAH**
Sultan of Brunei Darussalam

For the Kingdom of Cambodia:

**SAMDECH HUN SEN**
Prime Minister

For the Republic of Indonesia:

**DR. SUSILO BAMBANG YUDHOYONO**
President

For the Lao People's Democratic Republic:

**BOUASONE BOUPHAVANH**
Prime Minister

For Malaysia:

**DATO' SERI ABDULLAH AHMAD BADAWI**
Prime Minister

For the Union of Myanmar:

**GENERAL THEIN SEIN**
Prime Minister

For the Republic of the Philippines:

**GLORIA MACAPAGAL-ARROYO**
President

For the Republic of Singapore:

**LEE HSIEN LOONG**
Prime Minister

For the Kingdom of Thailand:

**GENERAL SURAYUD CHULANONT (RET.)**
Prime Minister

For the Socialist Republic of Viet Nam:

**NGUYEN TAN DUNG**
Prime Minister

# ANNEX 1: ASEAN SECTORAL MINISTERIAL BODIES

## I. ASEAN POLITICAL-SECURITY COMMUNITY

1. **ASEAN Foreign Ministers Meeting (AMM)**
   ASEAN Senior Officials Meeting (ASEAN SOM)
   ASEAN Standing Committee (ASC)
   Senior Officials Meeting on Development Planning (SOMDP)

2. **Commission on the Southeast Asia Nuclear Weapon-Free Zone (SEANWFZ Commission)**
   Executive Committee of the SEANWFZ Commission

3. **ASEAN Defence Ministers Meeting (ADMM)**
   ASEAN Defence Senior Officials Meeting (ADSOM)

4. **ASEAN Law Ministers Meeting (ALAWMM)**
   ASEAN Senior Law Officials Meeting (ASLOM)

5. **ASEAN Ministerial Meeting on Transnational Crime (AMMTC)**
   Senior Officials Meeting on Transnational Crime (SOMTC)
   ASEAN Senior Officials on Drugs Matters (ASOD)
   Directors-General of Immigration Departments and Heads of Consular Affairs Divisions of Ministries of Foreign Affairs Meeting (DGICM)

6. **ASEAN Regional Forum (ARF)**
   ASEAN Regional Forum Senior Officials Meeting (ARF SOM)

## II. ASEAN ECONOMIC COMMUNITY

1. **ASEAN Economic Ministers Meeting (AEM)**
   High Level Task Force on ASEAN Economic Integration (HLTF-EI)
   Senior Economic Officials Meeting (SEOM)

2. **ASEAN Free Trade Area (AFTA) Council**

3. **ASEAN Investment Area (AIA) Council**

4. **ASEAN Finance Ministers Meeting (AFMM)**
   ASEAN Finance and Central Bank Deputies Meeting (AFDM)
   ASEAN Directors-General of Customs Meeting (Customs DG)

5. **ASEAN Ministers Meeting on Agriculture and Forestry (AMAF)**
   Senior Officials Meeting of the ASEAN Ministers on Agriculture and Forestry (SOM-AMAF)
   ASEAN Senior Officials on Forestry (ASOF)

6. **ASEAN Ministers on Energy Meeting (AMEM)**
   Senior Officials Meeting on Energy (SOME)

7. **ASEAN Ministerial Meeting on Minerals (AMMin)**
   ASEAN Senior Officials Meeting on Minerals (ASOMM)

8. **ASEAN Ministerial Meeting on Science and Technology (AMMST)**
   Committee on Science and Technology (COST)

9. **ASEAN Telecommunications and Information Technology Ministers Meeting (TELMIN)**
   Telecommunications and Information Technology Senior Officials Meeting (TELSOM)
   ASEAN Telecommunication Regulators' Council (ATRC)

10. **ASEAN Transport Ministers Meeting (ATM)**
    Senior Transport Officials Meeting (STOM)

11. **Meeting of the ASEAN Tourism Ministers (M-ATM)**
    Meeting of the ASEAN National Tourism Organisations (ASEAN NTOs)

12. **ASEAN Mekong Basin Development Cooperation (AMBDC)**
    ASEAN Mekong Basin Development Cooperation Steering Committee (AMBDC SC)
    High Level Finance Committee (HLFC)

13. ASEAN Centre for Energy

14. ASEAN-Japan Centre in Tokyo

## III. ASEAN SOCIO-CULTURAL COMMUNITY

1. **ASEAN Ministers Responsible for Information (AMRI)**
   Senior Officials Meeting Responsible for Information (SOMRI)

2. **ASEAN Ministers Responsible for Culture and Arts (AMCA)**
   Senior Officials Meeting for Culture and Arts (SOMCA)
3. **ASEAN Education Ministers Meeting (ASED)**
   Senior Officials Meeting on Education (SOM-ED)
4. **ASEAN Ministerial Meeting on Disaster Management (AMMDM)**
   ASEAN Committee on Disaster Management (ACDM)
5. **ASEAN Ministerial Meeting on the Environment (AMME)**
   ASEAN Senior Officials on the Environment (ASOEN)
6. **Conference of the Parties to the ASEAN Agreement on Transboundary Haze Pollution (COP)**
   Committee (COM) under the COP to the ASEAN Agreement on Transboundary Haze Pollution
7. **ASEAN Health Ministers Meeting (AHMM)**
   Senior Officials Meeting on Health Development (SOMHD)
8. **ASEAN Labour Ministers Meeting (ALMM)**
   Senior Labour Officials Meeting (SLOM)
   ASEAN Committee on the Implementation of the ASEAN Declaration on the Protection and Promotion of the Rights of Migrant Workers
9. **ASEAN Ministers on Rural Development and Poverty Eradication (AMRDPE)**
   Senior Officials Meeting on Rural Development and Poverty Eradication (SOMRDPE)
10. **ASEAN Ministerial Meeting on Social Welfare and Development (AMMSWD)**
    Senior Officials Meeting on Social Welfare and Development (SOMSWD)
11. **ASEAN Ministerial Meeting on Youth (AMMY)**
    Senior Officials Meeting on Youth (SOMY)
12. **ASEAN Conference on Civil Service Matters (ACCSM)**
13. ASEAN Centre for Biodiversity (ACB)
14. ASEAN Coordinating Centre for Humanitarian Assistance on disaster management (AHA Centre)
15. ASEAN Earthquakes Information Centre

**16.** ASEAN Specialised Meteorological Centre (ASMC)

**17.** ASEAN University Network (AUN)

**20 November 2007**

Source: http://www.41amm.sg/amm/index.php/web/info_for_delegates/agreements/annex_1_asean_sectoral_ministerial_bodies
Accessed date: 2 October 2008
Publisher: ASEAN Secretariat
Country: Jakarta
Date of Publication: 2007

# ANNEX 2: ENTITIES ASSOCIATED WITH ASEAN

## I. PARLIAMENTARIANS

ASEAN Inter-Parliamentary Assembly (AIPA)

## II. BUSINESS ORGANIZATIONS

ASEAN Airlines Meeting
ASEAN Alliance of Health Supplement Association (AAHSA)
ASEAN Automotive Federation (AAF)
ASEAN Bankers Association (ABA)
**ASEAN Business Advisory Council (ASEAN-BAC)**
ASEAN Business Forum (ABF)
**ASEAN Chamber of Commerce and Industry (ASEAN-CCI)**
ASEAN Chemical Industries Council
ASEAN Federation of Textiles Industries (AFTEX)
ASEAN Furniture Industries Council (AFIC)
ASEAN Insurance Council (AIC)
ASEAN Intellectual Property Association (ASEAN IPA)
ASEAN International Airports Association (AAA)
ASEAN Iron & Steel Industry Federation
ASEAN Pharmaceutical Club
ASEAN Tourism Association (ASEANTA)
Federation of ASEAN Economic Associations (FAEA)
Federation of ASEAN Shippers' Council
**US-ASEAN Business Council**

## III. THINK TANKS AND ACADEMIC INSTITUTIONS

ASEAN-ISIS Network

## IV. ACCREDITED CIVIL SOCIETY ORGANIZATIONS

ASEAN Academics of Science, Engineering and Technology (ASEAN CASE)
ASEAN Academy of Engineering and Technology (AAET)

ASEAN Association for Clinical Laboratory Sciences (AACLS)
ASEAN Association for Planning and Housing (AAPH)
....
ASEAN Confederation of Employers (ACE)
ASEAN Confederation of Women's Organisation (ACWO)
ASEAN Constructors Federation (ACF)
....
ASEAN Council for Japan Alumni (ASCOJA)
ASEAN Council of Teachers (ACT)
....
ASEAN Federation of Accountants (AFA)
ASEAN Federation of Electrical Engineering Contractors (AFEEC)
ASEAN Federation of Engineering Organization (AFEO)
....
ASEAN Federation of Mining Association (AFMA)
ASEAN Fisheries Federation (AFF)
....
ASEAN Forest Products Industry Club (AFPIC)
ASEAN Forestry Students Association (AFSA)
ASEAN Handicraft Promotion and Development Association (AHPADA)
....
ASEAN Law Association (ALA)
ASEAN Law Students Association (ALSA)
ASEAN Music Industry Association (AMIA)
....
ASEAN NGO Coalition on Ageing
ASEAN Non-Governmental Organizations for the Prevention of Drugs and Substance Abuse
....
Asian Partnership for Development of Human Resources in Rural Asia (AsiaDHRRA)
Committee for ASEAN Youth Cooperation (CAYC)
Federation of ASEAN Consulting Engineers (FACE)
Federation of ASEAN Public Relations Organizations (FAPRO)
Federation of ASEAN Shipowners' Associations (FASA)
Medical Association of Southeast Asian Nations Committee (MASEAN)
....
Southeast Asia Regional Institute for Community and Education (SEARICE)
Southeast Asian Studies Regional Exchange Program (SEASREP) Foundation
....

# V. OTHER STAKEHOLDERS IN ASEAN

ASEANAPOL
Federation of Institutes of Food Science and Technology in ASEAN (FIFSTA)
Southeast Asian Fisheries Development Centre (SEAFDEC)
Working Group for an ASEAN Human Rights Mechanism

**20 November 2007**

Source: http://www.41amm.sg/amm/index.php/web/info_for_delegates/agreements/annex_2_entities_associated_with_asean
Accessed date: 2 October 2008
Publisher: ASEAN Secretariat
Country: Jakarta
Date of Publication: 2008

# ANNEX 3: ASEAN FLAG

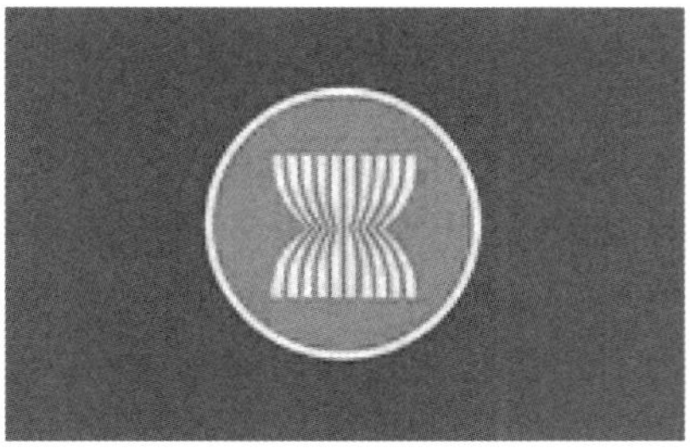

The ASEAN Flag represents a stable, peaceful, united and dynamic ASEAN. The colours of the Flag — blue, red, white and yellow — represent the main colours of the flags of all the ASEAN Member States.

The blue represents peace and stability. Red depicts courage and dynamism. White shows purity and yellow symbolises prosperity.

The stalks of padi represent the dream of ASEAN's Founding Fathers for an ASEAN comprising all the countries in Southeast Asia bound together in friendship and solidarity. The circle represents the unity of ASEAN.

The specification of Pantone Colour adopted for the colours of the ASEAN Flag are:

Blue: Pantone 19-4053 TC
Red: Pantone 18-1655 TC
White: Pantone 11-4202 TC
Yellow: Pantone 13-0758 TC

For the printed version, the specifications of colours (except white) will follow those for the colours of the ASEAN Emblem, i.e.:

Blue: Pantone 286 or Process Colour 100C 60M 0Y 6K
Red: Pantone Red 032 or Process Colour 0C 91M 87Y 0K
Yellow: Pantone Process Yellow or Process Colour 0C 0M 100Y 0K

The ratio of the width to the length of the Flag is two to three, and the size specifications for the following Flags are:

Table Flag: 10 cm × 15 cm
Room Flag: 100 cm × 150 cm
Car Flag: 10 cm × 30 cm
Field Flag: 200 cm × 300 cm

**20 November 2007**

Source: http://www.41amm.sg/amm/index.php/web/info_for_delegates/agreements/annex_3_asean_flag
Accessed date: 2 October 2008
Publisher: ASEAN Secretariat
Country: Jakarta
Date of Publication: 2008

# ANNEX 4: ASEAN EMBLEM

The ASEAN Emblem represents a stable, peaceful, united and dynamic ASEAN. The colours of the Emblem — blue, red, white and yellow — represent the main colours of the crests of all the ASEAN Member States.

The blue represents peace and stability. Red depicts courage and dynamism. White shows purity and yellow symbolises prosperity.

The stalks of padi represent the dream of ASEAN's Founding Fathers for an ASEAN comprising all the countries in Southeast Asia bound together in friendship and solidarity. The circle represents the unity of ASEAN.

The specification of Pantone Colour adopted for the colours of the ASEAN Emblem are:

Blue: Pantone 286
Red: Pantone Red 032
Yellow: Pantone Process Yellow

For four-colour printing process, the specifications of colours will be:

Blue: 100C 60 M 0Y 6K (100C 60M 0Y 10K)
Red: 0C 91M 87Y 0K (0C 90M 90Y 0K)
Yellow: 0C 0M 100Y 0K

Specifications in brackets are to be used when an arbitrary measurement of process colours is not possible.

In Pantone Process Colour Simulator, the specifications equal to:

Blue: Pantone 204-1
Red: Pantone 60-1
Yellow: Pantone 1-3

The font used for the word "ASEAN" in the Emblem is lower-case Helvetica in bold.

**20 November 2007**

Source: http://www.41amm.sg/amm/index.php/web/info_for_delegates/agreements/annex_4_asean_emblem
Accessed date: 2 October 2008
Publisher: ASEAN Secretariat
Country: Jakarta
Date of Publication: 2008

# CHAPTER 26

# SINGAPORE DECLARATION ON THE ASEAN CHARTER

**WE**, the Heads of State/Government of Brunei Darussalam, the Kingdom of Cambodia, the Republic of Indonesia, the Lao People's Democratic Republic, Malaysia, the Union of Myanmar, the Republic of the Philippines, the Republic of Singapore, the Kingdom of Thailand and the Socialist Republic of Viet Nam, Member Countries of ASEAN, on the occasion of the 40th Anniversary of ASEAN and the 13th ASEAN Summit in Singapore;

**REAFFIRMING** our conviction, as expressed in the Kuala Lumpur Declaration on the Establishment of the ASEAN Charter on 12 December 2005 and the Cebu Declaration on the Blueprint of the ASEAN Charter on 13 January 2007, that the Charter shall serve as a legal and institutional framework, as well as an inspiration for ASEAN in the years ahead;

**REITERATING** our full resolve and commitment to narrow the development gap and to advance ASEAN integration through the creation of an ASEAN Community in furtherance of peace, progress and prosperity of its peoples; and

**HAVING SIGNED** the ASEAN Charter;

## DO HEREBY DECLARE

To faithfully respect the rights and fulfil the obligations outlined in the provisions of the ASEAN Charter;

To complete ratification by all Member Countries as soon as possible in order to bring the ASEAN Charter into force; and

To undertake all appropriate measures in each Member Country to implement the ASEAN Charter.

**ADOPTED** in Singapore, this Twentieth Day of November in the Year Two Thousand and Seven.

Source: http://www.aseansec.org/21233.htm
Accessed date: 2 October 2008
Publisher: ASEAN Secretariat
Country: Jakarta
Date of Publication: 2007

# CHAPTER 27

# CHAIRMAN'S STATEMENT OF THE SECOND EAST ASIA SUMMIT

**15 January 2007**

1. The Second East Asia Summit chaired by H.E. Gloria Macapagal Arroyo, President of the Republic of the Philippines was held on 15 January 2007 in Cebu City, the Republic of the Philippines.
2. The Heads of State/Government of ASEAN, Australia, the People's Republic of China, the Republic of India, Japan, the Republic of Korea and New Zealand had a productive exchange of views on regional and international issues, as well as on issues of strategic importance to the East Asian region.

## POVERTY ERADICATION

3. We reaffirmed our commitment to the eradication of poverty in East Asia. We resolved that improving the standard of living for our people should remain a central focus of our regional cooperation efforts. We also confirmed our commitment to achieve the target and objectives of the Millennium Development Goals (MDG's).

## ENERGY

4. As a priority area for the second East Asia Summit, we convened a special session on energy to achieve our shared goal of ensuring affordable energy sources for development in our region. We expressed appreciation for the background paper prepared by the ASEAN Secretariat, and agreed that discussions should take into consideration:

   a. energy security
   b. renewable and alternative energy sources energy
   c. efficiency and conservation, and
   d. climate change

5. To this end, we signed the Cebu Declaration on East Asian Energy Security, which aims to achieve the following goals:

   a. Improve the efficiency and environmental performance of fossil fuel use;
   b. Reduce dependence on conventional fuels through intensified energy efficiency and conservation programs, hydropower, expansion of renewable energy systems and bio-fuel production/utilization, and for interested parties, civilian nuclear power;
   c. Encourage the development of open and competitive regional and international markets geared towards providing affordable energy at all economic levels;
   d. Mitigate greenhouse gas emission through effective policies and measures, thus contributing to global climate change abatement; and
   e. Pursue and encourage investment in energy resource and infrastructure development through greater private sector involvement

6. We welcomed the various project proposals made on cooperation in energy security, including Japan's four-pillar initiative entitled "Fueling Asia — Japan's Cooperation Initiative for Clean Energy and Sustainable Growth." We agreed to establish an EAS Energy Cooperation Task Force, based on the existing ASEAN Energy Sectoral mechanisms, to follow up on our discussion and report on its recommendations at our next Summit. We welcomed Singapore's offer to host an EAS Energy Ministers Meeting to consider ways to enhance energy cooperation.

## EDUCATION

7. We agreed to strengthen regional educational cooperation, noting that we could tap the region's centers of excellence in education for this purpose. Noting proposals to renew our historical ties, we welcomed initiatives such as the revival of the Nalanda University in India, to improve regional understanding and the appreciation of one another's heritage and history.

## FINANCE

8. We recognized that sustaining economic growth and stability in the region will require continued efforts to develop deeper, more diversified and better-integrated financial markets, and to strengthen regional mechanisms to prevent and manage financial crises. We welcomed closer cooperation among

EAS participating countries and agreed to task officials to develop proposals to this end for our consideration at our next Summit.

## AVIAN INFLUENZA

9. We recalled that at the First East Asia Summit in Kuala Lumpur, we adopted the EAS Declaration on Avian Influenza Prevention, Control and Response. We expressed concern over some continuing cases of avian influenza in the region, and we reaffirmed our commitment to coordinate efforts and to increase cooperation in addressing this challenge including ensuring the availability of medicine and health personnel protection measures.

## NATURAL DISASTER MITIGATION

10. Noting that natural disasters have caused tremendous loss of life and damage to property in the region in recent years, we agreed to strengthen our cooperation to improve our natural disaster response preparedness and mitigation. We identified closer coordination among our national emergency response and management mechanisms as a specific area for this cooperation.

## DOHA DEVELOPMENT AGENDA

11. We reaffirmed our commitment to the World Trade Organization's Doha Round and urged WTO members to restart negotiations as soon as possible. We called on all members to work towards the achievement of a balanced and ambitious outcome to expand opportunities in agriculture, industry and services, and to realize global development objectives.

## ECONOMIC DEVELOPMENT AND REGIONAL INTEGRATION

12. We welcomed ASEAN's efforts towards further integration and community building, and reaffirmed our resolve to work closely together in narrowing development gaps in our region. We reiterated our support for ASEAN's role as the driving force for economic integration in this region. To deepen integration, we agreed to launch a Track Two study on a Comprehensive Economic Partnership in East Asia (CEPEA) among EAS participants. We tasked the ASEAN Secretariat to prepare a time frame for the study and to invite all our countries to nominate their respective participants in it.

We welcomed Japan's proposal for an Economic Research Institute for ASEAN and East Asia (ERIA).

## INTERFAITH INITIATIVES

13. We welcomed the contribution of interfaith and intercultural dialogue in building mutual trust, respect and cooperation between our peoples, and in enhancing regional peace and security. The importance of educational material, including curriculums, and of training centers for promoting understanding across different religions, societies and cultures, was recognized. We welcomed the specific proposal made for a Dialogue among East Asian Cultures, Societies and Faith, as we expressed support for various initiatives in this area now underway in the region, including the Asia Pacific Regional Dialogue, the ASEM Interfaith Dialogue, and the UN's Alliance of Civilizations.

## DENUCLEARIZATION OF THE KOREAN PENINSULA

14. Reaffirming our views that the denuclearization of the Korean Peninsula in a peaceful and verifiable manner is a critical international objective, we expressed grave concern over the recent nuclear test conducted by the DPRK. We urged the DRPK to desist from conducting further tests, to take concrete and effective steps to fully implement the 19 September 2005 Joint Statement, and to rejoin, at an early date, the Nucelar Non-Proliferation Treaty. We also urged the DPRK to actively address the security and humanitarian concerns of the international community, including serious shortages of food, medical and other humanitarian services in North Korea, as well as the abduction issue.
15. We emphasized our strong support for the Six Party Talks, and reaffirmed our conviction that the Talks should result in more tangible progress in addressing outstanding issues.
16. While encouraging every diplomatic option remains a very high priority, we agreed on the need to remain consistent in conveying to the DPRK the international community's disapproval of actions that threaten the peace and security of our region and the world. In this regard, we reaffirmed our commitment to the full implementation of UNSC Resolutions 1695 and 1718, urged North Korea to respect these resolutions, and discussed how we could work together to ensure their effectiveness.

## FUTURE DIRECTION OF THE EAS

17. We agreed to initiate concrete projects in all the five priority EAS cooperation areas before our next Summit. We also agreed that our officials and the ASEAN Secretariat will use existing mechanisms to facilitate the implementation of these projects.
18. We recognized our progress in building confidence among EAS participants and encouraged an open and continuing exchange of views on issues of strategic importance to the region. We expressed our conviction that the EAS should remain outward looking, with ASEAN as the driving force working in close partnership with other participants of the East Asia Summit.
19. We reaffirmed our position that the East Asia Summit is an important component of the emerging regional architecture, and we confirmed our view that the EAS complements other existing regional mechanisms, including the ASEAN dialogue process, the ASEAN + 3 process, the ARF, and APEC in community building efforts. We underscored the value of open and spontaneous Leaders-led discussions on strategic issues of peace and stability in our region and in the world.
20. To implement our decisions, we tasked our Officials and the ASEAN Secretariat to continue coordination within the framework of existing ASEAN mechanisms. We commended the work of the ASEAN Secretariat in establishing the EAS electronic network to help ensure closer coordination and cooperation.
21. We agreed to convene the third East Asia Summit in Singapore on 21 November 2007.

Source: http://www.aseansec.org/19302.htm
Accessed date: 17 January 2008
Publisher: ASEAN Secretariat
Country: Jakarta
Date of Publication: 2007

# CHAPTER 28

# CHAIRMAN'S STATEMENT OF THE 3^RD^ EAST ASIA SUMMIT

**Singapore, 21 November 2007**

1. The Third East Asia Summit (EAS) chaired by H.E Lee Hsien Loong, Prime Minister of the Republic of Singapore, was held on 21 November 2007 in Singapore. The Heads of State/Government of ASEAN, the People's Republic of China, the Republic of India, Japan, the Republic of Korea and New Zealand, and the Foreign Minister of Australia, representing his Prime Minister, had a productive exchange of views on regional and international issues, as well as on the growing areas of cooperation within the EAS framework.

## REGIONAL AND INTERNATIONAL ISSUES

2. We welcomed recent progress made at the Six-Party Talks, in pursuit of a peaceful and comprehensive resolution to the nuclear issue on the Korean Peninsula. In this respect, we welcomed the DPRK's agreement to disable all existing nuclear facilities subject to abandonment under the September 2005 Joint Statement and the February 13 agreement, as well as the Inter-Korean Summit in October 2007. We look forward to the Six-Party Ministerial Meeting to be held in Beijing. We also emphasized the importance of addressing the issue of humanitarian concerns of the international community.
3. On the situation in Myanmar, we noted that the recent visits by UN Special Advisor Ibrahim Gambari had resulted in several steps in the right direction. We expressed the view that the process of national reconciliation had to move forward, and that the UN played a vital role in this process. We noted Myanmar's views about ASEAN's role, and ASEAN's decision to respect Myanmar's wishes and make way for Myanmar to deal directly with the UN and the international community on its own. We acknowledged that ASEAN had done its best to engage Myanmar and be helpful in Myanmar's efforts to move towards national reconciliation. We reaffirmed our commitment in continuing to give strong support to the UN's role and Gambari's mission, and encourage Myanmar to continue to work closely with the UN towards national reconciliation.

4. We reiterated our strong commitment towards an expeditious and successful conclusion of the Doha Development Round. Concluding the Round is essential to promote growth, opportunity, and prosperity. The primacy of the rules-based multilateral trading system is also vital to ensure a fair and predictable global market in which we can all participate. We firmly believe that a successful outcome is within our collective grasp if we all make the necessary sacrifices. We are prepared to make our contribution. We each know what we must do and we call on all WTO Members to do the same at this critical juncture. We have come too far to fail.

## ENERGY, ENVIRONMENT, CLIMATE CHANGE AND SUSTAINABLE DEVELOPMENT

5. We devoted a session to discuss "Energy, Environment, Climate Change and Sustainable Development", which are pressing and inter-related global concerns. We also signed the Singapore Declaration on Climate Change, Energy and the Environment, which affirmed our commitment to carry out collective action to address these challenges for mutual benefit and the common good.
6. Recognizing the adverse impact of climate change on socio-economic development, health and the environment, we expressed our support for the work to achieve a common understanding on a long-term aspirational global emissions reduction goal to pave the way for a more effective post-2012 international arrangement. In this regard, we appreciated the efforts of various EAS participating countries, including the "Cool Earth 50" proposal by Japan.
7. We also stressed the importance of developing an effective, comprehensive, and equitable post-2012 international climate change arrangement under the UNFCCC process. We thus agreed to participate actively in the process of establishing such an effective, flexible and equitable arrangement, involving all countries, and would achieve compatibility between environmental protection and economic growth, in accordance with our common but differentiated responsibilities and respective capabilities. In this context, we reiterated our strong support for the 13$^{th}$ session of the COP to the UNFCCC and the 3$^{rd}$ CMP to the Kyoto Protocol to be held in Bali, Indonesia in December 2007.
8. We were pleased to hear the many useful initiatives and ideas proposed by EAS participating countries to address the challenges of climate change, and instructed our Ministers and officials to follow up on these. In particular, we welcomed Viet Nam's proposal to host an EAS Environment Ministers' Meeting and Thailand's hosting of the 2$^{nd}$ EAS Energy Ministers' Meeting in 2008 to follow up on our discussions on Climate Change, Energy and the

Environment. We agreed that there was much scope for cooperation in the areas of protecting carbon-sinks, energy efficiency and conservation, sustainable forest management and ensuring afforestation/reforestation, technology transfer, adaptation measures.

9. We appreciated Japan's environmental cooperation initiative "Towards a Sustainable East Asia", through which it would contribute more than USD2 billion over the next 5 years to anti-pollution measures, and undertake a number of key proposals. We endorsed Singapore's proposal to convene an EAS Conference on Liveable Cities in June 2008 to address the inter-related issues of urbanisation, climate change, energy, and the environment. We also welcomed the proposals from Thailand and China to organise an EAS workshop on biofuels and a seminar on climate change adaptation capacity building respectively. We also affirmed our support for important forestry initiatives such as the Heart of Borneo conservation plan.
10. Reiterating our concern over the current oil price increases which could hurt all economies, especially those of developing countries; we agreed to intensify efforts to improve energy efficiency and conservation, increase the use of renewable energy sources, and explore alternative energy sources, including civilian nuclear energy for interested parties, while ensuring nuclear safety, security and non-proliferation, in particular, its safeguards, within the framework of the International Atomic Energy Agency (IAEA); so as to enhance the strength of our economies in coping with this challenge.
11. We expressed satisfaction with the follow-up to the Cebu Declaration on East Asian Energy Security that we had signed at our 2nd Summit in Cebu. We commended the work done by the EAS Energy Ministers at their inaugural meeting in Singapore on 22 August 2007, supported by the EAS Energy Cooperation Task Force; and tasked them to continue their good work. We appreciated, in particular, the EAS Energy Ministers' recommendations on future areas of cooperation, including:

    a. Formulating, on a voluntary basis, energy efficiency goals and action plans, with a view to presenting the first goals and action plans in 2009, followed by monitoring of progress towards each countries' own energy efficiency goals;
    b. Enhancing cooperation on biofuels in the region, including formulating principles for biofuels, and supporting cooperation in developing reference benchmarks for biofuels; and
    c. Promoting energy market integration.

We also exchanged further ideas on how to enhance regional energy cooperation such as through promoting the use of low-carbon and environmentally friendly technology, enhancing research and development, encouraging technology transfer, providing technical and financial assistance and enhancing the implementation of clean development mechanisms as well as developing carbon-trading mechanisms and looked forward to the EAS energy officials looking into these areas further.

## REVIEW OF EAS COOPERATION

12. Recognizing the potential of the EAS to build a united, stable and prosperous East Asia, we reaffirmed our determination to continue developing the EAS as an important forum for strategic dialogue and regional cooperation. We reiterated our decision at the 2nd EAS in Cebu to deepen cooperation in all the five priority EAS cooperation areas. In this regard, we welcomed the proposals presented by the ASEAN Secretariat on EAS cooperation in disaster management and education, as a means to begin initiating concrete cooperation in these two priority areas. We also looked forward to the broadening and deepening of EAS cooperation in other areas.
13. We agreed to the establishment of the Economic Research Institute of ASEAN and East Asia (ERIA) to be accommodated temporarily at the ASEAN Secretariat. We welcomed the report submitted to us by the Expert Group, which focuses on research topics of strategic interest to the EAS countries. We encouraged the Expert Group to continue its research work and we looked forward to practical policy recommendations to further regional integration and strengthen partnerships in East Asia.
14. We welcomed the progress report of the study by scholars and academics on a Comprehensive Economic Partnership in East Asia (CEPEA), and encouraged them to maintain good momentum in their work towards submitting a final report of recommendations through the Economic Ministers to us at the 4$^{th}$ East Asia Summit. It would be useful to incorporate the views of the private sector in the work process. The CEPEA should build upon and add value to our existing FTAs. We encouraged the expeditious conclusion of our ASEAN Plus 1 FTAs.
15. Given the importance of developing and diversifying financial markets, we welcomed closer cooperation among EAS participating countries. In particular, we welcomed the key recommendations made by our Finance officials, including that of an Informal Senior EAS Finance Officials' Dialogue.
16. Recognising that United Nations' Alliance of Civilizations (AOC) initiative was an important means of fostering dialogue among faiths, cultures and communities; we agreed that the implementation of its recommendations would improve relations and understanding between communities in East Asia and elsewhere. We further welcomed the intention of a number of East Asian

governments to collaborate on AOC-related projects, in areas such as youth exchanges, education and media training, and instructed our officials and the ASEAN Secretariat to follow up on these.

17. We welcomed the positive developments in India's Nalanda University initiative, including the inaugural meeting of the Nalanda Mentor Group chaired by Nobel Laureate Professor Amartya Sen in Singapore in July 2007 and Japan's offer to host its 2nd meeting as well as an associated Forum on Intercultural, Inter-societal and Interfaith dialogue next month. The revival of Nalanda University would create a centre for cultural exchange and inter-religious study and understanding in the region.
18. We noted with satisfaction, the progress of youth exchange in East Asia, including the steady implementation of the "Japan-East Asia Network of Exchange for Students and Youths" (JENESYS) Programme.

## FUTURE DIRECTION OF THE EAS

19. We recognised that deepening economic integration is a key element in promoting regional community-building, and that as the regional architecture evolves, it becomes even more pertinent that the relationship among the EAS countries strengthen.
20. Reaffirming our common desire to see continued progress in the various areas of cooperation under the EAS while maintaining the EAS' "leaders-led" and strategic nature, we recognised the practical need to coordinate such cooperation and ensure follow-up on our discussions. We tasked our officials, working with the ASEAN Secretariat, to consider possible structures to better coordinate the EAS process.
21. We stressed our conviction that the EAS should continue to help build a united and prosperous East Asia, with ASEAN as the driving force working in close partnership with other participants of the East Asia Summit. We reaffirmed that the East Asia Summit is an important component of the emerging regional architecture and would help build an East Asian community. It should play a complementary and mutually reinforcing role with other regional mechanisms, including the ASEAN dialogue process, the ASEAN Plus Three process, the ARF, and APEC in community building efforts.
22. We expressed our appreciation to ROK President Roh Moo-hyun for his contributions to the EAS process, and wished him all the best in his future endeavours. We also expressed our appreciation to ASEAN Secretary-General Ong Keng Yong for his service and contributions to the EAS.
23. We agreed to convene the Fourth East Asia Summit in Thailand.

Source: http://www.aseansec.org/21127.htm
Accessed date: 24 February 2009
Publisher: ASEAN Secretariat
Country: Jakarta
Date of Publication: 2007

# CHAPTER 29

# DECLARATION ON THE ASEAN ECONOMIC COMMUNITY BLUEPRINT

**WE**, the Heads of State/Government of Brunei Darussalam, the Kingdom of Cambodia, the Republic of Indonesia, the Lao People's Democratic Republic, Malaysia, the Union of Myanmar, the Republic of the Philippines, the Republic of Singapore, the Kingdom of Thailand and the Socialist Republic of Viet Nam, Member Countries of ASEAN, on the occasion of the 40$^{th}$ Anniversary of ASEAN and the 13$^{th}$ ASEAN Summit in Singapore;

**RECALLING** our earlier decision to establish by 2020 the ASEAN Community, including the ASEAN Economic Community (AEC), made in the Declaration of ASEAN Concord II in Bali, Indonesia, on 7 October 2003;

**DETERMINED** to achieve higher levels of economic dynamism, sustained prosperity, inclusive growth and integrated development of ASEAN;

**CONSCIOUS** of the increasing interdependence of the ASEAN economies within the region as well as with the rest of the world and stressing the importance of narrowing the development gap for accelerating the ASEAN Economic Community by 2015;

**RECOGNISING** that different levels of development within ASEAN require some flexibility as ASEAN moves towards a more integrated and interdependent future;

**REAFFIRMING** our collective commitment, made at the 12$^{th}$ ASEAN Summit in Cebu, the Philippines, on 13 January 2007, to accelerate the establishment of the ASEAN Community, including its AEC pillar, to 2015;

**COGNISANT** of the need to have a strengthened institutional framework and a unified legal identity as set forth in the ASEAN Charter by putting in place rules-based systems to realise the establishment of the AEC by 2015;

**EXPRESSING** satisfaction at the overall progress made and commitment shown by ASEAN in developing the AEC Blueprint and to ensure its timely implementation;

**REAFFIRMING** the ASEAN Economic Ministers (AEM) as the coordinator of all ASEAN economic integration and cooperation issues;

## DO HEREBY:

1. **ADOPT** the AEC Blueprint which each ASEAN Member Country shall abide by and implement the AEC by 2015. The AEC Blueprint will transform ASEAN into a single market and production base, a highly competitive economic region, a region of equitable economic development, and a region fully integrated into the global economy. The AEC Blueprint including its strategic schedule is annexed to this Declaration.
2. **TASK** concerned Ministers, assisted by the ASEAN Secretariat, to implement the AEC Blueprint and to report to us regularly, through the Council of the ASEAN Economic Community, on the progress of its implementation.

**DONE** in Singapore on the twentieth day of November in the Year Two Thousand and Seven, in single copy, in the English language.

For Brunei Darussalam:

**HAJI HASSANAL BOLKIAH**
Sultan of Brunei Darussalam

For the Kingdom of Cambodia:

**SAMDECH HUN SEN**
Prime Minister

For the Republic of Indonesia:

**DR. SUSILO BAMBANG YUDHOYONO**
President

For the Lao People's Democratic Republic:

**BOUASONE BOUPHAVANH**
Prime Minister

For Malaysia:

**DATO' SERI ABDULLAH AHMAD BADAWI**
Prime Minister

For the Union of Myanmar:

**GENERAL THEIN SEIN**
Prime Minister

For the Republic of the Philippines:

**GLORIA MACAPAGAL-ARROYO**
President

For the Republic of Singapore:

**LEE HSIEN LOONG**
Prime Minister

For the Kingdom of Thailand:

**GENERAL SURAYUD CHULANONT (RET.)**
Prime Minister

For the Socialist Republic of Viet Nam:

**NGUYEN TAN DUNG**
Prime Minister

Source: http://www.aseansec.org/21081.htm
Accessed date: 20 February 2009
Publisher: ASEAN Secretariat
Country: Singapore
Date of Publication: 2007

# CHAPTER 30

# JOINT DECLARATION OF THE ASEAN-EU COMMEMORATIVE SUMMIT

**Singapore, 22 November 2007**

**WE**, the Heads of State/Government of the Member Countries of the Association of Southeast Asian Nations (ASEAN) and the European Union (EU), gathered in Singapore on 22 November 2007 for the occasion of the ASEAN-EU Commemorative Summit;

**BUILDING** on the momentum of the 30th anniversary of ASEAN-EU relations, the 40th anniversary of the establishment of ASEAN and the 50th anniversary of the signing of the Rome Treaties to promote sustainable peace, security and prosperity through regional integration;

**RECALLING** the establishment of official relations between the EU's Permanent Representatives Committee (COREPER) and ASEAN in Brussels in February 1977, the Cooperation Agreement between Member Countries of ASEAN and European Community signed on 7 March 1980, the ASEAN-EU Joint Declaration on Cooperation to Combat International Terrorism endorsed on 27 January 2003 and the Nuremberg Declaration on an EU-ASEAN Enhanced Partnership endorsed on 15 March 2007;

**NOTING** with deep satisfaction that, over thirty years, ASEAN-EU relations have grown and expanded to cover a wide range of areas including political and security, economic and trade, social and cultural and development cooperation;

**DETERMINED** to deepen and broaden our cooperation, based on mutual trust and respect, with the ASEAN-EU Enhanced Partnership as a strong foundation for our relations and cooperation to ensure peace, stability, progress and prosperity in the region;

**COMMENDING** the adoption of the ASEAN Charter which marks a new level in ASEAN regional integration and sets a firm basis for its further community building;

**EXPRESSING** support for the realization of the ASEAN Community by 2015;

**WELCOMING** the adoption of the ASEAN Convention on Counter Terrorism at the 12th ASEAN Summit in Cebu, the Philippines;

**ACKNOWLEDGING** ASEAN's centrality and the leading role played by ASEAN in all ASEAN-related regional architecture, in particular the ASEAN Regional Forum (ARF) as the main forum for regional dialogue and political and security cooperation in the Asia Pacific;

**FURTHER** acknowledging the importance of the Treaty of Amity and Cooperation in Southeast Asia (TAC) as a milestone in the regional code of conduct for inter-state relations and promoting regional peace and stability;

**RECOGNIZING** the need to strengthen the promotion and the protection of human rights through practical steps and closer cooperation, including in international fora;

**RENEWING** our commitment to actively cooperate in addressing major global and transboundary problems such as climate change and its impact on socio-economic development and the environment, particularly in developing countries, as presented by the Fourth Assessment Report from the Intergovernmental Panel on Climate Change;

**RECOGNIZING** the need for all countries to participate in developing an effective, comprehensive, and equitable post-2012 international climate change arrangement, and in this regard, welcome Indonesia's efforts to host the 13th Session of the Conference of the Parties to the United Nations Framework Convention on Climate Change (UNFCCC) and the 3rd Session of the Conference of the Parties Serving as the Meeting of the Parties to the Kyoto Protocol;

**ACKNOWLEDGING** that all countries have common but differentiated responsibilities and respective capabilities in addressing the common challenge of climate change, and that developed countries should continue to play a leadership role in substantially reducing global emission of greenhouse gases and that developing countries should also play their part, supported by developed countries through positive incentives, including through a strengthened global carbon market;

**NOTING** the role of forests in mitigating and adapting to climate change, preserving biodiversity and sustaining the livelihoods of forest communities; and

**AFFIRMING** the need to take an effective approach to address interrelated challenges of climate change, energy security and other environmental issues, in the context of sustainable development.

## HEREBY DECLARE TO:

1. Commit to further enhance ASEAN-EU dialogue and cooperation and welcome the "ASEAN-EU Plan of Action to Implement the Nuremberg Declaration on an EU-ASEAN Enhanced Partnership" annexed herewith;
2. Continue ASEAN-EU dialogue and close coordination on regional and international issues so as to contribute to the maintenance of peace, security and prosperity;
3. Strengthen political dialogue between ASEAN and the EU as well as regional and political dialogue through the ARF for advancing the common interest of ASEAN and the EU in promoting peace, stability and prosperity in the Asia Pacific region, with ASEAN as the driving force;
4. Welcome the intention of the EU/EC to accede to the TAC;
5. Support the implementation of the UN Global Counter Terrorism Strategy, an early conclusion of a UN Comprehensive Convention on International Terrorism, the ASEAN Convention on Counter Terrorism, and the implementation of the ASEAN-EU Joint Declaration on Cooperation to Combat International Terrorism;
6. Explore cooperation to promote disarmament and non-proliferation of weapons of mass destruction and their means of delivery, as these represent serious threats to peace and security, according to the existing disarmament and non-proliferation conventions, treaties and instruments;
7. Enhance cooperation to support ASEAN's efforts in its community building through effective implementation of the Vientiane Action Programme;
8. Support the Initiative for ASEAN Integration (IAI) and other sub-regional endeavours to narrow the development gaps in ASEAN, as contributing to regional integration, through the EU's ongoing bilateral programmes with ASEAN countries;
9. In light of the recent events in Myanmar, the ASEAN and the EU actively support the good offices mission of the UN Secretary General and the efforts of the Secretary General's Special Advisor Ibrahim Gambari to bring about an inclusive and comprehensive process of genuine national reconciliation and peaceful transition to democracy;
10. Call for the release of political detainees in Myanmar, including those recently detained, and the early lifting of restrictions placed on political parties;

11. Welcome the decision of the Government of Myanmar to step up its engagement with the UN and to enter into a dialogue with Daw Aung San Suu Kyi, recalling that such a dialogue should be conducted with all concerned parties and ethnic groups;
12. Reaffirm the willingness of ASEAN and the EU to help address the humanitarian needs of the people of Myanmar and to respond constructively to political transformation and reform, including Myanmar's long-term development needs;
13. Enhance economic relations by expeditiously negotiating the ASEAN-EU Free Trade Agreement based on a region-to-region approach, mindful of the different levels of development and capacity of individual ASEAN countries, providing for comprehensive trade and investment liberalization and facilitation;
14. Agree to work closely to ensure an ambitious, balanced and comprehensive conclusion of the Doha Development Agenda, as priority for both ASEAN and the EU;
15. Intensify the implementation of the activities agreed under the Trans-Regional EU-ASEAN Trade Initiative (TREATI) and the Regional EU-ASEAN Dialogue Instrument (READI) in order to promote and broaden cooperation and relations between ASEAN and the EU in both trade and non-trade areas;
16. Enhance cooperation on Intellectual Property Rights in the fields of legislation, enforcement, and capacity building to build and strengthen awareness on intellectual property;
17. Commit to act with resolve to meet the interrelated multiple goals of addressing climate change, reducing air pollution and improving the global environment while contributing to sustainable development and improving energy security;
18. Commit to the common long-term goal of mitigating global emissions of greenhouse gases, so as to stabilise atmospheric greenhouse gas concentrations in the long run, at a level that would prevent dangerous anthropogenic interference with the climate system;
19. Strengthen cooperation to address the critical issue of climate change in accordance with the UNFCCC and the Kyoto Protocol, with particular emphasis on promoting energy efficiency and the use of cleaner and sustainable renewable energy, as well as promoting afforestation and reforestation and reducing deforestation, forest degradation and forest fires, and combating illegal logging and its associated trade; and in this regard, acknowledge sub-regional conservation initiatives such as the Heart of Borneo conservation plan and the Greater Mekong Programme and look forward to continuing the EC-ASEAN READI Dialogue on Climate Change;

20. Promote cooperation on the sustainable management and use of our biodiversity including forest, coastal and marine ecosystems and environments and other natural resources, taking into account the Convention on Biological Diversity to significantly reduce the rate of biodiversity loss by 2010; and support the ASEAN Centre for Biodiversity, as a regional centre for biodiversity conservation and management, noting the importance of various regional and international initiatives such as the Forestry Eleven Forum and Coral Triangle Initiative on Coral Reefs, Fisheries and Food Security;
21. Promote energy security, sustainable energy and multilateral measures for stable, effective and transparent global energy markets, through an ASEAN-EU policy dialogue on energy as well as through other regional fora such as the ARF, where appropriate;
22. Strengthen cooperation at the national, regional and international level to mobilise financial resources and to attract public and private finance for the deployment of technologies for clean and environmentally friendly energy investment;
23. Enhance cooperation in promoting the use of renewable and alternative energy sources such as solar, hydro, wind, tide, biomass, sustainable biofuels and geothermal energy, as well as, for interested parties, civilian nuclear energy; while giving careful and due regard to ensuring safety and security standards and exploring cooperation in this area;
24. Intensify cooperation in promoting, sharing and implementing environmentally sustainable practices, including the transfer of environmentally-sound technologies, the enhancement of human and institutional capacities and the promotion of sustainable production and consumption patterns; and in this regard, consider regional cooperation under the international Marrakesh Process on sustainable consumption and production (SCP);
25. Step up dialogue and cooperation at regional and global levels on disaster management including in the areas of preparedness, mitigation and emergency response as well as rehabilitation and reconstruction, and consider support for the implementation of the ASEAN Agreement on Disaster Management and Emergency Response;
26. Enhance cooperation in public health to address the threats of emerging infectious diseases such as avian influenza;
27. Strengthen our socio-cultural cooperation by encouraging greater interaction among our peoples, in particular youth, academics, media personnel and civil society, and by cooperating with the ASEAN Foundation in promoting public awareness on ASEAN-EU Dialogue Relations; and
28. Identify possible ways and mechanisms to cooperate to ensure the promotion and protection of the rights and welfare of migrant workers.

**Adopted** in Singapore on the Twenty-Second Day of November in the Year Two Thousand and Seven.

Source: http://www.aseansec.org/21120.htm
Accessed date: 2 October 2008
Publisher: ASEAN Secretariat
Country: Jakarta
Date of Publication: 2007

# CHAPTER 31

# JOINT COMMUNIQUE OF THE 40TH ASEAN MINISTERIAL MEETING (AMM) "ONE CARING AND SHARING COMMUNITY"

**Manila, 29–30 July 2007**

## INTRODUCTION

1. We, the Foreign Ministers of the Association of Southeast Asian Nations (ASEAN), met at the 40th ASEAN Ministerial Meeting on 29–30 July 2007 in Manila. His Excellency Alberto G. Romulo, Secretary of Foreign Affairs of the Philippines and Chairman of the 40th ASEAN Standing Committee, chaired the Meeting.
2. The Representatives of Timor-Leste and Papua New Guinea attended the Opening Ceremony of the 40th ASEAN Ministerial Meeting as Guest of the Chairman of the 40th ASEAN Standing Committee and as Special Observer in ASEAN, respectively.

## OPENING ADDRESS

3. Her Excellency President Gloria Macapagal-Arroyo, President of the Republic of the Philippines, addressed the Opening Ceremony of the 40th ASEAN Ministerial Meeting.
4. President Arroyo stated that ASEAN relations have never been stronger and recalled ASEAN achievements in cooperation, solidarity, fighting poverty and winning collective security. She called on ASEAN to carry forward the landmark commitments made at the 12th ASEAN Summit to create "one caring and sharing" community by 2015. She said such a community should be anchored on economic integration with a focus on social justice and raising the standards of living in the region.
5. To achieve that objective, President Arroyo urged ASEAN to build upon its bold decision to draft an ASEAN Charter that will strengthen ASEAN and deepen collaboration among its Member Countries. She said the ASEAN Charter should be a testament to ASEAN's commitment to become one, single united front.

6. President Arroyo said, furthermore, that developing ASEAN is more than creating a regional community and should also be a dynamic force in Asia that would maximize the benefits of globalization. For ASEAN to become a true expanding union, the President said ASEAN should continue nurturing its relations with key partners through, among other things, forging free trade agreements and engaging all parties that have a stake in the region to establish an East Asia community.
7. President Arroyo also called on ASEAN to point the way ahead in regional security cooperation. In this regard, she said that ASEAN welcomed the recent positive developments on the Korean Peninsula nuclear issue, including the shutdown of the Yongbyon reactor, and commended all parties for the progress they have made thus far. She said ASEAN must stand ready to advance regional security and stability and, in this connection, to strengthen our collective stake in a stable Korean Peninsula.
8. The President emphasized the achievements ASEAN has made in regional security, from the Treaty of Amity and Cooperation in Southeast Asia (TAC) to the ASEAN Regional Forum (ARF). The President said ASEAN has been a force for regional peace and progress for forty years and must find the means to sustain this role for the next forty years.
9. In conclusion, President Arroyo said ASEAN must be a community where all can grow and prosper together. If ASEAN succeeds in this respect, then future generations will look back on ASEAN's fortieth year, on the 12th ASEAN Summit and on the 40th ASEAN Ministerial Meeting, as the point where the region's effort to attain this aspiration was begun.

## THE ASEAN COMMUNITY

10. We welcomed the progress achieved in the implementation of the Leaders' decisions at the 12th ASEAN Summit on 13 January 2007 in Cebu, Philippines, in accelerating the establishment of an ASEAN Community to 2015 and in building a people-centred ASEAN, consistent with our commitment to establish "One Caring and Sharing Community". We reaffirmed our resolve to pursuing region-wide programmes and activities that would truly make ASEAN relevant, beneficial and meaningful to peoples of ASEAN.
11. We are encouraged by the advancement we have made in ASEAN regional integration, and agreed to further intensify our efforts to accelerate the narrowing of the development gap to ensure the realization of the ASEAN Community.
12. We recognized the need for synergy in enhancing our efforts and pooling our resources, as well as achieving effective coordination, so that ASEAN can be

more responsive to and consistent with the stated goals and objectives of an ASEAN Community.

13. To ensure that all three pillars of the ASEAN Community move in the same pace, we agreed to give particular attention to developing blueprints for each of the ASEAN Security Community and the ASEAN Socio-Cultural Community, similar to those of the ASEAN Economic Community.
14. We agreed in a Joint Statement issued on 30 July 2007 to recommend to our Leaders the endorsement of the proposal to observe ASEAN Day (8 August) as a special day in each of the ASEAN Member Countries with the objective of increasing ASEAN awareness among our people.

## 40th anniversary of ASEAN

15. We highlighted that the 40th anniversary of ASEAN on 8 August 2007 will be an historic milestone for our regional organization. We supported the various initiatives and activities carried out by Member Countries to commemorate this auspicious occasion, which would highlight ASEAN's achievements and develop ASEAN consciousness. We welcomed Malaysia's initiatives to convene an ASEAN Integrity Dialogue.

## Vientiane Action Programme (VAP)

16. We took note of the progress in the implementation of the Vientiane Action Programme (VAP). Reaffirming our commitment to the completion of the VAP by 2010, we agreed to mobilize financial resources for the remaining VAP programs, projects and activities. We resolved to strengthen coordination among the various ASEAN sectoral bodies carrying out the VAP and reiterated the importance of undertaking coordination among the three pillars of ASEAN Community.

## Initiative for ASEAN Integration (IAI)

17. We agreed to exert greater efforts on narrowing the development gap to enhance ASEAN integration and ensure equitable economic development for the well-being of the peoples of ASEAN.
18. We expressed support for the recommendations made at the Second Initiative for ASEAN Integration (IAI) Development Cooperation Forum in Ha Noi, Viet Nam, on 12–13 June 2007 on new and innovative strategies to narrow the development gap among the ASEAN Member Countries, including the proposed formulation of the Second IAI Work Plan for 2008–2015. To realize the

full ASEAN integration in compliance with ASEAN Community by 2015, we recognized the need to also address the "pockets of poverty and underdevelopment" in ASEAN Member Countries. The programmes for IAI should also be aligned with ASEAN's larger efforts to become an ASEAN Community by 2015.

19. We expressed appreciation to our Dialogue Partners and other international institutions for their support and contributions to the IAI. We are committed to sustain and accelerate our efforts to narrow the development gap in the region to make ASEAN more economically competitive and socially cohesive.

## The ASEAN Charter

20. We stressed the importance of codifying the principles, values and norms of ASEAN into a Charter and in sustaining the momentum towards transforming ASEAN into a rules-based organization with a legal personality, capable of performing a greater role in regional and international affairs.
21. We welcomed the submission of the first draft of the ASEAN Charter by the High Level Task Force on the Drafting of the ASEAN Charter (HLTF) and conveyed our appreciation for the HLTF's excellent work. We thoroughly discussed the draft ASEAN Charter and gave our views to the HLTF on the important aspects of the ASEAN Charter. We looked forward to the completion of the work of the HLTF and its submission of the final draft of the ASEAN Charter at the 13th ASEAN Summit in November 2007 in Singapore.

## ASEAN SECURITY COMMUNITY (ASC)

22. We stressed the importance of building the ASC as a backbone of the ASEAN Community. We noted the convening of the 2nd ASC Plan of Action Coordinating Conference (ASCCO) on 10–11 July 2007 and underscored the importance of coordination in the implementation of the Programme Areas and Measures of the ASC Plan of Action in the process of ASEAN Community building.

....

24. Consistent with our goal to build One Caring and Sharing Community, we are committed to the timely implementation of the provisions of the ASEAN Declaration on the Protection and Promotion of the Rights of Migrant Workers. We agreed to establish the ASEAN Committee on the Implementation of the ASEAN Declaration on the Protection and Promotion of the Rights of Migrant Workers that will lead and oversee the implementation of various activities

under this Declaration. We recognized that this Committee shall report to ASEAN Senior Labor Officials.

25. We reaffirmed our commitment to the protection and promotion of human rights under the Vientiane Action Programme (VAP). We also noted the convening of the 6th Workshop on ASEAN Regional Human Rights Mechanism in Manila on 16-17 July 2007 and the Working Session of National Human Rights Institutions Consultations Mechanism in Bali on 28 June 2007. We further noted the work carried out by the non-governmental Working Group for an ASEAN Human Rights Mechanism, including the meeting between the open-ended SOM Troika and the Working Group on the sidelines of the 40th AMM with the objective of facilitating the implementation of the activities under the promotion of human rights component of the VAP.

## Treaty on the Southeast Asia Nuclear Weapon-Free Zone (SEANWFZ)

26. We noted the results of the Meeting of the Commission on SEANWFZ in Manila on 30 July 2007 which reviewed the progress of the implementation of the Treaty since it came into force in 1997 and discussed ways for the Treaty to effectively contribute to ASEAN Security Community-building efforts.
27. We welcomed the adoption of the Plan of Action that would guide the future implementation of the SEANWFZ Treaty to ensure that we are able to respond to the evolving internal and external challenges and opportunities.

## Treaty of Amity and Cooperation in Southeast Asia

28. We welcomed the accessions to the TAC of the Republic of France and the Democratic Republic of Timor-Leste at the margins of the 12th ASEAN Summit on 13 January 2007 in Cebu, Philippines. We looked forward to the accessions of the Democratic Socialist Republic of Sri Lanka and the People's Republic of Bangladesh to the Treaty of Amity and Cooperation in Southeast Asia (TAC) on 1 August 2007 in Manila. We acknowledged the declarations of the United Kingdom and the European Union of their intent to accede to the TAC. We noted that the continuing interest in the TAC underscores its important role as a key code of conduct governing inter-state relations in Southeast Asia and its value as a major diplomatic instrument for the promotion of peace, security and stability in the region.
29. We called upon the other countries, particularly our Dialogue Partners and friends in the ARF, sharing ASEAN's aspirations for peace, security, stability and development in the region, to also accede to the TAC.

## South China Sea

30. We reaffirmed the continuing importance of the Declaration on the Conduct of Parties in the South China Sea of 2002 (DOC) as a milestone document between ASEAN and China, embodying their collective commitment to ensure the peaceful resolution of disputes in the area. We believed that the Declaration had been effective in building mutual trust and confidence among the claimants in the area and in maintaining peace and stability in the region. We underscored the need to intensify efforts to move forward the implementation of the Declaration and eventually conclude a Regional Code of Conduct in the South China Sea.
31. We encouraged the continued exercise of self-restraint by all the parties concerned and the promotion of confidence building measures in this area and welcomed their commitment to resolving disputes in the South China Sea by peaceful means in conformity with the spirit of the DOC and recognized principles of international law including the United Nations Convention on the Law of the Sea.

## ASEAN Regional Forum (ARF)

32. We reaffirmed the role of ASEAN as the primary driving force of the ASEAN Regional Forum (ARF) process and the ARF as the primary forum in enhancing political and security dialogue and cooperation as well as the fulcrum for building peace and security in the wider Asia-Pacific region.
33. We welcomed the Democratic Socialist Republic of Sri Lanka as the 27th participating country in the ARF and we looked forward to its attendance at the 14th ARF on 2 August 2007. We expressed confidence that the Democratic Socialist Republic of Sri Lanka would be able to contribute to the further enhancement of political and security dialogue and cooperation in the region.
34. We commended the steady progress and growing momentum generated in the implementation of ARF activities. We encouraged the forging of more concrete and practical cooperation among ARF countries in building capacity and capabilities in order to better cope with numerous challenges, including in counter-terrorism, disaster relief, maritime security, non-proliferation and disarmament of weapons of mass destruction and energy security, among others. We would discuss at the 14th ARF Meeting the elevation of the ARF to a premier forum for discussion of security issues of common concern affecting the region in the future.
35. While emphasizing that confidence building would continue to play a vital role in the ARF process, we welcomed the ARF's progress towards Preventive

Diplomacy (PD). We also commended the activities undertaken to enhance links between Track I and Track II in the ARF, and between the ARF and other regional and international security organizations. We noted with satisfaction the progress made in the implementation of the agreed ARF activities for the Inter-Sessional year 2006–2007.

## ASEAN ECONOMIC COMMUNITY (AEC)

36. We underscored ASEAN's commitment to establish a Single Market and Production Base characterized by a competitive economic region with equitable economic development and one that is fully integrated into the global economy.
37. We noted the finalization of the ASEAN Economic Community Blueprint and Strategic Schedule, which will serve as an integrated and coherent master plan with clearly defined measures and actions, milestones and timelines to establish the ASEAN Economic Community by 2015, for the consideration and signing by the ASEAN Leaders at the 13th ASEAN Summit in November 2007 in Singapore. This would reaffirm and reinforce ASEAN's collective will to deepen the economic integration of the region.
38. We supported the decision of the ASEAN Economic Ministers to recognize Viet Nam as a full market economy, taking into consideration its rate of economic progress and integration with the regional and global economies, and we encouraged our Dialogue Partners to make similar recognitions.

### Energy Cooperation

39. We agreed to implement projects and activities in line with the Cebu Declaration on East Asian Energy Security within ASEAN and the East Asia Summit (EAS). In particular, we welcomed the upcoming inaugural meeting of the EAS Energy Ministers in Singapore on 23 August 2007 as an important step towards fulfilling the Cebu Declaration and following-up on the Leaders' discussions during the 2nd EAS in Cebu. We are committed to improving energy efficiency and conservation, increasing the use of alternative and renewable sources of energy, expanding biofuel production/utilization, developing open and competitive energy markets, and encouraging greater private sector involvement in energy resource and infrastructure investment within the region.

### Sub-regional Cooperation

40. We recognized the positive contributions of sub-regional cooperation within ASEAN to the growth and development of the whole region. We supported the

initiatives and programmes currently being undertaken under these subregional arrangements within ASEAN: Ayeyawady-Chao Phraya-Mekong Economic Cooperation Strategy (ACMECS), Brunei-Indonesia-Malaysia-Philippines East ASEAN Growth Area (BIMP-EAGA), Indonesia-Malaysia-Thailand Growth Triangle (IMT-GT), Cambodia-Laos-Myanmar-Viet Nam (CLMV), and Cambodia–Lao–Vietnam Development Triangle (CLV-DT).

## ASEAN SOCIO-CULTURAL COMMUNITY (ASCC)

41. To ensure that all three pillars of the ASEAN Community move in the same pace, we agreed to paying particular attention to putting in place a mechanism for the socio-cultural community, similar to the SOM and SEOM, which coordinates the activities of the two other Communities. We tasked our senior officials to come up with a blueprint to ensure proper coordination of the ASEAN Socio-Cultural Community (SOC-COM).
42. We agreed that ASCC sectoral bodies should work together with those under the AEC in intensifying strategic focus, particularly on the core element pertaining to "Managing the Social Impact of Economic Integration." They should also focus on operationalizing the decisions and declarations of the 12th ASEAN Summit and consider possible thematic approach and cross-cutting programmes in the fields of migrant workers, women, education, ASEAN identity, disaster management, climate change and sustainable development, and communicable diseases. We encouraged ASEAN sectoral bodies to develop and implement some flagship projects under the ASCC.
43. To carry out the ASCC Plan of Action, particularly towards building a community of caring societies, we agreed on the need to draw up an ASEAN roadmap for the implementation of the Millennium Development Goals Plus (MDG Plus) by the concerned ASEAN sectoral bodies, particularly those involved in poverty reduction and social development.
44. We recognized the valuable contribution of the civil society organizations (CSO) in the building of an ASEAN Community and expressed our commitment to continue to engage with CSO representatives at various levels, programmes and meetings.
45. We acknowledged the Report of the Executive Director of the ASEAN Foundation. We noted ASEAN Foundation's 10th year anniversary in 2007 and encouraged it to continue its efforts in promoting ASEAN awareness in the region, especially among the youth and students, and in mobilizing funds to support its programmes and activities.

....

## Environment and climate change

48. We expressed concern over the impact of global warming and climate change and called on concerted efforts involving the international community, including the private sector and the civil society, in addressing these challenges in accordance with the principle of common but differentiated responsibilities.
49. We welcomed the proposal by Singapore, as the next Chair of ASEAN, to focus on "Energy, Environment, Climate Change and Sustainable Development" as the theme for discussions at the 13th ASEAN Summit and Related Summits in Singapore in November 2007. In line with this theme, we looked forward to the ASEAN Leaders' Declaration on Environmental Sustainability to be signed at the 13th ASEAN Summit. We also welcomed Singapore's proposal to work on a Singapore Declaration on the Environment to be issued at the 3rs East Asia Summit in Singapore. We also looked forward to the outcome of the Informal ASEAN Ministerial Meeting on Environment to be held in Bangkok in September 2007. We called on the international community to support the successful convening of the 13th Conference of Parties (COP) of the United Nations Framework Convention on Climate Change (UNFCCC) and the 3rd Meeting of Parties (MOP) of the Kyoto Protocol to be held in Bali on 3–14 December 2007. We also welcomed the Indonesian proposal to develop a draft declaration on the 13th COP to the UNFCCC and the 3rd MOP to the Kyoto Protocol to be signed by the Leaders at the 13th ASEAN Summit.
50. We reiterated the need to step up cooperation to prevent and mitigate transboundary haze pollution in the region and welcomed the efforts of ASEAN Member Countries to finalize the process of ratification of the ASEAN Agreement on Transboundary Haze Pollution. We called upon the ASEAN Member Countries to expedite the operationalization of the ASEAN Agreement on Transboundary Haze Pollution and for those that have not yet ratified to do so soon.
51. We welcomed the signing of the Host Country Agreement between the Republic of the Philippines and the ASEAN Centre for Biodiversity (ACB) on 8 August 2006 in Manila. We expressed support for the operations of the ACB and the implementation of various projects that would preserve and protect biodiversity areas in the region. We encouraged our Dialogue Partners to support the ACB in implementing key biodiversity projects.

## Disaster Management

52. Recognizing the fact that Southeast Asia is one of the most disaster-prone regions in the world, we committed to coordinate and cooperate during disaster emergencies to provide immediate relief, assistance and rehabilitation to disaster victims, and implement measures to reduce disaster losses in the ASEAN region. We called for the early ratification of the ASEAN Agreement on Disaster Management and Emergency Response (AADMER).
53. We endorsed the offer of Indonesia to host the ASEAN Coordinating Centre for Humanitarian Assistance on Disaster Management (AHA Centre) as recommended by the 4/40 Meeting of the ASEAN Standing Committee, held in Manila on 27–28 July 2007, and we tasked the relevant officials to work out the details.

## Health

54. We expressed support for the implementation of the Third ASEAN Work Programme (AWP) on HIV and AIDS for 2006–2010, following its adoption by the Leaders during the 12th ASEAN Summit Special Session on HIV and AIDS.

## Education

55. We expressed support for programmes undertaken by the ASEAN University Network in promoting ASEAN studies and ASEAN regional identity among the youth. We acknowledged the critical role that education plays in fostering greater inter-cultural, inter-religious and inter-racial understanding within and among societies in the region. We agreed on the need to provide broader access to education and more educational opportunities and scholarships for study in ASEAN universities.

## Labour

56. We welcomed the establishment on 30 July 2007 of the ASEAN Committee on the Implementation of the ASEAN Declaration on the Protection and Promotion of the Rights of Migrant Workers as the instrument for effectively implementing the provisions of the ASEAN Declaration on the Protection and Promotion of the Rights of Migrant Workers, which our Leaders signed on 13 January 2007 in Cebu, Philippines.
57. We expressed confidence that with the signing of the Cooperation Agreement between the ASEAN Secretariat and the International Labour Organization

(ILO) Secretariat on 20 March 2007, ASEAN and the ILO would collaborate more to address labour issues where they have common interests. We also welcomed the adoption of an ASEAN Plan of Action on National OSH Framework and the continued progress of the ASEAN Occupational Safety and Health Network.

## Youth

58. We recognized the importance of involving and engaging ASEAN youth to obtain their perspectives on the activities and programmes of ASEAN. We welcomed Singapore's announcement to launch a S$5million Singapore-ASEAN Youth Fund at the ASEAN Ministerial Meeting on Youth on 26 April 2007, which aims to foster greater understanding and friendship amongst the youth of the region through its support of ASEAN youth projects. We agreed to harness the capabilities, talents and potentials of the youth so that they could contribute more to ASEAN. We were encouraged by the interest of Dialogue Partners to undertake youth and student exchange programmes with ASEAN as a way of promoting cross-cultural understanding.

## Science and technology

59. We commended the initiative to strengthen science and technology cooperation between ASEAN and the Dialogue Partners, such as Australia, China, India, Japan, the Republic of Korea and New Zealand, through the holding of informal ministerial consultations held on 28–29 August 2006 in Kuantan, Malaysia. We also welcomed the efforts of ASEAN and the U.S. to forge dynamic and effective cooperation among scientific and technological organisations and individual scientists and technical experts in these countries through the establishment of the ASEAN-U.S. Science and Technology Agreement, which will be signed soon. We also look forward to the establishment of the ASEAN-India Science and Technology Development Fund, which will promote collaborative research and development activities between ASEAN and India.

## Rural Development and Poverty Eradication

60. We welcomed the development of the ASEAN Millennium Development Compact (AMDC) during the 5th ASEAN Ministerial Meeting on Rural Development and Poverty Eradication (5th AMRDPE) in Bangkok in January 2007. We looked forward to the adoption of the AMDC during the next Senior

Officials Meeting on Rural Development and Poverty Eradication (SOM-RDPE) in Singapore next year to pursue the priority projects under the ASEAN Framework Action Plan on Rural Development and Poverty Eradication in order to improve the economic conditions of people living in the rural areas.

## Culture and Information

61. We acknowledged the significance of a number of projects and activities that were implemented in the culture and information sectors to promote the rich and vast cultures of ASEAN and raise the level of ASEAN awareness among the peoples of ASEAN. We recognized the contribution of the ASEAN Committee on Culture and Information (COCI) in the implementation of these projects and activities. We supported the formulation of an ASEAN Communications Plan under the purview of the ASEAN Ministers Responsible for Information (AMRI) to promote ASEAN to the people in and outside the region. We underscored the importance of having more television programs about ASEAN in Member Countries as a communication tool to promote cross-cultural understanding among the people of ASEAN.

## EXTERNAL RELATIONS

62. We stressed the important role and contributions of our Dialogue Partners, namely Australia, Canada, China, the European Union (EU), India, Japan, New Zealand, the Republic of Korea, the Russian Federation, and the United States of America, in the building of an ASEAN Community. We were pleased with the progress in our cooperation with our Dialogue Partners over the past year and committed to moving these partnerships forward. We discussed regional and international issues that were of interest to ASEAN and our Dialogue Partners.
63. We looked forward to the signing of the Joint Declaration of the ASEAN-Australia Comprehensive Partnership on 1 August 2007 and the early finalization of the Plan of Action to Implement the Joint Declaration of the ASEAN-Australia Comprehensive Partnership (2007–2012). We expressed confidence that the implementation of the Joint Declaration would further broaden and enhance ASEAN-Australia Dialogue Relations covering political and security, economic and socio-cultural cooperation.
64. We agreed to adopt the 2007–2010 Second ASEAN-Canada Joint Cooperation Work Plan on 1 August 2007.

65. We also agreed to work expeditiously to complete the Plan of Action to Implement the Nuremberg Declaration on an ASEAN-EU Enhanced Partnership. We welcomed the launch of the ASEAN-EU FTA negotiations, on a region-to-region basis, during the 8th ASEAN Economic Ministers and EU Trade Commissioner Consultations in Brunei Darussalam in May 2007. In this regard, we welcomed the convening of the ASEAN-EU Commemorative Summit in Singapore on 22 November 2007 to further deepen and enhance the partnership.
66. We welcomed the Russian Federation's initial contribution to the ASEAN-Russian Federation Dialogue Partnership Fund, which would pave the way for the implementation of joint ASEAN-Russia projects. We noted the progress in the drafting of the ASEAN-Russia Agreement on Cultural Cooperation, and looked forward to its signing by the Ministers Responsible for Culture and Arts at an appropriate time, which will promote exchange and cooperation in various cultural and artistic fields between ASEAN and the Russian Federation.
67. We welcomed the conferment of observer status to ASEAN at the UN General Assembly and other main bodies in December 2006. We recalled our decision during our ASEAN Foreign Ministers Retreat in Siem Reap in March 2007 to explore the possibility to upgrade our relations with the UN. In this regard, we looked forward to conclude the ASEAN-UN Cooperation Agreement as soon as possible.
68. We acknowledged the interest of Pakistan, currently an ASEAN Sectoral Partner, to become a Full Dialogue Partner. We looked forward to implementing more cooperation projects and strengthening ASEAN-Pakistan relations. Towards this end, we welcomed the contribution from Pakistan to the ASEAN-Pakistan Cooperation Fund.
69. We were encouraged by the interest expressed by countries and regional and international organizations to forge relations with ASEAN. We agreed that ASEAN should work to promote greater interactions with those countries and organizations.
70. We took note that this year marks the 30th Anniversary of the establishment of ASEAN Dialogue Relations with the EU, the United States of America and Canada. We underscored the importance of these milestone events and agreed to conduct various commemorative activities in ASEAN and in the three Dialogue Partner countries this year.
71. We expressed satisfaction on the progress of partnership between ASEAN and the Plus Three Countries in the economic and financial area, particularly the multilateralization of the Chiang Mai Initiative and expansion of the Asian

Bond Market Initiative, as well as in new areas of cooperation, such as women, poverty alleviation, disaster management and minerals. We renewed our commitment to the ASEAN Plus Three process. We looked forward to the adoption of the Second Joint Statement on East Asia Cooperation and its accompanying Work Plan at the 11th ASEAN Plus Three Summit in Singapore, to mark the Tenth Anniversary of ASEAN Plus Three Cooperation. We reaffirmed that the Second Joint Statement should provide strategic guidance for the future direction of the ASEAN Plus Three Cooperation in the next ten years.

72. We welcomed the entry into force of the ASEAN-Korea Free Trade Agreement in Goods (FTA) on 1 June 2007 and the progress made in the FTA negotiations with Australia, India, Japan and New Zealand, as well as negotiations on services and investment agreements with the Republic of Korea and the investment agreement with China. These expansions in economic ties with Dialogue Partners would contribute positively to the economic development of the region and complement ASEAN's own internal integration process.

73. We recalled the successful convening of the 2nd EAS in Cebu on 15 January 2007 and noted that the EAS has carved for itself an important niche as a Leaders-led forum for dialogue on broad strategic, political and economic issues of common interest. We reaffirmed our commitment to intensify our cooperation in the priority areas of energy security, education, finance, avian influenza, poverty alleviation and natural disaster mitigation. We welcomed the progress in the cooperation made thus far in energy security and the work done on other important proposals and ideas endorsed by the EAS Leaders in Cebu, in particular, in financial integration, the proposal for a Comprehensive Economic Partnership in East Asia, and the revival of the Nalanda University. We agreed that progress reports on these projects should be submitted to the next EAS in Singapore. We noted the preparation of the EAS Regional Financial Cooperation and Integration (RFCI) Workshop to be held in Jakarta on 10 September 2007.

74. We noted the on-going 2nd Phase Study on the feasibility of establishing the East Asia Free Trade Area (EAFTA) and the commencement of the study of the Comprehensive Economic Partnership in East Asia (CEPEA) involving ASEAN, Australia, China, India, Japan, Korea, and New Zealand. We also noted the discussion among the experts on the establishment of the Economic Research Institute for ASEAN and East Asia (ERIA).

## DEVELOPMENTS IN MYANMAR

75. We took note of the briefing by Myanmar on the recent developments in the process of national reconciliation and peaceful transition to democracy as

envisaged in the Roadmap to Democracy. We expressed concern on the pace of the national reconciliation process and urged Myanmar to show tangible progress that would lead to a peaceful transition to democracy in the near future. We welcomed the convening of the final session of the National Convention, which commenced on 18 July 2007, and we were encouraged by the assurances of Myanmar that the National Convention process will be completed within two months. We also expressed the hope that it would allow Myanmar to move to the next steps of the Roadmap. While recognizing the steps taken by the Myanmar Government to release the leader of the NLD, we continue to express concern on the detention of all political detainees and reiterate our calls for their early release.

76. We recognized the fact that Myanmar has tried to address the many and complex challenges she is facing. We reaffirmed our commitment to remain constructively engaged with Myanmar as part of building "one caring and sharing" regional community together.

## REGIONAL AND INTERNATIONAL ISSUES

We exchanged views on the following issues:

....

### • World Trade Organization (WTO)

85. We recalled the ASEAN Leaders' declaration at the 12th ASEAN Summit calling for the resumption of the Doha Round. We reiterated ASEAN's preparedness to contribute constructively in all areas of the Doha negotiations, including the importance of the development dimension of the negotiations. We called on all WTO Members to push the Doha Development Agenda negotiations forward for the benefit of all Members, especially the developing Members.
86. We urged key members of the WTO to show the necessary leadership to hasten the negotiations and reiterated our commitment to support the efforts of the Chairs of the negotiating groups and the WTO Director-General to build consensus on an ambitious and balanced outcome. To this end, we strongly reaffirmed our commitment to a successful completion of the Doha round negotiations this year.
87. We reiterated our support for the early accession of Lao PDR into the WTO. We warmly congratulated Viet Nam's accession to the WTO as its 150th member.

## Cooperation with regional organizations

88. We agreed to pursue cooperation with other regional organizations that could complement ASEAN's objectives. We agreed to follow up on the results of the Meeting of the Foreign Ministers of ASEAN and the Gulf Cooperation Council (GCC) in September 2006 in New York, including the possible joint meeting of the Secretariats of ASEAN and the GCC and a study on the feasibility of having an ASEAN-GCC Free Trade Area. We further agreed to continue exploring concrete areas of cooperation with the Shanghai Cooperation Organization in line with the decision of the Leaders at the 12th ASEAN Summit. We welcomed the interest of the League of Arab Nations to engage ASEAN and agreed to explore possible areas of cooperation between the two organizations.

## INSTITUTIONAL MATTERS

## Streamlining of ASEAN Meetings

89. We agreed to rationalize and streamline the ASEAN Summit and ASEAN Ministerial Meeting to improve the substance of those meetings and ensure the effectiveness of its deliberations by holding all ASEAN Post-Ministerial Conferences Plus One Sessions with our Dialogue Partners immediately after the annual ASEAN Ministerial Meetings starting from July 2008 in Singapore. We recommended that rationalization and streamlining of the meetings be also applied to ASEAN sectoral bodies.

## Secretary-General of ASEAN

90. We expressed appreciation for the outstanding stewardship and contribution of H.E. Ong Keng Yong to ASEAN as the Secretary-General of ASEAN for the period 2003 to 2007. We endorsed Thailand's nomination of Dr. Surin Pitsuwan, former Foreign Minister of Thailand, for consideration of our Leaders at the 13th ASEAN Summit for his appointment as the new Secretary-General of ASEAN for the period 2008–2012.

....

Source: http://www.aseansec.org/20764.htm
Accessed date: 2 October 2008
Publisher: ASEAN Secretariat
Country: Jakarta
Date of Publication: 2007

# CHAPTER 32

# CHAIRMAN'S STATEMENT OF THE 6$^{TH}$ ASEAN-INDIA SUMMIT

**Singapore, 21 November 2007**

1. The 6$^{th}$ ASEAN-India Summit was held on 21 November 2007 in Singapore and was chaired by H.E. Lee Hsien Loong, Prime Minister of the Republic of Singapore. The Summit was attended by the Heads of State/Government of ASEAN Member Countries and H.E. Dr. Manmohan Singh, Prime Minister of the Republic of India.
2. We had a comprehensive review of ASEAN-India cooperation, as well as a wide-ranging exchange of views on regional and international issues. We welcomed India's rapid engagement with the region since becoming a sectoral dialogue partner with ASEAN in 1992, and a full dialogue partner with ASEAN in 1995. We expressed satisfaction with the overall progress of ASEAN-India dialogue relations and stressed our determination to strengthen and deepen our relations.
3. We recognised that India's engagement with ASEAN was a pillar of India's "Look East" policy, and that ASEAN's leading role and centrality in all ASEAN-related architecture facilitated India's rapid development of ties in the region. In this regard, we reaffirmed our commitment to the ASEAN-India dialogue partnership, the East Asia Summit, and the ASEAN Regional Forum (ARF) as integral components of an open and evolving regional architecture. We also highlighted the ASEAN-India dialogue partnership as a key building block for a robust architecture for regional cooperation.
4. We welcomed India's continued support for ASEAN's efforts to build an ASEAN Community by 2015. We also expressed our appreciation for India's support for the Vientiane Action Programme and to narrow the development gap within ASEAN through its various contributions, including the Initiative for ASEAN Integration and other sub-regional growth initiatives such as the Mekong-Ganga Cooperation Initiative.
5. We welcomed the Progress Report of Implementation of the Plan of Action (POA) to Implement the ASEAN-India Partnership for Peace, Progress and Shared Prosperity, and tasked our Ministers and officials to accelerate the implementation of the POA through concrete projects and practical cooperation.

6. We were pleased to note that ASEAN-India bilateral trade had already reached US$30 billion, and looked forward to achieve the target of US$50 billion in 2010. We recognised that the establishment of an ASEAN-India Free Trade Area (AIFTA) would anchor the strategic engagement between both sides and sustain the momentum of the relationship. We agreed that the AIFTA, when realised, would act as an important building block for a regional FTA in Asia.
7. We were heartened by the latest progress made in negotiations of the ASEAN-India Trade in Goods Agreement. We recognised that decisions on the Agreement must be made on a strategic basis, and urged that the remaining matters be handled with flexibility and resolved quickly. We agreed that ASEAN and India are committed to the speedy completion of negotiations, and look forward to the conclusion of the Agreement by March next year. Acknowledging the immense potential in ASEAN-India trade and investment relations, we re-affirmed our continuous work on the FTA, which when implemented, would further strengthen our economic partnership towards the shared goal of regional economic integration.
8. We recalled Prime Minister Manmohan Singh's proposal for dialogue on an Open Skies Agreement at the 5th ASEAN-India Summit in Cebu in January 2007 that would fully liberalise air services between ASEAN and India and foster greater interaction and movement between the peoples of Southeast Asia and India. We welcomed India's keen interest to join the ASEAN countries in an Open Skies regime, even as we look forward to the implementation of ASEAN's own liberalisation of air services within the ASEAN region from 2008.
9. We also looked forward to further integration of shipping, road and rail links between Southeast Asia and India to create an "Arc of Advantage" for our region. In this regard, we welcomed the proposal to construct the Indian-Myanmar-Thailand Trilateral Highway.
10. We further noted that there were more than 2 million tourists from India visiting ASEAN this year and 280,000 ASEAN tourists to India. There was huge potential for further growth and expansion. We noted India's proposal to set a target of 1 million tourist arrivals from ASEAN to India by 2010 and noted India's proposal for our officials to look into ways to facilitate bona fide business travel between ASEAN countries and India, including by simplifying the existing visa regime if feasible.
11. We were deeply concerned over the impact of climate change on socio-economic development and the environment, particularly in developing countries. We agreed to strengthen cooperation between ASEAN and India in addressing the critical issue of climate change, including participating actively and constructively

to ensure a successful outcome of the upcoming UNFCCC meetings in Bali, Indonesia.

12. We welcomed India's proposal to establish an ASEAN-India Network on Climate Change that would pool and share expertise and exchange best practices. In this regard, we welcomed India's offer to set up an "ASEAN-India Green Fund" with an initial contribution from India of US$ 5 million, and looked forward to its early operationalisation.
13. We noted that ASEAN and India shared common interests in managing transboundary issues such as maritime security, counter-terrorism and disaster relief. We agreed to increase our practical cooperation in these areas under the ASEAN-India dialogue as well as other forums such as the ARF. We highlighted the need for greater cooperation to implement the ASEAN-India Joint Declaration for Cooperation to Combat International Terrorism that was adopted in October 2003 in Bali, Indonesia.
14. We noted India's proposals to further extend cooperation in the field of healthcare, including: (i) making basic drugs available at low cost to public health systems; and (ii) developing a framework of cooperation in traditional medicine. We looked forward to increased cooperation between ASEAN and India in addressing the threat of avian influenza. We also noted that India would host an international conference on avian influenza in December 2007 in New Delhi, India.
15. We expressed our appreciation for India's contribution of US$1 million to operationalise the ASEAN-India Science & Technology Development Fund. The Fund would intensify research and development cooperation in science and information technology, and enable ASEAN to tap India's expertise in those fields.
16. We emphasised human resource development as another important area of cooperation to help narrow the development gap. The ASEAN Leaders expressed their appreciation to India for institutionalising the Special Course for Diplomats from ASEAN Countries, as well as for India's establishment of Entrepreneur Development Centres and Centres for English Language Training in Cambodia, Laos, Myanmar and Viet Nam. We also looked forward to the implementation of the ASEAN-India project on education fairs.
17. We underscored the importance of encouraging people-to-people exchanges to promote mutual understanding. We recalled PM Manmohan Singh's proposal at the 5th ASEAN-India Summit in Cebu, January 2007, to invite 100 students from ASEAN Member Countries to experience the sights and sounds of modern and ancient India, and looked forward to the visit that would be conducted in December this year.

18. We noted India's proposal to establish a special programme for regular exchanges among our parliamentarians and tasked our officials to follow up on the idea. We also noted Malaysia's proposal to explore innovative ways to encourage film production houses in ASEAN and India to jointly produce movies to promote our culture and historical background.

Source: http://www.aseansec.org/21133.htm
Accessed date: 24 January 2009
Publisher: ASEAN Secretariat
Country: Jakarta
Date of Publication: 2007

# CHAPTER 33

# CHAIRMAN'S STATEMENT, 15$^{TH}$ ASEAN REGIONAL FORUM

....

## OVERVIEW OF THE ARF PROCESS

4. The Ministers reaffirmed the importance of the ARF as the main multilateral political and security forum in the region, and reiterated their support for ASEAN as the primary driving force of the ARF. They encouraged the continued cooperation and contribution of all the ARF participants in moving the ARF process forward to the next stage of its development. The Ministers also agreed that confidence building and preventive diplomacy should be mutually reinforcing and parallel processes.
5. The Ministers noted with satisfaction the significant progress of the ARF and the role that it has played in enhancing political and security dialogue and cooperation as well as confidence building in the Asia-Pacific region. While acknowledging the importance of the basic principles of decision-making by consensus and non-interference, the Ministers agreed that the ARF should undertake more concrete cooperation to address both traditional and non-traditional security challenges confronting the region.
6. The Ministers recognised that the challenges facing the Asia Pacific region are becoming more complex and inter-related and require greater regional cooperation. Given the wide range of issues involved, such as counter terrorism, non-proliferation, disaster relief, maritime security, avian and pandemic influenza, human and drugs trafficking, the Ministers agreed on the need for the ARF to strengthen its efforts and carefully consider how to focus on those issues most relevant to its mandate, capabilities and membership.

## HIGHLIGHTS OF DISCUSSIONS ON REGIONAL AND INTERNATIONAL SECURITY ISSUES

7. The Ministers expressed their condolences to Myanmar and China over the loss of lives and devastation caused by Cyclone Nargis and the earthquakes in Sichuan, China. The Ministers noted with satisfaction that the ASEAN

Humanitarian Task Force had effectively delivered humanitarian assistance to the victims and survivors of Cyclone Nargis. This first ASEAN-led mechanism involving ASEAN Member States individually and collectively, as well as the United Nations and the international community, had brought positive results.

8. Recognising that many of the ARF countries are in a region prone to natural disasters, the Ministers emphasised the need for the forum to intensify cooperation in the areas of emergency preparedness, disaster relief and management, rehabilitation and recovery including with existing mechanisms and the United Nations. They agreed that there should be further training, technical assistance and coordination among ARF participants in advance of disasters. The Ministers considered the following areas of cooperation:

   a) The Ministers called for in greater civil-military coordination for major, multinational disaster responses through training, information sharing, and multinational exercises. They recognised that military assets and personnel, in full support and not in place of civilian responses, have played an increasingly important role in regional disaster responses.
   b) The Ministers instructed Senior Officials to continue work on developing the ARF Strategic Guidance for Humanitarian Assistance and Disaster Relief. Along with the General Guidelines on Disaster Relief Cooperation adopted at the 14$^{th}$ ARF, these operational procedures will facilitate better understanding and cooperation among the relief agencies of ARF participants.
   c) The Ministers tasked the Co-Chairs of the ARF ISM on Disaster Relief to work with ARF participants to draw up an ARF disaster relief Workplan aimed at coordinating ARF-wide or sub-regional training for disaster preparedness, and to explore the feasibility of an ARF humanitarian assistance military and civil defence assets template that could be utilised for disaster relief. This should be bilateral, voluntary, and only a tool that could be called upon for use between interested affected and assisting states as needed.
   d) The Minister also endorsed the proposal by the Philippines and the US to conduct an ARF Disaster Relief Exercise, termed Voluntary Demonstration of Response (VDR), in the next ARF Inter-Sessional year. The Philippines and the US have initiated discussions on potential sites and dates, identified logistical procedures and requirements, and draft proposed rules of participation.

9. In undertaking disaster relief cooperation, the Ministers agreed that several basic principles should continue to apply. These included the principle that the

affected country has the primary responsibility to respond to the humanitarian needs of its people following natural disasters occurring within its territory in a prompt and effective manner; where needed, the affected country should facilitate humanitarian assistance from other countries and international organizations to achieve the overall objective of coordinated, timely and effective disaster management and relief based on identified needs; and that external assistance should be provided in response to a request from the affected country, and the disaster relief efforts should be under its overall coordination.

10. The Ministers welcomed the convening of the informal meeting of the Foreign Ministers of the Six-Party Talks at the sidelines of the 15th ARF. They reiterated their support for the Six-Party Talks toward the verifiable denuclearization of the Korean Peninsula and the eventual normalisation of the relations between the relevant Six Party members through the full implementation of the Joint Statement of 19 September 2005. They welcomed the submission of the declaration by the DPRK on its nuclear programs and emphasised the importance of the early establishment of an effective verification and monitoring mechanism. They expressed their hope that the recent progress would contribute to an expedited completion of the Second-Phase actions.
11. The Ministers also emphasised the importance of addressing the issue of humanitarian and people concerns of the international community.

....

15. The Ministers expressed their concern over the continued danger of terrorism, and reaffirmed their commitment to countering it. They underlined the importance of inter-cultural and inter-civilisational dialogue in combating ideology of terrorism and called for greater involvement of civil society, private sector as well as mass media into its development. The Ministers also advocated active cooperation between the ARF and other international and regional organisations in fighting terrorism and transnational organised crime.

....

## REVIEW OF ACTIVITIES OF THE CURRENT INTER-SESSIONAL YEAR (AUGUST 2007–JULY 2008)

....

## PROGRAMME OF WORK FOR THE NEXT INTER-SESSIONAL YEAR

....

## FUTURE DIRECTION OF THE ARF PROCESS

32. The Ministers agreed to institute the ASEAN Vice-Chair as the ARF Vice-Chair. Accordingly, Thailand was appointed as the first ARF Vice-Chair at the 15th ARF. Subsequently, Thailand (incoming ASEAN Chair) will serve as ARF Chair and Vietnam (incoming ASEAN Vice-Chair) as ARF Vice-Chair from July 2008–December 2009.
33. The Ministers adopted the Singapore Declaration on the 15th ARF, which reaffirmed their individual and collective commitment to build upon the achievements of the ARF and strengthen dialogue and cooperation in existing and new areas to maintain and promote regional peace and security.
34. The Ministers had a comprehensive discussion on the Paper on the Review of the ARF, which provided a stocktake on the forum's progress and achievements, and outlined its future direction. The Ministers adopted the recommendations as contained in the Review of the ARF, including the need to strengthen the role of all ARF participants; enhance practical cooperation; maintain the moratorium on membership; focus on concrete areas of cooperation; enhance the role of the ARF Chair and the ARF Unit, develop an ARF Vision Statement, standardise the format of the voluntary Annual Security outlook, enhance cooperation with Track II organisations; and improve the ARF's operating mechanisms. The Ministers tasked the Senior Officials to implement the recommendations and report on the progress at the next ARF Ministerial.

....

39. The Ministers emphasised the need to continue strengthening ties with other regional and international security organisations as well as linkages between Track I and Track II. In this regard, the Ministers welcomed the participation of Track II and regional and international organisations in ARF meetings, where appropriate, as they could value add and enhance discussions. In this context, the Ministers also noted the CSCAP Memorandum on Human Trafficking, and instructed the ISM on CTTC to consider the recommendations put forth in the Memorandum.

....

Source: http://www.aseansec.org/21816.htm
Accessed date: 3 March 2009
Publisher: ASEAN Secretariat
Country: Jakarta
Date of Publication: 2008

# CHAPTER 34

# CO-CHAIRS' STATEMENT OF THE 4TH ASEAN-CANADA DIALOGUE

### Ottawa, Canada, 10–11 May 2007

1. The 4th ASEAN-Canada Dialogue was held in Ottawa, Canada on 10–11 May 2007. The Meeting was attended by representatives of ASEAN Member Countries, Canada and the ASEAN Secretariat.

....

5. ASEAN briefed Canada on the outcomes of the 12th ASEAN Summit and 2nd East Asia Summit (EAS) held in January 2007 in Cebu, Philippines, in particular, the ASEAN Declaration on the Protection and Promotion of the Rights of Migrant Workers, the Cebu Declaration on the Acceleration of the Establishment of an ASEAN Community by 2015, Declaration on the Blueprint of the ASEAN Charter and the on-going work of the High Level Task Force to draft the ASEAN Charter in time for the 13th ASEAN Summit in Singapore in November 2007. Canada welcomed the positive developments in ASEAN, and supported ASEAN's efforts towards narrowing the development gap, strengthening regional integration and establishing an ASEAN Community by 2015. Canada welcomed ASEAN to play a central role in the emerging regional architecture in East Asia and Asia-Pacific.

....

7. Canada briefed ASEAN on the results achieved to date under the auspices of the 1st ASEAN-Canada Joint Cooperation Work Plan (2005–07), notably the signing of the Joint Declaration for Cooperation to Combat International Terrorism at the Post Ministerial Conference in Kuala Lumpur, July 2006, and that Canada is sharing counter terrorism capacity building expertise in many countries throughout the region. In addition, effective collaboration has occurred in the following key areas:

   - Fighting disease: Canada funds $15 million for the Canada-Asia Regional Emerging Infectious Diseases project, implemented by the Public Health Agency of Canada and the World Health Organization, to reduce the threat of emerging infectious diseases in Southeast Asia and China. In support of the objective of strengthening Canada-ASEAN cooperation in international fora, Canada also has signed an agreement with the WHO regional offices to implement the Asia Pacific Strategy on Emerging Diseases, and works with various ASEAN countries to implement the UN Regional Strategy on mobility and HIV vulnerability.

- Promoting human rights: Canada is providing $1.7 million over five years to the Working Group for an ASEAN Human Rights Mechanism in support of ASEAN's human rights objectives to promote and protect the rights of women, children and migrant workers in the region as outlined in 1.1.4 of the Vientiane Action Programme. This support is part of a $9 million project named SEARCH which is supporting the Working Group, Forum-Asia and the Coordinated Mekong Ministerial Initiative Against Trafficking.
- Supporting communities: Canada provided $95,000 for the 5th ASEAN People's Assembly, held in December 2006 in the Philippines, in support of ASEAN's goal of building a people-centred community.
- Promoting gender equality: Canada is working with the ASEAN Secretariat to conduct regional analysis and prepare the third regional report on women's advancement in ASEAN countries.
- Fostering innovative information technology: The ASEAN Collaboratory, a three-year, $800,000 project established by the ASEAN Foundation and Canada's International Development Research Centre, promotes innovative "ICT for development" applications.

8. The Meeting noted that Canada is a long-standing development partner in the region. Canada briefed ASEAN on the Canadian International Development Agency's Southeast Asia Regional Program and noted that the Regional Program focuses on strengthening regional institutions, networks and organizations working on trans-boundary issues or development issues that are more effectively dealt with at a regional level. Canada supports ASEAN goals as outlined in the Vientiane Action Programme, the Initiative for ASEAN Integration (IAI), and Vision 2020, and will consider proper ways and means to collaborate with ASEAN in realizing the objectives of these important programs. Canada welcomes and hopes to attend the 2nd IAI Development Cooperation Forum, to be held in Ha Noi, 12–13 June 2007.

....

14. The Meeting commended Canada for its prompt and continuous assistance to the survivors of regional disasters. The Meeting viewed that, to deal with natural disasters, it was necessary to strengthen regional and global efforts in disaster risk reduction and response. ASEAN expressed its interest in cooperating with Canada in the areas of research and studies on these topics and would welcome the opportunity for ASEAN students to study weather forecasting and natural disasters. Canada stressed the importance of a disaster risk-reduction

approach and of working through the multilateral system, particularly the UN International Strategy for Disaster Reduction and the Hyogo Framework for Action.

15. The Meeting discussed the importance of the environment and natural resources, particularly recognizing the importance of these to the livelihoods of people in Southeast Asia, as well as for the broader global commons.

....

18. The Meeting noted that to effectively address HIV/AIDS, a priority should be placed on public education and renewed emphasis on prevention, anti-retro viral treatment as well as care and support to people living with HIV/AIDS. The Meeting welcomed continued and improved regional and cross-border approaches to HIV reduction, including addressing the vulnerabilities of migrant and mobile populations.
19. The Meeting emphasized the importance of promoting closer cooperation to deal with and prevent the spread of communicable diseases such as avian influenza, including through the training of personnel, establishment of information sharing systems and coordination of national pandemic preparedness plans. Canada commended efforts of countries in the region to overcome this disease, including identifying ways to develop an enhanced response.
20. ASEAN informed Canada on its economic outlook, trade and economic relations with trading partners, and developments in its regional economic integration processes, both internally and externally. Canada welcomed the strengthening of economic and trade cooperation under the framework of ASEAN Free Trade Agreement (AFTA) and advancing economic partnership with its other Dialogue Partners through the various FTAs. Canada informed ASEAN of its economic outlook, trade and economic relations with trading partners, particularly under the NAFTA. ASEAN and Canada exchanged views on measures to promote enhanced economic cooperation and closer commercial relations, particularly through the proposed Trade and Investment Framework Arrangement (TIFA) under the auspices of the ASEAN-Canada Senior Economic Officials Meeting (SEOM). The Meeting expressed the hope that such an arrangement could be finalized at the 3rd SEOM, which will be held in Canada in the fall of 2007, and that it could serve as a starting point for further discussion on trade expansion.

....

22. The Meeting recognized the role of the Asia Pacific Economic Cooperation (APEC) in promoting prosperity and fostering economic cooperation in the region and looked forward to the successful outcome of the APEC Leaders Meeting to be held in Sydney, Australia in September 2007. The Meeting welcomed the desire of ASEAN Member Countries who are non-APEC members

to join the forum when the moratorium is lifted, and took note of the proposed concept of a Free Trade Area of the Asia-Pacific discussed at the November 2006 meeting in Ha Noi.

....

26. ASEAN and Canada also undertook to explore developing a Declaration on Enhanced Partnership and a comprehensive Plan of Action.

....

Source: http://www.aseansec.org/20689.htm
Accessed date: 2 October 2008
Publisher: ASEAN Secretariat
Country: Jakarta
Date of Publication: 2007

# CHAPTER 35

# JOINT DECLARATION ON ASEAN-AUSTRALIA COMPREHENSIVE PARTNERSHIP

**WE**, the Foreign Ministers of Brunei Darussalam, the Kingdom of Cambodia, the Republic of Indonesia, the Lao People's Democratic Republic, Malaysia, the Union of Myanmar, the Republic of the Philippines, the Republic of Singapore, the Kingdom of Thailand and the Socialist Republic of Viet Nam and the Minister for Foreign Affairs of Australia gathered in Manila, Philippines, on 1 August 2007;

**NOTING** with satisfaction that since 1974 when Australia became the first Dialogue Partner of ASEAN, relations between ASEAN and Australia have grown from strength to strength, and have been nurtured through the annual ASEAN Post Ministerial Conferences, the ASEAN-Australia Forum as well as other relevant fora and further strengthened by the ASEAN-Australia and New Zealand Commemorative Summit;

**RECALLING** the Joint Declaration of the Leaders at the ASEAN-Australia and New Zealand Commemorative Summit, signed in Vientiane on 30 November 2004, the ASEAN-Australia Joint Declaration for Cooperation to Combat International Terrorism in 2004 and the accession of Australia to the Treaty of Amity and Cooperation in Southeast Asia in 2005 which reflected Australia's firm commitment to the promotion of peace and stability in the region;

**CONVINCED** that establishing a comprehensive ASEAN-Australia and New Zealand Free Trade Agreement (AANZFTA) would further deepen economic integration between ASEAN and Australia, promote growth and development, improve living standards of the people throughout the region, and provide a platform for economic engagement in the long term; WELCOMING the breadth, maturity and continuing progress of ASEAN-Australia cooperation, on political and security, economic, socio-cultural and development issues;

**ACKNOWLEDGING** Australia's significant and on-going efforts to support ASEAN's development and integration as envisaged in ASEAN Vision 2020 and the Declaration of ASEAN Concord II (Bali Concord II) through development cooperation both bilaterally and regionally, including the ASEAN-Australia

Development Cooperation Program (AADCP) and Australia's contribution to the ASEAN Development Fund (ADF);

**REAFFIRMING** the important role of ASEAN and Australia in maintaining sustainable peace and security in the region and reiterating Australia's and ASEAN's commitment to working together in this regard;

**REALIZING** that the multifaceted challenges and opportunities arising from globalization, regional integration and integration within ASEAN provide grounds for reinforcing on-going ASEAN-Australia cooperation and expanding into new areas of mutual interest and enhancing people-to-people contacts;

**SHARING** common values of justice, democracy, social equality, good governance, human rights and caring societies that are the foundation for lasting peace, stability, progress, and prosperity according to the Charter of the United Nations;

**ADHERING** to the principles and purposes of the Charter of the United Nations and other universally recognised principles of international law;

**REAFFIRMING** our faith in, and respect for, each other's independence, sovereignty, territorial integrity, the principles of non-interference in the internal affairs of other states, renunciation of threat or use of force, peaceful settlement of disputes, mutual respect and mutual benefit as enshrined in the Treaty of Amity and Cooperation in Southeast Asia;

**EXPRESSING** desire to continue working closely together on the basis of the friendship, goodwill and understanding for the realization of an ASEAN Community, comprising ASEAN Security Community, ASEAN Economic Community and ASEAN Socio-Cultural Community; and reducing the development gap within ASEAN through the implementation of the Vientiane Action Programme (VAP) and its appropriate successor programmes as well as the Initiative for ASEAN Integration (IAI);

## ASEAN AND AUSTRALIA HEREBY

Mutually decide to launch an ASEAN-Australia Comprehensive Partnership that is action-oriented, forward-looking and encompassing political and security cooperation, economic cooperation, socio-cultural cooperation and development cooperation at regional and international levels including, but not limited to, the following elements.

## Political and security cooperation

1. Engage in dialogue and support efforts to realise the ASEAN Security Community in order to help promote peace, stability, security, development and prosperity in the region;
2. Promote closer cooperation in order to address, prevent and combat transnational crimes, including terrorism, .... cyber crime and international economic crime by undertaking joint activities based on existing agreements and mechanisms;
3. Also collaborate to address other crimes, such as corruption, .... and illegal activities relating to fishing and encroachment and destruction of forest resources;
4. Cooperate in areas of disarmament, arms control and non-proliferation of Weapons of Mass Destruction (WMD);
5. Strengthen the various regional frameworks and fora, including the ASEAN Regional Forum (ARF), the East Asia Summit (EAS) and the Asia-Pacific Economic Cooperation (APEC), and ensuring their complementarity in advancing the common interests of ASEAN and Australia in promoting stability and security in the Asia-Pacific region, with ASEAN as the primary driving force in the ARF and the EAS;
6. Cooperate in multilateral frameworks, including the United Nations;

## Economic cooperation

7. Enhance cooperation in support of deeper economic integration between ASEAN and Australia and the realization of an ASEAN Economic Community within 2015;
8. Promote favourable environments for trade, investment and other economic linkages between ASEAN and Australia, which will help sustain and boost economic growth in ASEAN and Australia;
9. Fully commit to work towards concluding the negotiations of the AANZFTA by 2007 as well as to ensure full implementation of the Agreement thereafter;
10. Enhance cooperation in areas of mutual economic interest;
11. Strengthen cooperation in multilateral frameworks concerning regional and international trade and economy, including the World Trade Organization (WTO), APEC and EAS to ensure equitable benefits from globalization and economic liberalization and, towards this end, urge WTO Members to restart and complete the Doha Round negotiations as soon as possible;
12. Promote and strengthen financial cooperation in areas of mutual interest;

13. Support the early accession of the Lao PDR to the WTO;
14. Promote greater interaction between the private as well as public sectors in ASEAN and Australia and recognize the pivotal role of the business community;

## Socio-cultural cooperation

15. Enhance cooperation in support of mutual socio-cultural goals, such as by addressing poverty, equity, health and other social impacts of economic growth and integration; preserving and promoting the region's cultural heritage and cultural identity;
16. Strengthen collaboration to address the threat of communicable and emerging infectious diseases, including HIV/AIDS, SARS, and avian influenza at sub-regional, regional and global levels;
17. Foster greater cooperation in disaster preparedness, mitigation and emergency response as well as rehabilitation and reconstruction;
18. Promote closer cooperation in environmental conservation, including transboundary environmental pollution, and sustainable natural resources management;
19. Continue cooperation in science and technology in areas of mutual interest;
20. Enhance cooperation in education such as by encouraging and facilitating student and academic exchanges;
21. Promote people-to-people contacts, in particular among youths and the media, as well as interfaith dialogues and exchanges of cultural activities in order to further improve understanding between ASEAN and Australia;
22. Strengthen networking and interactions with and among private sectors, civil societies, experts and scholars in order to tap their expertise, initiatives and ideas, particularly with regard to policy planning and socio-economic development;

## Development cooperation

23. Further support, through the AADCP and other current and future development cooperation programmes, the foregoing as pillars of the VAP and its successor programme as well as the IAI aiming to alleviate poverty, to narrow the development gap and to promote sustainable development within ASEAN; and

## Follow-up

24. Call on ASEAN and Australian senior officials to coordinate with their relevant agencies to develop a Plan of Action to implement the ASEAN-Australia Comprehensive Partnership and annually review and report its progress to the PMC Session with Australia.

**Done** at Manila, Philippines, this First Day of August in the Year Two Thousand and Seven in two original copies in the English Language.

For Brunei Darussalam:

**MOHAMED BOLKIAH**
Minister of Foreign Affairs and Trade

For the Kingdom of Cambodia:

**HOR NAMHONG**
Deputy Prime Minister and Minister of Foreign Affairs
and International Cooperation

For the Republic of Indonesia:

**DR. N. HASSAN WIRAJUDA**
Minister for Foreign Affairs

For the Lao People's Democratic Republic:

**DR. THONGLOUN SISOULITH**
Deputy Prime Minister and Minister of Foreign Affairs

For Malaysia:

**DATO' SERI SYED HAMID ALBAR**
Minister of Foreign Affairs

For the Union of Myanmar:

**NYAN WIN**
Minister for Foreign Affairs

For the Republic of the Philippines:

**ALBERTO G. ROMULO**
Secretary of Foreign Affairs

For the Republic of Singapore:

**GEORGE YONG-BOON YEO**
Minister for Foreign Affairs

For the Kingdom of Thailand:

**NITYA PIBULSONGGRAM**
Minister of Foreign Affairs

For the Socialist Republic of Viet Nam:

**LE CONG PHUNG**
First Deputy Minister of Foreign Affairs

For Australia:

**ALEXANDER DOWNER**
Minister for Foreign Affairs

Source: http://www.aseansec.org/20786.htm
Accessed date: 2 October 2008
Publisher: ASEAN Secretariat
Country: Jakarta
Date of Publication: 2007

# CHAPTER 36

# CO-CHAIRS STATEMENT ASEAN-CANADA DIALOGUE

**Bandar Seri Begawan, 30–31 March 2004**

1. The ASEAN-Canada Dialogue was held on March 30–31, 2004 in Bandar Seri Begawan, Brunei Darussalam. The Meeting was attended by delegations from the governments of all ten ASEAN member countries and Canada, and the Secretary General of ASEAN, His Excellency Ong Keng Yong.

....

5. Canada welcomed the outcomes of the 9$^{th}$ ASEAN Summit, ASEAN Plus Three Summit and the ASEAN Plus One Summits with China, India, Japan and the ROK held in Bali, in October 2003. It particularly welcomed the establishment of the ASEAN Community with the objective of an integrated ASEAN in the political and security, economic and socio-cultural field. Canada also welcomed ASEAN's efforts to strengthen its relations with its Dialogue Partners such as through the accession of China and India to the Treaty of Amity and Cooperation in Southeast Asia (TAC), as well as the establishment of the ASEAN-India Framework Agreement on Comprehensive Economic Cooperation and the Framework on ASEAN Japan Comprehensive Economic Partnership. Canada expressed its commitment to work closely with ASEAN in support of its various initiatives particularly in implementing the Initiative for ASEAN Integration (IAI) and the realization of the ASEAN Community.

....

7. The Meeting had an extensive exchange of views on the future direction of ASEAN-Canada relations. ASEAN acknowledged that since the establishment of the dialogue relations, cooperation between both sides has developed very significantly contributing to the region's growth. ASEAN welcomed Canada's keen interest to have an enhanced dialogue with ASEAN. ASEAN affirmed its desire for a mutually rewarding ASEAN-Canada dialogue relationship. The Meeting agreed that there is considerable scope for cooperation

and therefore it is timely for the dialogue relations to move forward and explore ways to revitalize it.

8. ASEAN discussed future areas of cooperation including Canada's proposal for cooperation activities with ASEAN such as the idea of developing a trilateral development cooperation mechanism. The Meeting was of the view that the proposed trilateral cooperation would contribute to ASEAN's integration efforts including implementing the Work Plan on the Initiative of ASEAN Integration (IAI) and in the promotion of sub-regional growth areas. In this regard, ASEAN welcomed Canada's proposal to organise a Symposium to further develop the idea. Both sides agreed that cooperation should move forward in the spirit of dialogue, inclusiveness and respect.

....

14. The Meeting exchanged views on transnational issues, including transnational crimes such as human trafficking, money laundering and illicit trafficking of drugs, as well as transnational health threats such as HIV/AIDS, SARS and Avian Influenza.
15. The Meeting agreed to work together to address the problem of illicit drugs from both the supply and demand sides, taking into account ASEAN's goal to make the region free from drugs by 2015.

....

17. Canada commended regional efforts in addressing the Avian Influenza outbreak such as the Ministerial Meeting on the Current Poultry Disease Situation in Bangkok on 28 January 2004 and the ASEAN-China Special Meeting on Highly Pathogenic Avian Influenza (HPAI) Control in Beijing on 3 March 2004. ASEAN also expressed appreciation to Canada for its financial support to the World Health Organization's regional programs to combat SARS. The Meeting underlined the need to strengthen cooperation among the health and other relevant agencies to promote and facilitate the exchange and sharing of information, as well as strengthen the early warning system to deal with and prevent the spread of SARS and other communicable diseases.
18. The Meeting stressed the need for closer economic cooperation between ASEAN and Canada, which would contribute positively to the economic growth of both sides. The Meeting therefore welcomed Canada's proposal for enhancing economic cooperation between ASEAN and Canada. In this regard,

the Meeting welcomed the convening of the workshop on "Regionalisation in the 21st Century: A Canada-ASEAN Dialogue As Part of Opening Up of New Cross-Pacific Exchanges" held at the ASEAN Secretariat on 9 March 2004.

19. Canada welcomed the positive developments made by ASEAN in moving towards greater economic integration, both internally through AFTA and externally via comprehensive economic cooperation and partnership with its dialogue partners. Canada commended ASEAN's decisions to establish an ASEAN Economic Community, which aims to integrate the economies of ASEAN Member Countries into a single market and production base.
20. The Meeting noted that trade and investment between ASEAN and Canada had steadily increased over recent years and agreed that there is great potential to further expand and deepen their scope in the near future. The Meeting agreed to increase greater interaction between senior economic officials from ASEAN and Canada. The Meeting was also of the view that the sectoral experts from both regions could also increase their collaboration such as in the areas of customs, animal husbandry and sanitary and phytosanitary.

....

22. The meeting encouraged the participation of the Canadian Private Sector at the ASEAN Business Investment Summit in Vientiane, November 2004 as a means to promote business-to-business contacts between ASEAN and Canada.
23. The Meeting also exchanged views on WTO issues, and noted the importance of the Doha Round and of concluding the negotiations by the agreed deadline. The Meeting noted the results of the WTO Ministerial Conference in Cancun and concurred that to move the process forward, all Member Countries need to exercise flexibility and political will so as to re-energize the stalled multilateral negotiations towards the successful conclusion of the Doha Development Agenda. The Meeting also expressed continuing support for the early accessions of Lao PDR and Vietnam to the WTO.

....

25. The next ASEAN-Canada Dialogue will be held in Toronto, in April 2005.
26. The Meeting expressed its appreciation to the Government of Brunei Darussalam for its warm hospitality and for the excellent arrangements extended during the Meeting. The Meeting was conducted in a spirit of cooperation and cordiality under the chairmanship of Brunei Darussalam and Canada.

Source: http://www.aseansec.org/16019.htm
Accessed date: 24 February 2009
Publisher: ASEAN Secretariat
Country: Jakarta
Date of Publication: 2004

# CHAPTER 37

# SINGAPORE DECLARATION ON THE 15$^{TH}$ ASEAN REGIONAL FORUM

**Singapore, 24 July 2008**

**WE**, the Ministers of the Member States of the Association of Southeast Asian Nations (ASEAN), Australia, Bangladesh, Canada, People's Republic of China, European Union, India, Japan, Democratic People's Republic of Korea, Republic of Korea, Mongolia, New Zealand, Pakistan, Papua New Guinea, Russian Federation, Sri Lanka, Timor Leste, and the United States of America, on the occasion of the 15th ASEAN Regional Forum (ARF) in Singapore on 24 July 2008;

....

**COGNISANT** that the ARF and its working processes should evolve to ensure that it continues to be the main regional security forum in the Asia-Pacific region;

## HEREBY DECLARE TO:

1. Renew our individual and collective commitment to build upon the achievements of the ARF and strengthen dialogue and cooperation in existing and new areas to promote and maintain regional peace and security;
2. Further the development of appropriate Preventive Diplomacy concepts, in line with our decision in 2005 to move the ARF from the Confidence Building stage to the Preventive Diplomacy phase, while ensuring that future development would continue to be based on the values and roadmap contained in the 1994 ARF Concept Paper, 2001 ARF Concept and Principles of Preventive Diplomacy, and Paper on the Review of the ARF;
3. Strengthen the existing ARF's organisational mechanism, including that of the ARF Chair, Friends of the Chair (FOC), ARF Unit and ARF Fund, through the mobilization of more resources, manpower and expertise;
4. Commit to undertake concrete and practical cooperation to address issues of common interests, with the view to build capacity, develop expertise and enhance coordination in areas that can contribute to the region's collective security objectives;

....

6. Enhance further the engagement between Track I and Track II in the ARF, as well as partnership ties between the ARF and other regional and international organisations particularly by exchanging ideas, experiences and best practices;
7. Promote greater awareness and understanding of the ARF's achievements, and its relevance to people in the ARF region as well as enhance the visibility of the forum, its objectives and activities, in promoting regional peace and security; and
8. Further cooperate to strengthen and develop the ARF, its mandate, and its activities so that the ARF can serve as the premier regional security forum in the Asia-Pacific region.

Adopted in Singapore, this Twenty-Fourth Day of July in the Year Two Thousand and Eight.

Source: http://www.aseansec.org/21822.htm
Accessed date: 8 October 2008
Publisher: ASEAN Secretariat
Country: Jakarta
Date of Publication: 2008

# CHAPTER 38

# JOINT COMMUNIQUE OF THE 41ST ASEAN MINISTERIAL MEETING "ONE ASEAN AT THE HEART OF DYNAMIC ASIA"

**Singapore, 21 July 2008**

## INTRODUCTION

1. We, the Foreign Ministers of the Association of Southeast Asian Nations (ASEAN), met at the 41st ASEAN Ministerial Meeting (AMM) from 20–21 July 2008 in Singapore. His Excellency George Yeo, Minister for Foreign Affairs of Singapore and Chairman of the 41st ASEAN Standing Committee (ASC), chaired the Meeting. We had wide-ranging and productive discussions under the theme of "One ASEAN at the Heart of Dynamic Asia", during which we reaffirmed our common desire and collective commitment to the establishment of an ASEAN Community of peace, stability, prosperity and social progress.
2. His Excellency Lee Hsien Loong, Prime Minister of Singapore, addressed the Opening Ceremony of the 41st AMM. Noting that the celebration of ASEAN's 40th anniversary brought ASEAN closer to the people, Prime Minister Lee underlined that fostering our people's understanding of ASEAN's relevance to their well-being would nurture their sense of belonging to an ASEAN community. This in turn would be critical to our integration efforts.
3. Reviewing the past year under Singapore's Chairmanship of ASEAN, Prime Minister Lee raised two events which he believed would continue to define ASEAN in the years ahead. First, ASEAN's response to Cyclone Nargis demonstrated ASEAN's unity, and showed that ASEAN member countries recognised the responsibilities and obligations of membership. While not perfect, the ASEAN-led tripartite process bridged the gap of trust between the Myanmar authorities and the international community to facilitate the flow of emergency aid to the disaster victims. Only the international community had the capacity to address the effects of Cyclone Nargis, and ASEAN welcomed Myanmar's willingness to continue with the tripartite cooperation.
4. Prime Minister Lee also highlighted that the signing of the Charter would help realize the vision of a vibrant ASEAN Community by improving ASEAN's

record of implementation through a rules-based framework. He stressed that the timely ratification and implementation of the Charter would be a signal of ASEAN's resolve.

5. Prime Minister Lee underscored that ASEAN could not take its relevance as the preferred platform for regional interactions for granted. While ASEAN members may be pre-occupied with pressing domestic issues, it was vital that we continue to move forward on ASEAN cooperation and integration, even if the pace may sometimes vary. A thriving ASEAN would be courted by the major powers as an economic power and valued as a partner for cooperation to deal with larger regional and global issues.
6. Prime Minister Lee also launched the ASEAN Studies Centre in the Institute of Southeast Asian Studies in Singapore. The Centre would work closely with the ASEAN Secretariat to undertake policy research on ASEAN that would help the organisation grow new capabilities, strengthen its institutions, and enhance cooperation among its members.

## BUILDING AN ASEAN COMMUNITY

7. We are pleased with the progress in the implementation of the Leaders' decisions of the 13th ASEAN Summit in Singapore, and agreed to further intensify our integration efforts in all three pillars of the ASEAN Community to establish a people-oriented, caring and sharing ASEAN Community by 2015. We reaffirmed our resolve to pursue more region-wide cooperation programmes and activities geared towards accelerating the ASEAN Community-building process. We also reiterated the importance of maintaining ASEAN's central role in regional processes.

### The ASEAN Charter

8. We stressed our full commitment to the realization of the vision set out in the ASEAN Charter that was signed by our Leaders on the occasion of the 40th Anniversary of ASEAN last November. With our Statement on the ASEAN Charter issued on 21 July 2008, we reaffirmed the commitment by all Member States to ratify the ASEAN Charter by the 14th ASEAN Summit in Bangkok, and pledged to undertake all measures necessary to ensure expeditious implementation of the Charter.
9. We endorsed the Terms of Reference of the Committee of Permanent Representatives to ASEAN. We agreed that each ASEAN Member State would appoint their Permanent Representative to ASEAN at the level of Ambassador in Jakarta with effect from 1 January 2009.

10. We reaffirmed our commitment to the promotion and protection of human rights. We set up the High Level Panel on an ASEAN human rights body, and endorsed its Terms of Reference. We look forward to the High Level Panel's submission of its first draft of the Terms of Reference of an ASEAN human rights body at the 14th ASEAN Summit in December 2008 for our guidance and direction. We noted the reports of the 7th Workshop on ASEAN Regional Human Rights Mechanism in Singapore on 12–13 June 2008 and the Workshop on the Promotion and Protection of Human Rights in Bali on 15–17 May 2008. We further noted the work carried out by the non-governmental Working Group for an ASEAN Human Rights Mechanizm, including the meeting between the open-ended SOM Troika and the Working Group on the sidelines of the 41st AMM with the objective of facilitating the implementation of the activities under the promotion of human rights component of the VAP.
11. We are committed to make ASEAN a more rules-based organization. We established the High Level Legal Experts' Group on Follow Up to the ASEAN Charter and endorsed its Terms of Reference. We look forward to the first draft of recommendations on the legal personality of ASEAN, dispute settlement mechanisms and other legal issues by December 2008.
12. In view of the increase in ASEAN's activities with the coming into force of the ASEAN Charter, we noted the importance of strengthening the ASEAN Secretariat and agreed to provide it with adequate resources. We endorsed the recommendations of our Financial Experts Group. We requested for the Secretary-General to strengthen the Secretariat's internal systems, in particular its Staff Regulations and Financial Rules in order to put in place a more robust system of accountability and financial management. In addition, as one of the measures to strengthen the Secretariat, we agreed that the appointment of two additional Deputy Secretaries-General should be finalized by November 2008. We also tasked our officials to explore the idea of an ASEAN laissez-passer for ASEAN Secretariat staff as a valid travel document among ASEAN Member States.

## Narrowing the development gap and initiative for ASEAN integration

13. We agreed to intensify our cooperation to Narrow the Development Gap (NDG) with a view to supporting ASEAN's integration efforts, which is of paramount importance to ASEAN community-building. This would also help to ensure the equitable economic development of the region and facilitate the

attainment of the Millennium Development Goals (MDGs), which would in turn contribute to the well-being of the peoples of ASEAN. In this regard, we emphasised the key role of the Initiative for ASEAN Integration (IAI) in ASEAN's overall NDG efforts and look forward to the final draft of the 2nd IAI Work Plan for 2009–2015 by December 2008. We also noted with appreciation the support and contributions of ASEAN Member States and external partners to the implementation of the IAI.

14. We support programmes to uplift existing pockets of under-development in all parts of ASEAN, specifically in sub-regional areas including BIMP-EAGA and IMT-GT and Mekong sub-regional frameworks.

## Vientiane Action Programme

15. We welcomed the progress achieved in the implementation of the Vientiane Action Programme (VAP). We tasked our officials to prepare a comprehensive review of the implementation of the Vientiane Action Programme to be undertaken in 2008.
16. Noting the adoption of the ASEAN Economic Community Blueprint at the 13th ASEAN Summit in Singapore last year, and the ongoing work to draft the Blueprints for the ASEAN Political-Security Community and ASEAN Socio-Cultural Community as well as the 2nd IAI Work Plan, we agreed to recommend to the ASEAN Leaders that these documents be issued as part of a declaration at the 14th ASEAN Summit.

## ASEAN POLITICAL-SECURITY COMMUNITY

....

## Treaty of Amity and Cooperation in Southeast Asia

18. We warmly welcome the impending accession by the Democratic People's Republic of Korea (DPRK) to the Treaty of Amity and Cooperation in Southeast Asia (TAC) as a strong signal of the DPRK's commitment to the peace and security of the region. We noted that the continuing interest in the TAC underscores its important role as a key code of conduct governing interstate relations in Southeast Asia. We also called upon other countries, particularly our Dialogue Partners and other interested parties, to consider acceding to the TAC. In this regard, we will continue to work to facilitate the accession of the EU to the TAC in the near future.

## Treaty on the Southeast Asia Nuclear Weapon-Free Zone

19. At the Meeting of the Commission on Southeast Asia Nuclear Weapon-Free Zone (SEANWFZ) in Singapore on 21 July 2008, we welcomed the progress made in the implementation of the Plan of Action adopted by the SEANWFZ Commission in 2007, and reaffirmed the importance of persevering in our efforts to strengthen cooperation to implement the Treaty. We instructed our officials to continue to engage the Nuclear Weapons States, to secure their accession to the SEANWFZ Protocol as soon as possible. We elected Thailand as the incoming Chair of the Commission.

....

## ASEAN Regional Forum

22. We reaffirmed the role of ASEAN as the primary driving force of the ASEAN Regional Forum (ARF) process and the ARF as the primary forum in enhancing political and security dialogue and cooperation in the Asia-Pacific region. We agreed that the ARF should undertake concrete cooperation to address the increasingly complex and multi-faceted security challenges confronting the region, through cooperation in areas such as counter-terrorism and transnational crime, non-proliferation and disarmament, maritime security, disaster relief, and combating communicable diseases. We also looked forward to the discussions at the upcoming 15th ARF on 24 July 2008, in particular, to have a comprehensive review of the ARF process and consider its future direction.

## ASEAN Maritime Forum

23. We noted the Concept Paper for the Establishment of the ASEAN Maritime Forum, which could provide a platform for comprehensive deliberations and dialogues among relevant ASEAN bodies on maritime issues. We noted the offer by the Government of Indonesia to host the First Meeting of the ASEAN Maritime Forum in 2009.

....

## ASEAN ECONOMIC COMMUNITY

25. We underscored ASEAN's commitment to establish a single market and production base characterised by a competitive economic region, with equitable economic development and one that is fully integrated into the global economy.

26. We welcomed the ongoing implementation of the ASEAN Economic Community (AEC) Blueprint, which was adopted by the Leaders at the 13th ASEAN Summit in Singapore in November 2007, and the imminent launch of the AEC Scorecard, a monitoring mechanism intended to help ensure compliance with the provisions of the AEC Blueprint. We noted the significant progress made in the areas of trade in goods, services and investment. We viewed these developments with satisfaction, as proof of ASEAN's commitment to maintain and strengthen its credibility and effectiveness, by transforming itself into a rules-based organization.
27. We welcomed the progress in negotiations by the Transport Sectoral on the implementing Multilateral Agreements (MAs) for the Roadmap for the Integration of Air Travel Sector (RIATS). We welcomed the Joint Ministerial Statement of the 13th ASEAN Transport Ministers' Meeting in Singapore in November 2007, and looked forward to the signing of the ASEAN Multilateral Agreement on the Full Liberalisation of Air Freight Services and the Multilateral Agreement on Air Services by the ASEAN Transport Ministers.

## ASEAN SOCIO-CULTURAL COMMUNITY

28. We underscored the importance of the ASEAN Socio-Cultural Community (ASCC) to address the region's aspiration to further improve the well-being of its peoples through investing in human resource development, enhancing food security and safety, protecting the environment, protecting people from natural disasters and infectious diseases, and pursuing cooperative activities that are people-oriented. The ASCC shall lay the foundation for greater understanding and good neighbourliness, and build a shared sense of identity and responsibility in ASEAN. We were pleased with the progress made in the drafting of the ASCC Blueprint and looked forward to the adoption of an action-oriented and substantive document by the 14th ASEAN Summit in Bangkok, Thailand.
29. We expressed our satisfaction at the fast-growing people-to-people linkages, especially among our youths, as we continue to build deeper understanding, friendship and mutual respect among our countries. We commended the efforts and initiatives of the ASEAN Member States in promoting greater ASEAN awareness and strengthening existing cultural links through projects like the "ASEAN Quest" video game, the "Trail of Civilization" and the "Best of ASEAN Performing Arts", which aim to regularly showcase ASEAN's best arts and cultural performances to regional and international audiences. We looked forward to the celebration of ASEAN Day on 8 August by all ASEAN Member States.

30. We further stressed the need to integrate education priorities into ASEAN's development agenda, and hone the skills and talents of our peoples to boost the region's overall competitiveness, in order to reap the fruits of globalization.
31. We expressed our satisfaction with the progress made in the implementation of the Guidelines for the Provision of Emergency Assistance by ASEAN Missions in Third Countries to Nationals of ASEAN Member States in Crisis Situations, following our July 2006 Statement on this issue.

## Energy, environment, climate change and sustainable development

32. We stressed the need to address the issues of energy security, sustainable agriculture and environmental protection in a comprehensive manner. We expressed our appreciation for the efforts undertaken by the relevant ASEAN Sectoral Bodies to follow up on the outcomes of the Leaders' discussions at the 13th ASEAN Summit and related meetings on the theme of "Energy, Environment, Climate Change and Sustainable Development". We encouraged the relevant ASEAN Sectoral Bodies to develop concrete programmes and activities to implement measures and enhance international and regional cooperation to combat transboundary environmental pollution, including haze pollution, through, among other things, capacity building, enhancing public awareness, strengthening law enforcement, promoting environmentally sustainable practices, as well as combating illegal logging and its associated illegal trade.

## Disaster management

33. We are pleased to note that the ASEAN Humanitarian Task Force had effectively delivered humanitarian assistance to the victims and survivors of Cyclone Nargis. This first ASEAN-led mechanism involving ASEAN Member States individually and collectively, as well as the United Nations and the international community, had brought positive results. The post-cyclone emergency relief operations have underlined the urgency for ASEAN to further strengthen cooperation in mitigating large-scale disaster situations. As we strengthen our collective efforts in disaster management, we should maintain credibility by ensuring more open access and accountability. We acknowledged ASEAN Member States' contributions and sharing of experiences from the post-tsunami relief and recovery efforts in extending humanitarian assistance to Myanmar. We also expressed appreciation to the ASEAN Humanitarian Task Force and the Tripartite Core Group for their dedication

and hard work in discharging their tasks. We welcomed the release of the Post-Nargis Joint Assessment (PONJA) report. We agreed that the ASEAN-led mechanism should continue for another year until 2009 to support the humanitarian effort in Myanmar.

34. Recognizing Southeast Asia as one of the most natural disaster prone regions, we reaffirmed our commitment to intensify our cooperation as well as with other countries and international organizations in the areas of disaster relief and management. In this regard, we called for the full ratification of the ASEAN Agreement on Disaster Management and Emergency Response (AADMER), which provides for effective regional mechanisms to mitigate the impact of disasters in the region. We also looked forward to the operationalization of the ASEAN Standby Arrangements and Standard Operating Procedures and commended the efforts of the interim ASEAN Coordinating Centre for Humanitarian Assistance on Disaster Management (AHA Centre) in Jakarta. We called upon the relevant Sectoral Bodies and the ASEAN Secretariat to work towards the establishment of a fully functional AHA Centre.

....

## EXTERNAL RELATIONS

37. We agreed to continue strengthening ASEAN's relations with our external partners. We underscored the importance of further deepening and broadening our cooperation in various fields with our Dialogue Partners as a critical part of ASEAN's efforts to build a closely integrated community. In particular, we looked forward to the appointment of ambassadors to ASEAN from Dialogue Partners.
38. We agreed that our cooperation with Dialogue Partners should focus on key areas such as energy and food security, **....** poverty reduction, sustainable forest management and climate change, communicable diseases and disaster relief and response.
39. We reiterated our commitment to push ahead with the FTA negotiations with Australia and New Zealand, the EU and India. We also welcomed the progress made in the ongoing negotiations on the investment agreements with China and the Republic of Korea, and looked forward to the early entry into force of the ASEAN-Japan Comprehensive Economic Partnership Agreement. Besides economic benefits, the FTAs between ASEAN and its Dialogue Partners are also strategic linkages that will bind our regions even closer together.
40. We agreed that we should conclude as soon as possible the MOU on the Second Phase of the ASEAN-Australia Development Cooperation

Programme (AADCP II). We took note that the AADCP II would focus on strengthening the ASEAN Secretariat's institutional capacity to effectively implement its mandate as well as supporting regional mechanisms and capacity for implementation of ASEAN Economic Community Blueprint activities.

41. We looked forward to the finalization of the MOU on the establishment of the ASEAN-China Centre to further deepen our cooperation in all areas.
42. We looked forward to the launch of the ASEAN-Korea Centre to further enhance our cooperation in the areas of trade, investment, tourism and cultural exchange by end 2008. We supported the proposal to convene an ASEAN-ROK Commemorative Summit in 2009 to celebrate the 20th anniversary of relations between ASEAN and the Republic of Korea.
43. We also looked forward to adopting the Roadmap on the Implementation of the ASEAN-Russia Comprehensive Programme of Action, at this year's ASEAN Post Ministerial Session with Russia. We expressed confidence that this Roadmap will help to promote mutual understanding, increase people-to-people interaction and facilitate cooperation projects between ASEAN and Russia.
44. We noted the launch of the ASEAN Development Vision to Advance National Cooperation and Economic Integration (ADVANCE) programme initiated by the US in February 2008. The ADVANCE programme sets to implement the goals of the ASEAN-US Cooperation Plan, the ASEAN-US Enhanced Partnership, the ASEAN-US Trade and Investment Framework Arrangement (TIFA) and the Vientiane Action Programme (VAP). We also welcomed the appointment of the first US Ambassador for ASEAN Affairs.
45. We expressed our appreciation to India for its contribution of US$1 million to operationalize the ASEAN-India Science and Technology Fund, which demonstrated India's firm commitment to further its cooperation with ASEAN. We expressed our readiness to work closely with India to expeditiously establish the initiative on ASEAN-India Green Fund. We looked forward to the implementation of more collaborative projects between ASEAN and India in this area.
46. We recalled the adoption of the 2nd Joint Statement on East Asia Cooperation and the ASEAN Plus Three Cooperation Work Plan (2007–2017) at the 11th ASEAN Plus Three Summit in Singapore. In this regard, we welcomed the completion of the Terms of Reference for the ASEAN Plus Three Cooperation Fund and looked forward to the establishment of the Fund. We expressed confidence that the priority areas set out in the Cooperation Work Plan can be implemented without delay.
47. Recalling our Leaders' substantive discussions at the 3rd East Asia Summit in Singapore, we reaffirmed the value of continued cooperation within the EAS.

As the EAS develops, we stressed the importance of ensuring follow-up actions in areas as mandated by the Leaders. We looked forward to the upcoming EAS Foreign Ministers' Informal Consultations on 22 July 2008 as an opportunity to discuss regional and international issues, and consider the future direction of the EAS.

48. We welcomed the enhancement of the ASEAN-UN Partnership which has been marked by events such as the signing of the Memorandum of Understanding in September 2007 and the ASEAN-led humanitarian assistance for the victims of Cyclone Nargis. We recommended the convening of the 3rd ASEAN-UN Summit back-to-back with the 14th ASEAN Summit in Bangkok in December 2008.
49. We agreed to pursue cooperation with other regional organizations that could complement ASEAN's objectives. In this regard, we welcomed the invitation from Brazil, the pro tempore president of MERCOSUR, to attend the inaugural ASEAN-MERCOSUR Ministerial Meeting in Brasilia on 24 November 2008. We looked forward to the meeting that would deepen the engagement between both sides. We also looked forward to the convening of a full-fledged ASEAN-Gulf Cooperation Council Ministerial Meeting in Thailand in 2009 to take ASEAN-GCC relations in the areas of inter alia, trade and investment, tourism, and energy security to a higher plane.

## Developments in Myanmar

50. We took note of the briefing by Myanmar on the recent developments in the process of national reconciliation and its peaceful transition to democracy, as envisaged in the roadmap to democracy; in particular, the adoption of the State Constitution of 2008 by referendum. We urged Myanmar to take bolder steps towards a peaceful transition to democracy in the near future, and working towards the holding of free and fair General Elections in 2010. While recognising the steps undertaken by the Government of Myanmar to conduct meetings with all concerned parties, including the NLD leadership, we reiterated our calls for the release of all political detainees, including Daw Aung San Suu Kyi, to pave the way for meaningful dialogue involving all parties concerned.
51. We recognized the fact that Myanmar has tried to address many and complex challenges. We reaffirmed our commitment to remain constructively engaged with Myanmar as part of building the ASEAN Community. We encouraged Myanmar to continue to work closely with the Good Offices of the UN Secretary-General and his Special Advisor Ibrahim Gambari in ensuring an inclusive process towards national reconciliation. In this regard, we welcomed Myanmar's agreement to the upcoming visits of Mr. Tomas Ojea Quintana,

Special Rapporteur on the situation of human rights in Myanmar in August 2008, and Professor Ibrahim Gambari in August 2008, and reiterated our call for Myanmar to extend its full support for their missions.

## REGIONAL AND INTERNATIONAL ISSUES

### Food and energy security

52. We discussed how the mounting challenge posed by rising oil and food prices poses a serious challenge to our peoples' welfare as well as our countries' continued economic development. On the issue of food security, we affirmed that access to adequate and reliable supply of staples, and stable prices were fundamental to the region's economic and social well-being. To address rising food prices, we stressed the importance of regional and international efforts to ensure the efficient functioning of market forces, as well as to come up with longer term agricultural solutions. We encouraged all countries to do away with price-distorting export subsidies and other protectionist policies and to provide market access to competitive food exports.
53. We are concerned that the recent volatility and rise of oil prices has adversely affected our economies. We reiterated the need for regional and international efforts to ensure the efficient functioning of market forces and to enhance the region's energy security in a sustainable manner through greater cooperation measures such as improving energy efficiency and conservation.

....

Source: http://www.aseansec.org/21771.htm
Accessed date: 8 October 2008
Publisher: ASEAN Secretariat
Country: Jakarta
Date of Publication: 2008

# CHAPTER 39

# STATEMENT BY MR GEORGE YEO, MINISTER FOR FOREIGN AFFAIRS OF SINGAPORE AND CHAIRMAN OF THE 41ST ASEAN STANDING COMMITTEE AT THE CLOSING CEREMONY OF THE 41ST ASEAN MINISTERIAL MEETING AND HANDING OVER OF THE ASEAN STANDING COMMITTEE

**24 July 2008**

Dear ASEAN Colleagues,

Excellencies,

Ladies and Gentlemen,

1. The last year proved to be quite an eventful year for ASEAN. When Singapore took over the Chairmanship of ASEAN, we identified three key areas of work, what I then referred to as the 3 'C's. First, the ASEAN Charter; second, Community-building; and, third, common Challenges.
2. The Charter signed at the 13th ASEAN Summit in Singapore will help make ASEAN a more effective organization with clearer purposes, with a stronger legal framework and a better mechanism for dispute settlement. We must make sure that the Charter comes into force at the 14th ASEAN Summit in Bangkok this December. We have already started taking steps to implement its key provisions. At this AMM, two high-level expert groups were formed — the High-Level Panel (HLP) for the establishment of an ASEAN Human Rights Body and the High-Level Legal Experts' Group (HLEG) to establish a dispute settlement mechanism. ASEAN will also soon have its own Committee of Permanent Representatives based in Jakarta. We are also strengthening the Secretariat for which it will need additional resources.
3. On community-building, we have adopted the ASEAN Economic Community Blueprint. The Blueprint is a roadmap for the remaking of ASEAN into an Economic Community. We are working expeditiously to draft similar blue-prints for the ASEAN Political-Security Community and the ASEAN Socio-Cultural Community. They should be completed by the ASEAN Summit in

Thailand this December. We are also working on the 2nd IAI (Initiative for ASEAN Integration) Work Plan, mapping out our efforts over the next 7 years to narrow the development gap in ASEAN.

4. For ASEAN to succeed and endure, the peoples of Southeast Asia must increasingly internalize a sense of common ASEAN citizenship. This will naturally take time. We know we are succeeding if members of each younger generation feel more for ASEAN than their parents. ASEAN has to be built both top down and from the bottom up. Only then will we truly be an ASEAN Community. Recognizing this, ASEAN has organized in the past year a range of commemorative activities to celebrate ASEAN's 40th anniversary and raise general awareness about ASEAN.
5. This brings me to the last 'C', the challenges that the region face. The world is changing rapidly. We don't know how badly we will hit by the gathering financial storm in the US. China's and India's growth will provide us some buffer. There is however little doubt that the global economic centre of gravity will shift across the Pacific in the coming decades. Such a major shift is never smooth and we must expect problems of various kinds to surface. Building a robust regional political architecture must be our key priority. We must also respond to trans-boundary challenges from climate change, natural disasters and the threat of pandemics to global terrorism and food/energy security. At the ASEAN Summit in Singapore, we agreed that sustainable development, protection of the environment and climate change should be high up on our list of priorities. After Cyclone Nargis, ASEAN played a critical role in building a bridge of trust between the Myanmar Government and the international community.
6. Looking ahead, implementing the Charter, forging ahead with Community-building and dealing with common Challenges will remain key tasks, the three C's which guide our work. In carrying them out, we should always bear in mind three other C's — **c**redibility, **c**ompetitiveness and the **c**entrality of ASEAN.

## Credibility

7. First, credibility. We must always ensure that our words are backed up by our actions. Only then will others believe us and take us seriously. We must always fulfil our obligations and honour our commitments.

## Competitiveness

8. Second, competitiveness. The test of ASEAN's success is whether it enhances the competitiveness of each and every one of its member states. In a globalised world, each of us is stronger being part of ASEAN than not. The purpose of

integration is to enhance our competitiveness, not reduce it. ASEAN helps us each of us to secure our place in the sun.

## Centrality of ASEAN

9. With the rise of China and India changing the polarity of the world, we must make sure that the political, economic and security architecture of the region takes into account the interest of ASEAN. Over the years, ASEAN, in a peaceful, non-threatening way, has helped to bring countries in the region together. We have been able to do this through enlightened diplomacy and by offering our hand of friendship to all the major powers. We must never lose this position. We must take an active interest in regional and global affairs and play a role which is helpful to others. We ensure the centrality of ASEAN in the evolving regional architecture, not by force or assertion but by the openness and neutrality of our position and by our usefulness to others.
10. Let me conclude by thanking all our ASEAN colleagues for your support and cooperation in the last year. I apologise for all our shortcomings. It was Singapore's honour to take its turn in the Chair. ASEAN is a work-in-progress which we took over from the Philippines and now hand over to Thailand.

Source: http://www.41amm.sg
Accessed date: 2 October 2008
Publisher: ASEAN Secretariat
Country: Jakarta
Date of Publication: 2008

# CHAPTER 40

# ASEAN CHARTER ENTERS INTO FORCE NEXT MONTH

**Bangkok, 15 November 2008**

Thailand delivered the tenth and final instrument of ratification of the ASEAN Charter today with Dr Surin Pitsuwan, Secretary-General of ASEAN.

"This is certainly an occasion to celebrate for the 570 million people of ASEAN," said a beaming Secretary-General, upon receiving the Thai document.

"This means that when the ASEAN Leaders gather at their annual Summit in mid December, the ASEAN Charter will have come into force," Dr Surin told reporters.

Philippines deposited its instrument of ratification of the ASEAN Charter on 3 November and Indonesia deposited its instrument of ratification on 13 November.

The ASEAN Leaders signed the ASEAN Charter last November at the 13th ASEAN Summit. They urged their member states to fully ratify it by the end of 2008. All member states have now responded to their call.

When they meet again in Chiang Mai, Thailand for their 14th ASEAN Summit on 15–18 December, they will celebrate not only the full ratification of the ASEAN Charter but also the entering into forcem of the new basic law of ASEAN. It will be a rules-based and people-oriented organisation with its own legal personality.

Source: http://www.aseansec.org/22072.htm

# CHAPTER 41

# CHAIRMAN'S STATEMENT OF THE 14TH ASEAN SUMMIT "ASEAN CHARTER FOR ASEAN PEOPLES"

**Cha-am, 28 February–1 March 2009**

1. We, the Heads of State/Government of ASEAN Member States, gathered in Cha-am Hua Hin, Thailand, for the first time under a new Charter, for the 14th ASEAN Summit on 28 February–1 March 2009. We had extensive, open and fruitful discussions under the theme of "ASEAN Charter for ASEAN Peoples".

## ASEAN CHARTER

2. We celebrated the entry into force of the ASEAN Charter on 15 December 2008. The Charter provides the legal and institutional framework for ASEAN to be a more rules-based, effective and people-centred organisation paving the way for realising an ASEAN Community by 2015. This ASEAN goal is made even more urgent by the global financial crisis. ASEAN needs to respond effectively to this financial crisis in order to retain its central position in the regional architecture. In this connection, we mandated all ASEAN organs to be guided by and to fully implement the ASEAN Charter.
3. We were pleased with the fruitful meeting between our Foreign Ministers and Members of the High Level Legal Experts' Group on Follow-up to the ASEAN Charter, during which recommendations were made particularly on the issues of the legal personality of ASEAN, the establishment of dispute settlement mechanisms and other legal issues under the ASEAN Charter.
4. We welcomed the progress made in the establishment of the Committee of Permanent Representatives (CPRs) in Jakarta. Once operationalised, the CPRs will be instrumental in strengthening cooperation among ASEAN Member States, improving coordination with the ASEAN Secretariat and enhancing relations with our external partners.
5. We also welcomed the progress made by the High Level Panel on an ASEAN Human Rights Body, which has already submitted the first draft of the Terms of Reference of an ASEAN human rights body (TOR of AHRB) to the ASEAN Foreign Ministers' Meeting on 27 February 2009. We noted that the

establishment of the AHRB to promote and protect human rights of ASEAN's peoples would be one of the most important undertakings to make ASEAN a genuinely people-oriented community. We therefore agreed that this body should be inaugurated and operationalised by the 15th ASEAN Summit at the end of 2009.

6. We emphasised the need to allocate sufficient resources, including budget and personnel, to strengthen the ASEAN Secretariat so that it can fulfill its additional responsibilities and functions as required by the Charter.

## BUILDING REGIONAL RESILIENCE

### Economic and Financial Stability

7. We discussed extensively the global economic and financial crisis and its adverse impact on our region. We were concerned that global economic prospects continue to deteriorate as the major economies plunge deeper into recession. We stressed the importance of deepening ASEAN integration to maintain its resilience while remaining open to global and regional trade.

....

10. At the global level, we agreed to work in tandem with the G20, particularly on the reform of the international financial institutions and markets. We welcomed the informal meeting between ASEAN Foreign Ministers and Lord Mark Malloch-Brown, the British Government's envoy for the London Summit, on 27 February 2009 at the sidelines of the 14th ASEAN Summit and appreciated the invitation extended by the London Summit host to Thailand as the ASEAN Chair to attend the Summit on 2 April 2009. We looked forward to sharing ASEAN's views and working together with other major economies to address the current global economic and financial crisis.

### Food and Energy Security

11. We recognised the importance of addressing the challenge of climate change and the need for ASEAN to work closely together and with other Partners for a successful Copenhagen Conference of States Parties.
12. We recognised the need to address the inter-related issues of food and energy security in a comprehensive manner. We pledged to strengthen our cooperation to enhance food security on both production and distribution fronts. We would make sure that resources and technology be sufficiently provided to

increase food productivity, while appropriate mechanisms need to be developed to eliminate market distortions for food trade. To ensure food security in time of crisis, we welcomed the on-going effort to establish an ASEAN Plus Three Emergency Rice Reserve (APTERR) as a permanent mechanism in the region.

13. We noted the importance of ASEAN energy cooperation to ensure greater security and sustainability of energy through diversification, development and conservation of resources, the efficient use of energy as well as the wider application of environmentally-sound technologies. In this connection, we welcomed the signing of the ASEAN Petroleum Security Agreement (APSA) which will help contribute to energy security.
14. We stressed the need to strengthen our cooperation on the development of renewable and alternative energy including hydropower and bio-fuels. We underlined the need to promote more use of renewable energy in our total energy mix. In this connection, we urged the ASEAN Energy Ministers to set a collectively quantitative target for renewable energy in the total mix of energy for the next five years. We also agreed to promote the development of centers for research and development on renewable energy in the region. We stressed the need to ensure that these sources are sustainable. We agreed to pay attention to the security, environmental, health and safety dimensions of the energy sector.

## Disaster Management

15. We welcomed the success of the ASEAN-led mechanism to help the victims of Cyclone Nargis and pledged to continue supporting Myanmar in its recovery efforts following the launching of the Post-Nargis Recovery and Preparedness Plan (PONREPP). We also welcomed the decision of our Foreign Ministers to extend the mandate of the ASEAN Humanitarian Task Force and the Tripartite Core Group until July 2010. In order to enhance our disaster relief capacity, we were encouraged to develop a regionally integrated system to respond to future large scale disasters. We also took note of Thailand's offer to provide training and capacity building facilities on disaster management through the Asian Disaster Preparedness Centre (ADPC).
16. We agreed to entrust the ASEAN Secretary-General to serve as ASEAN's humanitarian assistance coordinator which can be activated any time at the request of the affected ASEAN Member State in the event of a major disaster, whether it be a natural disaster or a pandemic.

## Millennium Development Goals and Narrowing the Development Gap

17. We were pleased with the progress made in the attainment of the Millennium Development Goals (MDGs), particularly in primary education, gender equality and combating infectious diseases. We reiterated the need to strike a balance between economic growth and social development and environmental sustainability to further enhance our effort towards achieving the MDGs.
18. We highlighted the strategic importance of concerted efforts in narrowing the development gap in realising a people-oriented ASEAN Community. We approved the Second Initiative for ASEAN Integration (IAI) Work Plan II for the period 2009–2015 and noted that the Work Plan, together with the three Community Blueprints, would help move forward the community-building process in a more balanced, inclusive and sustainable manner.

## ASEAN COMMUNITY BUILDING

19. We signed the Cha-am Hua Hin Declaration on the Roadmap for the ASEAN Community (2009-2015), comprising 3 pillars, namely, Political-Security Community, Economic Community and Socio-Cultural Community, all of which are closely intertwined and mutually reinforcing for the purpose of ensuring durable peace, stability and shared prosperity in the region.
20. In this regard, we tasked the Ministers and the Secretary-General of ASEAN to explore ways and means as well as long term strategy to further mobilise resources from Member States, Dialogue and Sectoral Dialogue Partners, Development Partners of ASEAN as well as from other external Parties to implement the Cha-am Hua Hin Declaration in an effective, timely and sustainable manner.

## ASEAN POLITICAL-SECURITY COMMUNITY

21. We adopted the ASEAN Political-Security Community (APSC) Blueprint which envisaged ASEAN to be a rules-based Community of shared values and norms; a cohesive, peaceful, stable and resilient region with shared responsibility for comprehensive security; as well as a dynamic and outward-looking region in an increasingly integrated and interdependent world.
22. We called for full implementation of the Blueprint in order to help promote peace, stability and prosperity in our region and to protect the interests and welfare of peoples of ASEAN. In this connection, we tasked the ASEAN Political-Security Community (APSC) Council to set priorities for actions and

activities to realise the objectives of the APSC in accordance with the principles and purposes of the ASEAN Charter.

23. We welcomed the results of the 3rd ASEAN Defense Ministers' Meeting (ADMM) convened in Pattaya, Thailand on 25–27 February 2009 which contributed towards the strengthening of the ASEAN Political-Security Community, reinforced ASEAN's ability to deal with non-traditional security challenges such as disasters, including in cooperation with civil society organisations, and strengthened the framework for future dialogue and cooperation with ASEAN Dialogue Partners and friends.

## ASEAN ECONOMIC COMMUNITY

24. We welcomed the outcomes of the Inaugural ASEAN Economic Community Council Meeting, particularly the AEC Scorecard mechanism that tracks the implementation of our commitments and the AEC Communication Plan that contributes to greater awareness of AEC.
25. We appreciated the progress made following the signing of the Declaration on the AEC Blueprint at the 13th ASEAN Summit in Singapore on 20 November 2007 and underscored the importance of timely integration of ASEAN economies under the theme "Walk together, work together toward AEC".
26. We agreed that in order to facilitate trade liberalisation in ASEAN in order to expand intra-ASEAN trade, the ASEAN Secretary-General could engage in cooperation with the private sector, for example, in championing a certain project.

### Goods

27. We appreciated the conclusion of the ASEAN Trade in Goods Agreement (ATIGA) and its signing by the ASEAN Economic Ministers at the sidelines of this Summit. We recognised that ATIGA contains a number of key features that would enhance transparency, certainty and predictability in the ASEAN legal framework and enhance AFTA's rules-based system, which is of importance to the ASEAN business community and consumers.
28. We welcomed the finalisation of the Sectoral Mutual Recognition Arrangement (MRA) on Good Manufacturing Practice (GMP) Inspection of Manufacturers of Medicinal Products and looked forward to its signing by the ASEAN Economic Ministers at the earliest opportunity.

### Services

....

## Investments

30. We welcomed the signing of the ASEAN Comprehensive Investment Agreement (ACIA) at the sidelines of this year's Summit. We appreciated the timely introduction of ACIA as this new comprehensive agreement makes ASEAN more attractive as an investment destination and enhance further expansion of intra-ASEAN investment which would stimulate ASEAN economy.

## Tourism

31. We appreciated the commitments and efforts of ASEAN Tourism Ministers in further integrating tourism towards the establishment of the ASEAN Economic Community by formulating an ASEAN Tourism Strategic Plan 2011–2015 and developing ASEAN Tourism Connectivity Corridors. We also acknowledged counter measures in response to economic downturn by declaring the years 2009–2010 as the Youth Travellers' Years with ASEAN Tourism Incentives.

## Doha Development Agenda

32. We reaffirmed our commitment to a successful conclusion of the Doha Round. We urged all Members of the World Trade Organisation, especially the major players, to expeditiously reengage and exercise flexibility to bring about an early conclusion of the Round. We believe that an early conclusion to the modalities negotiations, and thereafter, the Doha Round, would help to restore confidence and growth in the global economy. A successful Doha Round would provide a "stimulus package" at a multinational level to help mitigate the negative effects of this current global economic crisis.
33. We propose to preserve the progress that had been achieved in 2008, especially in the areas of agriculture and industrial goods modalities, so that we can focus on narrowing our remaining differences.
34. We called on developed countries to increase assistance to developing countries, and in particular to Least Developed Countries, with a view to increasing their participation in the global trade and alleviate the effects of the current global crisis.
35. We urged that the accession process of the Lao PDR to the World Trade Organisation be facilitated and expedited with special emphasis on their development.

### Small and Medium Enterprises (SMEs)

....

37. We also underlined the need to foster partnership between the private sector and the ASEAN Secretariat to act as a driving force to accelerate implementation of the Priority Integration Sectors (PIS).

## ASEAN SOCIO-CULTURAL COMMUNITY

38. We adopted the ASEAN Socio-Cultural Community (ASCC) Blueprint to serve as the roadmap to realise an ASEAN Community that is people-centred, socially responsible with a view to achieving solidarity, unity and a common identity and building a sharing and caring society which is inclusive and harmonious where the well-being, livelihood, and welfare of the peoples are enhanced. In view of this, we emphasised the importance of enhancing cooperation in human development; promoting social welfare, justice and rights; ensuring environmental sustainability; building the ASEAN identity and narrowing the development gap.
39. We encouraged ASEAN Member States to continue promoting ASEAN awareness among our peoples particularly the youths through education and culture. Under education, we viewed that the development of national ASEAN curriculum for all educational levels would prepare our youths to reap the benefits as well as contribute to the ASEAN Community building process. We also encouraged the development of life-long education as well as the use of ICT as a means to promote ASEAN education and ASEAN awareness particularly for those living in underprivileged and marginalised areas.
40. We stressed the importance of enhancing people's participation in the ASEAN Community building process. We therefore welcomed Thailand's initiative in establishing the ASEAN-Association of Thailand which would provide a platform for engagement with representatives from governmental agencies, educational institutes and civil society organisations on ASEAN Community building.
41. We welcomed 'The ASEAN Way' as the official ASEAN Anthem which is the concrete outcome of the implementation of the ASEAN Charter. The ASEAN Way is under the copyright of ASEAN with the ASEAN Secretariat as the main body to oversee its proper use. We encouraged The ASEAN Way to be used within ASEAN formal meetings and related activities as well as with

ASEAN Dialogue Partners. We encouraged ASEAN Member States to promote The ASEAN Way within their countries through translation into local languages as well as adaptation into various versions as a way to promote ASEAN awareness. We also highlighted the need to develop the idea and sense of ASEAN citizen, who has greater awareness of ASEAN and of its values and principles.

## REGIONAL AND INTERNATIONAL ISSUES

### Myanmar

....

### Illegal Migrants in the Indian Ocean

....

### Situation in the Gaza

....

## ASEAN'S EXTERNAL RELATIONS

46. We welcomed the appointments of non-ASEAN Ambassadors to ASEAN who will be instrumental in closer relations and cooperation between ASEAN and our external partners.
47. We welcomed the upcoming ASEAN-ROK Commemorative Summit to be held on 1–2 June 2009, on Jeju Island, the ROK, to celebrate the 20th Anniversary of ASEAN-ROK Dialogue Partnership. We shared the view that the Summit would be a good opportunity to review the 20-year-long dialogue partnership and map out future directions of cooperation between ASEAN and the ROK.
48. We recognised that ASEAN's existing Free Trade Agreements with Dialogue Partners are important in enhancing market access for ASEAN products and services and laying the foundation for ASEAN to forge stronger links with the other Asian economies and the rest of the global economy.
49. In this connection, we welcomed the progress made in the implementation of the ASEAN-China Trade in Goods Agreement, ASEAN-China Trade in Services Agreement, ASEAN-ROK Trade in Goods Agreement, and ASEAN-Japan

Comprehensive Economic Partnership Agreement. We also noted with pleasure the conclusion of the ASEAN-China Investment Agreement, which is targeted to be signed during the upcoming Related Summits with Dialogue Partners in April 2009.

50. We congratulated the signing of the Agreement Establishing the ASEAN-Australia-New Zealand Free Trade Area (AANZFTA). The Leaders urged both sides to explore ways to resolve remaining technical issues under the ASEAN-India Free Trade Agreement.
51. We supported Thailand's proposal to convene the ASEAN Plus One, ASEAN Plus Three and East Asia Summits in Thailand during 10–12 April 2009.

....

## OTHER MATTERS

52. We renewed our commitment to build a people-centred ASEAN through greater peoples participation in our community-building process. In this connection, we were pleased with the outcomes of our Informal Meetings with representatives from various groups, namely the ASEAN Inter-Parliamentary Assembly (AIPA), ASEAN Youth and ASEAN civil society. We also appreciated the useful insights provided by the ASEAN Business Advisory Council (ABAC) Leaders during our Working Lunch.

Source: http://www.aseansec.org/22328.htm
Accessed date: 3 March 2009
Publisher: ASEAN Secretariat
Country: Jakarta
Date of Publication: 2009

# PART II

# GENERAL LEGAL FRAMEWORKS ON THE ENVIRONMENT

# A. General: Programmes, Strategies, Plans of Action and Blueprints

# CHAPTER 42

# ASEAN SUB-REGIONAL ENVIRONMENT PROGRAMME

## PHASE I

### 1978–1982

## I. GOALS OF THE ASEAN ENVIRONMENT PROGRAMME (ASEP)

### Environmental Management including Environmental Impact Assessment

*Goal No. 1:*

Development of tested methodologies in integrating environmental aspects into development plans and project evaluation. These methodologies should be applicable to the regional situation and based on the experience of the ASEAN region.

### Nature Conservation and Terrestrial Ecosystems

*Goal No. 1:*

Development and promotion of a regional network of selected protected areas of significance for conservation of nature, including genetic resources, with emphasis on proper management of these reserves to ensure the conservation of wild flora and fauna of the region.

*Goal No. 2:*

Implementation of a regional instrument in regulating international trade in endangered species of flora and fauna.

### Marine Environment

*Goal No. 1:*

Implementation of the Action Plan for the development and protection of the marine environment and the coastal areas of the ASEAN Seas, with early attention to oil pollution control, waste management, and information exchange. This includes the establishment of institutional and financial arrangements for the implementation of the Action Plan.

## Industry and Environment

### *Goal No. 1:*

Enhancement of regional capability in pollution control, with emphasis on residue utilization, particularly for those industries which are of significance to the ASEAN region such as agro-industry and mining industries.

### *Goal No. 2:*

Establishment of adequate urban air and water quality monitoring systems to serve as an indicator of the status of environmental quality.

## Environmental Education and Training

### *Goal No. 1:*

Promotion of environmental education and training in the ASEAN region through the development of:

(a) suitable national programmes at school, out-of-school and other levels; and
(b) a network of institutions of higher learning offering environmental education training and research programmes.

## Environmental Information

### *Goal No. 1:*

Establishment of an information dissemination network among ASEAN governments, non-governmental organizations and the public at large in order to increase the awareness and broaden the knowledge base of the ASEAN people on environment.

## II. ANTECEDENTS

1. The Association of Southeast Asian Nations (ASEAN) since its inception in 1967 has advocated collaboration among its members for the attainment of peace, progress and prosperity of the region. Technical collaboration among member countries has been progressively promoted throughout the years resulting in a continuing exchange of information and expertise for the benefits of all members.

2. In this decade of the eighties, the ASEAN region has the potential of becoming one of the fastest growing economies of the world. The region itself is endowed with natural tropical resources. The ASEAN countries are determined to pursue the development pattern which would elevate the standard of living of the majority of their people.
3. In order to ensure sustainable development, countries of the region have taken cognizance of environmental issues. Governmental mechanisms have been established at the ministerial level in all ASEAN countries to co-ordinate and supervise environmental activities viz: the Office of the Minister for Development Supervision and Environment in Indonesia, the Ministry of Science, Technology and Environment in Malaysia, the Ministry of Human Settlements in the Philippines, the Ministry of the Environment in Singapore and the Ministry of Science, Technology and Energy in Thailand.
4. In the spirit of ASEAN, member countries of the region share the feeling that there are common and similar environmental issues which would benefit from vigorous technical co-operation among themselves. At the same time, ASEAN would like to avail themselves of the technical collaboration of international and bilateral agencies.
5. In 1977, the United Nations Environment Programme (UNEP) commissioned its Regional Advisory Team to visit ASEAN countries to confer with governmental authorities resulting in a draft ASEAN Sub-Regional Environment Programme. This Draft Programme identified thirty-two possible collaboration activities encompassing the whole gamut of environmental issues of the region.
6. The First Meeting of the ASEAN Experts Group on Environment which was held in Jakarta in December 1978 served as the first forum where national experts from all five ASEAN countries had the opportunity to comprehensively discuss all the environmental issues of the region. As a major item on the agenda, The First Meeting considered the UNEP Draft Programme in depth. From the proposed list of collaboration activities, it had selected four areas which the ASEAN experts felt should be pursued as a matter of urgency viz. regional seas, environment and development especially the development of methodologies for environmental impact assessment and for quantifying environmental parameters for development planners, urban air and water quality monitoring and pollution control technology.
7. In the ensuing period, UNEP commenced the first phase of its East Asian Seas Programme which was aimed at the compilation, evaluation and systematic analysis of available data on the seas of the ASEAN countries which would lead towards the formulation of an action plan to conserve the marine environment

of the region. Within this first phase, UNEP provided financial support to UN agencies, with the collaboration of ASEAN countries, to conduct studies on various aspects of marine environment, inter alia:

i) River inputs to South-East Asian Seas, UNESCO/UNEP.
ii) Overview of land-based sources of marine pollution in South-East Asia, WHO/UNEP.
iii) Assessment of oil pollution and its impact on living aquatic resources in South-East Asia, FAO/IOC/UNEP.
iv) Research into toxicity of oil dispersant chemicals on tropical and sub-tropical marine species, IMCO/UNEP.
v) Impact of pollution on the mangrove ecosystem and its productivity in South-East Asia, FAO/UNESCO/IUCN/UNEP.
vi) Research on degradation problems of the coral reefs of East Asia, FAO/UNEP.
vii) Workshop on coastal area development and management, UNTCD/CCOP/UNEP.
viii) Regional Seminar on Environmental Impact Assessment, WHO/UNEP.
ix) Review of environmental management needs related to coastal area development and coastal water pollution problems in the East Asian Region, WHO/UNEP.
x) Development of sub-regional oil spill contingency arrangements in the Celebes (Sulawesi) sea, IMCO/UNEP.
xi) Comparative study of national legislations for protection of the marine environment in the ASEAN sub-region, ESCAP/UNEP.

8. Concurrently, UNEP upon request of ASEAN, had prepared a draft project proposal on ASEAN Case Studies on Environmental Assessment and submitted to ASEAN for its consideration.
9. The Second Meeting of the ASEAN Experts on the Environment which was held in Penang in September 1979 further elaborated on the priority areas identified in the First Meeting, resulting in the following conclusions:

i) The Meeting agreed in principle on the approach undertaken by UNEP in its East Asian Seas Programme. It called for the convening of an expert group to study the result of the first phase of this Programme and to consider the draft action plan to be formulated by UNEP.
ii) The Meeting endorsed the project "ASEAN Case Studies on Environmental Assessment". In this connection, it recommended that a

workshop should be held on the institutional aspect of environmental impact assessment in ASEAN countries, to be followed by technical workshop on specific development sectors.

iii) The Meeting recommended that all ASEAN industrial projects be submitted to detailed environmental impact assessment.

iv) The Meeting recommended that a workshop on nature conservation should be convened for national experts to discuss common issues and major problems in the Field of wildlife management and nature conservation. In this connection, an inventory of endangered species of flora and fauna in the region should be prepared.

10. In the ensuing period leading towards the Third Meeting, the first phase of the East Asian Seas Programme continued to be executed vigorously. At the same time, the Philippines Government in collaboration with UNEP was preparing to organize the UNEP-ASEAN Workshop on EIA for Decision-Maker as a follow-up of the Second Meeting's recommendations.
11. The Third Meeting of the ASEAN Experts on Environment was held in Manila in May 1980. The Meeting felt that the thrust of the ASEAN Environment Programme should base on strong technical collaboration among ASEAN countries to be complemented by inputs from international and bilateral agencies. The Meeting emphasized on pursuing the ASEAN Environment Programme along the outlines agreed upon in previous meetings.
12. In the ensuring period leading to the Fourth Meeting, two meetings of experts were held to review the UNEP Draft Action Plan of East Asian Seas.
13. A Workshop on Nature Conservation was held at Bali, Indonesia, in September 1980 which led to the preparation of a Draft Action Plan (DAP) for the Conservation of Nature in the ASEAN Region by the International Union for the Conservation of Nature and Natural Resources (IUCN) with financial assistance from UNEP.
14. Two ASEAN-UNEP Workshops on Environmental Impact Assessment were also held. The Workshop on EIA for Decision-Makers was held in Baguio City, Philippines in June 1980 and the Workshop on EIA for Water Resources Development Projects was held at Kanchanaburi, Thailand in February 1981.
15. Upon the request of the Interim Coordinator, UNEP provided assistance in preparing the First Draft of the ASEAN Environment Programme dated August 1980.
16. A Report on the Urban Air and Water Quality Monitoring in ASEAN Countries was completed in December 1980 by a UNEP Consultant after visiting ASEAN environment focal points.

17. The first issue of the ASEAN Environment Newsletter was published in December 1980 and closely followed by a second issue in February 1981.
18. The recommendation of the Third Meeting to elevate the Experts Group to a level of a sub-committee was considered at the Meeting of ASEAN COST held in Singapore in August 1980 and referred to the Working Committee of high-level officials currently studying the overall restructuring of the entire ASEAN organisational machinery.
19. At the ASEAN-EEC Dialogue held in Brussels, Belgium, environmental pollution control technology was identified as a possible area of cooperation. ASEAN COST at its Fifth Meeting had also given its support within the framework of the ASEAN procedure instituted by the ASEAN Standing Committee for a regional seminar on "Environmental Protection" to be funded under the ASEAN-EEC Cooperation Programme.
20. A sum of US$800,000 was allocated by UNDP in support of ASEAN science and technology programmes for the period 1982 to 1986.
21. ASEAN COST has agreed to the setting up of a Trust Fund with financial assistance from third countries, UN Interim Fund and from other third parties to support priority projects.
22. The Fourth Meeting of the ASEAN Experts on Environment was held in Singapore from 8–10 April 1981. The Meeting reviewed recent actions and developments and agreed to further develop and promote regional cooperation in the various environmental fields. Towards this end the following recommendations were made:

## Nature Conservation

### *Recommendation No. 1*

That the Interim Coordinator request the Draft Action Plan for The Conservation of Nature in the ASEAN Region (DAP) to be further developed by IUCN on the areas of common interest, setting aside for the time being Item 13.4 (Accession to Global Conservation Convention), Item 15.3 (Control of International Trade and Wildlife) and Item 17.2 (ASEAN Convention on Nature Conservation).

### *Recommendation No. 2*

That a Workshop for National Experts by convened to discuss the revised DAP and formulate recommendations for consideration by the Expert Group.

The Interim Coordinator should seek funds from UNEP/IUCN to hold the Workshop.

## Environmental Impact Assessment

### *Recommendation No. 3*

That the Interim Coordinator request UNEP to sponsor workshops to discuss, develop and try out new methodologies in EIA, which should be relevant and meaningful in the regional context.

### *Recommendation No. 4*

That member countries submit project proposal on post-mortem EIA case study in the areas of:

(1) Trans migration;
(2) Industrial estate development;
(3) Road and highway construction; and
(4) Mining

to the Interim Coordinator by July 1981 for collation and submission to UNEP for the preparation of the Report. The UNEP Report should consider and highlight the following:

(a) whether EIA had increased the cost of the project;
(b) whether EIA had caused any delay in the implementation of the project; and
(c) whether there were other problems in carrying out the EIA.

## Urban Air and Water Quality Monitoring

### *Recommendation No. 5*

That the Interim Coordinator seek financial assistance from UNEP and other possible funding sources, for the projects according to their priorities.

### *Recommendation No. 6*

That the Interim Coordinator communicate to the consultant the desire of the member countries to hold separate workshops on air and water quality monitoring and to re-compute the budget so that there would be no contribution from the countries involved.

## Environmental Education and Training

### *Recommendation No. 7*

That each member country submit in an agreed common format to the Interim Coordinator by end of July 1981 its requirements and priorities in environmental education and training. The Interim Coordinator would then formulate, if necessary, with the assistance of a Consultant from UN or other UN agency, a Draft Action Plan to be presented to the Fifth Meeting of the ASEAN Experts Group on the Environment.

## ASEAN Sub-Regional Environment Programme (ASEP)

### *Recommendation No. 8*

That the Interim Coordinator update the draft ASEP to prepare it for consideration at the forthcoming ASEAN Ministerial Meeting on the Environment. The Interim Coordinator will send a copy of the revised ASEP to all ASEAN member countries as soon as possible.

### *Recommendation No. 9*

That all member countries submit to the Interim Coordinator by October 1981 their proposals of new projects. The Interim Coordinator will collate and submit these project proposals for consideration at the next meeting of ASEAN Experts on the Environment.

23. On the UNEP Regional Seas Programme it was agreed that the final resolution of the financial and institutional arrangements be deferred to the forthcoming Inter-Governmental Meeting to be held at Manila, Philippines in April 1981.

## III. CHARACTERISTICS OF THE ASEAN SUB-REGIONAL ENVIRONMENT PROGRAMME

1. The ASEAN Experts on the Environment in its Third Meeting in Manila has agreed on the following criteria for consideration of a project for the ASEAN Environment Programme:

   (1) It is participated by at least three countries
   (2) It is endorsed by all ASEAN members

(3) It benefits the ASEAN region
(4) It strengthens national capabilities
(5) It develops ASEAN cooperation

2. The ASEAN Environment Programme (ASEP) is an on-going programme which was set in motion in December 1978. It contains the following salient characteristics:

   (a) ASEP is based on existing situation and needs of the region. It has identified specific priority areas which would benefit from regional collaboration.
   (b) The nature and scope of ASEP are comprehensive covering major regional environmental issues and aiming at achieving both short-term and long-term results.
   (c) ASEP emphasizes regional self-reliance. This can be achieved through technical cooperation among its member countries with complementary input, wherever necessary, from external sources.
   (d) ASEP is action-oriented. It is expected to lead towards concrete governmental actions. Its intention is to transform the agreement of regional meetings into national programmes of action drawing, wherever appropriate, upon full; cooperation of governmental agencies, non-governmental organizations, private sectors and related international agencies.
   (e) ASEP is dynamic in nature. It is designed as a flexible programme with room for incorporating new emerging issues which would merit regional attention.

## IV. PRIORITY AREAS

From the list of activities endorsed by the previous three meetings of the ASEAN Experts on Environment, priority areas of ASEP could be categorized as:

(1) Marine Environment (East Asian Seas programme)
(2) Environmental Management including Environmental Impact Assessment
(3) Nature Conservation and terrestrial ecosystems
(4) Industry and Environment
(5) Environmental Education and Training
(6) Environmental Information

### A. Marine Environment (East Asian Seas Programme)

1. The principal objective of the East Asian Seas Programme is to formulate and implement, in a consistent manner, a commonly agreed upon Action Plan for

the development and protection of the marine environment and the coastal areas of the East Asian Seas, starting with the ASEAN Seas, for the health and well-being of present and future generations. The Action Plan is intended to provide a framework for an environmentally-sound and comprehensive approach to coastal area development particularly appropriate to the needs of the region.

2. In developing the Action Plan, UNEP had provided direct financial support to various UN agencies such as FAO, UNESCO, WHO, IMCO, ESCAP to undertake studies on various aspects of the marine environment. The assessment of the status of marine environment conducted under these studies serve as vital input to the preparation of a Draft Action Plan which was considered by the Meeting of Experts to review the Draft Action Plan for the East Asian Seas held in Baguio in June 1980.
3. In principle, the Draft Action Plan consists of four major components: Environmental Assessment is conducted to identify the present quality of the marine environment and the coastal areas, the factors currently affecting its quality and having an impact on human health, and the assessment of future trends. The subject areas which require and would benefit from technical environmental assessment had already been agreed upon by the ASEAN experts.
4. To ensure the viability and practicality of the Action Plan, the Environmental Management component would be introduced which would stress on strengthening institutional capabilities of participating governments and the assessment of present and future developing activities and their impact to the marine environment. The success of such an effort would definitely depend on the concerted effort of all participating parties.
5. Regional legal agreements provide a fundamental basis for regional co-operation to protect the marine environment and adjacent coastal areas. The Legal component then would be introduced whenever appropriate, taking into consideration the existing working relationship among members of ASEAN and the tradition and practices of the region.
6. Lastly, the Institutional and Financial arrangements which would ensure the continuity of the Action Plan would be established. The input from international agencies might be necessary and vital at the beginning stage of such a programme. However, it is expected that all coastal states benefiting from the Action Plan would gradually assume institutional and functional responsibilities in pursuing the Plan in the long run.
7. The Fourth Meeting of Environment Experts expressed general agreement with the DAP. However, the final resolution of the financial and institutional arrangement of the DAP was deferred to the forthcoming Inter-Governmental Meeting which would be held in Manila, Philippines in April 1981.

8. The Action Plan of the East Asian Seas Programme will incorporate the following activities:

    i) Assessment of oceanographic phenomena with particular reference to hydrography, water masses, water circulation and their effects on pollution dispersion patterns including detailed oceanographic surveys;
    ii) Assessment of oil pollution and its impact on living aquatic resources;
    iii) Assessment on non-oil pollutants, especially metals, organics, nutrients and sediments, and their environmental impact, and
    iv) Assessment of the impact of pollution on, and habitat degradation of, mangrove and coral ecosystems.

9. For future expansion of the environmental assessment programme the following components may be considered:

    i) Assessment of the environmental impact of offshore seabed exploration and exploitation, including petroleum mining and dredging;
    ii) Assessment of thermal pollution in coastal waters and its impact on marine biota;
    iii) Assessment of the nature and magnitude of pollution reaching the marine environment through the atmosphere.

## B. Environmental Management including Environmental Impact Assessment

1. Environmental management as an integrated component in economic development and project evaluation has been endorsed by ASEAN countries. The ultimate goal of this concept is to ensure sustainable development by optimizing the utilization of natural resources taking into consideration the benefit of the majority of the people and the long-term impact to the well-being of future generations.
2. ASEAN seeks to adapt appropriate environmental management tools and technology to serve the needs of the region. The ASEAN/UNEP Workshop on Environmental Impact Assessment (EIA) for Decision-Makers held in Baguio in June 1980 verified the beneficial role of EIA as an environmental management tool. Although the Workshop concluded that it is still too early to assume the overall benefit of EIA, ASEAN countries are determined to apply this tool, wherever appropriate, to safeguard the quality of their environment.
3. As a follow-up to the Workshop at Baguio City, Philippines, Thailand successfully hosted an ASEAN/UNEP Workshop on Environmental Impact

Assessment for Water Resources Development Projects in February 1981 at Srinakarin Dam, Thailand. The Workshop identified the various problems in the assessment and management of environmental impacts associated with water resource development projects.

4. The EIA case study on the ASEAN Urea Project in Sumatra is under active consideration and would be implemented in 1982.

## C. Nature Conservation and Terrestrial Ecosystems

1. The ASEAN region is endowned with diverse species of flora and fauna. In fact, the region possesses thirty per cent of the world's tropical rain forest. Not only that the ecological assets of the tropical rain forest are invaluable, they also serve as sources of economic development in terms of timber production. Unfortunately due to unchecked exploitation of forest resources and population pressure, deforestation in the region is increasing at an alarming rate. If deforestation cannot be arrested by the turn of the century forest area in some parts of the region may be totally and irreversibly damaged.
2. Luxuriant tropical forest has more species of wild flora and fauna than any other ecosystems of equal size. However many of the endangered species are being put to extinction through illegal trade. ASEAN countries are conscious of the need for a regulating system to control illegal trade of endangered species.
3. One effective method in the protection of wild flora and fauna is the establishment of natural parks and wildlife sanctuaries. This approach, however, entails substantial investment not only in terms of financial input but in training of wardens and park managers. In ASEAN countries, where population pressure has led to the transformation of virgin forests into cash crop plantations, the setting up of restricted areas for nature and wildlife conservation may be the most effective way to protect nature, although on a limited scale. This approach will also ensure the survival of ecologically undisturbed areas for scientific studies.
4. At the same time, proper management of other terrestrial ecosystems particularly land and water is vital to the economic well-being of ASEAN countries which are agriculture-based. The problem of soil erosion and its concomitant effects on reforestation, agricultural activity, marine environment, (through sedimentation, mining activities) and siltation is recognized as an environmental problem of the ASEAN region.
5. As a follow-up to the Third Meeting of ASEAN Experts on the Environment, Indonesia organised a Workshop on Nature Conservation which was held in Denpasar, Bali, Indonesia in September 1980. Financial assistance was

provided by UNEP, Geneva for a consultant from IUCN to attend the meeting and to provide follow-up action. Following the Consultant's visit to ASEAN countries, a Draft Action Plan (DAP) for the Conservation of Nature in the ASEAN Region was prepared.

6. The Draft Action Plan is oriented at regional level and it incorporates the following activities:

   (1) Establishment of a network of ASEAN Reserves;
   (2) Institution of measures to protect endangered species;
   (3) Establishment of mechanism for information exchange on research and management; and
   (4) Establishment of a regional training programme on conservation management.

7. At the Fourth Meeting it was agreed to request IUCN to further develop the areas of common interest in the DAP.

## D. Industry and Environment

1. The deteriorating environmental quality in urban areas due particularly to air and water pollution is most perceptible and is well recognised as an environmental problem in ASEAN countries. Emissions from automobiles and industry in urban areas release toxic gases and dust into ambient air which are not only a nuisance but also detrimental to the health of the citizen of these cities. Any pollution control programme, to be effective, must be complemented with a vigorous environmental quality monitoring system to pinpoint the areas and sources of pollution. This requires substantial governmental investment in terms of equipment and training of technical manpower. As a complementary measure, ASEAN thus intends to strengthen national activities on air and water quality monitoring through regional collaboration.
2. Another main source of pollution are residues of those industries which are characteristic of developing countries such as agro-industry and mining industry. Although these residues are not necessarily toxic in nature, their quantum alone may cause serious pollution and result in the depletion of riverine and marine biota. Western technology to abate such pollution is normally available, but most options are too costly or too technically complicated for the needs of ASEAN. Fortunately, each ASEAN country has on-going government-supported research institutes involving in the research on residue utilization and pollution control technology. By taking

advantage of the local situation, such as the availability of land for water treatment, regional technology more appropriate to solving local problems could be developed. It would also serve in strengthening regional capability in science and technology. The strengthening of regional capability in pollution control technology thus is selected as a prominent component of ASEP.

3. As a follow-up of the Third Meeting of ASEAN Experts on the Environment, a UNEP Consultant visited ASEAN environment focal points, and completed a Draft Report on Assessment of Capabilities and Needs in Urban Air and Water Quality Monitoring in ASEAN countries.
4. The Report recommended that the following proposals could be considered for implementation in the region:

   (1) Technical Workshop on Quality Assurance for Air and Water Quality Monitoring Programme;
   (2) Technical Workshop in Air and Water Quality Management for Small and Medium Scale Industries;
   (3) Development and Implementation of a National Action Programme on Air and Water Quality Management and Monitoring;
   (4) Study Tour on the Control of Domestic Sewage and Industrial Effluents in Singapore and Malaysia;
   (5) Emission Standards and Test Procedures for Used and New Motor Vehicles.

## E. Environmental Education and Training

1. Although manpower requirements vary from country to country, there is a general need for more qualified personnel in most areas related to environment. Environmental education and training serve as a long-term approach in strengthening the awareness of the public at large on environmental issues and in leading towards the scientific solutions for technical environmental issues. Through appropriate environmental education and training programmes, trained professionals could effectively carry out their functions in management supervision, research and support services.
2. National training programmes are annually conducted by governments on various disciplines related to the environment such as public health, pollution control. In this area, international agencies have long been in association with ASEAN countries. However, due to the fact that environmental issues only come to prominence since the past decade, there is still a lack of permanent

mechanisms in ensuring the integration of the environmental dimension in the training programmes of professionals.

3. At the tertiary level, universities in ASEAN countries in recent years have actively introduced environmental curricula into their programmes. However, contact among universities of the region are still on ad hoc basis. Since many of the research conducted by universities have regional implications, it would be beneficial to establish a permanent linkage among various universities and higher learning institutes of ASEAN to ensure the flow of communication and knowledge.
4. Malaysia submitted a project proposal to the Interim Coordinator with the help of the Regional Institute for Higher Education (RIHED) to obtain funds for the holding of a Regional Seminar on Environmental Education. This proposal has been submitted to EEC for funding.

### F. Environmental Information

1. Since environment is the subject which concerns all human beings, environmental programmes cannot be successful without enthusiastic support from the people at large. At times, due to the technical nature of environmental programmes, solution to environmental issues can become incomprehensible or even confusing to the public. The principal objective of environmental information is to disseminate knowledge on environmental issues and to strengthen the linkage among governmental agencies, non-governmental organizations and the public.
2. Ironically, although published environmental documents based on national experience are sometimes available, they are generally not well-known to neighbouring countries. ASEAN is determined to strengthen its environmental exchange programme in order to enhance the sharing of regional expertise. This in itself, will promote regional collaboration and mutual understanding among scientists and the people of ASEAN.
3. The first issue of the ASEAN Environment Newsletter was published in December 1980 and closely followed by a second issue in February 1981.

## V. PROJECTS UNDER THE ASEAN ENVIRONMENT PROGRAMME

1. This chapter is intended not only to provide a compendium of projects agreed by ASEAN, but also to identify potential collaborating international and bilateral agencies, and the status of the implementation of such projects. The tabulation is designed for easy reference in following up on particular projects under ASEP (See Table 1).

Table 1.

| Priority Area and Project | Nature and Objectives | Major Collaborating Countries and International Agencies | Schedule and Status |
|---|---|---|---|
| A. Marine Environment (East Asian Seas Programme) | To implement an Action Plan for the development and protection of the marine environment and coastal areas of the East Asian Seas, starting with the ASEAN Seas, for the health and well-being of present and future generations. | UNEP/UNDP/UNESCO/WHO/ FAO/IMCO/IUCN/ESCAP/ UNTCD/ASEAN | 1979–present<br><br>The preliminary phase of the East East Asian Seas Programme which consisted of the compilation, evaluation and systematic analysis of available data on the seas of ASEAN was launched in 1979 and completed by June 1980. The Draff Action Plan (DAP) was reviewed by experts in Baguio, June 1980 and Bangkok, December 1980. This DAP will be presented to the Inter-Governmental Meeting to be held at Manila in April 1981. Some elements of the DAP have already been implemented by some member countries. |

(*Continued*)

Table 1. (*Continued*)

| Priority Area and Project | Nature and Objectives | Major Collaborating Countries and International Agencies | Schedule and Status |
|---|---|---|---|
| B. Environmental Management including Environmental Impact Assessment | | | |
| 1. Development of a Test Model for Environmental Assessment Statements | To develop a novel environmental impact statement format centred on resources and based on tested case studies from the region. | UNEP together with seven participating countries in Asia including Indonesia, Malaysia and Philippines | 1979–1980; completed. |
| 2. ASEAN/UNEP E1A Workshop for Decision Makers | To assess the pros and cons of introducing EIA in ASEAN countries and the existing institutional set-ups in implementing EIA. | UNEP/Philippines | Baguio, June 1980; completed. |
| 3. Quantification of Environmental parameters | To develop methodology and techniques for the identification of environmental dimensions in development planning | UNEP/UNAPDI | May 1979; completed.<br>A meeting related to this topic was organized by UNEP/ UNAPDI in Bangkok. |

(*Continued*)

Table 1. (*Continued*)

| Priority Area and Project | Nature and Objectives | Major Collaborating Countries and International Agencies | Schedule and Status |
|---|---|---|---|
| 4. Case Studies on Environmental Assessment | To develop environmental impact assessment guidelines based on actual case studies in ASEAN Countries in the areas of<br><br>i) transmigration<br>ii) industrial estate development<br>iii) road and highway construction<br>iv) mining | UNEP/ASEAN | At the Fourth Meeting of the ASEAN Experts on the Environment, it was decided that member countries submit project proposals on post-mortem EIA case study in the four areas of concern to the Interim Coordinator by July 1981 who will then collate and submit the cases to UNEP for the preparation of a Report. |
| 5. Introduction of EIA in ASEAN Industrial Projects | To minimize any adverse environmental impact from ASEAN Industrial projects | Indonesia | 1980–present<br><br>Indonesia volunteers to conduct EIA on its ASEAN urea project in Sumatra. COST was approached by the Interim Coordinator to put up to COIME to ascertain that the ASEAN Industrial Projects will be subjected to EIA Studies. The Interim Coordinator was requested to take up the matter with COST again. |

(*Continued*)

Table 1. (*Continued*)

| Priority Area and Project | Nature and Objectives | Major Collaborating Countries and International Agencies | Schedule and Status |
|---|---|---|---|
| 6. Information Exchange in EIA Case Studies | To share information and experience among ASEAN countries on EIA particularly those related to port and harbour development, mining industry, water resources development and the development of non-conventional energy sources | ASEAN | 1980 onwards;<br>ASEAN national focal agencies on environment are requested to provide the Interim Coordinator with a list of documented EIA Case Studies for circulation among Member Countries. |
| 7. Workshop on Environmental Impact Assessment for Water Resource Development Projects | To address technical problems which hinder the effectiveness of EIA as a planning tool for environmental management of water resources development project | UNEP/Thailand | Completed<br>Thailand hosted the workshop in February 1981 at Srinakarin Dam. |
| 8. Workshop on Environmental Impact Assessment | To exchange experiences on EIA | UNEP/Indonesia,<br>UNEP/Malaysia | Late 1981, Malaysia<br>Early 1982, Indonesia |
| 9. Formulation of technical guidelines on E1A of specific selected industries | To minimize adverse environmental impact from industrial development activities, particularly chemical industry, agro-industry and mining industry. | UNEP | 1980 onwards;<br>Project endorsed by ASEAN but not yet implemented. |

(*Continued*)

Table 1. *(Continued)*

| Priority Area and Project | Nature and Objectives | Major Collaborating Countries and International Agencies | Schedule and Status |
|---|---|---|---|
| C. Nature Conservation and terrestrial ecosystems | This workshop will consider major common issues on wildlife and nature conservation in ASEAN, in particular: | UNEP/IUCN/WWF/Indonesia | Completed<br><br>Workshop held in Denpasar, Bali in September 1980. |
| 1. Workshop on Conservation of Nature in ASEAN | i) Draft ASEAN Convention on Endangered Species — to regulate trade in endangered species of flora and fauna<br>ii) The establishment of ASEAN natural heritage reserves<br>iii) Education and training for nature conversation and wildlife management in ASEAN countries | | |
| 2. Inventory of endangered species in ASEAN countries | To build up an inventory of endangered species as one of the measures to protect these species | ASEAN | Completed |
| 3. Convention on International Trade of Endangered Species of Flora and Fauna (CITES) | To protect endangered species of Flora and Fauna in ASEAN | IUCN/UNEP/ASEAN | On-going;<br>National environmental agencies of ASEAN will explore with their respective governments on the ratification of this convention. |

*(Continued)*

Table 1. *(Continued)*

| Priority Area and Project | Nature and Objectives | Major Collaborating Countries and International Agencies | Schedule and Status |
|---|---|---|---|
| 4. Soil Erosion Control | To preserve the quality of topsoil from degradation due to erosion | ASEAN | On-going;<br>Indonesia is preparing project proposals on this topic. |
| 5. ASEAN School of Environmental Conservation | To prepare ASEAN curriculum and stages of training for ASEAN Conservation Programme | ASEAN | Draft completed |
| D. Industry and Environment | | | |
| 1. Technical Workshop on Agricultural and Agro-Industrial Residue Utilization | To promote the utilization of agricultural and agro-industrial residues | UNEP/ESCAP/FAO | Completed<br>The Workshop which was held in December 1979 at Pattaya was attended by twelve countries including Indonesia, Malaysia, Philippines, Thailand. |
| 2. Pollution Control Technology | To develop appropriate pollution control technology emphasizing low-waste, and non-waste technology and waste-recycling to the extent possible and take into consideration the nature of pollution in ASEAN countries.<br>To facilitate exchange of expertise through study tour. | UNDP/UNEP/ASEAN | Pending;<br>Project proposal for UNDP and UNEP consideration is needed |

*(Continued)*

Table 1. *(Continued)*

| Priority Area and Project | Nature and Objectives | Major Collaborating Countries and International Agencies | Schedule and Status |
|---|---|---|---|
| 3. Urban Air and Water Quality Monitoring | To strengthen urban air and water quality monitoring activities of governments through:<br>i) National survey of existing monitoring capabilities<br>ii) Regional collaboration through study tour to Singapore<br>iii) Technical collaboration with international programmes particularly those of UNEP such as INFOTERRA, GEMS | ASEAN/UNEP/WHO | On-going;<br>It was decided at the Fourth Meeting of the ASEAN Experts on the Environment that the Interim Coordinator seek financial assistance from UNEP and other possible funding sources for the projects mentioned in the Draft Report on Assessment of Capabilities and Needs in Urban Air and Water Quality Monitoring in ASEAN countries prepared by Mr. B N Garcia, UNEP Consultant. |

*(Continued)*

Table 1. (*Continued*)

| Priority Area and Project | Nature and Objectives | Major Collaborating Countries and International Agencies | Schedule and Status |
|---|---|---|---|
| E. Environmental Education and Training | | | |
| a. Environmental Training | To develop regional environmental training programme for ASEAN, the programme may cover training courses, seminar, workshops, study tours etc. and emphasize on the priority subjects as identified by ASEAN viz. environmental impact assessment, pollution control technology, nature conservation, environmental quality monitoring, marine environment, environmental education. | UNEP/UNESCO/WHO/FAO/ESCAP/SEAMEO/USAID/RIHED | At the Fourth Meeting of the ASEAN Experts, it was decided that each member country should submit to the Interim Coordinator its requirements and priorities in environmental education and training. A Draft Action Plan is to be formulated by the Interim Coordinator, with the assistance of a Consultant from UNEP or other UN agency. |
| b. Environmental Education | | | |
| 1. Meeting on Environmental Education for Asia and Oceania | To promote environmental education in Asia with emphasis on primary, secondary, non-formal and out-of-school education | UNESCO/UNEP | Completed<br>Meeting held in September 1980 in Bangkok. |

(*Continued*)

Table 1. *(Continued)*

| Priority Area and Project | Nature and Objectives | Major Collaborating Countries and International Agencies | Schedule and Status |
|---|---|---|---|
| 2. Asia-Oceania Regional Workshop on Higher Environmental Education | To promote a regional programme on tertiary and post-graduate environmental education | UNESCO/Australia | Completed<br>Workshop organized in Melbourne and Canberra, August 1979; 10 countries were represented including all members of ASEAN. |
| 3. Regional Seminar on Higher Education and Environment | To promote environmental education, training and research in ASEAN Universities | UNEP/RIHED/Malaysia | Planned for 18–21 August 1981 Malaysia will host a Seminar on "Environmental Education in ASEAN Universities and its Transfer" in collaboration with UNESCO/RIHED. |
| F. Environmental Information | | | |
| 1. Country Profile (PPCR) | To prepare documents providing a synoptic overview of environmental situation and needs of a country. | UNEP/ASEAN | Counting;<br>UNEP has on hand country profiles on each ASEAN country except Indonesia, which were prepared in collaboration with ASEAN Countries |

*(Continued)*

Table 1. (*Continued*)

| Priority Area and Project | Nature and Objectives | Major Collaborating Countries and International Agencies | Schedule and Status |
|---|---|---|---|
| 2. Collaboration with International Environmental Information Collection and Dissemination Programmes | To participate and benefit from existing international programmes on environmental information such as INFOTERRA, IRPTC | UNEP/ASEAN | On-going;<br>ASEAN countries to play an active role in INFOTERRA, IRPTC |
| 3. Publication of ASEAN Newsletter | To promote regional activities through dissemination of information and the publication and dissemination of technical research on environment | ASEAN/UNEP | On-going;<br>Philippines as the Interim Coordinator has published two issues of newsletter on ASEAN environment. (Asia Journal on Environment shall carry a column on development in environmental activities of ASEAN.) |
| 4. World Environment Day (WED) | To promote regional themes on WED | ASEAN/UNEP | Planned;<br>ASEAN countries to develop a common theme for WED in 1982. |

*Source*: Prepared by the ASEAN Experts Group on the Environment in, collaboration with the United Nations Environment Programme (1981–1988).

# CHAPTER 43

# ASEAN SUB-REGIONAL ENVIRONMENT PROGRAMME

# PHASE II

## 1983–1987

## FOREWORD

This revised version of the ASEAN Environment Programme II (ASEP Il/Rev. 1) for the period 1983–1987 is based on the decisions taken at the Seventh Meeting of the ASEAN Experts Group on the Environment (AEGE) which met at Genting Highlands, Malaysia, 2–4 April 1984. The revised version reflects the present status of the activities which have been undertaken under ASEP I and II as well as incorporates the amendments made at the Sixth Meeting of the AEGE.

As the new member country of ASEAN, Brunei Darussalam, joined the Seventh Meeting for the first time and agreed to consider participating in the various activities of the Programme, the revised version contains very little changes.

## I. PRINCIPLES OF ASEP II

In March 1983, the ASEAN Environment Programme (ASEP) reached another milestone by which the first cycle of its programme was completed. This programme was inaugurated at the First Meeting of the ASEAN Experts Group on the Environment (henceforth to be referred to as "the Group") in Jakarta in December 1978. Since then, the Group was permanently established within the umbrella of ASEAN under its Committee on Science and Technology (COST) and each country took turn, in alphabetical order, to serve as the Interim Co-ordinator in executing this programme.

The First Ministerial Meeting on the Environment of ASEAN, Manila, April 1981, endorsed ASEP I and its eight goals. Priority areas were established in accordance with the common interest of the region, viz. Marine Environment (East Asian Seas Programme), Environmental Management including Environmental Impact Assessment, Nature Conservation and Terrestrial Ecosystems, Industry and Environment, Environmental Education and Training, and Environmental Information.

Under ASEP I, emphasis was given to the formulation of action plans identifying those common activities which would benefit ASEAN. At the same time, series of technical meetings on specific priority areas were organised providing opportunity for ASEAN environmentalists to discuss technical and policy issues on environment and to get acquainted with each other's national activities. The full participation of national and regional experts in such meetings had ensured that collaborative activities formulated are conducive to the need of ASEAN and are supportive to national environment programmes.

The definite nature, reaching for the eight established goals, had led the execution of ASEP I in a coherent manner. Technical assessments on environmental situation and existing institutional capabilities were undertaken. As an outstanding example, ASEAN felt the compelling need to establish a co-operative programme on marine environment on a continuing basis. Thus the East Asian Seas Trust Fund was established in co-operation with UNEP, with direct financial contributions from ASEAN countries. In the priority area of Nature Conservation and Terrestrial Ecosystems, the establishment of ASEAN Heritage Parks and Reserves is becoming a reality. Concurrently, the benefit of EIA practices in ASEAN was analysed in-depth and regional collaboration on air and water quality monitoring and management and pollution control technology was carried out.

In each and every ASEAN country, there is now a ministry in charge of environment. At the conceptual level, such ministries have been successfully spreading the gospel of environmentally-sound development and pressing for greater awareness of the importance of the environmental dimension in national development activities, both public and private. Guidelines on environmental considerations have been prepared and disseminated. However, although so much have been achieved, the task is far from over. It is regionally recognized that environmental issues are complex and require continuing attention by all parties concerned.

With this background in mind, ASEP II is designed to be action-oriented, emphasizing on demonstration projects. It will pay less attention to esoteric environmental issues but more to solving immediate regional needs. There will be less meetings since the regional environmental scene is now well understood. Wherever possible, regional experts and their regional higher learning institutes will be consulted and invited to participate in the Programme. ASEP II will promote demonstration projects in order to serve as pilot studies to verify the benefit of environmentally-sound development at the field level. By so doing, it will hopefully assist national environmental agencies in the integration of environmental concepts in development activities at the implementation level. It is envisaged that this will eventually lead to investment-type projects in the future phases of ASEP, which may include full-scale area development taking advantage of the results of demonstration projects to be accomplished under ASEP II.

In those cases where ASEP wishes to give selected existing centres the regional mandates, such as the Biotrop in Bogor to serve as the ASEAN Information Centre on Nature Conservation, ASEP II will ensure that such centres will be duly strengthened to carry out their entrusted responsibilities. At the same time, action plans and programmes will be formulated for those remaining priority areas which still lack one, including the additional area of Remote Sensing.

In the past, although ASEP was comprehensive in nature, the implementation of which had been ad hoc depending mostly on the contribution of UNEP as the only major external financial source. To rectify this constraint, ASEP II is intended to project a more systematic approach to reflect the maturity of the programme as a whole. Contact with potential donor sources will be broadened both on technical and financial grounds. To this end, ASEAN itself has established formal dialogues with various bilateral and multilateral sources resulting in multi-million dollar collaborative programmes. It is thus envisaged that COST should be in the position to share the responsibility of the Group in acquiring additional external financial resources to implement parts of ASEP II.

To optimize the programming effort, activities under ASEP II are designed to cover a five-year period from 1983 to 1987. A rolling programming approach is followed by which activities are mainly identified for the first three-year period of 1983 to 1985. It is envisaged that after eighteen months of the implementation of ASEP II, the experience gained will be utilized as the basis for the modification and extension of the Programme to cover the entire five-year cycle.

As a regional grouping, the success of ASEAN is indisputable. With fifteen years of mutual collaboration as its history and four and a half years of collaborative programmes on environment, ASEP II is definitely on a solid foundation. ASEP II is intended for strengthening regional collaboration on environment aiming at regional self-reliance to benefit all participating countries.

## II. ENVIRONMENTAL SITUATION AND TRENDS IN ASEAN

Since the commencement of ASEP I in December 1978, one can say that there is a general increase in the awareness of environmental issues in ASEAN countries.

The public at large are more conscious of environmental problems, and are often exposed to discussions related to environment, mainly through mass media.

In the past six years, Governments in ASEAN have made headways in tackling their environmental problems. The man-made environment in Singapore is well managed and under control, serving as a model urban environment. In Malaysia, the Government is winning the war on controlling palm oil mill effluents which were singled out as the most important pollution sources in the country. In Thailand, the Government decided to impose EIA on major development activities. The wisdom of adopting such an approach is now being tested in the field. The Philippines has one of the most comprehensive sets of Environmental laws, whereas Indonesia's approach in promoting environmental education in its major universities is worth emulating.

This section is intended to highlight major environmental issues in the ASEAN region in the 1980s covering present situation and the future prospects to come.

## Population

In terms of population, Indonesia alone is the fifth largest country of the world, whereas Thailand and Philippines both rank among the top twenty. The present total population of ASEAN is more than 250 million. With such a large population base, one can surmise that the prevailing high growth in population is the root cause of environmental degradation. Population pressure is often cited as the major cause of encroachment into forest areas by landless farmers. At the same time, the imbalance in demographic patterns often exacerbate environmental problems. In Indonesia, the islands of Java and Madura support 65 per cent of the people with only seven per cent of the land area of the country.

The World Bank in its World Development Report 1980 made a hypothetical projection of the population of the world up to the stationary level. The figures projected for ASEAN are:

(a) Indonesia, 350 million by the year 2155, estimated year 2000 population 204 million.
(b) Malaysia, 30 million by the year 2070, estimated year 2000 population 20 million.
(c) Philippines, 126 million by the year 2075, estimated year 2000 population 75 million.

(d) Singapore, 4 million by the year 2065, estimated year 2000 population 3 million.
(e) Thailand, 103 million by the year 2095, estimated year 2000 population 68 million.

Based on this projection, three out of five ASEAN countries will end up with more than 100 million people each. An increase of such a magnitude will assert more pressure on the resources available in these countries. Even in the present situation, due to the uneven distribution of population in the country, Indonesia has already had to spend substantial amount of governmental resources in its huge "transmigrasi" programme. In the present five-year plan from 1979–1984, Indonesian Government plans to relocate half a million families or 2.5 million people from Java, Bali, Madura, Lombok to other outer islands of Sumatra, Kalimantan and Sulawesi.

The impact to the environment from such a massive resettlement scheme could not be ignored. Fortunately, the Government fully understands the probable environmental damages particularly from the clearing of primary forests. Based on its past experience, the Indonesian Government has prohibited clear cutting of primary forests for transmigration and has shifted the resettlement areas to grass lands.

Population pressure, thus, will likely continue to be the most important factor causing environmental degradation. The success of family planning programmes will contribute significantly towards the improvement of human environment in a country. The adverse impacts from population pressure both to the national environment and to society should be fully understood so that ways and means to effectively mitigate them can be gainfully employed.

## Urban Congestion

The Global 2000 Report prepared by the Council on Environmental Quality of the U.S.A. projected that by the year 2000, Jakarta will have 16.9 million and Manila 12.7 million. As for Bangkok, its population will at least double the present number of 5.5 million. Such a tremendous pressure exerted by the increase in population will stretch the carrying capacity of any urban environment to its limits.

Even with the existing situation, there is a widespread shortage of housing which leads to the expansion of slums and other forms of marginal settlements.

Municipal authorities normally lack the financial means to invest on necessary infrastructures such as sewerage treatment systems. Only a few cities in ASEAN countries are adequately served by appropriate sewerage system.

The influx of migrants from rural to urban areas is difficult to control due to the economic superiority which urban centres normally provide. Long-term solutions definitely lie with the success of rural development programmes of a country. One of the more viable intermediate solutions is the promotion of secondary cities or satellite towns at the peripheries of urban centres.

With the increasing population, the traffic congestion tends to become worse. In cities such as Bangkok, Manila, Jakarta, traffic congestion has cut down on productivity. It is not uncommon for a commuter to waste at least a few hours every day on the road. With the increase in the number of motor vehicles, the level of air pollution will get worse. Even at present, there are indications that air pollution is stepping beyond the safety thresholds.

Similarly, the issues of water pollution and solid waste management deserve more attention. It could no longer be considered as the sole responsibility of the State to provide these services. The public should be mobilized to join the governmental effort in managing urban environmental quality. On top of this, other urban environmental problems such as shortage of water supply and land subsidence will become more pronounced in the future. Governments are often constrained by the urban-rural imbalance in the existing development patterns. Any additional allocation for investment in urban infrastructures and public utilities means a reduction in the rural development fund. It is thus the responsibility of these urban population, both morally and financially, to contribute to the governmental effort in solving urban environmental problems.

## Tropical Forests and Nature Conservation

ASEAN is fortunately well endowed with diverse species of flora and fauna with one-third of the world's tropical forests. It is universally recognized that tropical forests contain more species of wild flora and fauna than any other ecosystem of equal size. Economically, they are productive in serving as renewable sources of timber production. Scientifically, tropical forests offer many environmental services due to their existence alone. They safeguard natural hydrological system, regulate climate, protect existing soils and form new soils, supply habitats for wildlife and serve as genetic reservoirs, and maintain ecosystem nutrients.

Unfortunately, forests in many parts of ASEAN are fast dwindling. Deforestation has become a common problem in the ASEAN countries except, of course, Singapore.

It is well known that deforestation stems mainly from three causes: the encroachment of forest land by farmers, swidden cultivation practices, and illegal logging. Aside from vigorous regulatory measures, proper forest management requires sound scientific studies and planning. Technical studies conducted in the region have confirmed the importance of maintaining forest lands particularly in the watershed areas. A recent study by the Kasetsart University conducted in Northern Thailand shows that shifting cultivation can cause up to four times more sediment yield comparing with natural soil erosion.

Natural forests also serve as repositories of invaluable wild fauna and flora, both for present and future generations. Realizing the value of these resources, the ASEAN countries have developed their own systems of protected areas. In Indonesia, the system comprises 160 nature reserves and 54 game reserves covering a total area of 7.6 million hectares. In Malaysia, the national parks, wildlife reserves and sanctuaries cover a total of 801,150 hectares in Peninsular Malaysia, 162,240 hectares in Sabah and 67,831 hectares in Sarawak. The Philippines has established 11 national parks, 11 recreation areas, two strict nature reserves and seven wildlife sanctuaries. Singapore, though a city-state, possesses three nature reserves of which the Bukit Timah still holds a sizeable area of high Dipterocarp forest. Thailand has 21 sanctuaries and 17 national parks, one of which is marine.

What is needed therefore is a regional nature conservation programme. Fortunately, a network of reserves serving as regional heritage parks and reserves is being contemplated by ASEAN. Species conservation programmes including research and training for wildlife and nature conservation management, and information dissemination on nature conservation are major components of this regional nature conservation programme. This will contribute significantly to the regional effort in ensuring the conservation of its dwindling forest resources.

## Marine Environment

As a regional "common", marine environment is regarded as valuable source of food in terms of fisheries production, as a mode of transportation particularly for bulk carriers, and as recreational grounds. The most serious marine environment risk nowadays is marine pollution caused by the transportation of petroleum products and offshore exploration and production. The Straits of Malacca and Singapore, with the highest number of Very Large Crude Carriers (VLCC) passing per average 24-hour period than any comparable stretch of water, have been subjected to a number of accidents involving tankers resulting in oil spillages. Accidents of tankers Showa Maru (5,000 ton spillage, Malacca Strait 1975), Mysella (2,000 ton spillage, Singapore 1976), and Diego Silang (6,000 ton spillage, Malaysia 1976) all raise the level of concern of Governments in the region on the serious environmental damage which may be afflicted by oil pollution.

Aside from oil pollution, heavy metals have been identified as a serious threat in the region. Pesticides and petroleum hydrocarbons are problems common in almost all ASEAN countries while domestic sewerage causes serious problems in coastal zones adjacent to urban areas. Potential problem areas are found near industrial centres by virtue of the concentration of polluting sources.

The ASEAN countries cover 4.8 million ha of mangrove areas, which represent 1.6 per cent of the total land area of the five ASEAN countries. Most of the mangrove forests are found in Indonesia (about 75 per cent), while the remaining 25 per cent are in Malaysia, Philippines and Thailand. Mangroves are known to protect marine organisms in the food chain vital to the survival of marine life. Mangroves serve in protecting coastal erosion and if properly cultivated, carry sustainable economic value in terms of firewood production. However, for the ASEAN region, ecological studies in relation to mangroves are few and very little is known on the impact of land, coast and sea-based pollution on the mangrove ecosystem.

Proper management of marine environment calls for concerted effort among neighbouring countries. Fortunately, ASEAN has established good precedent in the collaboration for the management of its seas. The Traffic Separation Scheme adopted by Indonesia, Malaysia and Singapore being implemented in the narrow Malacca Straits which has become effective since 1 May 1981, could serve as a good example. Moreover, ASEAN countries are collaborating in a more comprehensive programme on the East Asian Seas. This programme aims at promoting scientific studies and the implementation of a viable management programme for the protection and development of the ASEAN marine resources. With the catalytic and supportive role of UNEP, the ASEAN countries had adopted an Action Plan for the Protection and Development of the Marine Environment and Coastal

Areas of the East Asian Region. This Action Plan has specified priority areas which require technical studies, viz.:

(a) Assessment of the oceanographic phenomena with particular reference to hydrography, water masses, water circulation and their effects on pollution dispersion patterns;
(b) Assessment of oil pollution and its impact on living aquatic resources;
(c) Assessment of non-oil pollutants, especially metals, organics, nutrients and sediments, and their environmental impact;
(d) Assessment of the impact of pollution on, and habitat degradation of, mangrove and coral ecosystems.

The implementation of the Action Plan is being undertaken by U.N. agencies together with the marine science institutes of ASEAN. It is expected that local marine scientists will play a leading role in undertaking various scientific studies necessary for the success of this Action Plan.

## Public Awareness and Environmental Impact Assessment

Environmental awareness in the region is on the rise due partly to governmental effort and partly to the role of non-governmental organizations (NGOs) and the mass media. Environmental education has been gradually introduced in formal education at all levels from primary up to tertiary. In most of the major universities of the region, there is an environmental programme offering integrated and comprehensive environmental research and degree courses.

Aside from serving as centres of excellence with their own pools of expertise, ASEAN universities serve as intellectual bases and breeding grounds for conservation activities. Various conservation groups have been formed in these universities with students and faculty staff as members. Such groups have been instrumental in promoting environmental awareness and at times have been successful in introducing changes in governmental policies regarding environment. However, it should be recognized that many environmental issues are technically complicated without clear-cut solutions. Comprehensive studies on the scientific and technical impacts of development schemes should thus be carried out in advance so that sound alternatives may be developed for policy decision-making. This will help governments avoid conflicting and protracted controversies which may delay development.

In the existing situation, public sentiment has become a decisive factor in governmental decision. Nam Choan Dam in Thailand and Tembeling Dam in Malaysia are cases in point. In present-day governance, popular support has become a prerequisite in determining the viability of a major development project. To cultivate public participation, ASEAN countries except Singapore are employing environmental impact assessment as a management tool in which comprehensive environmental studies are conducted prior to actual development of major projects. At times, such practice can be time-consuming and expensive. The next couple of years will confirm either the justification or the wastefulness of such practice.

In the ASEAN region, environmental impact from hydropower generation continues to elicit special attention. The most serious environmental impact from dam construction is undoubtedly the forced migration of inhabitants in inundated areas. Without proper planning and fair compensation, experience in the region has shown that these migrants ended up poorer. It is not uncommon to find corollary irrigation schemes many years behind schedule after the completion of a dam. To avert such pitfalls, governments must ensure that benefits accrued from multipurpose water resources development programmes be effectively channelled to rural people to raise their standard of living.

The impact to health due to the spread of contagious water-borne diseases particularly schistosomiasis deserves special attention. This debilitating disease, once propagated, is extremely difficult to control. Careful preventive measures to prevent its outbreak must thus be incorporated into dam construction investment plans.

On the cultural front, ASEAN region possesses invaluable archaeological sites. Excavations in northeast Thailand have discovered prehistoric artifacts dating back to 3600 BC. Such historic treasure must be carefully preserved. Due to limited budget, field archaeology survey has not been carried out extensively enough in this part of the world. Once inundated, a land is lost forever. Hence, it is of utmost importance to ensure that any inundated area will be free from such hidden treasures.

In this region, the adverse impact of dam construction in terms of loss of forest lands and their indigenous wildlife is most controversial. It is even more so, considering the issue of dwindling tropical forest resources already acknowledged. The only viable solution calls for a concerted effort by both Government and NGOs in preparing reliable environmental impact studies which could serve as bases for decision-making.

## Other Issues

The environmental issues cited so far in this chapter are not meant to be exhaustive. They are intended to project coming environmental scenarios of the region. Nevertheless, emerging new issues such as the management of hazardous substances are gaining due attention. Such an issue is technically complicated and requires integrated programmes to cover all aspects of hazardous substances: importation, transportation, uses, and disposal among others. For a Government to come up with a sound policy, detailed study of existing situation is a prerequisite.

Other environmental issues such as soil erosion are not new but have always been parts of the recurring problems of agricultural development. This aptly amplifies the catalytic nature of environment which is a dimension in all development activities. Environmental issues thus are dynamic depending on the state of development of a country and depending on the natural resources available at a point in time.

## III. THE PAST AND THE PRESENT — ACHIEVEMENTS UNDER ASEP I AND PROGRAMMES OF ASEP II

The past six years has reconfirmed the exemplary spirit of cooperation among ASEAN countries on environment. During this period, action plans have been formulated for the areas of Marine Environment, Nature Conservation and Environmental Education Training, whereas extensive programmes have been established under the priority areas of Environmental Management including Environmental Impact Assessment, Industry and Environment, and Environmental Information and Environmental Data.

ASEP I witnessed many gatherings of environmentalists of all professions on different environmental fora. Such association has fostered regional collaboration. This trend was continued during ASEP II and through such fora, environmentalists were given opportunity to discuss and got acquainted with their counterparts in other ASEAN members. It could definitely be said that ASEP I succeeded in establishing the necessary groundworks vital for future regional collaboration. Institutionally, ASEAN by itself had established a permanent Experts Group on the Environment serving as a viable vehicle in propelling environmental collaboration for the benefit of all.

## Environmental Management Including Environmental Impact Assessment (EIA)

Under ASEP I, emphasis was given to verifying the value of environmental impact assessment as a management tool. The ASEAN/UNEP Environmental Impact Assessment Workshop for Decision Makers held in Baquio in June 1980 had initiated this process. The Workshop succeeded in confirming the interest and willingness of ASEAN countries in employing EIA as a management tool. This was confirmed, for example, by the EIA completed in 1983 for the ASEAN-Ache Fertilizer (AAF) as well as the EIA for the ASEAN-Bintulu Fertilizer (ABF) plant in Malaysia which was completed in 1984 and the report under review.

In Thailand, Government had issued proclamation on types and sizes of projects which require environmental impact assessment and is vigorously enforcing this proclamation since July 1981. The Philippines has the most comprehensive environmental legislation with various Presidential Decrees and Proclamations. Proclamation number 2146 specifies areas and types of projects which are classified as environmentally critical and thus would fall under the requirement of environmental impact assessment. Indonesia has very recently, in March 1982, passed a landmark act on Basic Provisions for the Management of the Living Environment under which environmental impact analysis is called for every plan which may have significant impact to the environment. In the case of Malaysia, Government is following a gradual approach by which it is envisaged that environmental impact assessment would be fully incorporated in the implementation of the Fifth Malaysia Plan 1986–1990.

Following the Baguio Workshop, Thailand hosted the Workshop on Environmental Impact Assessment for Water Resources Development Project at Srinakarin Dam in February 1981. This was a useful training exercise to share its experience with other countries on the impact of water resources development projects, particularly dam construction.

In early 1982, a comparative study was commissioned on the practices of EIA in Thailand and the Philippines. At the national level, guidelines were issued by Governments in various ASEAN countries stipulating the nature and scope of environmental impact assessment. The National Environment Board of Thailand published a useful manual on Guidelines for Preparation of Environmental Impact Evaluations aiming at familiarizing other implementing agencies on environmental impact assessment, covering major development sectors. Another approach in environmental management worth citing is the tax incentive programme offered by the Philippines on the importation of pollution control equipments. On environmental planning, various studies on soil erosion control, coastal zone management, river quality management, watershed management have been carried out in the Philippines, Thailand, Indonesia and Malaysia.

In retrospect, environmental management is by now well recognized at the conceptual and policy level. Taking advantage of various guidelines formulated, national environmental agencies have been engaging in direct dialogues with implementing agencies on their development programmes. However, there is still prevailing lack of actual integration of the environmental dimension in development activities at the field level. The next logical step thus would seem to be the execution of demonstration and pilot projects, the main objective of which is to ensure that environmentally sound development can be carried out in a manner beneficial to all and also to verify the guidelines and the concepts already developed by national environmental agencies.

In this regard, a number of projects which have been implemented were reported at the Seventh Meeting. These include, environmental planning methodologies for the Sungai Linggi water resources and water quality management in Malaysia, and ecological mapping in Pangasinan in the Philippines. As the ASEAN countries continue to use EIA as a management tool and accumulate more case experience, the Seventh Meeting decided that it was necessary to carry out an evaluation to assess to what extent EIA carried out in ASEAN countries has succeeded/failed to produce desired results. Hence, a workshop to be hosted by Indonesia and in collaboration with UNEP will be organized for this purpose.

This would eventually lead towards future phases in which investment may be induced to support large-scale projects which are environmentally sound based on the experience to be accumulated from the demonstration projects under ASEP II.

## Nature Conservation

With 30 per cent of the world tropical forest in the ASEAN region, the significance of ASEAN as one of the three major repositories of tropical ecosystems of the world is well-recognized. It is thus opportune that ASEP I had identified nature conservation a one of its priority areas and had established as one of its goals the conservation of flora and fauna of significance to the region.

The Workshop on Nature Conservation organized by Indonesia in Bali in September 1980 served as the first milestone for regional collaboration on nature conservation. Arising from the Workshop, an Action Plan for Conservation of Nature in the ASEAN Region was prepared by IUCN and UNEP and formally adopted at the Fourth Meeting of the ASEAN Experts Group on the Environment in Singapore in 1981.

ASEAN is progressing smoothly in achieving its established goals under this priority area. The five member countries had agreed on ten selected sites to be established as ASEAN Heritage Parks and Reserves. It is envisaged that the proclamation of ASEAN Heritage Parks and Reserves would contribute to the development of an appropriate management plan for each selected site which would induce adequate fund from national government and external sources to ensure the conservation of important flora and fauna of these heritage areas.

On the other established front, a Draft ASEAN Agreement on the Conservation of Nature and Natural Resources was prepared by the IUCN Commission on Environmental Policy, Law and Administration. ASEAN had agreed to continue its discussion on this issue in order to seek a common consensus. A meeting of legal experts was hosted by the Philippine Government in Manila in November 1982. The Ninth Meeting of COST held in Phuket, Thailand in September 1983 and also the Tenth Meeting in Baguio City, Philippines in March 1984, considered and adopted the Draft ASEAN Agreement. It is now envisaged that the ASEAN Agreement on the Conservation of Nature and Natural Resources will be officially accepted in the near future.

Recognizing the importance of nature conservation, Singapore hosted the First Meeting of the ASEAN Experts on Nature Conservation in March 1982 which highlighted future areas for regional collaboration. The Second Meeting was held in Manila, Philippines in October 1983 to discuss further steps that need to be taken in the implementation of activities in nature conservation. At the Seventh meeting of the ASEAN Experts Group on the Environment, it was recommended that each country should encourage the establishment of a wildlife society, and a list of professionals in wildlife management be provided to the Interim Co-ordinator for further action. It was agreed that BIOTROP in Bogor, Indonesia, will serve as the ASEAN Information Centre on Nature Conservation. A questionnaire was prepared by Indonesia on the training needs of ASEAN on nature conservation and is being circulated to ASEAN members. At the same time, lists of endangered species of fauna (mammals, aves, reptiles) and flora are being compiled in each country. These lists are being harmonized with a view of producing one consolidated list.

Regarding forestry, a Co-ordination Group on Forestry was established under the Committee on Food, Agriculture and Forestry of ASEAN. This Group has established direct dialogues with donor sources in implementing various joint programmes aiming at forestry management such as the ASEAN/New Zealand Project on Afforestation, ASEAN/USA Project on ASEAN Watershed Conservation and Management Research Programme, ASEAN/Canada dialogue on ASEAN Institute of Forest Management.

Looking into the future, it appears that the groundwork has already been established by the Group. ASEAN may thus concentrate on accomplishing the identified needs such as the establishment of an ASEAN training programme on nature conservation for game wardens and superintendent-level staff. The other activities which elicited the interest of ASEAN are wildlife research and management which Malaysia, Philippines and Indonesia all expressed their keen interest in, and the actual implementation and dissemination of information on ASEAN nature conservation.

## Industry and Environment

ASEAN can point to regional success cases as far as environmental quality management is concerned. The urban environmental quality management of Singapore, particularly its air, water and solid waste management, could serve as a model for other countries; whereas Malaysia can be cited as a success case in its stage-wise control of palm oil mill and rubber mill effluents. However, this should not be construed as the overall picture since the degradation of urban environmental quality in most ASEAN cities is still too obvious to be disregarded.

Under ASEP 1, ASEAN emphasized the strengthening of air and water quality management. It thus initiated a study on the capability and needs in urban air and water quality management. Resulting from this study, two workshops were hosted by Singapore on urban air and water quality monitoring and management which succeeded in sharing the Singapore experience with other ASEAN countries. A project on air quality monitoring and management submitted to the EEC was approved under the ASEAN-COST/EEC Co-operation on the subject of "Upgrading ASEAN Capabilities in Urban Air Pollution Control and Monitoring". The project package comprised workshop/seminar, training course-cum-study tour and a four to five weeks mission of one EEC expert.

Other established goal of ASEP I under this priority area is the promotion of pollution control technology, recognizing the fact that organic residues comprise the majority of wastes generated in ASEAN countries. These residues are not toxic in nature and could in fact be turned to useful resources. A project on pollution control technology with the objective to utilize residues generated from agricultural and industrial activities for beneficial purposes was formulated and earmarked for funding by UNDP. This has been secured and the project on Technology Transfer in Organo-Industrial Pollution Control will be implemented.

Also under this priority area, a comparative study on small and medium scale industries in urban areas of ASEAN was completed. It had identified small electroplating plants, battery manufacturing, foundries, and paint factories as the most important targets to be dealt with. As a follow-up measure, a manual on the design and operation of wastewater treatment facilities for small electroplating plants was completed.

With the increasing number of people clustered in urban centres of ASEAN, the issue of environmental quality management will be more and more pronounced in the coming years. One new emerging issue is hazardous substances which itself is technically complicated, difficult to handle, and requires concerted and well-planned management schemes. Special attention in handling such problem is called for and regional programmes on such subject area will serve the interest of ASEAN.

## Environmental Education and Training

In the period of ASEP I, ASEAN countries continued to strengthen their environmental education programmes at all levels. Emphasis was given to the introduction of environmental courses in formal education, the development of environmental curricula and the training of teachers. At the tertiary level, all major universities of ASEAN have established their own environmental education programmes.

Malaysia hosted the Regional Conference on Environmental Education in Kuala Lumpur in August 1981 which served as the first forum of its kind, organized regionally for ASEAN environmentalists and educators, to discuss common areas of interest on environmental education and research. For its part, the Regional Institute of Higher Education and Development (RIHED) with financial support of UNEP prepared a survey on environmental education and research in each country of ASEAN.

With the existing programme on environment in each ASEAN university, it may thus be opportune to establish a network of universities on environmental education and research for ASEAN. Such network could be instrumental in sharing the fruits of research being conducted simultaneously by various universities in the region. It will also serve in assuring continuing dialogues among various scientists and researchers sharing the same interest.

At the request of ASEAN, UNESCO/UNEP formulated and submitted an action plan on environmental education and training. At the primary and secondary levels, training of teachers has been identified as most important. Teachers serve as important media in conveying environmental knowledge to students, and in turn, to the public. In this connection, the development of teaching curricula and demonstration aids as instruction tools should be widely promoted.

The Sixth Meeting of the ASEAN Experts Group on the Environment adopted the draft action plan submitted. Priority areas of activities were identified and UNESCO, EEC assistance for funding was solicited. Following this development, UNESCO with UNEP support held a workshop for the Transfer of Environmental Education to Planners and Decision-Makers in South East Asia in Quezon City, Philippines in December 1983. The objectives of the Workshop were to serve as a forum for the exchange of ideas and experiences between academics and practitioners on the various strategies/programmes on the role of universities in environmental education, research and training and to discuss the feasibility of establishing a council or conference of ASEAN institutions of higher learning on environmental education.

Every country of ASEAN can rightfully claim that there exists a core group of environmentalists in each country. The next step is to convince other professionals on the value of the environmental dimension. Among professionals, undoubtedly economists and development planners should be given priority, due to the omnipotent nature of planning agencies in this part of the world.

Education and training are continuing processes. To be effective, both instructors and receptors must be in continuing touch with the changing environmental scenes and be exposed to the latest technical development on environment. Environmental Education and Training thus constitutes an indispensable priority area of ASEP II.

## Environmental Information and Information Data

It is widely recognized by now that information dissemination is vital in eliciting the support of the public on environmental programmes. Public relations and information dissemination have become major functions of national environmental agencies. For example, it is a regular practice in ASEAN countries to organize special exhibitions on World Environment Day. Publicity and education campaigns are not only limited to urban areas. Thailand has initiated a project aiming at providing information directly to the rural people at the village level. Mobile units were established and sent to remote villages to work with local schools in organizing demonstration courses on environment.

At the regional level, ASEAN felt the need to develop common interest and common themes. As a starter in 1982, ASEAN selected the theme of "Education for Better Environment" as its common theme of the year. In 1984, "Save Our Soils" was selected. This was closely linked to UNEP's global theme on Desertification.

The training of mass media professionals such as journalists and broadcasters is emerging as an important activity. Newspapers in ASEAN countries have always highlighted environmental issues of local and international interest. It is thus important that these issues be fully understood by media professionals so that the views expressed would be unbiased and factual in nature.

Under the sponsorship of UNEP and the Press Foundation of Asia, a workshop for Asian journalists was held in Manila in December 1983. Similar training courses for radio announcers and television broadcasters are being planned.

Another target group as mentioned earlier is the NGOs. These non-profit organizations have been actively performing the watchdog functions and must be given due credit. In the past, they have been instrumental in pressing for the passage of important legislations and regulatory measures to protect the environment. There must be a rapport between governmental agencies and these citizen groups who have more direct access to the people at the grassroots level. One way to strengthen such dialogues is to organize workshops on specific environmental issues so that open and full discussions could be exchanged which may contribute to mutual understanding vital to reducing any unnecessary potential conflicts.

On environmental data, it is often the feeling in ASEAN countries that there is a need for easier access to environmental information particularly those available in developed countries. What is needed is a retrieval system which could provide not only sources of information but the information itself upon request. This however could entail exorbitant cost and expensive secretariat.

## Marine Environment

The Sixth ASEAN Standing Committee in Manila in June 1981 decided that the East Asian Seas Programme should be considered as a UNEP programme. Nevertheless, the Fifth ASEAN Experts Group on the Environment, Bangkok, April 1982 felt that it is the responsibility of this Group to monitor the progress of the East Asian Seas Programme for reporting to COST.

Under Phase I of the East Asian Seas Programme, various studies were conducted mainly by U.N. agencies, the results of which provided background information necessary for the formulation of the programme in the present phase which is covering the biennium 1982–1983. Emphasis is now given to continuing environmental assessment by local universities and research institutes. Priority research areas include the assessment of oceanographic phenomena, oil pollution, non-oil pollutants, coral ecosystems and information exchange.

Institutionally, a Co-ordinating Body on the Seas of East Asia (COBSEA) was formally established to co-ordinate this programme. More important, a Trust Fund for the East Asian Seas Programme came into existence with contributions from ASEAN countries and UNEP. Such collaboration reflects the genuine willingness of ASEAN countries to tackle common issues such as marine environment. With the accumulation of basic information and data from various assessment activities mentioned earlier, it is envisaged that ASEAN will eventually institutionalize its common activities through the establishment of regional machineries and, as necessary, through regional conventions.

## Remote Sensing

This new priority area was discussed during the Fifth Meeting of the Group in Bangkok in April 1982. It was agreed that the feasibility of this priority area should be further studied. In principle; such high technology programme could be made more cost-effective by common utilization of existing facilities and exchange of expertise. Potential areas of collaboration include a systematic dissemination of satellite imageries available from ground receiving station in Bangkok; the exchange of expertise in the application of remote sensing to solving environmental problems in land use planning, forest survey, and coastal zone management, and the training of scientists in the applications of remote sensing taking advantage of existing training facilities and national programmes being offered in Philippines and Thailand.

## IV. THE FUTURE — PRIORITY AREAS AND ACTIVITIES OF ASEP II GOALS OF ASEP II

### Environmental Management including Environmental Impact Assessment

***Goal No. 1 (new):***

Implementation of demonstration projects on (new) environmentally-sound development to verify the established environmental concepts and guidelines on environmental management and to serve as pilot projects in integrating the environmental dimension in development activities at the field level.

***Goal No. 2:***

Development of tested methodologies in integrating environmental aspects of development plans and project evaluation. These methodologies should be applicable to the regional situation and based on the experience of the ASEAN region.

***Goal No. 3 (new):***

Enhancement of regional capability in environmental legislation through the development of a regional network of institutions, including institutions of higher learning, offering joint research programmes as well as education and training in environmental law, leading towards manpower development and instructional material development.

### Nature Conservation

***Goal No. 4:***

Development and promotion of a regional network of selected protected areas of significance for conservation of nature including genetic resources with emphasis on proper management of these resources to ensure the conservation of wild flora and fauna of the region.

***Goal No. 5 (new):***

Promotion of scientific and systematic regional (new) nature conservation programmes on training of park and reserve wardens, wildlife research and management, and information dissemination on nature conservation.

### *Goal No. 6*:

Implementation of a regional instrument in regulating international trade in endangered species of flora and fauna.

## Industry and Environment

### *Goal No. 7*:

Enhancement of regional capability in pollution control with emphasis on residue utilization particularly for those industries which are of significance to the ASEAN region such as agro-industry and mining industry.

### *Goal No. 8 (revised)*:

Establishment of adequate urban air and water quality monitoring and management systems, including the control of effluents from small and medium scale industries, in order to improve urban environmental quality.

### *Goal No. 9 (new)*:

Establishment of proper management programmes for the control of hazardous substances.

## Environmental Education and Training

### *Goal No. 10*

Promotion of environmental education and training in the ASEAN region through the development of:

(a) suitable national programmes at school, out-of-school and other levels; and
(b) a network of institutions of higher learning offering environmental education, training, and research programmes.

## ASEP I and II Projects Summary

The various activities under ASEP I and II and their current status are presented in tabulated from in Table 2. It shows that of a total of 101 activities and projects, 37 have been completed, 19 are on-going national or regional activities, 31 project proposals are in various levels of development, and only 14 projects have not been implemented. Thirty-two projects in ASEP II will be carried over to ASEP III.

As envisaged in ASEP II, a rolling programming approach was followed in its implementation using the experience gained during the first eighteen months of implementation to modify the Programme to cover the entire five-year cycle. Consequently, 17 projects not listed in the original ASEP II document have been proposed during the latter part of the cycle. These projects are among the 32 projects in ASEP II that will be carried over to ASEP III.

Table 2.

| Activity | Nature | Status | Major Collaborating and Potential Donor Agency | Period to Start Activity 1983–1985 | Period to Start Activity 1986–1987 |
|---|---|---|---|---|---|
| **Priority Area: Environmental Management including Environmental Impact Assessment** | | | | | |
| 1. Development of Environmental Planning Methodologies suitable for ASEAN | Case studies on environmental planning methodologies covering: | Projects ongoing and will be reported at the Eighth Meeting of the ASEAN Experts Group on the Environment. | UNEP, COST bilateral aid | × | |
| | (a) integrated watershed development planning for Citanduy in West Java. | 1983–1986 | | | |
| | (b) Sungei Linggi water resources and water quality management In Malaysia. | 1982–1984 | | | |
| | (c) Ecological mapping in the Philippines. | Completed in Pangasinan in 1983 | | | |
| | (d) Water resources development planning for | 1984–1985 | | | |

*(Continued)*

Table 2. (*Continued*)

| Activity | Nature | Status | Major Collaborating and Potential Donor Agency | Period to Start Activity 1983–1985 | Period to Start Activity 1986–1987 |
|---|---|---|---|---|---|
| | Rayong River basin, Eastern Thailand. | | | | |
| 2. Demonstration Projects on Environmentally Sound Development | Pilot projects verify the environmental guidelines developed by national environmental agencies on: | Projects ongoing and will be reported at the Eight Meeting of the ASEAN Experts Group on the Environment. | UNEP, COST | × | |
| | (a) Rehabilitation of "Critical land" through integrated development in Cigaru and Sagalaherang communities, West Java. | Partially completed, being monitored and evaluated in 1982–1985. | | | |
| | (b) Environmentally sound development through soil erosion control in Malaysia. | In the Federal Territory (Kuala Lumpur only) 1984–1986. | | | |

(*Continued*)

Table 2. (*Continued*)

| Activity | Nature | Status | Major Collaborating and Potential Donor Agency | Period to Start Activity 1983–1985 | Period to Start Activity 1986–1987 |
|---|---|---|---|---|---|
| | (c) Rehabilitation strategies in critically eroded watersheds of lemery, Batangas, the Philippines. | 1983–1985 | | | |
| | (d) Appropriate technology for rural development of Ban Na, Nakorn Nayok, Thailand. | 1983–1985 | | | |
| 3. EIA in ASEAN Industrial Projects | To ensure that EIA will be undertaken in the ASEAN Industrial Projects namely: | | COST/COIME | × | |
| | (a) ASEAN-Aceh Fertilizer (AAF) Indonesia. | Completed (1982–1983) | | | |
| | (b) ASEAN-Bintulu Fertilizer (ABF) Plant, Malaysia. | EIA completed in 1984, being reviewed. | | | |

(*Continued*)

Table 2. (*Continued*)

| Activity | Nature | Status | Major Collaborating and Potential Donor Agency | Period to Start Activity 1983–1985 | Period to Start Activity 1986–1987 |
|---|---|---|---|---|---|
| | (c) Copper Fabrication Project, the Philippines. | Project under review | | | |
| | (d) Rocksalt Soda Ash Project in Thailand. | Project under review | | | |
| 4. Case studies on Environmental Impact Assessment | To develop EIA guidelines based on actual case studies in ASEAN countries on. | | EEC, Canada, UNEP | × | |
| | (a) Transmigration in Indonesia | On-going 1983–1985 | | | |
| | (b) Industrial estate development in Malaysia. | Not Started | | | |
| | (c) Mining and quarrying industries in the Philippines. | Partially completed (1983–85) | | | |
| | (d) Road and highway construction in Thailand. | Under preparation (1984–85) | | | |

(*Continued*)

Table 2. (*Continued*)

| Activity | Nature | Status | Major Collaborating and Potential Donor Agency | Period to Start Activity 1983–1985 | Period to Start Activity 1986–1987 |
|---|---|---|---|---|---|
| 5. Seminar for National Industrial Development Banks on Loan Policy for Industrial Pollution Control. | To prepare comparative study on industrial pollution control and the role of national industrial development banks, and to organize a seminar with national development bank as the target group. | New activity | UNEP, ADB, IBRD | | |
| 6. Seminar for Local Environment Consulting Firms | To provide a forum for national environmental consulting firms to discuss their association with international consulting companies, and any actions needed to strengthen their role in serving ASEAN countries. | Completed in 1984 | World Environment Center, New York | | |

(*Continued*)

Table 2. (*Continued*)

| Activity | Nature | Status | Major Collaborating and Potential Donor Agency | Period to Start Activity 1983–1985 | Period to Start Activity 1986–1987 |
|---|---|---|---|---|---|
| 7. National Workshop on the Application of Extended Benefit Cost Analysis | Organization of national workshop to test the applicability of such methodology of ASEAN. | Completed in the Philippines and Thailand | EWC, UNEP | × | |
| 8. Information Dissemination on EIA. | Strengthening exchange of information on EIA reports conducted in ASEAN countries, e.g. through listing of titles in ASEAN Environment Newsletter. | Starting 1984 | | × | |
| 9. Enhancement of Regional Capability in Environmental Legislation | To develop a regional network of institution of higher learning offering:<br><br>(1) joint research programmes, and | Indonesia to initiate | UNEP, IUCN | × | |

(*Continued*)

Table 2. (*Continued*)

| Activity | Nature | Status | Major Collaborating and Potential Donor Agency | Period to Start Activity 1983–1985 | 1986–1987 |
|---|---|---|---|---|---|
| | (2) education and training in environmental law. | | | | |
| 10. Workshop on Evaluation of EIA Applications in ASEAN Countries | To assess to what extent EIA carried out in the ASEAN region has succeeded/failed to produce desired results.<br>To identify technical, legal, administrative, institutional and other constraints.<br>To recommend ways and means including the formulation of an Action Plan to overcome these constraints. | New activity. Workshop to be held in Indonesia in January–February 1985 | UNEP | × | |

(*Continued*)

Table 2. (*Continued*)

| Activity | Nature | Status | Major Collaborating and Potential Donor Agency | Period to Start Activity 1983–1985 | Period to Start Activity 1986–1987 |
|---|---|---|---|---|---|
| 11. Environmental Impact Study on Coal Fired | Project activities consist of on-site and off-site studies as well as epidemiological studies to correlate health effects and the amount of pollution emanating from the plants. To be carried out in the Philippines. | Approved by COST for third country funding. | COST | × | |
| **Priority Area: Nature Conservation** | | | | | |
| 1. Establishment of ASEAN Heritage Parks and Reserves | To upgrade selected national sites with regional significance into regional heritage parks and reserves. | ASEAN Heritage Parks and Reserves was formally adopted in the Sixth | UNEP, IUCN | × | |

(*Continued*)

Table 2. (*Continued*)

| Activity | Nature | Status | Major Collaborating and Potential Donor Agency | Period to Start Activity 1983–1985 | Period to Start Activity 1986–1987 |
|---|---|---|---|---|---|
| | | Meeting of the ASEAN Experts Group on the Environment, March 1983. The Heritage Sites will be jointly declared by the Second ASEAN Ministerial Meeting to be held in Thailand, 1984, as well as the master plan for each site is on-going. | | | |
| 2. Establishment of ASEAN School of Nature Conservation | To establish a regional training school for park wardens and superintendent-level staff by upgrading | The Seventh Meeting of the ASEAN Experts Group on the Environment, | Netherlands, Indonesia | × | |

(*Continued*)

Table 2. (*Continued*)

| Activity | Nature | Status | Major Collaborating and Potential Donor Agency | Period to Start Activity 1983–1985 | Period to Start Activity 1986–1987 |
|---|---|---|---|---|---|
| | the School of Environmental Conservation Management in Ciawi. | Malaysia, 1984, decided to forward this activity for funding through ASEAN-COST. | | | |
| 3. Wildlife Research and Management | To promote wildlife research and management in the region either through the establishment of an ASEAN centre or the formulation of a network of national centres. This activity includes studies on wildlife in captivity management. | Ditto | IUCN, UNEP | × | |
| 4. Establishment of an ASEAN Information | To strengthen BIOTROP to serve as the Centre. One of the first projects | Ditto | IUCN, BIOTROP, COST | × | |

(*Continued*)

Table 2. *(Continued)*

| Activity | Nature | Status | Major Collaborating and Potential Donor Agency | Period to Start Activity 1983–1985 | Period to Start Activity 1986–1987 |
|---|---|---|---|---|---|
| Centre on Nature Conservation | that it may undertake is to prepare a booklet on endangered species of fauna and flora of ASEAN. | | | | |
| 5. Meeting of ASEAN Experts on Nature Conservation | To continue providing a forum for ASEAN counterparts to discuss their programmes on nature conservation. | On-going, Indonesia offered to host the third meeting in October 1984. | UNEP | × | |
| 6. ASEAN Agreement on the Conservation of Nature and Natural Resources | To adopt a workable instrument in regulating international trade in endangered species of flora and fauna. | This activity has been approved by ASEAN COST in Spetember 1983. | | | |
| 7. Conservation of Tropical Forests | To ensure that tropical forests of ASEAN will be properly managed. | COFAF has an extensive programme on tropical forests, the ASEAN Experts Group on the | COFAF | × | |

*(Continued)*

Table 2. (*Continued*)

| Activity | Nature | Status | Major Collaborating and Potential Donor Agency | Period to Start Activity 1983–1985 | Period to Start Activity 1986–1987 |
|---|---|---|---|---|---|
| | | Environment thus felt that it should monitor the activities of COFAF for possible collaboration. | | | |
| 8. Training in the Recovery of Tropical Forest following Disturbance | To promote manpower development for the management of tropical forestry in ASEAN. | New activity | EEC | × | |
| 9. Establishment of ASEAN Wildlife Society | To promote professional exchange of communications of wildlife specialists and supporters. | New activity. The Second Meeting of the ASEAN Experts on Nautre Conservation in October 1983 and the Seventh Meeting of ASEAN Experts Group on the Environment | | × | |

(*Continued*)

Table 2. (*Continued*)

| Activity | Nature | Status | Major Collaborating and Potential Donor Agency | Period to Start Activity 1983–1985 | Period to Start Activity 1986–1987 |
|---|---|---|---|---|---|
| | | in April 1984, recommended that ASEAN Wildlife Society ought to constitute itself as a Non-Governmental Organization and each participating country should encourage the establishment of such a society at national level. A list of professionals in wildlife management be provided to the Interim Co-ordinator for further action. | | | |
| 10. Regional Project on Wildlife Resources | To promote rural programme on wildlife resources management. | Indonesia will formulate the project proposal | | × | |

(*Continued*)

Table 2. (*Continued*)

| Activity | Nature | Status | Major Collaborating and Potential Donor Agency | Period to Start Activity 1983–1985 | Period to Start Activity 1986–1987 |
|---|---|---|---|---|---|
| Development and Utilization for Rural People in Southeast Asia | | for consideration in the Third Meeting of ASEAN Experts on Nature Conservation. | | | |
| 11. (a) Urban Park Development and greenery | To promote establishment and programme management of urban parks. | Ditto | | | × |
| (b) Wildlife in Captivity Management | | New activity | | | |
| 12. ASEAN Workshop for Park Managers | To share experiences among national park executives of ASEAN. | New activity. The workshop is to be held in a national park in Indonesia in October 1984. | UNEP | × | |
| 13. ASEAN Park Study Tour | | | | | × |

(*Continued*)

Table 2. (*Continued*)

| Activity | Nature | Status | Major Collaborating and Potential Donor Agency | Period to Start Activity 1983–1985 | Period to Start Activity 1986–1987 |
|---|---|---|---|---|---|
| **Priority Area: Industry and Environment** | | | | | |
| 1. Technology Transfer in Organo-Industrial Pollution Control | Promotion of utilization of organic residues from agro-industry for beneficial purposes and as a means of pollution control. | Ongoing. Funding has been secured from UNDP. | UNEP | × | |
| 2. Upgrading ASEAN Capability in Air Pollution Control and Monitoring | ASEAN to strengthen its air quality control and management through a collaborative project with EEC including consultancy, training workshop, and travel fellowships. | On-going. Funding has been secured from EEC. Training course-cum-study tour is proposed to be implemented in Spring 1985 in Italy. | EEC | × | |
| 3. Preparation of Policy Guidelines on Transportation, | To assist Governments in preparing action programmes on | New activity | COST/Australia WHO (PEPAS), UNEP | × | |

(*Continued*)

Table 2. (*Continued*)

| Activity | Nature | Status | Major Collaborating and Potential Donor Agency | Period to Start Activity 1983–1985 | Period to Start Activity 1986–1987 |
|---|---|---|---|---|---|
| Collection Treatment and Disposal of Hazardous Substances | management of hazardous substances. | | | | |
| 4. Workshop-cum-Study Tour on Solid Wastes Management | To learn from the experience of Singapore on its solid wastes management programmes particularly incineration. | The Interim Co-ordinator is seeking for funds. Singapore will hold a workshop as soon as funding is made available. | UNDP, Singapore | × | |
| 5. Preparation of Manuals on Environmental Quality Management of Selected Small- and Medium-Scale Industries | Manuals will cover the design and operation of waste treatment facilities for various small- and medium-scale industries. | The Seventh Meeting of the ASEAN Experts Group on the Environment, April 1984, Malaysia, agreed to evaluate the extent of its use before initiating further action on | UNEP, WHO (POEPAS) | × | |

(*Continued*)

Table 2. (*Continued*)

| **Activity** | **Nature** | **Status** | **Major Collaborating and Potential Donor Agency** | **Period to Start Activity** | |
|---|---|---|---|---|---|
| | | | | **1983–1985** | **1986–1987** |
| | | similar manuals for other industries. | | | |
| 6. Workshop-cum-Study Tour on Environmental Quality Management of Palm Oil and Rubber Mils | To learn from the success of Malaysia in managing palm oil and rubber effluents. | New activity. The Interim Co-ordinator is seeking for funds. Malaysia is ready to host a study tour-cum-training course as soon as funding is made available. | UNEP, Malaysia | × | |
| 7. Training Programme for Water Quality Monitoring and Management | To conduct regional training programme on standardized methods for water quality monitoring, laboratory procedures, establishment of computerized water quality data system. Such programme should | New activity. Thailand proposed a Regional Training Course in Water Quality Management in Tropical Regions in the Seventh Meeting of the | AIT, WHO (PEPAS), APO, UNEP, Australia | × | |

(*Continued*)

Table 2. (*Continued*)

| Activity | Nature | Status | Major Collaborating and Potential Donor Agency | Period to Start Activity 1983–1985 | Period to Start Activity 1986–1987 |
|---|---|---|---|---|---|
| | be about 4 weeks in duration. | ASEAN Experts Group on the Environment, April 1984, Malaysia. | | | |
| 8. Air Quality Monitoring and Management | Specific activities may include:<br>(1) Technical workshop on design of urban air pollution monitoring programme.<br>(2) On-the-job training in ambient air monitoring.<br>(3) Technical workshop on statistical management of air quality data. | This is a follow-up of the ASEAN/UNEP Study Tour and Technical Workshop on Air Quality Monitoring and Management, Singapore, November 1982. | EEC | × | |

(*Continued*)

Table 2. (*Continued*)

| Activity | Nature | Status | Major Collaborating and Potential Donor Agency | Period to Start Activity 1983–1985 | Period to Start Activity 1986–1987 |
|---|---|---|---|---|---|
| | (4) On-the-job training in stock taking procedures in an advanced country.<br>(5) Technical workshop on industrial processes and control techniques of industrial emission.<br>(6) On-the-job training in control of pollution from motor vehicles. | | | | |
| **Priority Area: Environment Education and Training** | | | | | |
| 1. Development of Prototype Curriculum Materials for Environmental Education (in-school) | To promote curriculum development through regional and national workshops | New activity | UNESCO, EEC | × | |
| 2. Development of Curriculum Materials for Non-Formal Education | To organize a series of workshops, both regional and national, to promote such activity. | New activity | UNESCO, EEC | × | |

(*Continued*)

Table 2. (*Continued*)

| Activity | Nature | Status | Major Collaborating and Potential Donor Agency | Period to Start Activity 1983–1985 | Period to Start Activity 1986–1987 |
|---|---|---|---|---|---|
| 3. Training on Development of Institutional Materials for Environmental Education (in-school) | | New activity | UNESCO, EEC | | |
| 4. Training on the Integration of Environmental Education Concepts in Various Disciplines as well as on the Development of Prototype Institutional Materials for Out-of-School Environmental Education | | New activity | UNESCO, EEC | | |
| 5. Training on Wastewater Control, Planning and Management | To strengthen manpower development for wastewater management. | New Activity | WHO (PRPAS), APO, UNEP | × | |

(*Continued*)

Table 2. (*Continued*)

| Activity | Nature | Status | Major Collaborating and Potential Donor Agency | Period to Start Activity 1983–1985 | Period to Start Activity 1986–1987 |
|---|---|---|---|---|---|
| 6. Training Programme for Water Quality Monitoring and Management | Same as Activity (7) under Industry and Environment. | New Activity | AIT, WHO (PEPAS), APO, UNEP, Australia | × | |
| 7. Training on Technology, Treatment and Disposal of Toxic and Hazardous Wastes | This is complementary to Activity (3) under Industry and Environment. | New Activity | WHO (PEPAS), APO, UNEP | × | |
| 8. Training on Nature Conservation | Same as Activity (2) of Nature Conservation | New Activity | Netherlands, Indonesia | × | |
| **Priority Area: Environment Information and Environmental Data** | | | | | |
| 1. Workshop for Journalists | To organize regional and national training workshops on specific issues on environment for journalists such as:<br>(a) tropical forests;<br>(b) hazardous substances; | The Workshop for Asian Journalists was held under the joint sponsorship of UNEP and the Press Foundation of Asia (PFA) at Manila in | UNEP, ESCAP, PFA | × | |

(*Continued*)

Table 2. (*Continued*)

| Activity | Nature | Status | Major Collaborating and Potential Donor Agency | Period to Start Activity 1983–1985 | Period to Start Activity 1986–1987 |
|---|---|---|---|---|---|
| | (c) environmental impact of water resources development | December 1983. A training course for broadcasters is planned to be organized in conjunction with the Asian Institute of Broadcasting Development (AIBD). | | | |
| 2. Strengthening Public Awareness on Environment at the Village Level | Development of demonstration materials on environment for use by community schools both for teaching students and the rural public. This is complementary to Activity (2) under Environmental Education and Training. | New activity | UNEP, UNESCO | × | |

(*Continued*)

Table 2. (*Continued*)

| Activity | Nature | Status | Major Collaborating and Potential Donor Agency | Period to Start Activity 1983–1985 | Period to Start Activity 1986–1987 |
|---|---|---|---|---|---|
| 3. Acquisition of Environmental Information and Data | (a) Establishment of a regional environmental information retrieval scheme by which environmental information may be acquired and disseminated.<br>(b) Promotion of pilot projects on systematic collection and use of environmental statistics. | New activity. The Seventh Meeting of the ASEAN Experts Group on the Environment, Malaysia, April 1984 agreed that assistance be sought from UNEP for an expert to review present status on the current use of computer-based information systems in ASEAN countries. | UNSO, UNEP, UNESCO | × | |
| 4. ASEAN Newsletter | Continuation of publication of ASEAN Newsletter | On-going | | × | |

(*Continued*)

Table 2. (*Continued*)

| Activity | Nature | Status | Major Collaborating and Potential Donor Agency | Period to Start Activity 1983–1985 | Period to Start Activity 1986–1987 |
|---|---|---|---|---|---|
| 5. World Environment Day (WED) | Continuation of regional collaboration on WED activities. | On-going. The third theme selected for the year 1984 was "Save Our Soils". | | × | |
| 6. Traning of NGOs | To organize technical training workshops, for NGOs based on scientific and technical studies | New activity | UNEP | | × |
| **Priority Area: Marine Environment** | | | | | |
| 1. East Asian Seas Action Plan | To protect the marine environment of ASEAN through joint collaboration. The present phase of the programme covers | On-going | UNEP and other U.N. agencies (ESCAP, FAO, WHO, UNESCO, etc.) | × | |

(*Continued*)

Table 2. (*Continued*)

| Activity | Nature | Status | Major Collaborating and Potential Donor Agency | Period to Start Activity 1983–1985 | Period to Start Activity 1986–1987 |
|---|---|---|---|---|---|
| | 1982–1983 and emphasizes: (a) Assessment of Oceanographic Phenomena; (b) Assessment of Oil Pollution; (c) Assessment of Non-Oil Pollutants; (d) Assessment of the Impact of Pollution on, and Habitat Degradation of Coral Ecosystems; (e) Information and Data Exchange | | | | |
| 2. ASEAN Guidelines on the Development and Management of Coastal Area | | | | | |

(*Continued*)

Table 2. (*Continued*)

| Activity | Nature | Status | Major Collaborating and Potential Donor Agency | Period to Start Activity 1983–1985 | Period to Start Activity 1986–1987 |
|---|---|---|---|---|---|
| 3. Island Ecosystems Development Approach | | | | | |
| 4. Symposium on Marine Pollution in Shallow Waters | | | | | |
| **Priority Area: Remote Sensing** | | | | | |
| 1. Formulation of an ASEAN Action Plan on Remote Sensing | Areas of collaboration may include:<br>(a) Systematic dissemination of satellite imageries received by existing ground station.<br>(b) Research and training programmes taking advantage of existing facilities and experience in the region. | New activity. The. Seventh Meeting of the ASEAN Experts Group on the Environment, Malaysia, April 1984 agreed that Interim Coordinator should approach U.S.A. for technical assistance to assess ASEAN capabilities and to formulate guidelines for the application and | UNEP, AIT, ESCAP, U.S.A. | × | |

(*Continued*)

Table 2. (*Continued*)

| Activity | Nature | Status | Major Collaborating and Potential Donor Agency | Period to Start Activity 1983–1985 | Period to Start Activity 1986–1987 |
|---|---|---|---|---|---|
| | (b) Research and training programmes taking advantage of existing facilities and experience in the region.<br>(c) Pilot projects on environmental assessment using satellite imageries in land-use planning, coastal management, forest survey, etc. | systematic development of this activity. | | | |
| 2. Workshop of ASEAN Experts to Consider the Action Plan on Remote Sensing | To organize a Workshop for ASEAN experts to consider the Action Plan to be formulated by (1) above. | New activity | EWC, UNEP | × | |

# CHAPTER 44

# ASEAN SUB-REGIONAL ENVIRONMENT PROGRAMME

# PHASE III

## 1988–1992

## PREFACE

The ASEAN Experts Group on the Environment prepared the ASEAN Environment Programme III (1988–1992) with the assistance of the United Nations Environment Programme Regional Office for Asia and the Pacific and the Bureau of Science and Technology of the ASEAN Secretariat.

This document has been circulated to all ASEAN member countries, considered and endorsed by the Tenth Meeting of the ASEAN Experts Group on the Environment, and adopted by the Third ASEAN Ministerial Meeting on the Environment.

## I. BACKGROUND AND REVIEW

The year 1987 marks the end of two decades of cooperation among the members of the Association of Southeast Asian Nations (ASEAN) which was established when the ASEAN Declaration was signed in Bangkok on 8 August 1967. It also marks the beginning of a new era of cooperation with the holding of the Third Summit of the Heads of Governments of ASEAN countries in Manila in December 1987.

In the field of the environment, the year 1987 marks the end of the first decade of ASEAN cooperation as formulated in the ASEAN Environment Programme I (1978–1982) and the ASEAN Environment Programme II (1983–1987). It also marks the start of the implementation of the ASEAN Environment Programme III (1988–1992) which is designed to provide a firm base for the launching of a new era of cooperation into the 1990s and the next century.

ASEAN cooperation in the environment field was initiated in 1977 when the draft ASEAN Sub-Regional Environment Programme (ASEP I) was prepared with the assistance of the United Nations Environment Programme (UNEP). The ASEAN Committee on Science and Technology (ASEAN COST) recommended that a meeting of ASEAN experts on the environment be convened to consider the proposed Programme. Consequently, the First Meeting of the ASEAN Experts Group on the Environment (AEGE) was held in Jakarta on 18–20 December 1978 to consider ASEP I. Since then, the AEGE has met regularly each year and has become a permanent body under the purview of ASEAN COST.

ASEP I identified six priority programme areas for cooperation, namely, Environmental management Including Environmental Impact Assessment, Nature Conservation and Terrestrial Ecosystem, Industry and Environment, Marine Environment, Environmental Education and Training, and Environmental Information. It established eight goals within the six programme areas and emphasized the identification of common activities which would benefit ASEAN, the assessment of the environmental situation and the existing institutional capabilities in ASEAN; and the holding of meetings and workshops to discuss technical and policy issues on environment and to learn about the national activities of each member country.

The First ASEAN Ministerial Meeting on the Environment held in Manila on 30 April 1981 endorsed ASEP I and adopted the following objective and policy guidelines on the ASEAN environment:

## Objective

To ensure the protection of the ASEAN environment and the sustainability of its natural resources so that it can sustain continued development with the aim of eradicating poverty and attaining the highest possible quality of life for the people of the ASEAN countries.

## Policy Guidelines

Foster a common awareness among the people of the ASEAN countries of the biological, physical and social environment and its vital significance for sustained development to proceed apace;

> Ensure, as far as practicable, that environmental considerations are taken into account in development efforts, both on-going and future;

> Encourage the enactment and enforcement of environmental protection measures in the ASEAN countries; and
> Foster the development of environmental education programmes.

In the context of the restructuring of ASEAN, the meeting also recommended the establishment of an ASEAN Committee on Environment.

The ASEAN Environment Programme II (ASEP II) retained the six programme areas of ASEP I and added another, namely, Remote Sensing. Thirteen goals were established within the seven programme areas: five new ones, two revised from ASEP I, and six goals remaining unchanged. Emphasis was given to the promotion of demonstration projects to solve immediate regional needs, the formulation of action plans and programmes for all the priority areas, and the strengthening of regional collaboration.

The Second ASEAN Ministerial Meeting on the Environment held in Bangkok on 29 November 1984, adopted ASEP II and noted with satisfaction the progress of the implementation of projects under the ASEAN Environment Programme. The Meeting also adopted the new objective on the ASEAN environment as follows:

> To implement the ASEAN Development Strategy through an integrated approach entailing advance or forward planning in the environmentally related activities with a view to incorporating environmental dimension in development planning right at the base level in order to achieve sustained development and long-term conservation of environmental assets and at the same time improving the quality of life for all.

Detailed policy guidelines outlining the specific steps to be taken by ASEAN member countries with respect to environmental management. Nature conservation, marine environment, industry, urban environment, environmental education and training, environmental information systems, wider involvement in environmental management, environmental legislation, and international cooperation on environmental management were also adopted.

To achieve the objective of ASEP II, various projects were implemented and numerous proposals were developed within the seven priority programme areas. These are reviewed briefly here.

## Environmental Management Including EIA

One of the most significant developments in ASEAN during the past decade was in the field of environmental management. During this period, the value of environmental impact assessment was recognized and the EIA system became an integral part of the planning and evaluation of major development projects. In Indonesia, EIA studies were conducted on the Saguling Hydro-Electric Power Plant and the Kujang Fertilizer Plant Projects; in Thailand, a comprehensive environmental impact assessment was made on the Chiew Larn Multipurpose (Hydro-Electric Dam) Project; in Malaysia, on the Bintulu Regional Development; and in the Philippines, on the North Davao Mining Corporation Amacan Copper Project. These were among the case studies presented during the Workshop on Evaluation of Environmental Impact Assessment Applications in ASEAN Countries which was held in Bandung on 4–7 March 1984.

The importance that ASEP II gave to EIA is reflected in the number of project proposals developed since 1983 under this subject. In this regard, a number of project proposals in varying levels of development have been reported at the Ninth Meeting of the AEGE in Singapore in April 1986. These include: Assessment of Environmental Impacts of Coal-Based Electric Power Plants and Other Industries, approved by ASEAN COST and accepted by Australia for third party funding support; EIA of Mini-Hydro Plants, approved by ASEAN COST and awaiting third party funding support; Developing Environmental Guidelines for Development Planning, approved in principle by the AEGE and ready for submission to ASEAN COST; EIA Training, a revised proposal is awaited by the AEGE; and Information Dissemination on EIAs, all member countries are requested to submit articles on EIA for publication in ASEAN Newsletter. Most of these projects, particularly those in an advanced stage of development and awaiting third party funding support, will be carried over to ASEP III.

Substantial progress has also been achieved in two major activities under this priority programme area. With respect to the activity on the development of environmental planning methodologies suitable for ASEAN, Indonesia has continued to pursue the Watershed Development Project and during the Ninth Meeting of the AEGE, Indonesia reported on the Sub-Watershed Kali Konto Experience. The Philippines has completed the ecological profiles of several selected provinces while a number are in varying stages of completion. Thailand has also completed its report on the Water Resources Development Planning for Rayong River Basin Project. However, Malaysia had to suspend work on the

Sungai Linggi Water Resources and Water Quality Project due to manpower problem and has instead carried out a special study on water quality criteria and standards.

On the activity on Demonstration Projects on Environmentally-Sound Development, Indonesia is actively conducting a project on the Rehabilitation of Critical Land Areas. Malaysia has a project on Soil Erosion Control; the Philippines on Rehabilitation Strategies in Critically-Eroded Watersheds in Lemery, Batangas which is expected to be completed in 1987; and Thailand has completed a project on Appropriate Technology for Rural Development and has started to apply the technology to specific target groups.

Because of their importance to ASEAN and of the need to further integrate economic and environmental planning and development, demonstration projects on environmentally-sound development and the development of environmental planning methodologies suitable for ASEAN will continue to be pursued in ASEP III. Future efforts will be guided by the experience obtained during the past decade of ASEAN cooperation.

## Nature Conservation

After that landmark ASEAN Declaration on Heritage Parks and Reserves in Bangkok on 29 November 1984, ASEAN cooperation in nature conservation reached another milestone with the approval of the ASEAN Agreement on the Conservation of Nature and Natural Resources at the Eighteenth ASEAN Ministerial Meeting in Kuala Lumpur in July 1985. Then at the Ninth Meeting of the AEGE, the recommendations of the Ad-Hoc Working Group on the Harmonization of the List of Endangered and Threatened Species of ASEAN Countries were adopted. This should pave the way for the ratification by each ASEAN government of the ASEAN Agreement on the Conservation of Nature and Natural Resources.

At the national level, conservation efforts have intensified over the last half decade. In the Philippines, a Task Force Pawikan has been created to conserve the dwindling population of economically important marine turtle species and marine turtle sanctuaries have been established in Taganak, Baguan, and Bancauan islands. The Philippine eagle conservation project has been launched to manage the remaining population of the Philippine eagle and its habitat. Marine sanctuaries have been established in sixteen areas, with the Sumilon Marine Park providing an excellent example for the genetic conservation of marine species. In Malaysia, 5.8% of the land in Peninsular Malaysia, 0.63% in Sarawak and 1.4% in Sabah have been set aside as national parks and wildlife reserves. Similar efforts are found in Thailand, Indonesia, and Brunei.

At the regional level, the ASEAN Meeting on Nature Conservation (formerly, ASEAN Experts on Nature Conservation) has met regularly to consider projects of regional interest. An ASEAN Workshop for Park Managers was held in Baluran, East Java, Indonesia on 26–29 October 1984. Working under the purview of the AEGE, the ASEAN Meeting on Nature Conservation has prepared and developed a number of project proposals. The Regional Project on Wildlife Resources Development and Utilization for the Rural People in South East Asia has been approved by the AEGE and the ASEAN COST while two project proposals are under consideration, namely, Protected Areas Training and Technical Assistance, and the Development of Master Plan for ASEAN Heritage Parks and Reserves.

The ASEAN Declaration on Heritage Parks and Reserves and the ASEAN Agreement on the Conservation of Nature and Natural Resources are outstanding achievements of ASEP I and ASEP II. But to ensure effective nature conservation, the multifarious roles of the forest ecosystem need to be recognized and forest conservation need to be integrated with wildlife conservation, agriculture, and rural development.

## Industry and Environment

Although the goals of ASEP II under this programme area are spread out into three areas of concern, namely, the enhancement of regional capability in pollution control with emphasis on residue utilization, the establishment of adequate urban air and water quality monitoring and management systems, including the control of effluents from small and medium industries, and the establishment of proper management programmes for the control of hazardous substances, more emphasis was placed by ASEAN member countries on the upgrading of ASEAN capability on air pollution monitoring and control. This is apparent in the number of projects carried out and the number of project proposals prepared in this area.

Two projects have been completed, namely, a Training Course Cum Study Tour on Air Pollution Control and Monitoring which was held in Italy on 15 April to

7 June 1985 and an ASEAN-EEC Workshop/Seminar on Air Pollution Monitoring which was held in Bangkok on 17–26 June 1985.

The ASEAN member countries have also prepared and developed a number of project proposals in this field which are presently in varying levels of development. These include the ASEAN-EC Project on Urban Air Quality Monitoring and Management, which has been approved by ASEAN COST and accepted by the EC for possible third party funding support, and three projects which have been approved at the 15th Meeting of ASEAN COST in October 1986, namely, Application of Meteorological Data in Air Pollution Monitoring and Control in the ASEAN Region, Air Pollution Control and Management in Flue Gas Desulphurization and Denitrification, and Vehicle Exhaust Emission in the ASEAN Region.

In line with the goal of establishing management programmes for the control of hazardous substances, an ASEAN-UNEP-CDG Workshop on Developing Policies and Strategic Guidelines for Managing Hazardous Wastes was held in Singapore on 7–9 May 1986. An ASEAN project on the Study of the Management and Control of Hazardous Materials in the United States has also received favorable response from the United States for possible third party funding support.

Towards the latter part of ASEP II, there was a discernible shift in emphasis from small and medium scale industries to organo-industrial industries. The ASEAN-UNDP project on Technology Transfer in Organo-Industrial Pollution Control and Monitoring was completed with the holding of a meeting in Thailand on 3–4 October 1985 and a new ASEAN project on Technology Transfer in the Treatment of Effluents From Palm Oil and Rubber Industries has been approved for funding by the United Nations Development Programme (UNDP) under the Third Cycle.

Water quality monitoring and management was also given some attention. An ASEAN-Australia Regional Training Course in Water Quality Management in Tropical Regions was held in Thailand on 25 June–10 July 1986.

As ASEAN countries continue to industrialize, the problem of industrial pollution will increasingly become more important. And as more industries are established outside of urban centers, following the programme on the regional dispersal of industries in most ASEAN countries, the problems of industrial pollution will increasingly become more distinct and separate from the problems of the urban environment. This aspect will be considered in ASEP III.

## Marine Environment

Cooperation among the ASEAN countries in the field of marine science and marine environment is carried out through three distinct regional bodies, namely, the Coordinating Body on the Seas of East Asia (COBSEA), the ASEAN Experts Group on the Environment (AEGE), and the Working Group on Marine Science (WGMS). While the AEGE and the WGMS are official ASEAN bodies under the purview of the ASEAN Committee on Science and Technology (COST), COBSEA is not. It comes under the purview of the United Nations Environment Programme (UNEP).

COBSEA was established in December 1981 by the Government of Indonesia, Malaysia, the Philippines, Singapore, and Thailand to co-ordinate the Action Plan for the Protection and Development of the Marine and Coastal Areas of the East Asian Region. Through annual meetings of COBSEA (Bangkok, 3 April 1982; Yogyakarta, 25–26 March 1983; Genting Highlands, 5–6 April 1984; Manila 22–23 April 1985; Singapore, 25–26 April 1986) the progress of the Action Plan was reviewed.

On 8–12 December 1986, a meeting of experts on the East Asian Seas Action Plan was held in Bangkok to review the development and achievements of the East Asian Seas Action Plan. Among the projects reviewed were the following: Cooperative Research on Oil and Oil Dispersant Toxicity; Study on Coral Resources and the Effects of Pollutants and Other Destructive Factors on Coral Communities and Related Fisheries; Study of the Maritime Meteorological Phenomena and Oceanographic Features; Survey and Monitoring of Oil Pollution and Development of National Co-ordinating Mechanisms for the Management and Establishment of a Regional Data Exchange System; Assessment of Concentration Levels and Trends of Non-Oil Pollutants and Their Effects on the Marine Environment; and Implementation of a Technical and Scientific Support Programme for Oil Spill Contingency Planning.

On January 14–16, 1986, a UNEP-COBSEA Workshop on Cleaning Up of Urban Rivers was held in Singapore. A number of measures were recommended to solve short and long term urban river pollution problems in ASEAN countries.

Under the AEGE, two projects are on the pipeline, namely, the ASEAN-UNDP Project on the Development of Cooperative Action Plan for Oil Pollution Combat (South China Sea) and the ASEAN-UNDP Project on Environmental Guidelines for Coastal Zone Management. Both projects will be funded from the UNDP Fourth Cycle. A third project proposal has been approved by ASEAN COST for submission to UNDP, namely, the Integrated Island Ecosystems Development Approach in ASEAN Countries.

## Environmental Education and Training

The Eighth Meeting of the AEGE held in Manila on 17–20 April 1985 noted that there had been no progress in the implementation of the ASEAN Action Plan on Environmental Education and Training and noted that the Action Plan had not been the subject of any experts meeting in a manner similar to that on nature conservation. However, on 11–14 November 1985, a meeting of Experts on Environmental Education and Training and Public Awareness in the Asia-Pacific Region was held in Bangkok to formulate a list of recommendations for formal and informal education and training, and to prepare an Action Plan for Environmental Education and Training for the Asia-Pacific Region. The Ninth Meeting of the AEGE agreed that Thailand be the coordinator for the ASEAN Action Plan on Environmental Education and Training and requested Thailand to inform the other ASEAN countries regarding follow up actions.

In line with the Programme goal of promoting environmental education and training through the development of suitable national programmes at school, out-of-school and other levels, a Regional Programme for the Training of Trainers on Environmental Education in the ASEAN Region has been prepared by the AEGE. This Programme has been approved by the ASEAN COST and will receive third party funding support from the Fourth Inter-Country Programme Cycle of the UNDP.

As stated in ASEP II, education and training are continuing processes. Thus it will remain a priority programme area in ASEP III and beyond.

## Environmental Information and Data

Majority of ASEAN member countries participate in UNEP's INFOTERRA Programme and in the activities of the International Register of Potentially Toxic Chemicals (IRPTC).

The ASEAN Environment Newsletter and the celebration of the World Environment Day in ASEAN countries are continuing activities that foster exchange of information and public awareness on issues related to the environment.

In support of the programme goal of increasing the awareness and broadening the knowledge base of the ASEAN people on environment, the AEGE has prepared a project proposal on the Development of Communication Media and Materials for Enhancing Environmental Awareness in ASEAN. The Fifteenth Meeting of ASEAN COST has approved the proposal for submission to UNDP for funding support.

In ASEP III, education, training, and information will be integrated to make the programme more effective and the implementation more cohesive.

## Remote Sensing

Although remote sensing has been added as a new priority area in ASEP II, there has not been much progress in regional cooperation in this area. However, an ASEAN proposal on Regional Technical Cooperation Programme for Improving Environmental Monitoring and Surveillance through Remote Sensing has been prepared by the AEGE and approved by ASEAN COST for possible funding by the UNDP.

Among the ASEAN countries, Thailand appears to be at the forefront in the use of remote sensing techniques for environmental planning and management. Being the location of the Landsat Satellite Ground Receiving Station, Thailand, through its National Research Council, serves as the focal point for distribution of Landsat satellite imageries to neighboring countries. Remote sensing techniques have been and are being used in the study and classification of land use patterns in the Eastern Seaboard and the Upper South Region of Thailand; in classifying forest cover types in the northern region; in studies on Chiangmai watershed management classification; in the monitoring of tailings from offshore mining activities in the southern region; and in the study of location and relocation of hilltribe settlements in northern Thailand.

Both Thailand and Indonesia have remote sensing projects supported by UNEP GRID (Global Resources Information Data Base). In Thailand, the UNEP GRID project is concerned with the analysis of environmental changes due to deforestation in Chiang Mai province. Digitized forest cover maps, as well as soils, geology, and political boundaries have been processed into polygons and now require rasterizing and verifying.

In Indonesia, UNEP GRID is concerned with the analysis of the environmental carrying capacity of selected outer islands, West Java, and possibly Sumatra.

A GRID mission has been to Jakarta to identify problem area and national capabilities.

Since remote sensing is now widely recognized as a technological tool for planning and management, it will not be listed as a separate priority area but subsumed under environmental management.

## II. OBJECTIVE AND POLICY GUIDELINES

In formulating environmental policies, it is useful to recognize that environmental problems are multi-faceted and can assume different dimensions or forms. The direct externalities of economic activities, such as, the emissions and effluents from industrial plants, are the more readily recognizable forms of environmental problems. The depletion of natural resources due to overuse constitutes yet another dimension of the problem. Desertification, deforestation, salinization, and soil erosion are examples of environmental problems resulting from the excessive exploitation of natural resources. Conflicts arising from the different uses of the environment are another facet of environmental problems. Thus, large water resources projects, such as the building of dams for hydroelectric power generation, may conflict with other uses of the environment, such as, for human settlements, agriculture, or conservation.

During the last decade, the salience of environmental issues within ASEAN has grown and the multifarious nature of environmental problems has been recognized. Nonetheless, environmental policy formulation and implementation continue to be ensnared in a host of other political and economic issues. The prominence of political and economic considerations in both national and regional policy formulation is understandable in the light of ASEAN's desire to maintain peace and attain prosperity for the region. Unfortunately, this situation has resulted in the episodic nature of environmental policy making and planning and has given rise to the apparent conflict between economic development and environmental protection.

Among the major challenges confronting ASEAN today, and perhaps up to the next century, is the problem of providing its people the basic human needs in the face of increasing pressures from a rapidly growing population. The World Development Report 1986, a publication of the World Bank, projects that the population of Indonesia will increase from 159 million in 1984 to 212 million in year 2000 and will reach the hypothetical size of stationary population of 361 million by the year 2010. The population of the Philippines will reach 76 million in year

2000 and 137 million in year 2015 from 53 million in 1984. The figures for Thailand and Malaysia are 50 million (1984), 66 million (2000) and 101 million (2005) and 15 million (1984), 21 million (2000) and 33 million (2005), respectively. In less than two decades, the population of ASEAN is projected to increase by 35% from 280 million in 1984 to 378 million in year 2000. This represents an increase of about 98 million, a figure that is more than six times the 1984 population of Malaysia.

The response of ASEAN to the aforementioned problem is to accelerate its development activities. This means rapid industrialization, more intensive and extensive agriculture, and increased exploitation of natural resources. While these efforts have made ASEAN among the fastest developing regions in the world, they have also resulted in industrial and agricultural pollution, depletion of natural resources, and conflicts in the use of the environment. If the adverse environmental impacts of these development activities are not avoided or mitigated, the environment's ability to sustain its productivity will decline resulting in long-term, permanent damage.

To resolve the apparent conflict between economic development and environmental protection, ASEAN will adopt the principle or philosophy of environmentally-sound and sustainable development which seeks to systematically integrate environmental considerations into all aspects of development and into all relevant sectoral activities. Consequently, the harmonization of economic development with environmental protection, the integration of economic and environmental planning at all levels, and the implementation of environmentally-sound and sustainable development strategies will constitute the central theme of the ASEAN objective and policy on the environment for the coming years.

Mindful of the objectives adopted in the Manila Declaration on the ASEAN Environment on 30 April 1981 and the Bangkok Declaration on the ASEAN Environment on 29 November 1984, and recognizing the need for systematic integration of environmental concerns at all stages of economic development efforts, ASEP III sets the following programme objective:

> To promote the proper management of the ASEAN environment so that it can sustain continued economic development while maintaining a high quality of life for the people of the ASEAN countries.

To achieve this objective, the following policy guidelines are formulated for the implementation of ASEP III:

1. Cooperation among its member countries in the field of the environment shall be promoted, with emphasis on the following six priority areas: environmental management, nature conservation and terrestrial ecosystem, industry and environment, marine environment, urban environment, and environmental education, training, and information.
2. The environmental dimension shall be integrated, at an early stage, into regional and national development planning and implementation in order to attain an environmentally-sound and sustainable economic development.
3. The regional and national institutional structures shall be strengthened to make them more responsive to the needs of ASEAN in implementing programmes and projects aimed at protecting the ASEAN environment.
4. Cooperation with other countries outside of ASEAN and with international agencies shall be encouraged for the purpose of sharing experiences in the management of the environment, promoting transfer of technology, and solving common global environmental problems.

These policy guidelines respond to and recognize the following realities: that environmental problems do not cease at national boundaries; that there are existing conflicts between economic development and the regenerative capacities of natural systems; that implementation is normally the weakest link in the operationalization of policies; and, that the environment is a global common.

## III. PRIORITY AREAS AND GOALS

In accordance with the first policy guideline for the implementation of ASEP III, six areas will be afforded high priority, namely, environmental management, nature conservation and terrestrial ecosystem, industry and environment, marine environment, urban environment, and environmental education, training, and information. The first area deals with the overall and integrated approach to the problems of the environment and the use of management tools, such as environmental impact assessment, and the application of advanced technologies, such as remote sensing, to solve these problems or at least mitigate their adverse impacts. The next four areas represent four selected sectors of the ASEAN environment in which there are increasing pressures resulting from continued economic development and population growth. Finally, the sixth area represents the human resources development aspect of ASEP III.

Human resources development is the bottom line in all planning processes since effective implementation can be achieved only if competent individuals are available to do the job and there is a political will to do it.

## Environmental Management

Environmental management is now well recognized at both the conceptual and policy levels. The interdependence between environment and development, that one cannot be sustained without the other, is now widely accepted by policy makers. That this is true in ASEAN is apparent in a number of national programmes and projects. The Kelang Valley, the Songkhla Lake, and the Integrated Palawan Environmental Management Projects in Malaysia, Thailand and the Philippines, respectively, are examples of environmental management plans prepared for specific areas earmarked for development. The Songkhla Lake Basin Planning Study is the first project in ASEAN to incorporate the environmental dimension in the overall planning process. The Jakarta-Puncak Corridor Environmental Management Strategy: UNEP Clearing House Program in Indonesia is an example of an environmental management program for an area which is under considerable environmental stress resulting from urbanization and development. However, there is still much to be done in actually integrating the environmental dimension into development activities at the implementation level.

In the long term, the best approach for ensuring environmental protection is through the integration of economic and environmental planning at all levels. This requires the application of evaluation techniques, such as the EIA, from the earliest stage of the planning process. It may also necessitate the use of advanced technologies, such as remote sensing, to ensure that a comprehensive picture of the environmental conditions is taken into consideration.

The integration of environmental concerns into economic development during the planning and design stages of programmes and projects is rendered ineffective if measures to monitor and manage the environmental effects are not incorporated. For this reason and to further foster regional cooperation and enhance the development of environmental management, the following goals have been set in ASEP III:

### *Goal No. 1:*

Implementation of demonstration projects on environmentally-sound development to verify the established environmental concepts and guidelines on environmental management and to serve as pilot projects in integrating the environmental dimension in economic planning and in development activities at the field level.

### *Goal No. 2:*

Application of developed methodologies, particularly environmental accounting and EIA methodologies, and use of advanced technologies, such as remote sensing, in development planning and project evaluation, implementation, and monitoring.

### *Goal No. 3:*

Enhancement of regional capability in environmental legislation and environmental accounting procedures through joint research programmes, and sharing of information, experience, and expertise.

## Nature Conservation and Terrestrial Ecosystem

The ASEAN region has abundant natural resources and has thirty percent of the world tropical forest. During the last two decades, ASEAN countries have embarked on massive economic development activities aimed at raising the standard of living of the ASEAN people. These activities have exerted considerable pressures on the region's natural resources since large outputs from primary industries like forestry, agriculture, and energy were required. The cutting of valuable timber for export was increased to earn much needed foreign exchange. Large tracts of land have been submerged to produce hydroelectric power or cleared for the construction of roads, industrial plants, housing, and other infrastructures. These activities have brought some wealth to the region but some of the economic successes have been at the expense of much priceless and rich genetic resources.

The interdependence between environment and development is most pronounced in the area of nature conservation and terrestrial ecosystem management. This fact has been recognized in the formulation of ASEP I and ASEP II, and ASEAN cooperation in this area has progressed well as evidenced by the ASEAN Agreement on the Conservation of Nature and Natural Resources and the ASEAN Declaration on Heritage Parks and Reserves. However, there is need to integrate conservation with development.

Deforestation is among the most serious environmental concerns of all ASEAN countries except Singapore and Brunei. The apparent lack of concern on the severity of this problem can be traced back to its two major causes, namely, excessive commercial logging, on one hand, and shifting cultivation and fuel wood gathering, on the other. The former is normally in the hands of the very rich while the latter is a preoccupation of the very poor. The middle class and the professionals are not directly affected by the adverse consequences of deforestation, hence the apparent weakness in the overall effort to solve the problem. A possible solution is the preparation and implementation of a comprehensive development plan for the rational exploitation and use of the ASEAN forests taking into consideration the needs of all sectors of society.

In line with the overall objective of ASEP III of integrating environmental protection, economic development, and quality of life, and in accordance with the second policy guideline for the implementation of ASEP III, this programme area does not limit itself to conservation, per se, but includes a rational and integrated approach to conservation and development. This concept is reflected in the following goals under this programme area:

### *Goal No. 4:*

Implementation of a regional programme on nature conservation with emphasis on the conservation of wild flora and fauna of the region; the harmonization of the list of endangered species of ASEAN countries; and the training of park and reserve wardens.

### *Goal No. 5:*

Development of regional programmes on the management of wetland ecosystems; management of wildlife species of economic importance; and the protection of migratory species that cross ASEAN borders.

### *Goal No. 6:*

Development and implementation of a regional programme for the development, protection, and rational exploitation of forest resources of the ASEAN region; and the establishment of adequate and proper monitoring, management and information system for the control of soil erosion and the practice of shifting cultivation.

## Industry and Environment

The ASEAN is among the world's most rapidly industrializing regions. The 1986 World Development Report published by the World Bank reports that for the five ASEAN member countries the industry's share in Gross Domestic Product (GDP) increased, between 1965 and 1984, from 12% to 40% for Indonesia, from 24% to 35% for Malaysia, from 28% to 34% for the Philippines, from 23% to 28% for Thailand, and from 24% to 39% for Singapore, or an arithmetic average increase from 22% to 35% for ASEAN. Industrial growth and economic development are further reflected in the huge increases in per capita energy consumptions of ASEAN countries. In terms of kilogram oil equivalent, the per capita consumptions between 1965 and 1984 increased from 91 to 205 for Indonesia, from 312 to 716 for Malaysia, from 160 to 271 for the Philippines, from 80 to 320 for Thailand, and from 670 to 2520 for Singapore.

Among the major industrial pollution problems in ASEAN countries are those coming from the palm oil and rubber industries in Malaysia, the coconut and sugar processing industries in the Philippines, and the tapioca processing industries in Thailand. The magnitude of the pollution load is evident from the figures for palm oil in Malaysia. In 1985, a total of 224 mills were in operation with sizes ranging from 10 to 60 tonnes FFB per hour. The mills generated 1640 tonnes BOD per day or a population equivalent of 33 million, more than twice the entire population of Malaysia. Substantial progress have been achieved by Malaysia, the Philippines, and Thailand in solving these industrial pollution problems and emphasis has shifted to the recovery and utilization of by-products from these enormous amounts of wastes. ASEAN cooperation in this area is aimed at promoting intra-ASEAN transfer of technology through the implementation of demonstration projects.

The recent and rapid development of low- and non-waste manufacturing technologies, the change in industry's perception of what constitutes waste and what could be a potential source of raw materials, and the tragic incident in Bhopal have also influenced the thinking of ASEAN with respect to the relationship between industry and environment. The impact of these recent events and developments and the desire of ASEAN to find feasible solutions to the pollution problems brought about by its traditional industries are reflected in the following goals for ASEP III:

### *Goal No. 7:*

Implementation of demonstration projects in industrial pollution control with emphasis on clean technologies in specific industries, resource recovery, waste recycling and utilization, and proper waste disposal.

### *Goal No. 8:*

Establishment of proper management programmes for the control of hazardous substances and wastes.

### *Goal No. 9:*

Development and implementation of a regional programme on the prevention of industrial accidents which may have adverse environmental consequences through proper risk assessment, adequate handling procedures, safety measures, emergency plan, and the like.

### *Goal No. 10:*

Development of methods for the assessment of highly pollutive industries and potentially harmful chemicals entering ASEAN.

## Urban Environment

In both ASEP I and ASEP II, the environmental problems in the urban environment are considered as a mere sector of industry and environment. ASEP I confined its attention to the establishment of adequate urban air and water quality monitoring systems to determine the quality of the urban environment. ASEP II expanded the scope somewhat by including urban air and water quality management systems, including the control of effluents from small and medium scale industries.

ASEP III recognizes that there are multifarious environmental problems in the urban centers of ASEAN which are not necessarily related to industry. On one hand, there are the problems of air and water pollution, solid wastes, inadequate urban parks and greenery, and the presence of slums and other forms of marginal settlements; and, on the other hand, there are the problems associated with development, like traffic noise and congestion and the new bio-physical problems associated with the construction of high-rise structures in the principal cities of ASEAN.

The principal cities of ASEAN, like Jakarta, Kuala Lumpur, Manila, and Bangkok, are reeling under increasing pressures from a rapidly increasing population. In 1984, 39% of the entire population of the Philippines live in the urban areas. For Malaysia, Indonesia, and Thailand the corresponding figures are 31%, 25%, and 18%, respectively. In the case of Thailand, 69% of the urban population are found in Bangkok, the country's capital and largest city. In the Philippines, 30% are in Manila, in Malaysia, 27% are in Kuala Lumpur, and in Indonesia, 23% are in Jakarta.

Traffic noise and congestion, inadequate sewerage system, poor garbage collection and disposal, heavily polluted urban rivers, and air pollution from dust, smoke, and other particulates seem to pervade the urban centers of ASEAN. In this regard, Singapore seems to be an exception. Aside from a few problem areas, like vehicle exhaust emission and noise pollution, Singapore has successfully implemented measures to create a clean urban environment. Extensive water pollution control and solid waste management programmes have resulted in the cleaning up of the Kallang Basin and the Singapore River. Singapore has also constructed an extensive network of sewerage facilities which in 1986 had 1,925 km of public sewer network serving 95% of the population, six sewage treatment works which can handle 835,000 $m^3$/day, and 123 sewage pumping stations. A fleet of 270 refuse collection vehicles and 60 mechanical sweepers, a solid waste transfer station in Kim Chuan, and two incineration plants in Ulu Pandan and Tuas have kept Singapore's streets garbage-free.

Since a large proportion of the population in ASEAN countries live in the urban areas, the urban environmental problems are really what most people perceive as "the problems of the environment". Consequently, ASEP III addresses this problem and has established the following goals:

### *Goal No. 11:*

Integration of the experience gained in air and water quality monitoring and management to serve as bases for decision making and to provide inputs for public information.

### *Goal No. 12:*

Development of an integrated approach to the management of the urban environment with emphasis on noise, water and air pollution, solid wastes, and heat islands and temperature effects arising from high-rise structures.

### *Goal No. 13:*

Implementation of demonstration projects to upgrade urban parks and to improve urban environmental quality, particularly in the slum areas and marginal settlements.

## Marine Environment

The marine environment is an ASEAN regional common, a fact that has been recognized from the very beginning of ASEAN cooperation. For this reason, among the first items to be adopted by ASEAN countries, with the catalytic and supportive role of UNEP, was the Action Plan for the Protection and Development of the Marine Environment and Coastal Areas of the East Asia Region.

The Philippines, Indonesia, Malaysia, and Thailand have extensive fishing industries. Thailand's national waters in the Andaman Sea and the Gulf of Thailand, for instance, have a maximum sustainable yield of 1.5 million metric tonnes. Singapore has one of the world's leading shipyards and the coastal waters of Brunei Darussalam are occupied by many oil rigs and production platforms while their associated pipelines criss-cross the seabed.

In line with the central concept of ASEP III of fully integrating environment and development, the Action Plan for the Protection and Development of the Marine Environment and Coastal Areas of the East Asian Region will be revised and implemented. The marine environment is recognized not only as a common regional heritage which needs to be conserved and protected, but also as an abundant source of resources which, if used rationally, can help foster economic development and improve the quality of life in ASEAN. With this in mind, ASEP III aims to accomplish the following goal:

### *Goal No. 14:*

Implementation of the revised Action Plan for the development, protection, and rational exploitation of the marine environment and resources and the coastal areas of the ASEAN region.

## Environmental Education, Training, and Information

After ASEP I and ASEP II, there now exist in all ASEAN countries groups of individuals and institutions well-versed in the environment field and aware of the value of environmental protection and management. Consequently, there are now a few NGOs in ASEAN that advocate environmentalism. These include the Sahabat Alam Malaysia and Nuclear-Free Philippines. Together with other NGOs, Sahabat Alam Malaysia has been able to mobilize public opinion to resist a hydroelectric development project in a national park. Nevertheless, much still needs to be done to promote environmentalism in ASEAN. In the Philippines, the Haribon Foundation can count on a membership of less than 200 out of a population of nearly 55 million. In contrast, environmental NGOs in the United States, like the Defenders of Wildlife, Friends of the Earth, and the National Audobon Society, have a total membership of nearly two million.

In Australia, environmental NGOs number more than 11,000 out of a population of only 25 million.

ASEP III is therefore aimed at sustaining the groups that have developed under ASEP I and II, at promoting environmental awareness in other sectors, and further enhancing information exchange among member countries of ASEAN. These are apparent in the following goals:

### *Goal No. 15:*

Preparation of regional and national action plans in environmental education and training with emphasis on the primary level and on specific priority groups.

### *Goal No. 16:*

Implementation of a regional programme leading to the establishment of an information network among ASEAN countries and the publication of regular reports on the status of the environment in member countries using a common format for areas of common concern.

### *Goal No. 17:*

Implementation of a regional programme to promote environmental awareness among the general public.

## IV. INSTITUTIONAL FRAMEWORK AND ORGANIZATIONAL STRUCTURE

ASEAN cooperation in the field of the environment has been carried out through the ASEAN Experts Group on the Environment (AEGE), a body under the purview of the ASEAN Committee on Science and Technology (COST). In the present organizational structure of ASEAN COST, as well as the other non-economic or functional committees, is under the purview of the ASEAN Standing Committee and the ASEAN Ministerial Meeting. The five economic committees, on the other hand, are under the purview of the ASEAN Economic Ministers Meeting.

Under the ASEAN COST, there are ten official regional bodies consisting of two sub-committees, seven working groups, and one experts group. These are: Sub-Committee on Climatology, Sub-Committee on Protein: Food Habits, Working Group on Food Waste Materials, Working Group on Food Technology Research and Development, Working Group on Non-Conventional Energy Research, Working Group on Marine Sciences, Working Group on Microelectronics, Working Group on Materials Science, Working Group on Biotechnology, and the Experts Group on the Environment.

The AEGE became a permanent ASEAN body shortly after the ASEAN COST recommended that a meeting of ASEAN experts on the environment be convened to consider the proposed ASEAN Sub-Regional Environment Programme (ASEP), a document prepared by UNEP, and to discuss other areas of possible cooperation including follow-up action on the UN Conference and Exhibition on Human Settlements: Habitat held in Vancouver in 1976. This First Meeting of the ASEAN Experts on the Environment took place in Jakarta on 18–20 December 1978 and was attended by experts on the environment from the ASEAN member countries and by representatives from the ASEAN Secretariat and the UNEP.

The First Meeting of the AEGE agreed to recommend the creation of a Sub-Committee on Environment under the ASEAN Committee on science and Technology. It was envisioned that the Sub-Committee will have the following functions: to co-ordinate and promote ASEAN cooperation in the field of the environment; to incorporate the environmental dimension in all aspects of planning and formulation of policies and programmes of other ASEAN Committees and related bodies; and to assist in seeking bilateral and multilateral financial support for projects that are ASEAN in character. Unfortunately, the Fifth Meeting of the ASEAN Standing Committee held in Bali on 27 June 1979 did not approve the recommendation. As a result, the AEGE remained as the regional body to co-ordinate ASEAN cooperation in the field of the environment. It has met regularly once a year since then.

At the Fourth Meeting of the AEGE held in Singapore on 8–10 April 1981, the Meeting recommended that a meeting of ASEAN experts be convened to consider the draft Action Plan on Nature Conservation in the ASEAN Region which was prepared by the International Union for the Conservation of Nature and Natural Resources (IUCN) with financial assistance from UNEP. The First Meeting of the ASEAN Experts on Nature Conservation (AENC) took place in Singapore on 25–26 March 1982 and the group has met regularly every year since then. Working under the purview of the AEGE, the ASEAN Meeting on Nature Conservation has become another formal venue for ASEAN cooperation in the environment field.

In the context of the restructuring of ASEAN and recognizing that environmental concerns are interactive with multifarious human activities that go beyond mere scientific and technological pursuits, the First ASEAN Ministerial meeting on the Environment held in Manila on 30 April 1981 recommended the establishment of an ASEAN Committee on Environment. In consonance with this recommendation, the Second Ministerial Meeting on the Environment held in Bangkok on 29 November 1984 recognized the need to include the environmental dimension as "an integral aspect of project development planning and implementation" and resolved that "environmental dimension be integrated into other activities of the ASEAN functional committees."

In view of the central role that the ASEAN environment plays in the quest for economic growth and development in ASEAN and having regard to the multifarious regional activities envisioned in ASEP III, there is need to further strengthen the regional institutional framework and organizational structure to make it more responsive to the needs of ASEAN during the next five years and beyond. The regional body on the environment must be high enough in the organizational hierarchy of the ASEAN so that it can effectively carry out the following functions, among others:

(i) to promote, co-ordinate, and implement ASEAN cooperation in the field of the environment;
(ii) to insure that the environmental dimension is incorporated in the plans, programmes, and projects of other ASEAN bodies;
(iii) to promote cooperation with other countries outside of ASEAN and with international agencies for the purpose of sharing experiences in the management of the environment, promoting transfer of technology, and solving common global environmental problems; and
(iv) to assist in obtaining financial support to ASEAN activities from within and from without of ASEAN.

The new ASEAN institutional framework and organizational structure in the environment field must also seek to rationalize the roles and functions of various ASEAN bodies concerned with the environment, namely: the ASEAN Experts Group on the Environment; the ASEAN meeting on Nature Conservation; the Coordinating Body on the Seas of East Asia; the ASEAN COST Working Group on Marine Science; and the ASEAN COFAF Coordinating Group on Forestry.

## V. PROGRAMMES AND PROJECTS

The sixty projects in ASEP III are divided into six priority areas, namely, environmental management, nature conservation and terrestrial ecosystem, industry and environment, urban environment, marine environment, and environmental education, training, and information. These projects are selected on the basis of three criteria: one, they are regional in character; two, they are relevant to the overall objective and the seventeen programme goals of ASEP III; and three, they are mutually supportive of and related to each other.

While the projects are divided into six areas, they are not, however, compartmentalized with little or no relevance to each other. On the contrary, the projects are interactive, integrative, and mutually supportive. To cite an example, the project on Environmental Management in the Agro-Industry (Area 1) can use inputs from three projects in Area 3 (Industry and Environment), namely, Technology Transfer on the Treatment of Effluents From Palm Oil and Rubber Industries, Anti-Pollution Technologies for Urban and Rural Areas, and Development Plan, Feasibility Study, and Demonstration Projects on Waste Utilization in the ASEAN Region. These projects can also provide very useful materials for the projects on Development of Communication Media and Materials for Enhancing Environmental Awareness in ASEAN (Area 6), as well as, provide inputs to the project on Formulation of Agreement for the Protection and Preservation of Marine Environment: Regional Agreement on the Use of Slop Reception and Treatment Facilities (Area 5). With these projects, four areas are interlinked and integrated.

Another example is the project on Case Studies on Environmental Impact Assessment (Area 1) which has five sub-projects. The five sub-projects can use inputs from the following other projects: Research on and Development of Management Plan for Water Birds and Wetlands (Area 2); Air Pollution Control and Management in Flue Gas Desulphurization and Denitrification (Area 3); Vehicle Exhaust Emission in the ASEAN Region (Area 4); and Urban Air Quality Monitoring Through the Establishment of Networks (Area 4). Subsequently, these projects can provide inputs into the following projects: Development of Communication Media and Materials for Enhancing Environmental Awareness in ASEAN (Area 6) and Development of Techniques for Promoting Environmental Awareness for Specific Target Groups (Area 6).

As in ASEP II, ASEP III will adopt a dynamic programming approach by which projects will be reviewed annually and modified, if necessary, to ensure that projects in any priority area remain regional in character, relevant to the overall objective of ASEP III, and related to the programmes and projects in the other priority areas.

The implementation of ASEP III must not be fragmented into six, unrelated areas. On the contrary, it must be integrated, with the six parts forming a cohesive whole. Fragmented, the six areas may be likened to the six blind men of Indostan. The legend tells the story of six blind men describing an elephant while limiting their individual observation to single parts of the animal's anatomy. Hence, the six blind men described the side of the elephant as a wall; the tusk, as a spear; the trunk as a snake; the knee, as a tree; the ear, as a fan; and the tail, as a rope. John Godrey Saxe caught the very essence of the legend in the following verses:

"It was six men of Indostan
To learning much inclined
Who went to see the elephant
(Though all of them were blind);
To each by observation
Might satisfy his mind
And so these men of Indostan
Disputed loud and long
Each in his opinion
Exceedingly stiff and strong
Though each was partly in the right
And all were in the wrong."

In ASEP I and II, 37% of all projects were completed within the planning cycle and 14% were not implemented. For ASEP III, the goal is to implement at least 90% of all projects and to complete at least 60% within the planning cycle, 1988–1992.

When completed, the 60 projects will result in the production of five guidelines, two manuals, one textbook, six management plans, and three sets of various teaching/visual aids. Thirteen regional seminars/workshops and thirteen different regional training courses will be conducted. These outputs, as well as the reports generated by the pilot/demonstration projects and the EIA studies, will contribute towards the attainment of the overall programme objective of promoting the proper management of the ASEAN environment so that it can sustain continued economic development while maintaining a high quality of life for the people of the ASEAN countries.

# CHAPTER 45

# ASEAN STRATEGIC PLAN OF ACTION ON THE ENVIRONMENT

**1994–1998**

## EXECUTIVE SUMMARY

The UN Conference on Human Environment held at Stockholm in 1972 provided a strong stimulus for the development of regional and sub-regional environmental programmes with a view to dealing with environmental problems in a cooperative framework. The ASEAN Environment Programme I (ASEP I), initiated in 1977 through the catalytic support of the United Nations Environment Programme (UNEP), marked the beginning of regional environmental cooperation in ASEAN.

ASEP I described the extent of regional cooperation and listed the different priority areas and projects/activities on environment. On the recommendation of the ASEAN Committee on Science and Technology, the first meeting of the ASEAN Experts Group on the Environment (AEGE) was held in Jakarta in December 1978 to consider ASEP I. The First ASEAN Ministerial Meeting on the environment which was held in Manila in April 1981 endorsed ASEP I, thereby adopting its objectives and guidelines.

In 1981, the first ASEAN declaration on cooperation on the environment was made. It defined the broad objective of cooperation as being to "ensure the protection of the ASEAN environment and the sustainability of its natural resources so that it can sustain continued development with the aim of eradicating poverty and attaining the highest possible quality of life for the people of the ASEAN countries". It enumerated a number of policy guidelines enjoining member countries to: develop a common awareness of the environment, enact and enforce environmental protection measures, ensure that environmental considerations are taken into account in development efforts, and foster the development of environmental education programmes. Subsequently, two other environment programmes were developed and implemented, namely, ASEP II covering the period 1982–1987, and ASEP III covering the period 1988–1992.

The Fourth Meeting of the ASEAN Senior Officials on the Environment held in July 1993 in Bangkok, agreed that a new ASEAN Action Plan should be developed taking into account new developments following the outcome of UNCED which adopted Agenda 21. The plan should take into consideration the need to harmonize the working groups' objectives, strengthen the existing institutional arrangements, identify priority regional issues including environmentally related implications of the ASEAN Free Trade Agreement (AFTA), as well as establish ASOEN's position in international fora such as the Commission on Sustainable Development (CSD) and Inter-Governmental Committee on the Convention on Biological Biodiversity (ICCBD). The Meeting requested the ASEAN Secretariat to initiate action to prepare such a plan.

This Strategic Plan of Action on the Environment has the following five objectives:

a. to respond to specific recommendations of Agenda 21 requiring priority action in ASEAN;
b. to introduce policy measures and promote institutional development that encourage the integration of environmental factors in all developmental processes both at the national and regional levels;
c. to establish long term goals on environmental quality and work towards harmonized environmental quality standards for the ASEAN region;
d. to harmonise policy directions and enhance operational and technical cooperation on environmental matters, and undertake joint actions to address common environmental problems; and
e. to study the implications of AFTA on the environment and take steps to integrate sound trade policies with sound environmental policies.

To attain these objectives, the following strategic thrusts and actions will be pursued.

### *Strategy 1*: Support the development of a regional framework for integrating environment and development concerns in the decision making process

Integrating environment and development concerns in decision making has been long recognized as a key element for promoting sustainable development. Successive ASEAN resolutions, declarations and decisions refer to this element as of vital significance. Efforts therefore have been initiated to meet these directives. But these efforts need to be consolidated and further refined if the intention is to apply them uniformly in the region. There is a necessity to develop a regional framework that will ensure the integration of environment and development concerns in the respective national decision-making processes. The elements of that framework include the following:

a) institutional capability to make an integrated, forward looking and cross-sectoral approach in making decisions;
b) appropriate policies and legal frameworks in place to undertake the task;
c) sufficient technological base for use in decision making; and
d) sound information and database derived from monitoring and research.

***Actions*:**

1.1 *Continue support in the documentation of regional EIA experiences leading towards the harmonisation of procedures.*
1.2 *Initiate activities that will make use of natural resource and environmental accounting studies and approaches.*
1.3 *Establish procedures that would initiate the integration of environmental concerns in the various ASEAN programmes and activities.*

### *Strategy 2*: Promote government-private sector interactions that lead towards the development of policies that mutually support the thrust of each sector

The recent decision of ASEAN to establish AFTA underscores the prevailing trend in regional trade cooperation embracing a liberal and market oriented system. This decision, however, has implications on the environment. The challenge for ASEAN is how to reinforce AFTA with sound environmental policies. In this regard, government institutions and industries would play major roles in developing sustainable societies. There should be consensus in the framing of policies that reinforce the thrust of each sector.

***Actions*:**

2.1 *Initiate studies on development of environmental and trade policies which are supportive to the principles of sustainable development*
2.2 *Establish mechanisms that encourage government and private sectors to adopt appropriate environmental standards backed up by sufficient economic incentives*
2.3 *Set up government private sector information linkages/networks to include information on technology, expertise and facilities for environmental management*

### *Strategy 3*: Strengthen the knowledge and information database on environmental matters

Environmentally sound and sustainable development requires that action is taken on the basis of objective, reliable and comparable environmental information. This calls for enhanced capability at national and regional levels to obtain sound environmental data, transform these data into meaningful information and share this knowledge among the various actors involved in implementing actions. This also implies that new demands will be placed on monitoring and information gathering systems on the basis of harmonised database and inter-calibration of existing monitoring systems. ASEAN should now start strengthening its capacity to collect, store and exchange information database and knowledge on environmental matters.

### *Actions*:

3.1 *Pursue the establishment of basic environmental quality standards leading to the setting up of harmonised quality standards in the region*

3.2 *Identify centres of excellence for environmental R&D and eventually build them as focal points of environmental networks*

3.3 *Establish a mechanism for the preparation of periodic reports on the state of the region's environment*

### *Strategy 4*: Strengthen institutional and legal capacities to implement international agreements on environment

Agenda 21 identifies, as a prerequisite to global participation on sustainable development, the strength of institutional and legal capacities of national and regional entities. As environmental issues now transcend beyond regional boundaries, the need to develop these capabilities in order to implement international agreements on environment as well as effectively participate in the negotiation of new international treaties, and the review of existing ones, cannot be overemphasized. There are still many aspects of international law on sustainable development that still merit development and appropriate interpretation to make them effective and binding. ASEAN, from a regional standpoint, should strengthen its institutional capacities to implement, and its legal capacities to present its concerns and interests in international legal discussions on the environment.

### *Actions*:

4.1 *Undertake a comparative study on the institutional structure and legislation on environmental management*

4.2 *Establish capacities to support regional efforts to implement international agreements and participate effectively in the negotiation of new or revised agreements*
4.3 *Enhance collaboration with international bodies overseeing the implementation of international agreements and cooperation.*

### *Strategy 5*: Establish a regional framework on biological diversity conservation and sustainable utilisation of its components

The ASEAN region has invaluable biodiversity and abundant natural resources comprising 30% of the world's tropical forests. During the last two decades, ASEAN countries have embarked on massive economic development activities aimed at raising the standard of living of its people. Consequently, however, the impacts of these activities have affected the region's biodiversity. Thus, capacities for assessment, study and systematic observation and evaluation of biodiversity need to be reinforced at national and regional levels. An effective national and regional action supported by international cooperation is required for the *in situ* protection of the ecosystems and the *ex situ* conservation of biological and genetic resources. Similarly, the establishment of a regional centre on biodiversity conservation should be actively supported.

### *Actions*:

5.1 *Promote the development of a framework for the protection and conservation of heritage areas and endangered species*
5.2 *Strengthen capacities for R&D to enhance biodiversity conservation in the region*

### *Strategy 6*: Promote the protection and management of coastal zones and marine resources

The marine environment is truly an ASEAN regional heritage, a fact that has been recognized from the very beginning of ASEAN cooperation. Among the first actions by the ASEAN countries, with catalytic support from UNEP, was the adoption of an Action Plan for the Protection and Development of the Marine Environment and Coastal Areas of the East Asia Region. The Southeast Asian seas are natural habitat for about 2500 species of fish and invertebrates. They provide 11% of the world's supply of marine products and are a source of livelihood for many of the region's fishermen. All ASEAN countries have extensive fishing industries. Yet, many of the major near-shore fishing areas in the region are over-fished and polluted from land-based sources and oil spills. The Straits of Malacca, for example, is one of the major shipping lanes for crude oil transport and is vulnerable to oil spills. There has been a notable increase in the occurrence of red tides which is attributed to domestic sources of pollution. This incidence poses not only a health hazard but also affects export earnings. Similarly, many mangroves are disappearing to make room for brackish water prawn farming, housing and industrial development. Coral reefs are also being degraded and require rehabilitation. Accordingly, there is an urgent need for a more coordinated, pro-active and collective action to protect ASEAN's coastal zones and marine resources.

### *Actions*:

6.1 *Improve regional marine and coastal environmental coordination*
6.2 *Develop a framework for the integrated management of regional coastal zones*

### *Strategy 7*: Promote environmentally sound management of toxic chemicals and hazardous wastes, and control of transboundary movement of hazardous wastes

With the continued rapid industrialization of the ASEAN economies and the trend in the transfer of highly polluting industries from developed to developing countries, the flow of toxic chemicals and dangerous products is bound to increase in the region. There is worldwide recognition that chemical contamination may result in grave damage to human health and the environment. It is therefore necessary to have good knowledge and assessment of these risks which is a prerequisite to planning for their safe and beneficial use, recycling and disposal. However, for a great number of high volume production chemicals, even basic data for risk assessment is generally lacking. ASEAN should now initiate action on effecting a regional management guide for the safe management of toxic chemicals and hazardous waste.

### *Actions*:

7.1 *Establish regional guidelines for assessing highly pollutive industries and safe handling of potentially harmful chemicals entering the ASEAN region*
7.2 *Strengthen the information network on the transboundary movement of toxic chemicals and hazardous waste*

### *Strategy 8*: Develop a system for the promotion of environmentally sound technologies

Since the region is likely to face increasing challenges for controlling pollution and resource degradation, it is necessary to evolve a system for the promotion of environmentally sound technologies in the region. Pollution control techniques tend to transfer pollution from one medium to another, rather than eliminating it. Therefore, although these technologies may reduce some risks from certain factories, large scale transfer of such techniques may not prove beneficial to promoting regional environmental quality. Environmentally sound technologies are less polluting, use resources in a more sustainable manner and recycle more of their by-products, residues and waste than the traditional technologies they replace.

### *Actions*:

8.1 *Establish linkages with existing clearing houses on environmentally sound technologies*
8.2 *Establish mechanisms that identify end users of R&D results and encourage the participation of private sector*
8.3 *Strengthen linkage and coordination with other ASEAN committees such as COST doing related R&D work on the environment*
8.4 *Support the promotion of indigenous technology or technologies that have been adapted to regional needs*

## *Strategy 9*: Promote regional activities that strengthen the role of major groups in sustainable development

The region's ability to develop sustainably depends on the capability and capacity of its people to understand complex environment and development issues and choose the best development alternative. As people would need to have the information and expertise to understand the potential limits of the environment, institutions have the responsibility of making these information available and easily understood. The mechanisms for achieving this objective vary depending on the level of information required. Nonetheless, efforts should be made by ASOEN to bring the result of its various programmes to the ASEAN public either in formal approaches or on an informal basis. ASOEN in general should establish mechanisms that will motivate, educate, train and build capacities especially among the major groups identified in Agenda 21.

### *Actions*:

9.1 *Support the publication of regional environmental magazine and newsletters*
9.2 *Strengthen regional information network and promote exchange of expertise on environmental education programmes*

9.3 *Develop strategic programmes of action that will strengthen the role and participation of major groups on environmental management and decision making*

## *Strategy 10*: Strengthen the coordinative mechanism for the implementation and management of regional environment programmes

As mandated by the Jakarta Resolution on Sustainable Development, ASOEN should facilitate the incorporation of environmental considerations into the programmes and activities of ASEAN committees. This would require a review of all ASEAN committees' activities and projects to assess their environmental implications and suggest measures for environmental protection and improvement. To be able to do this and at the same time implement programmes of this Plan of Action, ASOEN would need strong coordinative support from the ASEAN Secretariat. This will require substantial time on the part of the professional staff of the Secretariat. Since ASOEN's activities are expected to increase in the near future, support should be given to the ASEAN Secretariat to enable it to upgrade its capacities. This may mean augmenting the existing number of professional staff in the environment unit.

### *Actions*:

10.1 *Establish an operational system at the ASEAN Secretariat that could plan, monitor and facilitate the implementation of environmental projects*
10.2 *Source and match funding requirements for proposed projects*

As an initial step to operationalize the recommended thrusts, the following institutional measures should be taken:

a. Strengthen the capacity of the ASEAN Secretariat as discussed in Strategy 10. The ASEAN Secretariat should play an active supportive and coordinative role in the implementation of all actions in this Plan. While it is recognized that the Secretariat may not have sufficient resources to augment its present staff, it could explore arrangements with multilateral agencies supportive to the organization to have professionals seconded to the Secretariat to help ensure the implementation of this Plan.
b. The ASOEN Working Groups should start preparing the necessary adjustments in their programmes and activities consistent with the identified strategic thrusts.

To implement the Plan of Action, various funding sources and schemes should be explored. These include: cost-sharing arrangements among participating ASEAN member countries for selected priority projects; the ASEAN Fund which gives priority to urgent, short-term projects of strategic or confidential nature and which are considered fundamental in building a stronger cooperative ASEAN infrastructure; the ASEAN Sub-regional Environment Trust (ASSET); and other project-related sources of funding such as ASEAN's Dialogue Partners, the Global Environment Facility (GEF) and the Asia Sustainable Development Fund.

## 1. INTRODUCTION

### 1.1 The Emergence of Environmental Concerns in Development

The UN Conference on Human Environment held at Stockholm in 1972 provided a strong stimulus for the development of regional and sub-regional environmental programmes with a view to dealing with environmental problems in a cooperative framework. The ASEAN Environment Programme I (ASEP I), initiated in 1977 through the catalytic support of the United Nations Environment Programme (UNEP), marked the beginning of regional environmental cooperation in ASEAN. Since then, two more programmes have been developed and implemented, namely, ASEP II covering the period 1982–1987, and ASEP III covering the period 1988–1992. Together with new developments worldwide, they provide a firm basis for launching a new era of cooperation in the field of the environment in ASEAN.

The concept of environmental management and sustainable development was put on a firm footing with the report and recommendations of the World Commission on Environment and Development in 1987. The said report underscored two significant developments in thinking: firstly, the concept of environmental management has evolved from a localized issue to a global perspective highlighting the urgency of taking collective actions to address the ever threatening environmental issues; and secondly, it recognized the cross-sectoral nature of environmental problems which require comprehensive solutions. Agenda 21, adopted by the UN Conference on Environment and Development (UNCED) at Rio de Janeiro in June 1992, embodies these emerging views and lays down a comprehensive blueprint for action in all areas relating to sustainable development. These world events have a profound impact on the environmental programmes at all levels: governments, private sector, NGOs and other interest groups and regional and international bodies including ASEAN.

## 1.2 Rationale

Recognizing UNCED's importance, the Fourth Meeting of the ASEAN Senior Officials on the Environment held in July 1993 in Bangkok, agreed that there was a need for developing an ASEAN Action Plan in response to its outcome. The Plan should take into account the need to harmonise the working groups' objectives, strengthen the existing institutional arrangements, identify priority regional issues including environmentally related implications of AFTA, as well as establish ASEAN's common stand in international fora such as the Commission on Sustainable Development (CSD) and Inter-Governmental Committee on the Convention on Biological Diversity (ICBD). The Meeting requested the ASEAN Secretariat to initiate action to prepare such a plan. This document was prepared in pursuant to this decision. The ASEAN Strategic Plan of Action on the Environment has been structured in the following manner: Section I is the introduction. Section II reviews the mandates and policy guidelines as provided by past ASEAN declarations, resolutions and decisions; assesses the existing institutional arrangements; and presents a brief summary of the implementation of ASEP III and activities of the six ASOEN Working Groups. Section III describes the new directions, objectives and strategic thrusts and the proposed actions and activities. Section IV presents the institutional and financial mechanisms to operationalize the Plan.

# 2. MANDATE AND POLICY GUIDELINES

## 2.1 Background: Mandate for Environmental Cooperation

The first ASEAN declaration on cooperation on the environment, the "Manila Declaration on the ASEAN Environment of 1981" defined the broad objective of cooperation as being to ensure the protection of the ASEAN environment and the sustainability of its natural resources so that it can sustain continued development with the aim of eradicating poverty and attaining the highest possible quality of life for the people of the ASEAN countries. It enumerated a number of policy guidelines urging member countries to: develop a common awareness of the environment, enact and enforce environmental protection measures, ensure that environmental considerations are taken into account in development efforts, and foster the development of environmental education programmes.

Actual cooperation on the environment started in 1977 when the ASEAN Sub-Regional Environment Programme (ASEP) was drafted with assistance from the United Nations Environment Programme (UNEP). ASEP I described the extent of regional cooperation and listed the different priority areas and projects/activities on environment. On the recommendation of the ASEAN Committee on Science and Technology, the first meeting of the ASEAN Experts Group on the Environment (AEGE) was held in Jakarta on 18–20 December 1978 to consider ASEP I. AEGE, which became a permanent body under ASEAN COST, has met every year since. The First ASEAN Ministerial Meeting on the Environment, which was held in Manila on 30 April 1981, endorsed ASEP I, thereby adapting its objectives and guidelines.

Since 1989, the status of AEGE has been upgraded and called the ASEAN Senior Officials on the Environment (ASOEN). ASOEN has assumed all the activities, tasks, responsibilities and commitments of AEGE. ASOEN meets annually and is assisted in its work by six Working Groups which meet regularly.

## 2.2 Policy Guidelines

In the Bangkok Declaration on the ASEAN Environment of November 1984, the Ministers noted with satisfaction the progress made in the implementation of ASEP I. They also noted the establishment during the past decade of environmental protection agencies in ASEAN countries and their successes in initiating environmental protection measures and in developing their respective capabilities in environmental technology. The Ministers adopted a number of policy guidelines on: environmental management, nature conservation, marine environment, urban environment, environmental education and training, environmental information systems, involvement of NGOs and other organizations, and international cooperation.

In the Jakarta Resolution on Sustainable Development of October 1987, the Ministers recognized that developmental processes can only be sustained if the availability of natural resources is similarly ascertained. They resolved to adopt the principle of sustainable development, focus on common resources and issues that affect the common well-being of the ASEAN people and strengthen the institutional arrangements for ASEAN cooperation on environment. They stated that the strengthened arrangement should work on facilitating the incorporation of environmental considerations into the programmes and activities of ASEAN committees, monitoring the quality of environment and natural resources to enable periodic compilation of ASEAN state of environment reports, and enhancing cooperation on environmental matters.

The Kuala Lumpur Accord on Environment and Development issued by the ASEAN Ministers for the Environment in June 1990 agreed to focus on initiating efforts to enhance environmental management including formulation of an

ASEAN strategy and action plan for sustainable development, harmonisation of environmental quality standards as well as transboundary pollution prevention and abatement practices and promotion of the use of clean technologies. They also agreed to initiate efforts to develop and harmonise natural resources assessment and natural resource and environment accounting systems.

The most recent statement on the environment was embodied in the Singapore Resolution on Environment and Development, which was adopted a month after the Singapore Summit in January 1992. The Resolution spelled out the different policies and strategies that each ASEAN member country must pursue in order to advance regional cooperation for sustainable development. More specifically, the Ministers agreed that each country should:

a) introduce policy measures and promote institutional development that will encourage the integration of environmental factors in all developmental processes;
b) work closely on the inter-related issues of environment and development;
c) cooperate in setting basic environmental quality standards and regulations at national level, work towards harmonised quality standards in the region, and adopt long term quantitative goals relating to ambient air quality and river water quality; and
d) harmonise policy directions and enhance operational and technical cooperation on environmental matters, and undertake joint actions to address the anti-tropical timber campaign.

The last policy underscores the necessity for joint regional action to counter the anti-tropical timber campaign launched by environmental NGOs and governments in the more developed countries to stop the importation of tropical timber. The success of such campaign would have a very adverse effect on the timber and wood industries of the region.

The Ministers likewise agreed that regional cooperation aimed at institutional development should include: the strengthening of the institutional and technical capability of national agencies to enable them to integrate environmental considerations in their development plans; cooperation in capacity building through regional training assistance programmes, regular exchange of information, and more frequent exchange of visits among officials and experts; and provision of adequate training to public and private organizations, including NGOs, to enhance their environmental management expertise and skills.

On technology cooperation, the Ministers agreed to continue cooperation on environmental technology by sharing technical information, undertaking joint training and research programmes, and exchanging expertise, and to promote appropriate and environmentally sound technologies as well as encourage support for such effort from the business and public sectors. They also agreed that efforts to promote public awareness on environmental issues should be continued in order to elicit broader public participation and support.

In light of the UN Conference on Environment and Development (UNCED), the Ministers also agreed to adopt an ASEAN common stand for the conference, which dealt among others, with ASEAN's position on the issues of climate change; implementation of the Montreal Protocol on Ozone Depleting Substances; protection of the oceans and seas; protection of freshwater resources; and sustainable management of all forests.

## 2.3 Institutional Arrangements

The objective of ASEAN is to promote regional cooperation to accelerate economic growth, social progress and cultural development and peace and stability, and to provide assistance to each other in the form of training and research facilities and collaborate more effectively on issues of common regional interest such as trade and industry, transportation and communication and improvement of the living standards of the people.

The simplified organizational structure for ASEAN cooperation in the field of the environment is shown in Figure 1. It consists of the Heads of Government, the ASEAN Ministerial Meeting on the Environment (AMME), the ASEAN Senior Officials on the Environment (ASOEN), the six ASOEN Working Groups and the ASEAN Secretariat.

### *The Heads of Government*

The Heads of Government of member countries are the highest authority in the ASEAN structure. In the last Meeting of the ASEAN Heads of Government held in Singapore in January 1992, it was decided that the Heads of Governments would meet formally every three years with informal meetings in between to give guidance on ASEAN's policy directions. The Singapore Summit likewise agreed that member countries should continue to play an active part in protecting the environment by continuing its cooperation in promoting the principles of sustainable development and integrating it into all aspects of development.

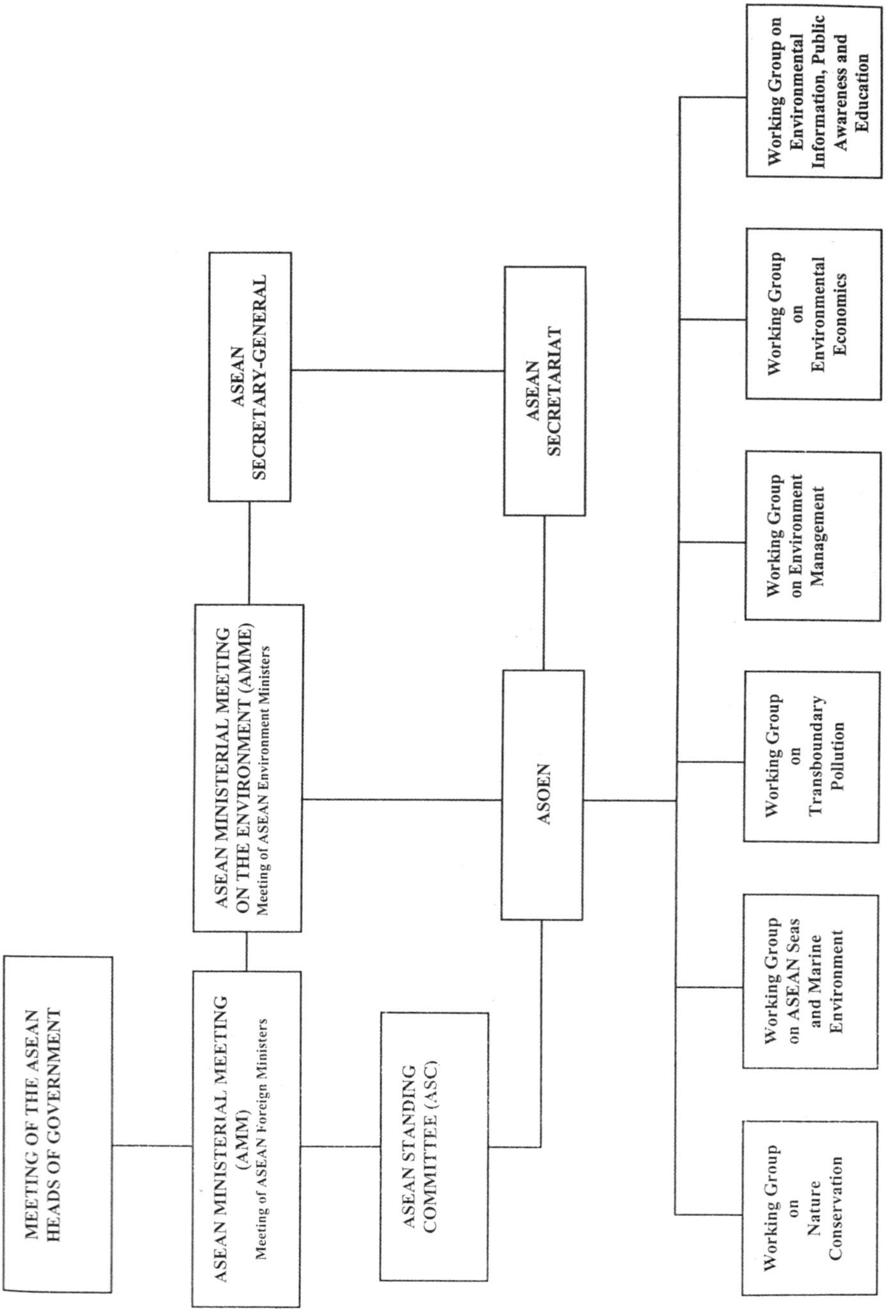


**Figure 1.** Organisational Structure of ASEAN

## ASEAN Ministerial Meeting on the Environment (AMME)

To promote ASEAN cooperation and ensure that the decisions of the Heads of Government relating to environment are carried out, the ASEAN Ministers for the Environment meet regularly at least once every 3 years. So far, the ASEAN Environment Ministers have met five times.

## ASEAN Senior Officials on the Environment (ASOEN)

The ASEAN Senior Officials on the Environment (ASOEN) has the following functions and responsibilities:

a) recommend policy guidelines and, in general, provide "catalytic impetus" towards the implementation of the principles of sustainable development to ASEAN Governments and relevant ASEAN committees;
b) facilitate the incorporation of environmental considerations into the programmes and activities of ASEAN committees;
c) monitor the state of ASEAN's natural resources and the quality of the ASEAN environment;
d) promote ASEAN cooperation on regional environmental matters, focusing upon ASEAN's common seas and resources, land resources and land-based pollution, tropical forest, air quality, urban and rural pollution; and maintenance of genetic diversity;
e) promote ASEAN cooperation in international fora through a common stand for the purpose of promoting the transfer of clean technology and solving common global environmental problems, in cooperation with other government agencies, the private/business sectors, professional associations, NGOs, and other organisations; and
f) assist in obtaining financial support for ASEAN activities from within and outside ASEAN.

The ASOEN meets once a year to consider the reports of the Working Groups and provide operational policy guidance on the various environmental programmes being pursued.

## The ASOEN Subsidiary Bodies

The cooperative programmes and projects of ASOEN are carried out through six Working Groups in the following areas: ASEAN Seas and Marine Environment, Environmental Economics, Nature Conservation, Environmental Management,

Transboundary Pollution, and Environmental Information, Public Awareness and Education. The Working Groups meet annually.

### *The ASEAN Secretariat*

The ASEAN Secretariat was established in 1976 to provide for greater efficiency in coordinating the implementation of policies, projects and activities of the various ASEAN bodies. With the growing realization that ASEAN cooperation would have to be enhanced, the Singapore Summit decided that the ASEAN Secretariat should be strengthened and provided more resources. Accordingly, the Secretary General of the Secretariat has been designated as the Secretary General of ASEAN with ministerial status and an enlarged mandate to initiate, advise, and implement ASEAN activities.

The ASEAN Secretariat has four Bureaus, namely, Economic Cooperation, Economic Research, Functional Cooperation and General Affairs, each headed by a Director, Issues on the environment fall under the purview of the Functional Cooperation Bureau along with science and technology, culture and information, social development, and drug abuse prevention. With the expected increase in the coordinative activities of the Bureau, especially in the field of environment, there is need to further strengthen its present professional capabilities.

## 2.4 Brief Review of ASEP III

ASEP III, covering the period 1988–1992, succeeded ASEP II and continued some of the latter's projects as well as goals. It had the following overall objective: to promote the proper management of the ASEAN environment so that it could sustain continued economic development while maintaining a high quality of life for the people of the ASEAN countries. This objective was to be achieved by strengthening the institutional framework and organisational structure of ASEAN cooperation on the environment.

Thus, ASEP III adopted the following policy guidelines:

a) the promotion of cooperation on the environment among member countries, especially in identified priority areas;
b) integration of the environmental dimension into regional and national development planning and implementation;
c) strengthening of regional and national institutions to enhance their capability to implement environmental programmes and projects; and

d) cooperation with other countries and with international agencies for the purpose of promoting the transfer of technology and sharing experiences in the management and solution of environmental problems.

Included under ASEP III were 17 programme goals and 60 regional projects, divided, as in ASEP I and ASEP II, into six priority programme areas as follows:

a) Environmental management — This area dealt with the overall and integrated approach to the problems of the environment and the use of management tools such as environmental impact assessment and the application of advanced technologies, such as remote sensing, to solve these problems or at least mitigate their adverse impacts. It recognized the interdependence between environment and development and that one could not be sustained without the other.
b) Nature conservation and terrestrial ecosystems — This area derived its urgency from the abundance of natural resources in the region and the need to conserve them in the face of rapid economic growth in ASEAN, particularly in the manufacturing sector, but to a lesser extent also in the agricultural sector. Such development, while it had undoubtedly resulted in increased output and higher standards of living in ASEAN, had also exerted tremendous pressure on the region's forest, marine, water and other resources. Hence, it emphasized on the need for a rational and integrated approach to development and conservation.
c) Industry and environment — Rapid industrialization in ASEAN, with its concomitant energy consumption, has not only strained the region's natural resources but has also contributed to the growing pollution problem, particularly in the urban areas. Some of the major products in the region such as palm oil, rubber and sugar, involve manufacturing processes that release considerable amounts of pollutive substances into the atmosphere. Collaboration among ASEAN member countries and between ASEAN and its Dialogue Partners was therefore necessary in order to promote intra-ASEAN transfer and development of anti-pollution technology and the transfer of clean technology from the Dialogue Partners to ASEAN.
d) Urban environment — Related to, but separate from, the immediately preceding priority area was urban environment. Rapid population growth as well as uncontrolled migration from the rural to the urban areas has resulted to housing and traffic congestion, noise, dust, inadequate water and sewerage systems as well as garbage disposal facilities, and related urban problems. This situation in most urban areas in ASEAN was the rationale for the inclusion of urban environment as a fourth priority area of ASEAN cooperation.

e) Marine environment — This area was a recognition of the fact that the marine environment was under serious stress in ASEAN, whether it was for ship-building in Singapore, oil exploration and extraction in Brunei, or fishing in the Philippines, Malaysia and Thailand. ASEAN cooperation was (and still is) necessary for the development, protection and rational exploitation of the region's marine resources and coastal areas.
f) Environmental Education, Training and Information — Ultimately, the most sound and solid basis for the protection of the environment and the conservation or rational exploitation of resources are people who are aware of the possible negative environmental implications of their actuation, not only for the present generation but for future generations as well, hence the importance of this area of cooperation.

Projects were selected and included in the above programmes on the basis of their relevance, regional character and relation to other projects. They were also selected on the basis of their being "interactive, integrative, and mutually supportive" of each other.

To further rank which projects could be funded under ASEP III, very high priority projects were subsequently identified using these criteria:

a) the project met the goal of sustainable development;
b) availability of project funding;
c) project did not require excessive resources;
d) project was carried over from ASEP II; and
e) project was goal-oriented as specified in ASEP III.

On this basis, twelve very high priority projects were selected. The list appears as Table 3.

ASEP III set as its target to implement 90% or more of its 60 projects, with at least 60% of them to be completed within the planning cycle 1988–1992. When completed, the 60 projects under ASEP III were expected to yield the following physical outputs:

- five guidelines;
- two manuals;
- one textbook;
- six management plans; and
- three sets of teaching/visual aids.

Table 3. Very High Priority Projects Under ASEP III

| | |
|---|---|
| 1. | Comparative study of environment law in ASEAN Countries |
| 2. | ASEAN waterbirds and wetlands |
| 3. | Integrated hydrological technology for water resources |
| 4. | Development of risk analysis guidelines and technologies for ASEAN Countries |
| 5. | Adaptation of environmental education materials for primary and secondary schools |
| 6. | Introduction of modern industrial effluent treatment technologies in ASEAN Countries |
| 7. | Impact of human activities on the productivity of mangrove ecosystems |
| 8. | Establishment of ASEAN information centre on national parks and reserve management |
| 9. | Monitoring of erosion intensity and sedimentation rate in rivers related to erosion control efforts |
| 10. | Strengthening public awareness at village level |
| 11. | Urban parks development and greenery |
| 12. | Consultant mission to national industrial development banks on loan policy for industrial development |

Other expected outputs include the conduct of thirteen regional training courses and numerous reports to be generated by the various pilot-demonstration projects and EIA studies.

A number of projects carried over from ASEP II were completed under ASEP III, namely:

a) Environmental Impact Study on Coal Fired Power Plants (renamed Programme Assessment of the Environmental Impact of Coal-Fired based Power Plants);
b) Technology Transfer on the Treatment of Effluent from Palm Oil and Rubber Industries;
c) Anti-pollution Control and Management in Fuel Gas Desulphurization and Control in ASEAN Region;
d) Development of Cooperative Action for Oil Pollution Combat;
e) Seminar on Toxic and Hazardous Waste; and
f) Regional Programme for the Training of Trainers on Environmental Education in the ASEAN Region.

## 2.5 Assessment of the Achievements

A review of ASEAN's environmental collaborative efforts indicates that ASOEN has substantially accomplished its mandate. For one, the development and evolution of ASEP Programmes provided a solid basis and further enhanced regional environmental cooperation. Perhaps the most significant contribution of the previous programmes was the maturing of the environmental agencies in the respective ASEAN countries. These accomplishments should be sustained and further developed in order to make them more attuned to the times.

Much work, however, would have to be done in the design, selection and prioritisation of programmes and projects as most of the previous activities were "stand-alone" projects which have not fully contributed to long term ASEAN objectives. Partly contributory to the short-term nature of previous projects was the inadequacy of financing to support ASOEN's activities and also institutional deficiencies. As there was inadequate follow up mechanisms in the development of projects, proposals had a tendency to have long gestation periods. These shortcomings must be addressed by ASOEN through this Strategic Plan of Action on Environment. Focus will have to be on activities which are truly regional in character and can contribute to the long-term overall objectives of ASEAN.

## 3. NEW DIRECTIONS, OBJECTIVES AND STRATEGIES

### 3.1 New Directions

#### 3.1.1 *ASEAN Free Trade Area (AFTA)*

The January 1992 Meeting of the ASEAN Heads of Government in Singapore decided to establish an ASEAN Free Trade Area (AFTA) over the next 15 years. AFTA will cover trade in manufactures, including capital goods and processed agricultural products. A Common Effective Preferential Tariff (CEPT) scheme will be established leading to a progressive reduction of tariffs to a 0–5 percent level by the year 2008. There are two programmes of tariff reduction under the CEPT Scheme: the fast track programme which targets the reduction of tariffs to 0–5 percent within 7 to 10 years; and the normal track programme which targets tariff reduction to 0–5 within 10 to 15 years. The 15 groups of commodities included in the fast track programme are: vegetable oils, cement, chemicals, pharmaceuticals, fertilizers, plastics, rubber products, leather products, paper pulp, textiles, ceramics and glass products, gems and jewellery, copper cathodes, electronics, and wooden and rattan furniture.

The link between international trade and sustainable development, where the latter is understood as development that meets the needs of the present without compromising the ability of future generations to meet their own needs, is not always obvious. But there is such a link, namely, the common concern for improving resource allocation and quality of life.

Reduced tariff rates would increase ASEAN's competitiveness as a production base and stimulate intra-ASEAN trade in the 15 commodity groups. Increased trade would, in turn, improve the allocation of resources and increase output, employment and incomes.

But AFTA may not come as an unmixed blessing. Among the 15 commodities in the fast track, whose rates are to be reduced, are highly pollutive and/or natural resource consuming industries–to the former belong chemicals, fertilizers, plastics, cement, paper and pulp, and leather and rubber products, and to the latter belong copper cathodes and wooden and rattan furniture. To the extent that increased intra-ASEAN trade in these commodities will lead to the more intensive exploitation of resources and/or the release of greater quantities of pollutants into the atmosphere as a result of increased manufacturing activities, to that extent the implementation of AFTA may not advance the goal of environmentally sound and sustainable development to which ASEAN also aspires.

Indeed, there is a potential development dilemma that needs to be carefully addressed. On the one hand, the goal of sustainable development requires that poverty — which, despite progress made during the past two decades, remains a problem in ASEAN — be reduced if not eradicated. Persistent poverty is one of the major causes of environmental degradation, as it increases pressure on natural resources (e.g. through deforestation, cultivation of marginal lands) and strains to limit the carrying capacity of urban ecosystems. Increased trade, through the higher incomes and greater employment that it provides, is a potentially powerful poverty-reduction measure, as the experience of the Newly Industrialized Economies (NIE) would show. However, where such trade involves natural resources either as traded goods or as inputs to manufacturing industries, it carries with it the danger of rapid resource depletion and increased pollution, and hence an unsustainable development.

How ASEAN policy-makers will resolve this dilemma will determine how the next generation will judge the recent decision to implement AFTA. The solution lies in translating the principle of environmentally sound and sustainable development into concrete policies and implementable programmes, inter alia, the application of environmental planning and assessment techniques and use of low- and non-waste manufacturing technologies.

### 3.1.2 *ASEAN Common Stand on UNCED*

During the ASEAN Ministerial Meeting on the Environment in Singapore in 1992, ASEAN declared its common stand on UNCED. The declaration called for: urgent measures to combat climate change; immediate implementation of the Montreal Protocol Interim Multilateral Fund; protection of the ecosystems of oceans and seas from pollution; greater efforts to protect freshwater resources and ensure access for all people; sustainable management of all forests; conservation of biological diversity, support for the Basel Convention on the Transboundary Movement of Hazardous Wastes and their Disposal; and support for the objective of the Prior Informed-Consent (PIC) system under the Amended London Guidelines for the Exchange of Information on Banned or Severely Restricted Chemicals in International Trade.

To achieve the above, ASEAN has called for new and additional financial resources to meet the incremental cost of protecting the global environment; and for more funding for implementing sustainable development policies at the regional and national levels to be provided by developed countries. The establishment of basic environmental protection is also required. Appropriate technologies to achieve environmental standards must be identified and all means, financial as well as legal, to overcome patent laws should be made available to enable the transfer of such technologies.

### 3.1.3 *Agenda 21 Programme Areas Relevant to ASEAN*

Agenda 21 is an action plan for the 1990s and into the 21st Century. It reflects a global consensus and political commitment at the highest level in the government on development and environment cooperation and is intended to serve as basis for global partnership. Its successful implementation rests with the governments. However, international and regional cooperation and efforts are necessary to support its national implementation. It has been suggested that the broadest public participation and the active involvement of non-governmental organizations are essential prerequisites to these efforts.

Agenda 21 covers 115 programme areas. Since it is a distilled wisdom of all the governments, and the ASEAN region embodies a wide spectrum of environment and development issues, it is understandable that almost all the programme areas will have some relevance to ASEAN. It is however, impossible to capture all the issues and dimensions of Agenda 21 in this document. Hence

Table 5 summarizes the more relevant chapters of Agenda 21 in the context of ASEAN collaboration.

## 3.2 Objectives

This Strategic Plan of Action on the Environment has the following five objectives:

a) to respond to specific recommendations of Agenda 21 requiring priority action in ASEAN;
b) to introduce policy measures and promote institutional development that encourage the integration of environmental factors in all developmental processes both at the national and regional levels;
c) to establish long term goals on environmental quality and work towards harmonised environmental quality standards for the ASEAN region;
d) to harmonise policy directions and enhance operational and technical cooperation on environmental matters, and undertake joint actions to address common environmental problems; and
e) to study the implications of AFTA on the environment and take steps to integrate sound trade policies with sound environmental policies.

## 3.3 Strategic Thrusts

To attain the objectives, the following strategies and actions will be pursued:

### *Strategy 1*: Support the development of a regional framework for integrating environment and development concerns in the decision making process

Integrating environment and development concerns in decision making has been long recognized as a key element for promoting sustainable development. Successive ASEAN resolutions, declarations and decisions refer to this element as of vital significance. Efforts therefore have been initiated to meet these directives. But these efforts need to be consolidated and further refined if the intention is to apply them uniformly in the region. There is a necessity to develop a regional framework that will ensure the integration of environment and development concerns in the respective national decision-making processes. The elements of that framework include the following:

a) institutional capability to make an integrated, forward looking and cross-sectoral approach in making decisions;

b) appropriate policies and legal frameworks in place to undertake the task;
c) sufficient technological base for use in decision making; and
d) sound information and database derived from monitoring and research.

## *Actions*:

1.1 *Continue support in the documentation of regional EIA experiences leading towards the harmonisation of procedures*

Increasing efforts are being made by all countries to strengthen environmental impact assessment procedures and practices. Institutional and legislative frameworks have also been improved. There is a need to continue this process. Exchange of information and experience among ASEAN could provide a solid foundation for further work. With the launching of AFTA and the implementation of the Common Effective Preferential Tariff (CEPT) Scheme and the improved prospects for attracting greater investment flows in the region as a whole, increasing efforts should be focused on the harmonisation of procedures in EIA. It would entail studies on the EIA procedures in different countries, identifying common and conflicting issues, proposing principles of harmonisation and coming up with a harmonised framework on EIA.

Responsible Working Unit: Environmental Management

1.2 *Initiate activities that will make use of natural resource and environmental accounting studies and approaches*

In recent years, governments and international organizations have made increasing efforts to collect environmental data. Most of these data are given in physical terms and some in monetary values. However, the gap between environmental data and macro-economic accounting systems remains almost unchanged. An important issue is how to expand existing systems of national economic accounts in order to integrate environmental and social dimensions in the accounting framework, including the use of satellite systems for natural resources. The resulting system of Integrated Natural Resources and Environment Accounting (INREA) to be established in ASEAN countries should be seen as complementing the existing national income accounting practices. INREA would be designed to play an integral part in national decision-making process. Some work in this field are being done in Indonesia and the Philippines. Based on international efforts and work done in ASEAN countries, guidelines may be prepared. These guidelines may be used for undertaking sectoral pilot studies in ASEAN countries and the system may be refined as necessary for wider application.

Responsible Working Unit: Environmental Economics

1.3 *Establish procedures that would initiate the integration of environmental concerns in the various ASEAN programmes and activities*

Another important issue in this area is the integration of environmental concerns in the programmes and activities of ASEAN. While it would be desirable to integrate environmental dimensions in the various ASEAN committees and other bodies, it may be difficult at this stage to undertake such a task, because of the complexity of the organisational structure and the limited technical and infrastructural support available from the ASEAN Secretariat.

It may, however, be possible to examine proposed projects and activities for the purpose of integrating environmental concerns. The mechanism for such an integration should be developed. One such mechanism could be the examination of relevant project proposals by the relevant sections of the ASEAN Secretariat with a view to providing inputs on environmental dimensions and likely mitigating measures. In any case, guidelines for integration of environmental concerns into ASEAN's activities will have to be prepared.

Responsible Working Units: Environmental Management

## *Strategy 2*: Promote government-private sector interactions that lead towards the development of policies that mutually support the thrust of each sector

The recent decision of ASEAN to establish AFTA underscores the prevailing trend in regional trade cooperation embracing a liberal and market oriented system. The theory is that regional trade cooperation promotes efficiency in the allocation of resources and provides economies of scale and competition which induce increase in output, income and standard of living. Prior to AFTA, the region registered one of the highest GDP growth performance globally. The creation of AFTA will further accelerate this trend. The challenge ASEAN faces now is how to reinforce the AFTA decision with mutually supportive environmental policies. In this regard, government institutions and industries would play major roles in developing sustainable societies. There should be consensus in the framing of policies that reinforce the thrust of each sector.

## *Actions*:

2.1 *Initiate studies on development of environmental and trade policies which are supportive to the principles of sustainable development*

The implications of AFTA on sustainable development have already been cited. AFTA should seek to promote an open and non-discriminatory trading system that is consistent with the goals of sustainable development. Improved market access for ASEAN's export, in conjunction with sound macro-economic and environmental policies, should result in positive environmental impacts; and environment and trade policies should be made mutually supportive.

The commodity sector dominates the economies of ASEAN countries in terms of production, employment and export earnings. An important feature of the world commodity trade in the 1980s was the prevalence of very low and declining real prices for ASEAN commodities in international markets resulting in increased exploitation of natural resources to maintain commodity export earnings for some countries. The ability of these countries to mobilize, through international trade, the resources needed to finance investments required for sustainable development may be impaired by this development and by tariff and non-tariff barriers. The international trading environment has been affected by a number of regional developments that have created new challenges, such as the establishment of the North American Free Trade Agreement (NAFTA) and the Single European Market (SEM). These developments will have profound impact on development and environment in the ASEAN countries.

Therefore, studies should be initiated to better understand the relationship between trade and environment for the promotion of sustainable development in the ASEAN region. This should be reinforced with the establishment of a platform for dialogue between trade, investment, development and environment sectors of the ASEAN region. ASEAN has already developed excellent cooperation with the private sector through the ASEAN Chamber of Commerce and Industry (ASEAN-CCI), the Business Council for Sustainable Development (BCSO), and the implementation of the ASEAN-US Environmental Improvement Programme (EIP).

Responsible Working Unit: Environmental Economics

2.2 *Establish mechanisms that encourage government and private sectors to adapt appropriate environmental standards backed up by sufficient economic incentives*

The responsibility for ensuring industrialization that adheres to sustainable development principles rests between institutions, as regulators, managers and economic policy framers, and industry, as the implementation and principal source of technological know-how. These roles must be respected and supported by each other. Governments, as an institution, must establish environmental goals that do not retard growth but create the right climate that encourages industry to comply. The standards, while it can be updated regularly, should allow industry to seek the best practicable environmental alternative which technology can provide. This approach can bend businesses that enhanced by reviewing existing policies and introducing incentives to industries and businesses that ensure sustainable industrial processes, such as the promotion on the use of cleaner technologies, and waste minimization techniques, to mention a few. On the part of the industry, there should be commitment to sustainability and environmental excellence. They should show the public their desire to comply with the standards of environmental performance which they themselves could set voluntarily.

Responsible Working Unit: Environmental Economics

*2.3 Set up government-private sector information linkages/networks to include information on technology, expertise and facilities for environmental management*

Access to information on technology and expertise is crucial if industry is to comply with environmental standards. While there is no dearth of information that could be used by industry, the availability of that information and its quality are impediments that hinder the selection of appropriate alternatives to sustainable industrial processes. The government and private sector should collaborate in setting up information networks that can make the needed information readily available. The academic and the scientific community could be harnessed to play a role in this endeavor.

Responsible Working Unit: Environmental Information, Public Awareness and Education

## *Strategy 3*: Strengthen the knowledge and information database on environmental matters

Environmentally sound and sustainable development requires that action is taken on the basis of objective reliable and comparable environmental information. This calls for enhanced capability at national and regional levels to obtain sound environmental data, transform these data into meaningful information and share this knowledge among the various actors involved in implementing actions. This also implies that new demands will be placed on monitoring and information gathering systems on the basis of harmonized database and inter-calibration of existing monitoring systems. There is an effort by UNEP, through its Global Resource Information Database (GRID), to open a subregional window on environmental information collection and dissemination. ASEAN should take advantage of this opportunity and coordinate with UNEP in setting up this system with information stored at the ASEAN Secretariat and disseminated to member countries.

## *Actions*:

3.1 *Pursue the establishment of basic environmental quality standards leading to the setting up of harmonised quality standards in the region*

The indicators of environmental quality could serve as good indices or guideposts for the state of the environment. With AFTA and the implementation of the CEPT, it is likely that industrialization in the ASEAN region will accelerate. If the environmental standards for air and water quality continue to be widely different in the region, it may lead to development of pollution havens or hot-spots. Anticipating the most likely impact of unsustainable industrialization, it may be prudent to already consider the establishment of long term goals for ambient air and water quality (both river and coastal). The major vehicle for achieving this will be the harmonisation of environmental quality standards in the region. This activity entails a substantial amount of capacity building through: training and the building up of an extensive network of monitoring stations; inventory of polluting sources; identification of the most pollutive industries; economic and industrial growth modeling; and institution building to enable exchange of information among member countries.

Responsible Working Unit: Environmental Management

3.2 *Identify centres of excellence for environmental R&D and eventually build them as focal points of environmental networks*

Support should be given to the identification of centres of excellence undertaking environmental research and development (R&D) activities. This can be done by assessing the capacities and capabilities of existing scientific and research institutions dealing with environmental work and ascertaining their competencies. Once determined, programmes could be designed to upgrade these institutions with a view to eventually establishing them as focal points of environmental networks which could provide basic environmental information, training of human resources and strategic environmental research studies for policy formulation.

Responsible Working Unit: Environmental Management

3.3 *Establish a mechanism for the preparation of periodic reports on the state of the region's environment*

Periodic environmental performance reviews would help in promoting policy dialogue and exchange of information on national approaches and experiences in improving collective and individual performance regarding the attainment of national and regional goals vis-a-vis the international agreements. It could also assist in the identification of priority activities for regional action, help in strengthening national and regional capabilities for environmental management and policy evaluation, and play a useful role in monitoring and assessing regional and national environmental quality. The preparation of this report should be seen in the light of the requested submission of national reports by the Commission on Sustainable Development (CSD).

Responsible Working Units: Environmental Information, Public Awareness and Education

## *Strategy 4*: Strengthen institutional and legal capacities to implement international agreements on environment

Agenda 21, identifies as a prerequisite to global participation on sustainable development, the strength of institutional and legal capacities of national and regional entities. As environmental issues now transcend beyond regional boundaries, the need to develop these capabilities in order to implement international agreements on environment as well as effectively participate in the negotiation of new international treaties and the review of existing ones, cannot be overemphasized. There are still many aspects of international law on sustainable development that merit development and appropriate interpretation to make them effective and binding. ASEAN, from a regional standpoint, should strengthen its institutional capacities to implement and its legal capacities to present its concerns and interests in international legal discussions on the environment.

### *Actions*:

4.1 *Undertake a comparative study on institutional structures and legislations on environmental management*

There have been previous efforts to document and compile the various legislations of ASEAN relating to the environment. This documentation should be consolidated and be further expanded to cover the undertaking of a comparative study on the various institutional structures and legislations on environmental administration. ASOEN should seek financial support and assistance to undertake and complete this project.

Responsible Working Units: Environmental Management

4.2 *Establish capacities to support regional efforts to implement international agreements and participate effectively in the negotiation of new or revised agreements*

There are a large number of international environmental treaties and conventions aimed at protecting the global commons, such as marine environment biodiversity and the atmosphere, which ASEAN member countries have signed. Its effective implementation, however, is hampered owing to the various administrative, technical, economic and financial obstacles within ASEAN. While the individual countries are encouraged to study the implications of ratification, there may be a need to look into the regional ramifications of the treaties. ASOEN should build its capacities that would enable it to participate effectively in the negotiation of new or revised agreements.

Responsible Working Units: All Working Groups

4.3 *Enhance collaboration with international bodies overseeing the implementation of international agreements and cooperation*

As countries in the region implement the various international agreements, they are likewise becoming actively involved in international discussions such as in APEC and OECD. Hence, ASEAN needs to promote greater regional visibility with concerned international bodies or organizations. This could be achieved by strengthening its linkages and networking with these institutions and actively participate in activities that have relevance to the region. Depending on how ASEAN would be invited in these collaborative discussions, there could be a need to present a common ASEAN stand to enhance its regional position.

Responsible Working Units: All Working Groups

## *Strategy 5*: Establish a regional framework on biological diversity conservation and sustainable utilization of its components

The ASEAN region has invaluable biodiversity and abundant natural resources comprising 30% of the world's tropical forests. During the last two decades, ASEAN countries have embarked on massive economic development activities aimed at raising the standards of living of its people. Consequently, however, the impacts of these activities have affected the region's biodiversity. Thus, capacities for assessment, study and systematic observation and evaluation of biodiversity need to be reinforced at national and regional levels. An effective national and regional action supported by international cooperation is required for the in situ protection of the ecosystems and the ex situ conservation of biological and genetic resources. Similarly, the establishment of a regional center on biodiversity conservation should be actively supported.

## *Actions*:

5.1 *Promote the development of a framework for the protection and conservation of heritage areas and endangered species*

ASEAN has long recognized the importance of nature and biodiversity, and thus has designated areas that are to be preserved as national parks, nature reserves and heritage areas. Despite these management and monitoring efforts, the threat to these identified areas persists owing to continued habitat destruction, overharvesting, pollution and threats posed by the introduction of exotic species (both plants and animals) which either replaces or competes with the endemic species. The absence of a regional framework for the protection and conservation of heritage areas and endangered species, only exacerbates the situation as management efforts are left to individual member countries. There is a need to develop a framework for the protection of these areas and species so as to ensure that conservation approaches are rationalized.

Responsible Working Unit: Nature Conservation

5.2 *Strengthen capacities for R&D to enhance biodiversity conservation in the region*

Supportive to the identification of areas designated for biological diversity conservation are efforts to improve the knowledge and understanding of species found in these areas. It is accepted that knowledge on the status and distribution of many animal and plant species is still poor and inadequate. As a result, effective conservation measures cannot be implemented. ASOEN should invest n this field and seek assistance from the international community both in public and private sectors. Strong support to systematic and taxonomic research which ranges from undertaking surveys and inventories to monitoring wildlife movement and control should be pursued by the region.

Responsible Working Unit: Nature Conservation

## *Strategy 6*: Promote the protection and management of coastal zones and marine resources

The marine environment is truly an ASEAN regional heritage, a fact that has been recognized from the very beginning of ASEAN cooperation. Among the first actions by the ASEAN countries, with catalytic support from UNEP, was the adoption of an Action Plan for the Protection and Development of the Marine Environment and Coastal Areas of the East Asia Region. The Southeast Asian seas are natural habitat for 2500 species of fish and invertebrates. They provide 11% of the world's supply of marine products and source of livelihood for many of the region's fishermen. All ASEAN countries have extensive fishing industries. Yet, many of the major nearshore fishing areas in the region are over-fished and polluted from land based sources and oil spills. The Straits of Malacca, for example, is one of the major shipping lanes for crude oil transport and is vulnerable to oil spills. There has been a notable increase in the occurrence of red tides which is attributed to domestic sources of pollution. This incidence poses not only a health hazard but also affects export earnings. Similarly, many mangroves are disappearing to make room for brackish water prawn farming, housing and industrial development. Coral reefs are also being degraded and require rehabilitation. Accordingly, there is an urgent need for a more coordinated, pro-active and collective action to protect ASEAN's coastal zones and marine resources.

### *Actions*:

6.1 *Improve regional marine and coastal environmental coordination*

Cooperation among the ASEAN countries in the field of marine science and marine environments have been carried out through three distinct regional bodies, namely, the Coordinating Body on the Seas of East Asia (COBSEA), the ASOEN Working Group on ASEAN Seas and Marine Environment (WGASME) and the COST Sub-committee on Marine Science (SCMS). While the WGASME and the SCMS are official ASEAN bodies, the latter being under the purview of the ASEAN Committee on Science and Technology (COST), COBSEA comes under the purview of the United Nations Environment Programme (UNEP). There is a need to streamline these cooperative mechanisms, as they create unnecessary overlaps and confusion and fritter away scarce technical and-financial resources.

Responsible Working Units: ASEAN Seas and Marine Environment Nature Conservation

6.2 *Develop a framework for the integrated management of regional coastal zones*

It is recognized that while several programmes have been developed on a bilateral and regional basis to protect and manage coastal zones in the region, these developments are not tied to any framework that could integrate its approaches on a regional basis. The impacts, therefore, of these programmes have been localized and its regional benefits have not been fully appreciated or felt. In order to enhance the effects of these activities, ASOEN could initiate the development of a framework for the integrated management of regional coastal zones. This framework could serve as a guide in the development of the respective coastal zone management interventions by member countries.

Responsible Working Units: ASEAN Seas and Marine Environment Nature Conservation

## *Strategy 7*: Promote environmentally sound management of toxic chemicals and hazardous wastes and control of transboundary movement of hazardous wastes

With the continued rapid industrialization of the ASEAN economies and the trend in the transfer of highly polluting industries, the flow of toxic chemicals and dangerous products is bound to increase in the region. There is worldwide recognition that chemical contamination may result in grave damage to human health and the environment. It is therefore necessary to have good knowledge and assessment of these risks which is a prerequisite to planning for their safe and beneficial use, recycling and disposal. However, for a great number of high volume production chemicals, even basic data for risk assessment are generally lacking. ASEAN should now initiate action on effecting a regional management guide for the environmentally sound management of toxic chemicals and hazardous wastes.

### *Actions*:

7.1 *Establish regional guidelines for assessing highly pollutive industries and safe handling of potentially harmful chemicals entering the ASEAN region*

The information exchange on toxic chemicals is of particular importance. In this regard, the UNEP London Guidelines for the Exchange of Information on Chemicals in International Trade is a useful instrument, in particular those relating to the information on banned and severely restricted chemicals. Work carried out under the International Register of Potentially Toxic Chemicals (IRPTC) and the International Programme on Chemical Safety (IPCS) should also be used.

However, there is a need for greater national vigilance in controlling the relocation of toxic chemical industries into the ASEAN region. There may be a case for developing a regional guideline on assessing highly polluting industries and potentially harmful chemicals entering ASEAN.

Responsible Working Units: Transboundary Pollution

7.2 *Strengthen the information network on the transboundary movement of toxic chemicals and hazardous waste*

There has been a notable achievement in this area within the ASEAN region over the past few years as evidenced by a number of cases relating to intra-ASEAN transboundary movement of hazardous waste. The identification of focal points helped in monitoring and regulating the movement of hazardous waste. This network should be further strengthened as movement of these substances is expected to increase. A regional protocol for the movement of toxic chemicals and hazardous substances consistent with the provision of the Basel Convention could be established.

Responsible Working Unit: Transboundary Pollution

## *Strategy 8*: Develop a system for the promotion of environmentally sound technologies

Since the region is likely to face increasing challenges for controlling pollution and resource degradation it is necessary to evolve a system for the promotion of environmentally sound technologies in the region. Pollution control techniques tend to transfer pollution from one medium to another, rather than eliminating it. Therefore, although these technologies may reduce some risks from certain factories, large scale transfer of such techniques may not prove beneficial to promoting regional environmental quality. Environmentally sound technologies are less polluting, use resources in a more sustainable manner, and recycle more of their by-products, residues and waste than the traditional technologies they replace.

### *Actions*:

8.1 *Establish linkages with existing clearing houses on environmentally sound technologies*

There is currently no comprehensive, independent and reliable mechanism for obtaining information on technologies which can help governments evaluate environmental impacts of investments. Although activities have been initiated to set up international clearing houses for identifying dirty technologies or preventing their transfer, its network has not yet been fully operationalized. Under these circumstances, investors present their own technologies as environmentally advanced, even though these may be discredited in other countries. ASOEN should therefore take the initiative in linking with these clearing houses on environmentally sound technologies available in the market so as to enable member countries to choose which appropriate technologies can be allowed in the region.

Responsible Working Unit: Environmental Information, Public Awareness and Education

8.2 *Establish mechanisms that identify end users of R&D results and encourage the participation of private sector*

These actions have bearing on the efforts of the ASEAN-COST to identify end-users of R&D outputs and to entice private sector involvement. Researches on environmental or environmentally friendly technologies may also be considered as part of the science and technology agenda. ASOEN through its Working Groups in collaboration with COST, should initiate discussions with industry and solicit their support to co-finance environmental R&D projects that have potential for commercialization.

Responsible Working Unit: Environmental Information, Public Awareness and Education

8.3 *Strengthen linkage and coordination with other ASEAN committees such as COST doing related R&D work on the environment*

As there are common interests between COST and ASOEN, these two bodies of ASEAN should interact more often to mutually support its respective thrusts. The Working Groups and Sub-committees should develop mechanisms to jointly pursue complementary programmes which would benefit ASEAN as a whole.

Responsible Working Unit: Environmental Information, Public Awareness and Education

8.4 *Support the promotion of indigenous technologies or technologies that have been adapted to regional needs*

There are existing environmentally friendly technologies utilized by industry which have been locally adapted from foreign technologies or indigenously developed.

Its widespread application, however, is hampered by the inadequacy of support in promoting its use. ASOEN in collaboration with COST may develop mechanisms whereby these technologies can be made available to the regional market.

Responsible Working Unit: Environmental Information, Public Awareness and Education Environmental Management

## *Strategy 9*: Promote regional activities that strengthen the role of major groups in sustainable development

The region's ability to develop sustainably depends on the capability and capacity of its people to understand complex environment and development issues and to choose the best development alternative. As people would need to have the information and expertise to understand the potential limits of the environment, institutions have the responsibility of making these information available and easily understood. The mechanisms for achieving this objective vary depending on the level of information required. Nonetheless, efforts should be made by ASOEN to bring the result of its various programmes to the ASEAN public either through formal approaches or on an informal basis. ASOEN should establish mechanisms that will motivate, educate, train and build capacities especially among the identified major groups under Agenda 21.

### *Actions*:

9.1 *Support the publication of regional environmental magazines and newsletters*

There is a need to increase public sensitivity to environment and development issues and involvement in finding solutions to environmental problems. Further, the sense of personal environmental responsibility and the desire for greater involvement and commitment need to be fostered towards sustainable development. Increased public awareness and participation in environmental decision making are important for the success of environmental policies. It is therefore necessary to make available accurate and authentic information on ASEAN environment and development issues to all sectors of the society. This can be achieved through the regular publication of regional newsletters and information materials. The ASEAN Secretariat should be provided with the needed resource to enable it to collect and edit articles, monographs and papers for the ASEAN Environment Newsletter to be issued on a bi-annual basis.

Responsible Working Unit: Environmental Information, Public Awareness and Education

9.2 *Strengthen regional information network and promote exchange of expertise on environmental education programmes*

Environmental education is very important in sensitizing people, particularly students, as it helps in developing the right environmental ethic and building environmentally responsive and responsible society. There should be initiatives taken to share environmental education modules that have been developed at the national levels to enrich the knowledge of environmental educators and trainers in the region. To enhance their capabilities exchange programme of environmental education, experts could be established. ASOEN may consider tapping potential public and private institutions who have expressed willingness to support this endeavor.

Responsible Working Unit: Environmental Information, Public Awareness and Education

9.3 *Develop strategic programmes of action that will strengthen the role and participation of major groups on environmental management and decision making*

As recommended in Agenda 21, the region should evolve a strategy for effectively involving NGO's, local bodies and other sectors in promoting sustainable development. As a start, ASOEN should consider representation of some of the major groups in a number of its programmes.

Responsible Working Units: All Working Groups

## *Strategy 10*: Strengthen the coordinative mechanism for the implementation and management of regional environment programmes

As mandated by the Jakarta Resolution on Sustainable Development, ASOEN should facilitate the incorporation of environmental considerations into the programmes and activities of ASEAN committees. This would require a review of all ASEAN committees' activities and projects to assess their environmental implications and suggest measures for environmental protection and improvement. To be able to do this and at the same time implement programmes of this Strategic Plan of Action on Environment, ASOEN would need strong coordinative support from the ASEAN Secretariat. This will require substantial time on the part of the professional staff of the Secretariat. Since ASOEN's activities are expected to increase in the near future, support should be given to the ASEAN Secretariat to enable it to upgrade its capacities. This may mean augmenting the existing number of professional staff in the Environment Unit.

***Actions*:**

10.1 *Establish an operational system at the ASEAN Secretariat for planning, monitoring and facilitation of the implementation of environmental projects*

While the Plan of Action identifies several programme areas, projects will need to be developed in all areas. The various Working Groups have already done some work in this direction, but these will have to be refined into a harmonized framework. With the expansion of mandate of the ASEAN Secretariat, these projects will have to be monitored and some coordinated and implemented by the Secretariat. This will require strengthened in-house project management capability.

Responsible Working Unit: ASEAN Secretariat

10.2 *Source and match funding requirements for proposed projects*

Agenda 21 recognizes that very large investments are needed to implement its sustainable development programmes. Since financial resources are scarce, it is imperative that a set of criteria for selecting and prioritizing programme areas and projects under this plan be developed. It is noted that under ASEP III a set of criteria was used to rank projects. There may be a need for ASOEN to review this ranking criteria. This would also mean that the necessary network and linkages with financing institutions and sectors should be developed and enhanced.

Responsible Working Unit: ASEAN Secretariat

## 4. INSTITUTIONAL AND FINANCIAL MECHANISMS

### 4.1 Institutional Requirement

Ten strategic thrusts and twenty-seven actions have been identified. Many of these actions have strong inter-linkages and the activities should be implemented in close coordination with one another. Indeed, the approach to environmental issues should be cross-sectoral and comprehensive. To operationalize these strategic thrusts and actions, institutional adjustments should be undertaken, namely:

a) The capacity of the ASEAN Secretariat should be strengthened as discussed in Strategy 10. The ASEAN Secretariat should play an active supportive and coordinative role in the implementation of all actions identified in this Plan. While it is recognized that the Secretariat may not have sufficient resources to augment its present staff, it could explore arrangements with multilateral agencies supportive to the organization to have professionals seconded to the Secretariat to help ensure the implementation of this Plan.

b) ASOEN Working Groups should start preparing the necessary adjustments in their programmes and activities consistent with the identified strategic thrusts. Table 4 is a summary matrix of working groups vis a vis the strategic thrusts.

## 4.2 Financing the Strategic Plan of Action on the Environment

### 4.2.1 *Cost-sharing Arrangements*

The inadequacy of funds to support the various programmes and projects of ASOEN remains the main limiting factor in attaining its objectives. As evident from the previous plans, while many project proposals were developed, donors did not support the proposals either due to limited funds or they did not fall within the donors' priority areas for assistance. On the other hand, these proposals were developed precisely on the basis of their importance to the region. Some of these project proposals could be important enough to be considered for implementation even without external funding. Accordingly, ASOEN should explore ways of generating funds to support such priority regional activities. A cost-sharing scheme or arrangement among participating member countries should be explored and devised to make these funds available. The ASEAN Secretariat should initiate studies to look into the feasibility of the cost-sharing scheme.

### 4.2.2 *The ASEAN Fund*

The ASEAN Fund was established in 1969 to finance ASEAN collaborative projects, programmes and activities approved by the ASEAN Foreign Ministers. Since its establishment, the Fund has been largely unutilized owing to the complex and cumbersome procedures stipulated in the 1969 Agreement governing the Fund. The ASEAN Standing Committee (ASC) has taken initiatives to address these problems and has most recently asked the ASEAN Secretariat to come up with recommendations to improve the utilization of the Fund. The Fund will initially consist of US$6 million with contributions of US$1 million from each member country. In general, ASEAN collaborative projects approved by the ASEAN Foreign Ministers through the ASC are eligible for financing under the Fund. More specifically, the four categories of activities eligible for financing under the Fund are those that:

a) promote ASEAN cooperation or perspective;
b) are confidential or strategic in nature;
c) require co-financing and counterpart funding from ASEAN; and
d) are priority projects not qualified for Dialogue Partner funding.

Table 4. Matrix of Actions to be Covered by the Working Groups

| Strategic Thrust | Actions | Working Groups |
|---|---|---|
| 1. Support the development of a regional framework for integrating environment and development concerns in the decision making process | 1.1 Continue support in the documentation of regional EIA experiences leading towards the harmonisation of procedures | Environmental Management |
| | 1.2 Initiate activities that will make use of natural resource and environmental accounting studies and approaches | Environmental Economics |
| | 1.3 Establish procedures that would initiate the integration of environmental concerns in the various ASEAN programmes and activities | Environmental Management |
| 2. Promote government private-sector interactions that lead towards the development of policies that mutually support the thrust of each sector | 2.1 Initiate studies on development of environmental and trade policies which are supportive to the principles of sustainable development | Environmental Economics |
| | 2.2 Establish mechanisms that encourage government and private sector to adopt appropriate environmental standards backed up by sufficient economic incentives | Environmental Economics |

(*Continued*)

Table 4. (*Continued*)

| Strategic Thrust | Actions | Working Groups |
|---|---|---|
| | 2.3 Set up government-private secto information linkages/networks to include information on technology, expertise and facilities for environmental management | Environmental Information, Public Awareness and Education |
| 3. Strengthen the knowledge and information data base on environmental matters | 3.1 Pursue the establishment of basic environmental quality standards leading to the setting up of harmonised quality standards in the region | Environmental Management |
| | 3.2 Identify centres of excellence for environmental R & D and eventually build them as focal points of environmental networks | Environmental Management |
| | 3.3 Establish a mechanism for the preparation of periodic reports on the state of the region's environment | Environmental Information, Public Awareness and Education |

(*Continued*)

Table 4. *(Continued)*

| Strategic Thrust | Actions | Working Groups |
|---|---|---|
| 4. Strengthen institutional and legal capacities to implement international agreements on environment | 4.1 Undertake a comparative study on the institutional structure and legislation for environmental management | Environmental Management |
| | 4.2 Establish capacities to support regional efforts to implement international agreements and participate effectively in the negotiation of new or revised agreements | All Working Groups |
| | 4.3 Enhance collaboration with international bodies overseeing the implementation of international agreements and cooperation | All Working Groups |
| 5. Establish a regional framework on biodiversity conservation and sustainable utilisation of its components | 5.1 Promote the development of a framework for the protection and conservation of heritage areas and endangered species. | Nature Conservation |
| | 5.2 Strengthen capacities for R & D to enhance biodiversity conservation in the region | Nature Conservation |

*(Continued)*

Table 4. (*Continued*)

| Strategic Thrust | Actions | Working Groups |
|---|---|---|
| 6. Promote the protection and management of coastal zones and marine resources | 6.1 Improve regional marine and coastal environmental coordination | ASEAN Seas and Marine Environment Nature Conservation |
| | 6.2 Develop a framework for the integrated management of regional coastal zones | ASEAN Seas and Marine Environment Nature Conservation |
| 7. Promote environmentally sound management of toxic chemicals and hazardous wastes, and control of transboundary movement of hazardous wastes | 7.1 Establish regional guidelines for assessing highly pollutive industries and safe handling of potentially harmful chemicals entering the ASEAN region | Transboundary Pollution |
| | 7.2 Strengthen the information network on the transboundary movement of toxic chemicals and hazardous waste | Transboundary Pollution |
| 8. Develop a system for the promotion of environmentally sound technologies | 8.1 Establish linkages with existing clearing houses on environmentally sound technologies | Environmental Information, Public Awareness and Education |
| | 8.2 Establish mechanisms that identify end users of R & D results and encourage the participation of private sector | Environmental Information, Public Awareness and Education |

(*Continued*)

Table 4. *(Continued)*

| Strategic Thrust | Actions | Working Groups |
|---|---|---|
| | 8.3 Strengthen linkage and coordination with other ASEAN committees such as COST doing related R & D work on the environment | Environmental Information, Public Awareness and Education |
| | 8.4 Support the promotion of indigenous technology or technologies that have been adapted to regional needs | Environmental Information, Public Awareness and Education<br>Environmental Management |
| 9. Promote regional activities that strengthen the role of major groups in sustainable development | 9.1 Support the publication of regional environmental magazine and newsletters | Environmental Information, Public Awareness and Education |
| | 9.2 Strengthen regional information network and promote exchange of expertise on environmental education programmes | Environmental Information, Public Awareness and Education |
| | 9.3 Develop strategic programmes of action that will strengthen the role and participation of major groups on environment management and decision making | All Working Groups |

The Fund will give priority to urgent, short-term activities of a strategic or confidential nature and which are considered fundamental in building a stronger cooperative ASEAN infrastructure. There are some possibility in attracting this Fund in specific strategic areas such as trade and environment issues.

### 4.2.3 *The ASEAN Sub-regional Environment Trust (ASSET)*

The ASOEN and the World Wildlife Fund (WWF) have signed a Memorandum of Understanding which authorizes WWF to develop proposals, enter into discussions with donors on behalf of ASOEN, and later on to provide assistance in the actual establishment and implementation of ASSET. ASSET could be designed along the lines of the more than 15 Trust Funds that were established with the technical assistance of WWF. Two avenues are being explored for ASSET: a free-standing trust fund that is not related to any project and one that is dedicated to the financing of the ASEAN Strategic Plan of Action of the Environment. The first approach is similar to the ASEAN Cultural Fund. For the second approach, it is advisable to explore the pooling of contributions of ASEAN Dialogue Partners into ASSET with projects based on the Strategic Plan of Action on the Environment. The ASEAN Plan of Action on the Environment would attract donor support since attention has been given to transboundary protected areas, migratory terrestrial and marine species, and GIS-based biodiversity information systems.

### 4.2.4 *Project-related Funds*

a) Funding from Dialogue Partners

The support of Dialogue Partners to ASEAN's environmental programmes has not been as strong as would have been expected, considering their overall commitment to environmental protection. UNEP and UNDP have been generally instrumental in getting many ASEAN projects off the ground and completed. UNEP catalysed the preparation of ASEP documents and funded many workshops, seminars, study tours and training programmes. UNDP supported projects on transboundary pollution problems and environmental education. Australia, the U.S. and New Zealand have also supported ASEAN's environment programmes. Australian assistance was provided to projects under the Working Groups on Environmental Management and ASEAN Seas and Marine Environment, while US support focused on projects of the Working Group on Environmental Management. New Zealand assistance was obtained for projects of the Working Group on Transboundary Pollution.

Despite UNDP and other Dialogue Partners support for ASEAN efforts on the environment, implemented and completed projects have fallen short of the goals of the various programmes and the sense of urgency expressed in several resolutions on the environment. Percentage of funds earmarked for environmental programmes by the Dialogue Partners against their total contribution to the Functional Cooperation programmes and projects have been very low, for instance, Australia 5%; USA 9% and UNDP 12%. As cited in the Report on the UN ESCAP Mission to ASEAN Member Countries in September 1991 "the uncertainty of the source of funds for ASEAN regional environmental projects has consistently afflicted ASEAN cooperation in the environmental field".

It may, however, be noted that with regard to Dialogue Partner funding, it has become clear that donors are moving away from the traditional donor-recipient relationship into one of mutual and equal partnership with preference for supporting projects from which economic benefits can flow to the industrial and private sectors. Some Dialogue Partners have also expressed the need for ASEAN countries to increase their contribution to collaborative projects through cost-sharing or cc-financing schemes. This notwithstanding, there is some scope for enhancing the assistance from the Dialogue Partners to fund this Strategic Plan of Action on the Environment, including the possibility of establishing a trust fund with Japanese support similar to the existing ASEAN Cultural Fund.

b) Global Environment Facility (GEF)

The Global Environment Facility was conceived to support projects that address global environmental issues, particularly ozone depletion, climate change and biodiversity. The Facility is currently managed by the World Bank, UNDP and UNEP. Discussions are now underway on the second phase of the GEF, i.e. GEF 11, to make it a more democratic environmental funding mechanism with universal membership, a voting arrangement acceptable to both developed and developing member countries, and — if current expectations are met — a budget nearly double that of its three-year pilot phase. ASOEN should tap the GEF for funding its projects.

c) Asia Sustainable Development Fund

The Asian Development Bank has established the *Asia Sustainable Development Fund* which will have US$100 million capital to invest in companies undertaking sustainable development projects in the Bank's developing and newly-industrialized member countries. ASEAN should similarly tap this Fund for its projects, particularly those that involve the private sector.

## 5. CONCLUSION

The past economic performance of the ASEAN countries have indicated its capacities to achieve growth. This trend is likely to continue as these countries industrialize, especially with the implementation of the ASEAN Free Trade Agreement (AFTA), ASEAN as a whole is conscious that growth without due regard to environment cannot be sustained in the long term. Thus, environment ranks high in the priority of ASEAN leaders and officials. As proof of this, ASEAN has made seven major declarations/resolutions an the environment in just slightly over a decade since the first one in Manila in 1981. ASEAN has come out with three major programmes (ASEPs I to III) of regional cooperation on the environment. But the environmental challenge remains; more so as ASEAN endeavors to maintain its competitive edge in the global economic area. The impetus provided by the Earth Summit, the mandate from the Rio Declaration on Environment and Development, the leadership provided by the Commission on Sustainable Development, and the guidance from Agenda 21, provide reason that ASEAN can meet these challenges. The Strategic Plan of Action on the Environment reflects these perspectives. Its objectives could only be achieved through the strong commitment and continued support of the Governments of ASEAN member countries.

Source: http://www.aseansec.org/l814.htm; Selected ASEAN Documents on the Environment (APCEL Document Services; 1996)
Accessed date: 7 February 2006
Publisher: ASEAN Secretariat
Country: Jakarta
Date of Publication: 1994

Table 5. ASEAN

| Section | Relevant Chapters for ASEAN |
|---|---|
| **Section I:**<br>Social and Economic Dimensions | **Chapter 2: International Cooperation**<br><br>Essentially deals with fostering partnership amongst the world's nations which promotes efficient and equitable economy aimed at helping countries achieve sustainable development. Of the several strategies identified under this chapter an area which has relevance to the ASEAN relates to the<br><br>a) promotion of sustainable development through trade and<br>b) ensuring that trade and environment policies support sustainable types of development.<br><br>With the decision of creating the ASEAN Free Trade Area (AFTA) within the next fifteen (15) years, the region's environmental policies should complement this effort.<br><br>**Chapter 4: Changing Consumption Patterns**<br><br>Is a chapter that focuses on changing unsustainable patterns of production and consumption. To attain this goal, policies and development strategies should be developed along the lines of requiring efficiency in production processes and changes in the consumption patterns that encourages resource optimization and waste minimization. Areas that may have significant interest in the ASEAN Region are in the following:<br><br>a) greater efficiency in the use of energy and resources<br>b) minimizing the generation of waste |

*(Continued)*

Table 5. (*Continued*)

| Section | Relevant Chapters for ASEAN |
|---|---|
| | c) capturing full environmental costs through proper pricing and<br>d) reinforcing values towards supporting sustainable consumption. |
| | **Chapters: 6 Protection and Promoting Human Health** |
| | Seeks to meet the urban health challenge and reduce the risks arising from environmental pollution and hazards. The chapters advocates for a strong collaboration among government, private sector and international organizations in addressing human health issues. Of interest to the region are health issues relating to the effects and mitigating measures to combat: |
| | a) air pollution<br>b) indoor air pollution<br>c) water pollution<br>d) unsafe use of pesticides and<br>e) solid wastes |
| | **Chapter 7: Promoting Sustainable Human Settlements Development** |
| | Relating to the integrated provision of environmental infrastructure; water, sanitation sewerage and solid waste management systems. The objective is to ensure that adequate environmental facilities are provided in all settlement particularly urban areas. While the identified programme areas are general concerns of particular interest to the region will be that of reducing risk of damage from natural disasters, flooding, earthquakes and landslides. Human settlement policy must go hand in hand with other development policies discussed in the other chapters of Agenda 21. |

(*Continued*)

Table 5. (*Continued*)

| Section | Relevant Chapters for ASEAN |
|---|---|
| | **Chapters 8: Integrating Environment and Development in Decision Making** |
| | This chapter underscores the necessity of understanding the links between environment and development in order to generate options that will balance the two. The ASEAN Region have long recognized the importance of integrating environment in the decision making process and this has established environmental impact assessment procedures at certain levels. The emergence of new techniques, methodologies and approaches, however, needs to be considered in the present processes in order to enrich it. Among the several programme areas identified under this Chapter, interest will be focused on the following: |
| | a) Integrating environmental development policies at management levels<br>b) Making effective use of economic instruments and other market based incentives<br>c) Development of systems that integrate environmental and economic accounting<br>d) Establishment of a common EIA framework for the regions |
| **Section II:** | **Chapter 9: Protecting the Atmosphere** |
| Conservation and Management of Resources | Chapter 9 raises one of the major issues which the ASEAN region has long recognized. In the region itself owing to the increasing economic activity taking place, there has likewise been a notable increase in the emission of greenhouse gases and chemicals that threaten to change the climate and damage the ozone layer. In fact, some parts of the ASEAN region is very vulnerable to climate change which is now being more frequently noticed. The chapter identified four key programme area which the region would very much support viz; |

(*Continued*)

Table 5. (*Continued*)

| Section | Relevant Chapters for ASEAN |
| --- | --- |
| | a) Improving the scientific basis for predicting levels of atmospheric pollutants and greenhouse gas concentrations<br>b) Promoting sustainable development practices in the sector of energy; transport; industrial development; and terrestrial, marine and land use<br>c) Prevent stratospheric ozone depletion by actively supporting all of the major agreements and conventions e.g. Vienna Convention; Montreal Protocol; Convention on Climate Changeto mention a few<br>d) and measures to stop/prevent Transboundary Atmospheric Pollution |
| | **Chapter 10: Managing Land Sustainability**<br>**Chapter 11: Combating Deforestation**<br>**Chapter 12: Combating Desertification and Drought** |
| | Are three related chapters that deals with land degradation. While the specific programme areas may be within the purview of other committees in the ASEAN Institution e.g. Committee on Food, Agriculture and Forestry (COFAF), the ASOEN, through the ASEAN Secretariat may endorse a particular programme of action which can be considered by these committees. The ASEAN Secretariat can even ensure the consideration of the programme of actions embodied in the three chapters to the various programmes which the appropriate committees are developing or may have developed. |

(*Continued*)

Table 5. *(Continued)*

| Section | Relevant Chapters for ASEAN |
|---|---|
| | **Chapter 15: Conservation of Biodiversity**<br><br>Is aimed at improving the conservation of biological diversity, its sustainable use and support action to the Convention on Biodiversity. The ASEAN region is recognized to be one of the regions where biodiversity is abundant and thus is expected to prominently lead. Identified programme areas where the ASEAN will have significant involvement will on the following:<br><br>a) establishment or strengthening of networks for exchange of data and information<br>b) promotion of in situ and ex situ conservation efforts<br>c) programmes and action plans that promote international coordination for the effective conservation and management of protected areas<br><br>**Chapter 17: Protecting and Managing the Oceans**<br><br>Focuses on the development of new approaches to marine and coastal area management and development at the national, subregional, regional and global levels. Of the seven (7) programme areas identified under this chapter, three (3) are considered to have significant impact in the region viz; |

*(Continued)*

Table 5. (*Continued*)

| Section | Relevant Chapters for ASEAN |
|---|---|
| | a) Integrated management and sustainable development of coastal areas which covers activity measures in exclusive economic zones, inventory of endangered species, maintenance of biological diversity and protection of coastal and marine habitats to mention a few<br>b) Marine environmental protection which recommends priority alternative be given to prevention, reduction and control of degradation of marine environment from land based activities taking into account the implementation of the various treaties and conventions that have been effected and<br>c) Strengthening of subregional and regional coordination and cooperation in the sustainable management of regional marine ecosystems. |
| | **Chapter 18: Protecting and Managing Freshwater Resources** |
| | This chapter highlights the needed measures to protect and sustainably manage fresh water resources through the proper planning and assessment with the preparation of an integrated water resources development and management plan. Said plan should at least cover the following areas of concern: |
| | a) water pollution, prevention and control applying environmentally acceptable approaches and technologies<br>b) conservation of freshwater ecosystem such as wetlands<br>c) equitable provision of safe water in urban areas within the local governments, private and business sector actively involved. |

(*Continued*)

Table 5. *(Continued)*

| Section | Relevant Chapters for ASEAN |
|---|---|
| | **Chapter 19: Safer Use of Toxic Chemicals and Management of Hazardous Waste**<br>**Chapter 20**<br><br>Covers six programme areas which have relevance to the regions activities viz;<br>a) acceleration of assessment of chemical risks<br>b) harmonization of classification and labelling of chemicals<br>c) information exchange on toxic chemicals and chemical risks<br>d) establishment of risk reduction programmes<br>e) strengthening of national capacities for the management of chemicals<br>f) prevention of illegal international traffic in toxic and dangerous products. All said programme areas would require closer collaboration and linkage of the ASEAN member countries as the region is exposed to the threats of toxic chemicals plying in its seas.<br><br>**Chapter 21: Management of Solid Wastes**<br><br>While it is recognized that solid waste management is generally a national issue, its occurrence has become a common concern among the ASEAN member countries. As covered by its programme areas, much can be learned through sub-regional coordination and cooperation information networking on the following aspects: waste minimization techniques, promotion of waste reuse, recycling; development of environmentally sound waste disposal and treatment. |

*(Continued)*

Table 5. (*Continued*)

| **Section** | **Relevant Chapters for ASEAN** |
|---|---|
| **Section III:** | |
| Strengthening the Role of Major Groups | This Section covers 7 chapters dealing on the role of major groups in the general sustainable development and management strategies. Each of the section highlights the essential participation of citizens clustered as NGOs, women, youth and children, indigenous people, local governments, business and private sectors, academe etc. in the planning, decision making and implementation processes for a sustained economic development. It is accepted that as the sub-region/region develop its respective programmes along the areas discussed in Sections I and II of A21, the increasing involvement of these groups must be prominently seen. |
| **Section IV:** | |
| Means of Implementation | Deals with the strategic operationalization of Agenda 21 identifying the programme cases that will support and ensure its implementation. Under this section are chapters that touches on the financial requirements, transfer of environmentally sound technologies, role of science in SD; promotion of public awareness and training; capacity building strategies; international institutional arrangement; legal instruments and information networking for decision-making. Of significant development that would have important being to the sub-regional/regional cooperation is the establishment of a commission on Sustainable Development that will periodically review the progress of implementation of Agenda 21. Generally, the programme areas that are most likely to impact on ASEAN undertakings are the following: |
| | a) Development of international information network, procedure and methodologies which can be easily accessed and shared |

(*Continued*)

Table 5. *(Continued)*

| Section | Relevant Chapters for ASEAN |
| --- | --- |
| | b) Establishment of collaborative network of research centers<br>c) Influencing the reorientation of education towards sustainable development<br>d) Increasing public awareness<br>e) Promotion of training and capability upgrading of institutions that are in forefront of implementing sustainable development strategies<br>f) Capacity building that relates to improved regional and sub-regional consultative process |

# CHAPTER 46

# HANOI PLAN OF ACTION

## INTRODUCTION

The Second ASEAN Informal Summit, held in Kuala Lumpur on 15 December 1997, adopted the ASEAN Vision 2020 which sets out a broad vision for ASEAN in the year 2020: an ASEAN as a concert of Southeast Asian Nations, outward looking, living in peace, stability and prosperity, bonded together in partnership in dynamic development and in a community of caring societies.

In order to implement the long-term vision, action plans are being drawn up to realize this Vision. The Hanoi Plan of Action (HPA) is the first in a series of plans of action building up to the realization of the goals of the Vision.

The HPA has a six-year timeframe covering the period from 1999 to 2004. The progress of its implementation shall be reviewed every three years to coincide with the ASEAN Summit Meetings.

In recognition of the need to address the current economic situation in the region, ASEAN shall implement initiatives to hasten economic recovery and address the social impact of the global economic and financial crisis. These measures reaffirm ASEAN commitments to closer regional integration and are directed at consolidating and strengthening the economic fundamentals of the Member Countries.

## I. STRENGTHEN MACROECONOMIC AND FINANCIAL COOPERATION

. . . .

## II. ENHANCE GREATER ECONOMIC INTERGRATION

. . . .

### 2.10.3 *Energy*

a. Ensure security and sustainability of energy supply, efficient utilization of natural energy resource in the region and the rational management of energy demand, with due consideration of the environment; and

b. Institute the policy framework and implementation modalities by 2004 for the early realization of the trans-ASEAN energy networks covering the ASEAN Power Grid and the Trans-ASEAN Gas Pipeline Projects as a more focused continuation of the Medium-Term Programme of Action (1995–1999).

### 2.10.4 *Water utility*

c. Cooperate on a regular basis, exchange of information, knowledge, and experiences among Member States as means to improve water resources management and water supply system within the region; and
d. Support the development of Trans-ASEAN land and submarine pipeline for conveyance of raw water between ASEAN Member States.

....

## VI. PROTECT THE ENVIRONMENT AND PROMOTE SUSTAINABLE DEVELOPMENT

6.1 Fully implement the ASEAN Cooperation Plan on Transboundary Pollution with particular emphasis on the Regional Haze Action Plan by the year 2001.
6.2 Strengthen the ASEAN Specialized Meteorological Centre with emphasis on the ability to monitor forest and land fires and provide early warning on transboundary haze by the year 2001.
6.3 Establish the ASEAN Regional Research and Training Centre for Land and Forest Fire Management by the year 2004.
6.4 Strengthen the ASEAN Regional Centre for Biodiversity Conservation by establishing networks of relevant institutions and implement collaborative training and research activities by the year 2001.
6.5 Promote regional coordination for the protection of the ASEAN Heritage Parks and Reserves.
6.6 Develop a framework and improve regional coordination for the integrated protection and management of coastal zones by the year 2001.
6.7 Strengthen institutional and legal capacities to implement Agenda 21 and other international environmental agreements by the year 2001.
6.8 Harmonize the environmental databases of Member Countries by the year 2001.
6.9 Implement an ASEAN regional water conservation programme by the year 2001.

6.10 Establish a regional centre or network for the promotion of environmentally sound technologies by the year 2004.

6.11 Formulate and adopt an ASEAN Protocol on access to genetic resources by the year 2004.

6.12 Develop a Regional Action Plan for the Protection of the Marine Environment from Land-based and Sea-based Activities by the year 2004.

6.13 Implement the Framework to Achieve Long-Term Environmental Goals for Ambient Air and River Water Qualities for ASEAN Countries.

6.14 Enhance regional efforts in addressing climatic change.

6.15 Enhance public information and education in awareness of and participation in environmental and sustainable development issues.

## VII. STRENGTHEN REGIONAL PEACE AND SECURITY

....

7.9 Promote efforts to secure acceptance by Nuclear Weapon States of the Treaty on Southeast Asia Nuclear Weapon-Free Zone (SEANWFZ), including their early accession to the Protocol to the SEANWFZ Treaty.

7.10 Convene the Commission for SEANWFZ Treaty to oversee the implementation of the Treaty and ensure compliance with its provisions.

7.11 Support and participate actively in all efforts to achieve the objectives of general and complete disarmament, especially the non-proliferation of nuclear weapons and other weapons of mass destruction.

....

## VIII. ENHANCE ASEAN'S ROLE AS AN EFFECTIVE FORCE FOR PEACE, JUSTICE, AND MODERATION IN THE ASIA-PACIFIC AND IN THE WORLD

8.1 Maintain ASEAN's chairmanship in the ASEAN Regional Forum (ARF) process.

8.2 Undertake, actively and energetically, measures to strengthen ASEAN's role as the primary driving force in the ARF, including directing the ASEAN Secretary-General to provide the necessary support and services to the ASC Chairman in coordinating ARF activities.

8.3 Formulate initiatives to advance, on a consensus basis and at a pace comfortable to all, the ARF process from its current emphasis on confidence-building to promoting preventive diplomacy.

8.4 Promote public awareness of the ARF process and the need for ASEAN's role as the primary driving force in respective ASEAN Member Countries.
8.5 Continue the involvement of ASEAN defense and security officials together with foreign affairs officials in ARF activities.
8.6 Develop a set of basic principles based on TAC as an instrument for promoting cooperative peace in the Asia-Pacific region.
8.7 Enhance consultation and coordination of ASEAN positions at the United Nations and international fora.
8.8 Revitalize ASEAN's relations with Dialogue Partners on the basis of equality, non-discrimination and mutual benefit.

## IX. PROMOTE ASEAN AWARENESS AND ITS STANDING IN THE INTERNATIONAL COMMUNITY

9.1 Support the activities of the ASEAN Foundation and other available resources and mechanisms to promote ASEAN awareness among its people.
9.2 Launch, within ASEAN's existing resources, a concerted communications programme to promote ASEAN's standing in the international community and strengthen confidence in ASEAN as an ideal place for investment, trade and tourism.
9.3 Establish and operate an ASEAN satellite channel by year 2000.
9.4 Provide and disseminate materials on ASEAN's efforts to cope with the financial and economic crisis.
9.5 Publicise ASEAN's HPA priorities through ASEAN's external mechanisms with its Dialogue Partners.
9.6 Develop linkages with mass media networks and websites on key areas of ASEAN cooperation to disseminate regular and timely information on ASEAN.
9.7 Prepare and adopt an ASEAN Declaration on Cultural Heritage by year 2000.
9.8 Mount professional productions of ASEAN performances and exhibitions within and outside ASEAN and provide adequate mass media coverage on such activities.
9.9 Organize art and cultural immersion camps and exchange programmes for the youth and encourage their travel to other ASEAN Member Countries.
9.10 Establish an ASEAN Multi-Media Centre by the year 2001 to conduct professional training programmes and provide production facilities and services for mass media and communication practitioners.

## X. IMPROVE ASEAN'S STRUCTURES AND MECHANISMS

10.1 Review ASEAN's overall organisational structure in order to further improve its efficiency and effectiveness, taking into account the expansion of ASEAN activities, the enlargement of ASEAN membership, and the regional situation.

10.2 Review and streamline ASEAN external relations mechanisms with its Dialogue Partners, regional organisations and other economic groupings.

10.3 Review the role, functions and capacity of the ASEAN Secretariat to meet the increasing demands of ASEAN and to support the implementation of the Hanoi Plan of Action.

Source: http://www.aseansec.org/8754.htm
Accessed date: 7 February 2006
Publisher: ASEAN Secretariat
Country: Jakarta
Date of Publication: 2003

# CHAPTER 47

# VIENTIANE ACTION PROGRAMME (VAP)

## 2004–2010

## I. PREAMBLE

***Theme:*** ***Towards shared prosperity and destiny in an integrated, peaceful and caring ASEAN Community***

**WE** the Heads of State and Government of the Association of Southeast Asian Nations (hereinafter referred to as "ASEAN"), gathered here in Vientiane, Laos, on 29 November 2004 for the Tenth ASEAN Summit;

**NOTING** that ASEAN Vision 2020 envisions ASEAN as a concert of Southeast Asian Nations, outward-looking, living in peace, stability and prosperity, bonded together in partnership in dynamic development and in a community of caring societies;

**NOTING FURTHER** that the Hanoi Plan of Action (HPA), the first in a series of action plans or programmes leading to the end-goal of ASEAN Vision 2020, ends in 2004 and that a successor action plan or programme is needed to guide further progress towards ASEAN Vision 2020;

**RECALLING** the Declaration of ASEAN Concord II, which elaborates on the themes of ASEAN Vision 2020 by setting concrete milestones to reach the goals of a broad and comprehensive ASEAN Community, founded on the three pillars of political and security cooperation, economic integration, and socio-cultural cooperation, to form the ASEAN Security Community, the ASEAN Economic Community and the ASEAN Socio-Cultural Community by 2020;

**ACKNOWLEDGING** that the global and regional economic environment has changed and is continuously challenged by new developments which have an impact on the trade and investment flows, and the economic competitiveness of ASEAN, and that ASEAN now has to work within a new strategic context;

**RECOGNISING** that deepening and broadening the integration of ASEAN must be accompanied by technical and development cooperation to address the development gap among the Member Countries so that the benefits of ASEAN integration are shared and which will enable all ASEAN Member Countries to move forward in a unified and cohesive manner;

**REITERATING** our commitment to strengthen efforts to narrow the development gap in ASEAN by building upon existing initiatives such as the Initiative for ASEAN Integration (IAI), the Roadmap for the Integration of ASEAN (RIA), the Ha Noi Declaration on Narrowing Development Gap for closer ASEAN Integration of 23 July 2001 and the Vientiane Declaration on Enhancing Economic Cooperation and Integration Among Cambodia, Lao PDR, Myanmar and Viet Nam of 28 November 2004.

## Do Hereby Declare That:

1. We agree to pursue the comprehensive integration of ASEAN towards the realisation of an open, dynamic and resilient ASEAN Community by 2020 as envisioned in the Declaration of ASEAN Concord II and its annexes in the form of the action plans of the ASEAN Security Community (ASC), the ASEAN Socio-Cultural Community (ASCC) and the Recommendations of the High-level Task Force on ASEAN Economic Integration;
2. We shall address, by various ways and means, the development issues and special needs of the less developed ASEAN Member Countries and sub-regional areas of ASEAN, including the implementation of the concept of "Prosper Thy Neighbour" by instituting programmes to narrow the development gap, reducing socio-economic disparities and eradicating poverty within ASEAN, and by doing so, move forward in a unifying and cohesive manner to prosper ASEAN. We also recognise the contributions of sub-regional arrangements such as, the Brunei, Indonesia, Malaysia, Philippines — East ASEAN Growth Area (BIMP-EAGA), Indonesia, Malaysia, Thailand-Growth Triangle (IMT-GT), Indonesia, Malaysia, Singapore-Growth Triangle (IMS-GT), ASEAN Mekong Basin Development Cooperation (AMBDC), Greater Mekong Sub-region (GMS) and the Ayeyawady-Chao Phraya-Mekong Economic Cooperation Strategy (ACMECS) to reducing the development gap within the region;
3. We shall strengthen further ASEAN's institutional framework both in terms of its structure and process to ensure that it is responsive to the challenges and needs of moving towards an ASEAN Community, including in terms of coordination and efficiency as well as in strengthening its ability to shape events in Southeast Asia and beyond;
4. We shall adopt greater outward-looking external relation strategies with our Dialogue Partners and friends in building a peaceful, secure and prosperous ASEAN, strengthening our economic linkages and deepening our socio-cultural cooperation with East Asia and beyond;

5. We recognise the need to strengthen ASEAN and shall work towards the development of an ASEAN Charter;
6. We shall, first and foremost, work closely between and among ourselves to generate our own indigenous resources as well as reach out to our Dialogue Partners and all others who wish to engage ASEAN on the basis of equality, non-discrimination and mutual benefit, to build bridges between the public sector and all other sectors of society within and outside ASEAN in order to facilitate a synergy of experience, expertise and resources available thereof for the attainment of the ASEAN Community;
7. We shall promote an ASEAN cultural heritage as a creative expression of the ASEAN spirit, and as a basis for an enduring bond of an ASEAN regional identity, since it originates from common ties throughout history and a shared aspiration for peace and prosperity;
8. We hereby endorse the Vientiane Action Programme (VAP), the successor to the HPA, to be implemented for the period 2004–2010, as an instrument to unify and cross-link the strategies and goals of the three pillars of the ASEAN Community and as an integral part of the action plans and programmes building up to the realisation of the goals of ASEAN Vision 2020;
9. As the process leading to the establishment of the ASEAN Community is continuously evolving, the VAP should therefore be perceived as an evolving document. Therefore, the lists of activities that are envisaged as being implementable in the period of 2004–2010, as contained in the various annexes to the VAP, are non-exhaustive; and
10. We commit ourselves, therefore, to implement the VAP paying attention to its two dimensions, the first being the broader integration of the ten Member Countries into one cohesive ASEAN Community, and the second being the identification of new strategies for narrowing the development gap to quicken the pace of integration, and working closely among ourselves, with our Dialogue Partners and others, to mobilise political will and generate the required resources for the effective implementation of the VAP.

## II. GOALS AND STRATEGIES TOWARDS REALISING THE ASEAN COMMUNITY

### 1. ASEAN Security Community

....

### 2. ASEAN Economic Community

....

## 2.9 *Energy*

Pursue sustainable energy development through the implementation of the ASEAN Plan of Action for Energy Cooperation for 2004–2009, based primarily on individual sectoral plans of action and roadmaps, including but not limited to the ASEAN Power Grid, the Trans-ASEAN Gas Pipeline (TAGP), Coal, Energy Efficiency and Conservation, Renewable Energy, and Regional Energy Policy and Planning, focusing on cooperation activities, including with the ASEAN Dialogue Partners, to enhance the integration of the regional energy infrastructures, promote energy security, create responsive policies to progressively enhance market reforms and liberalisation, as well as preserve the sustainability of environment.

## 2.10 *Food, Agriculture and Forestry Sectors*

Enhance the competitiveness of the food agriculture and forestry sectors through developing appropriate technologies to increase productivity and by promoting inter-and extra-ASEAN trade and greater private sector investment in the food, agriculture and forestry sectors.

## 2.11 *Institutional Strengthening*

### 2.11.1 Dispute Settlement Mechanism

Establish an effective system to ensure proper implementation of all economic agreements and expeditious resolution of any disputes through appropriate advisory, consultative, and adjudicatory mechanisms.

The feasibility of establishing a common legal framework for the incorporation or registration of ASEAN companies to assist in dispute settlement would also be explored.

### 2.11.2 Statistics

Provide the necessary statistical support for ASEAN initiatives, planning and policy making through improved quality and availability of important statistics, adoption of international good practices, promotion of greater awareness of statistics, enhanced networking and close partnership between users in policy areas and statistical systems, and wider dissemination of ASEAN statistics through the annual publication of the ASEAN Statistical Yearbook and a continuous expansion of statistical coverage on Member Countries and the ASEAN Secretariat's Websites.

## 2.12 *Economic Relations with Dialogue Partners*

The economic growth of the ASEAN region in past decades has been largely driven by FDI flows and exports. While exports have stabilised and are again beginning to expand, ASEAN has experienced a sustained decline in FDI flows since the 1997–1998 economic and monetary crisis. Since internal measures, aimed at creating a single ASEAN market and production base, may not be sufficient to attract the volume of investment required to sustain economic growth, efforts will be made to strengthen external economic relations and the terms of trade with major Dialogue Partners through the establishment of Free Trade Areas (FTAs) and Closer Economic Partnerships (CEPs).

The strategy for ASEAN external economic cooperation will involve strengthening linkages and promoting the coherence of agreements with major trading partners such as China, Japan, Korea, the US, Australia, New Zealand, the EU and emerging economies such as India. The promotion of the coherence of agreements might include increasing coordination of extra-ASEAN economic agreements and the closer alignment of MFN tariffs.

## 3. ASEAN Socio-Cultural Community

***Theme:*** ***Nurturing human, cultural and natural resources for sustained development in a harmonious and people-centred ASEAN***

### *Strategic Thrusts*

The ASEAN Socio-Cultural Community (ASCC) represents ASEAN's aspirations to lift the quality of life of its peoples, sustainably use natural resources and strengthen its cultural identity towards a people-centred ASEAN. The roadmap for the Community focuses on four strategic thrusts to support other ASEAN Community goals: strong and functional systems of social protection that address poverty, equity and health impacts of economic growth; promoting environmental sustainability and sustainable natural resource management that meets current and future needs; social governance that manages impacts of economic integration; and the preservation and promotion of the region's cultural heritage and cultural identity.

Since economic growth could be threatened by social inequities that could in turn undermine political stability, the ASEAN socio-cultural action programme is linked inextricably with the economic and security pillars of the ASEAN

Community. The establishment of the ASCC stems from the premise that economic integration and security alone will not be sufficient to realise the vision of an ASEAN Community.

The human, natural and cultural resources of ASEAN provide the means for economic growth. The sustainable development and conservation of these resources allows for the region to prosper now and into the future, thereby enabling people to uplift their living standards and have a decent and healthy lifestyle. Measures taken to promote social protection, cultural identity, the conservation of natural resources and the protection of the environment fuel economic growth and sustain life.

### 3.1 *Building a Community of Caring Societies*

The hallmark of a strong and resilient community of caring societies is its commitment and capability to address the core issues of poverty, equity and health. National initiatives will fundamentally drive the manner and extent to which these issues are addressed. However, the Member Countries can gain significant leveraging of political commitment and goals at the national level through regional advocacy.

The regional interventions that will complement the national actions include:

i. Raising the standard of living of marginalised, disadvantaged groups by strengthening the capacity of officials in rural development and poverty alleviation administrations and promoting approaches that engage these groups in society;
ii. Facilitating universal access to education and promoting high standards through networking and institutional collaborations.
iii. Reducing the social risks faced by children, women, elderly and persons with disabilities, by supporting programmes consistent with international conventions and promoting services such as aged care, health care and education;
iv. Increasing the effective participation of family, civil society and the private sector in tackling poverty and social welfare issues through the establishment of networking and exchange programmes, and promoting the professions involved in poverty and social welfare issues;
v. Increasing the participation of women and youth in the productive workforce through skills training and increasing access to microfinance and information systems;

vi. Addressing health development concerns;
vii. Preventing the spread and reducing the harm of HIV/AIDS and other infectious diseases;
viii. Enhancing food security, in particular the establishment of food security information systems;
ix. Ensuring a region of disaster-resilient nations by minimising the adverse effects of disasters in pursuit of safer communities and sustainable development.
x. Ensuring a Drug Free ASEAN by 2015 through prevention, treatment and community-based control of drug abuse, including the promotion of alternative development, as well as the elimination of drug trafficking; and
xi. Promoting science and technology in ASEAN to improve regional human resources by developing science and technology culture and increasing usage of applied science and technology in socio-economic activities.

### 3.2 *Managing the Social Impact of Economic Integration*

Domestic policy adjustments and emerging regional production arrangements from economic integration will have a profound social impact that will be felt mostly in the labour market. Consequently there is a need to:

i. Enhance human resource development through the networking of skills training institutions, and the development of regional assessment and training programmes;
ii. Strengthen the capacity of governments to monitor labour markets and monitor human resource indicators; and
iii. Promote social protection and social risk management systems.

The inclusion of health services as one of the eleven priority sectors for vertical integration will require strategies to address the impact of liberalisation in the health sector. In addition, the development of mutual recognition arrangements shall facilitate labour mobility in the region and will support the realisation of the AEC.

### 3.3 *Promoting Environmental Sustainability*

The ASCC promotes a clean and green ASEAN with fully established mechanisms for sustainable development to ensure the protection of the region's environment, the sustainability of its natural resources and the high quality of life of its people.

The medium-term strategies and milestones in pursuit of this goal are:

Environmental Management

i. Effectively address global environmental issues without impinging on competitiveness, or social and economic development based on the principle of common but differentiated responsibility;
ii. Prevent transboundary haze pollution as a result of land and/or forest fires through concerted national efforts and intensified regional action and international cooperation, pursued in the context of sustainable development and in accordance with the provisions of the ASEAN Agreement on Transboundary Haze Pollution;
iii. Establish a clean and green ASEAN, rich in cultural traditions (where the values and practices of the people are in accord with the rhythm and harmony of nature), with citizens who are environmentally literate, imbued with the environmental ethic, and willing and capable to ensure the sustainable development of the region through environmental education and public participation efforts;
iv. Aim for zero waste and minimal impact on the environment, and promote business opportunities in environmental goods and services, through relevant environmentally sound technologies;
v. Ensure cities/urban areas in ASEAN are environmentally sustainable, while meeting the social and economic needs of the people; and
vi. Strive for harmonisation of environmental policies, legislation, regulations, standards and databases, taking into account the national circumstances of Member Countries, to support the integration of the environmental, social and economic goals of the region.

Natural Resource Management

i. Ensure ASEAN's coastal and marine environment are sustainably managed, representative ecosystems, pristine areas and species are protected; economic activities are sustainably managed, and public awareness of the coastal and marine environment instilled;
ii. Ensure ASEAN's rich biological diversity is conserved, and sustainably managed, and the benefits arising from these biological and genetic resources are fairly and equitably shared toward enhancing social, economic and environmental well-being;
iii. Promote sustainability of water resources to ensure sufficient water quantity of acceptable quality to meet the needs of the people of ASEAN in terms of

health, food security, the economy and the environment, taking into consideration the strong linkage between water, health and poverty;

iv. Ensure sustainable management of land-based resources while enhancing optimum agricultural production;

v. Promote the sustainable management of forest resources and critical ecosystems through the eradication of unsustainable practices as well as strengthening the preservation and management of the ASEAN Heritage Parks; and

vi. Promote environmentally sound and socially responsible mineral development practices in the sustainable management and optimum utilisation of mineral resources.

### 3.4 *Promoting an ASEAN Identity*

Amidst the diversity of their historical experience and cultural heritage, common threads of historical ties, habitation of a geographical area and aspirations for peace and prosperity weave the ASEAN nations together and form the foundations of an ASEAN identity. The strategies to foster ASEAN awareness and build an ASEAN identity are:

i. Mainstream the promotion of ASEAN awareness and regional identity in national communications plans and educational curricula, people-to-people contact including through arts, tourism and sports, especially among the youth, and the promotion of ASEAN languages learning through scholarships and exchanges of linguists;

ii. Preserve and promote ASEAN cultural heritage through the promotion of exchanges, meetings of experts and the implementation of the ASEAN Declaration on Cultural Heritage;

iii. Encourage dialogue amongst Member Countries to promote a deeper understanding of the regions' civilisation, cultures and religions; and

iv. Further promote ASEAN's standing in the international community through the proactive engagement of ASEAN in international issues and strengthening communication mechanisms.

## 4. Goals and Strategies for Narrowing the Development Gap

***Theme: Progressing together through cooperation in development***

We have explicitly and repeatedly declared the need to narrow the development gap if ASEAN Member Countries are to move forward in a unified manner to realise Vision 2020. This need was first recognised and officially announced in the

Hanoi Declaration on Narrowing Development Gap for Closer ASEAN Integration of 2001. It was reaffirmed in the Bali Concord II of 2003.

The development gap is often manifested by disparity in per capita GDP (income). It can also be manifested by disparities in other dimensions of human development, such as life expectancy and the literacy rate. The gap can also be measured by disparity in poverty incidence.

The gap must be narrowed as an end in itself, if the principle that development is a fundamental human right is to be followed. It must also be narrowed, as a necessary condition for realising the end goal of economic integration: one community of ten nations functioning as a single market and production base. Indeed, efforts to narrow the development gap would be self-reinforcing. They would help remove the biggest constraint to the formation of the AEC, which in turn would help narrow that gap.

### 4.1 *Goal*

The practical goal of the VAP for narrowing the development gap is to reduce the large disparities in terms of per capita GDP as well as other human development dimensions. The development gap exists between the ASEAN-6 and the CLMV countries, and within the ASEAN-6 countries, where some isolated pockets of underdevelopment persist.

To realise this goal, ASEAN Member Countries will determine and agree, at an appropriate forum the extent to which the gap could be realistically narrowed through the VAP by 2010 and its successor programmes or plans of action by 2015 and by 2020. By sharing experiences on how they have planned and implemented their development policies, strategies and programmes, Member Countries can draw lessons from one another and apply these to their own development strategies.

### 4.2 *Strategy*

To achieve the goal, technical and development cooperation among ASEAN Member Countries and with Dialogue Partners will be intensified as the main strategy to help less developed Member Countries accelerate the process of economic integration, but in a way that leads to equitable and inclusive development. A key element is to ensure that regional cooperation supplements rather than supplants national efforts.

The Initiative for ASEAN Integration (IAI), ASEAN's main instrument for narrowing the development gap, will be strengthened to address development needs of the CLMV and other sub-regional areas. This will include broadening and deepening the scope of the IAI CLMV Work Plan as well as developing innovative modalities for resource mobilisation. For the other sub-regional areas, it will involve strengthening the framework for sub-regional cooperation within ASEAN's covering policy, coordination mechanisms and work programme.

Addressing both the benefit and cost of economic integration is another important feature of the strategy. To help narrow the development gap, it will seek to ensure that the benefit of economic integration is maximised and equitably distributed across and within Member Countries. It will also seek to ensure that the cost of integration in terms of economic dislocation and disruption arising from market adjustments is minimised and the burden is equitably shared across and within Member Countries. Intensification of regional cooperation to prevent or mitigate the social costs of integration would also contribute directly towards the realisation of the two other pillars of the ASEAN Community.

The programme for narrowing the development gap will include specific regional cooperation activities aimed at assisting less developed Member Countries in removing tariff, non- tariff and physical barriers to the free flow of goods and services in the product and factor market. The programme will also include activities that supplement national efforts directly aimed at poverty reduction and the promotion of equitable and inclusive development.

## 5. Implementation Mechanisms

The attainment of the Bali Concord II goals does not simply mean strengthening existing cooperation activities among the ASEAN Member Countries. Deepening integration, especially in the economic sphere, will also require the Member Countries to intensify dialogue, make binding commitments, identify appropriate implementing timetables and mechanisms, extend national and regional capacities and competences, and develop institutional frameworks, responses and human resources in a range of areas that extend far beyond the existing scope of ASEAN integration.

Three major issues have to be addressed. First, resource mobilisation to support the various programmes and projects required to attain the targets; second, strengthening existing institutions and, as necessary, the establishment of appropriate institutional arrangements to facilitate coordination among the various implementing bodies and with external partners; and third, developing a monitoring and evaluation framework to track progress with regard to the attainment of integration objectives, and to assess the outcomes of programmes and projects directed towards them.

There are potentially five levels of cooperation among the ASEAN Member Countries in moving towards the ASEAN Community. The levels are:

i. Confidence-building, an initial step characterised by understanding common problems, exploring common interests and identifying mutual gains of cooperating on a regional basis;
ii. Harmonisation, which aims to achieve compatible national approaches by ASEAN Member Countries;
iii. Special assistance, which focuses on capacity building to bridge development gaps across Member Countries, in particular, for less developed countries;
iv. Joint efforts, which are about developing regional approaches and regional institutions; and
v. Regional integration and expansion, where regional institutions can act in unison to further the ASEAN cause on behalf of Member Countries to attain the intended goals and objectives.

Within each level, there are three types of development cooperation interventions that may be carried out. These three types of interventions are the formulation of regional policy initiatives, the development of regional implementation mechanisms and human capacity building.

Accordingly, the implementation and coordination mechanisms for the VAP, the resource mobilisation strategy and the success measures to be used for monitoring and evaluating a project under the VAP should be fine-tuned to fit the level of cooperation and the type of development intervention.

## 5.1 *Resource Mobilisation*

ASEAN is entering a resource-intensive period in its progress towards the ASEAN Community. The period covered by the HPA saw the implementation of many activities intended to lay the groundwork for the more substantive measures to deepen integration that would be undertaken during the period of the VAP. Thus, it is anticipated that the VAP would essentially need more resources than the HPA.

With respect to the five levels of cooperation described above, the VAP operates mainly at the first three levels, and shall also aim toward strategies involving action at the fourth level.

There are three broad sources of funding for the implementation of the VAP. These are direct contributions from all or some Member Countries towards specific activities; ASEAN pooled resources, and external funding. ASEAN will adopt a mix of these approaches towards resource mobilisation, so that internal ASEAN resources and external funding complement each other.

Member Country contributions will be enhanced to form a predictable and reliable resource to facilitate implementation of the VAP. While Member Countries will continue making "in-kind" contributions to ASEAN activities and directly finance the implementation of activities at the national level, ASEAN will ensure the availability of a common pool of financial resources by establishing an ASEAN Development Fund, to be made up from contributions of Member Countries, based on a mutually acceptable scheme.

The ASEAN Development Fund shall serve as ASEAN's common pool of financial resources to support the implementation of the VAP through the following roles:

a) For complex projects of relatively large scale, the Fund will provide seed funding for some initial activities such as feasibility studies, meetings with donor institutions, project design development, etc., leading towards obtaining major funding to implement the full project, from a Dialogue Partner or donor institution; and
b) The fund can fully support small scale projects of a confidential or strategic nature.

Another important strategy to promote the commitment of national funding to regional programmes is to mainstream the ASEAN agenda into national development programmes. In this way, the allocation of national funds to implement regional initiatives could be more easily secured.

Contributions from Dialogue Partners and other donor institutions will remain an important funding source for ASEAN, especially for funds intended to support very specific programmes and activities.

Another possible source of complementary funding for ASEAN activities is the private sector. ASEAN will embark on a fund-raising programme to encourage and generate private sector support for ASEAN activities, especially those that would result in direct benefits to business and industry.

Resource mobilisation from both internal and external sources to support the VAP could be undertaken through, among others, the convening of an ASEAN development cooperation forum.

## 5.2 *Institutional Arrangements*

The VAP has been designed along thematic lines to minimise the risk of fragmentation that may arise from a sectoral approach. Thus, there may be projects that have to be implemented jointly by two or more ASEAN bodies, or multi-component programmes where different ASEAN bodies are responsible for individual components.

In such cases, the current mechanisms for closer coordination of inputs in project design and efficiency in joint management and implementation of projects need to be strengthened to ensure better coherence, complementation, efficiency, flexibility, transparency and accountability, without unduly creating additional complexity to the overall ASEAN cooperation structure.

The ASEAN Secretariat will facilitate the consultation process among ASEAN bodies and seek the most efficient modality in setting up the appropriate institutional arrangement at the programme/project level.

Approaches and mechanisms to closely involve other ASEAN stakeholders, including the private sector and civil society, must also be addressed.

## 5.3 *Monitoring and Evaluation*

The VAP needs to have a mechanism for monitoring and evaluation to ensure that targets are achieved, timely corrective measures are undertaken if needed, and that initiatives and activities remain consistent with the stated goals of the VAP and are responsive to emerging issues and priorities. The monitoring and evaluation mechanism should also fulfil the principles of transparency and accountability.

For this purpose a monitoring and evaluation framework for the VAP has been developed, using a VAP scorecard as a basic tool. The scorecard offers the possibility of both quantitative ratings at the project level as well as qualitative assessment of impact at higher levels, and allows aggregation across diverse elements, sectors and countries to form an overall picture of VAP performance.

Thus, the monitoring and evaluation process will be undertaken at two levels:

- At the micro level, with a monitoring and evaluation plan built into each project; and
- At the macro level, with a consolidated assessment mechanism introduced to help ensure that the overall VAP is on track in achieving its agreed objectives.

At the micro level, different projects will have their own set of success indicators, depending on their stated objectives. At the macro level, to permit aggregation, a generic set of criteria will be used.

The generic criteria include:

Appropriateness/Relevance:

— Conformity with VAP priorities
— Sectoral need
— Contribution to Millennium Development Goals

Quality of Desgin:

— Objectives
— Programme logic
— Performance indicators
— Risks

Effectiveness:

— Achievement of planned processes and results
— Outputs delivered
— Outcomes achieved

Efficiency:

— Level of resources needed to achieve outputs and targets

Impact:

— Contribution to VAP goals
— Avoidance of negative consequences

Sustainability:

— Retention of knowledge gained (knowledge management)
— Risk management plan in place
— On-going resources available
— Political will to sustain momentum
— Continuity of flow of benefits

The baseline situation at the beginning of the implementation of the VAP must be established to have a reference or benchmark for the periodic monitoring and evaluation exercises to be undertaken.

One important issue to be addressed is defining which stakeholder perspectives would form part of the scorecard assessment. It is suggested that, to obtain a balanced view, the widest range of stakeholder views be obtained, i.e. the beneficiaries, the implementing bodies, the programme managers and the sponsoring ASEAN bodies should all be invited to participate in the assessment.

Whenever possible, over the longer term, the review should take in relevant inputs from Dialogue Partners or their specialist agencies with interest in the project. The information gathered from the views of external evaluators would be useful in the development of new cooperation programmes and formulation of new projects with Dialogue Partners.

Progress in the implementation of the VAP shall be reported annually by the Secretary-General to the ASEAN Summit through the ASEAN Ministerial Meeting (AMM) after consideration by the ASEAN Standing Committee. Formal reviews shall be undertaken by the ASEAN Secretariat every two years. Any recommendations for revisions or updating the VAP arising from the formal review shall likewise be submitted to the Summit so that guidance for the relevant sectoral bodies can be issued accordingly. A final review will be conducted in 2010 and reported to the Summit. This review will guide the preparation of the next action programme for the medium-term period of 2010–2015.

We charge our Ministers and Senior Officials to begin the implementation of the VAP.

**DONE** at Vientiane, Lao PDR, on the Twenty Ninth Day of November, Two Thousand and Four.

For Brunei Darussalam

**HAJI HASSANAL BOLKIAH**
Sultan of Brunei Darussalam

For the Kingdom of Cambodia

**SAMDECH HUN SEN**
Prime Minister

For the Republic of Indonesia

**DR. SUSILO BAMBANG YUDHOYONO**
President

For the Lao People's Democratic Republic

**BOUNNHANG VORACHITH**
Prime Minister

For Malaysia

**DATO' SERI ABDULLAH AHMAD BADAWI**
Prime Minister

For the Union of Myanmar

**LIEUTENANT GENERAL SOE WIN**
Prime Minister

For the Republic of the Philippines

**GLORIA MACAPAGAL-ARROYO**
President

For the Republic of Singapore

**LEE HSIEN LOONG**
Prime Minister

For the Kingdom of Thailand

**DR. THAKSIN SHINAWATRA**
Prime Minister

For the Socialist Republic of Viet Nam

**PHAN VAN KHAI**
Prime Minister

# ANNEX 1

## ASEAN SECURITY COMMUNITY

....

# ANNEX 2

## ASEAN ECONOMIC COMMUNITY

....

| Ref. No. | Programme Areas and Measures |
|---|---|
| **2.9** | **Energy** |
| 2.9.1 | Operationalisation of the ASEAN Memorandum of Understanding (MOU) on the Trans-ASEAN Gas Pipeline (TAGP) Project with a fully functional ASEAN Gas Consultative Council and ASEAN Council on Petroleum (ASCOPE) Gas Centre in place |
| 2.9.2 | Significant implementation of the ASEAN Power Grid Project with an established policy framework and modalities for power inter-connection and trade |
| 2.9.3 | Enhanced energy infrastructure facilities in ASEAN with the commissioning of three gas pipelines under the TAGP Project and five power inter-connections under the ASEAN Power Grid |
| 2.9.4 | Comprehensive institutional arrangement for enhanced security and stability of energy supply in ASEAN |
| 2.9.5 | Enhancing sustainable energy development through the expanding markets for renewable energy technologies and energy-efficient products |
| 2.9.6 | Increase the share of renewable energy in power generation in ASEAN region to at least ten per cent |
| **2.10** | **Food, Agriculture and Forestry Sectors Develop and Adopt Existing and New Technologies** |
| 2.10.1 | Conduct collaborative research to develop new/improved technologies in food, agriculture and forestry production, post-harvest and processing activities and sharing of research results and available technology |

(*Continued*)

2.10.2 Conduct Research and Development (R&D) in critical areas to reduce the cost of inputs for food, agriculture and forestry production

2.10.3 Strengthen programmes in food, agriculture and agro-forestry technology transfer, training and extension to increase productivity

**Enhance the Marketability of ASEAN Food, Agriculture and Forestry Products/Commodities**

2.10.4 Develop, harmonise and adopt quality standards and regulations for food, agriculture and forestry products

2.10.5 Promote trade, investment and services incidental to agriculture and forestry to increase trade in agro-based and wood-based products in ASEAN and ASEAN Trade in these products with the rest of the world

**Enhance Private Sector Involvement**

2.10.6 Establish networking and strategic alliances with the private sector to promote investment and joint venture opportunities in ASEAN

**Enhance ASEAN Cooperation and Joint Approaches in International and Regional Issues**

2.10.7 Strengthen ASEAN's cooperation and joint approaches in addressing issues and problems affecting trade in the region's food, agriculture and forestry products including environment and labour issues

2.10.8 Seek closer cooperation and negotiate, through relevant ASEAN bodies, with trading partners on market access for ASEAN products

....

# ANNEX 3

# ASEAN SOCIO-CULTURAL COMMUNITY

| Ref. No. | Programme Areas and Measures |
|---|---|
| **3.1** | **Building A Community of Caring Societies** |
| **3.1.1** | **Raising the standard of living of marginalised, disadvantaged groups** |
| 3.1.1.1 | Increase the instances of economic entrepreneurship in rural enterprises |
| 3.1.1.2 | Build the capacity of officials in rural development and poverty alleviation administration |
| 3.1.1.3 | Raise ICT awareness and ICT utilisation rates among the poor |
| 3.1.1.4 | Develop a programme to increase capacity for producing prostheses and other assistive devices for persons with disabilities (access to research and production methods, joint procurement) |
| 3.1.1.5 | Develop and strengthen regional cooperation for promoting self-reliance of elderly and disabled people to be productive members of the community |
| **3.1.2** | **Facilitating universal access to education and promoting high standards** |
| 3.1.2.1 | Develop collaboration on educational systems in the region through comparative studies with a view to ensure quality education in the region |
| 3.1.2.2 | Promote education information networking in various levels of institutions in the region |
| 3.1.2.3 | Initiate collaboration with other regional and international educational organisations to develop a concerted effort in provision of education in the region |
| **3.1.3** | **Reducing the social risks faced by children, women, the elderly and persons with disabilities** |
| .... | |
| 3.1.3.7 | Develop and implement regional activities that assist Member Countries to strengthen capacity to facilitate access by all members of society, especially the vulnerable groups, to education, consistent with the UN Millennium Development Goals |
| 3.1.3.8 | Promoting equitable participation of women in the development process by eliminating all forms of discrimination against them |

(*Continued*)

*(Continued)*

| Ref. No. | Programme Areas and Measures |
|---|---|
| **3.1.4** | **Increasing the effective participation of family, civil society and the private sector in tackling poverty and social welfare issues** |
| 3.1.4.1 | Establish an ASEAN Social Workers Exchange Programme |
| 3.1.4.2 | Establish an ASEAN Network for Family Development |
| 3.1.4.3 | Promote regional networking of professional social workers, NGOs and private sector groups involved in social services education or provision of care |
| 3.1.4.4 | Facilitate a rural volunteers movement, and the exchange of young professionals in rural development in ASEAN |
| **3.1.5** | **Increasing the participation of women and youth in the productive workforce** |
| 3.1.5.1 | Develop a skills training curricula on specific skills and accreditation systems for skills training programmes for youth |
| 3.1.5.2 | Conduct skills training for out-of-school youth and disadvantaged women |
| 3.1.5.3 | Increase women's access to micro-credit, information systems and basic social services |
| 3.1.5.4 | Use ICT to enable more effective youth work and networking among youth in the region |
| 3.1.5.5 | Promote employability of youth by mainstreaming youth into the national development agenda |
| 3.1.5.6 | Develop a consolidated plan for regional cooperation mechanisms on skills development, taking into account the skills training programmes under ASEAN cooperation on labour, women and youth, to ensure relevance with the AEC's priority sectors |
| **3.1.6** | **Addressing health development concerns** |
| 3.1.6.1 | Develop strategies for ASEAN to strengthen capacity and competitiveness in health-related products and services, including:<br>• harmonisation of standards and regulations for health services and greater coordination with policy makers in the trade sector<br>• enhancing human resources for health in the area of globalisation and trade liberalisation |
| 3.1.6.2 | Strengthen ASEAN capacity for good clinical practice (GCP) and clinical trials |
| 3.1.6.3 | Develop and operationalise a framework of cooperation on integration of traditional medicine/complementary and alternative medicine (TM/CAM) into national health systems |

*(Continued)*

(*Continued*)

| Ref. No. | Programme Areas and Measures |
|---|---|
| 3.1.6.4 | Complete regional surveillance of risk factors for priority health issues identified in the Regional Action Plan on Healthy Lifestyles |
| 3.1.6.5 | Formulate detailed work plans for implementing technical cooperation in pharmaceuticals phase VI in the plan's identified areas |
| **3.1.7** | **Preventing the spread and reducing the harm of HIV/AIDS and other infectious diseases** |
| 3.1.7.1 | Reduce new infection and transmission rate of HIV in ASEAN Member Countries, consistent with the UN Millennium Development Goals |
| 3.1.7.2 | Increase access to affordable anti-retroviral treatment and opportunistic disease treatment as well as testing reagents |
| 3.1.7.3 | Integrate HIV/AIDS impact assessment into the feasibility study phase for development projects, particularly in the countries of the Greater Mekong Sub-region |
| 3.1.7.4 | Conduct research on the socio-economic impact and trends of HIV/AIDS in ASEAN, with a view to mitigating the negative impacts |
| 3.1.7.5 | Establish regional mechanisms to proactively reduce HIV/AIDS vulnerability arising from development-related mobility and in the workplace |
| 3.1.7.6 | Strengthen capacity of ASEAN Member Countries to reduce the vulnerability of drug users to HIV/AIDS and other blood-borne infectious diseases |
| 3.1.7.7 | Develop and implement the Third ASEAN Work Programme on HIV/AIDS (AWPIII) with a time-frame of 2005–2010 |
| 3.1.7.8 | Put into place regional systems, networks and procedures for communicable diseases (including animal disease) surveillance, early warning and response |
| 3.1.7.9 | Formulate and work for the adoption of a ministerial agreement to facilitate the deployment of multinational ASEAN outbreak response teams |
| 3.1.7.10 | Activate regional simulation exercises of an outbreak response |
| 3.1.7.11 | Involve the Plus Three partners in sharing expertise and in strengthening networks for outbreak response |
| 3.1.7.12 | Complete Phase I of the ASEAN + 3 Emerging Infectious Diseases (EID) programme and convene a donors' forum to mobilise resources to develop and implement Phase II of the ASEAN + 3 EID Programme |
| 3.1.7.13 | Establish a regional veterinary surveillance network with linkages to public health surveillance mechanisms as a strategy for combating zoonotic diseases |

(*Continued*)

(*Continued*)

| Ref. No. | Programme Areas and Measures |
|---|---|
| **3.1.8** | **Enhancing food security and safety** |
| 3.1.8.1 | Complete an analysis of long-term supply and demand prospects of major food commodities (to include rice, corn, soybean, sugar, pulses and oilseeds) |
| 3.1.8.2 | Develop and adopt a common framework for analysing food trade policies in Member Countries |
| 3.1.8.3 | Establish a food security information system for ASEAN to allow Member Countries to forecast, plan and manage their food supplies and utilisation of basic commodities as well as provide information to investors on potential ventures in food production and related areas |
| 3.1.8.4 | Develop model food legislative framework and guidelines from farm to table |
| 3.1.8.5 | Harmonise related protocols on food safety and organise a network of food laboratories in ASEAN |
| 3.1.8.6 | Develop a mechanism for region-wide recognition of food safety assurance systems including certification such as HACCP and GMP |
| 3.1.8.7 | Adopt mutual recognition agreements to facilitate trade in food products |
| 3.1.8.8 | Develop and implement a work plan to involve the food industry and the agriculture sectors in the implementation of the ASEAN Food Safety Implementation Plan (AFSIP) |
| 3.1.8.9 | Establish centres of excellence among ASEAN Member Countries in various analytical services/fields: training-centres, joint training programmes, etc. taking into account the existing models and institutions |
| **3.1.9** | **Disaster Management** |
| 3.1.9.1 | Fully implement the ASEAN Regional Programme on Disaster Management 2004–2010 emphasising the following actions:<br>• Establishing a fully functional regional mechanism for disaster management, response and relief<br>• Institutionalising capacity building programmes for enhancing skills in disaster management<br>• Establishment of an ASEAN Disaster Information Sharing and Communication Network and promoting research capability<br>• Promoting public awareness and participation in disaster management programmes |
| **3.1.10** | **Ensuring a Drug Free ASEAN by 2015** |
| .... | |

(*Continued*)

(*Continued*)

| Ref. No. | Programme Areas and Measures |
|---|---|
| **3.1.11** | **Promote science and technology in ASEAN** |
| 3.1.11.1 | Develop and implement programmes to enhance science and technology culture in the society through participation of related and interested elements in the community, such as private sectors |
| 3.1.11.2 | Implement applied science and technology in relevant lectors for social and economic benefit |
| **3.2** | **Managing the Social Impacts of Economic Integration** |
| **3.2.1** | **Developing and enhancing human resources in the workforce** |
| 3.2.1.1 | Establish a network of skills-training institutions and a programme on vocational skills-training methodology |
| 3.2.1.2 | Promote life-long learning as a means of personal development and integration into the working life and society |
| 3.2.1.3 | Develop a regional assessment and training programme in the informal sector to promote employment and self-employment |
| 3.2.1.4 | Enhance capacity of governments to monitor labour markets and human resource indicators, and design social impact policies |
| 3.2.1.5 | Develop a programme on overseas employment administration |
| 3.2.1.6 | Develop ASEAN human resources in applied research concentrating on micro-electronic, new materials, bio-technology, telecommunication and other high value-added industries that enhance ASEAN's global competitiveness |
| 3.2.1.7 | Develop joint certification and accreditation of science and technology in the region |
| **3.2.2** | **Strengthening systems of social protection and social risk management** |
| 3.2.2.1 | Establish an integrated social protection and social risk management system in ASEAN |
| 3.2.2.2 | Conduct research on the impact of globalisation and regional integration on labour and unemployment |
| 3.2.2.3 | Strengthen systems of social protection at the national level and work toward adoption of appropriate measures at the regional level to provide a minimum uniform coverage for skilled workers in the region |

(*Continued*)

(*Continued*)

| Ref. No. | Programme Areas and Measures |
|---|---|
| **3.2.3** | **Addressing health development issues from liberalisation** |
| 3.2.3.1 | Develop strategies to:<br>• ensure coordination between policy makers, practitioners and users in rationalising health delivery<br>• enhance human resources for health to respond to globalisation and trade liberalization |
| 3.2.3.2 | Complete regional surveillance of risk factors for priority health issues identified in the Regional Action Plan on Healthy Lifestyles |
| **3.3** | **Promoting Environmental Sustainability** |
| **3.3.1** | **Global environmental issues** |
| 3.3.1.1 | Promote national and regional cooperation to address measures related to the cluster of multilateral environmental agreements addressing atmospheric issues such as Climate Change and Vienna Conventions and its Protocols |
| 3.3.1.2 | Promote national and regional cooperation to address measures related to the cluster of multilateral environmental agreements addressing chemical and chemical wastes such as the Basel, Stockholm and Rotterdam Conventions |
| **3.3.2** | **Land and forest fires and transboundary haze pollution** |
| 3.3.2.1 | Undertake appropriate measures to set in place legislative, administrative and/or other measures to implement the relevant preventive, monitoring, and mitigation measures under the ASEAN Agreement on Transboundary Haze Pollution |
| 3.3.2.2 | Operationalise the ASEAN Coordinating Centre for Transboundary Haze Pollution Control to effectively implement the provisions of the ASEAN Agreement on Transboundary Haze Pollution |
| 3.3.2.3 | Operationalise the ASEAN Transboundary Haze Pollution Control Fund to provide the required resources for regional and national level action |
| **3.3.3** | **Public awareness and environmental education** |
| 3.3.3.1 | Further expand and intensify the implementation of the ASEAN Environmental Education Action Plan 2000–2005, targeting measures in four |

(*Continued*)

(*Continued*)

| Ref. No. | Programme Areas and Measures |
|---|---|
| | target areas: formal education, non formal education, manpower capability building and networking, collaboration and communication |
| 3.3.3.2 | Further promote the ASEAN Environmental Education Inventory Database as a primary means of communication, networking, sharing resources and experiences, and capacity building |
| **3.3.4** | **Promotion of environmentally sound technologies** |
| 3.3.4.1 | Operationalise an appropriate ASEAN-level regional mechanism (centre/network) to promote environmentally sound technologies |
| 3.3.4.2 | Foster effective government-business-innovative financial mechanisms to promote environmentally sound technologies especially among the SMEs |
| 3.3.4.2 | Adopt region wide environmental management/labeling schemes to promote economic growth and environmental protection |
| **3.3.5** | **Urban environmental management and governance** |
| 3.3.5.1 | Clean Air — Achieve ASEAN long-term goal of maintaining good ambient air quality of PSI (Pollutant Standard Index) <100 to safeguard public health |
| 3.3.5.2 | Clean Water — Achieve ASEAN long-term goals for water quality intended for various uses, and move towards sustainable supply and use of water |
| 3.3.5.3 | Clean Land — Ensure that waste is properly collected and disposed of in an environmentally sustainable manner |
| **3.3.6** | **Sustainable development, monitoring and reporting/database harmonisation** |
| 3.3.6.1 | Implement the thirteen priority environmental parameters and ensure region-wide harmonisation in terms of measurement (methodology), monitoring and reporting |
| 3.3.6.2 | Consolidate and promote synergy in the reporting requirements under the various multilateral environmental agreements, aiming for consolidated region-wide reporting |
| 3.3.6.3 | Produce informative periodical state of the environment reports for policy-making and addressing impacts on the environment |

(*Continued*)

(*Continued*)

| Ref. No. | Programme Areas and Measures |
|---|---|
| **3.3.7** | **Coastal and marine environment** |
| 3.3.7.1 | Enhance inter-agency and inter-sectoral coordination at the national, regional and international levels for achieving sustainable development of the ASEAN's coastal and marine environment |
| 3.3.7.2 | Further expand and implement the ASEAN Marine Water Quality Criteria |
| 3.3.7.3 | Implement the ASEAN Criteria for Marine Heritage Areas, and ASEAN Criteria for National Protected Areas to establish a representative network of protected areas to protect critical habitats |
| **3.3.8** | **Nature conservation and biodiversity** |
| 3.3.8.1 | Significantly reduce the current rate of loss of biological diversity by 2010 (WSSD target) |
| 3.3.8.2 | Promote further listing and coordinated management of ASEAN Heritage Parks as a platform for ecosystem-based protected areas management |
| 3.3.8.3 | Facilitate access and fair and equitable sharing of benefits arising from the region's biological and genetic resources, by effectively implementing the ASEAN Framework Agreement on Access to, and Fair and Equitable Sharing of Benefits Arising from the Utilisation of Genetic and Biological Resources |
| 3.3.8.4 | Set in place measures to minimise impacts of transboundary movement of living modified organisms in accordance with the ASEAN Guidelines on Risk Assessment of Agricultural GMOs |
| 3.3.8.5 | Promote national and regional cooperation to address measures related to the cluster of multilateral environmental agreements addressing biological diversity such as the Convention on Biological Diversity, CITES, Ramsar Convention |
| 3.3.8.6 | Establish a functional regional database or network of national databases containing inventory of the biological resources of the ASEAN Region |
| 3.3.8.7 | Enhance the role and capacity of the ASEAN Centre for Biodiversity to function as an effective regional centre of excellence in promoting biodiversity conservation and management |
| 3.3.8.8 | Address issues pertaining to invasive alien species |
| **3.3.9** | **Freshwater resources** |
| 3.3.9.1 | Halve by 2010 the proportion of people without sustainable access to safe drinking water (WSSD target by 2015) |
| 3.3.9.2 | Manage water resources efficiently and effectively |

(*Continued*)

(*Continued*)

| Ref. No. | Programme Areas and Measures |
|---|---|
| 3.3.9.3 | Promote integrated river basin management |
| 3.3.9.4 | Promote awareness to enhance integrated water resources management |
| **3.3.10** | **Ensuring sustainable management of land-based resources while enhancing optimum agricultural production** |
| Crops: | |
| 3.3.10.1 | Strengthening national frameworks for pest risk analysis |
| 3.3.10.2 | Bio-security planning |
| 3.3.10.3 | Harmonisation of maximum residue limits of commonly used pesticides for vegetables |
| 3.3.10.4 | Establishment of ASEAN pesticide database network |
| 3.3.10.5 | Identification and adoption of improved production/post-harvest technologies |
| 3.3.10.6 | Establishment of ASEAN-AVRDC regional network for vegetable research and development |
| 3.3.10.7 | Intensification of integrated pest and crop management practices |
| Livestock: | |
| 3.3.10.8 | Establishment of accreditation schemes for good practices in livestock production |
| 3.3.10.9 | Strengthening animal diseases control programmes among ASEAN Member Countries |
| 3.3.10.10 | Establishment of an information network for the sharing of information on animal health and production |
| Fisheries: | |
| 3.3.10.11 | Implementation of ASEAN-SEAFDEC's Resolution and Plan of Action Sustainable Fisheries |
| 3.3.10.12 | Utilisation of good production practices for aquaculture farming |
| 3.3.10.13 | Establishment of village-fish ponds and school fish ponds in rural community in selected ASEAN Member Countries |
| 3.3.10.14 | Development of disease surveillance system of aquatic animals |
| 3.3.10.15 | Promotion of mangrove-friendly aquaculture in Southeast Asia |
| 3.3.10.16 | Regionalisation of the Code of Conduct for Responsible fisheries |

(*Continued*)

(*Continued*)

| Ref. No. | Programme Areas and Measures |
|---|---|
| **3.3.11** | **Promoting forest management as a model in sustainable development by harmonising environmental, social and economic policies** |
| 3.3.11.1 | Enhance the capacities and human resources, including research and development in the forestry sector to achieve Sustainable Forest Management (SFM) |
| 3.3.11.2 | Strengthen ASEAN cooperation and joint approaches in addressing international and regional forestry issues to participate in the development of a global partnership for development |
| 3.3.11.3 | Establish policy and planning documents that promote the sustainable management and conservation of forest resources for socio-economic development while ensuring environmental sustainability |
| 3.3.11.4 | Promote multi-stakeholder participation to support development of regional partnership for development |
| 3.3.11.5 | Promote the sustainable management of forest resources, which include protection of forests in an ecologically sound and integrated manner by developing and adopting common criteria for sustainable forest management in ASEAN, and eradicating unsustainable practices and related activities |
| **3.3.12** | **Strengthen cooperation in the rational utilisation of mineral resources** |
| 3.3.12.1 | Intensify cooperation in strengthening institutional and human capacities to facilitate research, innovation and application of emerging and advanced technologies in mineral resources development and geosciences, including environmental management, minerals processing and rehabilitation, among others |
| 3.3.12.2 | Engage ASEAN Dialogue Partners and relevant international and regional organisations in the promotion of responsible mineral resources development, research and development, and technology transfer cooperative programmes and activities |
| 3.3.12.3 | Conduct safe, environmentally friendly and socially responsible mineral resource development in ASEAN |

(*Continued*)

*(Continued)*

| Ref. No. | Programme Areas and Measures |
|---|---|
| **3.4** | **Promoting an ASEAN Identity** |
| **3.4.1** | **Promoting ASEAN awareness and an ASEAN regional identity** |
| 3.4.1.1 | Implementation of the Memorandum of Understanding on the Implementation of National Communication Plans to Promote ASEAN Awareness and Understanding (signed by the ASEAN Ministers Responsible for Information in 2000) |
| 3.4.1.2 | Production of visual arts and showcases as well as performing arts that promote interaction among artists |
| 3.4.1.3 | Production of performing arts |
| 3.4.1.4 | Conduct of youth camps and similar activities involving youth exchanges |
| 3.4.1.5 | Promote shared values |
| 3.4.1.6 | Promote ASEAN languages learning |
| **3.4.2** | **Preserving and promoting ASEAN cultural heritage** |
| 3.4.2.1 | Implementation of the work programme on the ASEAN Declaration on Cultural Heritage to cover the following areas:<br>• National and regional protection of ASEAN cultural heritage<br>• Protection of national treasures and cultural properties<br>• Sustentation of worthy living traditions<br>• Preservation of past and living scholarly, artistic and intellectual cultural heritage<br>• Preservation of past and living popular cultural heritage and traditions<br>• Enhancement of cultural education, awareness and literacy<br>• Affirmation of ASEAN cultural dignity<br>• Advancement of cultural heritage policy and legislation<br>• Recognition of communal intellectual property rights<br>• Prevention of illicit transfer of ownership of cultural property<br>• Economic and commercial utilisation of cultural heritage and resources<br>• Integration of culture and development<br>• Development of national and regional networks on ASEAN cultural heritage |

*(Continued)*

(*Continued*)

| Ref. No. | Programme Areas and Measures |
|---|---|
| 3.4.2.2 | Exchange of visits among representatives of arts and culture |
| 3.4.2.3 | Build capacity, both people and facilities, within each country to develop and implement sustainable cultural conservation management plans and systems |
| **3.4.3** | **Fostering dialogue for a deeper understanding of ASEAN civilisation, cultures, and religions** |
| 3.4.3.1 | Organise dialogues for interaction and exchange among all individuals from various societies and civilisations in the region |
| 3.4.3.2 | Promote mutual visits and meetings of experts in various fields from different civilisations |
| 3.4.3.3 | Develop curricula materials suitable for each national education system |
| 3.4.3.5 | Clarify and publicise framework for cooperation with Dialogue Partners |
| 3.4.3.6 | Increase number of cooperative programmes with Dialogue Partners within framework |
| 3.4.3.6 | Identify existing networks and encourage cooperation |
| 3.4.3.7 | Increase ASEAN cultural and information cooperation to expose and disseminate the rich and vast culture of ASEAN through effective and efficient programmes, not only within ASEAN but also outside the region |
| **3.4.4** | **Promoting ASEAN's standing in the international community** |
| 3.4.4.1 | Advance and reinforce a positive international image of ASEAN supportive of its interests, policies programmes and goals |
| 3.4.4.2 | Undertake proactive communication measures to promote the realisation of the ASEAN Community |
| 3.4.4.3 | Improve the quality of mechanisms that disseminate news on ASEAN |
| 3.4.4.4 | Develop and implement a mechanism for engaging with the media |

# ANNEX 4

# NARROWING THE DEVELOPMENT GAP

| Ref. No | Programme Areas and Measures |
|---|---|
| **4.1** | **General Framework** |
| **4.1.1** | **Conduct a deeper analysis of the development gap in its various dimensions and manifestations and set realistic targets for the medium and long-term:** |
| 4.1.1.1 | Complete a study to analyse the nature, manifestations and magnitude of the development gap in ASEAN |
| 4.1.1.2 | Convene fora/workshops to set regional targets and milestones |
| **4.1.2.** | **Accord preferential consideration or special treatment in the form of more opportunities or greater resource allocation, for the participation of CLMV in all cooperation programmes and activities under the mainstream ASEAN agenda:** |
| 4.1.2.1 | Accord special consideration for the participation of CLMV built into the design of all ASEAN cooperation programmes, projects and activites |
| **4.2** | **Initiative for ASEAN Integration (IAI)** |
| **4.2.1** | **Strengthen the existing mechanisms to assist the CLMV grow at an accelerated rate, including broadening and deepening the scope of the IAI CLMV Work plan as well as developing innovative modalities for resource mobilisation:** |
| 4.2.1.1 | Completion and approval by the Leaders of the mid-term review of the IAI CLMV Work Plan |
| 4.2.1.2 | Innovation modalities for resource mobilisation |
| **4.2.2** | **Strengthening the framework for sub-regional cooperation within ASEAN:** |
| 4.2.2.1 | Strengthening coordinating mechanisms within the existing sub-regional arrangements in ASEAN |
| 4.2.2.2 | Development and launching of a work programme to address development needs of sub-regions |
| 4.2.2.3 | Providing a policy environment to encourage sub-regional cooperation |

(*Continued*)

*(Continued)*

| Ref. No. | Programme Areas and Measures |
|---|---|
| **4.3** | **Economic Integration Activities** |
| **4.3.1** | **Develop a conducive policy environment to support infrastructure development in CLMV:** |
| 4.3.1.1 | Study to identify policy incentives to attract FDI in infrastructure development in CLMV |
| 4.3.1.2 | Series of workshops organised to review the recommendations of the study and formulate an implementation strategy |
| **4.4** | **Social Development** |
| **4.4.1** | **Complement national poverty reduction programmes with regional advocacy efforts** |
| 4.4.1.1 | Adoption and implementation of regional advocacy programme areas to include, among others, agriculture, agro-based industry, integrated rural development |

# CHAPTER 48

# ASEAN SECURITY COMMUNITY PLAN OF ACTION

## INTRODUCTION

Leaders at the Ninth ASEAN Summit in Bali adopted the Declaration of ASEAN Concord II (Bali Concord II), which stipulated the establishment of an ASEAN Community resting on three pillars: an ASEAN Security Community, an ASEAN Economic Community and an ASEAN Socio-Cultural Community.

These three pillars shall be developed and implemented in a parallel and balanced manner.

Recognising the strong interconnections among political, economic and social realities, the ASEAN Security Community acknowledges the principle of comprehensive security, and commits to address the broad political, economic, social and cultural aspects of building an ASEAN Community. It is also acknowledged that political and social stability, economic prosperity, narrowed development gap, poverty alleviation and reduction of social disparity would constitute strong foundation for a sustained ASC given its subscription to the principle of comprehensive security.

The realisation of an ASEAN Security Community would ensure that countries in the region live at peace with one another and with the world at large in a just, democratic and harmonious environment. The ASC would be based on shared norms and rules of good conduct in inter-state relations; effective conflict prevention and resolution mechanisms; and post-conflict peace building activities.

The ASC promotes an ASEAN-wide political and security cooperation in consonance with the ASEAN Vision 2020 rather than a defence pact, military alliance or a joint foreign policy. The ASC Plan of Action is mutually-reinforcing with bilateral cooperation between ASEAN Member Countries while recognising the sovereign rights of the Member Countries to pursue their individual foreign policies and defence arrangements. In addressing future security challenges, ASEAN Member Countries share the responsibility for strengthening peace, stability and security of the region free from foreign military interference in any form or manifestation.

The ASC shall contribute to the further promotion of peace and security in the wider Asia Pacific region. In this regard, the ASC is open and outward looking, engaging ASEAN's friends and Dialogue Partners to promote peace and stability in the region. The ASC will reflect ASEAN's determination to move forward the stages of ASEAN Regional Forum (ARF) at a pace comfortable to all. In this regard, the ASC will strengthen ASEAN's role as the driving force in the ARF.

Since its inception in 1967, ASEAN has developed confidence and maturity to address issues of common concern as one ASEAN family. The ASC process shall therefore be progressive. This process shall be guided by well-established principles of non-interference, consensus based decision-making, national and regional resilience, respect for the national sovereignty, the renunciation of the threat or the use of force, and peaceful settlement of differences and disputes which have served as the foundation of ASEAN cooperation. ASEAN shall strengthen existing initiatives, launch new ones and set appropriate implementation frameworks.

The ASC upholds the existing ASEAN political instruments such as the Declaration on ZOPFAN, the TAC and the SEANWFZ Treaty, which shall play a pivotal role in the area of confidence building measures, preventive diplomacy and the approaches to conflict resolution. It shall abide by the UN Charter and other principles of international law.

ASEAN shall explore innovative ways to implement the Plan of Action which comprises six components, but not limited to, as follows: political development, shaping and sharing of norms, conflict prevention, conflict resolution, post-conflict peace building, and implementing mechanisms. A list of areas of activities, which is non-exhaustive, is provided to ensure a coordinated process of cooperation towards an ASEAN Security Community.

## I. Political Development

One of the main objectives of the ASEAN Security Community as envisaged in the Bali Concord II is to bring ASEAN's political and security cooperation to a higher plane.

In working towards this objective, ASEAN Member Countries shall promote political development in support of ASEAN Leaders' shared vision and common values to achieve peace, stability, democracy and prosperity in the region. This is the highest political commitment that would serve as the basis for ASEAN political cooperation. In order to better respond to the new dynamics within the respective ASEAN Member Countries, ASEAN shall nurture such common socio-political values and principles. In this context, ASEAN Member Countries shall not condone unconstitutional and undemocratic changes of government or the use of their territory for any actions undermining peace, security and stability of other ASEAN Member Countries.

A conducive political environment will ensure continued peace, security and stability in the region, in which member countries shall rely exclusively on peaceful processes in settling intra-regional differences and disputes and consider their individual security as fundamentally linked together and bound by geographic location, common vision and objectives.

## II. Shaping and Sharing of Norms

Shaping and sharing of norms aim at achieving a standard of common adherence to norms of good conduct among members of the ASEAN Community; consolidating and strengthening ASEAN's solidarity, cohesiveness and harmony (the "we feeling"); and contributing to the building of a democratic, tolerant, participatory and transparent community in Southeast Asia.

These norms setting activities shall adhere to the following fundamental principles:

1. Non-alignment;
2. Fostering of peace-oriented attitudes of ASEAN Member Countries;
3. Conflict resolution through non-violent means;
4. Renunciation of nuclear weapons and other weapons of mass destruction and avoidance of arms race in Southeast Asia; and
5. Renunciation of the threat or the use of force.

ASEAN Member Countries shall therefore engage in such activities as strengthening the ASEAN Declaration of 1967, the ZOPFAN, the TAC and the SEANWFZ regimes, developing regional legal frameworks, and establishing a Code of Conduct in the South China Sea.

## III. Conflict Prevention

Based on the principles contained in the TAC, which is the key code of conduct governing relations between states and diplomatic instrument for the promotion of peace, security and stability in the region, the objectives of conflict prevention shall be:

1. To strengthen confidence and trust within the Community;
2. To mitigate tensions and prevent disputes from arising between or among member countries as well as between member countries and non-ASEAN countries; and
3. To prevent the escalation of existing disputes.

ASEAN Member Countries shall enhance security cooperation by strengthening confidence building measures; carrying out preventive diplomacy; resolving outstanding regional issues; as well as enhancing cooperation on non-traditional security issues.

## IV. Conflict Resolution

It is essential that any disputes and conflicts involving ASEAN Member Countries be resolved in a peaceful way and in the spirit of promoting peace, security and stability in the region. While continuing to use national, bilateral and international mechanisms, ASEAN Member Countries shall endeavour to use the existing regional dispute settlement mechanisms and processes in the political and security areas and work towards innovative modalities including arrangements to maintain regional peace and security so as to better serve theirs as well as collective interests of all members for peace and security.

## V. Post-conflict Peace Building

Post-conflict peace building seeks to create the conditions necessary for a sustainable peace in conflict-torn areas and to prevent the resurgence of conflict. It is a process involving broad-based inter-agency cooperation and coordination across a wide range of issues. ASEAN activities related to post-conflict peace building shall include the establishment of appropriate mechanisms and mobilisation of resources. As an ASEAN family, members should assist each other in post-conflict peace building efforts, such as humanitarian relief assistance, reconstruction and rehabilitation.

## VI. Implementing Mechanisms

To ensure the effective implementation of this Plan of Action, the following measures will be undertaken:

1. The AMM shall take necessary follow-up measures to implement this Plan of Action including consultation and coordination with other relevant ASEAN

ministerial bodies; to set up ad-hoc groups as appropriate; and to report annually the progress of implementation to the ASEAN Summit; as well as to introduce new measures and activities to strengthen the ASEAN Security Community as appropriate;

2. The AMM shall undertake overall review of progress of this Plan of Action. The AMM shall inscribe permanently an agenda item entitled "Implementation of the ASC Plan of Action" in the agenda of its meetings; and
3. The Secretary-General of ASEAN shall assist the ASEAN Chair in monitoring and reviewing the progress of implementation of this Plan of Action.

## VII. Areas of Activities

To realise the ASEAN Security Community by 2020, ASEAN shall endeavour to work towards the implementation of the areas of activities in the following **Annex**. It is acknowledged that some of these activities are already ongoing and at various stages of implementation. Additional activities could also be implemented in the future. ASEAN will make every effort to promptly carry out activities which gain consensus support.

Source: http://www.aseansec.org/16826.htm
Accessed date: 16 January 2009
Publisher: ASEAN Secretariat
Country: Jakarta
Date of Publication: 2004

# ANNEX

# ACTIVITIES

## I. POLITICAL DEVELOPMENT

1. Promotion of a just, democratic and harmonious environment:

   a. Strengthening democratic institutions and popular participation;
   b. Promoting understanding and appreciation of political system, culture and history of ASEAN Member Countries;
   c. Strengthening the rule of law and judiciary systems, legal infrastructure and capacity building;
   d. Promoting free flow of information among and within ASEAN Member Countries;
   e. Enhancing good governance in public and private sectors;
   f. Strengthening effective and efficient civil services; and
   g. Preventing and combating corruption.

2. Promotion of human rights and obligations:

   a. Establishing a network among existing human rights mechanisms;
   b. Protecting vulnerable groups including women, children, people with disabilities, and migrant workers; and
   c. Promoting education and public awareness on human rights.

3. Promotion of people-to-people contacts:

   a. Encouraging the role of ASEAN Inter-Parliamentary Organisation (AIPO) in political and security cooperation;
   b. Promoting public participation and the contribution of the ASEAN People's Assembly (APA) to the ASEAN community building;
   c. Strengthening the role of the ASEAN Foundation;
   d. Encouraging the contribution of ASEAN-ISIS to political development;
   e. Strengthening the role of the ASEAN Business Advisory Council (ABAC); and
   f. Supporting the activities of the ASEAN University Network.

## II. SHAPING AND SHARING OF NORMS

1. Strengthening the TAC regime:
    a. Accession to the TAC by non-ASEAN countries; and
    b. Periodic assessment of the implementation of the TAC and exploration of ways and means for its effective implementation.
2. Working towards development of an ASEAN Charter which will *inter alia* reaffirm ASEAN's goals and principles in inter-state relations, in particular the collective responsibilities of all ASEAN Member Countries in ensuring non-aggression and respect for each other's sovereignty and territorial integrity; the promotion and protection of human rights; the maintenance of political stability, regional peace and economic progress; and the establishment of effective and efficient institutional framework for ASEAN.
3. Resolving all outstanding issues to ensure early signing of the Nuclear Weapon States to the Protocol to the SEANWFZ Treaty.
4. ASEAN Treaty on Mutual Legal Assistance (MLA) Agreement:
    a. Compilation of existing bilateral MLA Agreements among ASEAN Member Countries and between ASEAN and other countries;
    b. Identification of issues relating to the establishment of an ASEAN MLA Agreement; and
    c. Conclusion of ASEAN MLA Agreement.
5. ASEAN Extradition Treaty as envisaged by the 1976 Declaration of ASEAN Concord:
    a. Identification of ASEAN political decisions to establish Extradition Treaty and bilateral Extradition Treaties between ASEAN Member Countries; and
    b. Establishment of a working group on ASEAN Extradition Treaty under the purview of ASEAN Senior Law Officials Meeting (ASLOM).
6. Ensuring the implementation of the Declaration on the Conduct of Parties in the South China Sea (DOC) through, *inter alia*:
    a. Establishing an ASEAN–China Working Group on the Implementation of the DOC;
    b. Establishing a review mechanism on the implementation of the DOC; and
    c. Working towards the adoption of the Code of Conduct in South China Sea (COC).

7. ASEAN Convention on Counter Terrorism:

   a. Identification and analysis or assessment of documents and relevant instruments related to counter terrorism;
   b. Working towards accession to and ratification of the relevant UN conventions on counter terrorism; and
   c. Preparation, negotiation and conclusion of an ASEAN convention on counter terrorism.

## III. CONFLICT PREVENTION

1. Strengthening Confidence Building Measures:

   a. Organising and conducting regional military exchanges among high-ranking officials, military academies, and staff colleges of ASEAN Member Countries, apart from increasing bilateral visits and exchanges;
   b. Periodic publication of strategic assessments on the security environment, defence policies, and other security issues, such as Defence White Papers and equivalent documents;
   c. Working towards convening of an annual ASEAN Defence Ministers Meeting (ADMM);
   d. Promoting exchange of observers at military exercises;
   e. Establishment of an ASEAN Arms Register to be administered by the ASEAN Secretariat, in line with a similar activity being conducted in the ARF;
   f. Utilising military and civilian personnel in disaster relief operation;
   g. Promotion of civil-military relations; and
   h. Exploring joint development and sharing of resources.

2. Strengthening Preventive Measures:

   a. Publishing an ASEAN Members Annual Security Outlook;
   b. Voluntary briefing by ASEAN Member Countries on national security issues; and
   c. Developing an ASEAN early warning system based on existing mechanisms to prevent occurrence/escalation of conflicts.

3. Strengthening the ARF process in support of the ASEAN Security Community:

   a. ARF Unit within the ASEAN Secretariat;
   b. Enhanced role of the ARF Chair;
   c. Strengthening ASEAN's role in addressing the four overlapping issues of CBMs and Preventive Diplomacy (Enhanced role of the ARF Chair,

Annual Security Outlook, Register of Experts/Eminent Persons, Voluntary Briefing on Regional Issues); and

d. Moving the ARF to the preventive diplomacy stage and beyond (implementation of the Concept Paper on Preventive Diplomacy, establishment of an Intersessional Support Group on Preventive Diplomacy).

4. Enhancing cooperation on non-traditional security issues:

   a. Combating transnational crimes and other trans-boundary problems, including money laundering, illegal migration, smuggling and illegal trade of natural resources, trafficking in persons, drugs and precursors, as well as communicable diseases;
   b. Promoting ASEAN maritime security cooperation;
   c. Strengthening law enforcement cooperation; and
   d. Promoting cooperation on environmental issues including haze, pollution and floods.

5. Strengthening efforts in maintaining respect for territorial integrity, sovereignty and unity of member countries as stipulated in the Declaration on Principles of International Law Concerning Friendly Relations and Cooperation among States in Accordance with the Charter of the United Nations:

   a. Strengthening cooperation on the state's obligation not to intervene in the affairs of other neighbouring states, including refraining from the use of military, political, economic or other form of coercion aimed against the political independence or territorial integrity of other neighbouring states;
   b. Enhancing cooperation among ASEAN Member Countries to prevent the organisation, instigation, assistance and participation in terrorist acts in other neighbouring ASEAN Member Countries;
   c. Preventing the use of territory of any ASEAN Member Country as base for any activities against security and stability of neighbouring ASEAN Member Countries; and
   d. Strengthening cooperation to address subversive and insurgency activities aimed at neighbouring ASEAN Member Countries.

6. Strengthening cooperation to address threats and challenges posed by separatism.

## IV. CONFLICT RESOLUTION

1. Strengthening Dispute Settlement Mechanisms:

   a. The use of existing modes of pacific settlement of disputes such as negotiations and consultations, good offices, conciliation and mediation by all

ASEAN Member Countries, or use of the High Council of the TAC as a preferred option; and

b. If the High Council so requires, it may establish on an *ad hoc* basis an Experts Advisory Committee (EAC) or an Eminent Persons Group (EPG), which may extend assistance to the High Council to provide advice or counsel on the settlement of disputes upon request, in accordance with the Rules of Procedure of the High Council of TAC.

2. Developing regional cooperation for maintenance of peace and stability:

   a. Promoting technical cooperation with the UN and relevant regional organisations in order to benefit from their expertise and experiences;
   b. Establishing/assigning national focal points for regional cooperation for maintenance of peace and stability;
   c. Utilisation of national peace keeping centres which currently exist, or are being planned, in some ASEAN Member Countries to establish regional arrangement for the maintenance of peace and stability; and
   d. Establishing a network among existing ASEAN Member Countries' peace keeping centres to conduct joint planning, training, and sharing of experiences, with a view to establishing an ASEAN arrangement for the maintenance of peace and stability.

3. Developing Supporting Initiatives:

   a. Promoting exchange and cooperation among ASEAN centres of excellence on peace, and conflict management and resolution studies; and
   b. Considering the establishment of an ASEAN Institute for Peace and Reconciliation.

## V. POST-CONFLICT PEACE BUILDING

1. Strengthening ASEAN humanitarian assistance:

   a. Providing safe havens in conflict areas;
   b. Ensuring the delivery of basic services or assistance to victims of conflict;
   c. Orderly repatriation of refugees/displaced persons and resettlement of internally displaced persons;
   d. Ensuring safety of humanitarian relief assistance workers;
   e. Promoting the role of humanitarian relief assistance organisations;
   f. Considering the establishment of an ASEAN Humanitarian Assistance Centre; and

g. Intensifying cooperation with the United Nations and other organisations/donor countries.

2. Developing cooperation in post-conflict reconstruction and rehabilitation in affected areas by:

   a. Undertaking human resources development and capacity building;
   b. Assisting in institutional building and promoting popular participation;
   c. Reducing inter-communal tensions through educational exchanges and curriculum reform; and
   d. Increasing cooperation in reconciliation and promotion of a culture of peace.

3. Establishing a mechanism to mobilise necessary resources to facilitate post-conflict peace building (e.g. a Stability Fund), including through cooperation with donor countries and international institutions.

Source: http://www.aseansec.org/16829.htm
Accessed date: 16 January 2009
Publisher: ASEAN Secretariat
Country: Jakarta
Date of Publication: 2004

# CHAPTER 49

# THE ASEAN SOCIO-CULTURAL COMMUNITY (ASCC) PLAN OF ACTION

## INTRODUCTION

## THE VISION OF AN ASEAN SOCIO-CULTURAL COMMUNITY

1. Embedded in ASEAN Vision 2020, Declaration of ASEAN Concord I (1976), Declaration of ASEAN Concord II (2003) and the Hanoi Plan of Action (HPA) is ASEAN's goal of a community of cohesive, equitable and harmonious societies, bound together in solidarity for deeper understanding and cooperation. Its key features are:

- Equitable access to opportunities will be universal — rising above the barriers of religion, race, language, gender and social and cultural background;
- Human potentials are nurtured to the fullest, so that all individuals can participate meaningfully in a competitive world in a manner that gives paramount importance to their welfare and dignity;
- Norms of social and distributive justice are upheld by addressing issues of poverty and equity, and special care is given to vulnerable groups — children, youth, women, the elderly, and persons with disabilities — who could be the subject of abuse, neglect and discrimination;
- The environment and natural resources are protected and managed to sustain development and as a legacy for future generations;
- Civil society is engaged in providing inputs for policy choices;
- People are healthy in mind and body and living in harmony in safe environments; and
- ASEAN citizens interact in a community conscious of its ties of history, aware of its cultural heritage and bound by a common regional identity.

## THE IMPERATIVES OF THE ASEAN SOCIO-CULTURAL COMMUNITY

2. The ASCC reflects ASEAN's social agenda that is focused on poverty eradication and human development. It is linked inextricably with the economic and security pillars of the ASEAN Community. Social inequities can threaten

economic development and in turn undermine political regimes. Economic instability can exacerbate poverty, unemployment, hunger, illness and disease. Social instability can emerge from environmental scarcity or the inequitable distribution among stakeholders of the use of environmental assets. Failure to address these critical and persistent social issues can further cause both economic and political dislocations.

3. The ASCC will evolve amidst profound changes that are taking place in ASEAN's social landscape. These include: (i) the rise of consumerism and lifestyle changes resulting from rapid economic growth; (ii) increased personal mobility resulting from advances in infrastructure and more open regimes; (iii) transformation of the family roles and structures, with implications on the care of children and the elderly; (iv) the potential of information technology to enhance the speed and quality of learning and development of human skills, thus narrowing the digital divide; (v) the rapid pace of urbanisation and its impact on employment and the delivery of basic services; (vi) shifts in the labour market resulting from economic integration; and (vii) unsustainable exploitation of natural resources in the process of meeting developmental needs.

## THE ASEAN SOCIO-CULTURAL COMMUNITY PLAN OF ACTION

4. This ASCC Plan of Action (PoA) will have four core elements:

- **Building a community of caring societies** to address issues of poverty, equity and human development;
- **Managing the social impact of economic integration** by building a competitive human resource base and adequate systems of social protection;
- **Enhancing environmental sustainability** and sound environmental governance; and
- **Strengthening the foundations of regional social cohesion** towards an ASEAN Community in 2020.

## BUILDING A COMMUNITY OF CARING SOCIETIES

5. Poverty alleviation, equity and human development lie at the very core of a strong and resilient ASEAN Socio-Cultural Community. Poverty reduction is fundamental to the development of the human potential, allowing people to participate fully in the mainstream of economic life and contribute to society. A community of caring societies in ASEAN can enhance the potential for

production, consumption and wealth creation, thus ensuring the benefits from economic integration. ASEAN Member Countries will therefore strive, individually and collectively, to build caring societies concerned with, committed to, and capable of addressing fundamental issues of poverty, equity and human development. Governments, private sector and civil society will work in partnership to address these concerns.

6. Under the ASCC PoA, the goal of building an ASEAN community of caring societies will address the following concerns:

- Accelerating the goal of poverty reduction within the framework of the Millennium Development Goals (MDGs);
- Facilitating universal access to education for increased employability, good citizenship, and as a means of empowerment and life-long learning;
- Promoting the welfare of children by safeguarding their rights, ensuring their survival and full development, and protecting them from abuse, neglect and violence;
- Promoting improved standards and access to education through networking and institutional collaboration, using existing regional bodies;
- Enabling youth to have a better future by developing their leadership skills, entrepreneurship, and technical and vocational abilities;
- Promoting equitable participation of women in the development process by eliminating all forms of discrimination against them;
- Ensuring that the elderly are adequately cared for by promoting community-based support systems to supplement the role of the family as primary caregiver;
- Augmenting and supporting the efforts of sectoral bodies to prevent and combat human trafficking, particularly in women and children, through comprehensive policies and measures;
- Strengthening the system of social welfare through the enhancement of national capacities in responding to emerging social issues;
- Promoting health and nutrition, including through advocacy on health-related issues and healthy lifestyles;
- Preventing the spread of HIV/AIDS and other infectious diseases (including SARS and Avian influenza) through, among others, sharing of experiences and best practices and systems of surveillance;
- Ensuring access to safe, quality and affordable medicines by building ASEAN capacity and competitiveness in pharmaceutical as well as traditional medicines and complementary and alternative medicines;
- Enhancing food security and safety as a fundamental requirement of human security;

- Ensuring a drug-free ASEAN by 2015 through community-based drug prevention, treatment and control of drug abuse in parallel with eliminating drug-trafficking and illicit drug supply through law enforcement and alternative development for the sustainability of drug control; and
- Promoting a culture of science and technology and enhancing cooperation in the utilisation of appropriate applied science and technology in socio-economic activities to improve social well-being;
- Establishing efficient and well-functioning regional mechanisms for disaster prevention and relief that are fully compatible with global disaster management systems.

## MANAGING THE SOCIAL IMPACT OF ECONOMIC INTEGRATION

7. ASEAN Member Countries, as a community of caring societies, are committed individually and collectively, to address the impact of economic integration to minimise its social costs and ensure its benefits. Domestic policy adjustments and emerging regional production arrangements from economic integration will have profound social impact that will be felt mostly in the labour market.
8. To manage the social impact, the following key goals will be pursued under the ASCC PoA:

- Promoting human resource development to build a competitive labour force, through, among others, closer cooperation among existing regional centres in the area of education;
- Promoting an efficient labour market through mutual skills recognition arrangements to enhance regional mobility so that ASEAN's workforce are prepared for and benefit from economic integration; such efforts would enable labour markets to operate efficiently with appropriate matching of jobs and skills;
- Strengthening systems of social protection at the national level and working towards adoption of appropriate measures at the regional level to provide a minimum uniform coverage for skilled workers in the region;
- Addressing the impact of liberalisation in the health sector to meet the needs of ASEAN; and
- Promoting joint certification and accreditation of science and technology at the regional level to improve science and technology competence of ASEAN's human resources.

## ENHANCING ENVIRONMENTAL SUSTAINABILITY

9. A clean and green ASEAN, with fully developed mechanisms for environmental governance, is both a shared goal and responsibility of ASEAN Member Countries. ASEAN commitments to the Johannesburg Plan of Implementation of the World Summit for Sustainable Development (WSSD) have provided the framework for ASEAN cooperation on the environment which currently focuses on ten priority areas: (i) global environmental issues: (ii) land and forest fires and transboundary haze pollution; (iii) coastal and marine environment; (iv) sustainable forest management; (v) sustainable management of natural parks and protected areas; (vi) freshwater resources; (vii) public awareness and environmental education; (viii) promotion of environmentally sound technologies and cleaner production; (ix) urban environmental management and governance; and (x) sustainable monitoring and reporting, and database harmonisation.
10. Under the ASCC PoA, the following goals for promoting environmental sustainability will be pursued:

- Building national capacities to address issues and commitments to multilateral environmental agreements through awareness raising and informed policy choices;
- Effectively managing transboundary haze in accordance with the ASEAN Agreement on Transboundary Haze Pollution;
- Promoting the sustainable use of ASEAN's coastal and marine environment as a source of food supply and natural heritage;
- Conserving ASEAN's rich biological diversity and the fair and equitable sharing of the benefits from these biological and genetic resources;
- Promoting the sustainable management of forest resources and conserving critical ecosystems through the eradication of unsustainable practices and related activities, as well as strengthening preservation and management of ASEAN Heritage Parks;
- Promoting the sustainability of water resources to ensure adequate and quality water supply to meet ASEAN health and food needs;
- Promoting environmental education with the view to developing ASEAN citizens who are environmentally conscious;
- Promoting environmentally-sound technologies in partnership with the private sector;
- Ensuring quality living standards in ASEAN cities and urban areas;
- Augmenting and supporting the efforts of the ASEAN Economic Community through the energy sector in developing alternative fuels in order to prevent environmental devastation and resource exhaustion; and

- Promoting environmentally sound and socially responsible mineral development practices in the sustainable management and optimum utilisation of mineral resources.

## STRENGTHENING THE FOUNDATIONS OF REGIONAL SOCIAL COHESION

11. With globalisation, many of the region's traditional societies, with their cherished cultural norms and practices, are facing new challenges. As ASEAN continues in its community-building efforts, the concern is how to fulfill its aspirations for progress and prosperity while at the same time preserving its rich cultural heritage. Thus, the ASEAN Community envisaged to emerge from regional integration by 2020 is where people, amidst the diversity of their historical and cultural experience, are conscious of a common regional identity. This sense of regional identity and solidarity will have been built on years of cumulative interaction in all facets of social and economic life and at all levels — communities, governments and civil society.
12. Under the ASCC PoA, the goal of creating an ASEAN identity involves:

- Mainstreaming the promotion of ASEAN awareness, regional identity and values in national communications plans, educational curricula, people-to-people contact mainly through culture, arts and sports, especially among the youth, and the promotion of ASEAN languages learning through scholarships and exchanges of linguists;
- Preserving and promoting ASEAN cultural heritage and living traditions, as a vehicle to better understand the link between culture and development, and as a source of inspiration for future endeavours;
- Fostering dialogues among civilisations, cultures and religions as a means to foster better understanding, build confidence, and address threats to peace and security; and
- Promoting ASEAN's standing in the international community.

## IMPLEMENTATION MODALITIES

13. Specific measures envisaged under each of the four elements of the ASCC PoA are in **Appendix A**. These measures will be translated into more concrete projects and activities in the Vientiane Action Programme (VAP) covering the medium-term period 2004–2010. In general, ASCC activities fall into three categories: (i) nationally-driven initiatives: (ii) regional activities that enhance or complement national initiatives through sharing of experiences, information

and knowledge; establishment of regional networks; and joint regional approaches (e.g. the development of regional work programmes); and (iii) regional activities that involved setting up of regional mechanisms or standards.

14. For nationally-driven initiatives, ASEAN Member Countries shall prepare individual action plans for the period 2005–2010 consistent with their respective national policies and development priorities, and taking into account implementation capacity, including the availability of budgetary resources. Peer review and monitoring of these individual action plans will be done at the level of the relevant ASEAN body, consolidated by the ASEAN Secretariat, and reflected in the Secretary-General's report card to the ASEAN Summit.
15. The AMM shall take necessary follow-up measures to implement this Plan of Action including consultation and coordination with other relevant ASEAN Ministerial bodies; setting up ad-hoc groups as appropriate; reporting annually the progress of implementation to the ASEAN Summit; as well as introducing new measures and activities to strengthen the ASEAN Socio-Cultural Community as appropriate.
16. Self-reliance, shared responsibility and ownership are the principles that will guide the implementation of ASCC projects. The discipline of mainstreaming regional goals and commitments into the national plans and priorities will be of paramount importance in order to secure the resources required for implementation. Regional advocacy can provide the leverage to help drive national level actions and secure the necessary budget resources.
17. For regional level activities, particular attention will be given to activities that are best achieved through regional cooperation because of resulting economies of scale, value-added, or strategic interests. These activities will be implemented primarily through the relevant ASEAN bodies or through the ASEAN Secretariat.
18. Implementing the ASCC PoA will require intensive and sustained capacity building at the national and regional levels in a wide range of areas. Active participation of various stakeholders in ASCC activities will also be encouraged to draw from their wealth of expertise and experience and to promote a strong sense of commitment and ownership of projects and activities. Building region-wide networks of NGOs, training centres, academic institutions and other ASEAN organisations will gradually weave into the fabric of the ASEAN Community and help to strengthen social cohesion.
19. Mobilisation of resources will remain to be a key challenge for implementing various activities under the ASCC PoA. Resource mobilisation, however, should increasingly be viewed as a process of mobilising national, regional

and external resources — intellectual, technical and financial — in support of ASEAN priorities.

20. Finally, the ASEAN Foundation, with the full support of the Member Countries, should play a more active role in supporting the implementation of the ASCC PoA. Activities where the ASEAN Foundation could play an active role include: promoting access to ICT resources of differently advantaged groups (youth, women, persons with disabilities, and rural communities); promoting ASEAN awareness through language training and mass media; and youth exchange activities (such as through volunteer programmes and youth camps) with the view to facilitating greater awareness among ASEAN youth of the region's vision of a cohesive community of caring societies.
21. To realise the ASEAN Socio-Cultural Community by 2020, ASEAN shall endeavour to work towards the implementation of the areas of activities in the following Appendix. It is acknowledged that some of these activities are already ongoing and at various stages of implementation. Additional activities could also be implemented in the future. ASEAN will make every effort to promptly carry out activities, which gain consensus support.

Source: http://www.aseansec.org/16832.htm
Accessed date: 12 January 2009
Publisher: ASEAN Secretariat
Country: Jakarta
Date of Publication: 2005

# APPENDIX A

# SPECIFIC MEASURES

## I. BUILDING A COMMUNITY OF CARING SOCIETIES

a) Implement an "MDG Plus" initiative to accelerate poverty reduction in ASEAN;
b) Facilitate universal access to education for vulnerable groups (youth, women, persons with disabilities) to obtain the skills and knowledge necessary for gainful employment and meaningful participation in society;
c) Strengthen educational networks and institutional collaboration to improve standards of, and access to, education;
d) Ensure a better future for children by safeguarding their rights, ensuring their survival and development, and protecting them from abuse, neglect and violence;
e) Create enabling environments to prepare the youth for their future role as ASEAN citizens equipped with the necessary skills in leadership, entrepreneurship, and technical and vocational abilities;
f) Promote the equitable and effective participation of women in all fields both as agents and beneficiaries of development;
g) Promote community-based support systems for the elderly to supplement the role of families as primary caregiver and to build the capacity of health care professionals to address the needs of the elderly;
h) Ensure access of persons with disabilities to opportunities and protection against all forms of discrimination;
i) Strengthen social welfare mechanisms to make them more responsive to emerging social issues resulting from globalisation as well as demographic shifts;
j) Strengthen regional mechanisms and networks for combating human trafficking;
k) Ensure a healthy ASEAN Community living in harmony and safe environments;
l) Promote an enabling environment for the prevention of HIV/AIDS and for the comprehensive treatment, care and support for people living with HIV/AIDS in ASEAN;
m) Enhance the effectiveness of regional surveillance, preparedness, early warning, and response to emerging and resurging infectious diseases;

n) Ensure access to safe, quality and affordable medicines by building ASEAN capacity and competitiveness in pharmaceuticals as well as traditional medicines/complementary and alternative medicines;
o) Promote an enabling environment that allows ASEAN citizens to make healthy lifestyle choices accessible, affordable and sustainable and consistent with their views, beliefs, and culture in supportive environments;
p) Strengthen food security by enhancing stability in food production and supply and protect the region against fluctuations in production of basic commodities;
q) Strengthen food safety systems to ensure the protection of consumers' health by increasing the level of credibility and competency of regulatory authorities, and enhancing industry and consumer awareness and participation in food safety;
r) Promote activities related to community-based drug prevention aimed at families, schools and youth through publications, campaigns and training;
s) Strengthen cooperation with the private sector, in creating a science and technology community in the region;
t) Promote applied science and technology in socio-economic activities to improve social well-being; and
u) Establish efficient and well-functioning regional mechanisms for disaster prevention and management, including a coordinated response action plan in ASEAN and a network of training institutes.

## II. MANAGING THE SOCIAL IMPACT OF ECONOMIC INTEGRATION

a) Support the efforts of the ASEAN Economic Community to facilitate the movement of professional and skilled persons, including mutual skills recognition arrangements for qualification in professional services to realise regional economic integration in ASEAN;
b) Develop a well-prepared labour force in ASEAN that would benefit from and cope with the challenges of regional economic integration;
c) Establish a technologically competitive ASEAN, competent in strategic and enabling technologies, with an adequate pool of technically trained manpower, strong networks of scientific and technical institutions and centres of excellence;
d) Strengthen systems of social protection at the national level and work towards adoption of appropriate measures at the regional level to provide a minimum uniform coverage for skilled workers in the region;
e) Promote sound industrial relations, industrial harmony, high productivity and social practice through tripartite cooperation;

f) Secure the benefits of trade liberalisation in healthcare services in terms of increased availability and better accessibility to quality and affordable health-related products and services;
g) Enhance the competitiveness of ASEAN health and related industries;
h) Strengthen regional training on management of innovation and technology, and establish a mechanism for its regional certification and accreditation; and
i) Consider the establishment of centres for training and research to support the development of human resources and institutional capacity in regional as well as international cooperation.

## III. ENHANCING ENVIRONMENTAL SUSTAINABILITY

a) Effectively address global environmental concerns by building national capacities to address issues and commitments to multilateral environmental agreements through awareness-raising and informed policy choices;
b) Effectively manage transboundary haze pollution resulting from land and/or forest fires through concerted national efforts and intensified regional action and international cooperation in accordance with the provisions of the ASEAN Agreement on Transboundary Haze Pollution (the Haze Agreement), including the operationalisation of the ASEAN Centre for Transboundary Haze Pollution Control and the ASEAN Haze Fund;
c) Promote the sustainable use of ASEAN's coastal and marine environment through the implementation of the ASEAN criteria for marine waters, and marine heritage and protected areas;
d) Ensure the conservation of ASEAN's rich biological diversity through the implementation of the ASEAN Framework Agreement on Access to, and Equitable Sharing of Genetic and Biological Resources (expected to be concluded in 2004);
e) Promote the sustainable management of forest resources, which include protection of forests in an ecologically sound and integrated manner by developing and adopting common criteria for sustainable forest management in ASEAN, and eradicating unsustainable practices and related activities;
f) Promote the preservation of ASEAN Heritage Parks through coordinated systems of management;
g) Promote sustainability of water resources to ensure sufficient water quantity of acceptable quality to meet the needs of ASEAN in terms of health, food security and environmental sustainability through among others, the promotion of integrated river basin management and awareness promotion;
h) Promote environmental education through formal and non-formal education systems, capacity building and networking;

i) Promote environmentally-sound technologies in active partnership with the business sector through innovative financial mechanisms and labelling schemes;
j) Promote quality living standards in ASEAN cities/urban areas by achieving standards for environmental pollution reduction, including ensuring good ambient air and water quality, and minimum solid waste disposal;
k) Establish parameters for harmonising environmental policies, legislation, regulations, standards and databases, and preparing regular state of the environment reports; and
l) Pursue joint research in developing alternative fuels in order to prevent environmental devastation and resource exhaustion.

## IV. STRENGTHENING THE FOUNDATIONS OF REGIONAL SOCIAL COHESION

a) Promote ASEAN awareness with the ultimate goal of fostering an ASEAN regional identity by promoting interactions and exchanges among artists, writers, media practitioners, scholars, students, cultural entrepreneurs, professionals, experts in culture and sports and others;
b) Promote people-to-people contact, especially among the youth through youth volunteer programmes and youth camps;
c) Promote ASEAN languages learning through scholarships and exchange of linguists;
d) Coordinate efforts for the documentation, preservation and safeguarding of national and regional treasures and other properties, antiquities, and works of historic, archaeological, anthropological and scientific significance;
e) Enhance ASEAN cooperation in culture and information to formulate and implement effective and efficient programmes in a concerted manner in order to promote the rich and vast cultures of ASEAN;
f) Promote confidence-building at the national and regional levels by promoting the learning of core values, customs and traditions and integrating multiple perspectives on civilisations through regular dialogue mechanisms; and
g) Promote an image of unity, stability and dynamism of ASEAN by strengthening contacts with mass media, the international fora and other channels of communication.

Source: http://www.aseansec.org/16835.htm
Accessed date: 16 January 2009
Publisher: ASEAN Secretariat
Country: Jakarta
Date of Publication: 2005

# CHAPTER 50

# 2ND ASEAN-CANADA JOINT COOPERATION WORK PLAN (2007–2010)

Cooperation between ASEAN and Canada is guided by the *ASEAN-Canada Joint Cooperation Work Plan,* a framework for cooperation developed and initiated in 2005, under the auspices of the ASEAN-Canada Dialogue.

## OBJECTIVES:

Through the *ASEAN-Canada Joint Cooperation Work Plan*, ASEAN and Canada seek to:

- *enhance ASEAN-Canada relations through comprehensive dialogue and cooperation agenda over the next three years on a range of areas of mutual interest such as political-security, economic, socio-cultural and development areas as resources permit.*
- *support ASEAN's regional integration efforts, including through the implementation of the Vientiane Action Programme (VAP), the ASEAN Millennium Development Compact initiative, and the Initiative for ASEAN Integration (IAI) and other sub-regional growth arrangements in ASEAN designed to narrow the development gaps in ASEAN.*

In 2007–10, ASEAN and Canada cooperation initiatives will build on the progress achieved under the 1st ASEAN-Canada Joint Cooperation Work Plan (2005–07), including in thematic areas such as: health security, counter-terrorism and transnational crime, good governance, inter-faith/inter-cultural dialogue, sustainable development/environment, disaster risk management/preparedness, gender equality, trade and investment and other areas.

ASEAN and Canada also seek to strengthen cooperation in the context of enhanced collaboration in international fora, such as the ASEAN Regional Forum, APEC and within the United Nations. Furthermore, Canada and ASEAN encourage efforts to foster increased people-to-people and institutional linkages and to engage civil society in developing a people-centered ASEAN Community.

....

## PRIORITIES FOR ASEAN-CANADA COOPERATION IN 2007–08 INCLUDE:

- **Counter-Terrorism and Transnational Crime:** Implement a workshop on preventing bioterrorism and a workshop on forging cooperation among anti-terror agencies.
- **Economic Cooperation:** Reach agreement on ASEAN-Canada Trade and Investment Framework Arrangement.
- **Health Security:** Cooperate in the implementation of Canada-Asia Regional Emerging Infectious Diseases such as avian influenza and pandemic influenza.
- **Interfaith Dialogue:** Organize an event to explore potential areas for ASEAN-Canada cooperation on matters related to interfaith dialogue.
- **Technical assistance and capacity building with the ASEAN Secretariat:** Identify a process for initiating short-term technical assistance and capacity building (i.e., short-term experts) for the ASEAN Secretariat.

A. Under the Framework of the ASEAN-Canada Dialogue

| Areas of Cooperation/ Interest | Proposed Action/Initiative |
|---|---|
| **1. Official dialogue** | |
| 1.1 Enhanced senior-official-level dialogue with ASEAN on a broad range of political, security, development cooperation and economic issues. | 1.1.1 Hold annual ASEAN-Canada Dialogues. |
| 1.2 Follow-up mechanism | 1.2.1 Hold annual meetings of the ASEAN-Canada Informal Coordinating Mechanism (ICM) to monitor, coordinate and review the implementation of the Work Plan, including a time frame for implementation of the Work Plan. The ICM will be at the level of Director-General/Director comprising the ASEAN Country Coordinator, Canada and the ASEAN Secretariat. The ICM will be open to participation of other ASEAN Member Countries. The ICM will report to the ASEAN-Canada Dialogue. |

## 2. Thematic Issues

| | | |
|---|---|---|
| 2.1 Health security | 2.1.1 | Collaborate on health security issues with ASEAN, through the Canada-Asia Regional Emergency Infectious Diseases (CAREID) project, being implemented by the World Health Organization's regional offices and the Public Health Agency of Canada (PHAC), with funding from the Canadian International Development Agency (CIDA). |
| | 2.1.2 | Exchange information on infectious diseases and emergent public health incidents as appropriate. |
| | 2.1.3 | Work together on health security capacity building projects in ASEAN, including on Avian Influenza, HIV/AIDS prevention and education, and impact alleviation responses by addressing relevant priorities of the Vientiane Action Programme and the Third ASEAN Work Programme on HIV and AIDS (2006–2010)s, while exploring ways to enhance cooperation with ASEAN on health-related issues and initiatives. |
| 2.2 Counter-Terrorism and Transnational Crime | 2.2.1 | Implement, in a systematic and comprehensive manner, the ASEAN-Canada Joint Declaration for Cooperation to Combat International Terrorism. |
| | 2.2.2 | Continue to strengthen and deepen cooperation with ASEAN Member Countries in support of international counter-terrorism through signing, ratification or accession to, and implementation of relevant UN conventions, protocols, resolutions related to terrorism. |
| | 2.2.3 | Strengthen and deepen cooperation with ASEAN Member Countries against other transnational crimes inter alia, through encouraging signature, ratification or accession to, and implementation of the UN Convention Against Transnational Organized Crime. |
| | 2.2.4 | Cooperate and support ASEAN's efforts in implementing the ASEAN Convention on Counter Terrorism, signed in January 2007. |
| | 2.2.5 | Strengthen cooperation among law enforcement agencies and relevant authorities, in accordance with applicable treaties and domestic legislation, with respect to extradition and mutual legal assistance in criminal matters, including the confiscation of proceeds of crime and, where |

appropriate, the repatriation/sharing of confiscated proceeds of crimes.

2.2.6 Explore the possibility for cooperation, especially in capacity building and professional development in various areas related to transnational crime, such as illicit drug trafficking, money laundering, international economic crime and cybercrime.

....

2.2.10 Strengthen regional capacity, as appropriate, to prevent and respond to terrorism, which includes terrorist financing and weapons of mass destruction, including chemical, biological, radiological or nuclear materials as agents.

2.2.11 Strengthen efforts to prevent terrorists from acquiring weapons of mass destruction by promoting implementation of United Nations Security Council Resolution 1540 (2004), including through the sharing of best practices.

2.2.12 Expand Canada's engagement in the region on counter-terrorism through bilateral and multilateral fora which will include counter-terrorism capacity building program. These include support for training activities related to bio-terrorism and enhancing cooperation between national counter-terrorism units in the region. CTCBP Programming will also focus on current and possible future engagement with existing centres such as the International Law Enforcement Academy (ILEA) in Bangkok, the Southeast Asia Regional Centre for Counter Terrorism (SEARCCT) in Kuala Lumpur, and the Jakarta Center for Law Enforcement Cooperation (JCLEC).

2.3 Good Governance

2.3.1 In the framework of applicable national and international law, intensify cooperation to combat corruption, including denying a safe haven to those guilty of public corruption and cooperate in the recovery and return of the proceeds of corruption, as well as cooperate in the extradition and prosecution of those engaged in bribery, including in international business transactions.

| | | |
|---|---|---|
| | 2.3.2 | Promote and develop capacity building programmes on best practices in civil/public service management to create a professional and modern bureaucracy mechanism in ASEAN countries. |
| | 2.3.3 | Advocate for and support the enhancement of women's leadership role and participation in all levels of decision making and in the promotion of good governance. |
| 2.4 Sustainable Development/ Environment | 2.4.1 | Enhance cooperation in capacity building for ASEAN through the exchange of knowledge and experience between government authorities and experts. |
| | 2.4.2 | Examine scope for exchange of information on climate change, including land use, land use change and forestry aspects, noting the link between emissions reduction and poverty reduction. |
| | 2.4.3 | Undertake consultations on a regular basis and forge closer cooperation on environmental and related matters as well as to explore the opportunity to cooperate in joint research and development in protecting the environment and in promoting the efficient and sustainable use of natural resources. |
| | 2.4.4 | Enhance cooperation in capacity building for ASEAN in mitigating global environmental problems such as climate change and long-range transport of air pollutants. |
| | 2.4.5 | Promote and develop cooperation multilaterally, regionally and bilaterally, as appropriate, in areas such as:<br>a. Transboundary environmental pollution reduction, particularly transboundary haze pollution;<br>b. Biological diversity and natural heritage conservation, including implementation of obligations under the Convention on Biological Diversity;<br>c. Application of advance and environmentally-friendly technologies and best practices;<br>d. Sustainable water resource management, including groundwater;<br>e. Coastal and marine resource management/ environment; |

f. Sustainable forest management;
g. Urban environmental management and governance, including the ASEAN Initiative on Environmentally Sustainable Cities.
h. Responsible mining and minerals development;
i. Public awareness and environmental education;
j. Multilateral environmental agreements, in particular climate change, chemicals and chemical waste related conventions and partnerships, and
k. Air quality management;
l. Solid waste management.

| | |
|---|---|
| | 2.4.6 Promote cooperation towards achieving sustainable development and energy security goals, where applicable in research, development, production and use of alternative, renewable and other low emitting energy sources that could possibly include solar, wind, tides and waves, hydro, geothermal, biofuel, biomass, marsh gas etc. as well as in areas such as energy conservation, energy efficiency, clean energy and related capacity building. |
| | 2.4.7 Strengthen the knowledge and information database on environmental matters. |
| 2.5 Disaster Risk Management/ preparedness | 2.5.1 Strengthen existing national capabilities, build capacity and raise public awareness on disaster risk-management and emergency response as envisaged in the ASEAN Agreement on Disaster Management and Emergency Response (AADMER). |
| | 2.5.2 Support cooperation on emergency relief, rehabilitation and reconstruction process in the aftermath of natural disasters, such as typhoons, tsunamis and earthquakes. |
| | 2.5.3 Promote disaster risk reduction as a cross-cutting priority into development programming and institutional capacity building, at all levels of governance. |
| | 2.5.4 Cooperate with ASEAN Member Countries on the development and maintenance of early warning systems taking into consideration existing systems to ensure sustainability. |
| | 2.5.5 Share experience and best practices in the field of advance technologies in relation to public warning |

| | |
|---|---|
| | during natural, man-made and technological disasters or other major incident. |
| | 2.5.6 Initiate training and capacity building for personnel involved in emergency and disaster response and management of major incidents. |
| | 2.5.7 Encourage efforts to implement, as appropriate, the 2005 United Nations Commission on the Status of Women (UNCSW) Resolution on "Integrating a Gender Perspective in Post-disaster Relief, Recovery, Rehabilitation and Reconstruction Efforts, Including in the Aftermath of the Indian Ocean Tsunami Disaster." |
| | 2.5.8 Share public health experiences and expertise in disaster risk reduction. |
| | 2.5.9 Conduct joint training programmes and exchange information on new techniques on disaster risk management and emergency response, to enhance capacity of government authorities concerned. |
| 2.6 Gender Equality | 2.6.1 Assist the ASEAN Committee on Women (ACW)'s efforts to promote the full implementation of the Millennium Development Goals (MDG) and to accelerate the full and effective implementation of the Beijing Declaration and Platform for Action, the Convention on the Elimination of all forms of Discrimination against Women (CEDAW), as well as the Declaration on the Elimination of Violence Against Women in the ASEAN Region. |
| | 2.6.2 Explore opportunities to assist with regional priority projects as outlined in the 3rd Report on the Advancement of Women in ASEAN. |
| 2.7 People-to-people and institutional linkages | 2.7.1 Explore opportunities for Canada and other interested ASEAN partners to offer professional training to Government officials in public policy areas of mutual interest. |
| | 2.7.2 Explore the opportunity for university linkages between ASEAN Member Countries and Canada and to cooperate in joint research, including through the ASEAN University Network (AUN). |
| | 2.7.3 Work together with the ASEAN Senior Officials on Youth in addressing priorities for youth leadership development and greater involvement of youth in national and regional development processes. |

2.7.4 Support the ASEAN Millennium Development Compact initiative, and develop joint activities to sustain partnership for regional integration.

2.7.5 Promote interaction and networking between government authorities involving culture, cultural institutions, museums, archives and libraries as well as artist and experts.

2.7.6 Share Information on preservation and restoration of cultural and historical heritage, both tangible and intangible.

2.7.7 Strengthen and deepen cooperation with ASEAN Member Countries in support of cultural relations, inter alia, through encouraging signing, ratification or accession to, and implementation of relevant UN conventions, protocols, resolutions.

2.7.8 Establish an ASEAN-Canada fellowship programme similar to the SEAMEO-Jasper Research Award in 2007 to commemorate 30th anniversary of Canada-ASEAN relations. (The Jasper Award was established in 1990 with the support of the Government of Canada as a way of recognizing exemplary research conducted by Southeast Asian Nationals in the region. The yearly award seeks to encourage young scholars to conduct research on a relevant theme on social development in Southeast Asia and to stimulate continued interaction and knowledge-sharing among Southeast Asian and Canadian researchers.)

2.7.9 Support efforts to establish a network among existing human rights mechanisms in response to ASEAN's Vientiane Action Programme.

2.7.10 Encourage efforts to promote and protect the rights of women and children, persons with disabilities and older persons in line with the Vientiane Action Programme.

2.7.11 Encourage efforts to promote and protect the rights of migrant workers in Southeast Asia in compliance with the Cebu Declaration on the Protection and Promotion of the Rights of Migrant Workers adopted at the 12th ASEAN Summit in Cebu, Philippines.

2.7.12 Exchange best practices on investigation of international crimes relating to women and children.

| | | |
|---|---|---|
| | 2.7.13 | Assist and support efforts to increase effective participation of civil society and private sector in tackling poverty and social welfare issues. |
| | 2.7.14 | Exchange information about mutual recognition of skills and qualifications between ASEAN Member Countries and Canada. |
| | 2.7.15 | Collaborate as appropriate with the ASEAN Foundation in strengthening cooperation between Canada and ASEAN especially in promoting people-to-people interaction and awareness between the two sides. |
| 2.8 Interfaith/Inter cultural Dialogue | 2.8.1 | Explore potential areas for ASEAN-Canada cooperation on matters related to interfaith dialogue to further promote peace, understanding and tolerance. |
| | 2.8.2 | Encourage international/multilateral efforts promoting and advocating interfaith dialogue such as the Tripartite Forum on Interfaith Cooperation for Peace (TFICP) in New York. |
| 2.9 Initiative for ASEAN Integration (IAI) | 2.9.1 | Encourage ASEAN's regional integration efforts, including through the implementation of the Vientiane Action Programme (VAP), the Initiative for ASEAN Integration (IAI) and sub-regional growth areas, which are designed to narrow the development gaps in ASEAN, including Cambodia, Laos, Myanmar and Vietnam (CLMV), and to expedite regional integration. |
| | 2.9.2 | Enhance the ASEAN Secretariat's capacity in the formulation, implementation, monitoring and evaluation of the Narrowing the Development Gap (NDG) projects, and in other areas where appropriate, such as through the provision of short-term technical assistance. |
| 2.10 Expanded education, science and technology (S&T) cooperation | 2.10.1 | Seek ways to engage in the development of human infrastructure and resources through educational exchange, joint research and training programmes, including through the ASEAN University Network. |
| | 2.10.2 | Identify and promote S&T cooperative activities such as ASEAN-Canada virtual academic networks in key mutual sectors including alternative and clean energy; health and life sciences, pandemic diseases; environment; agriculture and bio-agriculture; marine science; biotechnology; |

| | |
|---|---|
| | food science; microelectronics and information technology; materials science; earth science; technology transfer and management in collaboration and with the participation of the private sector. |
| | 2.10.3 Engage with ASEAN in joint research activities, organization of scientific seminars, conferences, symposia and workshops; facilitate visits and exchange of experts and scientists; and, encourage awareness and advocacy strategies to popularize science and technology. |
| | 2.10.4 Design and implement training design and implement training programmes to address the needs of high value-added industries that enhance ASEAN global competitiveness. |
| 2.11 Food, Agriculture and Forestry | 2.11.1 Promote networking between government authorities concerned, together with agriculture and food experts, laboratories, and agriculture and food-related academic institutions of ASEAN and Canada. |

B. Under the Framework of the ASEAN-Canada Senior Economic Officials' Meeting (SEOM)

| | |
|---|---|
| 1 Enhanced senior-official-level dialogue with ASEAN on trade and investment issues | 1.1 To engage ASEAN Economic Ministers and Canadian Trade Ministers, where appropriate, to enhance trade and investment linkages. |
| | 1.2 Hold annual ASEAN-Canada Senior Economic Officials' Meetings (SEOM), with the 3rd ASEAN-Canada SEOM scheduled for fall 2007 in Canada. |
| | 1.3 Explore convening SEOM-Canada meetings back-to-back with Canada-ASEAN trade/investment missions, where possible, as a strategy to generate increased involvement of the business community towards achieving a more robust ASEAN-Canada economic partnership. |
| 2 Expanded collaboration in international fora on trade and investment issues | 2.1 Strengthen cooperation in multilateral trading system, especially the World Trade Organization (WTO) and support the early accession of Lao PDR to the WTO. |
| | 2.2 Determine ways in which Canada can work with ASEAN Member Countries in sharing information and advancing common WTO and Doha Round |

| | |
|---|---|
| | objectives (e.g., progressing the Doha Development Agenda, collaboration on Agriculture issues in the Cairns Group etc.). |
| | 2.3 Support ASEAN's efforts towards a strengthened rules-based multilateral trading system by taking full account of the special needs and concerns of developing countries to better integrate development dimensions into the multilateral trading system. ASEAN notes the importance of WTO capacity building as a means to permit developing countries to reap the full benefits of their membership in the WTO. |
| 3 Trade and investment capacity building | 3.1 Share Canadian expertise in customs and border control practices (e.g., training and information sessions via video-conferencing or appropriate working-level visits including the possibility of appropriate working-level visits of ASEAN's customs and border control agencies to Canada, as resources permit).<br>3.2 Promote trade and investment promotion best practices with ASEAN Member Countries through possible Canadian participation in international and regional meetings/seminars held on this subject.<br>3.3 Consider ASEAN requests to share information and provide assistance on the technical aspects of trade and investment arrangements operating under the North America Free Trade Agreement (NAFTA) including: (a) the treatment of rules of origin; (b) the treatment of services; (c) dispute settlement/resolution mechanisms; and (d) Canadian standards in food safety.<br>3.4 Support capacity-building on investment protection and promotion with ASEAN Member Countries.<br>3.5 Cooperate to overcome existing trade and investment obstacles. |
| 4 Increased business community involvement in promoting two-way trade and investment relations | 4.1 Encourage greater participation and interest from small and medium enterprises (SMEs) in ASEAN-Canada trade promotion events.<br>4.2 Collaborate as appropriate on outreach organized by Canadian or ASEAN foreign missions (embassies/high commissions), with private sector participation, both in Canada and ASEAN Member Countries to expand the breadth of two-way commercial engagement. |

| | |
|---|---|
| | 4.3 Liaise as appropriate with the various Southeast Asia-focused bilateral business associations in ASEAN and Canada to brainstorm on future initiatives that could be undertaken collectively to promote two-way trade and investment relations. |
| | 4.4 Work with business organizations such as the Canadian Commercial Corporation; Export Development Canada; the Canadian-Council of Chief Executives, the Canadian Chamber of Commerce; and Canadian Manufactures and Exporters, to identify and track opportunities to increase business community involvement. |
| | 4.5 Promote practical measures to encourage greater private sector interaction in order to promote two-way trade and investment flows. |
| | 4.6 Continue efforts to organize Trade Missions as part of efforts to strengthen ASEAN-Canada business alliances. |
| | 4.7 Encourage greater private sector interaction with ASEAN-Canada SEOM. |
| 5 Increased cooperation on trade and investment policy | 5.1 Engage in preliminary discussions with individual ASEAN Member Countries on investment protection provisions as appropriate. |
| | 5.2 Consider opportunities for further cooperation on trade and investment policy, including through a proposed ASEAN-Canada Trade and Investment Framework Agreement (TIFA). |
| | 5.3 Encourage cooperation between ASEAN Coordinating Committee on Investment (CCI) and Canadian business organizations. |

C. Broader International Collaboration

| | |
|---|---|
| 1 Expanded collaboration in international fora. | 1.1 Strengthen cooperation with ASEAN Member Countries in the context of the ASEAN Regional Forum (ARF) and develop joint activities, as appropriate, in support of shared objectives in promoting peace and security in the region. [For e.g., Canada and Brunei intend to co-host the ARF ISG process during the 2007–2008 ARF Intersessional year.] |

| | |
|---|---|
| | 1.2 Expand and deepen interaction and coordination within multilateral frameworks, including the United Nations system, the WTO, and when deemed appropriate, carry out consultations between ASEAN and Canada at the margins of those fora. |
| | 1.3 Working through our respective constituency offices to the Asian Development Bank to support the ADB's efforts at refocusing its regional cooperation and integration strategy on four key pillars: regional infrastructure and interconnectivity; the provision of regional public goods; and support for regional trade and financial integration issues, with inclusive growth as an over-arching goal. |
| | 1.4 Enhance the information-sharing process with ASEAN members regarding the G8 Summit agenda and related policies and initiatives prior to and/or after key G8 events (e.g., briefing Ottawa-based ASEAN officials and/or ASEAN officials attending the ASEAN-Canada SOM.) |
| 2 Track II/civil society engagement | 2.1 Support efforts to engage civil society in developing a people-centered ASEAN Community. |

*Source*: http://www.aseansec.org/20800.pdf

# CHAPTER 51

# ASEAN PLUS THREE COOPERATION WORK PLAN (2007–2017)

To realize the goals and objectives set forth in the Second Joint Statement on East Asia Cooperation: "Building on the Foundations of ASEAN Plus Three Cooperation", adopted by the Heads of State/Government of ASEAN Plus Three countries on 20 November 2007, this Work Plan is formulated to serve as the master plan to enhance ASEAN Plus Three relations and cooperation in a comprehensive and mutually beneficial manner for the next ten years (2007–2017). This Work Plan shall also support the establishment of the ASEAN Community by 2015.

In light of the above, the ASEAN Plus Three countries shall pursue the following joint actions and measures as well as capacity building activities, through closer consultation and coordination with sectoral bodies, in accordance with their respective laws and regulations:

## SECTION A: POLITICAL AND SECURITY COOPERATION

### 1. Deepen political and security cooperation

1.1. Utilise the ASEAN Plus Three process as the framework for building mutual understanding, confidence and solidarity. The ASEAN Plus Three countries are encouraged to constructively undertake, with increasing candor and transparency, exchanges on their strategic outlooks, assessments of national and regional developments and briefings on their respective strategies and plans on vital issues.

1.2. Continue to hold the ASEAN Plus Three Summit annually in conjunction with the ASEAN Summit.

1.3. Continue high-level consultations and increase exchanges between officials of the ASEAN Plus Three countries in the political and security areas.

1.4. Cooperate to strengthen the multilateral system as well as expand and deepen interaction and coordination, within multilateral frameworks, including the United Nations.

1.5. Cooperate to promote good governance, including strengthening the rule of law, promoting human rights, enhancing administrative effectiveness, efficiency, transparency through policy dialogue and capacity building activities and participation by relevant segments of society in policy-making process.

1.6. In the framework of applicable national and international law, intensify cooperation to combat corruption, including denying a safe haven to those guilty of public corruption.

....

1.8. Strengthen cooperation through exchanges of experts, joint research projects and joint seminars in order to strengthen the linkages between ASEAN Plus Three government-affiliated policy and strategic research institutes.

1.9. Enhance technical assistance and capacity building in support of efforts to address traditional and non-traditional security issues.

## 2. Peace and stability cooperation in the region

2.1. Strengthen cooperation and increase consultations through the ASEAN Regional Forum (ARF) and the ASEAN Plus Three process with the view to ensuring peace, security and stability in the region.

2.2. Promote peace building through, inter alia, sharing of experiences on peace building operations and exchanges of experts and academics on peace studies.

2.3. Enhance multilateral and regional cooperation in disarmament and non-proliferation of weapons of mass destruction and their means of delivery and related materials.

2.4. Cooperate closely on action-oriented measures including participation of civil society and industrial sectors in opposing the proliferation of WMD by adopting and enforcing effective export controls, and on disarmament issues with the objective of total elimination of all WMD including nuclear weapons, in accordance with their national legislation and consistent with international law.

## 3. Counter-Terrorism

3.1. Strengthen cooperation in the field of border management to jointly address matters of common concern, including forgeries of identification and travel documents, by enhancing the use of relevant technologies to effectively stem the flow of terrorists and criminals, to monitor and curb their means of operations as well as enhancing cooperation to prevent the organisation, instigation and support for groups that carry out acts detrimental to the security and stability of ASEAN Plus Three countries.

3.2. Enhance cooperation in information sharing on terrorists and transnational criminal organisations, including their leaders and members, operational methods and supporting infrastructures, linkages, as well as criminal activities.

3.3. Implement measures to combat money laundering and terrorist financing, in accordance with the recommendations of the Financial Action Task Force (FATF).

3.4. Work towards the elimination of smuggling of small arms and light weapons, as a major contribution to the national and international efforts of counter terrorism.

3.5. Support the implementation of the ASEAN Convention on Counter Terrorism.

3.6. Support the implementation of and the accession to relevant international conventions and protocols on counter terrorism and the finalisation of a UN comprehensive convention on international terrorism.

3.7. Ensure that any measures taken to combat terrorism are implemented in accordance with international laws, in particular, regarding human rights, displaced persons and humanitarian concerns.

3.8. Cooperate to support development initiatives aimed at enhancing quality of life, rule of law, good governance and community awareness in order to reduce the conditions that terrorists seek to exploit.

## 4. Maritime Cooperation

4.1. Enhance maritime cooperation on safety of navigation, such as through implementation of relevant international and regional treaties and agreements and through, inter alia, the promotion of information sharing, and technology cooperation projects such as through exchanges of visits of authorities concerned, training of personnel in search and rescue and other areas, where applicable.

4.2. Forge closer cooperation in fighting against sea piracy, armed robbery against ships, hijacking and smuggling, in accordance with international laws and without impinging on the sovereignty and territorial integrity of ASEAN Plus Three countries.

## 5. OTHER NON-TRADITIONAL SECURITY ISSUES

....

5.4. Strengthen cooperation and render mutual assistance in combating and suppressing cyber crimes including cooperation among law enforcement agencies, taking into account the need of each country to develop laws to address cyber crimes.

## SECTION B: ECONOMIC AND FINANCIAL COOPERATION

### 1. Trade and investment

1.1. Conclude the ASEAN+1 FTAs according to their schedules and to ensure their smooth implementation in order to enhance overall economic growth and development conducive to businesses.

1.2. Continue efforts towards promoting and strengthening economic cooperation in the East Asian region, including an idea of region-wide FTAs, taking into account the recommendations of various studies that have been completed or are currently being undertaken.

1.3. Phase out tariffs and non-tariff barriers to ensure free flow of goods in ASEAN Plus Three countries, in accordance with the results of WTO negotiations and relevant FTA/EPA negotiations and continue to accord Generalised System of Preference (GSP) status and preferential treatment for Developing and Least Developed Countries.

1.4. Encourage discussion on mobility of labor and its influence on economies and other related issues, taking into account the respective circumstances of each country.

1.5. Strengthen cooperation in the multilateral trading system, especially in the World Trade Organization (WTO) and support the early accession of Lao PDR to the WTO.

1.6. Jointly pursue the successful conclusion of the negotiations of the Doha Development Agenda (DDA) and endeavour to ensure that the development dimension of the DDA is embodied in a comprehensive package that would deliver tangible, fair and effective development benefits to all developing member countries.

1.7. Strengthen efforts to facilitate trade through improving customs procedures such as promotion of pre-arrival customs processing/clearance of goods, audit-based practices of customs control, standardisation of practices to assess customs value and origin determination.

1.8. Work towards expediting customs clearance and release, using ASEAN Single Window as a basis.

1.9. Promote the application of information and communication technology (ICT) in the field of customs for better management and service.

1.10. Promote the transparency of policies to facilitate trade and investment expansion, including those enhancing conducive business environment, business mobility and trade financing.

1.11. Encourage free flow of services and progressively liberalise trade in services in accordance with the results of WTO negotiations and relevant FTA/EPA negotiations consistent with the WTO rules and principles.

1.12. Strengthen the role of the East Asia Business Council (EABC) in pushing forward economic cooperation in East Asia and to encourage appropriate activities aimed at promoting business interaction in the region.

1.13. Provide regional support to foster an attractive investment climate through sharing best practices, giving mutual encouragement, responding to the requirements of investors, extending technical assistance and exchanging statistical information.

1.14. Consider conducting comprehensive studies on the possible establishment of an East Asia Investment Area by expanding the ASEAN Investment Area.

1.15. Promote cooperation between investment promotion agencies and facilitate mutual investment promotion missions by respective business communities.

1.16. Promote understanding of each other's policies, regulations and legislations pertaining or related to trade, competition policy, services, investment and industry as well as the sharing of experiences and best practices among ASEAN Plus Three countries.

## 2. Financial cooperation

....

## 3. Standards and conformance

3.1. Cooperate to support ASEAN's efforts to adopt and use international standards as the basis for technical regulations, conformity assessment procedures and Sanitary and Phytosanitary Measures (SPS) standards, as appropriate and consistent with WTO principles.

3.2. Promote information exchange with ASEAN regarding development standards, technical regulations and conformity assessment procedures, including the domestic implementation of WTO TBT agreements.

3.3. Undertake appropriate measures to ensure greater participation and contribution of ASEAN Member Countries in the international and regional bodies related to standards and conformance.

## 4. Intellectual Property Rights

4.1. Promote the exchange of views, experiences and information in the creation, utilization, protection, commercialization and enforcement of intellectual property rights and related issues of mutual concern.

4.2. Undertake appropriate measures to strengthen IP systems and promote greater public awareness of IP and IPR issues in the field of education and industries, the commercialisation of IP, the utilisation of IP information, and technology transfer, in accordance with the relevant provisions in the WTO TRIPS Agreement.

4.3. Promote the harmonization of IP laws and systems, where possible, to enhance trade and investment in the region and facilitate intellectual property rights registration.

4.4. Promote cooperative activities to increase the level of knowledge among a broader section of government officials and IP professionals so that they may contribute to business growth and development.

4.5. Endeavour to encourage technology-transfer policies on the part of multinational corporations operating in the region.

## 5. Transport

5.1. Forge closer cooperation to enhance transport infrastructure, networks and operations, including air, maritime, road, rail, and multi-modal transport, for fast, efficient and safe movement of people and goods, as well as for clean urban transport, in and among ASEAN Member Countries and between ASEAN and the Plus Three Countries.

5.2. Enhance cooperation in the development of new transportation systems, such as "intelligent Transportation Systems-ITS," promotion of public transport, road networks and structures, environment-friendly maintenance, technological development and regulations, road safety management.

5.3. Enhance cooperation in capacity-building and human resources development, in the areas of transport policy, planning and regulation and in transferring and sharing of technology as mutually agreed.

5.4. Enhance cooperation in observing international rules on safety and security in air, land, and maritime transport, taking into account relevant international laws and in accordance with the domestic laws of the ASEAN Plus Three countries.

5.5. Enhance cooperation to promote transport linkages, focusing on air connectivity, among ASEAN Plus Three Countries, as appropriate.

5.6. Expedite the completion of the Singapore-Kunming Rail Link (SKRL) project.

## 6. Tourism

6.1. Promote the development of quality tourism through, where appropriate, the promotion of ASEAN's environmental management standards and certification programmes for sustainable tourism, and forge concrete collaboration in cultural and eco-tourism, cruise tourism, youth exchange, manpower development, joint tourism marketing and promotion, and quality assurance, as well as safety measures for tourists.

6.2. Promote linkages and strengthen cooperation among national tourism organisations and training institutions, covering areas such as tourism information exchange, human resource development and crisis communications, and encourage the involvement of the private sector in such cooperation.

## 7. Food, agriculture, fisheries and forestry

7.1. Forge closer cooperation in agriculture in key areas of mutual interests, including research and development, technology transfer, crops, horticultural plants cultivation, biotechnology application, fertiliser, agricultural infrastructure, post-harvest technology, livestock, fisheries, aquaculture, organic farming, as well as agricultural cooperatives.

7.2. Promote networking in areas of key mutual interest between government authorities concerned, as well as between agricultural and food-related research institutions of ASEAN Plus Three Countries.

7.3. Cooperate in strengthening agricultural markets and promoting linkages and cooperation between relevant agriculture authorities to enhance accessibility of ASEAN agricultural products into global markets.

7.4. Promote cooperation in rural financial institutions, such as agricultural banks and micro-financing arrangements.

7.5. Provide opportunities for ASEAN farmers, including young farmers, and those engaged in agribusiness to learn and develop more efficient farming practices and management skills through training and information sharing with Plus Three Countries farmers.

7.6. Enhance capacity-building and human resources development in areas of agriculture where there is key mutual interest through training courses, seminars, workshops, job attachment and scholarship schemes.

7.7. Promote closer cooperation in food security, including exchange of information on major food commodities, food handling and food safety.

7.8. Enhance cooperation in sustainable forest management, and deepen cooperation in the Asian Forest Partnership (AFP) as an effective way to tackle the challenges of forest management in Asia through collaborative efforts, especially law enforcement mechanisms of illegal logging and its associated trade, prevention of forest fires, reforestation of degraded lands, and a phased approach to certification.

7.9. Cooperate on fisheries and forest products development and promotion schemes.

7.10. Promote regionalization of the code of conduct for responsible fisheries.

## 8. Minerals

8.1. Facilitate trade and investment in the mineral sector for mutual benefits, as well as forge closer cooperation in capacity building in the mineral sector.
8.2. Enhance collaboration in research and development activities for the sustainable development of the mineral sector.
8.3. Encourage private sector participation and public-private sector collaboration in the development and/or implementation of joint cooperation in programmes and activities related to the sustainable development of mineral resources in the region.
8.4. Promote technical information exchange, experience and best practices on, among others, the development of the ASEAN Mineral Database, scientific and technological research and development of geosciences, the sustainable development of mineral resources.

## 9. Small and medium enterprises (SMEs)

....

## 10. Information and communication technology (ICT)

10.1. Promote cooperation activities, particularly in the areas of bridging the digital divide, telemedicine, e-government, e-commerce, distance education, cyber security and network monitoring, and for mutual recognition of electronic signatures for cross-border transactions.
10.2. Enhance cooperation and development of interconnected, high-capacity and resilient information infrastructure between ASEAN and the Plus Three Countries through various measures, e.g., policies and regulations for next generation network (NGN), Ipv6, wireless broadband, and applications of the suitable, new and emerging technologies.
10.3. Facilitate cooperation in regulatory framework to support trade, investment and business activities in ICT sector, harmonization of frequency, standards and interoperability of products/services, and consumer protection.

## 11. Development cooperation

11.1. Support the Initiative for ASEAN Integration (IAI) and other sub-regional endeavours such as the Ayeyawady-Chao Phraya-Mekong Economic Cooperation Strategy (ACMECS), the ASEAN-Mekong Basin Development Cooperation (AMBDC), the Brunei Darussalam-Indonesia-Malaysia-Philippines East ASEAN Growth Area (BIMP-EAGA), the Cambodia-Lao

PDR-Viet Nam (CLV) Development Triangle, the Greater Mekong Sub Region (GMS), the Indonesia-Malaysia-Thailand Growth Triangle (IMT-GT) and the East-West Economic Corridor (EWEC) to narrow the development gaps in ASEAN in order to expedite regional integration.

11.2. Continue to develop resources and infrastructure jointly for growth areas and to continue mobilizing and exploring the expansion of financial resources for development with active participation of the private sector.

11.3. Promote development cooperation in accordance with international norms, rules and disciplines.

## SECTION C: ENERGY, ENVIRONMENT, CLIMATE CHANGE AND SUSTAINABLE DEVELOPMENT COOPERATION

### 1. Energy Cooperation

1.1. Pursue energy security, sustainable development and economic growth in an integrated approach taking into account specific and diverse national circumstances.

1.2. Promote energy diversification through information exchanges and researches on alternative, new and renewable energy development such as solar, wind, sea tides and waves, hydro, geothermal, clean coal technology, biofuels, biomass, gas and marsh gas, and others, taking into consideration each country's specific national circumstances; and for those Member countries which choose to do so, the use of civilian nuclear energy, while giving careful and due regards to the security, environmental, health and internationally-recognized safety standards of the energy source.

1.3. Promote energy conservation and energy efficiency as well as the use of clean and environment-friendly technologies such as new vehicle technologies.

1.4. Endeavour to create a more favourable market environment with a view to creating efficient energy market, facilitating regional energy production and trade, promoting investment in energy infrastructure and facilities.

1.5. Improve energy efficiency, where possible, in all sectors, such as the industrial, transport, residential/commercial and power sectors, through setting individual goals and formulating action plans.

1.6. Enhance cooperation on emergency preparedness by making full use of the ASEAN Plus Three Energy Security Communication System.

1.7. Promote greater cooperation and market transparency, including through the Joint Oil Data Initiative, and intensify the exchange of energy data, where possible, and the sharing of national energy policies on a voluntary basis.

1.8. Explore means of supporting the national rural electrification programmes of concerned ASEAN member countries.

1.9. Support the work of the ASEAN Centre for Energy.

1.10. Consider specific projects and proposals on energy issues raised within various regional processes such as the EAS and APEC.

1.11. Promote dialogue with Middle East oil and gas producing countries to enhance mutual understanding and cooperation between oil-producing and oil-consuming countries.

1.12. Promote cooperation for diversification of energy transportation routes to enhance energy security.

## 2. Environment and sustainable development

2.1. Forge closer cooperation in protecting the environment and promoting sustainable use of natural resources.

2.2. Forge closer cooperation among ASEAN Plus Three countries to mitigate and adapt to climate change.

2.3. Strengthen cooperation, among others, in the development, transfer and diffusion of technologies to raise the capacity of ASEAN Plus Three countries to respond to climate change.

2.4. Forge closer cooperation in the following areas:

(a) transboundary environmental pollution reduction, particularly transboundary haze pollution,
(b) biological diversity and natural heritage conservation,
(c) application of advanced and environment-friendly technologies and best practices,
(d) sustainable water resource management, including groundwater,
(e) coastal and marine environment,
(f) sustainable forest management, including combating activities associated with illegal encroachment and destruction of forest resources,
(g) Urban environmental management and governance, especially the ASEAN Initiative on Environmentally Sustainable Cities,
(h) responsible mining and minerals development,
(i) public awareness and environmental education,
(j) multilateral environmental agreements, in particular climate change and chemical and chemical waste related conventions and partnerships, and
(k) air quality management.

2.5. Enhance cooperation in capacity building in the area of environment through the following:

(a) exchanges of information and experiences between and among government authorities, institutions and experts,

(b) provision of training courses and scholarships,
(c) undertaking joint research and development and networking among research/academic institutions, and
(d) technology transfer.

2.6. Promote 3R (Reduce, Reuse and Recycle) and environmental sound management of waste.
2.7. Promote sustainable development as a means to reduce negative aspects of development on the environment.

## SECTION D: SOCIO-CULTURAL AND DEVELOPMENT COOPERATION

1. Develop cooperative activities towards realising the UN Millennium Development Goals.
2. Strengthen the Networking of East Asian Cultural Heritage (NEACH), the East Asia Forum (EAF), the Network of East Asian Think Tanks (NEAT) and the Network of East Asian Studies (NEAS), and consider their recommendations as supplementary source of inputs for policy formulation that is based on research and inter-sectoral consultations.

## 3. Poverty alleviation

3.1. Open ASEAN Plus Three countries' markets to the products of their poorer citizens, including assistance in marketing their products, in accordance with multilateral or bilateral agreements and arrangements, and provide assistance to education, skills training, public health, the protection of their work environment and the building of effective national and community institutions.
3.2. Establish benchmarks and monitoring mechanisms to measure progress toward the Millennium Development Goals, extending assistance to enable such progress to be made, such as networks among "poverty alleviation facilitators", poverty-related data collection systems and monitoring systems for poverty alleviation programmes.
3.3. Forge closer cooperation in capacity building in the area of rural development and poverty eradication for government officials, experts, practitioners through information and experience sharing activities, people-exchange programme, training courses.
3.4. Monitor the effects of trade liberalization and economic integration on rural development and poverty alleviation programme, including social protection systems and ICT as a tool for rural development and poverty alleviation.

## 4. Promoting development of vulnerable groups

4.1. Support efforts to provide care to and promote empowerment of vulnerable groups, such as children, youth, women, the elderly and persons with disabilities.

4.2. Support efforts to ensure access of persons with disabilities to opportunities and protection against all forms of discrimination, including the promotion of their human rights.

4.3. Support efforts to promote equitable participation of and equitable distribution of benefits for women in the development process by eliminating all forms of discrimination against them.

4.4. Strengthen cooperation in addressing violence against women and children.

## 5. Culture and people-to-people contact

5.1. Cooperate in the promotion of people-to-people contacts involving, inter alia, parliamentarians, government officials, academia, youth, media, cultural experts, sports persons and representatives of business, industries, and think tank institutions.

5.2. Promote education, access to justice, and the empowerment of moderates in various religions as well as promote inter-faith and inter-cultural dialogue to enhance mutual understanding among different cultures and religions, as well as promote universal ideals of religious moderation and tolerance.

5.3. Support efforts to engage civil society in developing a people-centered ASEAN Community.

5.4. Promote cultural understanding and greater awareness of each other's culture, through regularly held cultural festivals, film festivals, art exhibitions, workshops and other events, such as the East Asia Week.

5.5. Promote interaction, networking, and exchange of visits between government authorities involved in cultural affairs, as well as between cultural institutions, museums, archives and libraries, as well as artists, experts, practitioners in theatre, music, acrobatics, dance, folk art, and cinematography.

5.6. Render mutual assistance and cooperation for the protection, preservation, and restoration of cultural and historical heritage, both tangible and intangible, according to the laws and regulations of each country, enhance cooperation to combat pillage, illicit trafficking and smuggling of moveable cultural property.

5.7. Promote closer cooperation and collaboration between cultural, creative and design industries including joint venture and co-production.

5.8. Promote exchanges and cooperation in the area of journalism, including press, radio, and television.
5.9. Promote research and policy dialogue on the impact of globalization, modernization and ICT revolution on youth with a view to exchanging lessons learned and best practices.
5.10. Intensify youth exchanges, for deeper mutual understanding and forging a sense of commonality, as well as continue to hold the ASEAN Plus Three Young Leaders Forum.

## 6. Education

6.1. Encourage investments in education and training to accelerate learning opportunities for out-of-school children and youth and to upgrade the quality of educational institutions, including human resources development for teachers, lecturers and administrative personnel.
6.2. Promote collaboration, networking, and research and development among institutions and authorities involved in education.
6.3. Promote higher education cooperation, increase linkages between universities through the ASEAN University Network (AUN) and encourage credit transfers between universities ASEAN Plus Three countries.
6.4. Support research activities and exchanges of ASEAN Plus Three scholars and professionals interested in the ASEAN Plus Three relationship.
6.5. Continue to make efforts to expedite visa application procedures for students and intellectuals of ASEAN Member Countries who travel to the Plus Three countries for academic purposes, in accordance with existing national regulations.
6.6. Cultivate an East Asian identity through promotion of ASEAN Studies and East Asian Studies in the region.

## 7. Science and technology

7.1. Broaden and expand exchanges and cooperation between the scientific and technological communities in ASEAN Plus Three countries.
7.2. Cooperate in the fields of technology transfer and technology management on issues covering R&D and IPR management, technology commercialization, public-private sector collaboration, and science, technology and innovation indicators.
7.3. Promote research and technology development in areas of having potential for commercial applications such as biotechnology, food technology, new

materials, microelectronics and Information technology, marine resources, new and renewable energy, and space technology.

7.4. Strengthen cooperation in meteorology addressing climate information and prediction services, weather observations and climate change.

7.5. Promote the awareness of specific elements of community such as private sector and youth in science and technology through the participation in various activities such as ASEAN Food Conference, ASEAN Science and Technology Week, S&T Youth Camp and other relevant events.

## 8. Public health

8.1. Strengthen cooperation in capacity building and enhance cooperation and technical assistance for government authorities and members of the private sector, civil society institutions, laboratories, and experts in the area of public and environmental health.

8.2. Strengthen cooperation in capacity building of government staffs in public health emergency disaster management.

8.3. Promote networking among government authorities and members of the private sectors (of ASEAN Plus Three countries, including between laboratories, research institutions and experts.

8.4. Promote research and development and human resources development in the areas related to public health, including joint research and development, seminars, workshops, training courses and study tours as well as exchange of visits and scholarships for officials, health professionals and experts.

8.5. Enhance cooperation, research and technical assistance at the global and regional levels to prevent, control and reduce the impact of communicable and pandemic diseases, such as HIV/AIDS, SARS, avian influenza, tuberculosis and dengue hemorrhagic fever, and also to increase health and well-being of mother, children and newborns.

8.6. Effectively implement the ASEAN Plus Three Emerging Infectious Diseases Programme and continue supporting the Global Fund to Fight AIDS, Tuberculosis and Malaria.

8.7. Continue to improve ASEAN's emergency preparedness against the outbreak of pandemic influenza, including information sharing and early warning systems, immediate transfer from the existing ASEAN stockpile of antiviral and personal protection equipment to the sites of pandemic influenza outbreak, and establish a network of antiviral drug stockpiles.

8.8. Increase accessibility to safe, non-counterfeit, affordable and effective medication.

## 9. Disaster management and emergency response

9.1. Strengthen cooperation in the fields of floods, landslides, earthquakes and other disasters such as assistance to support national and regional network of early warning systems for tsunamis and other disasters, including through real-time information sharing and public awareness campaigns.

9.2. Render assistance to the implementation of the ASEAN Agreement on Disaster Management and Emergency Response.

9.3. Enhance civil-military cooperation in disaster relief.

## SECTION E: INSTITUTIONAL SUPPORT AND FOLLOW-UP MECHANISM

1. Develop the modalities of an ASEAN Plus Three Cooperation Fund.
2. Continue to strengthen the ASEAN Plus Three Unit at the ASEAN Secretariat to improve consultation and coordination among the ASEAN Plus Three countries.
3. Conduct joint projects to advance the objectives of this Plan, and, where appropriate, sub-regional activities and cooperative efforts that further the goals and objectives set forth in this Work Plan will be encouraged.
4. The ASEAN Secretariat to develop a schedule and time frame for implementation of the Work Plan to be endorsed by the ASEAN Plus Three countries.
5. Regularly review this Work Plan through the existing mechanisms, with the ASEAN Plus Three Directors-General Meeting as the monitoring mechanism.
6. Submit concise progress reports on the implementation of the Work Plan to the annual ASEAN Plus Three Summit.

# CHAPTER 52

# PLAN OF ACTION TO IMPLEMENT THE JOINT DECLARATION ON ASEAN-AUSTRALIA COMPREHENSIVE PARTNERSHIP

This Plan of Action will implement over the next five years (2008–2013) the Joint Declaration on the ASEAN-Australia Comprehensive Partnership signed in Manila, the Philippines on 1 August 2007.

In implementing this Plan of Action, ASEAN Member Countries and Australia commit to support ASEAN integration, including narrowing the development gap, to attain the end goal of the establishment of an ASEAN Community by 2015, consisting of three pillars, namely security, economic and socio-cultural, and to support enhanced Australian engagement with the region, in ways which are mutually agreed by all parties.

ASEAN Member Countries and Australia commit to implement the Plan in accordance with our international legal obligations and the laws, regulations and national policies of ASEAN Member Countries and Australia.

## I. POLITICAL AND SECURITY COOPERATION

....

5. Deepen and broaden cooperation in response to common security interests in terrorism, other transnational crime, non-proliferation and non-traditional security threats within the framework of national legislation and applicable international laws, agreements and protocols by:

   a. continuing cooperation in the fight against terrorism including technical cooperation and exchange of information on the organisation, activities, methods, financing, and movement of terrorists;
   b. continuing cooperation on the development of appropriate legislative and regulatory frameworks;
   c. strengthening links between relevant agencies in ASEAN Member Countries and Australia;
   d. providing technical assistance and capacity-building activities to ASEAN Member Countries through regional training centres such as the Jakarta

Centre for Law Enforcement Cooperation (JCLEC), the Southeast Asia Regional Centre for Counter-Terrorism (SEARCCT) in Kuala Lumpur and the International Law Enforcement Academy (ILEA) in Bangkok and other regional facilities;

e. strengthening law enforcement cooperation between ASEAN Member Countries and Australia including in the areas of extradition and mutual legal assistance, where applicable;

....

g. increasing cooperation in the ASEAN Regional Forum (ARF), in particular to move the ARF process from Confidence Building Measures to Preventive Diplomacy through information sharing, capacity building and cooperative activities; and

h. increasing cooperation in APEC, the East Asia Summit (EAS), the United Nations (UN) and other regional and international fora;

6. Promote cooperation in human rights through consultation, information sharing and capacity building;
7. Strengthen collaboration and assist ASEAN's efforts in implementing the ASEAN Declaration against Trafficking in Persons particularly Women and Children, including cooperation among law enforcement agencies as called for under the relevant and applicable UN conventions;
8. In the framework of applicable national and international law, intensify cooperation to combat corruption, including denying a safe haven to those guilty of public corruption and those who corrupt them, and cooperate in the recovery and return of the proceeds of corruption, as well as cooperate in the extradition and prosecution of those engaged in bribery, including in international business transactions, according to the means of each concerned country;
9. Deepen understanding of the Treaty of Amity and Cooperation in Southeast Asia (TAC), noting that Australia's accession reflects our firm commitment to the promotion of peace and stability in the region;

## II. ECONOMIC COOPERATION

10. Foster favorable environments for trade, investment and other economic linkages between ASEAN and Australia;
11. Maintain and enhance cooperation under the ASEAN-Australia Development Cooperation Program (AADCP) and, where applicable, other regional and sub-regional development programmes to assist ASEAN members with their trade and investment liberalization efforts consistent with their commitments under the WTO, bilateral and regional FTAs as well as within APEC, taking

into account ASEAN's efforts for regional integration and narrowing the development gap within ASEAN;

12. Encourage greater communication among stakeholders in government, industry and academia to support the successful establishment and implementation of the ASEAN Australia and New Zealand Free Trade Area (AANZFTA); including support to allow the less developed and the developing ASEAN Member Countries to meaningfully participate in and benefit from the AANZFTA;
13. Continue to provide technical support, especially to the CLMV, for ASEAN's regional economic integration objectives, particularly the establishment of ASEAN Economic Community (AEC) by 2015;
14. Improve flows of goods, services and investment between ASEAN Member Countries and Australia by:

    a. improving domestic business environments through improved transparency of laws and regulations as well as promoting understanding of each other's legislation and regulations on trade and investment, including anti-dumping, tariff and non-tariff measures;
    b. cooperating in the World Trade Organization (WTO) to ensure a successful conclusion of the Doha Round which results in new commercial opportunities across all areas of the negotiations agriculture, Non-Agricultural Market Access and services, taking into account the importance of ensuring that development aspects are integrated in the outcome; to address the special concerns of developing and less-developed countries;
    c. strengthening cooperation in areas of mutual interest at the regional and multilateral levels to create more trade and investment opportunities; and

....

    e. enhancing capacity building on competition policy and sanitary and phytosanitary
    f. exchanging information on mutual recognition arrangements to further enhance the existing trade exchanges and exports of products and services between ASEAN and Australia;
    g. encouraging cooperation and interaction between the business communities of ASEAN Member Countries and Australia through regional initiatives, such as Business Summits and trade fairs held in ASEAN Member Countries and Australia, investment missions, seminars, business linkages and other initiatives which bring together potential business partners; and
    h. developing cooperative measures and activities for promoting mutual investment, including exchanges of experts and information on investment opportunities;

15. Promote further cooperation and linkages, through seminars, workshops, technical assistance, scholarship schemes, training, joint research and development projects, and institutional linkages so as to exchange information, experience, know-how, technology, and best practices, where appropriate, in the following areas:

    a. trade and investment promotion and facilitation;
    b. regional financial development and integration;
    c. food safety;
    d. emergency food supplies;
    e. agriculture, fisheries, livestock, animal health and forestry;
    f. mineral resources;
    g. transport;
    h. customs procedures;
    i. tourism;
    j. Small and Medium Enterprises (SMEs) development;
    k. Information Communication Technology (ICT); and
    l. standards and conformance;

16. Promote energy diversification through information exchanges and research on alternative, low emission, new and renewable energy development such as solar, wind, tidal and waves, hydro, geothermal, clean coal technology, natural gas, sustainable biofuels, biomass, marsh gas, and others, taking into consideration each country's specific national circumstances; and as appropriate for those Member Countries which choose to do so, the use of civilian nuclear energy, while giving careful and due regards to the security, environment, health, and internationally-recognized safety standards of the energy source;
17. Continue to support the early accession of the Lao PDR to the WTO;

## III. SOCIO-CULTURAL COOPERATION

18. Strengthen cooperation in the achievement of the United Nations Millennium Development Goals (MDGs);
19. Assist ASEAN's efforts in implementing the ASEAN Agreement on Disaster Management and Emergency Response and continue cooperation activities, including capacity building in disaster response and preparedness, disaster prevention, mitigation and rehabilitation, records recovery plan, and consider support for the operationalization of the ASEAN Coordinating Centre for Humanitarian Assistance on Disaster Management (AHA Centre);

20. Continue strengthening networks of tsunami early warning systems (including the Indian and Pacific Ocean Tsunami Warning and Mitigation Systems) and other hazards at scales appropriate to each hazard. In addition, support regional networks for disaster risk management and records recovery plan, including information sharing, exchange of best practices, capacity building and transfer of sustainable, advanced technology;
21. Strengthen collaboration on research and development and human resources development in the areas related to public health, including joint research and development, seminars, workshops and training courses both in scientific and management aspects of public health, exchange of visits and scholarships for officials and experts;
22. Continue to cooperate to address the threat of communicable and emerging infectious diseases, including HIV/AIDS, SARS and avian influenza, at sub-regional, regional and global levels, including through:

    a. technical assistance and capacity-building activities;
    b. sharing information, best practices and experiences;

    ....

    e. supporting ASEAN's efforts in providing better accessibility to safe, non-counterfeit, affordable and effective medication;

23. Continue cooperation in education, including through scholarship programmes, and by encouraging and facilitating regional student and academic mobility and exchange, and addressing any barriers to these. In particular, promote cooperation in the following areas:

    a. raising quality assurance frameworks and standards, including courses delivered online;
    b. recognition of education and professional qualifications;

    ....

    e. development of common recognition of technical skills across the region in order to meet the overall skills needs of the economic base of the region;
    f. cooperative programmes and activities through linkages between ASEAN University Network (AUN) universities and Australian universities through Universities Australia;
    g. enhance cooperation in human resources development, especially, academic scientists, technologists and administrative personnel of ASEAN Member Countries, through fellowship programmes, training courses, field trip studies, seminars and exchange of visits, professional exchanges and grassroots interactions;

h. continue to provide undergraduate and graduate scholarships for each ASEAN Member Country;

24. Continue cooperation in science and technology, including through the exchange of information, knowledge, and researchers, the adoption of best practices, the development and application of technology, joint research and development, specialized training and workshop and institutional linkages, especially in the fields of:

a. biotechnology;
b. food technology;
c. geoinformatics;
d. information technology;
e. renewable energy;
f. meteorology;
g. water resource management;
h. marine sciences;
i. space technology;
j. material science;
k. mineral resources development; and

....

25. Forge closer cooperation in environmental protection and the promotion of sustainable use of natural resources including through public awareness and environmental education, the exchange of information and best practices, specialized training and workshops and enhanced institutional linkages, especially in the following areas:

a. sustainable forest management;
b. biological diversity and natural heritage conservation;
c. application of advanced and environmental-friendly technologies and best practices;
d. responsible mining and mineral development;
e. public awareness and environmental education; and
f. multilateral environmental agreements; in particular climate change and chemical and chemical waste related conventions and partnerships;

26. Consider closer cooperation in environmental protection and the promotion of sustainable use of natural resources, especially in the following areas:

a. transboundary environmental pollution reduction, particularly transboundary haze pollution;

b. sustainable water resource management, including ground water;
c. coastal and marine environment;
d. urban environmental management and governance; and
e. air quality management;

27. Strengthen cooperation to combat illegal logging, promote afforestation and reforestation and avoiding deforestation and forest degradation; and in this regard, express appreciation for regional forest initiatives such as the Heart of Borneo Initiative and Indonesia's Forestry Eleven Forum Initiative;
28. Cooperate to support the implementation of the Convention on International Trade in Endangered Species (CITES), and cooperation in migratory species and wetlands management;
29. Support ASEAN's efforts to strengthen the capabilities of the ASEAN Specialised Meteorological Centre (ASMC) and ASEAN Earthquake Information Centre (AEIC) and other regional facilities in providing services to communities through rapid dissemination of weather-related and seismic-related information, training of specialists and joint research in the areas of meteorology and seismology;
30. Cooperate in the acquisition, protection, preservation, management and promotion of cultural heritage, including through programmes of visits and exchanges between ASEAN and Australian archivists, librarians, and curators;
31. Conduct activities to promote tolerance of racial, religious and cultural diversity in the region, including through regional interfaith dialogue, performing arts exchanges, exchanges of arts experts and other visit and exchange programmes between ASEAN Member Countries and Australia;
32. Support the activities and projects of the ASEAN Foundation in promoting ASEAN integration and ASEAN awareness, including through the publishing of information on ASEAN in native languages of the ASEAN Member Countries, as well as people-to-people contacts among ASEAN Member Countries and with Australia; and

## IV. DEVELOPMENT COOPERATION

33. Continue to support efforts to reduce poverty, narrow the development gap and promote sustainable development in ASEAN, through the ASEAN-Australia Development Cooperation Program (AADCP), other current and future programmes, and ongoing policy dialogue;

## V. FOLLOW-UP

34. The ASEAN Secretariat and Australia mutually determine to develop a schedule and projects for the implementation of the Plan of Action. This Plan of Action will be reviewed through existing mechanisms, including at the annual Joint Planning Committee (JPC) Meeting and the biennial ASEAN-Australia Forum (AAF). Ministers will be updated regularly on the progress of the implementation of the Plan of Action.

Source: http://www.aseansec.org/21373.htm
Accessed date: 2 October 2008
Publisher: ASEAN Secretariat
Country: Jakarta
Date of Publication: 2008

# CHAPTER 53

# INITIATIVE FOR ASEAN INTEGRATION (IAI) STRATEGIC FRAMEWORK AND IAI WORK PLAN 2 (2009–2015)

## Part I — IAI Strategic Framework

## MANDATE

1. The ASEAN Heads of State/Government at their Summit in 2000 launched the Initiative for ASEAN Integration (IAI) to narrow the development divide and enhance ASEAN's competitiveness as a region to provide a framework for regional cooperation through which the more developed ASEAN members could help those member countries that most need it. The following year the ASEAN Foreign Ministers adopted the Hanoi Declaration on Narrowing the Development Gap (NDG) for Closer ASEAN Integration. The ASEAN Leaders in their 2003 Declaration of the ASEAN Concord (Bali Concord II) stressed that the deepening and broadening of ASEAN integration shall be accompanied by technical and development cooperation to address the development divide and accelerate the economic integration of Cambodia, Laos, Myanmar and Viet Nam (CLMV) through the road map for the integration of ASEAN to enable all member states to move forward in a unified manner and that the benefits of ASEAN integration are shared. In this regard, the Vientiane Action Programme 2004–2010, a medium-term development plan to realize ASEAN Vision 2020, highlighted the strategic importance of narrowing the development gap to realize the ASEAN Community, and that the IAI be strengthened to address the needs of CLMV and sub-regional areas.
2. The 13$^{th}$ ASEAN Summit in 2007 agreed that narrowing the development gap remains an important task which will ensure that the benefits of ASEAN's integration efforts are fully realized. The Leaders further noted that efforts to narrow the development gap should be aligned with the broader aspects of ASEAN's integration initiatives. With the acceleration of the realization of the ASEAN Community to 2015, these efforts have become even more urgent.

## GOAL

3. The overall goal of the NDG is to promote, through concerted efforts, effective cooperation and mutual assistance to narrow the development gap among ASEAN Member States (AMS) and between ASEAN and the rest of the world.
4. In operational terms, NDG efforts shall assist the CLMV countries to meet ASEAN-wide targets and commitments towards realizing the ASEAN Community.
5. This will include specific regional cooperation activities aimed at assisting the less developed member states to achieve closer economic integration, to benefit from ASEAN schemes for regional economic integration activities, to supplement national efforts directly aimed at poverty reduction and the promotion of equitable and inclusive development.

## IAI WORK PLAN

6. The efforts to narrow the development gap will be driven mainly by the IAI Work Plan. The first IAI Work Plan for the period 2002–2008 accomplished implementation of a total of 134 projects/programs attracting a total investment of about USD 191 million from ASEAN-6, and about USD 20 million by dialogue partners, development agencies and other partners. This does not include the other IAI related substantive support given to the CLMV, nor other projects implemented in the CLMV sub-region.
7. The IAI Strategic Framework provides the policy direction for the formulation, implementation, monitoring, and reporting of the IAI Work Plan for the period 2009–2015.

## GENERAL PRINCIPLES FOR FORMULATION OF THE IAI WORK PLAN

8. The NDG efforts in general, and the IAI in particular, are aligned with the three Community Blueprints namely the ASEAN Economic Blueprint, ASEAN Socio-Cultural Blueprint and the ASEAN Political Security Blueprint. Therefore the IAI Work Plan for the period 2009–2015 has been formulated based on the key program areas in each of the three Blueprints, the 1st IAI Work Plan 2002–2008, and the project ideas contained in the Mid-Term Review of the 1st IAI Work Plan 2002–2008.
9. While it is acknowledged that all AMS will benefit from the Blueprint actions and that CLMV countries may be accorded additional attention in the implementation

of these actions, the programs to be included in the IAI Work Plan are those that are critical and necessary to hasten the integration process and to move forward in a unified manner in the implementation of the Blueprints.

10. Criteria for projects in the IAI Work Plan include identification of the precise needs of CLMV in terms of external assistance, the importance of a project's role in national development plans, its effectiveness in building CLMV capacity for participation in ASEAN programs, long term continuity and sustainability, and absorptive capacity of CLMV countries. This will ensure that IAI projects have coherence, focus, ensure adequate coverage, reflect substantive gaps in priority sectors and activities essential for integration, and more importantly are responsive to CLMV needs.
11. While capacity building and human resource development is key to IAI efforts, there is a need to encourage the development of infrastructure as a means to promote ASEAN integration.

## IMPLEMENTATION/MANAGEMENT ARRANGEMENTS

12. The ASEAN Summit will provide overall guidance and advice on the implementation of the NDG initiative, and in particular approve the IAI Work Plan.
13. The ASEAN Coordinating Council in consultation with relevant ministerial bodies will provide recommendations to the ASEAN Summit with regard to the implementation of the NDG initiatives.
14. The IAI Task Force will provide policy guidelines, directions, and general advice on the IAI Work Plan; ensure coordination among the AMS; assist in formulation, implementation and design of the IAI Work Plan; seek funding and work closely with dialogue partners, development agencies and other partners in the implementation of the IAI Work Plan.
15. The co-shepherds mechanism shall continue to operate to foster greater collaboration in the formulation and implementation of ASEAN-6 assistance to the CLMV countries.
16. The ASEAN Secretariat, in particular through the IAI Unit, shall support the above bodies in the implementation of the IAI Work Plan and activities of other sub-regional frameworks. This will include servicing the meetings, assist in formulation, implementation, monitoring and reporting of projects, resource mobilization and overall operational coordination among the various bodies.

## RESOURCE MOBILIZATION

17. New, additional and innovative resource mobilization shall be a key aspect of the implementation of the IAI Work Plan. The assistance and resources shall

come from the following sources: ASEAN; ASEAN Dialogue Partners and Sectoral Partners, and Development Partners (ASEAN Partners); regional and international financial institutions; and private sector, foundations, and non-governmental organizations (NGOs).

## ASEAN

18. The Leaders have stressed that the IAI shall essentially be a mechanism for ASEAN-6 to help the CLMV countries. In that sense, ASEAN-6 shall continue to support and provide assistance and resources through ASEAN-6 contribution to the IAI Work Plan, and through bilateral initiatives. In addition, ASEAN-6 promoting joint projects with partial funding, in line with their more developed status, will be an attractive proposition to dialogue partners and other partners. By its very nature, projects sponsored by ASEAN-6 would acquire greater coherence and a higher degree of organization, strengthen ASEAN solidarity and present an image of doing something for itself and of other ASEAN countries as helping one another, and therefore attract outside funding and support.
19. The ASEAN Development Fund may be used to leverage funding of regional cooperation programs and projects from dialogue partners and other donors, provide seed funding for initial activities of large scale projects, and to provide full funding support to small and short-term projects of a confidential or strategic nature.

## ASEAN Partners

20. The NDG has revitalized the development-cooperation dimension of ASEAN's partners and made its projects the focus and center of development cooperation between ASEAN and its partners. Therefore, in addition to the on-going support provided to ASEAN, the partners should be encouraged to provide additional funding for the IAI activities. As explained above, partners should also explore joint projects with ASEAN-6 that will enhance collaboration beyond aid to joint partners for IAI activities. Special consideration for the participation of CLMV ought to be built into the design of all ASEAN cooperation programs, projects, and activities.

## Private enterprises, Foundations and NGOs

21. The private enterprises, foundations and NGOs make substantial contributions to the socio-economic development of the CLMV countries. In fact, the IAI

Work Plan cannot match the much needed funding for physical infrastructure projects of the private sector. The IAI Work Plan should therefore adopt a strategy to promote private sector investment, to expand their scope on a sub-regional scale by providing assistance in drawing feasibility studies for such infrastructure, conduct studies that are needed in seeking financing from international financial institutions or from private investors, organizing CLMV-wide investment and trade promotion fora, exhibitions etc.

## MONITORING/REPORTING ARRANGEMENTS

22. Regular monitoring and implementation of IAI Work Plan will be undertaken by the various institutional mechanisms outlined above.
23. Specifically, (i) the CLMV countries shall report annually on the assistance they have received from all sources concentrating on the utility, impact and effectiveness of the projects (ii) ASEAN-6 shall submit annual reports on their assistance programs for the CLMV countries, and (iii) the ASEAN Secretariat shall consolidate these reports together with its own account of IAI support from ASEAN partners.
24. A set of key parameters representative of narrowing the development gap shall be adopted to monitor its progress. For this purpose a study will be undertaken to determine these key parameters, building upon the ASEAN Baseline Report conducted by the ASEAN Secretariat.
25. The IAI Work Plan 2 (2009–2015) shall be reviewed periodically to take into account ASEAN Community building process and emerging needs of CLMV countries.

# Part II — IAI Work Plan 2 (2009–2015)

## ASEAN ECONOMIC COMMUNITY (AEC)

### A. Single Market and Production Base

### A1. *Free Flow of Goods*

Actions:

i. Conduct a study by 2009 to analyze the state, in each of the CLMV countries, of each of the relevant priority sectors and how the sector would benefit from or be affected by more rapid regional integration within ASEAN, proposing measures to undertake adjustments to reap the benefits and mitigate the costs.

ii. Implement the agreed measures recommended by the above study.

iii. Conduct a study by 2009 to identify obstacles encountered by CLMV exporters to or through ASEAN-6 countries and vice versa.

iv. Conduct a review by 2010 with a view to implement effectively the ASEAN Integration System of Preferences.

v. Conduct a study by 2009 of ways in which the ASEAN-6 can help strengthen the export competitiveness of the CLMV countries.

vi. Implement the agreed recommendations of the study, completed in 2004, on managing the revenue losses and adjustment costs arising from CLMV participation in AFTA.

vii. Assist CLMV in capacity building to ensure the implementation of National Single Window by 2012.

viii. Conduct attachment programs and other methods of improving the familiarity of the customs and other agencies of the CLMV countries with the CEPT scheme and other integration measures and strengthening their capacity to implement them.

ix. Conduct programs to familiarize the private sector in the CLMV countries with ASEAN Trade in Goods Agreement (ATIGA) and other integration measures.

x. Continue implementation of the IAI training and institution-building programs in customs administration and operations.

xi. Continue implementation of additional programs on the basis of a coherent capacity building program adopted by the ASEAN customs authorities, including training in the application of rules of origin, risk assessment, and enforcement of agreements related to customs.

xii. Provide assistance to those CLMV countries that need assistance in drafting or amending customs-related legislation.

xiii. Implement programs on customs-related information on transparency, appeal mechanism and access to information.

xiv. Implement programs on customs automation.

xv. Provide support for implementation of CLMV national master plans on standards and conformity assessment, including the improvement of technical infrastructure and equipment.

xvi. Conduct capacity-building projects for the improvement of technical infrastructure, on-the-job training in laboratories, product certification, implementation of ISO directives, technical training for regulatory bodies, and accreditation and certification within the framework of a capacity-building program adopted by ACCSQ.

xvii. Provide technical assistance in the establishment of national standards for those CLMV that needs it.
xviii. Provide technical assistance in the harmonization of standards and technical regulations primarily in the 12 priority sectors of the AEC.
xix. Strengthen strategic alliance between agricultural cooperatives in CLMV through bilateral and regional cooperation and promote business linkages among the potential agricultural cooperatives within ASEAN.

## A2. *Free Flow of Services*

Actions:

....

iii. Provide technical assistance by 2012 in formulating services related policy measures in tourism sector including air transport services, liberalization of tourism services, and the use of tourism professionals.
iv. Provide joint training by 2011 in tourism services sector to strengthen the capacity of government officials and private sectors in charge of services in CLMV countries.

## A3. *Free Flow of Investment*

Actions:

i. Conduct a research study to identify the difficulties encountered by investors in their operations in CLMV countries.
ii. Undertake a review on possible strategies to attract investment, improve the investment climate, build capacities and maximize the benefits of FDI for development.
iii. Conduct capacity building programs to review, streamline and simplify procedures for investment applications and approvals.
iv. Provide technical assistance in strengthening databases, such as on rules and regulations and incentives, for investments covering goods and services to facilitate policy formulation, and dissemination of investment information.
v. Conduct a study of the human resource requirements of the sectors to which the CLMV countries seek to draw investments, including reforms in the educational system and short-term vocational training.
vi. Conduct programs to familiarize the private sector in the CLMV countries with ASEAN Comprehensive Investment Agreement (ACIA) and other integration measures.

## A4. *Freer Flow of Capital*

Actions:

....

## A5. *Free Flow of Skilled Labour*

Action:

....

## A6. *Priority Integration Sectors*

Actions:

i. Assist CLMV to implement measures identified in the Roadmaps for Integration of Priority Sectors.
ii. Develop capacity building programs for CLMV authorities involved in the implementation of the measures identified in the Roadmaps for Integration of the PIS.

## A7. *Food, Agriculture and Forestry*

Actions:

i. Conduct capacity building for harmonization and inspection/sampling procedures.
ii. Provide assistance to harmonize the Maximum Residue Limits (MRLs) of commonly used pesticides for widely traded crop products in accordance with international standards/guides.
iii. Conduct a study by 2011 on how to increase competitiveness of food, agriculture and forestry products/commodities including addressing gap among CLMV and other ASEAN Member States in relation to food, agriculture and forestry related issues.
iv. Provide assistance to CLMV by 2011 in implementing Good Agriculture/Aquaculture Practices (GAP) for agricultural and food products and develop national GAP.
v. Provide assistance to each CLMV country to harmonise Sanitary and Phytosanitary (SPS) measures for agricultural, food and forestry products with significant trade/trade potential.
vi. Conduct training by 2011 on Criteria and Indicators for Forest Certification for each CLMV country.

vii. Develop collaborative research and technology transfer in food, agriculture and forestry products including training and extension programmes for CLMV countries.
viii. Establish strategic alliances and joint approaches with the private sectors in promoting food safety, investment and joint venture opportunities, promotion of agricultural products and market access in each CLMV country.
ix. Conduct study to empower and enhance market access of agricultural products and to build a network mechanism linking agricultural cooperatives among CLMV and other ASEAN Member States.
x. Organize workshops on strengthening efforts to combat illegal logging and its associated trade for the CLMV countries.
xi. Organise training workshops on Good Manufacturing Practices/Good Hygiene Practices and Sanitation Standard Operating Procedures for small and medium enterprises (SMEs) in relation to food, agriculture, aquaculture and forestry products.

## B. Competitive Economic Region

### B1. *Competition Policy*

Actions:

i. Conduct programs to strengthen rule of law in CLMV through capacity building, including the enforcement of contracts, competition policy, dispute settlement, and government policy reform.
ii. Provide support for CLMV in developing competition policy.

### B2. *Consumer Protection*

Actions:

i. Provide technical assistance by 2011 for CLMV countries on policy formulation, development and improvement of consumer protection guidelines and legal framework.
ii. Implement capacity building programs by 2011 on consumer protection through organising seminars, workshops, study visits and training courses.
iii. Provide assistance to those CLMV countries that need assistance in drafting protection-related registration especially with regard to unfair and deceptive practices including false and deceptive advertising, abusive sales tactics, consumer fraud and other unfair business practices.

### B3. *Intellectual Property Rights (IPR)*

Actions:

i. Organize training and workshops by 2010 on implications of IPR in regional FTAs.
ii. Provide necessary technical assistance to CLMV countries in the implementation of the ASEAN IPR Action Plan 2004–2010 and the Work Plan for ASEAN Cooperation on Copy Rights.
iii. Assist CLMV countries to enhance their IPR systems.

### B4. *Infrastructure Development*

Actions:

i. Continuation, intensification and expansion of training in multimodal transport.
ii. Provide training by 2011 in multimodal transport, logistics, and supply chain management .
iii. Provide technical assistance and training for CLMV in establishing and operating their segments of the Singapore-Kunming Rail Link.
iv. Conduct a feasibility study on the upgrading of secondary roads in each of the CLMV countries for connection to the ASEAN Highway Network.
v. Undertake activities on the application of information and communications technology to transportation.
vi. Conduct training projects for container transport, urban transport planning, traffic management, and transport engineering.
vii. Conduct a capacity building project on traffic safety in inland waterways.
viii. Consider implementation of Viet Nam's proposal to convert the Inland Waterways College in Ho Chi Minh City into a regional training center for inland waterways.
ix. Provide support to amend the road transport law and road traffic law for CLMV by 2010 to comply with regional obligations.
x. Provide training on railway operation for CLMV.
xi. Implement projects to build CLMV capacity to participate in ASEAN energy schemes, primarily the ASEAN Power Grid.
xii. Provide training by 2011 in high-voltage inter-connection and in power-systems planning.
xiii. Provide training in fuel quality testing, fuel transport safety, power trading and negotiations on transboundary power tariffs.
xiv. Develop a program of fuel conservation and renewable energy, with a training component by 2010.

xv. Provide support for formulation of national ICT master plans by 2010.
xvi. Provide support for formulation of e-government master plans.
xvii. Provide support for formulation of national action plans for human resource development in ICT.
xviii. Provide support to review telecommunications regulations to support liberalization (and development) of the telecom sector with an integrated approach on regulation and policy reform (on competition policy, foreign investment, licensing, allocation of resources such as frequencies and access facilities).
xix. Provide support to complete the GMS Information Superhighway to provide the telecom backbone network and connectivity to all parts of CLMV.
xx. Conduct a study and implement measures to implement CLMV ICT manufacturing bases/clusters (and to be connected to other IT parks in ASEAN).
xxi. Conduct training programs on the basis of a coherent program for the ICT focal points of CLMV.

### B5. *Taxation*

Actions:

....

### B6. *E-Commerce*

Actions:

....

## C. Equitable Economic Development

### C1. *SME Development*

Actions:

i. Conduct a study by 2009 to determine how the rural areas of each of the CLMV countries could benefit from the integration of each of the 12 priority sectors.
ii. Implement the agreed measures recommended by the above study.

....

## D. Integration into the Global Economy

### D1. *Coherent Approach Towards External Economic Relations*

Actions:

i. Conduct training programs for the CLMV countries in the application of the rules of origin of trade agreements concluded or being negotiated by ASEAN.
ii. Conduct capacity building programs to provide policy advice to CLMV governments in the negotiations of free trade agreements in accordance with their respective needs and interest.
iii. Provide assistance to the CLMV governments in ensuring that their specific requirements are taken into account in the study on the investment elements of FTAs being negotiated between ASEAN and Dialogue Partners.

### D2. *Enhanced Participation in Global Supply Networks*

Actions:

....

## ASEAN SOCIO-CULTURAL COMMUNITY (ASCC)

## A. Human Development

### A1. *Advancing and Prioritising Education*

Action:

i. Conduct a program for training in the management of higher education for CLMV countries.

### A2. *Investing in Human Resource Development*

Actions:

i. Conduct a seminar by 2009 on strategic planning for skills development.
ii. Study the possibility of establishing vocational/university exchange programs or temporary training programs for certain skills sets that are needed for CLMV.

### A3. *Promotion of Decent Work*

Actions:

....

## A4. *Promoting Information and Communication Technology (ICT)*

Actions:

i. Provide expertise training in the management of large-scale ICT projects in CLMV countries.
ii. Provide support in building up and developing a group of CEOs for ICT.
iii. Provide support for CLMV countries in studying and building of structures and information standards serving e-government.
iv. Develop a standard ICT infrastructure of CLMV for their people, especially women, youth, elderly and persons with disability, to easily access ICT.
v. Provide ICT training for people in each CLMV country including women, youth, elderly and persons with disability.
vi. Provide support to implement capacity building programmes to increase ICT literacy in ASEAN, including women, children, elderly and people with disabilities.

## A5. *Facilitating Access to Applied Science and Technology*

Actions:

i. Provide support to implement the ASEAN-Help-ASEAN programme to address the S&T needs and strengthen the S&T infrastructure of CLMV.
ii. Design activities to improve the capabilities of CLMV to undertake collaborative research and development in enabling technologies.
iii. Provide assistance to CLMV to develop national S&T indicators that can serve as inputs in the development of human resource strategies by economic and industry players.

## A6. *Strengthening Entrepreneurship Skills for Women, Youth, Elderly and Persons with Disabilities*

Actions:

....

## A7. *Building Civil Service Capability*

Actions:

i. Invest in infrastructure of civil service in CLMV with due attention to gender responsive aspects by 2010.

ii. Strengthen the capability of ASEAN Resource Centers under the auspices of the ASEAN Conference on Civil Service Matters (ACCSM) to develop training for CLMV civil services by 2009.
iii. Provide "Train the Trainers" session for CLMV officials in their respective countries to develop skills and capability in real working environment by 2012.
iv. Develop and conduct a training program by 2009 for CLMV to promote effective and efficient civil service, public accountability and good governance.
v. Develop and conduct e-learning programs by 2009 on specific areas of public management among ASEAN civil services.

....

## B. Social Welfare and Protection

### B1. *Poverty Alleviation*

Actions:

i. Conduct workshops by 2010 for CLMV to review and assess the impact of numerous internationally funded poverty-reduction programs and to adopt best practices.
ii. Implement projects related to poverty alleviation in CLMV with due attention to female households in rural areas.
iii. Conduct workshops on economic development at grassroots level and in rural areas.

### B2. *Social safety Net and Protection from the Negative Impacts of Integration and Globalization*

Actions:

i. Conduct a study by 2012 for CLMV to assess the formal and informal mechanisms for social security and social protection, and if necessary to modify those mechanisms with due attention to gender responsive aspects.
ii. Conduct studies focusing on identifying the impact of labor emigration on various CLMV industries as well as on identifying the specific needs of those industries.

### B3. *Enhancing Food Security and Safety*

Action:

i. Conduct capacity building programs by 2011 on risk analysis including training for CLMV countries to support food safety measures.

## B4. *Access to Healthcare and Promotion of Healthy Lifestyle*

Actions:

i. Enhance quality of herbal medicine and prevent illegal importation by 2011.
ii. Develop and implement action plan under the new ASEAN-WHO Memorandum of Understanding (2009–2013) to include capacity building activities on Healthy Lifestyles for CLMV by 2013.

## B5. *Improving Capability to Control Communicable Diseases*

Actions:

i. Integrate responses to HIV epidemic under the Third ASEAN Work Programme on HIV and AIDS, 2006–2013.
ii. Employing existing mechanisms to control other Emerging Infectious Diseases (EID) including TB and Malaria.
iii. Integrate HIV and AIDS impact assessment into the feasibility study phase for development projects with due attention to gender responsive aspects.

## B6. *Ensuring a Drug-Free ASEAN*

Actions:

i. Provide support by 2011 in exchange of experiences, best practices and technical assistance to develop patterns for drug-replacement crops/alternative crops as substitute in the areas previously used for illicit drug crops.
ii. Enhance capabilities and provide technical assistance for the treatment and rehabilitation of addicted persons including synthetic drugs users.
iii. Provide advisory assistance to create linkages between government, non-governmental organizations and civil society to establish comprehensive system which can provide treatment, rehabilitation and aftercare services.
iv. Develop national public awareness strategy and implementation plan against the threat of illicit drug.

## B7. *Building Disaster-Resilient Nations and Safer Communities*

Actions:

i. Organize training courses and workshops for CLMV countries to enhance capabilities in disaster responses, and search and rescue.
ii. Provide support in terms of equipments and upgrading of infrastructure for search and rescue, and disaster responses by 2012.

iii. Provide more capacity building in disaster management and emergency response.

## C. Social Justice and Rights

### C1. *Promotion and Protection of the Rights and Welfare of Women, Children, the Elderly, and Persons with Disabilities*

Actions:

i. Develop and implement by 2011 capacity building activities (workshops, trainings and study tours) for CLMV on caring societies.
ii. Conduct an ASEAN Workshop to promote understanding, implementation, monitoring and evaluation of the rights of the child, based on the convention on the Rights of the Child.

### C2. *Protection and Promotion of the Rights of Migrant Workers*

Actions:

i. Provide advisory services to the CLMV countries for the purpose of developing their capacity to manage overseas employment programs.
ii. Provide training/technical assistance/capacity building by 2011 towards the establishment of clear and easily accessible emigration/immigration procedures and documentation, with a view to aid safe and regular migration.

### C3. *Promoting Corporate Social Responsibility (CSR)*

Actions:

i. Provide training on the concept of corporate social responsibility and its environment for effective implementation in national and international markets.
ii. Develop and implement a comprehensive program to build capacity of CLMV countries for effective implementation of international best practices on corporate social responsibility.
iii. Conduct reviews on the implementation and continual support for strengthening the capacity of CLMV and promoting the conformity assessment activities, and addressing issues of particular concern to international market access.

## D. Ensuring Environmental Sustainability

### D1. *Addressing Global Environmental Issues*

Action:

i. Develop and implement a comprehensive program to build capacity of CLMV for effective participation and negotiations in multilateral environmental agreements and implementation of their obligations to those agreements.

### D2. *Managing and Preventing Transboundary Environmental Pollution*

Actions:

i. Promote and share the experiences of ASEAN 6 in managing forest fires and transboundary haze pollution for CLMV through the Mekong Technical Working Group on Transboundary Haze Pollution.
ii. Promote capacity building on the management of Hazardous Chemicals and Substances as well as Persistent Organic Pollutants (POPs).

### D3. *Promoting Sustainable Development through Environmental Education and Public Participation*

Action:

i. Provide additional support by 2012 to CLMV countries in the implementation of the ASEAN Environmental Education Action Plan (2008–2012), addressing issues of particular concern to CLMV.

### D4. *Promoting Environmentally Sound Technology (EST)*

Actions:

i. Promote capacity building by 2012 on environment labelling and certification schemes, and use of alternate and renewable energies as well as Best Available Techniques and Best Environment Practices (BAT/BEP).
ii. Enhance the capacity of CLMV countries in managing environmental pollution in handicraft villages.

## D5. *Promoting Quality Living Standards in ASEAN Cities/Urban Areas*

Action:

i. Promote best practices through the ASEAN Environmentally Sustainable Cities (ESC) Award for urban centres in CLMV.

## D6. *Harmonizing Environmental Policies and Databases*

Actions:

i. Provide support to CLMV for producing state of the environment reports.
ii. Provide assistance to harmonize key environmental parameters, including capacity building for monitoring and analyzing environmental pollutants.

## D7. *Promoting the Sustainable use of Coastal and Marine Environment*

Actions:

i. Develop a program by 2010 to build capacity for the implementation of the ASEAN Marine Water Quality: Management Guidelines and Monitoring Manual.
ii. Develop the model of community's participation in environmentally sustainable coastal zone economic development in CLMV.

## D8. *Promoting Sustainable Management of Nature Conservation and Biodiversity*

Actions:

i. Provide support to encourage more natural conservation areas, including listing in the ASEAN Heritage Parks Programs and World Heritage Sites.
ii. The ASEAN Center for Biodiversity to provide additional support in all its activities to the CLMV countries with regard to sustainable management of biodiversity of the region.
iii. Strengthen biodiversity conservation and natural resources protection through the establishment of transboundary protected areas among CLMV countries.

## D9. *Promoting the Sustainability of Freshwater Resources*

Actions:

i. Provide more assistance to CLMV countries in the implementation of the ASEAN Strategic Plan of Action on Water Resources Management.

ii. Lend more support to the Mekong River Commission to enable comprehensive integrated water resources management of the region.

### D10. *Responding to Climate Change and Addressing its Impacts*

Action:

i. Assess the impact of climate change on biodiversity, water resources, climate related disasters such as floods and fires, and draw up adaptation and mitigation plans by 2012.

### D11. *Promoting Sustainable Forest Management (SFM)*

Actions:

i. Promote capacity building and strengthen joint efforts to combat illegal logging and its associated trade, forest fires and its resultant effects.
ii. Promote the development of eco-tourism through training activities and study tours.
iii. Promote information sharing on rearing and breeding of Wild Fauna and Flora.
iv. Promote exchange of experience and best practice on forest law enforcement and governance in the respective countries and strengthen activities to implement commitments to the Convention on International Trade in Endangered Species of Wild Fauna and Flora (CITES) and the ASEAN Wildlife Enforcement Network (ASEAN-WEN).
v. Provide assistance to CLMV countries in implementing the ASEAN criteria and indicators for sustainable management of tropical forest.
vi. Provide assistance to CLMV countries to implement the GMS Program on Reafforestation.

## E. Building ASEAN Identity

### E1. *Promotion of ASEAN Awareness and a Sense of Community*

Actions:

i. Provide assistance to CLMV countries in the writing, translation if necessary, production and distribution of textbooks on Southeast Asia and ASEAN for different educational levels and in developing courses on these subjects, and translation of ASEAN Documents.
ii. Conduct cultural activities in order to promote cultural awareness among the young people by 2011.

iii. Assist CLMV countries in the implementation of programs to promote public images and awareness of ASEAN.

### E2. *Preservation and Promotion of ASEAN Cultural Heritage*

Actions:

i. Organise workshops by 2012 on preservation and promotion of tangible and intangible cultural heritage.
ii. Conduct workshops on dissemination and preservation of cultural heritage at risk.

### E3. *Promotion of Cultural Creativity and Industry*

Action:

i. Organise study tour for people engaged in small and medium sized cultural enterprises from CLMV countries to other ASEAN member countries with good experience in cultural industry.

## ASEAN POLITICAL-SECURITY COMMUNITY (APSC)

### A. *A Rules-Based Community of Shared Values and Norms (Political Cooperation)*

Actions:

i. Develop capacity building programs to complement the existing CLMV countries' efforts in the areas of rule of law and judiciary systems and legal infrastructure, promotion and protection of human rights, political and social development, effective and efficient civil services, and good governance in the public and private sectors.
ii. Promote capacity building for CLMV countries in the implementation of the Convention on the Elimination of All Forms of Discrimination against Women (CEDAW).

### B. *A Cohesive, Peaceful and Resilient Region with Shared Responsibility for Comprehensive Security (Security Cooperation)*

Actions:

i. Provide capacity building to CLMV countries to better participate in ASEAN programs related to combating transnational crimes and terrorism.

ii. Develop capacity building programme in the areas of conflict resolution and pacific settlement of dispute.

## C. *A Dynamic and Outward-Looking Region in an Increasingly Integrated and Interdependent World (External Relations)*

Actions:

i. Provide capacity building to CLMV countries to better participate and engage in relevant multilateral initiatives.
ii. Provide support to CLMV countries to reap the full benefit of ASEAN's engagement with external partners.

## *General Enabling Actions*

i. Conduct projects to raise English-language efficiency of government officials and people of the CLMV countries.
ii. Provide further attachment to the ASEAN Secretariat of CLMV officials, from the ASEAN National Secretariat as well as from key ministries involved in ASEAN affairs.
iii. Provide training, including training-for-trainers, in the formulation and management of projects.
iv. Develop a set of indicators for measuring the progress of CLMV towards the narrowing the development gap.

Source: http://www.aseansec.org/22325.pdf
Accessed date: 3 March 2009
Publisher: ASEAN Secretariat
Country: Jakarta
Date of Publication: 2009

# CHAPTER 54

# ASEAN POLITICAL-SECURITY COMMUNITY BLUEPRINT

## I. INTRODUCTION

1. The ASEAN Political-Security Community has its genesis of over four decades of close co-operation and solidarity. The ASEAN Heads of States/Governments, at their Summit in Kuala Lumpur in December 1997 envisioned a concert of Southeast Asian nations, outward looking, living in peace, stability and prosperity, bonded together in partnership in dynamic development and in a community of caring societies.
2. To concretise the ASEAN Vision 2020, the ASEAN Heads of States/Governments adopted the Declaration of ASEAN Concord II (Bali Concord II) in 2003, which establishes an ASEAN Community by 2020. The ASEAN Community consists of three pillars, namely the ASEAN Political-Security Community (APSC), the ASEAN Economic Community (AEC) and the ASEAN Socio-Cultural Community (ASCC).
3. Conscious that the strengthening of ASEAN integration through accelerated establishment of an ASEAN Community will reinforce ASEAN's centrality and role as the driving force in charting the evolving regional architecture, the ASEAN Leaders at the 12$^{th}$ ASEAN Summit in the Philippines decided to accelerate the establishment of an ASEAN Community by 2015.
4. At the 13$^{th}$ ASEAN Summit in Singapore, the ASEAN Heads of States/Governments signed the ASEAN Charter, which marked ASEAN Member States' commitment in intensifying community-building through enhanced regional cooperation and integration. In line with this, they tasked their Ministers and officials to draft the APSC Blueprint, which would be adopted at the 14$^{th}$ ASEAN Summit.
5. The APSC Blueprint is guided by the ASEAN Charter and the principles and purposes contained therein. The APSC Blueprint builds on the ASEAN Security Community Plan of Action, the Vientiane Action Programme (VAP), as well as relevant decisions by various ASEAN Sectoral Bodies. The ASEAN Security Community Plan of Action is a principled document, laying out the activities needed to realise the objectives of the ASEAN Political Security Community, while the VAP lays out the measures necessary for 2004–2010. Both documents are important references in continuing political and security

cooperation. The APSC Blueprint provides a roadmap and timetable to establish the APSC by 2015. The APSC Blueprint would also have the flexibility to continue programmes/activities beyond 2015 in order to retain its significance and have an enduring quality.

## II. CHARACTERISTICS AND ELEMENTS OF THE APSC

6. It is envisaged that the APSC will bring ASEAN's political and security cooperation to a higher plane. The APSC will ensure that the peoples and Member States of ASEAN live in peace with one another and with the world at large in a just, democratic and harmonious environment.
7. The APSC shall promote political development in adherence to the principles of democracy, the rule of law and good governance, respect for and promotion and protection of human rights and fundamental freedoms as inscribed in the ASEAN Charter. It shall be a means by which ASEAN Member States can pursue closer interaction and cooperation to forge shared norms and create common mechanisms to achieve ASEAN's goals and objectives in the political and security fields. In this regard, it promotes a people-oriented ASEAN in which all sectors of society, regardless of gender, race, religion, language, or social and cultural background, are encouraged to participate in, and benefit from, the process of ASEAN integration and community building. In the implementation of, the Blueprint, ASEAN should also strive towards promoting and supporting gender-mainstreaming, tolerance, respect for diversity, equality and mutual understanding.
8. At the same time, in the interest of preserving and enhancing peace and stability in the region, the APSC seeks to strengthen the mutually beneficial relations between ASEAN and its Dialogue Partners and friends. In doing so, it also maintains the centrality and proactive role of ASEAN in a regional architecture that is open, transparent and inclusive, while remaining actively engaged, forward looking and non-discriminatory.
9. The APSC subscribes to a comprehensive approach to security, which acknowledges the interwoven relationships of political, economic, social-cultural and environmental dimensions of development. It promotes renunciation of aggression and of the threat or use of force or other actions in any manner inconsistent with international law and reliance of peaceful settlements of dispute. In this regard, it upholds existing ASEAN political instruments such as the Declaration on Zone of Peace, Freedom and Neutrality (ZOPFAN), the Treaty of Amity and Co-operation in South East Asia (TAC) and the Treaty on the Southeast Asian Nuclear Weapon-Free Zone (SEANWFZ), which play a pivotal role in the area of confidence building measures, preventive diplomacy

and pacific approaches to conflict resolution. It also seeks to address non-traditional security issues.

10. Based on the above, the ASEAN Political-Security Community envisages the following three key characteristics:

    a) A Rules-based Community of shared values and norms;
    b) A Cohesive, Peaceful, Stable and Resilient Region with shared responsibility for comprehensive security;
    c) A Dynamic and Outward-looking Region in an increasingly integrated and interdependent world.

11. These characteristics are interrelated and mutually reinforcing, and shall be pursued in a balanced and consistent manner. To effectively realise the APSC, the APSC Blueprint is an action-oriented document with a view to achieving results and recognises the capacity and capability of ASEAN Member States to undertake the stipulated actions in the Blueprint.

## A. A RULES-BASED COMMUNITY OF SHARED VALUES AND NORMS

12. ASEAN's cooperation in political development aims to strengthen democracy, enhance good governance and the rule of law, and to promote and protect human rights and fundamental freedoms, with due regard to the rights and responsibilities of the Member States of ASEAN, so as to ultimately create a Rulesbased Community of shared values and norms. In the shaping and sharing of norms, ASEAN aims to achieve a standard of common adherence to norms of good conduct among member states of the ASEAN Community; consolidating and strengthening ASEAN's solidarity, cohesiveness and harmony; and contributing to the building of a peaceful, democratic, tolerant, participatory and transparent community in Southeast Asia.
13. Moreover, cooperation in political development will bring to maturity the political elements and institutions in ASEAN, towards which the sense of interstate solidarity on political systems, culture and history will be better fostered. Such interstate solidarity can be achieved further through the shaping and sharing of norms.

### A.1. Cooperation in Political Development

14. Since the adoption of the ASC Plan of Action in 2003, ASEAN has achieved progress in different measures of political development. There was increased participation by organisations, such as academic institutions, think-tanks, and civil

society organisations in ASEAN meetings and activities. Such consultations and heightened interactions fostered good relations and resulted in positive outcomes for the region.

15. Efforts are underway in laying the groundwork for an institutional framework to facilitate free flow of information based on each country's national laws and regulations; preventing and combating corruption; and cooperation to strengthen the rule of law, judiciary systems and legal infrastructure, and good governance. Moreover, in order to promote and protect human rights and fundamental freedoms, the ASEAN Charter stipulates the establishment of an ASEAN human rights body.

### A.1.1. *Promote Understanding and Appreciation of Political Systems, Culture and History of ASEAN Member States*

Actions

i. Assign appropriate ASEAN sectoral bodies to take necessary measures to promote understanding and appreciation of political systems, culture and history of ASEAN Member States, which will undertake to:

   a. Encourage the holding of at least two track two events per year, including academic conferences, workshops and seminars;
   b. Release periodic publications on the dynamics of ASEAN Member States' political systems, culture and history for dissemination to the public;
   c. Intensify exchange of experience and training courses in order to enhance popular and broader participation.

ii. Hold seminars/workshops to share experiences on democratic institutions, gender mainstreaming, and popular participation

iii. Endeavour to compile best practices of voluntary electoral observations

### A.1.2. *Lay the Groundwork for an Institutional Framework to Facilitate Free Flow of Information for Mutual Support and Assistance Among ASEAN Member States*

Actions

i. Encourage the ASEAN Ministers Responsible for Information (AMRI) to develop an institutional framework to facilitate free flow of information, based on each country's national laws, by establishing an information baseline of these laws and to submit a progress report to the ASEAN Political-Security Community Council

ii. Request each ASEAN Member State to develop relevant media exchange programmes to aid free flow of information, starting within three months from the adoption of this Blueprint
iii. Enhance media capacity to promote regional-community building, explore the possibility of establishing an ASEAN media panel to boost cooperation and collaboration among the media-related institutions and organizations with emphasis on the process of the implementation of the APSC Blueprint
iv. Implement internships, fellowships, scholarships and workshops, study visits and journalist exchange programs to enhance media capacity and professionalism in the region with emphasis on the process of the implementation of the APSC Blueprint
v. Facilitate co-production and exchanges of films, TVs, animations, games and new media content to promote cultural exchanges with emphasis on the process of the implementation of the APSC Blueprint

### A.1.3. *Establish Programmes for Mutual Support and Assistance Among ASEAN Member States in the Development of Strategies for Strengthening the Rule of Law and Judiciary Systems and Legal Infrastructure*

Actions

i. Entrust ASEAN Law Ministers Meeting (ALAWMM), with the cooperation of other sectoral bodies and entities associated with ASEAN including ASEAN Law Association (ALA) to develop cooperation programmes to strengthen the rule of law, judicial systems and legal infrastructure
ii. Undertake comparative studies for lawmakers on the promulgation of laws and regulations
iii. Develop a university curriculum on the legal systems of ASEAN Member States by the ASEAN University Network (AUN) by 2010
iv. Enhance cooperation between ALAWMM and ALA and other Track II organisations through seminars, workshops and research on international law, including ASEAN agreements.

### A.1.4. *Promote Good Governance*

Actions

i. Conduct analytical and technical studies to establish baselines, benchmarks, and best practices in various aspects of governance in the region.

ii. Promote sharing of experiences and best practices through workshops and seminars on leadership concepts and principles with emphasis on good governance, and on developing norms on good governance
iii. Conduct a study by 2009 on partnership between public and private sectors and academia in creating a conducive climate for good governance to provide concrete recommendations to appropriate ASEAN sectoral bodies
iv. Promote dialogue and partnership among governments, private sectors and other relevant organisations to foster and enable new ideas, concepts and methods with a view to enhance transparency, accountability, participatory and effective governance

## A.1.5. *Promotion and Protection of Human Rights*

Actions

i. Establish an ASEAN human rights body through the completion of its Terms of Reference (ToR) by 2009 and encourage cooperation between it and existing human rights mechanisms, as well as with other relevant international organizations
ii. Complete a stock-take of existing human rights mechanisms and equivalent bodies, including sectoral bodies promoting the rights of women and children by 2009
iii. Cooperate closely with efforts of the sectoral bodies in the development of an ASEAN instrument on the protection and promotion of the rights of migrant workers
iv. Strengthen interaction between the network of existing human rights mechanisms as well as other civil society organisations, with relevant ASEAN sectoral bodies
v. Enhance/conduct exchange of information in the field of human rights among ASEAN countries in order to promote and protect human rights and fundamental freedoms of peoples in accordance with the ASEAN Charter and the Charter of the United Nations, and the Universal Declaration of Human Rights and the Vienna Declaration and Programme of Action
vi. Promote education and public awareness on human rights
vii. Cooperate closely with efforts of the sectoral bodies in the establishment of an ASEAN commission on the promotion and protection of the rights of women and children

### A.1.6. *Increase the Participation of Relevant Entities Associated with ASEAN in Moving Forward ASEAN Political Development Initiatives*

Actions

i. Develop modalities for interaction between relevant entities associated with ASEAN, such as the ASEANISIS network, and ASEAN sectoral bodies
ii. Promote research studies and scholarly publications on ASEAN political development initiatives
iii. Hold consultations between AIPA and appropriate ASEAN organs
iv. Revise the Memorandum of Understanding of the ASEAN Foundation to take into account the provisions of the ASEAN Charter

### A.1.7. *Prevent and Combat Corruption*

Actions

i. Identify relevant mechanisms to carry out cooperation activities in preventing and combating corruption and strengthen links and cooperation between the relevant agencies
ii. Encourage all ASEAN Member States to sign the Memorandum of Understanding (MoU) on Cooperation for Preventing and Combating Corruption signed on 15 December 2004
iii. Promote ASEAN cooperation to prevent and combat corruption, bearing in mind the above MoU, and other relevant ASEAN instruments such as the Treaty on Mutual Legal Assistance in Criminal Matters (MLAT)
iv. Encourage ASEAN Member States who are signatories to the United Nations Convention against Corruption to ratify the said Convention
v. Promote the sharing of best practices, exchange views and analyse issues related to values, ethics and integrity through appropriate avenues and fora and taking into account inputs from various seminars such as the ASEAN Integrity Dialogue

### A.1.8. *Promote Principles of Democracy*

Actions

i. Promote understanding of the principles of democracy among ASEAN youth at schools at an appropriate stage of education, bearing in mind the educational system in the respective ASEAN Member States

ii. Convene seminars, training programmes and other capacity building activities for government officials, thinktanks and relevant civil society organizations to exchange views, sharing experiences and promote democracy and democratic institutions
iii. Conduct annual research on experiences and lessons learned of democracy aimed at enhancing the adherence to the principles of democracy

### A.1.9. *Promote Peace and Stability in the Region*

Actions

i. Support the inclusion of culture of peace which includes, inter alia, respect for diversity, promotion of tolerance and understanding of faiths, religions and cultures in the curriculum of ASEAN academic institutions
ii. Develop programmes and activities aimed at the promotion of culture of peace, interfaith and intrafaith dialogue within the region
iii. Promote respect and appreciation for the region's diversity and harmony among the peoples of the region
iv. Promote dialogue and greater interaction among various religious and ethnic groups
v. Promote networking among schools in the region to develop peaceeducation in their respective curricula
vi. Support poverty alleviation and narrowing development gaps to contribute to promoting sustained peace and stability in the region

## A.2. Shaping and Sharing of Norms

16. ASEAN promotes regional norms of good conduct and solidarity, in accordance with the key principles enshrined in the ASEAN Charter. In this context, ASEAN also continues to uphold the Treaty of Amity and Cooperation in Southeast Asia (TAC), the SEANWFZ Treaty and other key agreements, as well as the Declaration on the Conduct of Parties (DOC) in the South China Sea.

### A.2.1. *Adjust ASEAN Institutional Framework to Comply with the ASEAN Charter*

Actions

i. Prepare and implement a transitional work plan on the necessary institutional reforms needed to comply with the ASEAN Charter

ii. Develop, as appropriate, supplemental protocols and/or agreements, including terms of references and rules of procedures, needed to implement the ASEAN Charter
iii. Develop a legal division to support the implementation of the ASEAN Charter

### A.2.2. *Strengthening Cooperation Under the TAC*

Actions

i. Convene workshops and seminars to assess the progress of the implementation of the TAC and explore ways to improve its mechanisms
ii. Convene a conference of High Contracting Parties to the TAC to review its implementation
iii. Encourage the accession to the TAC by non-ASEAN countries

### A.2.3. *Ensure Full Implementation of the DOC for Peace and Stability in the South China Sea*

Actions

i. Continue ASEAN's current practice of close consultation among Member States to achieve full implementation of the DOC
ii. Explore and undertake cooperative activities identified in the DOC and eventually explore other cooperative measures on the basis of close consultation among the member countries, while respecting sovereignty and integrity of each other
iii. Carry out on a regular basis the overview of the process of implementation of the DOC, thus ensuring timely and proper conducts of the Parties in the South China Sea in accordance with the DOC
iv. Work towards the adoption of a regional Code of Conduct in the South China Sea (COC)

### A.2.4. *Ensure the Implementation of South East Asian Nuclear Weapon Free Zone (SEANWFZ) Treaty, and its Plan of Action*

Actions

i. Comply with the undertakings in the SEANFWZ Treaty, including accession to the International Atomic Energy Agency (IAEA) safeguards agreements and related instruments

ii. Encourage Accession to the Protocol of the SEANWFZ Treaty by Nuclear Weapon States
iii. Cooperate to implement the Plan of Action and draw up specific work programmes/projects to implement the Plan of Action

### A.2.5. *Promote ASEAN Maritime Cooperation*

Actions

i. Establish the ASEAN Maritime Forum
ii. Apply a comprehensive approach that focuses on safety of navigation and security concern in the region that are of common concerns to the ASEAN Community
iii. Stock take maritime issues and identify maritime cooperation among ASEAN member countries
iv. Promote cooperation in maritime safety and search and rescue (SAR) through activities such as information sharing, technological cooperation and exchange of visits of authorities concerned

## B. A COHESIVE, PEACEFUL AND RESILIENT REGION WITH SHARED RESPONSIBILITY FOR COMPREHENSIVE SECURITY

17. In building a cohesive, peaceful and resilient Political Security Community, ASEAN subscribes to the principle of comprehensive security, which goes beyond the requirements of traditional security but also takes into account non-traditional aspects vital to regional and national resilience, such as the economic, socio-cultural, and environmental dimensions of development. ASEAN is also committed to conflict prevention/confidence building measures, preventive diplomacy, and post-conflict peace building.

### B.1. Conflict Prevention/Confidence Building Measures

18. Confidence Building Measures and Preventive Diplomacy are important instruments in conflict prevention. They mitigate tensions and prevent disputes from arising between or among ASEAN Member States, as well as between ASEAN Member States and non ASEAN member countries. They will also help prevent the escalation of existing disputes.

19. In the area of defence and regional political consultations, ASEAN Defence Officials have been involved in the ASEAN security dialogue since 1996. Under the framework of the ASEAN Regional Forum (ARF), ASEAN has made voluntary briefings on political and security developments in the region and regularized meetings of high-level defence officials under the ARF Defence Officials' Dialogue (DOD) and the ARF Security Policy Conference (ASPC). ASEAN has also established an annual ASEAN Defence Ministers Meeting (ADMM) and ASEAN Defence Senior Officials' Meetings.

### B.1.1. *Strengthen Confidence-Building Measures*

Actions

i. Organise regional exchanges among ASEAN Defense and military officials, at all levels, including among military academies, staff colleges and defence universities in the ASEAN Member States
ii. Promote the exchange of observers of military exercises, commensurate with the capability and condition of each ASEAN Member State
iii. Share information among ASEAN Member States on submissions to the UN Register of Conventional Arms
iv. Promote bilateral exchanges and cooperation between defence officials and exchange visits between military training institutions to promote trust and mutual understanding
v. Conduct joint research projects on defence issues between government affiliated policy and strategic research institutes in the region

### B.1.2. *Promote Greater Transparency and Understanding of Defence Policies and Security Perceptions*

Actions

i. Work towards developing and publishing an annual ASEAN Security Outlook
ii. Hold voluntary briefings on political and security developments in the region
iii. Develop an ASEAN early warning system based on existing mechanisms to prevent occurrence/escalation of conflicts
iv. Hold consultations and cooperation on regional defence and security matters between ASEAN and external parties and Dialogue Partners including through the ADMM Plus when it is operationalised.

### B.1.3. *Build up the Necessary Institutional Framework to Strengthen the ARF Process in Support of the ASEAN Political-Security Community (APSC)*

Actions

i. Followup on the recommendations of the Review of the ARF
ii. Implement the enhanced role of the ARF Chair, and activate the Friends of the ARF Chair mechanism as and when needed
iii. Implement the decision of the ARF Ministers to move the ARF towards the preventive diplomacy stage (PD)
iv. Expand the capacity of the ARF Heads of Defense Universities, Colleges and Institutions Meeting (ARF HDUCIM) to exchange best practices in defense policies and academic development
v. Compile best practices on confidence building measures, preventive diplomacy and conflict resolutions for further development by ARF
vi. Enhance the role of the Secretary General of ASEAN in the ARF including further strengthening the ARF Unit in the ASEAN Secretariat

### B.1.4. *Strengthen Efforts in Maintaining Respect for Territorial Integrity, Sovereignty and Unity of ASEAN Member States as Stipulated in the Declaration on Principles of International Law Concerning Friendly Relations and Cooperation among States in Accordance with the Charter of the United Nations*

Actions

i. Compile best practices and relevant international law to promote understanding and appreciation of best practices concerning friendly relations and cooperation among Member States of the United Nations,
ii. Convene consultation as well as a series of tract two activities to strengthen cooperation in addressing threats and challenges that may affect the territorial integrity of ASEAN Member States including those posed by separatism
iii. Further promote and increase awareness on these issues to help accelerate the pace of ASEAN Community building and elevate ASEAN's profile in the world

### B.1.5. *Promote the Development of Norms that Enhance ASEAN Defence and Security Cooperation*

Actions

i. Initiate preparatory work for the development of practical cooperation programmes among the militaries of ASEAN Member States

## B2. Conflict Resolution And Pacific Settlement Of Disputes

20. Convinced that the settlement of differences or disputes should be regulated by rational, effective and sufficiently flexible procedures, avoiding negative attitudes, which might endanger or hinder cooperation, ASEAN promotes the TAC, which seeks to preserve regional peace and harmony and prescribes that Member States refrain from threat or use of force.
21. The TAC gives provision for pacific settlement of disputes at all times through friendly negotiations and for refraining from the threat or use of force to settle disputes. The strategies for conflict resolution shall be an integral part of a comprehensive approach. The purpose of these strategies shall be to prevent disputes and conflicts from arising between ASEAN Member States that could potentially pose a threat to regional peace and stability.
22. ASEAN, the United Nations and other organisations have held a number of cooperation activities in the effort to promote peace and stability. More efforts are needed in strengthening the existing modes of pacific settlement of disputes to avoid or settle future disputes; and undertaking conflict management and conflict resolution research studies. Under the ASEAN Charter, ASEAN may also establish appropriate dispute settlement mechanisms.

### B.2.1. *Build Upon Existing Modes of Pacific Settlement of Disputes and Consider Strengthening them with Additional Mechanisms as Needed*

Actions

i. Study and analyse existing dispute settlement modes and/or additional mechanisms with a view to enhancing regional mechanisms for the pacific settlement of disputes

ii. Develop ASEAN modalities for good offices, conciliation and mediation
iii. Establish appropriate dispute settlement mechanism, including arbitration as provided for by the ASEAN Charter

### B.2.2. *Strengthen Research Activities on Peace, Conflict Management and Conflict Resolution*

Actions

i. Consider the establishment of an ASEAN Institute for Peace and Reconciliation
ii. Compile ASEAN's experiences and best practices on peace, conflict management and conflict resolution
iii. Identify priority research topics, with a view to providing recommendations on promoting peace, conflict management and conflict resolution
iv. Enhance existing cooperation among ASEAN think tanks to study peace, conflict management and conflict resolution
v. Hold workshops on peace, conflict management and conflict resolution with relevant regional and international organisations, including the UN
vi. Undertake studies to promote gender mainstreaming in peace building, peace process and conflict resolution
vii. Develop a pool of experts from ASEAN Member States as resource persons to assist in conflict management and conflict resolution activities

### B.2.3. *Promote Regional Cooperation to Maintain Peace and Stability*

Actions

i. Carry out technical cooperation with the UN and relevant regional organisations to exchange expertise and experiences in maintaining peace and stability
ii. Identify national focal points, with a view to promoting regional cooperation in maintaining peace and stability
iii. Establish a network among existing ASEAN Member States' peace keeping centres to conduct joint planning, training, and sharing of experiences, with a view to establishing an ASEAN arrangement for the maintenance of peace and stability, in accordance with the ASEAN Defence Ministers' Meeting (ADMM) 3-Year Work Programme.

## B.3. Post-Conflict Peace Building

23. ASEAN's efforts in post-conflict peace building shall complement other comprehensive approaches to: (a) ensure the complete discontinuity of conflicts

and violence and/or manmade disasters in affected areas; (b) facilitate the return of peace and/or normalisation of life as early as possible; and (c) lay the ground for reconciliation and all other necessary measures to secure peace and stability, thus preventing the affected areas from falling again to conflicts in the future.

24. Measures can be pursued in promoting humanitarian relief activities, including intensifying cooperation with the United Nations and other organisations, as well as capacity building for people in affected areas.

### B.3.1. *Strengthen ASEAN Humanitarian Assistance*

Actions

i. Provide basic services or assistance to bring relief to victims of conflict in consultation with the receiving State
ii. Promote cooperation for orderly repatriation of refugees/displaced persons and resettlement of internally displaced persons
iii. Promote the safety of the humanitarian relief assistance workers
iv. Develop common operating procedures for the provision of humanitarian assistance in the event of conflict
v. Intensify cooperation with the United Nations and promote the role and contributions of relevant international organisations on humanitarian assistance
vi. Promote civil military dialogue and coordination in humanitarian assistance
vii. Expand the role and contribution of women in field based humanitarian operations

### B.3.2. *Implement Human Resources Development and Capacity Building Programmes in Post-Conflict Areas*

Actions

i. Draw up guidelines for training and capacity-building needs assessment
ii. Identify priority training topics
iii. Design training programmes in the identified priority topics and development of training materials
iv. Implement annual programmes in each target area
v. Develop cooperation programmes with relevant external parties and financial institutions to promote Human Resources Development and capacity building in post-conflict reconstruction and peace building
vi. Work towards the development of a systematic training programme for formal and community educators in the field of peace education and reconciliation, which can be conceptualised and implemented

### B.3.3. *Increase Cooperation in reconciliation and Further Strengthen Peace-Oriented Values*

Actions

i. Undertake studies to increase cooperation in reconciliation and further strengthen peace-oriented values
ii. Promote public participation in the development of cooperation in post-conflict reconstruction and rehabilitation including the encouragement of comprehensive input of academia, media, nongovernmental organisations, civil society and community groups
iii. Promote inter-communal understanding through exchange activities

## B.4. Non-Traditional Security Issues

25. A key purpose of ASEAN is to respond effectively and in a timely manner, in accordance with the principles of comprehensive security, to all forms of threats, transnational crimes and transboundary challenges.

### B.4.1. *Strengthen Cooperation in Addressing Nontraditional Security Issues, Particularly in Combating Transnational Crimes and Other Transboundary Challenges*

Actions

i. Implement effectively eight priority areas in the Work Programme to Implement the Plan of Action to Combat Transnational Crime
ii. Endeavour to ratify the Treaty on Mutual Legal Assistance in Criminal Matters among ASEAN Member States and work towards elevating it to an ASEAN treaty
iii. Continue the work of the working group, as mandated by the ASEAN Law Ministers' Meeting, to enhance cooperation on the issue of extradition

....

vi. Work towards a drug-free ASEAN by 2015, in accordance with the ASEAN Work Plan for Combating Illicit Drug-Trafficking, by: strengthening measures to prevent the illicit production of drugs, import and export of controlled chemical precursors as well as regional cooperation in controlled delivery; and enhancing cross-border law enforcement cooperation through information sharing, best practices, and capacity building, in combating drug-trafficking

vii. Develop multilateral or bilateral legal arrangements towards combating drug and precursor chemical trafficking starting in 2008

viii. Provide assistance to ASEAN Member States in enhancing scientific laboratory capacity in precursor identification and drugs signature analysis for drug enforcement operation and intelligence

ix. Provide transfer of knowledge concerning the profile of drug crime syndicate groups as well as watch-list of their drug activities

x. Provide transfer of knowledge on best practices on the disposal of precursors and essential chemicals seized from clandestine laboratories

xi. Strengthen the capacity of the criminal justice system including judges, prosecutors and law enforcement officials on drug control

xii. Enhance cooperation with relevant external parties in combating transnational crimes, including countering terrorism

xiii. Enhance cooperation and coordination among existing ASEAN sectoral bodies in dealing with transnational crimes

xiv. Strengthen close cooperation among ASEAN Member States, to combat IUU fishing in the region and where applicable, through the implementation of the IPOA IUU fishing and work towards the establishment of ASEAN Fisheries Consultative Forum (AFCF)

xv. Promote full implementation by relevant sectoral bodies, to prevent, combat and eradicate the illicit trade in small arms and light weapons in all its aspects, in accordance with the UN Programme of Action to Prevent, Combat and Eradicate the Illicit Trade in Small Arms and Light Weapons in All its Aspects (UN PoA) and the International Instrument to enable States to Identify and Trace, in Timely and Reliable Manner, Illicit Small Arms and Light Weapons (International Tracing Instrument)

xvi. Strengthen cooperation and assistance in combating and suppressing cyber crimes including cooperation among law enforcement agencies, taking into account the need of each country to develop laws to address cyber crimes

....

xviii. Strengthen cooperation in the field of border management to jointly address matters of common concern, including forgeries of identification and travel documents, by enhancing the use of relevant technologies to effectively stem the flow of terrorists and criminals

### B.4.2. *Intensify Counter Terrorism Efforts by Early Ratification and Full Implementation of the ASEAN Convention on Counter-Terrorism*

Actions

i. Work towards the entry into force of the ASEAN Convention on Counter-Terrorism (ACCT) by 2009 its ratification by all ASEAN Member States, and promote effective implementation of the Convention
ii. Endeavour to accede and ratify the relevant international instruments on counter terrorism
iii. Promote effective implementation of the ASEAN Comprehensive Plan of Action on Counter-Terrorism
iv. Cooperate to support development initiatives aimed at addressing the root causes of terrorism and conditions conducive to terrorism

## B.5. Strengthen ASEAN Cooperation on Disaster Management and Emergency Response

Actions

i. Enhance joint effective and early response at the political and operational levels in activating the ASEAN disaster management arrangements to assist affected countries in the event of major disasters
ii. Enhance civilian-military coordination in providing effective and timely response to major natural disasters
iii. Finalise the SOP for Regional Standby Arrangements and Coordination of Joint Disaster Relief and Emergency Response Operations for establishing joint operations in providing relief aid to disaster affected areas of Member States in line with the ASEAN Agreement on Disaster Management and Emergency Response (AADMER)
iv. Work towards effective interface on disaster management between ASEAN and other ASEAN-related bodies such as the ASEAN Regional Forum (ARF), ASEAN Plus Three and East Asia Summit (EAS) in a manner that will enhance ASEAN's disaster management capacities
v. Develop ARF strategic guidelines for humanitarian assistance and disaster relief cooperation

### B.6. Effective and Timely Response to Urgent Issues or Crisis Situations Affecting ASEAN

Actions

i. Convene special meetings at the Leaders' or Ministerial levels in the event of crisis or emergency situations affecting ASEAN; and develop arrangements to address such situations in a timely manner

## C. A DYNAMIC AND OUTWARDLOOKING REGION IN AN INCREASINGLY INTEGRATED AND INTERDEPENDENT WORLD

26. ASEAN fosters and maintains friendly and mutually beneficial relations with external parties to ensure that the peoples and Member States of ASEAN live in peace with the world at large in a just, democratic and harmonious environment. ASEAN remains outward — looking and plays a pivotal role in the regional and international fora to advance ASEAN's common interests.
27. Through its external relations, ASEAN will exercise and maintain its centrality and proactive role as the primary driving force in an open, transparent and inclusive regional architecture to support the establishment of the ASEAN Community by 2015

### C.1. Strengthening ASEAN Centrality in Regional Cooperation and Community Building

Actions

i. Initiate, host, Chair and/or Co-Chair activities and meetings with Dialogue Partners, other external parties, and within the context of ASEAN Plus Three, EAS and ARF
ii. Explore, initiate and implement concrete cooperation activities on actions as stipulated in various agreed documents including the APSC Blueprint under the existing regional frameworks
iii. Advance the ARF towards Preventive Diplomacy in a phased and prudent manner while continuing with Confidence Building Measures; while also

engaging other regional and international organisations and Track II organisations in the process

iv. Enhance coordination in ASEAN's external relation and regional and multilateral fora

### C.2. Promoting Enhanced Ties with External Parties

Actions

i. Promote activities to raise awareness of ASEAN and enhance ASEAN's interests, including the establishment of ASEAN Committees in Third Countries where appropriate

ii. Explore cooperation projects with regional organisations such as the GCC, ECO, Rio Group, SAARC and SCO

iii. Develop cooperation projects to implement the ASEANUN Memorandum of Understanding (MOU)

### C.3. Strengthening Consultations and Cooperation on Multilateral Issues of Common Concern

Actions

i. Enhance consultations within ASEAN including by ASEAN Permanent Missions in United Nations and other International Organisations with the aim of promoting ASEAN's interests

## III. IMPLEMENTATION AND REVIEW OF THE APSC BLUEPRINT

### A. Implementation Mechanism

28. To ensure the success in implementing the APSC Blueprint, Member States shall integrate the programmes and activities of the Blueprint into their respective national development plans.
29. All relevant ASEAN senior official bodies or their equivalent shall be responsible in ensuring the implementation of the various elements, actions and commitments in the Blueprint by reflecting them in their respective work plans, mobilising resources for them, raising issues for the consideration of their respective ministerial bodies and the ASEAN Leaders, and undertaking national initiatives in order to meet these commitments.

30. The Coordinating Conference for the ASEAN Political-Security Community Plan of Action (ASCCO) shall continue to serve as the platform in coordinating the efforts of various sectoral bodies through exchanges of information, best practices, and lessons learned in the implementation of the APSC Blueprint. ASCCO's new initiatives and recommendations on emerging issues shall be reported to the ASEAN Political-Security Council.
31. The ASEAN Political-Security Community (APSC) Council shall be responsible for the overall implementation of the Blueprint and shall ensure coordination of efforts under its purview as well as those which cut across the other Community Councils.
32. Progress of implementation of the APSC Blueprint shall be reported annually by the Secretary-General of ASEAN to the annual ASEAN Summit, through the APSC Council.

## B. Resource Mobilisation

33. Financial resources to implement the Blueprint will be mobilised by ASEAN Member States, as well as from various facilities including the ASEAN Development Fund (ADF), Dialogue Partners, donor countries, international agencies, the private sector, and nongovernmental organisations.

## C. Communication Strategy

34. To ensure the success of establishing the APSC, a comprehensive communication plan will be developed and launched at the national and regional levels. This will not only create greater public awareness of the various initiatives, outcomes and issues of the APSC, but also enable all stakeholders to be involved in the process.

## D. Review Mechanism

35. The APSC Blueprint shall be reviewed and evaluated to ensure that all the activities are responsive to the needs and priorities of ASEAN, taking into account the changing dynamics of the region and the global environment. The review and evaluation shall be conducted biennially by the ASCCO, in coordination with the ASEAN Secretariat. In the course of the review and evaluation, ASEAN Member States are given the flexibility to update the Blueprint. As in the progress of implementation of the APSC Blueprint, the results of the

review and evaluation shall be reported by the Secretary-General of ASEAN to the ASEAN Summit through the APSC Council.

Source: http://www.reliefweb.int/rw/rwb.nsf/db900sid/MWAI-7PR32R/$File/full_report.pdf
Accessed date: 3 March 2009
Publisher: ASEAN Secretariat
Country: Jakarta
Date of Publication: 2009

# CHAPTER 55

# BLUEPRINT FOR THE ASEAN SOCIO-CULTURAL COMMUNITY (2009–2015)

## I. INTRODUCTION

1. The ASEAN Leaders adopted the Declaration of ASEAN Concord II (Bali Concord II) in Bali, Indonesia on 7 October 2003 to establish an ASEAN Community by 2020. The ASEAN Community shall be established comprising three pillars, namely political and security community, economic community, and socio-cultural community that are closely intertwined and mutually reinforcing for the purpose of ensuring durable peace, stability, and shared prosperity in the region.
2. At the 12th ASEAN Summit on 13th January 2007 in Cebu, the Philippines the Leaders, affirming their strong commitment to accelerate the establishment of the ASEAN Community by 2015, signed the Cebu Declaration on the Acceleration of an ASEAN Community by 2015.
3. The 13th ASEAN Summit held in Singapore on 20th November 2007, agreed to develop an ASCC Blueprint to ensure that concrete actions are undertaken to promote the establishment of an ASEAN Socio-Cultural Community (ASCC).

## II. CHARACTERISTICS AND ELEMENTS

4. The primary goal of the ASCC is to contribute to realising an ASEAN Community that is people-centred and socially responsible with a view to achieving enduring solidarity and unity among the nations and peoples of ASEAN by forging a common identity and building a caring and sharing society which is inclusive and harmonious where the well-being, livelihood, and welfare of the peoples are enhanced.
5. The ASCC will address the region's aspiration to lift the quality of life of its peoples through cooperative activities that are people-oriented and environmentally friendly geared towards the promotion of sustainable development. The ASCC shall contribute to building a strong foundation for greater understanding, good neighbourliness, and a shared sense of responsibility.
6. The ASCC is characterised by a culture of regional resilience, adherence to agreed principles, spirit of cooperation, collective responsibility, to promote human and social development, respect for fundamental freedoms, gender

equality, the promotion and protection of human rights and the promotion of social justice.

7. The ASCC shall respect the different cultures, languages, and religions of the peoples of ASEAN emphasise their common values in the spirit of unity in diversity and adapt them to present realities, opportunities and challenges.
8. The ASCC will also focus on the social dimension of Narrowing the Development Gap (NDG) towards bridging the development gap among Member States.
9. Based on the above, the ASCC envisages the following characteristics: (a) Human Development; (b) Social Welfare and Protection; (c) Social Justice and Rights; (d) Ensuring Environmental Sustainability (e) Building the ASEAN Identity; and (f) Narrowing the Development Gap.

## A. HUMAN DEVELOPMENT

10. ASEAN will enhance the well-being and livelihood of the peoples of ASEAN by providing them with equitable access to human development opportunities by promoting and investing in education and life-long learning, human resource training and capacity building, encourage innovation and entrepreneurship, promote the use of English language, ICT and applied science and technology in socio-economic development activities.

### A1. Advancing and Prioritising Education

11. ***Strategic objective***: Ensuring the integration of education priorities into ASEAN's development agenda and creating a knowledge based society; achieving universal access to primary education; promoting early child care and development; and enhancing awareness of ASEAN to youths through education and activities to build an ASEAN identity based on friendship and cooperation.

***Actions:***

....

### A2. Investing in Human Resource Development

12. ***Strategic objective***: Enhance and improve the capacity of ASEAN human resource through strategic programmes and develop a qualified, competent and well-prepared ASEAN labour force that would benefit from as well as cope with the challenges of regional integration.

***Actions:***

. . . .

## A3. Promotion of Decent Work

13. ***Strategic objective***: Incorporating decent work principles in ASEAN work culture, safety and health at work place and ensuring that the promotion of entrepreneurship becomes an integral part of ASEAN's employment policy to achieve a forward-looking employment strategy.

***Actions:***

. . . .

## A4. Promoting Information and Communication Technology (ICT)

14. ***Strategic objective***: Implement human resource development programme which will facilitate the implementation of regional ICT initiatives.

***Actions:***

. . . .

## A5. Facilitating Access to Applied Science and Technology (S&T)

15. ***Strategic objective***: Develop policies and mechanisms to support active cooperation in research, science and technology development, technology transfers and commercialisation and establishment of strong networks of scientific and technological institutions with the active participation of private sector and other relevant organisations.

***Actions:***

. . . .

## A6. Strengthening Entrepreneurship Skills for Women, Youth, Elderly and Persons with Disabilities

16. ***Strategic objective***: Increasing the participation of women, youth, elderly, persons with disabilities, vulnerable and marginalised groups in the productive

workforce by enhancing their entrepreneurial skills, particularly to improve their social well-being and contribute towards national development and regional economic integration.

***Actions:***

....

## A7. Building Civil Service Capability

17. ***Strategic objective:*** Establish effective, efficient, transparent, responsive and accountable civil service systems through increased capacity-building, enhancement of public human resource competencies among ASEAN bureaucracies, and increased collaboration among ASEAN Member States.

***Actions:***

....

## B. SOCIAL WELFARE AND PROTECTION

18. ASEAN is committed to enhancing the well-being and the livelihood of the peoples of ASEAN through alleviating poverty, ensuring social welfare and protection, building a safe, secure and drug free environment, enhancing disaster resilience and addressing health development concerns.

## B1. Poverty Alleviation

19. ***Strategic objective***: Fully address socioeconomic disparities and poverty that persist across ASEAN Member States including achieving the MDG goal of eradicating extreme poverty and hunger.

***Actions:***

i. Develop and implement an ASEAN Roadmap towards realising the UN Millennium Development Goals in consultation among concerned sectoral bodies with a view to identify and extend technical assistance required in the field of poverty reduction;
ii. Support ASEAN Member States' community-driven initiatives for poverty reduction towards narrowing the development gap within ASEAN;

iii. Intensify efforts to implement projects related to poverty alleviation particularly in area of rural infrastructure, water supply, sanitation under the Initiative for ASEAN Integration and other sub-regional cooperation frameworks;
iv. Improve ASEAN capacity in simple and applicable assessment and monitoring poverty reduction strategies through a targeting system that ensures low exclusion and leakage rates;
v. Families living under poverty to be aided with appropriate support system to enable them to become self-reliant;
vi. Strengthen ASEAN cooperation in microfinance, including strengthening cooperation and networking between microfinance institutions in poverty-stricken areas with due regard to local values and traditions as well as addressing the phenomenon of the feminisation of poverty;
vii. Work towards the establishment of an ASEAN data bank on poverty incidence and poverty reduction programme, which can be shared among Member States;
viii. Continue sharing experiences and best practices through regular holding of workshops and seminars on poverty alleviation in ASEAN Member States and its dialogue partners;
ix. Establish an ASEAN Network for Family Development; and
x. Facilitate the rural volunteers movement and the exchange of young professional in rural development in ASEAN.

## B2. Social Safety Net and Protection from the Negative Impacts of Integration and Globalization

20. ***Strategic objective***: Ensure that all ASEAN peoples are provided with social welfare and protection from the possible negative impacts of globalisation and integration by improving the quality, coverage and sustainability of social protection and increasing the capacity of social risk management.

### *Actions:*

i. Undertake a survey of existing social protection regimes in ASEAN;
ii. Enhance exchange of best practices in social security systems;
iii. Include social protection in ASEAN's cooperation in progressive labour practices;
iv. Explore the establishment of the social insurance system to cover the informal sector;

v. Establish a network of social protection agencies to promote the well-being and living conditions of the poor, vulnerable, underserved and disadvantaged groups affected by adverse impacts of integration process and globalisation;
vi. Study on enhancement of support for natural disaster risk safety mechanism in agriculture, forestry and fisheries;
vii. Conduct research studies on the impact of economic integration and globalisation from gender perspective in order to have concrete bases in formulating appropriate genderresponsive interventions;
viii. Develop appropriate actions and preventive measures against the use of the internet and pornography which exploit women, children, and other vulnerable groups;
ix. Develop appropriate actions and preventive measures against the use of the internet to disrupt social harmony by inciting hatred, discrimination, and intolerance; and
x. Strengthen ASEAN cooperation in protecting female migrant workers

## B3. Enhancing Food Security and Safety

21. ***Strategic objective***: Ensure adequate access to food at all times for all ASEAN peoples and ensure food safety in ASEAN Member States.

### *Actions:*

i. Harmonise national food safety regulations with internationallyaccepted standard, including quarantine and inspection procedures for the movement of plants, animals, and their products;
ii. Strengthen the work of ASEAN Coordinating Committee on Food Safety to better coordinate all ASEAN Food bodies/subsidiaries, and the implementation of their work programmes;
iii. Promote production of safe and healthy food by producers at all levels;
iv. Develop model food legislative framework and guidelines and strengthen food inspection and certification system from farm to table in ASEAN Member States;
v. Develop further the competency of existing network of food laboratories in ASEAN to facilitate the exchange of information, findings, experiences, and best practices relating food laboratories works and new technology;
vi. Strengthen the capability of ASEAN Member States to conduct risk analysis;

vii. Enhance consumer participation and empowerment in food safety;
viii. Enhance the roles of ASEAN Food Security Reserve Board (AFSRB) as well as increase regional staple food reserves;
ix. Strengthen the cooperation with regional and international institutions including private organisations to secure food for the region;
x. Establish a network to enhance intra and extra ASEAN food trade co-operation to ensure stability in regional food distribution;
xi. Ensure that food is available at all times for all ASEAN citizens;
xii. Encourage the application of environmentally sound technologies in farming and food processing;
xiii. Improve the quality of surveillance and the effectiveness of responses to foodborne diseases and food poisoning outbreaks through, among others, information sharing and exchange of expertise;
xiv. Enhance advocacy to promote production of safe and healthy food by producers and education and communication to communities for empowerment in food safety;
xv. Provide opportunities such as forums, meetings to facilitate coordinated actions among stakeholders geared for promotion of food security and safety; and
xvi. Integrate these actions into a comprehensive plan of action with the ultimate goal of improving health outcomes.

## B4. Access to Healthcare and Promotion of Healthy Lifestyles

22. ***Strategic objectives***: Ensure access to adequate and affordable healthcare, medical services and medicine, and promote healthy lifestyles for the peoples of ASEAN.

### *Actions:*

i. Promote investment in primary health care infrastructure, in a rational manner and likewise ensure adequate financing and social protection for the poor and marginalised populations for better access to services and achievement of health-related Millennium Development Goals (MDGs);
ii. Promote and undertake information and educational drive and public health policies' advocacy activities to encourage healthy lifestyle and behaviour change intervention including diet, physical activities and mental health, that are accessible, affordable, and sustainable;

iii. Employ strategies to strengthen integrated risk management, promotion of healthy lifestyle and behavioural change;
iv. Develop and adopt a framework for unhealthy food and beverages including alcohol similar to the Framework Convention on Tobacco Control (FCTC);
v. Enhance awareness on the impact of regional/global trade policies and economic integration on health and develop possible strategies to mitigate their negative impacts through regional workshops and seminars, advocacy, sharing of studies and technical documents;
vi. Develop strategies for ASEAN to strengthen capacity and competitiveness in health related products and services, including in the pharmaceutical sector;
vii. Facilitate research and cross-country exchange of experience in promoting the integration of safe, effective and quality Traditional Medicine, Complementary and Alternative Medicine (TM/CAM) into the national healthcare system, and across other sectors;
viii. Promote the application of biotechnology, food technology, and nanotechnology to assist in the sustainable use of biological resources, and design, production and delivery of drugs and other products;
ix. Promote e-health in facilitating timely sharing of appropriate, accurate and complete information for the benefit of public health;
x. Promote collaboration in Research and Development on health promotion, health lifestyles and risk factors of non-communicable diseases in ASEAN Member States;
xi. Promote the sharing of best practices in improved access to health products including medicines for people in ASEAN;
xii. Provide adequate incentives and better working conditions to ensure the retention of health workers within the region and develop, in close collaboration with WHO including relevant sectors, a fair code of practice on the international recruitment of health workers to resolve the critical shortage of health workers around the world;
xiii. Encourage exchange of experts in the field of public health, medicine, physical and health education, to promote sharing of knowledge and experience;
xiv. Encourage public-private partnership, community empowerment and gender sensitive policies in improving community health standard;
xv. Promote capacity building programmes such as improving pharmaceutical management capability; facilitating training courses and exchange of experience in researches on stability, bioavailability, bioequivalence, clinical studies, validation of manufacturing process, validation of analytical methods;
xvi. Establish and maintain an ASEAN Nutrition Surveillance System;

xvii. Promote the sharing of best practises in improving the access to primary health care by people at risk/vulnerable groups, with special attention to diabetes mellitus, cardiovascular diseases, cancers and disabilities through regional workshops, seminars, and exchange visits among the ASEAN Member States;

xviii. Empower consumers to become active participants in health care and to make informed choices to maximise the benefits and minimise the risks of use of Traditional Medicine/Complementary and Alternative Medicine (TM/CAM);

xix. Advocate policy makers to accelerate actions to increase accessibility to sexual and reproductive health information and friendly health services, and educate society especially parents and adolescent on reproductive and sexual health education;

xx. Develop programmes and improve surveillance of certain non-communicable diseases, including diabetes mellitus, cardiovascular diseases and cancers which are becoming more prevalent in the community due to changing lifestyles;

xxi. Strengthen existing health networking in ASEAN Member States in order to push forward an active implementation on health services access and promotion of healthy lifestyles, as well as continually exchange of knowledge, technology and innovation for sustainable cooperation and development;

xxii. Promote rational use of drug, especially on prescription of antibiotic;

xxiii. Exchange of information and experience on drug price control to access essential drug in all ASEAN Member States; and

xxiv. Promote the exchange of experiences among ASEAN Member States on public health policy formulation and management.

## B5. Improving Capability to Control Communicable Diseases

23. ***Strategic objective***: To enhance regional preparedness and capacity through integrated approaches to prevention, surveillance and timely response to communicable and emerging infectious diseases.

### *Actions:*

i. Consolidate, further strengthen and develop regional cooperative arrangements through multi-sectoral and integrated approaches in the prevention, control, preparedness for emerging infectious diseases in line with International Health Regulation 2005 and the Asia Pacific Strategy for Emerging Diseases (APSED);

ii. Establish/strengthen/maintain regional support system and network to narrow the gap among ASEAN Member States in addressing emerging infectious diseases and other communicable diseases;
iii. Ensure that stockpile of antivirals and Personal Protective Equipment (PPE) is maintained at regional level for all member states and for rapid response and rapid containment of potential pandemic influenza;
iv. Reduce the impact of HIV transmission and the impact of HIV epidemic, consistent with the Millennium Development Goals (MDGs), the UNGASS declarations on HIV and AIDS, ASEAN Commitments on HIV and AIDS, and Third ASEAN Work Programme on HIV and AIDS;
v. Improve better access to affordable antiretroviral treatment and opportunistic disease treatment as well as diagnostic reagents;
vi. Develop programme to improve 2$^{nd}$ generation HIV surveillance (risk factors and behaviour) and promote sharing of information and experience among ASEAN Member States;
vii. Promote the sharing of best practises in improving the access to primary health care by people at risk/vulnerable groups, with special attention to HIV and AIDS, malaria, dengue fever, tuberculosis, and emerging infectious diseases through regional workshops, seminars, and exchange visits among the ASEAN Member States;
viii. Strengthen regional clinical expertise through professional organisations networks, regional research institution, exchange of expertise and information sharing;
ix. Strengthen cooperation through sharing of information and experiences to prevent and control infectious diseases related to global warming, climate change, natural and manmade disasters;
x. To tackle the issues of clean water, hygiene, sanitation and waste management that have implications on infectious diseases;
xi. Strengthen cooperation among ASEAN Member States in contact tracing and health quarantine;
xii. Strengthen and maintain surveillance system for infectious diseases including HIV and AIDS, malaria, dengue fever, and tuberculosis; and
xiii. Promote the collaboration in Research and Development on health products especially on new medicines for communicable diseases including neglected diseases commonly found in ASEAN Member States.

## B6. Ensuring a Drug Free ASEAN

24. ***Strategic objectives***: Reduce significantly, the overall prevalence of illicit drug abuse in the general population, in particular students, youth and those in

high-risk and vulnerable groups through preventive measures and by increasing access to treatment, rehabilitation and aftercare services to ensure full reintegration into society as well as through enhanced partnership between the public and private sectors and civil society organizations.

### *Actions:*

i. Develop and widely implement family, school, workplace and community-based drug prevention and drug abuse control programmes;
ii. Promoting civic awareness and social response by proactively advocating advocacy against the damage and dangers of drugs;
iii. Reducing illicit consumption of drugs by building consensus and sharing of best practices in drug demand reduction programmes;
iv. Sharing of drug research data among ASEAN Member States;
v. Develop technical assistance that would help concerned countries identify alternative crops as substitute to illicit drug crops and institute sustainable policy reforms;
vi. Promote wider access to markets for alternative development (AD) products within the region consistent with national and international obligations and treaties applicable multilateral trade rules;
vii. Facilitate the establishment and maintenance of treatment and rehabilitation centre in any ASEAN Member States;
viii. Exchange of experience, expertise and best practice and lessons learned on the prevention and treatment of and aftercare drug users/addicts among both public and community-based organisations and NGOs; and
ix. Strengthen capacities of drug demand reduction workers and drug control officers; and develop pool of experts and trainers in the fields of drug demand reduction and drug control programme.

## B7. Building Disaster-Resilient Nations and Safer Communities

25. ***Strategic objective***: Strengthen effective mechanisms and capabilities to prevent and reduce disaster losses in lives, and in social, economic, and environmental assets of ASEAN Member States and to jointly respond to disaster emergencies through concerted national efforts and intensified regional and international cooperation.

### *Actions:*

i. Fully implement the ASEAN Agreement on Disaster Management and Emergency Response by 2015;

ii. Support the establishment and operationalisation of the ASEAN Coordinating Centre for Humanitarian Assistance on disaster management (AHA Centre) to facilitate cooperation and coordination among ASEAN Member States and with relevant UN agencies and international organisations;
iii. Institutionalise capacity building programmes in areas of priority concern of Member States by the year 2015, and promote technical cooperation, joint research and networking to increase the capacity and capability of Member States in responding to disasters and reducing losses from disasters;
iv. Establish a fully functioning ASEAN Disaster Information Sharing and Communication Network by the year 2010, to promote sharing of information and best practices and facilitate decision making process;
v. Implement or enhance public awareness and education programmes on a regular basis, and promote public participation in programmes related to disaster risk reduction and emergency response in order to promote community resilience to disasters;
vi. Promote partnership with relevant stakeholders, including local communities, nongovernmental organisations and private enterprises, and strengthen cooperation with United Nations and relevant international organisations;
vii. Carry both national and ASEAN flag or logo to promote the visibility of ASEAN among the first responders engaged in humanitarian missions;
viii. Promote sustainable livelihood options through socioeconomic development activities to minimise disaster risks and enhance community-coping capacities;
ix. Strengthen community-based disaster preparedness and participation through promotion of indigenous knowledge and practices, implementation of public awareness and education and sharing of best practices and lessons learnt to build a disaster-resilient community;
x. Promote wider utilisation of services of existing regional facilities, such as ASEAN Specialised Meteorological Centre (ASMC) and ASEAN Earthquake Information Centre (AEIC), in providing early warning information and technical advisories to enhance regional disaster preparedness;
xi. Establish an ASEAN volunteer programme to assist disaster stricken areas which will also enhance ASEAN togetherness; and
xii. Promote multi-sectoral coordination and planning on Pandemic Preparedness and Response at the regional level including development of a regional Multi-Sectoral Pandemic Preparedness and Response Plan.

## C. SOCIAL JUSTICE AND RIGHTS

26. ASEAN is committed to promoting social justice and mainstreaming people's rights into its policies and all spheres of life, including the rights and welfare of disadvantaged, vulnerable and marginalised groups such as women, children, the elderly, persons with disabilities and migrant workers.

### C1. Promotion and Protection of the Rights and Welfare of Women, Children, the Elderly, and Persons with Disabilities

27. ***Strategic objective***: Safeguard the interests and rights as well as provide equal opportunities, and raise the quality of life and standard of living, for women, children, the elderly, and persons with disabilities.

***Actions:***

i. Work towards the establishment of an ASEAN commission on the promotion and protection of the rights of women and children;
ii. Continue to implement the Work Plan to Operationalise the Declaration on the Elimination of Violence Against Women in the ASEAN Region;
iii. Implement programmes on child survival, development and protection consistent with the Convention on the Rights of the Child;
iv. Establish an ASEAN network of social workers by 2013;
v. Conduct regional capacity building programmes on social services and rehabilitation for persons with disabilities;
vi. Support activities in promoting and developing care and welfare and the quality of life and well being of the elderly, persons with disabilities, women and children living under poverty, vulnerable and disadvantaged groups, including by exchanging best practices in all related fields such as accessibility, rehabilitation, protection and care including medical care. This should also include volunteer home-based care and all other forms of alternative family and community care arrangements;
vii. Enhance support and commitment to improve social protection for the elderly in ASEAN Member States, through networking, and exchange of information;
viii. Develop social security standards in each ASEAN Member States;
ix. Facilitate and exchange research and studies in gerontology and medicine for the elderly;

x. Use sex-disaggregated data, among others, to promote awareness on gender equality, women's role and contribution in the development of the region at the policy level;
xi. Promote and enhance the percentage of women's participation in all fields and at all levels, including political, decision-making as well as socioeconomic empowerment of women;
xii. Incorporate a gender perspective into national and regional policies and enhance the participation of women in programmes and projects;
xiii. Promote and encourage participation of persons with disabilities in decision-making and recognise their accomplishments;
xiv. Develop and implement programme to assist children living under disadvantaged and vulnerable conditions; and
xv. Establish an ASEAN Consortium of Social Welfare Practitioners, Educators and Schools of Social Work.

## C2. Protection and Promotion of the Rights of Migrant Workers

28. ***Strategic objective***: Ensure fair and comprehensive migration policies and adequate protection for all migrant workers in accordance with the laws, regulations and policies of respective ASEAN Member States as well as implement the ASEAN Declaration on the Protection and Promotion of the Rights of Migrant Workers.[1]

### *Actions:*

i. Operationalise the ASEAN Committee on the Implementation of the ASEAN Declaration on the Protection and Promotion of Rights of Migrant Workers under the auspices of the SLOM to implement the provisions of the Declaration and work towards the development of an ASEAN instrument on the protection and promotion of the rights of migrant workers;
ii. Institutionalise and convene on a regular basis the ASEAN Forum on Migrant Labour as a platform for broad-based discussions on migrant labour issues under the auspices of the Committee, which reports to SLOM;
iii. Promote fair and appropriate employment protection payment of wages and adequate access to decent working and living conditions for migrant workers and provide migrant workers, who may be victims of discrimination, abuse, exploitation, violence, with adequate access to the legal and judicial system of the receiving states;

iv. Intensify efforts to protect the fundamental human rights, promote the welfare and uphold human dignity of migrant workers by, among others, facilitating the exercise of consular functions to consular or diplomatic authorities of states of origin when a migrant workers is arrested or committed to prison or custody or detained in any other manner, under the laws and regulation of the receiving state and in accordance with the Vienna Convention and Consular Relations;
v. Facilitate data-sharing on matters related to migrant workers for the purpose of enhancing policies and programmes concerning migrant workers in both sending and receiving states;
vi. Strengthen policies and procedures in the sending state to facilitate aspects of migration workers, including recruitment, preparation for deployment overseas and protection of the migrant workers when abroad as well as repatriation and reintegration to the countries of origin;
vii. Facilitate access to resources and remedies through information, training and education, access to justice, and social welfare services as appropriate and in accordance with the legislation and of the receiving state, provided that they fulfil the requirements under applicable laws, regulations, and policies of the said state, bilateral agreements and multilateral treaties;
viii. Establish and promote legal practice of the sending state to regulate recruitment of migrant workers and adopt mechanisms to eliminate recruitment malpractices through legal and valid contracts, regulation, and accreditation of recruitment agencies and employers, and blacklisting of negligent/unlawful agencies; and
ix. Promote capacity building by sharing of information, best practises as well as opportunities and challenges in relation to protection and promotion of migrant workers' rights and welfare.

## C3. Promoting Corporate Social Responsibility (CSR)

29. ***Strategic objective***: Ensure that Corporate Social Responsibility (CSR) is incorporated in the corporate agenda and to contribute towards sustainable socioeconomic development in ASEAN Member States.

### *Actions:*

i. Develop a model public policy on Corporate Social Responsibility or legal instrument for reference of ASEAN Member States by 2010. Reference may be made to the relevant international standards and guides such as ISO 26000 titled "Guidance on Social Responsibility";

ii. Engage the private sector to support the activities of sectoral bodies and the ASEAN Foundation, in the field of corporate social responsibility;
iii. Encourage adoption and implementation of international standards on social responsibility; and
iv. Increase awareness of Corporate Social Responsibility in ASEAN towards sustainable relations between commercial activities and communities where they are located, in particular supporting community based development.

## D. ENSURING ENVIRONMENTAL SUSTAINABILITY

30. ASEAN shall work towards achieving sustainable development as well as promoting clean and green environment by protecting the natural resource base for economic and social development including the sustainable management and conservation of soil, water, mineral, energy, biodiversity, forest, coastal and marine resources as well as the improvement in water and air quality for the ASEAN region. ASEAN will actively participate in global efforts towards addressing global environmental challenges, including climate change and the ozone layer protection, as well as developing and adapting environmentallysound technology for development needs and environmental sustainability.

### D1. Addressing Global Environmental Issues

31. ***Strategic Objective***: Effectively address global environmental issues without impinging on competitiveness, or social and economic development based on the principle of equity, flexibility, effectiveness and common but differentiated responsibility, respective capabilities as well as reflecting on different social and economic conditions.

***Actions:***

i. Intensify regional cooperation to enhance and strengthen national and regional capacities to address issues and commitments to relevant Multilateral Environmental Agreements (MEAs) through regional research, promoting awareness, capacity building programmes and informed policy choices;
ii. Promote synergies in the implementation of related MEAs through strengthening of regional cooperation to address measures related to the thematic clusters of MEAs on atmospheric issues such as climate change

and ozone depleting substances, and MEAs on chemicals and chemical wastes;

iii. Promote ASEAN common understanding/common position on relevant MEAs; and

iv. Adopt a holistic approach in fostering regional cooperation on environmental issues, with the participation of all relevant stakeholders including business, academics, NGOs and civil society organisations.

## D2. Managing and Preventing Transboundary Environmental Pollution

32. ***Strategic Objective***: Implement measures and enhance international and regional cooperation to combat transboundary environmental pollution, including haze pollution, transboundary movement of hazardous wastes through, among others, capacity building, enhancing public awareness, strengthening law enforcement, promoting environmentally sustainable practices as well as implement the ASEAN Agreement on Transboundary Haze Pollution.[2]

### D2.1. *Transboundary Haze Pollution*

Actions:

i. Operationalize the ASEAN Agreement on Transboundary Haze Pollution through the implementation of concrete preventive, monitoring and mitigation measures and to initiate the process of developing protocols for the implementation and operationalisation of the Agreement;

ii. Develop mutually beneficial cooperation amongst ASEAN Member States that acknowledge each country's laws, rules, regulations, and national policies, whether it is multilateral or bilateral cooperation, which put more focus on prevention activities;

iii. Operationalize the ASEAN Coordinating Centre for Transboundary Haze Pollution Control to facilitate cooperation and coordination, including joint emergency response among Member States;

iv. Secure funds for the ASEAN Transboundary Haze Pollution Control Fund, with voluntary contributions from the Parties, and in cooperation with ASEAN partners to provide additional resources for the effective implementation of the ASEAN Agreement on Transboundary Haze Pollution;

v. Control and monitor land and forest fire occurrence in the region and promote the sustainable management of peatlands in the ASEAN region to reduce risk of fire and associated transboundary haze pollution through the implementation of the ASEAN Peatland Management Initiative (APMI) by the year 2015;

### D2.2. *Transboundary Movement of Hazardous Wastes*

Actions:

i. Enhance regional coordination and exchange of information, experience and expertise in hazardous waste management;
ii. Optimize the existence of Basel Convention Regional Centre for Training and Technology Transfer for Southeast Asia (BCRCSEA) and the role of its Steering Committee in providing regional services of technology transfer and capacity building of hazardous waste management;
iii. Establish effective and fully functioning regional mechanisms to address transboundary hazardous wastes, including illegal traffic of hazardous wastes, in line with the Basel Convention Procedures and Modalities.

## D3. Promoting Sustainable Development through Environmental Education and Public Participation

33. ***Strategic Objective***: Establish a clean and green ASEAN, rich in cultural traditions where the values and practices of the people are in accordance with the rhythm and harmony of nature, with citizens who are environmentally literate, imbued with the environmental ethic, and willing and capable to ensure the sustainable development of the region through environmental education and public participation efforts.

### *Actions:*

i. Implement the ASEAN Environmental Education Action Plan (AEEAP) 2008–2012;
ii. Establish a baseline assessment on the extent to which national curricula in the basic education system include Environmental Education (EE) and Environmentally Sustainable Development (ESD) content;
iii. Establish a baseline assessment on the extent to which teacher education programmes and in-service and pre-service training address EE/ESD theory and practice;
iv. Ensure that Quality Assurance (QA) systems for formal education (that is, national standards) require the inclusion of EE/ ESD issues in the relevant disciplines;

v. Promote research on EE/ ESD issues to ensure continuing development in formal education;
vi. Promote sustainable schools (for example, eco-schools/green schools) concept and practice throughout ASEAN;
vii. Develop EE curricula, materials and resources that are locally relevant and complement ESD at the local/community level;
viii. Promote EE as a key integrating tool for the development of 'environmentally sustainable cities' in each ASEAN Member State;
ix. Use appropriately designed and targeted EE for promotion of environmentally sustainable business practices;
x. Promote ASEAN Environment Week which serves as platform for national level activities to celebrate and raise awareness of the region's environment with all stakeholders in each of the ASEAN Member States;
xi. Establish a baseline of EE for sustainable development training needs for stakeholders in both the formal and non-formal sectors;
xii. Provide EE and ESD training opportunities for key stakeholders;
xiii. Provide ASEAN EE for Sustainable Development Leadership Training Programmes for key target groups (e.g., government officials, members of parliament and other elected officials, media and communication professionals, youth, women, etc.);
xiv. Create an ASEAN EE/ ESD scholarship scheme for the region's stakeholders;
xv. Actively promote and manage the ASEAN Environmental Education Inventory Database (AEEID) as the central platform for information dissemination, exchange and learning for EE and ESD in ASEAN;
xvi. Develop an ASEAN-wide 'Youth for Sustainable Environment' Network;
xvii. Establish an ASEAN sustainable/green/eco-school network;
xviii. Establish an annual ASEAN EE Conference/ Forum for the region's EE stakeholders as a platform for the exchange of information, materials, experience, networking, etc;
xix. Build and strengthen existing networks of NGOs, universities and media throughout the region to be effective practitioners, promoters, communicators and agents of change for EE and ESD; and
xx. Enhance the participation of community leaders, such as those religious leaders who have close contact with local communities, in promoting public awareness on the importance of sustainable development and environmentally sustainable practices.

## D4. Promoting Environmentally Sound Technology (EST)

34. ***Strategic Objective***: Use environmentally sound technologies to achieve sustainable development with minimal impact on the environment

### *Actions:*

i. Operationalise the ASEAN Network on EST (ASEANNEST) by 2015;
ii. Work towards the adoption of region wide environmental management/labelling schemes to promote economic growth and environmental protection by 2015;
iii. Facilitate an EST Forum to develop technology need assessments and develop cooperation among ASEAN Member States;
iv. Enhance cooperation among ASEAN Member States within the framework of South-South and North-South cooperation to promote technology transfer;
v. Explore the establishment of a clearing house centre on EST for ASEAN Member States (i.e. Cleaner Production Centre); and
vi. Intensify cooperation on joint research, development, deployment and transfer of EST.

## D5. Promoting Quality Living Standards in ASEAN Cities/Urban Areas

35. ***Strategic Objective***: Ensure cities/urban areas in ASEAN are environmentally sustainable, while meeting the social and economic needs of the people.

### *Actions:*

i. Expand on the existing work under the ASEAN Initiative on Environmentally Sustainable Cities;
ii. Intensify individual and collective efforts to improve the quality of air and water within ASEAN through regional or national initiatives to reduce industrial and transportation pollutions;
iii. Share experiences, expertise and technology in areas such as urban planning including transportation, green building, water management, urban greenery and urban biodiversity conservation, sanitation and waste management, 3Rs (Reduce, Reuse and Recycle) and air, noise, water, and land pollution control, through among others twinning cities programme;

iv. Work towards initiatives such as "Low Carbon Society", "Compact Cities", "Eco-Cities" and "Environmentally Sustainable Transport";
v. Develop internationally comparable measures for environmental sustainability for major cities in ASEAN by 2015;
vi. Introduce and implement an ASEAN Environmentally Sustainable Cities (ESC) Award by 2008 as an incentive to promote ESC practices.

## D6. Harmonizing Environmental Policies and Databases

36. ***Strategic Objective***: Promote feasible efforts to harmonize on a step-by-step basis environmental policies, and databases, taking into account the national circumstances of Member States, to support the integration of the environmental, social and economic goals of the region.

### *Actions:*

i. Work towards the implementation of the thirteen priority environmental parameters and undertake efforts to ensure region wide harmonization in terms of measurement, monitoring and reporting by 2015;
ii. Strive for harmonization of standards and conformity assessment procedures for environmental performance/programmes by 2015;
iii. Continue producing informative periodical state of the environment reports for policy making and addressing impacts on the environment;
iv. Promote environmental sustainable/green procurement practices in ASEAN Member States and develop a region wide strategy for the ASEAN region by 2015; and
v. Encourage regional cooperation on Strategic Environmental Assessment of large-scale projects and other activities which may cause significant environmental impacts in the region.

## D7. Promoting the Sustainable Use of Coastal and Marine Environment

37. ***Strategic Objective***: Ensure ASEAN's coastal and marine environment are sustainably managed; representative ecosystems, pristine areas and species are protected; economic activities are sustainably managed; and public awareness of the coastal and marine environment instilled.

***Actions:***

i. Enhance interagency and inter-sectoral coordination at the regional and international levels for achieving sustainable development of ASEAN's coastal and marine environment;
ii. Build capacities to develop national marine water quality standards by 2015 using the ASEAN Marine Water Quality Criteria as a reference;
iii. Establish a representative network of protected areas to conserve critical habitats by 2015 through further implementation of the ASEAN Criteria for Marine Heritage Areas, and ASEAN Criteria for National Protected Areas;
iv. Promote conservation and sustainable management of key ecosystems in coastal and marine habitats, such as joint efforts to maintain and protect marine parks in border areas, and the "Coral Triangle Initiative on Coral Reefs, Fisheries and Food Security";
v. Enhance the capacity and capability of, as well as economic benefits for the fishery and other coastal community to encourage their active participation in promoting environmental sustainability;
vi. Promote the sustainable use of coastal and marine environment through public awareness campaign to highlight the global importance of coastal and marine environment in addressing food security, maintaining ecosystem services, as well as protecting marine environment;
vii. Promote collaboration among ASEAN Member States in responding to transboundary pollution due to the oil spill incidents; and
viii. Promote cooperation in addressing pollution of coastal and marine environment from land-based sources.

## D8. Promoting Sustainable Management of Natural Resources and Biodiversity

38. ***Strategic Objective***: Ensure ASEAN's rich biological diversity is conserved and sustainably managed toward enhancing social, economic and environmental wellbeing.

***Actions:***

i. Achieve by 2010, a significant reduction in the current rate of loss of biodiversity through implementing relevant national, regional and international programmes of work;

ii. Promote collaboration, sharing of lessons learnt on access and equitable sharing of genetic and biological resources by 2015;
iii. Promote further listing and coordinated management of ASEAN Heritage Parks as an effective platform for ecosystem-based protected areas management by 2015;
iv. Enhance cooperation in the management of transboundary protected areas between neighbouring ASEAN Member States;
v. Take appropriate measures to minimise impacts of transboundary movement of living modified organisms in accordance with the Cartagena Protocol on Biosafety by 2015;
vi. Establish a functional regional network to promote capacity building in developing inventory of the biological resources and biosafety measures of the ASEAN Region by 2015;
vii. Enhance the role and capacity of the ASEAN Centre for Biodiversity (ACB) to function as an effective regional centre of excellence in promoting biodiversity conservation and management;
viii. Promote the involvement of local community to maintain biodiversity conservation and forest health by 2015;
ix. Promote effective management policies and practices to reduce the impact of invasive alien species at the regional and international levels;
x. Promote regional cooperation on sustainable management of biodiversity such as sharing research and development experiences, exchange of experts, and training;
xi. Strengthen efforts to control transboundary trade in wild fauna and flora through the ASEAN Action Plan on Trade in Wild Fauna and Flora 2005–2010 and the ASEAN Wildlife Enforcement Network (ASEAN-WEN) to implement commitments to Convention on International Trade in Endangered Species of Wild Fauna and Flora (CITES);
xii. Explore cooperation among ASEAN Member States to conduct joint survey and monitoring of migratory wildlife; and
xiii. Promote cooperation among ASEAN Member States in combating land degradation for sustainable land management to support sustainable agriculture and environment.

## D9. Promoting the Sustainability of Freshwater Resources

39. ***Strategic Objective***: Promote sustainability of water resources to ensure equitable accessibility and sufficient water quantity of acceptable quality to meet the needs of the people of ASEAN.

***Actions:***

i. Continue implementation of the ASEAN Strategic Plan of Action on Water Resources Management;
ii. Endeavour to reduce by half the number of people without sustainable access to safe drinking water by 2010;
iii. Manage water resources efficiently and effectively in order to provide adequate and affordable water services by 2015;
iv. Promote the implementation of integrated river basin management by 2015;
v. Promote public awareness and partnership to enhance integrated water resources management; and
vi. Promote regional cooperation on water conservation measures and programmes as well as scientific and technological innovations in water quality improvement and supply.

## D10. Responding to Climate Change and Addressing Its Impacts

40. ***Strategic Objective***: Enhance regional and international cooperation to address the issue of climate change and its impacts on socioeconomic development, health and the environment, in ASEAN Member States through implementation of mitigation and adaptation measures, based on the principles of equity, flexibility, effectiveness, common but differentiated responsibilities, respective capabilities, as well as reflecting on different social and economic conditions.

***Actions:***

i. Encourage ASEAN common understanding on climate change issues and where possible, engage in joint efforts and common positions in addressing these issues.
ii. Encourage the efforts to develop an ASEAN Climate Change Initiative (ACCI);
iii. Promote and facilitate exchange of information/knowledge on scientific research and development (R&D), deployment and transfer of technology and best practices on adaptation and mitigation measures, and enhance human resource development;
iv. Encourage the international community to participate in and contribute to ASEAN's efforts in afforestation and reforestation, as well as to reduce deforestation and forest degradation;

v. Develop regional strategies to enhance capacity for adaptation, low carbon economy, and promote public awareness to address effects of climate change;
vi. Enhance collaboration among ASEAN Member States and relevant partners to address climate related hazards, and scenarios for climate change;
vii. Develop regional systematic observation system to monitor impact of climate change on vulnerable ecosystems in ASEAN;
viii. Conduct regional policy, scientific and related studies, to facilitate the implementation of climate change convention and related conventions;
ix. Promote public awareness and advocacy to raise community participation on protecting human health from the potential impact of climate change;
x. Encourage the participation of local government, private sector, non-governmental organisations, and community to address the impacts of climate change; and
xi. Promote strategies to ensure that climate change initiatives lead to economically vibrant and environment friendly ASEAN Community taking into account win-win synergy between climate change and the economic development.

## D11. Promoting Sustainable Forest Management (SFM)

41. ***Strategic Objectives***: Promote the implementation of sustainable management of forest resources in the ASEAN region and eradicating unsustainable practices including combating illegal logging and its associated trade through amongst others; capacity building, technology transfer, enhancing public awareness and strengthening law enforcement and governance.

### *Actions:*

i. Implement Strategic Plan of Action of the ASEAN cooperation in Forestry (2005–2010);
ii. Encouraging environmentally sustainable planning and management of the ASEAN region's forests;
iii. Strengthen to address social cultural aspect of illegal logging and its associated trade in particular poverty eradication and illicit practices such as corruption and money laundering;
iv. Support for global and regional initiatives to reduce emissions from deforestation and forest degradation, and to promote a reformed afforestation

and reforestation under the Clean Development Mechanism (A/R-CDM) effort and to identify and avail appropriate international incentives and assistance;

v. Support the implementation of regional forest related initiatives such as the "Heart of Borneo" initiative, the Asia Forest Partnership and Asia-Pacific Network for Sustainable Forest Management and Rehabilitation, as well as global efforts such as Forestry Eleven Forum;

vi. Enhance the capacities and human resources, including research and development in the forestry sector to achieve Sustainable Forest Management (SFM);

vii. Strengthen ASEAN cooperation and joint approaches in addressing international and regional forestry issues to participate in the development of a global partnership for development;

viii. Promote forest management involving the community living within and surrounding the forest for the sustainability of the forest and prosperity of the people;

ix. Promote the eradication of unsustainable practices and related illicit activities;

x. Strengthen the implementation of forest law enforcement and governance to achieve sustainable management of forest resources and to support the sustainable development objective of Millennium Development Goals, including eradicating and combating illegal logging and its associated trade as well as combating the issue of illicit practices such as corruption and money laundering; and

xi. Implement the work plan for strengthening forest law enforcement and governance in ASEAN (2008–2015).

## E. BUILDING ASEAN IDENTITY

42. The ASEAN identity is the basis of Southeast Asia's regional interests. It is our collective personality, norms, values and beliefs as well as aspirations as one ASEAN community. ASEAN will mainstream and promote greater awareness and common values in the spirit of unity in diversity at all levels of society.

### E1. Promotion of ASEAN Awareness and a Sense of Community

43. ***Strategic Objective***: Create a sense of belonging, consolidate unity in diversity and enhance deeper mutual understanding among ASEAN Member States about their culture, history, religion, and civilisation.

***Actions:***

i. Review and develop new Regional and National Communication Plan in each Member State to support ASEAN identity and awareness building efforts;
ii. Encourage all sectoral bodies to intensify their efforts in promoting ASEAN identity and awareness as well as enhance the roles of Senior Officials Responsible for Information (SOMRI), Senior Officials Meeting on Culture and Arts (SOMCA) and the ASEAN Committee on Culture and Information (COCI) in promoting ASEAN identity and awareness;
iii. Undertake a coordinated production of printed, broadcast and multimedia materials on ASEAN to be reproduced and disseminated by national information agencies and private agencies of ASEAN Member States starting in 2009;
iv. Engage the mainstream media in promoting, on a continuing basis, all ASEAN programmes and projects, including ASEAN's cultural heritage and arts and the work of COCI;
v. Increase media exchange and networking of communication personnel among ASEAN Member States and between ASEAN and its Dialogue Partners;
vi. Support school activities promoting ASEAN awareness, such as by encouraging the observance of the annual ASEAN Day;
vii. Initiate the establishment of linkages among ASEAN cities and townships, especially those with cultural arts and heritage elements;
viii. Support the ASEAN Foundation's mandate to promote ASEAN identity and awareness and people-to-people interactions, primarily within ASEAN, but also between ASEAN and its friends and partners;
ix. Promote ASEAN sporting events in the national and private media such as the SEA Games and PARA Games;
x. Encourage the use of ASEAN Anthem and other ASEAN Symbols to raise ASEAN awareness in ASEAN Member States;
xi. Encourage the establishment of ASEAN associations at national levels to promote awareness of ASEAN in ASEAN Member States;
xii. Encourage the deepening of understanding and tolerance among the peoples of ASEAN through interfaith dialogue and ensuring adequate exposure of these events in the media;
xiii. Promote a culture of tolerance among media personnel about the diverse culture, religion and ethnicity of ASEAN by conducting enhanced intermedia dialogue among ASEAN media and in cooperation with other international actors;

xiv. Enhance the use of and the capability to utilize new media technologies such as digital broadcasting to promote ASEAN awareness and identity and facilitating ASEAN media industry collaborations to showcase Member States' culture, developments and talents;

xv. Strengthen national capabilities in the preservation and promotion of audiovisual heritage;

xvi. Encourage active participation of ASEAN Media Editors through regular Meetings to promote ASEAN awareness;

xvii. Encourage cooperation and networking including book exchange programmes among libraries in ASEAN; and

xviii. Disseminate ASEAN culture, social traditions and values particularly among the young generation through the media.

xix. Promote exchanges of television programmes to enhance cross-culture understanding among ASEAN Member States;

xx. Mobilise the mass media and other cultural institutions to disseminate and share information on ASEAN culture, developments, accomplishments, benefits, and objectives to the people;

xxi. Encourage youth exchanges such as the conduct of youth camps and similar activities to promote ASEAN arts and culture performances, ASEAN awareness and a sense of community among the public; and

xxii. Include the studies on ASEAN arts and culture as well as their values in school curriculum.

## E2. Preservation and Promotion of ASEAN Cultural Heritage

44. ***Strategic Objective***: Promote the conservation and preservation of ASEAN cultural heritage to ensure its continuity to enhance awareness and understanding of the people about the unique history of the region and the cultural similarities and differences between and among ASEAN Member States as well as to protect the distinctiveness of ASEAN cultural heritage as a whole.

### *Actions:*

i. Develop or improve national legislations and regional instruments/mechanisms to protect, preserve and promote ASEAN cultural heritage and living traditions of each ASEAN Member State by 2015;

ii. Document and manage significant ASEAN cultural heritage in a whole of ASEAN context;

iii. Undertake risk assessments and prepare emergency response plans for rescuing threatened significant cultural heritage across ASEAN; Promote

ASEAN civilization studies, including through collaboration between the ASEAN culture officials and the members of the AUN;

iv. Promote cultural tourism and the development of related industries by establishing working relations between and among the ASEAN culture and tourism officials and the private sector;

v. Promote capacity building/human capital in heritage management by providing training, seminar, workshop, conferences, etc;

vi. Undertake studies on the establishment of an ASEAN Cultural Centre in each ASEAN Member State as well as ASEAN dialogue partner countries;

vii. Preserve and develop the traditional handicraft villages and occupations in the rural areas, particularly among ethnic minority groups;

viii. Develop national capabilities in the promotion, management and preservation of traditional cultural heritage and nontraditional cultural heritage such as audiovisuals;

ix. Encourage community participation in preservation cultural heritage through mass media;

x. Promote the protection of cultural properties against theft, illicit and illegal trade and trafficking, and transfer within and outside ASEAN;

xi. Promote regional cooperation on the acquisition, preservation and use of archives;

xii. Establish effective resource centre or portal for Records and Archives of ASEAN Secretariat;

xiii. Exchange of best practices and experts in the field of Archive and Records Management;

xiv. Nurture talents and promote interactions among ASEAN scholars, artists, and heritage media practitioners to help preserve and promote ASEAN Cultural Diversity while fostering regional identity as well as cultivating people awareness of ASEAN

## E3. Promotion of Cultural Creativity and Industry

45. ***Strategic Objective***: Enhance ASEAN identity and togetherness through cultural creativity and the promotion and cooperation on cultural industry.

### *Actions:*

i. Promote the development of cultural industry resources by facilitating collaborations and networking between and among small and medium-sized cultural enterprises (SMCEs);

ii. Promote and support the development of cultural industries through the exchange of knowledge and best practices by respecting branded national cultural industries;
iii. Develop and support young peoples capacity for original ideas and action in the area of culture and arts;
iv. Promote wider opportunities for cultural creativity among youth and all sectors of the population, including the ethnic groups;
v. Promote marketing and distribution of cultural products and services;
vi. Improve capacity of national institutions to manage and develop cultural industry enhancing employment activities and commercialisation of local cultural products/services in domestic and international markets;
vii. Encourage cooperation on culture industry and creative economy with the ASEAN partner countries;
viii. Organise regular joint training programmes, seminars, and workshops for SMCEs; and
ix. Enhance interactions between Government Sectors and Private Sectors Institution on SMCE's Development by convening annual conferences.

## E4. Engagement with the Community

46. ***Strategic Objective***: To inculcate an ASEAN identity and build a people-oriented ASEAN where people are at the centre of community building, through the participation of all sectors of society.

### *Actions:*

i. Engage ASEAN-affiliated nongovernmental organisations in ASEAN Community building process;
ii. Convene the ASEAN Social Forum and the ASEAN Civil Society Conference on an annual basis to explore the best means for effective dialogue, consultations and cooperation between ASEAN and ASEAN civil society;
iii. Explore the establishment of an ASEAN volunteers programme, to be composed of young professionals, with focus on supporting rural development and assisting communities to help themselves by 2009;
iv. Support youth volunteers undertaking emergency or humanitarian missions by giving them recognition; and
v. Share public information network and databases of ASEAN for a greater flow of useful information in the region.

## F. NARROWING THE DEVELOPMENT GAP

47. ***Strategic Objectives***: Strengthen cooperation to reduce the development gap in particular the social dimensions of development between the ASEAN-6 and the CLMV countries and within ASEAN where some isolated pockets of under development persist.

### *Actions:*

i. Mainstream social development issues in developing and implementing projects for the IAI and through various subregional cooperation frameworks such as the Brunei-Indonesia-Malaysia-Philippines East ASEAN Growth Area (BIMPEAGA), Greater Mekong Subregion (GMS), Ayeyawady-Chao Phraya-Mekong Economic Cooperation Strategy (ACMECS), Indonesia-Malaysia-Thailand Growth Triangle (IMTGT), and the interstate areas along the East-West Economic Corridor (EWEC) among Vietnam, Laos, Cambodia and Northeastern Thailand, and Myanmar, the ASEAN-Mekong Basin Development Cooperation Scheme, Cambodia, Lao PDR, and Viet Nam (CLV) Development Triangle, the Cambodia, Lao PDR and Thailand (CLT) Emerald Triangle, Cambodia, Lao PDR, Myanmar and Viet Nam (CLMV);
ii. Implement the Second IAI Work Plan for the period of 2009–2015;
iii. ASEAN-6 to continue their support and assistance for the Second IAI Work Plan;
iv. Continue to mobilise the resources from dialogue partners, international and regional organisations/institutions for the Second IAI Work Plan and projects to support and assist the CLMV countries;
v. Engage related development agencies in each Member State and ASEAN partners to undertake assessment studies on the social impact of regional integration for the purpose of developing appropriate policy responses starting in 2009;
vi. Adopt and implement regional advocacy programme to include, among others, agriculture, marine and fisheries, agro-based industry, integrated rural development;
vii. Continue to assist the governments of CLMV countries to build and strengthen capacities to develop/implement social policies that will mitigate and monitor the impact of the regional integration process;
viii. Conduct a comprehensive study on the impact on new Member States of ASEAN as a result of acceleration of ASEAN Community building from 2020 to 2015;

## III. IMPLEMENTATION AND REVIEW OF THE ASCC BLUEPRINT

### A. Implementation Mechanism

1. The ASEAN Socio-Cultural Community Council shall be accountable for the overall implementation of the Blueprint and shall ensure coordination of efforts under its purview as well as those which cut across the other Community Councils.
2. All relevant ASEAN ministerial bodies or their equivalent shall be responsible in ensuring effective implementation of the various elements, actions and commitments in the Blueprint by reflecting them in their respective work plans, mobilizing resources for them, and undertaking national initiatives in order to meet these commitments.
3. To ensure effective implementation of the ASCC Blueprint, the following measures are recommended.

***Actions:***

i. Mainstream the strategies, targets and actions of the ASCC Blueprint, and incorporate them in respective national development plans;
ii. Endeavour to ratify relevant ASEAN Agreements within a timeline in accordance with the internal processes of each ASEAN Member State;
iii. Engage the Dialogue Partners, the private sector, civil society organisations and other relevant stakeholders in ensuring timely implementation of agreed measures;
iv. Identify and implement technical studies or training programmes on issues, areas or topics where analytical as well as capacity building supports which are required;
v. Strengthen the capabilities of the ASEAN Secretariat in areas relevant to the ASCC;
vi. Strengthen the capabilities of each ASEAN Member State especially in research and human capital development; and
vii. Establish appropriate capacity building programmes to assist new Member States in enhancing the achievement of the ASCC.

4. The progress of implementation of the ASCC Blueprint shall be reported by the Secretary-General of ASEAN to relevant ministerial meetings and Councils, and to the ASEAN Summit.

## B. Resource Mobilisation

5. Financial resources, expertise, research and capacity building for the implementation of the ASCC Blueprint can be mobilized, among others, from the following:

    a. ASEAN Member States;
    b. Dialogue, Sectoral and Development Partners;
    c. Regional and International Institutions in particular the ADB, the World Bank/IFC, the UN;
    d. Regional and International Foundations; and
    e. Private Sectors.

## C. Communication Strategy

6. Success in building the ASCC requires involvement by all stakeholders in the integration process. A good communications programme is required to create greater public awareness of the ASCC in all ASEAN Member States as well as to keep all stakeholders, including the social/cultural communities and people of ASEAN, informed of the progress of this community building.

### *Actions:*

i. Launch a comprehensive communications plan to explain to government officials, key stakeholders and the general public the objectives, benefits and challenges of the ASCC;
ii. Undertake activities to promote open discussion and sharing of information in implementing the ASCC;
iii. Member States shall set up a mechanism at the national level to regularly report the outcome and issues of the integration process; and
iv. Create an ASCC communications website that would provide an additional channel to reach communities at large, where stakeholders can provide feedback and respond to ASEAN socio-cultural initiatives.

## D. Review Mechanism

7. The implementation of the ASCC Blueprint shall be monitored and reviewed by the ASEAN Secretariat to ensure that all the activities are responsive to the needs and priority of ASEAN.

8. The ASEAN Secretariat shall develop and adopt indicators and systems to monitor and assess the progress of implementation of the various elements and actions in the Blueprint.
9. The midterm review of the implementation of the ASCC Blueprint can be undertaken whenever necessary, taking into account the changing dynamics of the region and the global environment.

## End Notes

1. Nothing in this Blueprint shall contradict the general principles in the ASEAN Declaration on the Protection and Promotion of the Rights of Migrant Workers.
2. This applies to Member States which are parties to the Agreement.

## GLOSSARY

**A**

| | |
|---|---|
| ACB: | ASEAN Centre for Biodiversity |
| ACCSM: | ASEAN Conference on Civil Service Matters |
| ACMECS: | AyeyawadyChao PhrayaMekong Economic Cooperation Strategy |
| AD: | Alternative Development |
| ADB: | Asian Development Bank |
| AEEAP: | ASEAN Environmental Education Action Plan |
| AEEID: | ASEAN Environmental Education Inventory Database |
| AEIC: | ASEAN Earthquake Information Centre |
| AFSRB: | ASEAN Food Security Reserve Board |
| AHA: | ASEAN Humanitarian Assistance |
| AIDS: | Acquired Immune Deficiency Syndrome |
| APMI: | ASEAN Peatland Management Initiative |
| APSED: | Asia Pacific Strategy for Emerging Diseases |
| A/RCDM: | Afforestation and Reforestation under the Clean Development Mechanism |
| ARCs: | ASEAN Resource Centres |
| ASEAN: | Association of Southeast Asian Nations |
| ASMC: | ASEAN Specialised Meteorological Centre |
| ASCC: | ASEAN SocioCultural Community |
| ASTNET: | ASEAN Science and Technology Network |
| AUN: | ASEAN University Network |
| AVIST: | ASEAN Virtual Institute of Science and Technology |

**B**

BCRCSEA: Basel Convention Regional Centre for Training and Technology Transfer for Southeast Asia

BIMPEAGA: BruneiIndonesiaMalaysiaPhilippines East ASEAN Growth Area

**C**

CAM: Complementary and Alternative Medicine

CITES: Convention on International Trade in Endangered Species of Wild Fauna and Flora

CLMV: Cambodia, Lao PDR, Myanmar, and Viet Nam

CLT: Cambodia, Lao PDR and Thailand

CLV: Cambodia, Lao PDR, and Viet Nam

COCI: Committee on Culture and Information

CSR: Corporate Social Responsibility

**E**

EE: Environmental Education

ESD: Environmentally Sustainable Development

EST: Environmentally Sound Technology

EWEC: EastWest Economic Corridor

**F**

FCTC: Framework Convention on Tobacco Control

**G**

GAD: Gender and Development

GMS: Greater Mekong Subregion

**H**

HIV: Human Immunedeficiency Virus

**I**

ICT: Information and Communication Technology

IFC: International Finance Cooperation

IMT-GT: Indonesia Malaysia Thailand Growth Triangle

**M**

MEAs: Multilateral Environmental Agreements

MDGs: Millennium Development Goals

**N**

NDG: Narrowing the Development Gap

NGOs: Non-Governmental Organisations

**O**

OSHNET: ASEAN Occupational Safety and Health Network

**P**

PPE: Personal Protective Equipment

**Q**

| | |
|---|---|
| QA: | Quality Assurance |

**T**

| | |
|---|---|
| TM: | Traditional Medicine |

**S**

| | |
|---|---|
| S&T: | Science and Technology |
| SEAMEO: | Southeast Asia Ministers of Education Organization |
| SFM: | Sustainable Forest Management |
| SLOM: | Senior Labour Officials Meeting |
| SMCEs: | Small and Medium-sized Cultural Enterprises |
| SOMCA: | Senior Officials Meeting on Culture and Arts |
| SOMRI: | Senior Officials Responsible for Information |

**T**

| | |
|---|---|
| TAYO: | Ten Accomplished Youth Organisations |

**U**

| | |
|---|---|
| UN: | United Nations |

**W**

| | |
|---|---|
| WEN: | Wildlife Enforcement Network |

Source: http://www.aseansec.org/22336.pdf
Accessed date: 3 March 2009
Publisher: ASEAN Secretariat
Country: Jakarta
Date of Publication: 2009

# B. Declarations, Resolutions and Accord

# CHAPTER 56

# MANILA DECLARATION ON THE ASEAN ENVIRONMENT

**Manila, 30 April 198l**

**FURTHER NOTING** with satisfaction the substantial progress to date in the progressive implementation of projects under the ASEAN Environmental Programme (ASEP) with the support of UNEP and other international organizations and with goals as elaborated in the Document No. ASEAN/MME/4;

1. **DO HEREBY DECLARE** their agreement to strengthen regional cooperation and collaboration in the field of environment by adopting the following objective and policy sidelines;

**(a) Objective**

To ensure the protection of the ASEAN environment and the sustainability of its natural resources so that it can sustain continued development with the aim of eradicating poverty and attaining the highest possible quality of life for the people of the ASEAN countries.

**(b) Policy Guidelines**

(1) Foster a common awareness among the people of the ASEAN countries of the biological, physical and social environment and its vital significance for sustained development to proceed apace;
(2) Ensure, as far as practicable, that environmental considerations are taken into account in development efforts, both on-going and future;
(3) Encourage the enactment and enforcement of environmental protection measures in the ASEAN countries;
(4) Foster the development of environmental education programmes;

2. **DECIDES** to endorse and implement the adopted ASEAN Environmental Programme (ASEP) as annexed.

**CONCERNED** with the pressing problems of poverty and underdevelopment besetting the people of the ASEAN countries;

**RECOGNIZING** the need to continue and accelerate national development in order to, promote economic and social well-being of the people;

**FURTHER RECOGNIZING** that sustained development is dependent upon the continuous availability of natural resources;

**AWARE** of the common environmental issues faced by the people of the ASEAN countries;

**CONSIDERING** the need to safeguard the ASEAN environment and the natural resources, renewable and non-renewable, that are part of it;

**HAVING CONSIDERED** the Reports of the ASEAN Experts Group Meetings and the ASEAN Environment Programme Document prepared for this meeting as annexed in Document No. ASEAN/MME/4;

**HAVING FURTHER CONSIDERED** the priority areas comprising the Programme, namely:

(a) Environmental Management including Environmental Inpact Assessment;
(b) Nature Conservation and Terrestrial Ecosystems;
(c) Marine Environment;
(d) Industry and Environment;
(e) Environmental Education and Training; and
(f) Environmental information.

**NOTING** the sound preparatory work undertaken including the Meetings of the ASEAN Experts Group held at Jakarta (1978), Penang (1979), Manila (1980) and Singapore (1981).

3. **DECIDES** to recommend the establishment of an ASEAN Committee on Environment in the content of the restructuring of ASEAN.

**DONE** in Manila, Philippines, on the Thirteenth Day of April, 1981.

**For the Government of the Republic of Indonesia :**

**HON. EMIL SALIM**
**Minister of Development Supervision and Environment**

**For the Government of the Republic of Singapore :**

**HON. ONG PANG BOON**
**Minister of Environment**

**For the Government of Malaysia :**

**HON. TAN SRI ONG KEE HUI**
**Minister of Science, Technology and Environment**

**For the Government of the Kingdom of Thailand :**

**HON. THINAKORN BHANDHUGRAVI**
**Minister of Science, Technology and Energy**

**For the Government of the Republic of the Philippines :**

**HON. IMELDA ROMUALDEZ MARCOS**
**Minister of Human Settlements**

Source: http://www.aseansec.org/6077.htm
Accessed date: 25 January 2006
Publisher: ASEAN Secretariat
Country: Jakarta
Date of Publication: 2003

# CHAPTER 57

# BANGKOK DECLARATION ON THE ASEAN ENVIRONMENT

**Bangkok, 29 November 1984**

**The Government of Brunei Darussalam,**
**The Government of the Republic of Indonesia,**
**The Government of Malaysia,**
**The Government of the Republic of the Philippines,**
**The Government of the Republic of Singapore and**
**The Government of the Kingdom of Thailand,**

Member States of the Association of South East Asian Nations (ASEAN)

**CONCERNED** with the problem of environmental degradation of the region resulting from the stresses of accelerated population growth and development;

**HAVING RECALLED** the First ASEAN Ministerial Meeting on the Environment and the Meetings of the ASEAN Experts Group on the Environment which recognized the need for cooperation amongst ASEAN countries in order to safeguard the ASEAN Environment and in particular its natural resources;

**MINDFUL** of the Manila Declaration on the ASEAN Environment signed in Manila, Philippines, on 30 April 1981, which provides that Member Countries shall cooperate in the progressive implementation of projects under the ASEAN Environment Programme (ASEP);

**NOTING** with satisfaction the progress of the implementation of the projects under the ASEAN Environment Programme (ASEP);

**FURTHER NOTING** that the ASEAN countries, during the past decade, have accomplished the establishment of national environmental protection agencies, and that these agencies have now accomplished the important step in defining their missions, in gaining an understanding of how environment protection can feasibly be accomplished within the context of the socio-cultural and economic patterns of the region in initiating programmes aimed at implementing feasible protection measures, and in developing national capabilities in environmental technology;

**CONCERNED** with the need to take full advantage of this good beginning to continue the progress over the next decade on national policies in the planning and implementation of development projects;

**CONSIDERING** that the task of integrating environmental protection concepts into national development planning represents one of the most complex tasks ever faced by governments of the region;

**RECOGNIZING** the experience and confidence gained in managing the environment during this initial period both in their own countries and through ASEAN cooperation;

**DO HEREBY DECLARE** their desire to strengthen and enhance their regional cooperation in the field of environmental protection to meet the increasing and challenging environmental problems of the ASEAN region in the decade ahead, and to this end hereby adopt the following objective and policy guidelines;

## OBJECTIVE

To implement the ASEAN DEVELOPMENT STRATEGY through an integrated approach entailing advance or forward planning in the environmentally related activities with a view to incorporating environmental dimension in development planning right at the base level in order to achieve sustained development and long-term conservation of environmental assets and at the same time improving the quality of life for all.

## POLICY GUIDELINES

To achieve the objective noted above, the following policy guidelines shall be adopted for application throughout the ASEAN region:

(1) With respect to environmental management:

(i) Foster the development of macro cum-economic environmental development plans which can be accommodated by the environmental carrying capacity of the region.

(ii) Continue and strengthen the use of Environmental Impact Assessment (EIA) process and extended Cost-Benefit Analysis for minimizing the adverse effects and for ensuring proper consideration of environmental values in all projects and programmes under government that are likely to produce significant environmental impact and its gradual extension to the private sector including industry.

(iii) Develop a system of procedures for conducting ElAs and for their review which can be practically utilized within the ASEAN region.

(iv) Continue and increase efforts for establishing environmental units in the planning divisions of major project implementing agencies to ensure that environmental consciousness permeates government departments that development policy and planning in all sectors reflect systematic consideration of the environment.

(v) Establish techniques for quantifying the impact of development projects on environment both favourable and unfavourable.

(vi) Evolve criteria for augmentation of renewable resources and economical use of non-renewable resources.

(vii) Prepare an optimal land use pattern and zoning plan.

(2) With respect to nature conservation:

Develop new and practicable approaches for preserving forests wildlife, and other ecological systems in the face of continuing population pressure.

(3) With respect to marine environment:

Develop practicable methods for the management of pollution discharges so that economic development of coastal resources may proceed in coexistence with preservation of the quality of coastal beaches and resorts and the marine environment.

(4) With respect to industry:

(i) Adopt practicable methods for ensuring reasonable control of waste discharges from the earliest stages of project formulation.

(ii) Wherever practicable adopt low waste and non-waste technology and more effective re-use and recycling of wastes in production.

(iii) Develop a Toxic and Hazardous Waste Control Programme and stimulate efforts by government agencies and industry to develop suitable systems for control.

(5) With respect to urban environment: increase efforts to provide water-borne sewerage systems with central sewage treatment facilities at least for the major towns.

(6) With respect to environmental education and training:

- (i) Continue efforts to enhance public awareness in respect of the importance of environmental protection and support governmental actions in this regard.
- (ii) Provide environmental training of personnel involved in decision-making on projects, programmes, policies and plans with emphasis on cause and effect relationship that exist between an individual's environment and his health.
- (iii) Introduce stronger general environmental theme into school and university syllabi.
- (iv) Provide technical training for staff engaged directly in the work of environmental protection agencies and in environmental programmes of other agencies.

(7) With respect to environmental information systems:

- (i) Develop a comprehensive environmental system to facilitate decision-making;
- (ii) Initiate or strengthen efforts for establishment of suitable national data bank/storage and retrieval system;
- (iii) Intensify efforts for establishing monitoring programmes for continuing surveillance of sensitive environmental resources; and
- (iv) Promote increased use of remote sensing as a means of establishing environmental data bases.

(8) With respect to wider involvement in environmental management: Encourage and promote cooperation between Governments, Non-Governmental Organizations, Universities, Business Communities within ASEAN in the field of environmental management.

(9) With respect to environmental legislation: Develop appropriate legislation to support the proper management and development of the environment.

(10) With respect to international cooperation on environmental management in the ASEAN countries: Establish cooperation with developed and other developing countries and international agencies for transfer of technology and share experiences in the management of the environment.

**DECIDE** to adopt and implement the revised ASEAN Environment Programme II (ASEP II).

**IN WITNESS WHEREOF,** the undersigned, being duly authorized thereto by their respective Governments, have signed this Bangkok Declaration.

**DONE** in Bangkok, Thailand, this Twenty-Ninth Day of November in the year One Thousand Nine Hundred and Eighty-Four.

**On behalf of the Government of**
**Brunei Darussalam :**

**PEHIN DATO ABDUL RAHMAN TAIB**
**Minister of Development**

**On behalf of the Government of**
**the Republic of Indonesia :**

**EMIL SALIM**
**Minister of State for Population and Environment**

**On behalf of the Government of**
**Malaysia :**

**DATUK AMAR STEPHEN K.T. YONG**
**Minister of Science, technology and the Environment**

**On behalf of the Government of**
**the Republic of the Philippines :**

**RODOLFO P. DEL ROSARIO**
**Minister of Natural Resources**

**On behalf of the Government of**
**the Republic of Singapoe :**

**ONG PAG BOON**
**Minister for the Environment**

**On behalf of the Government of**
**the Kingdom of Thailand :**

**NARON WONGWAN**
**Minister of Agriculture and Cooperative**

Source: http://www.aseansec.org/6079.htm
Accessed date: 26 January 2006
Publisher: ASEAN Secretariat
Country: Jakarta
Date of Publication: 2003

# CHAPTER 58

# JAKARTA RESOLUTION ON SUSTAINABLE DEVELOPMENT

**Jakarta, 30 October 1987**

The Deputy Minister of Development of Brunei Darussalam, the State Minister for Population and the Environment of the Republic of Indonesia, the Minister of Science, Technology and the Environment of Malaysia, the Secretary of Environment and Natural Resources of the Republic of the Philippines, the Minister for the Environment of the Republic of Singapore, and the Minister of Science, Technology and Energy of the Kingdom of Thailand, in a meeting in Jakarta, Indonesia, on 29–30 October, 1987.

**CONVINCED** that it is imperative for the peoples of ASEAN to continue and accelerate their development processes in order to meet their growing needs and to provide them with a quality of life in accord with their dignity and well-being;

**RECOGNIZING** that these development processes can only be sustained if the availability of natural resources is similarly sustained;

**MINDFUL** that it utilizing our natural resources to meet the needs of the present generation, the ability of future generations to meet their needs should not be imperiled;

**CONSCIOUS** that the sustainability of development requires that development processes and environmental management be conducted in an integrated manner;

**AWARE** that the integration of environmental considerations into the development process requires that international and regional cooperation be further heightened and intensified;

## HEREBY RESOLVE:

I. That ASEAN member countries adopt the principle of sustainable development to guide and to serve as an integrating factor in their common efforts.

II. That ASEAN cooperative efforts be focused upon those common resources and issues that affect the common well-being of the people, of ASEAN, including, but not be limited to:

— the common seas;
— land-resources and land-based pollution;
— tropical rain-forces;
— air quality; and
— urban and rural pollution.

III. That ASEAN cooperation should encompass governments and government agencies as well as the private business sector, professional associations, educational and academic institutions and non-governmental organizations.

IV. That in affirming this Resolution, the ASEAN Environment Ministers are aware that the pursuit of sustainable development would be best served by the establishment of a regional body on the environment of sufficient stature whose task should include, but not be limited to:

(a) recommending policy guidelines on the implementation of the principle of sustainable development;
(b) facilitating the incorporation of environmental considerations into the programmes and activities of ASEAN committees;
(c) monitoring the quality of the environment and natural resources to enable the periodic compilation of ASEAN state of the environment reports; and
(d) enhancing the cooperation on environmental matters.

**DONE** in Jakarta, Indonesia, this Thirtieth Day of October in the year of One Thousand Nine Hundred and Eighty Seven.

For Brunei Darussalam:

**Sgd**
**DATO PADUKA HJ. SELAMAT HJ. MUNAP**
Deputy Minister of Development,

For Indonesia:

**Sgd**
**EMIL SALIM**
The State Minister for Population and
the Environment

For the Philippines:

**Sgd**
**FULGENCIO S. FACTORAN, JR**
Secretary of Environment and Natural Resources

For Malaysia:

**Sgd**
**DATUK AMAR STEPHEN K.T. YONG**
Minister of Science, Technology and
the Environment

For Singapore:

**Sgd**
**DR. AHMAD MATTAR**
Minister for the Environment

For Thailand:

**Sgd**
**BANYAT BANTADTAN**
Minister of Science, Technology
and Energy

Source: http://www.aseansec.org/6081.htm
Accessed date: 2 October 2008
Publisher: ASEAN Secretariat
Country: Jakarta
Date of Publication: 2003

# CHAPTER 59

# THE KUALA LUMPUR ACCORD ON ENVIRONMENT AND DEVELOPMENT ISSUED BY THE ASEAN MINISTERS FOR THE ENVIRONMENT AT THE FOURTH ASEAN MINISTERS FOR THE ENVIRONMENT MEETING

**Kuala Lumpur, 19 June 1990**

**AWARE** that the management of the environment and the pursuit of sustainable development are imperative to secure the well-being of the people of ASEAN today and in the future;

**FURTHER AWARE** that the management of the environment and the pursuit of sustainable development require close cooperation between the member-countries of ASEAN in particular and global cooperation in general, and that ASEAN should endeavour to strengthen such cooperation;

**CONSCIOUS** that the United Nations Conference on Environment and Development, to be held in 1992, provides a forum and an opportunity to further promote such cooperation and for ASEAN to assert its views on environmental management and sustainable development;

**RECOGNIZING** that the formulation of such views and practices would require preparatory steps and studies, jointly as well as separately;

**ALSO RECOGNIZING** that in such formulation, it would be beneficial to take note of:

(a) the Manila Declaration of 1981;
(b) the Bangkok Declaration of 1984;
(c) the Jakarta Resolution of 1987;
(d) the Manila Summit Declaration of 1987; and
(e) the Langkawi Declaration of 1989.

**WE, THE ASEAN MINISTERS FOR THE ENVIRONMENT HEREBY AGREE:**

1. To initiate efforts leading towards concrete steps pertaining to environmental management, including:

   a. the formulation of an ASEAN strategy for sustainable development and a corresponding action programme,
   b. the harmonization of environmental quality standards,
   c. the harmonization of transboundary pollution prevention and abatement practices,
   d. the undertaking of research and development and the promotion of the use of clean technologies.

2. To initiate efforts leading towards concrete steps pertaining to natural resource management, including:

   a. the harmonization of approaches in natural resource assessment,
   b. the development of joint natural resource management programmes,
   c. the development and harmonization of procedures aimed at obtaining a better reflection of the state of natural wealth in the context of the System of National Accounts.

3. To initiate efforts enabling the inclusion of environmental factors into economic calculations and thus providing a better base for international economic cooperation.
4. To develop and formulate a common ASEAN position to be presented to the Ministerial Level Conference on the Environment for Asia and the Pacific and later to the United Nations Conference on Environment and Development in 1992, including:

   a. affirming ASEAN's commitment to the pursuit of sustainable development,
   b. stressing the need to strengthen regional and international cooperation and proposing the principles upon which such cooperation should be based,
   c. emphasizing the importance of a global environmental agenda which reflects the priorities and concerns of all countries,
   d. calling attention to the patterns of international relations that inhibit the implementation of national environmental efforts in developing countries and their participation in global environmental efforts,

e. reiterating the urgency for a supportive and predictable international economic environment which promotes economic growth and development of all countries,
f. stressing the need for equitable sharing of responsibilities and allocation of liabilities in global environmental efforts,
g. stressing that although global environmental efforts will benefit the common good, such benefits should be shared equitably, including the benefits of Research and Development,
h. underlining the need for substantial additional resources to assist developing countries to pursue their goals of sustainable development as well as access to, and transfer of, environmentally sound technologies at affordable costs and the establishment of appropriate funding mechanisms.

Source: http://www.aseansec.org/1096.htm
Accessed date: 26 January 2006
Publisher: ASEAN Secretariat
Country: Jakarta
Date of Publication: 2003

# CHAPTER 60

# SINGAPORE RESOLUTION ON ENVIRONMENT AND DEVELOPMENT

**18 February 1992**

**AWARE,** that the pursuit of sustainable development is essential for a better quality of life for the people of ASEAN today and in the future;

**FURTHER AWARE,** that sustainable development, especially the management of the environment, requires close cooperation among and between the member countries of ASEAN in particular and global cooperation in general, and that ASEAN should therefore strengthen such cooperation;

**RECOGNISING,** that environmental and population factors must be integrated into developmental efforts in order to achieve sustainable development;

**FURTHER RECOGNISING,** that natural resources and environmental accounting and valuation of environmental and ecological factors are essential to the successful pursuit of sustainable development;

**CONVINCED,** that the outcome of the 4th ASEAN Summit in January 1992 has brought about immense opportunities for economic cooperation which promises regional growth and that such growth will have to be sustained through, inter alia, greater intra-ASEAN cooperation;

**REALISING,** that the United Nations Conference on Environment and Development (UNCED) to be held in Rio de Janeiro on June 1992 offers a unique opportunity to put into effect programmes for global environmental management and the achievement of sustainable development, and that ASEAN should therefore contribute its views to this forum; and

**FURTHER REALISING,** that being a grouping of dynamic developing countries, ASEAN should take a leading role towards achieving a proper balance between environmental protection and economic development and promote its common views on these issues at the 4th UNCED Preparatory Committee Meeting to be held in New York in March 1992 and the 2nd Ministerial Conference of Developing Countries on Environment and Development to be held in Kuala Lumpur in April 1992.

## IN THE TRADITIONAL ASEAN SPIRIT OF AMITY, FRIENDSHIP AND COOPERATION, WE, THE ASEAN MINISTERS RESPONSIBLE FOR THE ENVIRONMENT AGREE THAT:

1. ASEAN member countries shall intensify cooperation in environmental management and protection in their common pursuit of sustainable development. In this regard, member countries shall work collectively towards the improvement of environmental quality, harmonization of standards, and jointly promote the application, transfer and development of appropriate environmental technologies.
2. ASEAN shall continue to actively participate in and support international efforts in promoting the principles of sustainable development.

## Enhancing Regional Cooperation

3. To promote regional cooperation towards sustainable development, we agree that ASEAN member countries shall:

### *Policies*

(i) introduce policy measures and promote institutional development that will encourage the integration of environmental factors in all developmental processes;

(ii) work closely on the inter-related issues of environment and development;

(iii) cooperate in setting basic environmental quality standards and regulations at national level, work towards harmonized environmental quality standards in the region, and adopt long term quantitative goals relating to ambient air quality and river water quality;

(iv) harmonize policy directions and step up operational and technical cooperation on environmental matters such as transboundary air and water pollution, natural disaster, forest fires, oil spills, and the transboundary movements and disposal of toxic chemicals and hazardous wastes, and undertake joint actions to address the anti-tropical timber campaign;

## Information Exchange

(i) encourage greater information and data exchange, particularly in air and water quality as well as greenhouse gas monitoring;

## Institutional Development

(i) strengthen the institutional and technical capability of national agencies to enable them to effectively integrate environmental considerations into development plans;
(ii) cooperate in capacity building of national institutions responsible for the environment through regional training assistance programmes, regular exchange of information and management data and a greater exchange of visits among officials and experts;
(iii) work with and cooperate in providing adequate training at all levels in public and private sector organizations, including NGOs, with the aim of improving their environmental management expertise and skills;

## Technology Cooperation

(i) continue to enhance cooperation in the field of environmental technology through sharing of technical information, initiate joint training and research programmes, and exchange expertise in environmental management and technology;
(ii) promote the application of appropriate and environmentally sound technologies, as well as encourage support from the business sector and the public for clean production and industrial practices;

## Public Awareness

(i) continue to promote public awareness of environmental issues so as to bring about broader participation in environmental protection efforts, and to do so bring about greater exchange of information and experiences on approaches and strategies in environmental education; and

## Programmes

(i) undertake to develop and implement specific programmes relating to: haze caused by forest fires, air and water quality management, natural resources and environmental accounting, environmental economics, trans-frontier parks and other protected areas, a regional network for biological diversity conservation and protection of the marine environment in ASEAN seas.

**Addressing development and global environmental issues**

4. To address development and global environmental issues, we agree that ASEAN member countries shall:
   (i) adopt a common stand on UNCED and related issues as in the ANNEX, and endeavour to have it reflected in the outcome of UNCED;
   (ii) actively take part in international efforts to protect the global environment;
   (iii) emphasize the importance for developed countries to provide adequate, new and additional financial resources to the developing countries to help address the environmental and development problems confronting them;
   (iv) stress the need for developed countries to assist developing countries by transferring and providing access to environmentally sound technologies on concessional and preferential terms;
   (v) support the call for the developed countries to maintain an international environment which is supportive of economic growth and development;
   (vi) explore the desirability of having States to contribute to and help ensure safe navigation for the protection of the marine environment; and
   (vii) promote greater cooperation among and between developing countries in the field of environment and development, through information exchange and the sharing of experience and expertise.

Source: http://www.aseansec.org/6083.htm
Accessed date: 25 January 2006
Publisher: ASEAN Secretariat
Country: Jakarta
Date of Publication: 2003

# ANNEX

# ASEAN COMMON STAND ON THE UNITED NATIONS CONFERENCE ON ENVIRONMENT AND DEVELOPMENT (UNCED) AND RELATED ISSUES

**AWARE**, that the pursuit of sustainable development is essential for a better quality of life for the people of ASEAN today and in the future;

**FURTHER AWARE**, that the pursuit of sustainable development, especially the management of the environment, requires close cooperation among and between the member countries of ASEAN in particular and global cooperation in general, and that ASEAN should therefore strengthen such cooperation; and

**RECOGNISING**, that the United Nations Conference on Environment and Development (UNCED) to be held in Rio de Janeiro in June 1992 offers a unique opportunity to put into effect programmes for global environmental management and the achievement of sustainable development.

## WE, THE ASEAN MINISTERS RESPONSIBLE FOR THE ENVIRONMENT HEREBY CALL FOR:

**1.** ***Urgent measures to combat climate change.***

In this respect, the developed countries should stabilise and limit the emissions of all greenhouse gases.

However, any reductions in greenhouse gases must be made on an equitable basis, taking into consideration historical emissions and efficiency of energy use. In addition, adequate, new and additional funding must be provided by developed countries, especially those which have been emitting cumulatively large amount of $CO_2$, to enable developing countries to meet the full incremental costs of combating climate change. Technologies to reduce $CO_2$ emissions shall be made available to developing countries on concessional and preferential terms.

All sinks, in particular coastal waters, seas and oceans, should be protected.

**2. *The immediate implementation of the Montreal Protocol Interim Multilateral Fund.***

There should be expeditious transfer of environmentally sound alternative technologies from developed countries to developing countries, including building the capabilities of developing countries in research and development. Recognizing that the Montreal Protocol may have to be amended from time to time, any amendments must include adequate provisions to ensure the non-application of compliance procedure until the required technologies become freely and commercially available on concessions and preferential terms.

**3. *The protection of the ecosystems of oceans and seas from pollution.***

Due recognition must be given to the fact that land-based sources of pollution in particular sewage and wastewater discharge, and offshore sources such as oil spills are major causes of marine degradation. There is a need to modify the existing policies for concessional loans to developing countries on coastal and marine environmental management and protection projects. National capabilities for the acquisition of expertise in the implementation of international instruments for the protection of marine environment must be built up and strengthened.

The vital role of Antarctica in the global atmospheric, oceanic and ecological systems must also be recognized and efforts to protect and conserve its environment for the benefits of mankind must be fully supported within the UNCED process.

**4. *Greater efforts to protect freshwater resources and to ensure access of all people to this vital commodity.***

Freshwater resources should be conserved and protected and the capacity for developing countries to conserve, manage and develop these resources should be strengthened. To achieve these, there should be adequate provision of funds at concessional rates.

**5. *The sustainable management of all forests.***

Countries have the sovereign right to develop on a sustainable basis their forests in accordance with their needs and levels of socio-economic development.

Any agreement on forestry and all types of forests must be part and parcel of the global package to undertake specific actions to resolve problems relating to environment and development. Developed countries should cease all forms of unilateral measures to ban the importation of tropical timber particularly when discussions have begun within the UNCED preparatory process on a statement of principles on global forestry. In addition, developed countries should undertake specific and transparent measures to increase their forest cover as part of their global responsibilities to restore the balance between development and the need to protect the environment.

### 6. *The conservation of biological diversity.*

The sovereign rights of states over natural resources, including genetic resources, should be honoured and respected. Funding mechanisms to compensate developing countries for their sacrifices and opportunity costs forgone for conserving biological diversity should be established. New funding mechanisms for biodiversity conservation should also be created. However, the funds should not be sourced from levies imposed on the trade of natural resources from the developing countries. The burden of conservation should be shared equitably by the developed and developing countries, taking into account the financial capabilities of the developing countries.

Access to biological diversity should be based on mutually agreed terms and the principle of prior-informed-consent so that the countries providing the genetic resources have preferential access to the results of research, products developed, and benefits and profits from genetic resources. Mechanisms to define ownership of genetic materials should be ensured. Transfer of technologies relevant to the conservation and sustainable use of biological diversity, as well as transfer of technologies that make use of genetic resources, should be on concessional and preferential terms.

### 7. *Support for the Basel Convention on the Control of Transboundary Movements of Hazardous Wastes and their Disposal*

The Convention should be complemented by a Protocol on liability and compensation which must address the concerns of the developing countries, taking into account their views with regard to liability and compensation from damage resulting from transboundary movements and disposal of hazardous wastes.

**8. *Support for the objective of the Prior-Informed-Consent (PIC) system under the Amended London Guidelines for the Exchange of Information on Banned or Severely Restricted Chemicals in International Trade.***

A legal framework on the management of toxic chemicals in international trade should be formulated jointly by UNEP (United Nations Environment Programme), WHO (World Health Organisation), FAO (Food and Agriculture Organisation), and IMO (International Maritime Organisation).

## TO ACHIEVE THE ABOVE, WE, THE ASEAN MINISTERS RESPONSIBLE FOR THE ENVIRONMENT FURTHER CALL FOR:

1. ***New and additional financial resources to meet incremental costs of protecting the global environment.*** New and innovative methods for generating financial resources should be sought and agreed upon. More funding for implementing sustainable development policies at the regional and national levels should be provided by developed countries.
2. ***The establishment of basic environmental standards for a minimum level of quality of life and environmental protection***. Appropriate technologies to help countries achieve such standards must be identified and all means, financial as well as legal to overcome patent laws, should be made available to enable the transfer of such appropriate technologies to the developing countries.
3. ***Equitable, balanced and comprehensive solutions to the inter-related issues of economic development and environmental protection.***

## WE, THE ASEAN MINISTERS RESPONSIBLE FOR THE ENVIRONMENT FURTHER RECOMMEND THAT THE FOLLOWING BE REFLECTED IN THE PREPARATION OF THE EARTH CHARTER AND AGENDA 21:

1. ***Earth Charter.*** The title of the declaration should be "Rio de Janeiro Declaration on Environment and Development". The Declaration should contain the general principles outlining the rights and obligations of individuals and states with regard to environment and development. Although not legally binding, the Declaration must be a strong expression of political and moral commitments to sustainable development. Among other things, the Declaration should affirm the principles of sovereign rights of states over environment and

natural resources, the rights of all peoples and states to develop, equitable sharing of responsibility, and the principle that unilateral barriers to free trade should not be imposed under the guise of environmental concerns.

2. ***Agenda 21.*** Priorities should be set for the programmes, projects and activities of Agenda 21. The criteria and procedure in prioritization should be transparent and there must be a proper balance between development and environmental projects.

In the development of a funding mechanism to finance the activities and programmes under the Agenda 21, there is a need to ensure that funds are available for both development and environmental projects. The Global Environment Facility (GEF) should be reviewed and revised in both its scope and mandate. The disbursement of its funds should involve the participation of both the developed and developing countries. There is a need to create a general Fund to deal with programmes not covered by GEF or other funds created under specific international conventions.

# CHAPTER 61

# BANDAR SERI BEGAWAN RESOLUTION ON ENVIRONMENT AND DEVELOPMENT

**26 April 1994**

**RECOGNISING** that in line with the outcome of the United Nations Conference on Environment and Development, which provided the impetus for sustainable development, ASEAN should promote the principles contained in the Rio Declaration on Environment and Development and actively implement Agenda 21;

**CONSIDERING** that economic growth and environmental management are inseparable and crucial to sustaining and further improving the quality of life of the people of ASEAN;

**REALISING** that international and regional cooperation and efforts are necessary to support the national and regional implementation of Agenda 21;

**FURTHER REALISING** the necessity to strengthen and enhance regional cooperation in the management and control of transboundary movements of hazardous wastes into and within the ASEAN region; and

**CONSCIOUS** that ASEAN member countries share common environmental aims and objectives and that the state of the environment lies ultimately in the hands of the people of ASEAN themselves;

## WE, THE ASEAN MINISTERS FOR THE ENVIRONMENT, HEREBY AGREE:

1. To adopt and implement the ASEAN Strategic Plan of Action on the Environment to attain the following objectives:

    a. to respond to specific recommendations of Agenda 21 requiring priority action in ASEAN;

b. to introduce policy measures and promote institutional development that encourage the integration of environmental factors in all developmental processes both at the national and regional levels;
c. to establish long term goals on environmental quality and work towards harmonized environmental quality standards for the ASEAN region;
d. to harmonize policy directions and enhance operational and technical cooperation on environmental matters, and undertake joint actions to address common environmental problems; and
e. to study the implications of AFTA on the environment and take steps to integrate sound trade policies with sound environmental policies.

2. To declare 1995 as the ASEAN Environment Year to highlight ASEAN environmental issues and cooperative programmes, and to stimulate awareness of these issues among the ASEAN populace; broaden the participatory process in the area of the environment in ASEAN; and stimulate regional activities in the area of the environment.
3. To adopt a set of Harmonized Environmental Quality Standards for ambient air and river water quality and implement the needed measures to attain these standards by the year 2010.
4. To strengthen cooperation among ASEAN countries to ensure the effective implementation of the decision of the Second Conference of the Parties to the Basel Convention.

**DONE** in Bandar Seri Begawan, Brunei Darussalam, this Twenty-sixth Day of April in the Year One Thousand Nine Hundred and Ninety-four.

Source: http://www.aseansec.org/2172.htm
Accessed date: 26 January 2006
Publisher: ASEAN Secretariat
Country: Jakarta
Date of Publication: 2003

# CHAPTER 62

# JAKARTA DECLARATION ON ENVIRONMENT AND DEVELOPMENT

**18 September 1997**

**DEEPLY** appreciative of the statement made by H.E. President Soeharto at the official opening of the 7th ASEAN Ministerial Meeting on the Environment;

**AWARE** that prosperity, equity, and a safe and healthy environment are interrelated elements of the human dream for a better future in the next millennium;

**FURTHER AWARE** that economic, environmental and social goals are integrally linked and by having policies that reflect that interrelationship, the lives of each generation will be better than the last;

**RECOGNIZING** that continued, long-term economic growth is essential to the prosperity of the ASEAN people and is fundamental to sustainable development;

**FURTHER RECOGNIZING** that sustainable development is the framework that integrates economic, environmental and social goals in discourse and policies that enhance the quality of life for the people of ASEAN at present and in the future;

**CONCERNED** that global economic growth and environmental challenges have compelled us to seriously take into account the ecological impact on the national, regional and global economic growth;

**DEEPLY CONCERNED** that the world is gripped by the anxiety caused by fires, floods and typhoons, and that the ASEAN region is not spared from the threat of these natural disasters;

**FURTHER CONCERNED** on the ecological, economic, health and political impacts brought about by transboundary pollution caused by land and forest fires;

**CONSCIOUS** that industrialization will continue to be a critical part of the ASEAN economy into the foreseeable future;

**FURTHER CONSCIOUS** that the rapid industrial growth and resource use may increase the environmental pollution and destruction;

**COMMITTED** that to overcome these environmental problems, ASEAN nations must take more concrete joint action.

## WE, THE ASEAN MINISTERS FOR THE ENVIRONMENT, HEREBY AGREE:

1. To sustain a healthy economy based on eco-efficiency that grows sufficiently to create meaningful jobs, reduce poverty, and provide the opportunity for a higher quality of life and a high quality of environment for all ASEAN people in an increasingly competitive world;
2. To produce, use and export globally competitive goods and services that use resources efficiently and sustainably;
3. To cooperate and render assistance wherever available, to prevent and control all domestic sources of pollution and activities that could contribute towards transboundary pollution, including haze formation;
4. To welcome international cooperation and assistance to strengthen ASEAN capability to combat transboundary pollution, including haze;
5. To use, conserve, protect, restore and manage natural resources and the environment, including the conservation of biodiversity, in ways that help ensure long-term social, economic, and environmental benefits for current and future generations and in this regard to:

    5.1. Support the formulation of ASEAN initiatives to achieve the long term environmental goals for ambient air and river water qualities as declared in the Bandar Seri Begawan Resolution on Environment and Development of 1994.

    5.2. Endorse the following activities as flagship projects in the area of environmental cooperation in ASEAN and to facilitate their implementation:

        a. ASEAN Environment Year 2000
        b. ASEAN Environment Award
        c. ASEAN Regional Center for Biodiversity Conservation

6. To create a widely held ethic of stewardship that strongly encourages individuals, communities, institutions and corporations to take full responsibility for the economic, environmental and social consequences of their actions, leading towards a vision of a clean and green ASEAN with a safe, healthy, and high quality of life for its peoples by the year 2020;
7. To support, enable and empower individuals, communities, and corporate entities to achieve their eco-efficiency objectives in the most flexible, expeditious, and cost-effective manner possible;
8. To take leadership role in addressing global environmental issues to ensure that solutions adopted are fair and equitable to developing countries and would provide developing countries with adequate means to fulfill their obligations;

9. To reaffirm support for UNEP and its continued role as a forum for promoting global environmental well being, and hope that its restructuring would simplify the policy making process in order to expedite program implementation and enhance its regional roles;
10. To urge developed countries to fulfill their commitments made at UNCED by providing additional resources and transfer of technology for effective implementation of Agenda 21;
11. To urge developed countries to commit targets of limitation and reduction of greenhouse gas emissions under the Berlin Mandate;
12. To urge all parties to the Basel Convention on the Control of Transboundary Movement of Hazardous Wastes and their Disposal to expedite the ratification of the amendment to the convention (Decision III/1), on the banning of the export of hazardous wastes from Annex VII countries to developing countries.

**Done** in Jakarta, Indonesia, this Eighteenth Day of September in the year One Thousand Nine Hundred and Ninety-seven.

**YANG AMAT MULIA PENGIRAN INDERA WIJAYA PENGIRAN Dr. HAJI ISMAIL BIN PENGIRAN HAJI DAMIT**
Minister of Development, Brunei Darussalam

**Mr. SARWONO KUSUMAATMADJA**
State Minister for the Environment, Indonesia

**Dr. SIENE SAPHANGTHONG**
Minister of Agriculture and Forestry, Lao People's Democratic Republic

**DATUK LAW HIENG DING**
Minister of Science, Technology and the Environment, Malaysia

**Mr. VICTOR O. RAMOS**
Secretary, Department of Environment and Natural Resource, the Philippines

**Mr. YEO CHEOW TONG**
Minister for the Environment and
Minister for Health, Singapore

**Mr. KASEM SNIDVONGS**
Permanent Secretary, Minister of Science,
Technology and Environment, Thailand

**Prof. CHU TUAN NHA**
Vice Minister of Science, Technology and
Environment, Vietnam

Source: http://www.aseansec.org/6085.htm
Accessed date: 7 February 2006
Publisher: ASEAN Secretariat
Country: Jakarta
Date of Publication: 2003

# CHAPTER 63

# KOTA KINABALU RESOLUTION ON THE ENVIRONMENT Kota Kinabalu, Sabah, Malaysia,

**7 October 2000**

**CONCERN** that the issues on environment are becoming more complex and challenging;

**AWARE** that to meet these challenges, there is a need to strengthen the institutional and organizational capacity within the ASEAN member countries;

**REALISING** that the "Rio + 10" Conference on Environment and Development, will provide new driving force for achieving environmentally sound and sustainable development;

**EMPHASISING** the need for enhancing ASEAN cooperation to address common environmental problems, promote technology transfer, information networking and to deal with the negative impacts of globalization; and

**RECOGNISING** that the ASEAN Strategic Plan of Action on the Environment shall continue to be the guiding document for present and future initiatives toward achieving the balance between environmental protection and economic development.

## WE, THE ASEAN MINISTERS FOR THE ENVIRONMENT HEREBY AGREED TO:

- Synergize the ASEAN Strategic Plan of Action on the Environment with the Regional Action Plan for Environmentally Sound and Sustainable Development, 2001–2005 for Asia and the Pacific Region with a view to optimize the utilization of limited resources in the implementation of the planned activities;
- Adopt the approach of overcoming environmental pollution by working in collaboration with cities such as Kitakyushu which has successfully controlled pollution;

- Adopt and implement the ASEAN Environmental Education Action Plan 2000–2005 and task ASEAN to implement the Plan;
- Accelerate our efforts in the realization of the Regional Action Plan for the Protection of the Marine Environment from Land and Sea-based activities by the year 2004;
- Initiate the process of negotiation on the ASEAN Agreement on Transboundary Haze Pollution;
- Continue and further enhance our collaboration to implement the Regional Haze Action Plan (RHAP) coherently and effectively;
- Sustainably manage and wise use of our diverse biological resources and to exchange information on biodiversity conservation issues including biosafety and access to biological and genetic resources;
- Stand firm on the common understanding that the developed countries must fulfill their commitment under the United Nations Framework Convention on Climate Change and subsequently the Kyoto Protocol;
- Intensify our cooperation in enhancing national capacities in the negotiation and implementation of the multilateral environmental agreements;
- Reiterate ASEAN's support on the proposal by Indonesia to host the "Rio + 10" Conference on Environment and Development, as stipulated at the 9th Environmental Congress for Asia and the Pacific (ECO ASIA 2000) on 3rd September 2000 and the Ministerial Conference on Environment and Development in Asia and the Pacific in Kitakyushu, Japan, 4–5 September 2000;
- Support the proposal of Cambodia to host an Asia Pacific regional preparatory meeting in the run-up to the "Rio + 10" Conference on Environment and Development;
- Enhance environmental cooperation between ASEAN and the 3 East Asian countries namely, China, Japan and the Republic of Korea;
- Task ASEAN Secretariat to explore the possibility of establishing environmental cooperation between ASEAN and Central Asian countries;
- Support the proposal to organize an international forum on fire hazards arising from large-scale biomass burning; and
- Support to explore the possibility of setting up an Emergency Response and Rescue Institute.

Source: http://www.aseansec.org/650.htm
Accessed date: 7 February 2006
Publisher: ASEAN Secretariat
Country: Jakarta
Date of Publication: 2003

# CHAPTER 64

# YANGON RESOLUTION ON SUSTAINABLE DEVELOPMENT

**RECALLING** the Declaration of ASEAN Concord II (Bali Concord II) to establish an ASEAN Community for the purpose of ensuring durable peace, stability and shared prosperity with a view to realizing an ASEAN Community that is open, dynamic and resilient;

**EMPHASIZING** that sustainable development could be achieved by addressing environmental protection, economic growth, and socio-cultural development in an integrated and coordinated manner;

**RECOGNIZING** that effective environmental and natural resources management, and sustainable utilization of these resources are critical to alleviate poverty, promote healthy living, reduce the incidence of diseases, and enhancing economic growth in the ASEAN region;

**COGNIZANT** of the need to effectively address global and regional transboundary issues related to the environment without impinging on the competitiveness or growth of the region;

**AFFIRMING** that the Johannesburg Plan of Implementation of the World Summit on Sustainable Development (WSSD) provides an effective framework for international and regional cooperation based on the principle of common but differentiated responsibilities; and

**AFFIRMING** that ASEAN Vision 2020, the Hanoi Plan of Action, and its succeeding Plans of Action, among others, provide the regional framework for ASEAN cooperation in response to emerging needs and international developments.

## WE, THE MINISTERS RESPONSIBLE FOR ENVIRONMENT OF THE ASEAN MEMBER COUNTRIES, DO HEREBY:

**TASK** the ASEAN Senior Officials on the Environment to contribute actively in the process of formulating the Vientiane Action Plan, particularly on concrete and realistic strategies, and measures in addressing problems associated with environmental degradation and transboundary pollution, with a view to achieving the ASEAN Socio-Cultural Community which envisages a Southeast Asia bonded together in partnership as a community of caring societies.

**REITERATE** strong commitment and resolve to fulfill the obligations in the WSSD, and to meet the Millennium Development Goals and achieve meaningful cooperation in the ten priority areas* as agreed at the Seventh Informal ASEAN Ministerial Meeting on the Environment.

**CALL UPON** the developed countries to fulfill their commitments made in the Johannesburg Plan of Implementation particularly in providing financial resources, enhancing capacity building, and promoting technology transfer to developing countries;

**WELCOME** the entry into force of the ASEAN Agreement on Transboundary Haze Pollution on 25 November 2003, and resolve to further enhance cooperation under the Agreement;

**ENDEAVOUR** to conclude by 2004 the ASEAN framework agreement on access to, and fair and equitable sharing of benefits arising from the utilization of, biological and genetic resources, in order to sustainably manage the rich biodiversity resources of ASEAN;

**ADOPT** the revised ASEAN Declaration on Heritage Parks, which now includes all ten members of ASEAN, and resolve to further enhance cooperation through the mechanisms provided by this Declaration;

**ACKNOWLEDGE** the valuable contributions made by the ASEAN Regional Centre for Biodiversity Conservation, and agree to further enhance its role by reviewing its management structure and programmes and providing necessary support for the continued sustainability of the Centre, and note the expression of

---

* The ten priority areas as agreed are global environmental issues; land and forest fires and transboundary haze pollution; coastal and marine environment; sustainable forest management; sustainable management of natural parks and protected areas; freshwater resources; public awareness and environmental education; promotion of environmentally-sound technologies and cleaner production; urban environmental management and governance; and sustainable development monitoring and reporting, and database harmonization.

appreciation of the participating member countries to the European Union for its financial support for the first phase and welcome its continued support for the second phase;

**ADOPT** the Framework for "Environmentally Sustainable Cities" in ASEAN to address the challenges of environmental sustainability;

**ADOPT** the ASEAN Long Term Strategic Plan for Water Resources Management to meet the needs in terms of health, food security, economy, and environment;

**RECOGNIZE** the need to expeditiously implement the ASEAN Marine Water Quality Criteria;

**ACKNOWLEDGE** the importance of promoting environmentally sound technologies for effective environmental management and economic growth through appropriate regional mechanisms as envisaged in the Hanoi Plan of Action by the year 2004;

**AGREE** to work towards a plan of action with a definite timeframe to harmonize environmental policies, legislation, regulations, standards and databases, taking into account national circumstances of member countries;

**AGREE** to pursue the idea of creating an ASEAN Environment Fund and task the ASEAN Secretariat in consultation with the ASEAN Senior Officials on Environment to develop the modalities for setting up such a Fund;

**EXPRESS** appreciation to dialogue partners, international and regional organizations, and other countries who have collaborated with ASEAN in promoting sustainable development initiatives; and call upon these partners and other prospective partners to enhance their collaboration; and

**COMMIT** to enhance cooperation with the People's Republic of China, Japan and the Republic of Korea under the ASEAN + 3 Framework, through regular policy dialogues and programmes of common interest at the ministerial and senior official levels.

**DONE** at Yangon, Myanmar on the eighteenth day of December in the year two thousand and three.

**H.E. Dato Seri Setia Dr. Awang Haji Ahmad bin Haji Jumat**
Minister of Development
Brunei Darussalam

**H.E. Dr. Mok Mareth**
Minister of the Environment
Kingdom of Cambodia

**H.E. Mr. Nabiel Makarim, MPA, MSM**
Minister for Environment
Republic of Indonesia

**H.E. Prof. Dr. Bountiem Phissamay**
Minister to Prime Minister's Office
Chairman of Science, Technology and Environment Agency
Lao Peoples' Democratic Republic

**H.E. Dato' Seri Law Hieng Ding**
Minister of Science, Technology and the Environment
Malaysia

**H.E. U Win Aung**
Chairman of the National Commission for Environmental Affairs and
Minister for Foreign Affairs
Union of Myanmar

Source: http://www.aseansec.org/15522.htm
Accessed date: 17 October 2006
Publisher: ASEAN Secretariat
Country: Jakarta
Date of Publication: 2003

# CHAPTER 65

# CEBU RESOLUTION ON SUSTAINABLE DEVELOPMENT

**RECALLING** the Declaration of ASEAN Concord II (Bali Concord II) to establish an ASEAN Community comprising three pillars, namely political and security cooperation, economic cooperation, and socio-cultural cooperation that are closely intertwined and mutually reinforcing for the purpose of ensuring durable peace, stability and shared prosperity in the region;

**WELCOMING** the implementation of the Vientiane Action Programme (VAP), the medium-term roadmap for the period 2004–2010 which sets out specific programme areas and measures to achieve the goal of establishing the ASEAN Community;

**NOTING** the emphasis of the VAP towards nurturing human, cultural and natural resources of the region for sustained development in a harmonious and people-centred ASEAN through the socio-cultural pillar;

**ENCOURAGED** by the sustainable development approach of the VAP which stresses that ASEAN's social and environmental agenda is linked inextricably with the economic and security pillars of the ASEAN Community, that social instability can emerge from environmental scarcity or the inequitable use of environmental assets, and that failure to address these critical and persistent issues can further cause both economic and political dislocations;

**MINDFUL** of the need to address global environmental issues by all parties based on the principle of common but differentiated responsibility, so that these issues do not cause adverse impact to the prosperity of the region; and

**DETERMINED** to further enhance environmental cooperation in order to achieve an environmentally sustainable ASEAN Community.

**WE, THE MINISTERS OF ASEAN MEMBER COUNTRIES RESPONSIBLE FOR THE ENVIRONMENT, DO HEREBY:**

**EXPRESS** our satisfaction on the progress of implementation of environmental programmes and measures and related activities in the VAP, and resolve to further enhance regional cooperation;

**REITERATE** our commitment to address global environmental issues through national and regional cooperation and active participation at international fora, and call upon the global community to continue to work with us to enhance such collaboration;

**LAUNCH** the Third ASEAN State of the Environment Report 2006 which highlights the environmental conditions of the region, challenges faced and actions being taken to address them, while inviting all parties to foster greater collaboration to address these challenges;

**EXPRESS** our serious concern over the recurring transboundary haze pollution which was aggravated by the extended drier weather condition during El Ni̊ňo years, and resolve to further enhance preventive, monitoring and mitigation efforts to address land and forest fires;

**COMMIT** to continue assisting member countries affected by land and forest fires within the framework of the ASEAN Agreement on Transboundary Haze Pollution, and for this purpose encourage the remaining member countries to quickly ratify the Agreement;

**ESTABLISH** the Sub-regional Ministerial Steering Committee consisting of Ministers from the 5 most affected countries namely Brunei Darussalam, Indonesia, Malaysia, Singapore and Thailand to oversee the implementation of concrete actions to address land and forest fires and the resulting transboudary haze pollution.

**EXPRESS** our full support and commitment to the effective operations of the recently established ASEAN Centre for Biodiversity, located in the Philippines, to promote biodiversity conservation in the region, and in this respect express our appreciation to the EU for providing financial support to participating member countries for the first three-and-half years of operations of the Centre;

**AGREE** to expedite the respective national process for signing the ASEAN Framework Agreement on access to, and fair and equitable sharing of benefits arising from the utilisation of, biological and genetic resources, in order to sustainably manage the rich biological resources of the region;

**ENDORSE** the ASEAN Environmentally Sustainable Cities Award to recognise exemplary national efforts in Member Countries and to promote further efforts towards environmental sustainability in ASEAN cities;

**RECOGNISE** the importance of strengthening national efforts and regional cooperation for effective environmental law enforcement, to address issues such as illegal trade in wildlife. As for illegal logging, there is a need for effective enforcement of forestry law and other related laws, where appropriate;

**EXPRESS** concern over the impact of climate change on ecosystems, in particular water resources, which requires mitigation and adaptation measures to minimise the impacts particularly from flood, drought, landslide, and other water-related hazards;

**COMMIT** to enhance further cooperation with the People's Republic of China, Japan and the Republic of Korea under the ASEAN Plus Three Framework through regular policy dialogues and implementation of activities of common interest; and

**EXPRESS** our appreciation to dialogue partners, international and regional organisations, and other countries that have collaborated with us in promoting sustainable development initiatives, and call upon these and other prospective partners to further enhance their collaboration.

Source: http://www.aseansec.org/18811.htm
Accessed date: 7 February 2006
Publisher: ASEAN Secretariat
Country: Jakarta
Date of Publication: 2006

# CHAPTER 66

# ASEAN DECLARATION ON ENVIRONMENTAL SUSTAINABILITY

**WE,** the Heads of State/Government of Brunei Darussalam, the Kingdom of Cambodia, the Republic of Indonesia, the Lao People's Democratic Republic, Malaysia, the Union of Myanmar, the Republic of the Philippines, the Republic of Singapore, the Kingdom of Thailand and the Socialist Republic of Viet Nam, Member Countries of ASEAN, on the occasion of the 40th Anniversary of ASEAN and the 13th ASEAN Summit in Singapore;

**COGNISANT** of mounting global concern over the environment and ASEAN's obligations to its people in fulfilling the aims of the World Summit on Sustainable Development (WSSD) and to achieve the UN Millennium Development Goals (MDGs), in particular to ensure environmental sustainability in the context of sustainable development;

**DETERMINED** that ASEAN should complement and support the efforts of global and regional organizations to tackle environmental issues, and in this regard support the APEC Leaders' Declaration on Climate Change, Energy Security and Clean Development, and Indonesia's efforts to host the 13th Session of the Conference of Parties (COP) to the United Nations Framework Convention on Climate Change (UNFCCC) and the 3rd Session of the Conference of the Parties Serving as the Meeting of the Parties (CMP) to the Kyoto Protocol in December 2007;

**NOTING WITH CONCERN** the findings of the Inter-governmental Panel on Climate Change's (IPCC) Fourth Assessment Report (AR4) that the warming of the climate system is unequivocal;

**FURTHER NOTING WITH CONCERN,** the adverse impacts of climate change caused by global emissions of greenhouse gases, particularly to the developing countries, such as the loss of biodiversity and severe environmental, social, health and economic consequences;

**REITERATING** the need to build an ASEAN Community that is economically vibrant and environmentally friendly, so that the present and future generations can enjoy a clean and sustainable environment;

**FURTHER RECALLING** the 10 priority areas of environmental sustainability as agreed at the 7th Informal ASEAN Ministerial Meeting on the Environment, and the key areas of Environmental Management and Natural Resource Management outlined for the period 2004–2010 in the Vientiane Action Programme (VAP);

**REAFFIRMING** the goals of the Yangon Resolution on Sustainable Development, signed on 18 December 2003 and the Cebu Resolution on Sustainable Development, adopted on 10 November 2006, by the Ministers of ASEAN Member Countries responsible for the environment;

**ACKNOWLEDGING** that fossil fuels will continue to be part of the energy landscape, and that ASEAN Member Countries, who are at different stages of economic development, will face various environment challenges and levels of resources needed to effectively address global environmental issues without compromising competitiveness or social and economic development;

**FURTHER ACKNOWLEDGING** the efforts of ASEAN Member Countries to ratify the ASEAN Agreement on the Conservation of Nature and Natural Resources, signed on 9 July 1985, the ASEAN Agreement on Transboundary Haze Pollution, signed on 10 June 2002, and the Agreement on the Establishment of the ASEAN Centre for Biodiversity, signed on 27 September 2005;

**ENCOURAGING** the efforts to develop an ASEAN Climate Change Initiative;

**RECOGNISING** the importance of sustainable forest management in ASEAN, which will contribute significantly to the international efforts to promote environmental sustainability, and to mitigate the effects of climate change as well as transboundary environmental pollution;

**RECOGNISING** the partnership of the world community in combating land degradation in the context of the United Nations Convention to Combat Desertification (UNCCD), a global instrument which can make a lasting contribution to the achievement of sustainable land management and environment; and

**FURTHER RECOGNIZING** the importance of protecting the natural resource base for economic and social development, including the sustainable management and conservation of soil, water, mineral, coastal and marine resources as well as the improvement in water and air quality for the ASEAN region;

## HEREBY DECLARE:

### Environmental Protection and Management

1. **To honour and implement** commitments to multilateral and regional sustainable development and environmental agreements, so as to achieve the common goal of a clean and green ASEAN;
2. **To intensify** regional and international cooperation in promoting, sharing and implementing environmentally sustainable practices, including the transfer of environmentally-sound technologies, the enhancement of human and institutional capacities and the promotion of sustainable consumption and production patterns;
3. **To adopt** a holistic approach in fostering regional cooperation on environmental issues, with the participation of all relevant stakeholders; including business, academics, NGOs and civil society organizations;
4. **To expand** on the existing work under the ASEAN Initiative on Environmentally Sustainable Cities;
5. **To intensify** individual and collective efforts to improve the quality of air and water within ASEAN through regional or national initiatives to reduce industrial and transportation pollutions;
6. **To implement** measures and enhance international and regional cooperation to combat transboundary environmental pollution, including haze pollution, through, among other things, capacity building, enhancing public awareness, strengthening law enforcement, promoting environmentally sustainable practices, as well as combating illegal logging and its associated illegal trade;
7. **To endeavour to reduce** by half of the number of people without sustainable access to safe drinking water by 2010 in accordance with the VAP to meet the needs of ASEAN citizens, and significant improvement in the lives of slum dwellers by 2020 in ASEAN Member Countries in accordance with the UN MDGs;
8. **To promote** the sustainable management and use of our soil, forest, coastal and marine environments as part of regional and global efforts on biodiversity conservation, mindful of their important value as our natural heritage, and their contribution towards mitigating the effects of climate change and environmental degradation;
9. **To further promote** cooperation among ASEAN Member Countries in combating land degradation for sustainable land management to support sustainable agriculture and environment;

10. **To call upon** the international community to participate in and contribute to afforestation and reforestation, and to reduce deforestation, forest degradation, and forest fires, including by promoting sustainable forest management and development, and combating illegal logging;
11. **To also call** on the international community to implement debt-for-sustainable development swap arrangements;
12. **To forge** ASEAN-wide cooperation to establish a regional nuclear safety regime, in line with our discussions at the 12th ASEAN Summit in Cebu on 13 January 2007; the Southeast Asia Nuclear Weapon Free Zone (SEANWFZ) Plan of Action adopted by the SEANWFZ Commission in Manila on 29 July 2007; and the agreement of the 25th ASEAN Ministers on Energy Meeting (AMEM) on 23 August 2007;
13. **To contribute** to the UN Decade on Education for Sustainable Development through the ASEAN Environmental Education Action Plan to nurture environmentally conscious ASEAN citizens;

## Responding to Climate Change

14. **To work closely** with the international community to better understand and adapt to the adverse impacts of climate change, including, in particular, the related issues of greenhouse gas emissions and carbon sinks;
15. **To agree** that the pursuit of climate change and energy security policies should avoid introducing barriers to trade and investment;
16. **To intensify** cooperation on the joint research, development and deployment of low emission technologies for the cleaner use of fossil fuels, recognising that fossil fuels will continue to play a major role in our energy mix;
17. **To take** concrete measures to promote the use of renewable and alternative energy sources such as solar, hydro, wind, tide, biomass, biofuels and geothermal energy, as well as, for interested parties, civilian nuclear power, while ensuring safety and safeguards that are of current international standards, and environmental sustainability throughout the full life cycle of production and use;
18. **To improve** energy efficiency in key sectors of energy use through capacity building and information sharing of best practices in managing energy use and the adoption of appropriate technologies and practices;
19. **To undertake** effective measures towards open and competitive regional and international markets geared towards providing affordable energy at

all economic levels to facilitate the adoption of energy-efficient and low-emission technologies;

## Conservation of Natural Resources

20. **To achieve** by 2010, a significant reduction in the current rate of loss of biodiversity, as pledged by countries at the WSSD in 2002 and as envisaged by the Convention on Biological Diversity;
21. **To conserve** our rich biodiversity, by promoting access to, and sustainable utilisation of its components, and the fair and equitable sharing of the benefits from these biological and genetic resources;
22. **To take into account** biodiversity considerations in the mitigation of and adaptation to climate change;
23. **To promote and support** the ASEAN Centre for Biodiversity as a regional centre for biodiversity conservation and management;
24. **To strengthen** efforts to implement the ASEAN Regional Action Plan on Trade in Wild Fauna and Flora, 2005–2010 through mechanisms such as the ASEAN Wildlife Enforcement Network;
25. **To support** the conservation and management of ASEAN Heritage Parks and encourage ASEAN Member Countries to identify more Parks;
26. **To ensure** the effective implementation of the ASEAN Strategic Plan on Water Resources Management;
27. **To promote** conservation and sustainable management of key ecosystems, including forest, coastal, and marine habitats, such as coral reefs, through initiatives, in particular, the "Heart of Borneo", "Forestry Eleven forum", and the "Coral Triangle Initiative on Coral Reefs, Fisheries, and Food Security";
28. **To agree** to collectively work towards achieving an aspirational goal of significantly increasing the cumulative forest cover in the ASEAN region by at least 10 million hectares by 2020; and
29. **Foster** the sustainable management and efficient use of mineral resources and environmentally-sound mining practices.

**DONE** in Singapore, this Twentieth Day of November in the Year Two Thousand and Seven.

For Brunei Darussalam:

**HAJI HASSANAL BOLKIAH**
Sultan of Brunei Darussalam

For the Kingdom of Cambodia:

**SAMDECH HUN SEN**
Prime Minister

For the Republic of Indonesia:

**DR. SUSILO BAMBANG YUDHOYONO**
President

For the Lao People's Democratic Republic:

**BOUASONE BOUPHAVANH**
Prime Minister

For Malaysia:

**DATO' SERI ABDULLAH AHMAD BADAWI**
Prime Minister

For the Union of Myanmar:

**GENERAL THEIN SEIN**
Prime Minister

For the Republic of the Philippines:

**GLORIA MACAPAGAL-ARROYO**
President

For the Republic of Singapore:

**LEE HSIEN LOONG**
Prime Minister

For the Kingdom of Thailand:

**GENERAL SURAYUD CHULANONT (RET.)**
Prime Minister

For the Socialist Republic of Viet Nam:

**NGUYEN TAN DUNG**
Prime Minister

Source: http://www.aseansec.org/21060.htm
Accessed date: 18 January 2008
Publisher: ASEAN Secretariat
Country: Jakarta
Date of Publication: 2007

# CHAPTER 67

# CHA-AM HUA HIN DECLARATION ON THE ROADMAP FOR AN ASEAN COMMUNITY (2009–2015)

**WE**, the Heads of State or Government of the Association of Southeast Asian Nations (hereinafter referred to as "ASEAN"), namely Brunei Darussalam, the Kingdom of Cambodia, the Republic of Indonesia, the Lao People's Democratic Republic, Malaysia, the Union of Myanmar, the Republic of the Philippines, the Republic of Singapore, the Kingdom of Thailand and the Socialist Republic of Viet Nam, on the occasion of the 14$^{th}$ ASEAN Summit in Cha-am, Thailand;

**RECALLING** the spirit in which the ASEAN Founding Fathers gathered in Bangkok in 1967 to create an organisation that would help bring about a Southeast Asian region of peace, freedom and prosperity for their peoples;

**RECALLING ALSO** the ASEAN Vision 2020, which charts a future direction for ASEAN as a concert of Southeast Asian nations, outward-looking, living in peace, stability and prosperity, bonded together in partnership in a just, democratic, and harmonious environment, dynamic development and ever-closer economic integration and in a community of caring societies, conscious of its ties of history, aware of its shared cultural heritage and bound by a common regional identity;

**RECOGNISING** the Declaration of ASEAN Concord II (Bali Concord II), which seeks to bring the ASEAN Vision 2020 into reality by setting the goal of building an ASEAN Community by 2020 comprising three pillars, namely political-security community, economic community and socio-cultural community, all of which are closely intertwined and mutually reinforcing for the purpose of ensuring durable peace, stability and shared prosperity in the region;

**INSPIRED** by the spirit of a new ASEAN, as symbolised by the ASEAN Charter, we reaffirm our commitment to accelerating the establishment of the ASEAN Community, comprising the aforementioned three pillars, by 5 years to 2015, as agreed in Cebu, the Philippines in 2007;

**EMPHASISING** that narrowing the development gap shall remain an important task to ensure the benefits of ASEAN integration are fully realized through effective implementation of the Initiative for ASEAN Integration (IAI) and other subregional frameworks;

**NOTING** with satisfaction the progress made so far under the series of action plans or programmes adopted to guide progress towards the realisation of the ASEAN Vision 2020, for example, the Hanoi Plan of Action (HPA), the Initiative for ASEAN Integration (IAI) and the Vientiane Action Programme (VAP);

**COGNISANT** that the rapidly changing globalised world continues to present both opportunities and challenges to which ASEAN must proactively utilize and respond, keeping itself always relevant, while maintaining ASEAN's **RECALLING** the signing of the Declaration on the ASEAN Economic Community Blueprint and the adoption of the ASEAN Economic Community Blueprint at the 13th ASEAN Summit on 20 November 2007 in Singapore and the adoption of the ASEAN Political-Security Community Blueprint and the ASEAN Socio-Cultural Community Blueprint, and the Second IAI Work Plan at the 14th ASEAN Summit on 1 March 2009 in Thailand.

## DO HEREBY:

1. **AGREE** that the ASEAN Political-Security Community Blueprint, the ASEAN Economic Community Blueprint, the ASEAN Socio-Cultural Community Blueprint and the IAI Work Plan 2 (2009–2015), as annexed, shall constitute the Roadmap for an ASEAN Community (2009–2015), and each ASEAN Member State shall ensure its timely implementation.
2. **ALSO AGREE** that the Roadmap for an ASEAN Community (2009–2015) shall replace the Vientiane Action Programme.
3. **TASK** the concerned ASEAN Sectoral Ministerial Bodies and the Secretary-General of ASEAN to implement this Declaration as well as monitor commitments supported by the Committee of Permanent Representatives, and report to us regularly through the respective ASEAN Community Councils on the progress of its implementation;
4. **ALSO TASK** concerned Ministers and the Secretary-General of ASEAN to mobilise resources from Member States, Dialogue and Sectoral Partners, Development Partners of ASEAN as well as from other external parties to implement this Declaration; and
5. **PLEDGE** our resolve and commitment to promote ASEAN peoples to participate in and benefit fully from the process of ASEAN integration and community building.

**DONE** at Cha-am, Thailand, this First Day of March in the Year Two Thousand and Nine, in single copy, in the English Language.

For Brunei Darussalam:

**HAJI HASSANAL BOLKIAH**
Sultan of Brunei Darussalam

For the Kingdom of Cambodia:

**SAMDECH HUN SEN**
Prime Minister

For the Republic of Indonesia:

**DR. SUSILO BAMBANG YUDHOYONO**
President

For the Lao People's Democratic Republic:

**BOUASONE BOUPHAVANH**
Prime Minister

For Malaysia:

**DATO' SERI ABDULLAH AHMAD BADAWI**
Prime Minister

For the Union of Myanmar:

**GENERAL THEIN SEIN**
Prime Minister

For the Republic of the Philippines:

**GLORIA MACAPAGALARROYO**
President

For the Republic of Singapore:

**LEE HSIEN LOONG**
Prime Minister

For the Kingdom of Thailand:

**ABHISIT VEJJAJIVA**
Prime Minister

For the Socialist Republic of Viet Nam:

**NGUYEN TAN DUNG**
Prime Minister

Source: http://www.aseansec.org/22331.htm
Accessed date: 3 March 2009
Publisher: ASEAN Secretariat
Country: Jakarta
Date of Publication: 2009

# CHAPTER 68

# JOINT DECLARATION ON THE ATTAINMENT OF THE MILLENNIUM DEVELOPMENT GOALS IN ASEAN

**WE**, the Heads of State or Government of the Member States of the Association of Southeast Asian Nations (ASEAN), namely Brunei Darussalam, the Kingdom of Cambodia, the Republic of Indonesia, the Lao People's Democratic Republic, Malaysia, the Union of Myanmar, the Republic of the Philippines, the Republic of Singapore, the Kingdom of Thailand and the Socialist Republic of Viet Nam;

**RECALLING** the Bali Concord II establishing an ASEAN Community based on three pillars, namely ASEAN Political-Security Community, ASEAN Economic Community and ASEAN Socio-Cultural Community within 2020 and the decision of the ASEAN Leaders at the ASEAN Summit in Cebu, the Philippines to accelerate the realization of an ASEAN Community from 2020 to 2015;

**GUIDED** by the ASEAN Charter which aims to ensure sustainable development for the benefit of present and future generations and to place the well-being, livelihood and welfare of the peoples at the centre of the ASEAN Community building process;

**REAFFIRMING** that a stable, secure and prosperous ASEAN Community can be realized when our peoples are free from hunger and provided with primary education as well as adequate health care;

**ACKNOWLEDGING** the different levels of social and economic development among ASEAN Member States and the need to narrow the development gap within ASEAN;

**NOTING** that overall ASEAN Member States have made good progress towards the attainment of the Millennium Development Goals (MDGs) particularly in primary education, gender equality as well as combating some infectious diseases and in some ASEAN Member States additional goals and targets have been added specific to their own particular circumstances;

**CONCERNED** that there are still significant challenges that need to be overcome for some ASEAN Member States to fully achieve the MDGs and thereby narrow the development gap in ASEAN;

**NOTING** the efforts undertaken at the regional level to address the challenges faced by ASEAN Member States in achieving the MDGs and narrowing the development gap particularly through the implementation of the Framework Plan of Action on Rural Development and Poverty Eradication, the projects/programmes on poverty and quality of life in the Initiative for ASEAN Integration (IAl) Work Plan, the Joint Statement of the Third ASEAN Education Ministers' Meeting, the Work Plan for primary education, gender equality as well as combating some infectious diseases for Women's Advancement and Gender Equality (2005–2010) and the Work Plan to operationalise the Declaration on the Elimination of Violence against Women (2006–2010), the ASEAN Work programme on HIV/AIDS and the measures on health development and sustainable development in the Vientiane Action Programme as well as the ASEAN Declaration on Environmental Sustainability; and

**RECOGNIZING** the contribution of sub-regional cooperation frameworks, namely Ayeyawady-Chao Phraya-Mekong Economic Cooperation Strategy (ACMECS), Brunei-Indonesia-Malaysia-Philippines East ASEAN Growth Area (BIMP-EAGA), Indonesia-Malaysia-Thailand Growth Triangle (IMT-GT) and Greater Mekong Subregion (GMS), and CLMV Sub-regional Cooperation in narrowing the development gap among ASEAN Member States and building an ASEAN Community.

## DO HEREBY ADOPT AND PROCLAIM THAT WE WILL:

1. Make ASEAN a more dynamic, gender responsive, resilient and cohesive regional rganization for the well-being of its Member States and people;
2. Ensure a continuous effort towards a balance between economic growth and social development and environmental sustainability in order to reduce and not to create negative impacts to the attainment of the MDGs;
3. Further enhance coordination and cooperation within the IAl and subregional cooperation frameworks in order to narrow the development gap in ASEAN in particular through the establishment of a consultative mechanism between ASEAN and the sub-regional frameworks;
4. Continue to promote public awareness in ASEAN Member States on the attainment of MDGs and enhance public participation;
5. Share information, experiences and best practices in the attainment of the MDGs among ASEAN Member States through the relevant ASEAN bodies as well as through the ASEAN Centre of Excellence on MDGs set up in the Asian Institute of Technology and other regional institutions;

6. Develop and implement a Roadmap for the Attainment of the Millennium Development Goals as a framework for collective actions among ASEAN Member States to achieve the MDGs focusing on five key areas namely advocacy and linkages; knowledge; resources; expertise; and regional cooperation and regional public goods;
7. Establish a monitoring and evaluation system, including generation of gender statistics for the attainment of MDGs in ASEAN in collaboration with the UN specialized bodies; and
8. Encourage the close collaboration and create networks among the public and private sectors and civil society in addressing challenges and developing strategies on the MDGs.

**ADOPTED** in Cha-am, Thailand, on the 1st Day of March in the Year Two Thousand and Nine, in a single original in the English language.

Source: http://www.aseansec.org/22334.htm
Accessed date: 3 March 2009
Publisher: ASEAN Secretariat
Country: Jakarta
Date of Publication: 2009